Deepening Reconciliation

Reflections on Glencree Peacebuilding

Edited by Eamon Rafter

First published in 2014 by The Glencree Centre for Peace and Reconciliation

ISBN 978-1-903727-02-7

Typeset in Adobe Caslon Pro by Sinéad Rafferty, for and on behalf of,

Graphprint,
Unit A9 Calmount Park,
Ballymount, Dublin 12,
Ireland.

DEDICATION

This publication is dedicated to the memory of
Brendan Crowley,
Conn Mulvenna,
Geraldine Fitzgerald and
Mira Dabit
in acknowledgement of their lasting
contributions to Glencree.
They remain an inspiration to us.

Helping others find non-violent ways of resolving their own conflicts

Table of Contents

Acknowledgements 2

Message from President Michael D. Higgins 3

Introduction - *William Devas CEO* 5

Section 1: The Context

Facilitating Lasting Peace:
Acknowledging Glencree's 40th Anniversary - *Roelf Meyer* 9

The Elusive Search for Reconciliation - *Geoffrey Corry* 17

Section 2: Reflections on Glencree Peacebuilding

Learning Peace: Schools, Youth and Adults - *Eamon Rafter* 37

The Role of Women in Peacebuilding - *Phil Killeen* 55

Political Dialogue: Building Critical Relationships
- *Ian White & Geoffrey Corry* 75

LIVE: Let's Involve the Victim's Experience - *Jacinta De Paor* 115

Working with Former Combatants &
the Sustainable Peace Network - *Wilhelm Verwoerd* 131

Peacebuilding Possibilities for People of Faith - *Colin Murphy* 151

Sharing Lessons from Ireland in International Contexts - *Ian White* 171

The Role of International Volunteers - *Sorcha Tormey & Eamon Rafter* 195

Author Biographies 205

ACKNOWLEDGEMENTS

Our sincere thanks to all the Glencree contributors whose chapters on their programme work make up the core of this book. We are aware that it is difficult to encapsulate twenty years of work in one short chapter, so, hopefully we have done their initial drafts justice in this publication. We also want to acknowledge all the participants for their courage and engagement throughout our programmes as they are the focus of our work and the reason for our existence in the first place.

We are most grateful to all the individuals, businesses and funding bodies who have supported our programmes over many years. We particularly want to thank Special EU Programmes Body and IFI who supported many of the programmes documented here. Thanks also to Roelf Meyer who was kind enough to agree to write a chapter as a forward to the programme reflections. We are grateful to all staff, Board members and volunteers at Glencree, many of whom are not named in the reflections, who helped to make our programme work possible. Also to facilitators on all of the programmes who were essential to the quality of the work done and helping to shape its direction.

This publication has been very much a group endeavour and there have been many people involved in bringing it into being. Thanks to Paula Kandefer for the cover photo and those of the Glencree site and all the people whose photos have been used in the various chapters. Many of these are collected in the Glencree photo archive and we apologise for not being able to credit them individually. Thanks to Sarah Franklyn for her early contributions to the layout of this publication and to all current staff who offered suggestions and comments. We are also indebted to Richard Belton and Vawn Corrigan for their help with proofreading. Dominic Finnegan and Graph Print have been a pleasure to work with and offered their expertise and advice about the look of the publication, which we greatly value.

This publication was made possible by the financial support of the Irish Government, Department of Foreign Affairs and Trade, Reconciliation Fund and the Conflict Resolution Unit. We are most thankful for their ongoing support of our programme work. We are also grateful to our patron President Michael D. Higgins for agreeing to take on this role and for his kind endorsement of our work.

Uachtarán na hÉireann
President of Ireland

MESSAGE FROM PRESIDENT MICHAEL D. HIGGINS

The contribution of the Glencree Centre for Peace & Reconciliation to the promotion of peace-building on the Island of Ireland has been a significant one. For forty years, the Centre has been reaching right into the heart of the community; knowing that a journey to lasting peace can only be achieved if citizens learn to understand and respect each others differences, while recognising and appreciating all they share in common. By gaining access to the perspective of those whom they may once have regarded as enemies, many people have been enabled to realise the power of human empathy and shared solidarity, and to witness their great capacity to transcend boundaries built on bitterness, intolerance or prejudice.

I am very proud to be Patron of the Glencree Centre for Peace & Reconciliation and wish them every success as they continue with their vital and inspiring work.

Michael D. Higgins

Michael D. Higgins
Uachtarán na hÉireann
President of Ireland

We look forward to working with you, in seeking to build a peaceful future

Introduction *William Devas CEO*

Will Devas - Glencree CEO

2014 marks 40 years since the founding of The Glencree Centre for Peace and Reconciliation and I am delighted to welcome you to this publication reflecting on our work both on the island of Ireland and internationally in the last 20 years.

Central to Glencree's work in transforming violent conflict and building peace has been helping to build improbable relationships between people involved in and affected by violent conflict. Through skillful facilitation and the creation of a 'safe space' participants in Glencree's programmes have engaged in often challenging and difficult dialogue with 'others' that in turn has contributed to breaking down barriers to peace and reconciliation in both the political and community spheres. The nature of this work is necessarily 'under the radar' and therefore Glencree has deliberately been quiet on the nature of the work that it has done and continues to engage in.

However, whilst wishing to retain necessary confidentiality, a coherent documentation of our work reflecting on what we have done, the lessons learned, the challenges faced, the mistakes made and how our experiences could usefully help others was overdue.

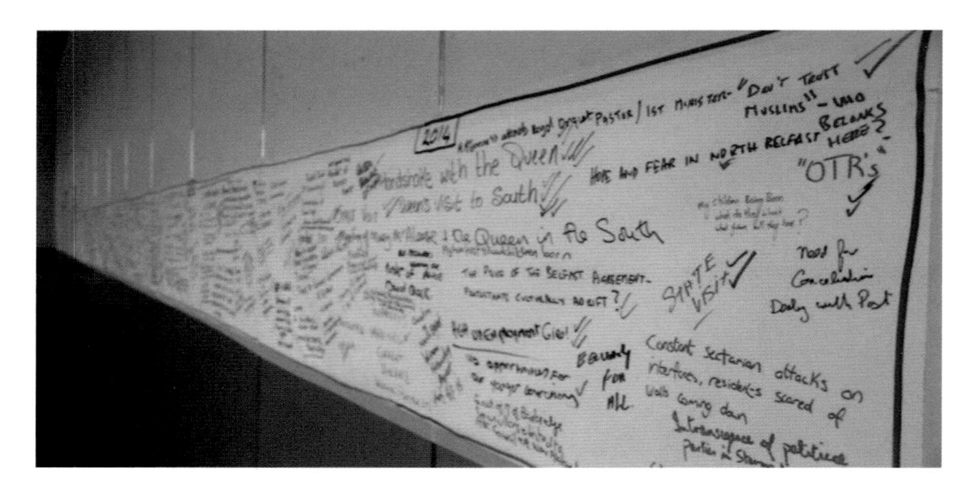

Timeline of the Troubles- Glencree Symposium, June 2014

Therefore in 2013, which marked 15 years since the signing of the Good Friday/ Belfast Agreement, we started on a process of internal reflection. This publication, a series of write ups that are both descriptive and reflective in nature, done by those that managed our various programmes, is the initial outcome. This is, for Glencree, a preliminary step in our commitment to be a better learning organisation, one that continually reflects on the effectiveness of our work and how our contribution to our mission of deepening reconciliation can be improved.

In 2013 Glencree also embarked on a strategic planning process considering whether there was still a significant role for the organisation and if so, define what that should be. We consulted widely and combined with events happening in Northern Ireland, whether expressions of dissident republican groups, flag protests or clashes during the marching season, we were left in no doubt about the need for our dialogue and capacity building work. More recent difficulties in reaching agreement on the three issues of flags, parades and how to deal with the legacy of violence and continued north-south disconnect demonstrate that there is still a great amount to be achieved for those that aspire to deeper reconciliation and a more cohesive and shared society irrespective of one's constitutional preferences. The horrors of violent conflict have become all too apparent in the last couple of years in other contexts further suggesting that lessons learned from our own peace process may be useful in helping others find non-violent ways of resolving their own conflicts.

Opening Session – Glencree Symposium, June 2014

Glencree, therefore, is committed, in partnership with others, to playing its part in helping deepen reconciliation on this island and sharing our experiences and expertise to aid peacebuilding in some other contexts overseas.

I hope you enjoy this publication and we look forward to working with you in seeking to build a peaceful future.

Glencree Mosaic – created by participants, volunteers and staff

Facilitating Lasting Peace: Acknowledging Glencree's 40th Anniversary

Roelf Meyer

> *'One of the things I learned when I was negotiating,*
> *was that until I changed myself, I could not change others'*
> *Nelson Mandela*

The decision to launch Glencree forty years ago followed a period of intense conflict in the Northern Ireland divide. That year, 1974, also marked a period of immense divide in my own country, South Africa. The white-only general election fixed the gaze of the world on the project of institutional apartheid, by then in its twenty-sixth year and abating none. Despite the global condemnation of social segregation, the racial lines that had been drawn in the 1650s were still firmly etched on to our social and political landscape.

Few, if any, of us on either side of that divide would have thought then that the change the late Nelson Mandela talks of in those inspiring lines above was possible. In 1974, he was a political prisoner, held in isolation on Robben Island off the coast of Cape

Town and would only begin secret talks with the apartheid leaders in later years. I was a practicing attorney and five years would pass before I would become an elected Member of Parliament for the ruling National Party.

Where I stood then, politically, was a very long distance from where I sit today and the intervening chapter recounts a years-long process of deep transformation and change. However, my personal story cannot be divorced from that of South Africa's and the 'struggle' we underwent collectively to shed the racial superiority that defined our outlook on life. Our search for peace is a fitting foreword for this commemorative book, dovetailing neatly with Glencree's ethos and philosophy.

My early life had been heavily influenced by the South Africa of the early 1970s and I belonged to a generation and racial grouping for whom opportunities were plentiful. As a young professional I was doing well, but at the same time, becoming increasingly uneasy with the injustices I encountered around me on a regular basis. As a lawyer, I was confronted with the sobering fact that constitutional rights were heavily skewed in one direction and in such a manner that the scales of justice could never possibly balance.

When I entered Parliament in my early thirties I was struck by how unreal the system was and how unreasonable was the book of statutes. I could not say to myself with any degree of honesty that as a member of the South African parliament I was representing all of the people of my country. I struggled with the unease intellectually, rather than emotionally or politically. But for as long as it burdened me at an intellectual level only, I know now that change would be a long time coming.

In 1986, President PW Botha appointed me deputy minister of law and order. That was at the height of apartheid repression and during a national state of emergency declared for the whole country.

South Africa was ablaze with rioting and I was given the unenviable task of spending prolonged periods in the black townships trying to understand who or what sparked the widespread violence and what could bring it to a halt. Not surprisingly, black townships were no place for white men in those years and for the 16 or so months I spent visiting those areas, I was essentially on enemy turf. And yet it was only by crossing that racial line that I truly came to appreciate the appalling conditions of black life in apartheid South Africa. That experience severely challenged my political beliefs. Henceforth I would find it difficult, if not impossible, to put a favourable construction on the reprehensible project of white superiority. Looking back, my emotional transformation was well under way by then.

When I stepped into the role of Deputy Minister of Constitutional Development under President de Klerk, in 1989, I publicly vowed to step down, if there was no move towards political change within a period of two years. It was a bold declaration but it was a vow that was underpinned by the personal change I had undergone and I clung dearly to that pledge. There was no turning back towards the old dispensation. I not only understood, but also embraced the need for change. Furthermore, I knew I could help change others, so profound was the change within myself. Ironically, or perhaps coincidentally, when I made that pledge in the late 1980s, the tide had already begun to turn within the ranks of the National Party.

Throughout the course of the eighties, it had become clear to President Botha and those around him that the policy of separate development, or apartheid as it was called, was not sustainable in the long term, though it was only when F.W. de Klerk took over in 1989 that the political process began to normalize. Provisions were finally made for mass, peaceful protests to take place around the country and some political prisoners were released later that year. Political parties and organisations were unbanned early the following year and Mr. Mandela walked free in February 1990.

Prior to that date, politics in South Africa was premised on race or colour, whilst thereafter we worked towards building a political system based on values. However, despite the far-reaching changes that were sweeping through the country, these were mainly for pragmatic reasons. These were for pragmatic reasons mainly. Pressure from the international community was mounting and UN-imposed sanctions had crippled the economy. The ANC had upped their game and made many parts of the country ungovernable; the extent to which we had lost control in some areas was evident by the presence of heavily armoured vehicles patrolling the streets. The country was bleeding and it had begun to dawn on many white South Africans that if they did not endorse a change they would face a bloody onslaught instead.

Though 1990 marked the beginning of the end, some critical back-channel talks had already begun many years earlier when Mandela entered into secret negotiations from his prison cell with some of Botha's men. Those talks about talks were immensely important not only in paving the way for the later talks about substance to begin but to help build and foster trust among the opposing sides during the formal negotiations.

As I have said many times before, a successful outcome can never be possible if there hasn't been a successful process and I would learn that trust goes a long way in this regard, as do the complimentary concepts of inclusiveness and ownership, which were to become the cornerstones of the South Africa talks.

In the dying days of 1991 we began to negotiate an end to apartheid and held the first plenary session of the Convention for a Democratic South Africa (CODESA). We chose to embark on the peace building process alone - with only the opposing sides gathered around the table - rather than rely on outside facilitators or mediators. That meant depending on one another to find the answers and lead the way, even when the going got tough, which it inevitably did.

Children in Kayamundi township, Stellenbosch during Journeys Out Project

Hence we had to develop a process of mutual understanding towards negotiations, mindful at all times that while we were working towards peace and partnership, we were opponents once we sat down at the negotiating table because we held different political aspirations and ideologies.

That was the sensitivity of our process; we had to become partners while we were essentially enemies and once again I recall the words of the late Mandela: 'If you want to make peace with your enemy, you have to work with your enemy. Then he becomes your partner.' In that would-be partnership, I headed the CODESA talks on the part of the National Party government, while Cyril Ramaphosa became my counterpart in the African National Congress (ANC).

It would take many failed attempts before we forged that partnership. In the South African negotiations there were essentially two main parties; the National Party government of the day and the ANC, though there were a total of two hundred and twenty eight delegates drawn from nineteen political parties, all told. In hindsight, we were merely trying to hammer out some pragmatic changes in those early days of CODESA. I speak here for many of us in the National Party who were informed by our minds in a calculated way, mindful of the factors that were inhibiting the apartheid system and which begged some sort of new dawn. If anything, it was but an intellectual mind-game that we played.

Therefore, there was no 'buy-in' without which a genuinely different outcome could ever be possible. Many of my former National Party colleagues were still advocating the retention of minority or group rights, or, at the very least, as much white power as they could possibly retain in a post-apartheid era. Not surprisingly, the talks floundered in 1992.

The breakdown in the talks forced us to return to the drawing board and ask ourselves what we really desired from a future constitution. It was only then that the protection of individual rights, as the foundation for a future constitution, became acceptable to my party colleagues. Once that milestone was overcome, we naturally conceded that reserved rights or group rights for minority protection simply could not and would not work. We agreed to work towards a united state with equality for all; and it was with that decision the paradigm shift finally began.

Though the deadlock was met with heavy disappointment on both sides, in hindsight it was what forced the National Party to turn that proverbial corner. Our willingness to return to the negotiating table was also a measure of our commitment to the process and it underscored the foundation of trust that had been invested in the process from both sides.

The breakdown lasted for a period of three months, though during that time Cyril and I maintained communication between the two sides, an open line that was later dubbed 'the channel'. As two individuals we had developed an excellent rapport.

Though we started out as strangers, we came to understand one another. We took the time to become acquainted. A mutual respect developed, out of which came trust and a knowing that neither one of us would let the other down.

And yet as crucial as that trust was, it was only an enabling factor. It alone could not have changed the course of South Africa's history or the mindset shift that was needed. A paradigm shift goes beyond the intellectual. It stems from an inner conviction to make that deep and meaningful change. It brings with it an emotional attachment that one has to learn and without which one cannot reach the other side.

Another key enabling factor in that paradigm journey is something as basic as ownership, which was a key factor in the South African story. As I explained above, we owned the peace talks process. It was entirely of our own making. But we also had to bring with us our constituencies, the white and Afrikaner communities, and they had to meaningfully and soulfully make that change, from believing they were better than the next person, to seeing that they were merely their equal.

That required dismantling centuries of white supremacy in the space of a few short years. In the main, it happened but it came from individual souls who took ownership of their own futures in a process that was facilitated by a group of political leaders, who in turn determined the path their country would take by designing its future themselves. If it was to become a future for all of us, it had to be created by us alone.

Talks, negotiations, peacebuilding, empowerment of civil society, leadership, political partnerships - these are the bread and butter of Glencree - a fine institution that has had much to do with the Northern Ireland process - but whose reputation and remit now extend well beyond the borders of the island.

We celebrate Glencree's fortieth anniversary in a post-Mandela era. My former president was a giant of a leader, an icon of peace and an excellent moral compass in conflict resolution. Over the years I have participated in various peacebuilding and conflict resolution processes around the world where delegates would inevitably throw their hands despairingly into the air and tell me, 'But we don't have a Mandela to pull us through'. Of course, it was not a Mandela they ever needed but instead the sheer will and determination to trust in their own process, their ability to own it and within it, find the way to transform the hearts and minds in the direction that is required.

Once again, I borrow Mandela's words: 'You don't negotiate with your friends, you negotiate with your enemies.' As I outlined above, from your enemies come partnerships but with those partners one must continue to work on an ongoing basis. Despite the success of the South African story, there remains an obstacle to lasting peace and true democracy in our path and that is racism. In Northern Ireland, I would venture to say it is sectarianism. Without doubt, they are the two most despicable 'isms' of them all. Regrettably, they will continue to challenge our respective countries for some time to come, but they in turn must be challenged through ongoing dialogue in centres such as Glencree that are dedicated to facilitating lasting peace.

What am I willing to give up so that others may live in peace?

The Elusive Search for Reconciliation: A utopian goal, symbolic action or a sustained relational journey?

Geoffrey Corry

'Reconciliation has multiple meanings which can vary from context to context. There is also often confusion between applying the term to the relationship between two individuals and to a broader political context of conflict between groups.'

Brandon Hamber & Grainne Kelly[1]

'Reconciliation is as old as the hills and at the same time in a pre-infancy stage.'

John Paul Lederach[2]

'Peacemaking requires a marathon mentality.....In working for peace, process and outcome walk hand in hand. Unless people own the process and help shape sustainable outcomes, it will indeed be difficult to provide human security or a meaningful future.'

Ed Garcia[3]

When Una O'Higgins O'Malley peered through the locked gates of the little used buildings at the top of the beautiful Glencree valley in 1973, there was a barely audible 'Wow'. What an incredible potential these buildings would have if they were converted into a reconciliation centre! It could be a place where Catholics and Protestants could meet together, build relationships of trust and begin an essential dialogue that would create peace and justice for all. The seed of that utopian vision lay in the inspirational work of Rev. Ray Davey, founder of the Corrymeela community, who opened a centre at Ballycastle in Northern Ireland. Una felt that something similar should be happening down south. She approached her family friend Dr Garret FitzGerald, then Minister for Foreign Affairs in the Coalition government (1972-1978), to make

[1] Brandon Hamber & Grainne Kelly, *A Place for Reconciliation?: Conflict and identity in Northern Ireland, Democratic Dialogue No 18 (2005)*, p19.

[2] John Paul Lederach, *'Five qualities of practice in support of reconciliation processes'* in RG HElmick & RI Petersen (eds), *Forgivenes and Reconciliation: Religion, Public Policy and Conflict Transformation*, Templeton Foundation Press (2002), p167.

[3] Accord 13, *Owning the Process: Public participation in peacemaking, Conciliation Resources* (2002), p5.

'Peace Wall' by artist Gerald Boyle with 1000 handprints from Belfast

inquiries through the Office of Public Works (OPW) whether the buildings would be available. They were being used as a storehouse for historic geological samples, old bicycles for postmen and as a film set. The challenge for the fledgling voluntary group would be whether their utopian goal of reconciliation would remain a fictional script to heal the past or become a real engagement with the protagonists to end the conflict.

Una was a member of a newly formed group called Working for Peace chaired by Dr Ivo O'Sullivan, a UCD chemistry lecturer. It was formed out of the small number of courageous people who turned up to protest outside the Sinn Féin Dublin offices in Kevin Street against the atrocities of Bloody Friday on Friday 21st July 1972. She held up a banner: 'You Don't do This in My Name' or on another day: 'Provos – Stop Bombing Families'.[4] At least 20 car bomb explosions had been set off by the Belfast IRA Brigade on the streets of Belfast in the space of an hour.[5] It caused mayhem. Two bus stations and two railway stations were chosen as targets where large numbers of people were bound to be congregating. Nine people were killed and 130 were injured, nearly all civilians. Kevin Myers reported for RTE that: '....terrified people skulked

[4] Una O'Higgins O'Malley, *From Pardon and Protest: Memoirs from the Margins,* Arlen House (2001), p108.

[5] Bloody Friday took place almost six months after Bloody Sunday when 13 men were shot dead by British paratroopers in Derry. It came two weeks after the ending of the IRA temporary ceasefire and it provoked a further escalation in the cycle of violence. It split the nationalist community, led to working class Protestants such as David Ervine joining the UVF and caused a strenghtening of the British military presence.

in clusters, paralysed, not knowing where to go, with hundreds of children screaming amid the acres of broken glass.'[6]

Ordinary people were outraged by the slaughter of innocent civilians. In Belfast, Rev. Joe Parker (Church of Ireland Chaplain to the Belfast Mission to Seamen) set up a personal vigil called 'Witness for Peace' to protest the death of his fourteen year old son, Stephen, killed by the Bloody Friday bombs. He mounted a scoreboard showing every day the rising numbers of people killed with the headline: 'What Price Peace?', a very sobering question indeed. It goes to the heart of the identity conflict in Northern Ireland between a besieged majority Protestant community who feared the threat coming from a substantial Catholic minority, who in turn felt treated as outsiders and second class citizens.

It can be followed by another question: 'What am I willing to give up so that others may live in peace?' What price would each community – northern unionists, all nationalists living on the island and Britain – be prepared to pay politically and economically to end the conflict? Unfortunately reconciliation does not come cheap or overnight. It would take the next thirty years of further political violence and over 3,500 lives lost to work through that question to get to some measure of resolution. It involves discovering how the behaviour of your own community affects and threatens the identity of others and what changes your community is prepared to make to live in a relationship of harmony.[7] It goes even deeper. Each community has to reckon with the other's memories of past glories (Battle of the Boyne) and chosen traumas (effects of the Ulster Plantation) that creates a sense of victimhood and humiliation on both sides.[8] Out of those struggles have come orange and green narratives that make enemies of the other and lead young men to take up arms to defend their community from attacks by the other. Compared to the provoke-react cycle of violence, peacemaking is a more complex and slower process of hearing each other's story and how each side has impacted the other. Flowing from that, the orange and green narratives created through past suffering face the challenge of altering and adjusting their understandings of themselves and others in the light of today's global realities and an interdependent world. Yet look at the peace dividend and human gains achieved when violence is ended and communities can put closure on the past.

[6] Daily Telegraph, 21 July 1972

[7] Alan Falconer (Ed), *Reconciling Memories*, Columba Press (1988), p5.

[8] Vamik Volkan, *Killing in the Name of Identity: A study of bloody conflicts*, Pitchstone Publishing (2006)

The carnage of Bloody Friday in Belfast and the loss of 13 lives on Bloody Sunday in Derry/Londonderry earlier that year on 30th January 1972 in effect triggered the peace movement, north and south. Civil Rights leaders and Nobel peace prize winner John Hume had to reconsider the strategy of bringing people out on the streets for fear of causing more deaths. The question bothered John Hume a lot: at what moment do you decide to come off the streets and try to get dialogue going? The civil rights movement in Northern Ireland decided to stop their protest. They no longer had the stomach for it.

Down in Dublin, Una was surprised at how few people turned up to protest outside the Sinn Féin offices. It was small in comparison to the numbers over the next twenty years that would come out on the streets against the bombings and atrocities. What was different was the way the media picked up the tragedy of civilian deaths leading to a much greater public response:

- in Belfast, the Peace People emerged in 1976 when the three Maguire children were killed by a car that went out of control after going through a security check point
- in Enniskillen on 8th November 1987, eleven people were killed and 63 injured when the IRA bomb exploded on Remembrance Day at the cenotaph
- in Warrington (England), Tim Parry (12) and Jonathon Ball (3) in 1993 died when an IRA bomb went off in a litter bin on Bridge Street, injuring another 54 people
- in Belfast on the Shankill Road, the Provisional IRA planted a bomb at Frizzell's fish shop on 23 October 1993 killing 8 Protestant civilians and wounding more than 50 people. In the week that followed, revenge attacks by loyalists took place in a number of places, one of which was a pub in Greysteel that killed 8 civilians and wounded 13.

Forty years later, Colin Parry (father of Tim Parry) believes that what began that day in Warrington 'as an act of terrorism, led to a sea change in attitudes on both sides of the divide'.[9] Such is the transforming power of people protest. However, public demonstrations have only short term impact. They get people thinking about the

[9] From the 2013 newsletter of the Tim Parry Jonathon Ball Peace Foundation Centre in Warrington founded by Colin and Wendy Parry to promote greater understanding between Great Britain and the two parts of Ireland. The Centre was opened in 1998.

futility of violence but deeper communal attitudes rarely get changed unless followed up by inter-community relationship building where people meet and understand the other's context.

Implementing a utopian goal

For any peace protest group that stands up against political violence, the first challenge that arises is: 'What do you do after the protest?' Do you keep protesting and gather as many people as possible under a simple demand to stop the violence? That's what a housewife and mother, Susan McHugh, did when she led a 'pop up' protest of ordinary people onto the streets of Dublin to express their anger and revulsion against what happened in Warrington. She kept the message simple: 'End the violence'. However, there is a shelf life for any protest group of several weeks. It is hard to keep it going after the first month. When a protest group attempts to turn itself into a peacemaking group, they will find the going difficult. That sense of solidarity forged on the peace line may not be sufficient to hold the group together over a longer period of time to work out a peace programme and form a community committed to the cause of

Geofrey Corry

reconciliation. It is much easier to say what you are against [negative identity] than what you are for. Unfortunately there is no such thing as simple peace and the beautiful goal of reconciliation is full of complexities. So any person willing to step forward to give leadership has a huge challenging job of bringing all of this together. Somehow they need vision with substance and a strategic programme of action.

> *'What began as an act of terrorism led to a sea change in attitudes on both sides of the divide'*

For those of us in the Glencree founding group [I joined in 1975 from the Dublin Methodist Church on returning from ecumenical work in London], it took some time to work out exactly what reconciliation meant in terms of practical peace action on the ground. It was intellectually beyond us to be able to come up with a vision of what a new agreed Ireland would look like and not necessarily our role. Neither were we able to grasp the kind of process needed if we wanted to build consensus on such a big question. Nevertheless, we were fortunate to have the help of Fr Frank Purcell, an Australian Columban priest, to devise the first programme of peace action and create the concept of Peace Week. Writing thirty years later, he comments on the prevalence at that time of an exclusivist theology within churches which fuelled division and hatred between Catholics and Protestants. 'All too many saw one another not as brothers and sisters in Christ but as enemies threatening the religious and national identities of one another. The 'others' were the enemy of God and of God fearing people.'[10]

For the Corrymeela community in Belfast, the leadership issue was easier because the founder, Rev. Ray Davey (a Presbyterian chaplain at Queen's University), was able to unite a group around him as a Christian community of reconciliation.[11] In contrast, Glencree started as a multidenominational committee of about ten people made up of clergy and lay people from different churches in Dublin as well as voluntary groups like Voluntary Service International and the Ballyfermot Peace Corps. Holding everyone together was not an easy task, made more difficult by the fact that many had strong convictions, each with a different approach to reconciliation. One Council member was Lil Collins (nee Hannigan) who worked as a governess with the Le Bret family on the western outskirts of Paris during the German occupation 1940-1944. Because she spoke fluent French, she was able to cycle incognito into the city and carried coded messages for the *maquis*, the French resistance movement. She avoided arrest many times and it was this low key role that she brought to Glencree, always available to welcome people to the centre with a cup of tea. This goes to the heart of reconciliation work – providing a safe welcoming space where everyone feels at home. By sharing a meal together, so much can be discerned from the other's story.

There was a Presbyterian connection through Rev. Alan Martin of Findlater's Church on Parnell Square who served as Chairman and provided real insight to southerners on the mindset and thinking of the northern unionist.[12] Another Chair of Glencree for a number of years was Lady Eleonor Wicklow, a former Labour Party Senator.[13]

[10] Frank Purcell, *"Sharing Una's Journey"* in Enda McDonagh (ed), *Remembering to Forgive: A Tribute to Una O'Higgins O'Malley*, Veritas (2007), p25.

[11] The Corrymeela Community was formed by Ray Davey in 1966 before the Troubles began. He had served in the British army during the second World War in Italy, became a prisoner of war and was inspired by the Iona Christian Community in Scotland. He had skills of enabling and listening to others. See chapter 5 in John Morrow, *On the Road of Reconciliation: A Brief Memoir*, Columba Press (2003).

[12] Later Alan joined the Faith and Politics group and was involved in writing a significant pamphlet that examined the Calvinist theology that underpins the Orange narrative: *"Boasting: Self-Righteous Collective Superiority as a Cause of Conflict"* (1999). They published a number of thought provoking pamphlets which still have currency today. See the archives section of the Corrymeela website: www.corrymeela.org.

[13] She served as a Senator under her maiden name, Eleonor Butler.

Eleonor's motivation came from the moral rearmament movement (MRA) based in Caux in Switzerland that arose out of the efforts to bring about Franco-German reconciliation after 1945. She believed that trust is built across divides through individual change of one high level leader speaking to another. This could be called 'heart' work on a private one-to-one basis, changing individual hearts by speaking the truth to them. It is similar to the Quaker movement started by George Fox who believed that the heart of reconciliation was building a personal relationship of respect, listening and understanding, enabling antagonists to get to the point where talk about delicate matters can happen. Rachel Bewley from the Society of Friends in Dublin represented that point of view on the Glencree Council. Yet this perspective may be blind to the many structural and political changes that have to happen for identity groups to live together in a harmonious way.

Another strong voice was Una herself, for whom forgiveness was quite personal and which she saw as a crucial ingredient of reconciliation. She was only six months old when her father, Justice Minister Kevin O'Higgins[14], was assassinated on his way to mass at the corner of Cross Avenue, Blackrock, by three anti-Treaty men in July 1927. She had no memory of the family catastrophe but was told he forgave his killers. In fact, it was not until 1987 on the sixtieth anniversary of the assassination that she found out precisely what her father had said in his dying moments.[15] She was approached by Roger Gannon to tell her what his own father, Bill Gannon (one of the three gunmen), had told him. It went along the following lines: 'I forgive my murderers. I can understand why you have done it. This must be the last of the killings.' This powerful message inherited by Una from her father was clear – it had to be only about forgiveness, there should be no bitterness and there should be no more revenge.[16] It showed the ability of Kevin to understand the reasons why his enemy resorted to violence and this allowed him to resist the instinctive temptation to retaliate, so that the cycle of violence gets stopped there and then. It placed a heavy responsibility on Una's shoulders as second generation and in turn her mission and ideals got transferred

[14] Kevin O'Higgins was a member of the Free State government that executed four anti-treaty prisoners in 1922, one from each province, in a calculated move to secure public order. O'Higgins did not agree with the shootings and was a close friend of Rory O'Connor, one of those executed who took the other side in the Civil War, but went along with the collective decision of the cabinet. A double price was paid for this act. Kevin's own father was murdered in his home some miles from Stradbally, Co Laois, weeks after the execution and his family also called for forgiveness. [Una O'Higgins O'Malley, op.cit., p17-21.] During his Boundary Commission speech in the Dail debate in 1925, O'Higgins forthrightly stated his views in a rhetorical fashion: "We stand not for the perpetuation of hatred, but for the rooting up and elimination of old hatreds, old furies and the quenching of old fires".

[15] Una also learned from Roger Gannon the identity of the other two gun men who killed her father - Tim Coughlin and Archie Doyle along with Bill Gannon – who all took the republican side of being against the Anglo-Irish Treaty of 1921. Also see Brian Frost, *Women and Forgiveness*, Fount Paperbacks/Collins (1990).

[16] Una O'Higgins O'Malley, op.cit., p15.

to the Glencree steering committee. The 1987 encounter between Roger Gannon and Una was in itself a profound moment of interpersonal reconciliation that happened out of the public eye and demonstrates the power of the second generation to heal the wounds of political violence. If it was not possible for Bill Gannon, who went to work in London after the event, to meet directly with the O'Higgins family, then his son found the courage to connect with Una. A memorial mass of reconciliation was celebrated in July 1987 by Fr Enda McDonagh at the Booterstown church for the families involved.

'I forgive my murderers. I can understand why you have done it. This must be the last of the killings.'

The task of understanding the true nature of reconciliation - the linkages between truth recovery and justice, the melting of hearts at the moment of mutual acceptance, the subtleties and experience of repentance and forgiveness - was more difficult in the seventies and eighties when peacemaking as a professional field was in its infancy. There were few books and institutes around at that time other than theological works to help get clarity of thought about such an intangible and often indefinable concept. At times this created a cloud of woolliness, vagueness and uncertainty. Yet it was a powerful aspiration that many of us yearned for against a background where Ireland was going through huge social change after Vatican II and having to cope with the Hunger Strikes in the Maze prison (1979-81). Educated young people who joined Glencree were antagonistic to a 'churchy' view of reconciliation and wanted something at a more human level without the religion that went with it. At the 1980 New Year's Day think-in, where members were free to speak their mind, one member said: 'It should not be Glencree's task to re-convert people to the Christian faith.'[17] Should we not also be drawing on the wisdom of the Hindu, Moslem and atheistic views of reconciliation?

Inevitable tensions grew between the different viewpoints in a healthy way and it took some time for cohesion to emerge. Every group needs someone to act as a facilitator either formally or informally if it wants to arrive at a shared common starting point. It

[17] Quoted in Geoffrey Corry, *The Priority of Reconciliation: Rediscovering our calling,* Paper prepared for Glencree Council, March 1983.

fell to Rachel Bewley to demonstrate a consensus approach to making decisions which was normal practice in the Society of Friends. For some, principles of inclusiveness, mutual acceptance and working with difference was not an easy experience because the flip side of consensus making, of course, is that it slows down decision making until there is a sense of agreement among all. We all had to discover how to be patient with each other.

The lack of consensus on whether Glencree Centre was a place of Christian worship,[18] a Christian community similar to Corrymeela, or a secular group committed to peacebuilding projects created much tension and began to immobilise the council. For those who were committed Christians, they felt inhibited when it came to prayer and were reluctant to worship at the Centre. It could have led to fragmentation were it not for the high level of respect and esteem built up between members and the solidarity they shared around the peace task. Fr Denis Greene, a Marist priest who joined in the late 70's, explained how he found Glencree in reality: 'Whatever about the intentions of some of the founders and the word 'Christian' in the constitution, Glencree was not *in fact* a Christian organisation. It was pluralist in respect to religious faith as with respect to many other aspects of life. The business of the community would be to enrich its members from their own diversity, to practice tolerance and mutual acceptance as equal human beings and to propagate this attitude.' He then went on to add an important caveat: 'So if we in Glencree stay at the level of getting people to discuss, to explore emotions and become more aware of themselves and each other.... and neglect to relate all that to the basic faith and aspirations of so many people, we are up a gum tree'.[19] Certainly Glencree was ahead of its time in exploring how pluralism works in practice - how different traditions could be at ease with each other in the same room rather than being a threat. Yet the point that Denis was making is that Glencree could not be so far ahead that it lost the connection with the mainstream Catholic and Protestant communities.

But what would happen if the differing positions did not blend – that people found they were not comfortable in being in the same room together? Una wrestled with this problem and reflected at the time: 'Are we to believe then that it is impossible to form a true community at Glencree, in the North, or in the whole of our island? Or to put

[18] Glencree was presented with the cross of nails by Coventry Cathedral to honour its work of reconciliation within the Christian tradition, along with Corrymeela.

[19] Geoffrey Corry, ibid 1983

things another way, if in Glencree an honest community could be formed from these two elements without damage to the integrity of either, could we begin to hope that we might have some suggestions to make to others who search for community across seemingly insoluble positions?'[20] Essential to a way out of the internal conflict was the realisation that the group had to have continued hope and belief in itself, to respect the other's expression of the truth as they see it and not feel the need for any apology from one group to the other for saying what was important for them. 'So when we meet', suggested Una, 'some will pray openly to God whom they know to be the truth supported by the accepted silence of others who will want to retire into themselves calling on their own reserves of fidelity to truth in the service of reconciliation. At other times, there will be special quiet periods when all together can search in their own hearts for truth in silence with no formal prayer being offered.'[21] The practice of meeting together in a reflective circle was introduced where all could be heard and acknowledged.

Little did we know at that time we were actually working with deep human themes - of holding the tension between distancing the other and mutual acceptance (Martin Buber [22]) and building the capacity in ourselves for processing exclusion and embrace (Miroslav Volf [23]). It would have been wonderful to have such mentors in the room with us as we struggled to name what was going on between us! The eventual outcome was to appoint Una O'Higgins O'Malley herself as the Leader of Glencree to bring cohesion to the effort to create a community of reconciliation and she served until the closure of the Centre in 1988 for financial reasons. Some of these issues were explored further by the Faith and Politics Group, of which Una was a member with Rev. John Morrow (also a Glencree Council member when he was Presbyterian Chaplain in Dublin and a future Corrymeela Leader).

Multiple dimensions of reconciliation

Having sat through many hours of discussions about reconciliation and engaged as a process facilitator with opposing groups, it remains a challenge to pin down the dimensions of this elusive concept that makes practical sense. Much of the literature on inter-group reconciliation describes it as a post-conflict activity that comes after an accord like the Belfast/Good Friday Agreement of 1998. Does that mean it cannot

[20] Geoffrey Corry, ibid 1983

[21] Geoffrey Corry, ibid 1983

[22] Martin Buber was a Viennese Jewish philosopher (1878-1965) committed to I-Thou dialogue and the mutuality of acceptance. Two of his books are *"Between Man and Man"* (1947) and *"I and Thou"* (1958).

[23] Miroslav Volf grew up in Croatia before the break up of Yugoslavia and was taught by the German theologian Jurgen Moltman in Tubingen. Often described as a theologian "on the bridge", his most important work is Í Abingdon Press (1996) which was written against the background of the Bosnian war.

happen in the pre-negotiation phase? This is where the South African definition is helpful. They describe it as both a goal and a process.[24] These two dimensions speak to my experience - a vertical goal that serves as an inspiration for those caught in violent conflict and a sustained horizontal process that is patiently built between estranged groups whenever circumstances allow them to meet. Diagram 1 below presents them as a reconciliation diamond to hold the active tension between these two dimensions.

Diagram 1: The Reconciliation Diamond: multiple dimensions

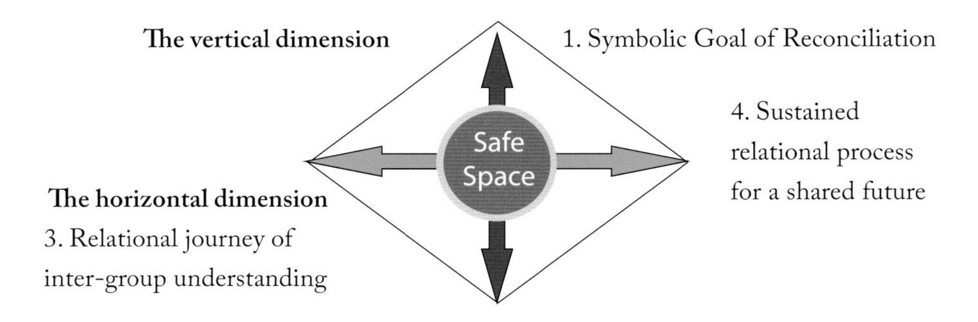

2. Symbolic action on the ground

Reflecting back on the first twenty years of Glencree's work in the seventies and eighties, the vertical dimension dominated because dialogue was not always possible. We probably were unaware of how the continued violence impacted on civil society, leaving us all in a place of 'learned helplessness'. This struck me forcibly when twenty years later I was in a local workshop with a group of Colombian *campesinos* who had to live with violence from all three sides at different times in their village – the Farc guerrillas, the AUC paramilitaries and the government troops. A farmer pondered the question: 'What can you do when there is nothing you can do?' A sense of powerlessness and hopelessness prevailed among them following years of brutalisation. Often we don't know what to do apart from providing emotional support and lighting a candle in the darkness – the ultimate symbol of hope. Holding on to the aspiration of reconciliation prevents groups from being dragged down into reactive conflict.

[24] Report of the Truth and reconciliation Commission of South Africa (1999), volume 1, p104. See other considerations of reconciliation in Hamber & Kelly (2005) and David Bloomfield, On Good Terms: Clarifying Reconciliation, Berghof Report No 14, available at www.berghof-center.org/

Reconciliation as symbolic action

I was involved with Una in organising two Walks of Remembrance through the streets of Dublin in 1981 and 1983 as part of Peace Week which was always held in the week before St Patrick's Day.[25] The walks started out at St Patrick's Cathedral where the dead of two world wars were remembered with the words: 'Though they were divided in life, let us remember them together in death.' Up to that point there was little official commemoration of the Irish men who gave their lives fighting for the various Irish regiments on the continent. The next stop was down the hill and across the river at the Four Courts to remember those who died on both sides of the Civil War. The final stop was the GPO in O'Connell Street where those killed in 1916 on both sides were remembered but also those who died in the War of Independence, those killed by the Dublin and Monaghan bombs in 1974 and finally those killed in the Troubles north and south. Several hundred people took part in the walk and wreaths of shamrocks in the form of a shamrock were laid in each place by distinguished people - General Collins-Powell, Siobhan McKenna and Cyril Cusack. It was the first time that all these wars and violent deaths were honoured together. Collins-Powell told Una: 'I always wanted to find a place to do it.' Today the Irish government has a national day of remembrance in July at Kilmainham to do something similar. It has often been described by participants as a deeply moving experience.

Another example of symbolic leadership was the ecumenical services of worship held in Leeson Park Church during Peace Week where church and civic leaders committed themselves to reconciliation. At a time when the Churches were exclusivist in Northern Ireland, not allowing their members to attend each other's services of worship, Una wanted to bring Catholics and Protestants together to build relationships of trust. It was a statement that in the face of the violence, Protestants and Catholics must work together to overcome the hatred between them, no longer seeing each other as enemies and threatening each other's religious and national identities.[26] When Una organised an ecumenical event in St Patrick's Cathedral in September 1979 on the day that Pope John Paul II was in Dublin, there was huge disappointment when he did not turn up, but it was not included in the official itinerary.

[25] Geoffrey Corry & Caroline Mitchell (eds), *Glencree Centre for Reconciliation: The first ten years, Glencree* (1984)

[26] Frank Purcell, *'Sharing Una's Journey'* in Enda McDonagh (ed), *Remembering to Forgive: A Tribute to Una O'Higgins O'Malley,* Veritas (2007). p21

Symbolic actions on the ground can therefore have a significant impact in keeping the vision and principle of reconciliation alive as well as keeping up the morale of peacemakers. Baby step actions like walks and ecumenical services are not only a sign of what could be in the future but they also show leaders representing different traditions cooperating together in public in a spirit of collegiality.

Reconciliation as a sustained relational journey

Moving to the second dimension, the horizontal process is more relational and interactive. It attempts to transform estrangement and enmity through the forging of new understandings and insights by hearing each other's stories. The visit by Dr Adam Curle (a veteran Quaker mediator and first head of Bradford University Peace Studies) to Glencree in 1981 switched on a new light for us. He said ever so quietly that 'reconciliation involved the building of a new relationship of understanding through an act of love, compassion or restitution'. It took some time for us to work out the meaning of that statement. What was different about Curle's definition was its emphasis on the horizontal process – the relational journey that each must make toward hearing the story of the other, to connect with the fears they have of the other and to their sense of historic suffering or grievance. Diagram 2 plots some of these essential steps. Reconciliation comes on foot of working through fear and hatred and addressing issues of past incidents of injustice and violent abuse. Protagonists are supported to reach out to their enemy, to listen to their story in the circle and hear the suffering that drives the hatred, bitterness and revenge.

Diagram 2: Steps and tasks of a horizontal intergroup reconciliation process

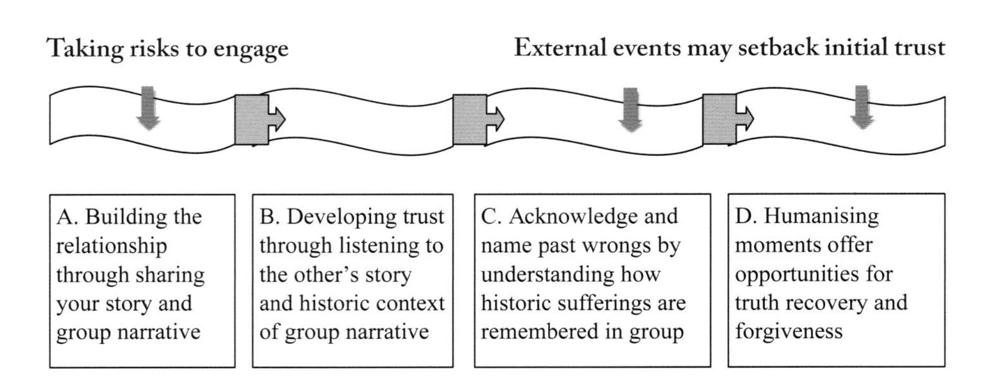

More discussion of Step D is required to break it down into sub-steps. For the moment, we will leave it to the poetic imagination of Nobel Laureate Seamus Heaney who not only believed politically but also urged and hoped 'for a great sea change/On the far side of revenge/...that a further shore is reachable from here.'[27] Forgiveness is a sea change moment and without it the longer journey to reconciliation is unlikely to happen.

Other peace groups tended to steer clear of engaging with politicians or controversial political issues but Judy Hayes, another leading member of the Council in the 70s, ensured that northern political voices were heard down south, particularly Unionist and Loyalist parties. This initiative was different to a faith-based approach working mainly with Protestant and Catholic issues. Panels of politicians were convened to update audiences in the south about party positions on the conflict. In 1980, she brought down Andy Tyrie and Glen Barr of the Ulster Political Research Group (UPRG) to present their document 'Beyond the Religious Divide' at a private meeting at Glencree. Among the politicians present was Dr Garret Fitzgerald, who made a serious economic critique of their case for Northern Ireland independence. Even though Fitzgerald discounted the economic viability of independence, he admired their new political thinking while the loyalist leaders were very impressed by his sincerity and honesty.

Glencree's inclusive dialogue work emerged out of these early events.[28] This represented a shift from the early years of being a protest group to one of facilitator of dialogue, which reflected my own journey in becoming a professional mediator from the late 80s onwards. At times it was not easy explaining to the international volunteers who came to live at the Centre for a year that Glencree could not protest on the streets about the latest atrocity or be an advocate for human rights. We stayed neutral, refrained from public comment but reflected among ourselves. Somehow, unknown to ourselves, we had slowly become incognito Quakers.

Ian White, the new Glencree CEO got the Centre re-opened in the summer of 1994 after Colin Murphy and his committee managed to get new funding from Atlantic Philanthropies, the Rowntree Trust and the Department of Foreign Affairs (ROI).

[27] From Seamus Heaney, *The Cure at Troy: A version of Sophocles' Philoctetes,* Faber (1990).

[28] In another political initiative, Judy found funding for a significant three day conference held in Belfast in March 1981 in association with Professor Des Rea and John Hunter of Corrymeela. It brought together political scientists to explore how the political themes of consociation and federalism, in operation in countries like Belgium, might be applied to Northern Ireland. It encouraged new thinking beyond the confines of the Westminster majoritarian model to see how minorities can become included in political structures. The papers were later published in a book. Desmond Rea (Ed), *Political Cooperation in Divided Societies: A series of papers relevant to the conflict in Northern Ireland,* Gill & Macmillan (1982).

The first Summer School was held in August with perfect timing. Within days there was the IRA ceasefire followed by the Loyalist ceasefire in October. Gusty Spence made a remarkable statement expressing 'true remorse'. The guns having been put down, it became more possible to have inclusive dialogue free from the fear of violence and intimidation.

There are descriptions elsewhere in this publication about the political dialogue workshops that got underway after the ceasefires of 1994 and the LIVE workshops with victims/survivors that happened after the Good Friday Agreement. Both created many humanising moments in the formal sessions as well as on the informal margins that led to opportunities for interpersonal forgiveness and intergroup reconciliation. Some experiences have been captured in the short film 'Brothers in Arms'[29] of those victims and ex-combatants who were willing to tell their story to camera. These personal journeys are never easy and they encounter ups and downs at regular intervals depending on what is happening in the external world. They also ebb and flow depending on the energy levels of people and their ability to work through past trauma. We came to realise over the years, 'the soft stuff is the hard stuff'. Wilhelm Verwoerd and Alastair Little found the following statement by Carl Jung helpful in motivating those who stepped out on the journey: 'The only way out is through'.[30]

Deeper layer of Reconciliation

While much progress has been made in implementing the Belfast/Good Friday Agreement at the high level, more work remains to be done in deepening the reconciliation process so that it reaches down to local communities. There is considerable despair at present among seasoned community workers in Belfast who have sought to build better relationships in interface areas, some of whom would have been to Glencree. One loyalist community worker has warned: 'There is a massive job of work to be done in tackling the root causes of sectarianism. And if we don't succeed, my fear is that a significant upturn in dissident republican violence will almost inevitably lead to a mirror-image response within the loyalist community. Parading is a massive issue for Protestants/unionists/loyalists and it could so easily be used as a catalyst for people opposed to a peace process.... Because if [the Assembly's Cohesion,

[29] A 20 minute film produced by Glencree (2008) showing the journey to South Africa of a joint group of victims/survivors and ex-combatants which took them to an overnight stay on Robben Island to visit Mandela's cell and a 5 day wilderness trail in the Drakensberg mountains.

[30] Alistair Little and Wilhelm Verwoerd, *Journey through Conflict Trail Guide: Introduction,* published online www.trafford.com (2013) p6.

Sharing and Integration document] is not brought forward and is not implemented on the ground, I have a fear that we will see a repeat of the cycle of Irish violence.'[31]

We still have a long way to go for local communities not to feel threatened but secure in their identity and in their local area, sufficient for the peace walls to come down. It begs the question: What is the link between sectarianism and continued segregation? Sectarianism and animosity remain systemic, pervasive and zero-sum, with a good deal of hate beneath the surface. Which is cause and effect? Does sectarianism drive segregation or is it the other way round? Liechty and Clegg remind us that sectarianism is deeply buried in communal memory where nationalism merged with religion on both sides.[32] Embedded within the orange and green narratives are collective memories attached to traumatic events in the life of each community. The story contains 'narrative truth' that helps us understand where each community comes from and where they stand in relationship to the other group.

A bottom down approach

Recently I was involved in a workshop where the Israeli Ambassador to the Vatican, 'Motty' Mordecai Lewy, talked about the top down approach of the Oslo peace accord had not been successful because it did not go deep enough to bring Israeli and Palestinian civil society into the political agreement. Coming at the end of his long diplomatic career, he believed that 'meeting the other' at civil society level was essential if you want to solve a protracted conflict as opposed to just managing it. He believed this was the missing bit – calling it the 'bottom down approach' – which was about going beyond politics to work at the sub-text of politics involving issues of religion and ethnic identity. He was not aware that he had made a Freudian slip until we pointed it out to him! He had meant to say a 'bottom up approach' which is known as Track III in the conflict resolution field. Yet the phrase stuck in my mind.

There is a need for much greater appreciation of how trauma is not just an individual experience arising out of personal injury and emotional shock. The collective hurt that is still there in both communities from past events gets transferred from one generation to another. We now know that if it is not addressed and processed in this generation, then the wounds will not heal and become recycled through pervasive

[31] Loyalist talking anonymously to Michael Hall, pamphlet 102, page 6

[32] Joseph Liechty and Cecelia Clegg, *Moving Beyond Sectarianism: Religion, Conflict and Reconciliation in Northern Ireland,* Columba Press (2001), Chapters 2 and 3.

sectarianism into the next generation. In an attempt to visualise this phenomenon, I have added a hidden underbelly to the reconciliation diamond [see Diagram 3]. In this basement area, painful memories and old hurts are locked away in the underworld of unconsciousness.

Diagram 3: The Underbelly of the Reconciliation Diamond

The two previous diagrams have shown the interconnection between the vertical and horizontal dimensions held together at the centre by safe space – like when Glencree was a community of reconciliation in its first phase (1974-1988) or a peacebuilding network hub in its second phase (1994-2008).

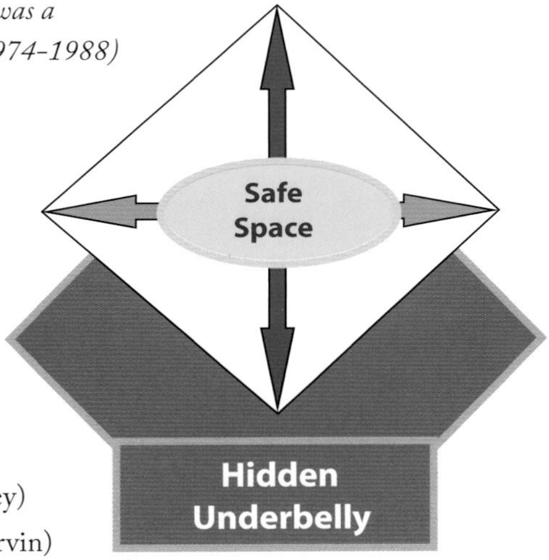

Deeper Reconciliation through the Bottom Down Approach

Overcoming and processing collective trauma held within a taught narrative:

- transgenerational nature of sectarianism
- historic resentments from past suffering
- 'the festering wound of memory' (Heaney)
- 'remembered history and bitterness' (Garvin)

Safe Space

Hidden Underbelly

Others have captured it better. In that same poem about the Trojan Horse of Troy, Heaney works with 'the festering wound of memory' and explores the tension of holding onto the wound and the hope for a cure.[33] In talking about the enormous gamble that Taoiseach Sean Lemass took in January 1965 to go north to meet Prime Minister Terence O'Neill, historian Tom Garvin wrote that Lemass 'was trying to transcend or bypass a considerable amount of remembered history, bitterness and political passion'.[34] The problem is that while politicians want to bypass it so as to get there quicker, the nature of the sectarian beast is that, in the words of the loyalist PUP leader, David Ervine, it is 'a taught process' of unwritten rules taught from an early age. In the deep political discussions that took place in the Maze prison with Gusty Spence, Davy discovered that political reality was more complex and what he needed

[33] I am grateful to Paul Arthur for this phrase from Heaney's poem, *The Cure at Troy.*

[34] Tom Garvin, *Judging Lemass, The Measure of the Man.* Royal Irish Academy (2009), p6.

was 'a thought process', to re-think what he had been taught. How could he hate a Catholic if he had never met one? It was a political journey he was prepared to make and he stands out as a hero in a land of limited political will.

Elusive yet attainable

A cornerstone of the Belfast Agreement is parity of esteem - a concept that means peaceful co-existence in a shared physical space based on respect for the other community. While the Haass/O'Sullivan proposals of December 2013 have not been accepted by the unionist parties, they provide a number of political solutions to the unfinished business of the peace process. There is still a lot of reconciliation work to be done to create the macro political infrastructure where estranged groups can work together on the legacy of the past and ensure the political violence does not happen again.

One of the great strengths of the Peace Education programme was its flexibility

Learning Peace: Schools, Youth and Adults

Eamon Rafter

'Peace education can definitely help to provide the requisite inspiration and direction to move beyond a culture of violence to envisioning and working toward a better world for all' [1]

Programmes and projects that emphasise learning have been a significant element of Glencree's work over the past fifteen years. As a way to offer the insights gained from other programmes to the wider society and present more general understandings of what might help peacebuilding at a civil society level, learning provides a way to

[1] Cabezudo, A & Haavelsrud, M. *'Rethinking Peace Education'* in *Handbook of Peace and Conflict Studies,* 2007. Ed Webel,C. & Galtung, J. Routledge, London/New York

broaden the impact of the work we have been involved in. It allows it to be presented in a way that is both relevant to specific groups and accessible in many different formats. Whether this takes the form of 'peace education', 'conflict transformation skills' or a presentation of the historical experience of the peace process on the island of Ireland, all these education initiatives have played a role in extending the reach of the organisation. We now need to reflect on what we have achieved in this area and what we have learnt that will inform future work. This overview of a varied body of work at schools, youth and adult levels, aims to describe some of this work and critically explore some of the key lessons learnt to inform our future work in this area.

Peace Education in Glencree

A definition of 'peace education' in a Glencree context and why we feel it is important to be engaged in this work is my starting point. Glencree's learning suggests that conflict is inevitable but violence is not, so we need to help people learn how to manage and even transform conflict through dialogue and other available means as part of the process of developing a 'culture of peace'.

Education has an important role to play in the creation of such a culture. In order to prevent or diminish the option of violence we need to offer young people and adults the understanding, knowledge and skills to help them deal with conflict creatively and in a non-violent way and explore ideas about 'peace' and 'reconciliation'. However, peace education is not only about different concepts of peace and what is taught, but also about how you teach and the context within which this takes place.[2] So, the Glencree context and values are very important as part of our understanding of peace education.

The rationale and need for peace education comes from the legacy of violence, historical divisions in Irish society in terms of north/south, segregation in Northern Ireland and the challenge of developing an increasingly multi-cultural society where inclusivity is seen as vital. Even in the context of moving beyond violence, through a peace process in Northern Ireland, we still have a long way to go to develop such a culture. Learning programmes are, therefore, a means to bring a wider participation into the process of healing and reconciliation. Peace education is also about providing a future

[2] Cabezudo, A & Haavelsrud, M. *'Rethinking Peace Education'* in Handbook of Peace and Conflict Studies, 2007. Ed Webel,C. & Galtung, J. Routledge, London/New York

The U.N. has defined a 'Culture of Peace' as:
'all the values, attitudes and forms of behaviour that reflect respect for life, for human dignity and for human rights, the rejection of violence in all its forms and commitment to the principles of freedom, justice, solidarity, tolerance and understanding between people.'

orientation about 'shared futures' where notions of interdependence and developing good relationships are central. Glencree is in a position to provide this experience at schools, community and university levels where trained facilitators are able to engage with real needs to provide a transformative experience. The development of critical thinkers who are curious and open to learning about how to deal with conflict in their own lives and how conflict can impact on communities locally and globally is at the heart of this.

Working with Schools & Youth Groups

Working with young people and 'peace education' had been central in the early days of Glencree. In the 1970s, schools and youth groups had come in significant numbers to the Centre and it was seen as essential to offer young people a say about the future world in which they would live. Later on, a newsletter from 1986 defined the aim as 'for each young person to realise his or her own potential as a peace worker for the peaceful future of the world' and it was mentioned that the 'harvest time of our endeavours at Glencree may not be for some years after'.[3] Have we now reached this harvest time and what are the achievements in this area that we can build on?

In the early 1990s, the formative years of the Peace Education Programme for Schools and Youth Groups, Glencree offered opportunities to learn about peacebuilding and reconciliation to primary and secondary schools as well as youth groups. There was a primary focus on Northern Ireland especially after the Good Friday Agreement and increasingly links were developed with schools north of the border. In those initial years, it was essential for Glencree to shine a light on the implications of the peace process which offered a way forward after so many years of the Troubles. For

[3] From *'Glencree News'* August 1986

reconciliation to become real, young people in the Republic of Ireland needed to be more aware of historical developments north of the border and cross-border work would also be essential.

In 2002, the goals of the Schools Programme were articulated as:

- To prepare young people for their role as young, autonomous, participative and responsible members of society

- To help young people develop inclusive mindsets, assist them in learning about their role in peacebuilding and facilitate them in addressing issues that must be confronted on the journey towards reconciliation

These objectives were taken on through visits to schools and overnight residential courses at Glencree, which, in 2002, were attended by 2,125 students. Skills development workshops were held with facilitators who also undertook study visits to Northern Ireland. Also in this period cross-border, cross-community youth weekends took place to develop this learning and bring people from different backgrounds together. In this way young people who had been involved at schools level could continue afterwards and gain further experience. Much of the methodology developed out of youth work approaches that allowed for active learning and specific activities that required participants to be directly engaged in the process were developed. The fact that many of the young people wanted to continue into the youth project suggests that there was a real desire to be involved in this kind of learning.

> 'Education for reconciliation is about learning self-respect and respect for other people especially if they come from different cultural traditions. It is also about understanding how individuals and communities depend on each other, how co-operation between them can be fostered in practical ways and how conflict can be resolved.'

Resources were required to cover such themes and these were developed to support the learning. Themes defined were: communication; problem-solving; identity and social action and these were related to the school curriculum at levels appropriate to the age and subject range of each group. Team-building and leadership were also areas that were considered important and these were covered in group-work settings. The first of these resources was *Worlds Apart?*, a comprehensive set of activities exploring elements of peacebuilding and reconciliation at personal, local, national and global levels. It also included conflict-related resources and action project ideas. The second resource was *Northern Ireland - A Place Apart?*, which was developed by Glencree and 80:20 to explore conflict, peace and reconciliation within and between these islands. The packs were also made available as a support to teachers who wanted to do class work on these themes. Ulster Bank had also sponsored the development of a resource centre in Glencree to provide a range of materials for students and teachers or researchers who wanted to access information on Northern Ireland or more general conflict-related themes.

Participants from Bridges Project in Belfast 2014

Some of the early youth work projects at this stage featured a Romanian exchange visit in 2001 and a multi-lateral exchange in Slovakia. Other countries taking part were Spain and Britain and one of the core themes was whether 'terrorists should be included or excluded in peace processes'. The Tim Parry Scholarship led to a project with what was then the Peace Centre in Warrington, UK, a partnership that was to develop over a number of years. There were also opportunities for young people from North and South to learn about Alternative Dispute Resolution with the Canadian practitioner Liz Iwaskiw.

Under the guidance of Hugh Doyle and Sean O'Boyle, Glencree developed sound foundations in peace education and the geographical spread of the work expanded to include schools throughout Ireland as well as cross-border work. A pilot scheme to allow follow-up visits to schools in the greater Dublin area was developed to deepen the experience of the students. Fund-raising was needed to meet the costs of the work, but it was clear that a strategic approach was emerging and the facilitators identified strongly with the broader mission of the organisation. There was a demand for the service offered as it was not easy to access such programmes elsewhere. International volunteers also played an important role as many came from education backgrounds or were interested in working with young people.

Consolidating the Peace Education Programme

In 2004, funding was secured from the International Fund for Ireland (IFI) through the Community Bridges Programme, to run a structured schools programme. Conn Mulvenna took over as manager to consolidate and build upon the significant achievements of the previous decade. A strong team of facilitators were supported by Claudia Bradshaw and later, Sorcha Tormey, as the programme developed high-quality, progressive learning opportunities in peace education that were relevant to the National Curriculum. Considerable work was done to make the workshops offered more relevant to subjects like Religion and CSPE, which made the one and two-day programmes more attractive to schools. The funding allowed for teacher substitution costs to be covered, which made it easier for schools to visit Glencree. One of the comments made about the new programme by a facilitator was *'There has been a dramatic transformation…it used to be a series of exercises with no purpose or learning objectives – it was very ad hoc but it has come on leaps and bounds – there are clear learning objectives now'.*

The development of clear guidelines and intended outcomes meant that the aims of the work were more defined and progress could be measured.

However, there were many elements of this more structured programme which required an emphasis on values that are a key characteristic of the Glencree methodology. The students remained very much at the centre of the process; their needs were the most important aspect of the work. Safety was inherent and ground rules agreed with the participants to ensure this safety. Garda vetting for all those working in the programme and child protection policy and training were also prioritised. The methodologies used meant that learners were active and engaged as much as possible and outdoor group activities were used where possible. This work could not have been done in the same way within schools and the site of Glencree offered something unique.

The IFI funding opportunity also extended to cross-border work. The programme provided appropriate and relevant cross-border learning opportunities for young people, their schools, their teachers and, to some extent, their communities through the North South Schools Link Programme. Although this took a while to get off the ground, significant progress was made in developing a good quality programme

> *'One of the great strengths of the Peace Education programme was its flexibility. There was scope for facilitators to adapt sessions on themes such as conflict resolution, social justice, or leadership and relate them to the issues emerging in that particular group of young people. Links were continually created between the interpersonal and the global. The programme drew on the diverse backgrounds of facilitators and international volunteers whilst maintaining adherence to the core values and methodologies that define the way we work at Glencree.'*
>
> Louise Keating (Schools & Youth Facilitator)

Conn Mulvenna at Art of Hosting 2008

in 2006-2008 and the two main links were Monaghan/Craigavon and Moville & Limavady/Letterkenny. Given that most of the other schools work was of a single identity nature, this aspect of the programme provided a much-needed opportunity to link schools across the border and develop relationships between the schools.

Youth work continued during the period with the continuation of the Tim Parry programme and groups coming to Glencree on a regular basis, through Northern Ireland youth organisations like Springboard. These workshops allowed for inputs from local youth groups and extended the idea of partnership through cross-border work, a key way of developing this dimension of learning.

An external evaluation of all the programme work was commissioned at the end of the IFI funding cycle. This was carried out by Tony Macaulay of Macaulay Associates in 2008 and evidenced many examples of high quality learning outcomes in the programme. The sustained nature of the work in the North/South Schools Link and the excellent cross-border learning opportunities were highlighted. Also, 'appropriate and relevant learning methodologies and materials on peace education suitable for a range of user groups and in a variety of formats were acknowledged. [4] However, it was noticed that Glencree had not managed to develop strategic relationships with other

[4] *PEP Final Evaluation,* 2008, Tony Macaulay

agencies to promote the mainstreaming of peace education and that the emphasis on short visits and high numbers - rather than more intensive whole schools initiatives - might need to be reconsidered. One of the challenges to the programme had always been this sense of working on the fringes while continuing to make the case for peace education. Schools could only make space for this where there was a route in from the curriculum and there was a need for agency support to broaden the basis for this. At the end of the funding cycle in 2008, Conn Mulvenna moved on to work with Kilcranny House. He had made a huge contribution to Glencree and there was great sadness on hearing of his premature death in 2012. It is so important that our tribute to him involves building on his achievements and continuing this work.

'We start with a contract of respect and confidentiality, so we feel safe to discuss openly, learn to trust each other, gain confidence'.

'Outdoor activities in beautiful Glencree grounds and surroundings encourage us to co-operate in teams, to rely on each other - we also have lots of fun'.

'We learn from Peace and Justice modules how much we need these in our world, our country, our communities our classrooms. We realise the value of understanding others, respecting different cultures, customs, beliefs, the need for mediation and conflict resolution'.

Notes from participants in Peace Education

Developing Learning at Glencree

I started working at Glencree in 2005 and one of the initial objectives was to develop the role of learning generally within the organisation. It was felt that we had a lot to share and that this could be made available to a wide range of groups through courses in Glencree and across the island. We also wanted to offer a better learning experience to the international volunteers who made such a contribution to the organisation. A programme was developed to offer them a learning space and also get direct access to programmes. Though such opportunities for volunteers remained limited due to other demands on their time, there was a growing acceptance in the organisation that learning should play a bigger role in the volunteer experience. Glencree needed to become a learning organisation and to place a greater value on education in the non-formal sense.

Not only did the students develop conflict resolution skills and gain a deeper knowledge of war and peace issues nationally and internationally, but many of them either initiated or got involved in youth projects aimed at connecting with young people in conflict situations and supporting peace and justice. A good example here is Ballinteer Community School which brought a group of students to Glencree for some workshops in 2006.

In the process, they learned about Gaza/Palestine and the impact of the conflict there on the lives of young people. Having done that and following the visit to the West Bank by some of their teachers, the students decided to work together and help raise the necessary funding to embark on a youth exchange programme with Palestinian students from the City of Jenin in the West Bank, which experienced horrific violence and destruction in 2002 by the Israeli army, and to link up also with other young participants from Belfast. The learning that the students gained first at Glencree about Palestinian youth and the conflict issues there, the peace project that developed after, and the lasting friendships and connections between the participants from Palestine and Ireland North and South all point clearly and significantly to the positive potential and achievements of the Peace Education Programme at Glencree

Yaser Alashqar (Schools & Youth Facilitator)

Accreditation was an issue in the delivery of programmes for adults at Glencree, so we applied for, and gained FETAC (Further Education & Training Awards Council) provider status, which allowed us to offer a recognised qualification for some of our courses. A number of volunteers took the Conflict Management module and this was also offered to individuals and groups through intensive courses at Glencree.

Courses in Facilitation Skills, Peace Journalism and Principled Negotiations were also offered. Geoffrey Corry's course in 'Conflict Resolution, Mediation and Peacemaking Skills' continued to be offered and many volunteers also participated in it. We were also able to tailor courses for the specific needs of organisations and community groups. As such, Glencree began to work with trainee teachers, social workers, drug workers and different state bodies working with young people at risk and also in school completion areas where conflict issues presented a challenge. The profile of the organisation was extended by providing training opportunities that involved wider groups of people. The methodology used was best practice in learner-centred adult education, where the experience of all participants offers something to the group and the critical reflective process creates new possibilities to apply the learning. Although the mission of the organisation did not emphasise education and facilities were often still inadequate, adult education offered a new dimension - especially with the possibility of residential programmes.

Another continuing aspect of training programmes at Glencree has been the programmes we run for university students at undergraduate and post-graduate levels. For many years, the School for International Training (SIT), based in Vermont, US, has run semester long courses in Transformation of Social and Political Conflict in Ireland with a residential element at Glencree and key input from our staff. We have provided inputs on approaches to Conflict Transformation, as well as insights based on the specific practical dimensions of our work.

Glencree offers a unique perspective on practical peacebuilding work that is valued by many universities. We deliver workshops and modules for Irish School of Ecumenics, Trinity College Dublin, and many other colleges from Ireland, European countries and the U.S. We also hope that our strategic partnership with universities will provide further opportunities to develop this aspect of our work with Irish and international students. This is a key part in sharing Glencree's learning from our programmes over the past twenty years.

Youth work and work with young adults continue to be important areas of engagement.

We have reconnected with the Foundation for Peace in Warrington in recent years in the Tim Parry Leadership Development Programme and done some focused work around identity, conflict resolution and leadership skills. We have also partnered with Corrymeela in the Bridges Programme to bring young people from north and south together to explore areas they have in common and understand some of their differences. Glencree provides an ideal location for this work and there is still something special about bringing groups together here.

Participants during visit to Flanders, Belgium, 2013

Schools work remains a priority and still takes place at Glencree, though in the last few years we have not been able to offer residential programmes and now have to pass on the full cost to the schools, which makes it more difficult for them to visit us. We have been offering workshops in leadership, mentoring and restorative practices and hope to work more intensively with some of the schools in the Dublin region with a view to linking them again with their northern counterparts. We may not be able to work with the numbers we used to, but hopefully there will be new opportunities to go into greater depth in the future. Collaborations such as with organisations like COMPASS, representing the minority religions' schools in Ireland have continued to be important. We are also able to visit schools in the Dublin region to talk about peacebuilding work and focus on specific themes of interest to them, which often tie in with development-related projects in which they are involved.

Partnership has been a key feature of the learning and training work we have been involved in, in recent years. Programmes like Journeys Out (2009 -11) connected us with INCORE (University of Ulster) PRG, Derry and INTERCOMM, Belfast. This was an EU PEACE III funded initiative aimed at building the capacity of emerging community leaders in NI and Border Counties to engage their communities in conversations about dealing with the past/legacies of the Troubles. It also aimed to filter the learning back to policy makers and a wider audience in Northern Ireland and Border Counties of the Republic. This programme involved two study visits to South Africa in 2010 and 2011, with the two separate groups and resulted in the production of a DVD to document the scope of the work done.

In January 2009, Glencree took part in a youth exchange on Active Citizenship with partner organisations: Leaders, from Ramallah in the West Bank, Palestine; Van Leer Institute in Jerusalem and Public Achievement from Belfast. The programme took place in Jerusalem and focused on active citizenship roles for young people in conflict situations, key issues that young people in Palestine and Ireland are faced with, and how, despite very different circumstances, they deal with these challenges. These partnerships were strong learning opportunities for Glencree and the participants involved, allowing us to link with organisations in Northern Ireland and wider, global contexts. International links such as that with Peaceboat, Japan brought diverse groups to Glencree and allowed us reach a broad range of people.

In May 2013, Glencree coordinated a visit to Messines in Belgium for a PEACE III-funded programme 'Leading the Way' based in Co. Louth through KW Research. The group of fifteen participants explored the legacy of the First World War and the role of the soldiers from Ireland who fought in it. This was another part of the strand of learning about the role of commemoration in reconciliation in which we have been involved. Individual participants found the process challenging, but very moving and an inspiring learning experience.

Glencree is available to a wide range of organisations, north and south, to help them develop capacity in dealing creatively with conflict. These may be community-based organisations working on specific issues, or partnerships in border areas where reconciliation is a key part of the programme objectives.

We have tried to develop programmes to meet the specific needs of these groups, even within our limited capacity. This is an important dimension of our work in the field of training, as we offer a practical approach to skills development that has a direct application in their work.

Key lessons to Inform Future Learning Projects

I want to finish by looking at some of the important things we have learnt about schools, youth and adult education work, which should guide us as we move into a new phase of Glencree's journey.

Schools and Youth

- While one-off visits by schools and youth groups to Glencree have provided good learning opportunities and there is evidence that individuals within these groups define this experience as influential in their life journey, progressive opportunities for deeper and more long lasting engagement are more desirable. This does not mean that we will not provide one-day programmes, but with limited resources we should prioritise working more intensively with specific schools. Working with teachers is an important element of this process to create a more sustainable impact and 'Peace Promoting Schools'. [5]

- North-South schools and youth work is considered a priority and key themes like dealing with the past, commemoration, identity, reconciliation and conflict resolution should be the focus of these programmes. Intensive work with schools on both sides of the border can be the basis for this work; supporting the development of good relations between these schools needs to be advanced. 'Learning together' is the key principle where we aim to move beyond tolerance, to openness and interdependence.

[5] This was emphasized in the PEP Final Evaluation by Macaualy Associates in 2008 and is still relevant

- Glencree is an advocate for peace education and developing strategic relationships with other agencies to promote its mainstreaming remains important. We have learnt that working in partnership and developing alliances with other organisations who share this goal makes progress in this area more realistic. There are people within schools and communities who value this contribution, so it is important to collaborate with them.

- Restorative Practice is an area that Glencree is committed to and we are in a position to be influential in supporting it. Initial learning opportunities have allowed schools especially to be more open to these practices and the contribution they can make to a positive culture in schools. We want to use the funding available for this in a strategic way, to allow us to make the most of it and gain experience to play a role in mainstreaming such practices in schools and communities.

- We have not yet found a strategic way to work with teachers at primary and secondary level, though we have engaged with them in a number of different projects and contexts. Working systematically with teachers in their initial training and ongoing professional development will be a major challenge for the future and this is a key area to consider now.

Adults and Third Level Students

- We have come to understand that Glencree's experience has a lot to offer professional and community groups about the practicalities of working with conflict. We feel that this is best done in a residential context where we have time and space to go into things in a deeper way. Though the group needs may not always refer to political conflict, there are skills and approaches that are relevant and Restorative Practices, ADR and facilitation skills are especially important. We have already been able to tailor these programmes for specific groups and can provide something that is not available elsewhere.

Palestinian and Peaceboat Participants at Glencree in 2006

- Students at third-level colleges often comment that a huge amount of the syllabus is based on theoretical understandings of peace and conflict. We offer something more practical and experiential, to which students respond well. University groups from Ireland and abroad are eager to access this learning, especially when we can offer it in partnership with colleges in Northern Ireland. Intensive residential programmes are the best way to do this as it allows students to have different learning experience that is both challenging and engaging. Partnerships with Irish universities can also allow for accreditation options here.

- A learning process that begins to deal with the past has something valuable to offer. The decade of commemoration we are now in provides an opportunity for Glencree to work with groups at different levels on ways to really 'learn together'. The First World War, Irish Revolution and Partition need to be understood in their multiple dimensions so that people north and south can really embrace reconciliation and move forward. Without learning, commemoration can be a divisive process so we are eager to make it central.

- Lessons learnt from other Glencree work such as the Sustainable Peace Programme suggest that we can make better use of our surroundings in the Wicklow Hills. There is great potential for outdoor work as an approach in itself or as an element in project work. We have not made as much use of this as we should have done, although we have introduced it in a small way. It should be developed as a way of working in the future that allows people to relate to each other and to nature in a more meaningful way.

Conclusion

Glencree has changed over the years, but in addition to its general programme development the organisation has continued to do significant work in the area of peace education. We hope that education will remain a way to broaden the reach of the organisation as learning programmes complement the front-line dialogue and relationship-building work which is the main mission of the organisation. It is important that the organisation defines education as a key part of its remit if reconciliation is to be better understood.

Reconciliation is a broad process, which applies to everyone, not just those who have suffered from or inflicted violence. David Bloomfield has commented: 'The attitudes and beliefs that underpin violent conflict spread much more generally through the community and must be addressed at that broad level'.[6] Education is a vital part of the reconciliation process and as such, should remain central to the future work of Glencree and continue to engage a wide range of people at different stages of their lives, from all parts of the island and internationally.

[6] David Blomfield in *'Reconciliation After Violent Conflict-A Handbook',* Ed. Bloomfield, D. Barnes, T & Huyse, L, IDEA, Stockholm, 2003

Without women, neither peace nor development is possible

The Role of Women in Peacebuilding

Phil Killeen

'We have seen first-hand in countries from every region the critical role women play as peace-builders, as community organizers, as voices for those who are marginalized. We are convinced that strengthening women's leadership at every level is key to advancing peace, sustainable development and human rights in the 21st century.'

Mary Robinson, Former President of Ireland and UN High Commissioner for Human Rights Ireland's National Action Plan for Implementation of UNSCR 1325, 2011 - 2014

Over the past seven years my work with the Glencree Women's Programme (GWP) has been a huge learning experience and it is a challenge to sum up in this short reflection. Although the Women's Programme is small in the face of current world problems, it points to many valuable lessons for challenging violence and building peace. It plays an important role in the capacity-building of women from different women's organisations and wider society in Northern Ireland. Women do not come to Glencree because they want qualifications or education credits, so there needs to be a different access point than that which is offered by many community-based learning programmes intended to help women access the labour market. The lens for this reflection is the politics of gender, which cannot be ignored; and this will be my starting point.

The twists and turns of social repression in Northern Ireland is also the story of the patriarchal nature of society in Northern Ireland. The story of pain and confusion with which women necessarily respond to the discrimination against them on grounds of their sex alone, is the story of patriarchy. It is the story of Irish history and the Celts, who were fiercely patriarchal and developed the cult of the hero, which defined the role of women quite specifically (Condren, 1989). To ignore this context would be to deny the facts that present themselves through the programme. So, I will start by offering a rationale for why we consider a women's programme to be an ongoing necessity.

Programme Background and Context

The GWP is a step to empower women through women-focused policies and programmes. It is not about marginalising women into 'special programmes' outside of the standard Glencree programmes. Equality between men and women is inextricably linked with peace and the underlying values of such equality promote respect for human rights and power-sharing. In a conflict situation, it is important to support moderate forces, and we know that such forces can be found in the role played by local women NGOs as peace builders. This role needs to be given more visibility and the recognition women's groups deserve. We know that without peace, development is impossible - and without women, neither peace nor development is possible. Yet, despite progress in policy, in practice, women worldwide are still marginalised in conflict prevention and peacebuilding. Women are not represented at negotiating tables, nor has violence against women substantially decreased.

Women's Programme participants receiving certificates at Corner House, Belfast in 2007

'An essential journey in developing women and their understanding of who they are, where they fit in the complex process of understanding the weave of a violent past, a contested present and realistic possibilities of an inclusive future, for me sums up the Glencree Women's Programme'.

Anne Carr, Facilitator on the GWP

It is difficult to solve the problems of humanity when our political, cultural and religious institutions are preoccupied with helping to create or prolong them. The main Western sources of cultural authority are the Christian and Jewish traditions. There is ample historical material documenting the rise of patriarchy and the role of Christianity - as the carrier of patriarchy in the West - that goes beyond anything the early Hebrews could have imagined.

Within a feminist framework, the relationship between church and state is seen as simply two alternative realms whose lifeblood has traditionally depended upon the subjugation of women. The patriarchal mindset and the sexual political struggle are demonstrated in the curious phenomenon of the ultimate respect for human life - in its foetal form - and the armaments shipments throughout the world in the interest of 'safeguarding democracy'. The two realms of church and state in Northern Ireland have played one off against the other and the problem is that far from failing, the political and religious leaders have succeeded in perpetuating the particular insanity that passes for normal life in NI today.

Gender is culturally and historically constructed and the embedding of gender in power relations has huge implications for peace work. The 'feminine' is devalued while 'masculinity' simultaneously tries to control it. This division, assignment, stratification and internalisation of gender identities are the gender myths that are hurting our relationships, our children, our jobs and destroying our world.

When we are living at a time of unprecedented personal success for women, why would women accept as immutable truth that they are less logical, emotionally weak, unambitious and more naturally dependent on men? There is no evidence that women's way of knowing is any different from men's, yet the 'otherness' of women has seeped so deep into the cultural consciousness that it remains stubbornly entrenched, affecting women's and men's jobs, relationships and personal and public decisions. The theoretical assumptions of innate and rigid ideas of 'essential differences' in gender that absolutely determine behaviour, as in Freud's 'anatomy is destiny', have real, practical consequences for the lives of men and women.

The gender difference story portrays women as paragons of care - empathising pacifiers with a degree of emotional intelligence that belittles their ability to use logic, understand facts, argue their point and stand their ground. The narrative that women have different capacities and inclinations (because of their genes, hormones, motivation or brain structure) is appealing in a patriarchal construct, because it helps to rationalise

Women's Programme: Shankill

the sex segregation and discrimination that pervades societies worldwide.

The very existence of two states in Ireland creates pressure, which pushes people apart, and the territorial border works to separate the 'we' inside from the 'they' beyond that naturalises the divisions. These man-made territories now seem like eternal features of the natural landscape and are so powerful because they are reproduced in everyday discourse. While Northern Ireland has welcomed peace, it is still busy trying to create an identity for itself. Understandably, there is a wariness that is natural due to events over the past decades. While the overwhelming majority did not participate in, or support the violence of the Troubles, the Troubles affected all, and in many cases, still affect the people of Northern Ireland.

Glencree Women's Programme History

The history of Glencree's early days tells the story of women like Una O'Higgins O'Malley, Lady Eleanor Wicklow and Rachel Bewley and their part in the formation of the organisation. Yet Glencree is itself part of the wider society and has been characterised by a significant lack of critique of the wider norms and patriarchal influence. The GWP was organised and run by volunteers from its inception in 1996 and unlike the other programmes, no specific funding was sought to run it on the same level as the other programmes. In 2008, Glencree underwent severe financial restructuring, which resulted in programmes and valuable programme staff being made redundant. However, 2008 was the year that the GWP received specific funding from DFA. This was probably due in no small way to UNSCR1325 and the Irish Government's commitment to the resolution, and this valuable support from DFAT has continued to maintain the Programme.

An evaluation of the work of the Women's Programme in 1999, indicated that those involved in the programmes to date, had been part of the political elite and were not representative of the issues affecting working-class women. In 2003 it was decided that a structured programme was needed, which was developed by an experienced UK-based trainer. Subjects covered included: equality, gender issues, self-development, conflict resolution and a taster course, which was to be the precursor to the current modular programme, was introduced. The development of a structured modular programme for women with each module as a building block was significant. It explored 'where women were at', starting from the personal, and going on to the role of women in their families, communities and in wider social and political arenas. The Programme was run on a voluntary basis with a Women's Programme Committee until 2007, when I was appointed as the part-time co-ordinator.

GWP works, specifically, with harder-to-reach communities and individuals, grassroots community-based groups who can effect change, and participants from diverse backgrounds in Northern Ireland and the Border Counties - and when the funding permits - with women from the Republic of Ireland. The Programme works at the personal level to produce deep change, addressing specific real-world problems and challenges faced by participants in their communities. It strives to equip them with the confidence, personal development resources, and the personal and community capacities to take on positive peacebuilding roles in their lives and their communities. The training has thus become more targeted at a deeper level; to generate the inner confidence to then take practical community initiatives. The programme has developed through the view that peacebuilding is a long-term process, requiring long-term commitment, with the focus on transformation through civil society involvement.

The following are the goals of the programme as it has evolved:

- To increase the influence of women on the development of Irish society, by helping them to understand political structures and systems of governance, and how to participate in these and demand accountability

- To develop their capacity to question traditional beliefs and practices, and critically analyse structures of oppression and exploitation

- To develop women's positive self-image by helping them to recognise their own strengths and value their existing knowledge and skills

- To build women's capacity in conflict resolution, mediation and negotiation skills, to increase their knowledge and their ability to engage effectively

Outline of the Programme

Basic Course: Gender, Peace and Conflict

This course explores the role gender plays in constructing cultures of peace or cultures of violence essential in peacebuilding. It comprises highly participatory, innovative and flexible methodologies designed to empower women to recognise, analyse and address gender issues at the grassroots level. Interpersonal skills that engage, not only the mind, but also the heart, provide the basic training technique. Peace is inextricably linked with equality between women and men and the underlying values of such equality promote respect for human rights and power-sharing. These are the values and attitudes that promote cultures of peace.

Advanced Course: Women in Decision-Making and Leadership

This programme consists of:

- Deeper understanding of the concepts and practices of nonviolence
- Developing self-awareness and analysing various aspects of our own identities

Journey of discovery rather than fixed destination

- Discussing the role of religion in gender structures
- Learning that religion, race, ethnicity, gender, sexuality, class and other factors of difference do not act independently of one another
- Further discussing the construction of masculinity and its connection to gender, peace and conflicts

It is important - not only for those who are discriminated against and marginalised in society - to acquire a critical consciousness and we do this through thinking critically about our own thinking. The concept of critical thinking is simple: we define it as 'the art of taking charge of our own mind'. If we can take charge of our own minds, we can take charge of our lives; we can improve them, bringing them under our self-command and direction.

By participating in the creative and critical thinking activities provided over the course and applying these ideas to their own experiences, participants find that their thinking and language abilities become sharper and more powerful. We begin with the participants - where they are and their life experiences and sharing these experiences in order to develop relationships. The emphasis is on learning-by-doing; means the participants are engaged in a variety of activities and are, in effect, thinking critically and creatively about their own thinking, so that their thinking and language abilities become sharper and more powerful.

We bring together a group of diverse people working together over a number of weekends. Each weekend has a particular theme, for example:

- Histories and Identities
- Self-esteem and Self-image
- Assertiveness
- Diversity
- Conflict Transformation

This model has a strong emphasis on personal development. A residential experience creates a new openness to deal with issues that people find difficult in their 'home' territory - often issues of reconciliation and community relations - and allows old patterns and ways of viewing one another to change. Such activity can bring challenge and even discomfort to some groups, but new ways can be opened up.

Key Elements in the Learning Process

The GWP has developed over time and we have now reached a point where we need to document how the process works in more detail. Ongoing learning informs the way we work and the content of the workshops. The starting point for this kind of work is the conviction that every adult is responsible for his, or her learning process. The facilitator initiates this process, guards it and tries to shape it. The goal of this learning process is to enable a person to make a contribution to social change and to the improvement of the situation in which they find themselves. The person is him/herself part of this process; the facilitators do not find any participant's contribution in, or out of order. The chaos is almost inevitably, the initial phase of learning to be confident enough to speak freely.

Gradually, the participants come to various realisations as it dawns on them they are really unfettered and as facilitators, we have learnt to manage this. Since the participants evaluate their own work, they can learn what they please, not simply the issues set forth in a text. They are discovering what it means to be autonomous, what it means to be responsible, free persons. They begin to rely on their own values rather

'I used to do what my parents did and vote the same as them, but now I'm going to start thinking for myself, see what I want and find out more about all that stuff'.

'I found the person within'

'To listen to myself'

'To trust myself - to value myself'

'Taking ownership of issues leads to collective action instead of pointing the finger of blame'

'Journey of discovery rather than fixed destination'

'Training the next generation'

'Have courage to work within your family, community - take a stand against wrong doing and injustice'

'Need to get politicians on our side -and use them - use ju-jitsu theory'

'Women shouldn't be afraid to approach them - they serve us'
'Kicking ass needs self-confidence'

'I know myself for the first time'

than imposed ones, get closer to their own feelings, learn to trust themselves more, and become less afraid of change.

The course is designed to provide experiential training to women, in a participative way, and enables the participants to take all opportunities to practice skills and get feedback during training. It enables participants to reason and reflect about life and the nature of society and culture by examining how attitudes and values are formed. They learn the practice of reconciliation in a place where people can experience trust and reconciliation. Another element we have found to be a common part of the process is that as individuals within the group, people develop a respect and a liking for each other, as they emerge in the group discussions. This kind of learning experience is incomplete without some mention of the effect upon the facilitators where we have been the agents for the release of such self-initiated learning. We have been inspired, stimulated, and left, at times, shaken and awed with the consequences for both ourselves and the participants.

The risk-accommodating 'safe space' provided by the GWP, enables women to tell the stories about their passions, their pains and to explore their collective possibilities. In creating this essential 'safe space' where we can tell our stories, we move through an organically-structured process that enables those stories to emerge. We tell our stories as a way of building relationships and to reframe the dimensions of 'difference', which have been represented almost as natural and inevitable. Stories are interwoven, and as emergent processes within different individual stories unfold, changes are produced in the everyday lives of the women and in the way the groups interact together. This could be described as spiralling outward, connecting women within and beyond the group.

'If I hadn't gone to Glencree I would be Orange and still living in the past'

'When I think of what my community and culture mean to me and then think if they feel as passionate about theirs, well that's scary. I don't know how to live with that'

'I have realised that in my home I am at times a peace creator and other times a peace destroyer. I need to put a few things right'

'I have learnt that I have to change my attitude and be a good listener. I will start listening to my friends and stop being judgemental'

Participants' comments

The women explore their varying understandings of confidentiality and its relationship to trust as it ranges from personal trust to the political complexities of trust in the community. The development of trust and group bonding fundamentally influences participation and willingness to explore issues based on their experience. This can be a difficult journey to make, involving issues of trust and safety not easily accessible in local communities. It is emotionally tough on all involved, including the facilitators.

In the workshops, there is an atmosphere of realness, of caring, and understanding. As the learning process continues, the learners increasingly provide it for themselves. Learning from one another in the workshops becomes as important as learning from books and other materials or community experiences. Self-discipline to reach goals becomes key. The evaluation of the extent and significance of each participant's learning is made primarily by the participants themselves.

Reflections on Learning in GWP

> *'We assess the value of education in the same manner as we assess the value of land or stocks in the stock-exchange market ... we hardly give a thought to the improvement of the character of the educated.'*
>
> Mahatma Gandhi

The importance of taking stock and assessing what we have learnt throughout the programme is at the heart of this reflection. There is a rich quality about this learning that is derived directly from the experiences and voices of the women involved. Key learning points that have emerged which will inform our future work include the following:

- The GWP enables participants to learn from each other to understand what makes us tick, how we think, how we feel, how we make sense of everyday life in the world around us. Participants in the GWP already bring evidence of considerable organisational and management skills so we, therefore, need to be able to make sense of complex realities and learn from the work in which we have been engaged

- Bringing women together, at the local, regional and international levels, so that they can listen and share their experiences, is a way of providing information and opportunities to link women with essential resources. Women learn from women's lives, and women's lives are different in many ways from those of men

Peacebuilding is a long-term process, requiring long-term commitment

- The participants are seeking a sense of control over their own lives, enabling them to make choices about where they want to focus their energy. The programme has to be about empowering the participants to engage directly in understanding and acting upon issues of concern in their own lives

- Evidence from the programme suggests that the home has a crucial role to play in ending the cycle of transmission of a sectarian culture (with loathing, fear and hatred at its core) which is still going on daily in many homes across Northern Ireland. It is clear to us that sectarianism still lies just below the surface. There is enduring hurt caused by what has happened in the past and the effects are being transferred to succeeding generations who bear the brunt of this legacy

- Participants on the programme say they want change but are still held back by the fear of public opinion in their own neighbourhoods, disapproval of people they love, or the threat of violence to their families. This fear isolates people and makes it hard to work with those who are longing for the same changes. People talk about helplessness and the difficulty of individuals standing up and speaking out

- Family needs, concerns and cares have a major influence over women's place in society, whether working inside or outside the home, across all social classes. Family, work and community all compete for women's devotion, time and energy; this needs to be factored into the way a programme works

- We try to make it easier for women to participate, as there are many conflicting demands on the women we want to engage. We have tried to place women's needs at the heart of this programme so that they can gain full advantage despite the conflicting demands that are placed on them

- We have learnt that women's socialisation in awareness of others and their listening skills can be affirmed and revalued by promoting participation, encouraging voices and valuing differences. We value lived experience as a source of constructed knowledge and draw, in part, on the women's movement of feminist consciousness-raising. Freire's concept of critical consciousness is, therefore, central to our work

- As the women tell their stories in the programme and are heard by other women, they develop a greater understanding of the political issues embedded in personal experiences and explore new perspectives that can help to influence change in the system

- Organisations that participate in the GWP workshops can be described as typical 'grassroots' organisations, that are located in communities and work with a local geographical focus. However, women who are not affiliated to any group or organisation have to be welcomed on the GWP as they represent a marginalised voice

- It is vital for women to understand that they, as group members on the programme, are part of a continual state of socio-political education and that it is possible to move, against the odds, from the personal to the political

- We need to be more aware of the international dimensions of women's role in peacebuilding. Though we feel that UNSCR1325 is a highly-biased gendered document, we see it as a first step towards recognising the need to ensure that women have a role in peace processes and in post-conflict reconstruction. UNSCR1325 is strictly concerned with a narrow definition of the role of women in peace processes and post-conflict reconstruction, it does not extend its reach to cover areas of social and economic policy that are essential for women's welfare

Acting on Learning: Broad Lessons

Eventually, the spotlight will not be on a leader just because she is a woman. But while the spotlight is on us, we will continue to use its power inclusively, to illuminate the great needs that still exist for women and children in the world.

What does the GWP mean for women? Why a Women's Programme? These are questions posed at the beginning of this piece and frequently, we are asked to elucidate. Here are some of our own broader reflections on this question based on facilitators' observations that will help us to build on our learning in the development of the programme:

- An important, intangible, asset of GWP is the goodwill and the recognition Glencree enjoys and the participants from NI frequently comment on this

- Being women-focused, a big issue is that it is mostly looked upon as a 'women's programme'. However, GWP has also much to contribute in relation to conflict, peace and reconciliation and if given the opportunity, the programme has the potential to deliver a much wider impact

- Awareness-raising of key international instruments such as CEDAW and UNSCR 1325 and UNSCR 1820, 1888, 1889 and now 2122, are valuable tools in exploring the role that gender plays in constructing cultures of peace or cultures of violence. These key Security Council resolutions are essential in understanding the role gender plays in peacebuilding

- Any action taken by civil society that promotes peace and reconciliation, gender equality (which is inscribed in the EU constitution) and poverty reduction, will facilitate European integration process general objectives of 'obtaining lasting peace', 'democratic development' and 'development of a multi- ethnic society'

- One of the priorities of GWP is to stimulate development activity and increase networking opportunities for women so that they can share experiences and work together on common issues. The strategy combines a focus on capacity-building in local areas and among target groups with promoting networking and identification of common policy issues

- The programme is seen as invaluable for women at the grassroots level to develop the space and tools to explore and articulate issues and to inform and influence national policy on responses needed. The participants are comfortable with the person-centred approach and feel that the process of challenging women's marginalisation has only begun to emerge at the grassroots level due to the preoccupation with the Troubles.

- As an Irish organisation, Glencree can be instrumental in supporting groups that work - or have the potential to work - across ethnic lines, and to bring organisations of different ethnic groups together

- There is the potential for Glencree to expand its support in gender mainstreaming beyond the grassroots women and focus on training for government counterparts to women's NGOs

- There is a failure in the public perception to link male violence in the home with the eradication of male domination and patriarchal thinking

- Male violence against women has received much ongoing media attention but awareness has not led to challenge the underlying causes of this violence, or to challenge patriarchy

- As a society, we must acknowledge that men and women have together made our country a culture of violence, whether in imaginary 'good guy'/'bad guy' fights or in the pursuit of nationalists / loyalists interests

- Even men who perpetuate patriarchal values are disturbed by the hatred and fear of women and male violence against women

- It is easier for men to support male domination passively than it is to face the fear of letting go of the benefits of the world they know; even when men know in their hearts and minds there is an imbalance that is wrong and needs to be changed

Conclusion

Since so many of the comments and reflections in this piece come from the collective learning on the Glencree Women's Programme, my debts are too diffuse and ordinary for acknowledgement. But I want to make it clear that I am in their debt, that their contribution has been extraordinary and I hope I have been able to do some justice to them here. We are often asked to rationalise why there is an ongoing need for a programme dedicated specifically to women. Tragically enough, each new conflict in the world constitutes an opening for GWP and provides a rationale for the expansion of its work to new areas and locations. I have tried to present the case for this here. The former participants on the GWP regularly encourage us to continue this work and we are determined to do this.

An open-ended process which entails deep listening, learning and a willingness to change perceptions and relationships

Political Dialogue: Building Critical Relationships

Ian White & Geoffrey Corry

Part One: Overview *Ian White*

Introduction

The Glencree Centre for Peace and Reconciliation has worked intensively to support the political dimension of the Irish Peace Process since 1991. During the last twenty years, Glencree held strong to its values on inclusivity and non-judgmentalism as it worked with prisoners, victims/survivors, former combatants, women's groups, religious hierarchies, cultural groups and young leaders. In parallel to, and yet interconnected with this range of activities, Glencree hosted a programme of political activity which aimed to complement the work of all governmental and non-governmental stakeholders in the conflict. Below is an outline of this phased political activity which developed organically over a number of years.

Glencree Summer School 2010

Initial Steps (1992-1994)

The involvement of Glencree in the political arena in Ireland North and South commenced in 1992 when the organisation hosted and provided a platform for a number of political speakers from Northern Ireland. The first speaker was John Hume, who addressed an audience of two hundred and fifty people in Jury's Hotel, Ballsbridge, as the facilities of the Glencree Centre were not sufficiently developed to host such meetings. By 1994, however, the facilities at Glencree - while still basic - had accommodated a range of speakers from Northern Ireland from both nationalist/ republican and unionist/loyalist parties in two series entitled 'Understanding Republicanism' and 'Understanding Unionism'. The broad purpose of these talks was to offer audiences in the south an opportunity to interact with, and gain a better understanding of Northern Irish politicians, but there were also more specific objectives.

Democratic Progress Institute Turkish group at DFAT, 2014

'Understanding Republicanism' was an attempt by Glencree to demonstrate to militant republicans that their political views were valid and, if a non-violent approach were to be adopted by them, the Irish public would create space for their inclusion in the political dynamics of the country.

At a time when political relationships were very raw and unionists did not, as a rule, cross the border, 'Understanding Unionism' was a vehicle through which Glencree could demonstrate to unionists that the people in the south were interested in their position. Following the formal sessions, private dinners involving Irish Government officials and one Glencree person together with the speaker, helped in a small way to build trusting relationships between the Department of Foreign Affairs (DFA) and at least some unionist representatives.

The two series of talks were not the only political activity in which Glencree engaged during the 1992-1994 period. Other, smaller political events were also taking place and included Councillor and UUP executive member Chris McGimpsey addressing an audience of TDs on the unionist response to the Downing Street Declaration. This interactive event took place at the same time as the Good Friday Agreement was signed and aimed to build understanding of, and support for the declaration across all parties. TDs had not yet seen the Good Friday Agreement, and Chris McGimpsey was very happy to circulate copies of it on UUP headed notepaper to the gathered audience.

Phase I (1994-1998)

While not all political parties found it easy to participate in the Glencree political programme during the early years, Glencree did detect from those who did engage, that they attached a high value to the work of the organisation. Direct feedback to Glencree was clear in its recognition that while political parties and governments can achieve great things, there were some initiatives which were required and that could be best delivered by a non-aligned NGO.

The ceasefires of 1994 created a new environment which brought with it new possibilities for Glencree to develop its role in the political arena. Up to this point, the work of Glencree in the political arena mainly took the shape of public talks. Possibilities for parties to meet each other away from the glare of the media were extremely limited and Glencree realised that relationships between the parties needed to be developed. In late 1994, Glencree hosted its first Political Dialogue Workshop which involved parties from the south, unionist and nationalist Parties from the north, but neither Sinn Féin (SF) nor the Democratic Unionist Party (DUP) found it possible to participate in the early events. By 1995, however, enough trust had been developed between Glencree and the other political parties to allow SF participate in the workshops without other parties excluding themselves.

Sinn Féin tested the integrity of Glencree by requesting a training programme for its youth membership which aimed to help them differentiate between a Protestant and a unionist. The delivery of this programme, which involved the moderator of the Presbyterian Church (John Dunlop), and unionist politicians and officials such as Stephen King and David Ervine, did much to build this relationship with Sinn Féin.

DUP involvement in the dialogue programme came much later, but with their exception, all other parties in Ireland north and south, actively engaged. The dialogue workshops were three-day residential gatherings based at Glencree, with the agenda being set by the participants, who were a mix of party officers and elected representatives. The purpose of the workshops was to build relationships between parties on a cross-border and cross-community basis and allow individual politicians to understand what rationale lay behind the positions of their political adversaries (they were familiar with the positions of others in most cases). The workshops catered for between twenty and thirty participants and took place at six to eight-week intervals. A version of the Chatham House Rule was adopted, which guided the workshops and protected the participants. While, publicly, the parties were not talking to each other, and megaphone diplomacy was very much the order of the day, unknown to most, the parties were quietly meeting at Glencree and slowly building some trust and new understandings between each other.

Officials from both the DFA and the British Embassy also attended the workshops on a regular basis, ensuring that up-to-date information about developments was available to participants and allowing new relationships to be developed between the officials and politicians with whom they may have had little contact. The workshops also included some who were non-aligned and un-elected, but nevertheless, were political activists who represented perspectives of institutions such as the Apprentice Boys, the GAA and the Orange Order.

While the political dialogue workshops were the core of Glencree peacebuilding in the political arena, it was not the only political activity in which Glencree engaged. During this phase, Glencree hosted a cross-party delegation of political leaders from South Africa, who addressed a gathering of fifty politicians from all parties that participated in the political workshop programme. The three-person delegation comprising Mac Maharaj, Leon Wessells and Constand Viljoen promoted the concepts of negotiation and out-of-the-box thinking, and spoke of the opportunities and challenges of the process in South Africa.

Mediation Event Dublin International Arbitration Centre, 2013

When the Forum for Peace and Reconciliation was convened in Dublin Castle, Glencree, at the request of the secretariat, collaborated to facilitate unionist participation in it, as their absence weakened the exercise and deliberations were limited to what the Forum perceived to be the opinions of unionists. Despite the best efforts of Glencree, unionists did not feel it appropriate to attend Dublin Castle, but after numerous meetings and negotiations, Gregory Campbell (DUP), Michael McGimpsy (UUP), David Ervine (PUP) and David Nichol (UDP) agreed to form a panel and make presentations to a semi-public event at Glencree, to which all members of the Forum for Peace and Reconciliation were invited and all parties attended. Such creative approaches to building the improbable relationships required for a sustainable peace process became standard as Glencree interacted with, and supported all political parties, both unilaterally and collectively as they developed the capacity to engage with each other within a positive framework.

Phase II (1999-2003)

The signing of the Good Friday Agreement and the ongoing release of political prisoners changed the context yet again and while the Political Dialogue workshop programme retained the same format as requested by the participants the programme was expanded to include three other dimensions:

- In addition to hosting political workshops in Glencree, some of the workshops were now able to take place in Belfast. This resulted in politicians from the Republic of Ireland (ROI) being invited to visit local loyalist and republican communities outside the official programme for the workshops. This by-product served to sensitise politicians from the south to the issues being faced by local communities in Northern Ireland (NI)

- In order to address the totality of relationships which impacted on the conflict and to complement Strand Three of the Good Friday Agreement, representatives of British Labour, Conservative and Liberal Democrats became part of the process

- The release of prisoners had a direct impact on the political environment with many of them moving towards political activity, even though the skill set for a politician was very different to the skill set required to be a paramilitary. Having observed high levels of frustration among former prisoners engaged in the dialogue programme, Glencree launched a political training programme for those wishing to transition from violence into politics. Trainers from Canada, US, South Africa and Ireland provided communications, negotiation and strategic thinking and analysis training to one hundred and fifty former prisoners to assist them with their transition to politics

Again, while the workshops were the core of the work during this phase, other activities were also undertaken. After discussions with the Department of Foreign Affairs Anglo Irish Division and British Embassy officials, it was agreed that Glencree would bring leading figures in the four main Unionist Parties together in an attempt to build consensus around their engagement in the peace process. A four-person delegation from both UUP and DUP including Danny Kennedy, David McNarry, Peter Robinson and Gregory Campbell was joined by two-person delegations from the PUP and UDP including the late David Ervine and Frankie Gallagher on a visit to South Africa. While there, the group was facilitated by Roelf Meyer and met with President Mbeki and former president De Klerk who encouraged them to work together in the peace process.

While there was consensus around a number of issues, total consensus was not achieved but again other by-products of this visit included:

- Introduction of Roelf Meyer to Peter Robinson, a relationship which continued with Roelf being invited to assist the DUP in their strategic thinking through three visits to NI where he worked with the DUP executive committee

- According to the late David Ervine, the event helped to bring an end to the loyalist feud

Phase III (2004-2010)

As the peace process continued to gather momentum and gain traction, a number of relationships were still extremely weak. One of these relationships which required support was that between the DUP and political parties in the Republic of Ireland. Glencree again adjusted the focus of its work to address this need. In addition to continuing to host inclusive political workshops in which all parties apart from the DUP participated, there was a parallel programme which engaged TDs from the main parties in the south with elected representatives from the DUP, in a set of workshops in both NI and ROI. One workshop in Belfast coincided with the 'Love Ulster Rally' in Dublin and this provided a stimulus for the participants to focus on victims' issues and dissatisfaction - particularly among members of the unionist victims community. One southern participant, Pat Carey - who, at the time was the co-chair of the British Irish Interparliamentary Body (BIIB) - used the workshop to get unionist input to the body. The attendance of Peter Robinson at the meeting of the BIIB was a direct result of the Glencree Political Dialogue Programme and the initiative taken by Pat Carey. A cross-party delegation of southern TDs and councillors visited Belfast for a workshop with the DUP and were invited to meet the party leadership at a fundraising function in East Belfast. The DUP was attempting to move its constituency towards a closer or, at least warmer relationship to the Republic and to the peace process. The attendance of the ROI participants at the dinner contributed in a small way to assisting the DUP leadership in moving its traditional followers, as Ian Paisley personally greeted the southern guests. The programme also facilitated a number of events in the ROI which brought senior DUP representatives into direct contact with the Minister for Foreign Affairs and as one DUP representative noted while being hosted to lunch in Iveagh House, the last time he visited the building he didn't enter and it was not during daylight hours.

Workshops in 2009 and 2010, while inclusive, focused on bringing the DUP in particular into contact with other political parties not in government in the south. These workshops also allowed Glencree to engage more senior politicians and every party involved in these workshops selected delegations comprising TD/MLA, local councillor and party activists.

The development of the Glencree International Programme (GIP) and its programme work benefits from the political relationships developed through the political programme, enabling senior political figures to share their experiences with others in conflicts internationally. Peter Robinson and Martin McGuinness agreeing to meet with a visiting delegation of Afghan parliamentarians, is a good example of this. Participation in the GIP by senior political actors helps develop new relationships and strengthen existing ones. An example of this is Alex Maskey and Jimmy Spratt collaborating to convey a meaningful message to actors in the southern Thailand conflict.

Glencree Summer School 2010

Positioning

By the end of 2010 Glencree had positioned itself in the political arena and was for many parties, clearly recognised as the main non-governmental actor in peacebuilding in that arena. Glencree had developed a high level of credibility with all political parties on the island. Furthermore, the physical space at Glencree was clearly recognised by these parties as a neutral space where they were respected and treated with fairness.

Phase IV (2011-2013)

In 2011 and 2012 the political dialogue workshop format changed from an open dialogue where the themes and subjects discussed reflected the interests of the participants, to one where Glencree, according to its assessment of the context, selected appropriate themes. In 2012, the theme was 'Commemoration'. From 2012 through to 2013, the programme moved towards building relationships between the parties and between them and civil society representatives. Given the difficulty that a minority of loyalists and republicans were experiencing with feeling included in the out-workings of the Good Friday Agreement, the participation in the workshops was now open to key civil society actors as well as politicians. The focus of each workshop was on how we might bring the groups who felt excluded into the peace process. Glencree is firmly of the opinion that ownership of the process must be held by all stakeholders in the conflict.

David Bloomfield chairing workshop 2010

Part Two: Reconciliation Lessons of Glencree's Political Dialogue Work

Geoffrey Corry

Political Dialogue Workshops: Enabling protagonists to build new relationships of trust and understanding

Between 1994 and 2007, over fifty residential three-day political dialogue workshops were held at the Glencree Centre during the negotiation phase of the Northern Ireland peace process. This article describes the structure and methodology of the workshops at second track level to support politicians from all the political parties in Ireland and Britain to arrive at new understandings and forge new relationships. It identifies the role of the facilitator in shaping an interactive dialogue space through four layers of dialogue over multiple encounters.

Political dialogue has been defined as 'an open-ended process which entails deep listening, learning and the willingness to change perceptions and relationships in addressing the root causes of the conflict, in order to achieve inclusive and sustainable positive change' (EU concept paper, 2009). The inspiration for the Glencree workshops lay in three significant events. First, Carl Rogers (1977) had demonstrated in The Steel Shutter film (1972) how Catholics and Protestants from Belfast could break through sectarian barriers, build their own interpersonal understanding and become human to each other. They had met for three days in a TV studio in Pittsburgh (Corry, 2004) made possible by funding from Irish Jesuits. I was fascinated and captivated by the power and potential of storytelling when the film was first shown in Dublin at Peace Week in 1974. That image of protagonists sitting in the circle and working through their trauma of the bombs that went off on Bloody Friday in July 1972 stayed with me for years. Fr. Shaun Curran SJ, who lived at Glencree in a caravan to look after the Centre, often spoke to me about his own part in editing the film.

Secondly, my visit to South Africa in 1985 at a time of great turmoil in the apartheid struggle, brought me in contact with Hendrik van der Merwe of the Centre for Intergroup Studies in Cape Town. He told me of his own work between the ANC and Afrikaners and introduced me to new thinking about conflict resolution emerging at that time in the USA. That led me in 1987 to get mediation training in San Francisco with the help of Ray Shonholtz of Community Boards. Sitting in those roleplays, I realised there was now available a step-by-step process to enable protagonists come to 'a new relationship of understanding' with each other through an interactive communication experience.

The third piece of the process jigsaw came together when Hugh O'Doherty, Glencree's first programme director, introduced me to Herb Kelman (1990 and 2003) at the Harvard Centre for International Affairs. He had spent ten years perfecting the problem-solving intergroup workshop in the years after the 1967 six-day war in Israel. Every few months he brought together about six Palestinians and six Israelis in a behind-the-scenes unofficial second track process. The workshops demonstrated that 'psychological barriers' of rigid assumptions rooted in past history, hate and fear - constituting seventy percent of the problem in identity conflicts - could be melted through residential workshops that laid the basis for mutual acceptance and meaningful negotiations. However, Kelman warned that overcoming these psychological barriers does not, of itself, resolve the conflict - that only comes through political negotiation and change. It was his emphasis on selecting participants who were influential within a political party at the sub-leadership level and who had access to the top leaders that proved to be innovative.

The first Glencree Workshops

With financial support from Chuck Feeney, the Irish-American philanthropist, Ian White was appointed on a full-time basis to get the Glencree Centre open again. In the summer of 1994, we cut through the cobwebs in the lower buildings and organised our first summer school for the last week in August. We tried out a 'listening circle' process with nationalists/republicans one day and with unionists the next day. Several days later, the IRA announced their ceasefire and in the following October, Gusty Spence led a combined loyalist group to announce their ceasefire. Suddenly, we were at the right time at the right place with the right programme to work with politicians in a post-ceasefire situation. What an opportunity! Ian and I immediately launched a political dialogue project based on the work of Herb Kelman, but shifted the emphasis away from problem solving to dialogue. We invited back the young unionists and young SDLP that had come to the summer school to engage with each other in a series of workshops that autumn. Little did we know in those months that this would be the start of thirteen years work from 1994 to 2007, taking us through the period of negotiations leading up to the Good Friday/Belfast Agreement of 1998 and all the way through the years of implementation. In total, Glencree organised fifty-five weekend dialogue workshops with a facilitation team led by the author of this piece. Workshop participants also took part in the annual, three-day residential summer school and many sessions of interest-based negotiation skills training.

Diagram 1: Positioning of political dialogue workshops at second track level within the peacemaking pyramid

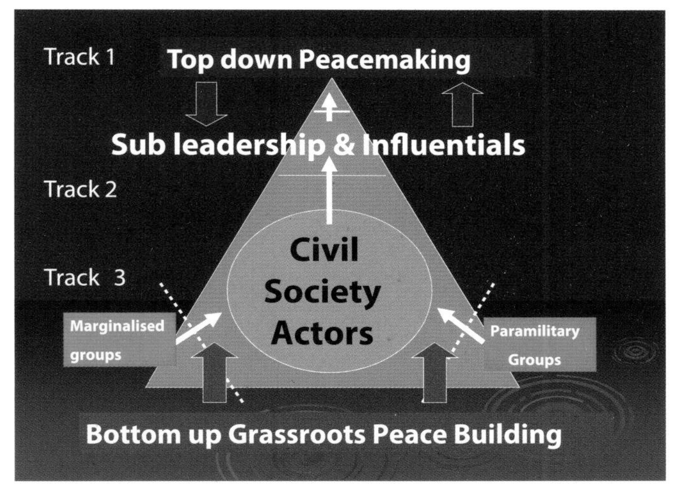

The workshops developed organically over that time. In putting an emphasis on interactive political dialogue, it was primarily an experiential learning circle with no formal presentations by the facilitation team or outside experts on conflict resolution. The dialogue ambience was aided by a relaxed atmosphere and it was possible to let sessions run on beyond the break times when significant dialogue moments arose.

Participants sat around the fire in a combination of comfortable seats and sofas with coffee/tea available. There was no table. Sometimes the workshops had as few as nine participants but most times there were twelve to fifteen people from a wide spectrum of political parties in the north and south of Ireland. Occasionally, we had up to twenty-five participants (and once, there were forty people in total), when parties came from England and Scotland. Workshops started on Friday evening at about 9pm (because people needed two hours or more to get to Glencree) and continued over two nights into Sunday afternoon. The residential nature of the weekend was crucial for people getting to know each other and in building relationships in the informal time. Most times, the Saturday evening dinner was held outside the Centre at a local restaurant or hosted occasionally by embassies in Dublin. The weekend normally had six sessions and the agenda was always shaped by the participants and connected to the negotiation phase of the political/peace process. The remote location of the Centre, not served by public transport, offered a safe space for confidential discussions and attracted political activists to get away from things for a weekend.

Diagram 2: Structure of a Residential Weekend Workshop

Friday	Saturday	Sunday
Morning	Agenda setting Dialogue on prioritised Topic 1	Dialogue on Topic 4 Closing circle
Afternoon	Dialogue on prioritised Topic 2 Dialogue on prioristised Topic 3	
Evening Bonding Session Informal social time	 Informal interaction at dinner More social interaction time	

The primary purpose of the workshops was relationship-building across the political parties. Political opponents were able to say what was important for their party at that point in the political peace process and to understand the needs and constraints of other parties. Through the robust face-to-face exchange and interactive analysis of party positions around particular topics, new understandings and new relationships of trust were built with each other. Facilitation was offered in a non-directive and non-judgemental approach because it was felt that overly structured sessions would not suit politicians. No pressure was placed on participants to come up with formal outcomes.

They were not about negotiation. At the same time, space was given to discuss possible points of agreement around emerging crunch issues in the peace process. There were times when the workshops reached some general conclusions and these were written up for all participants.

Workshop methodology

The two-hour session on the Friday evening opened with a 'bonding session' where an atmosphere of welcome was created to put people at ease. The ground rules were introduced: confidentiality/anonymity along the lines of the Chatham House rules where comments are not attributed to named individuals; one voice at a time; respect for each other; and the right to say 'pass' in any go-round. There was usually enough time to do two go-rounds of the circle with everyone speaking once. The first go-round was sequential where each participant in turn gave their name, where they grew up and where they live, their role or position in the party and level of responsibility [elected or not]. We did not use the stone/feather/talking stick of talking circles, partly because politicians don't necessarily like that kind of thing and may be put off right at the start of the weekend. This technique is best used with healing circles for victims and offenders/ex-combatants. One additional task was thrown in to encourage some personal storytelling around likes/dislikes as politicians. A different question was asked at each session and invariably included one of the following:

- Which politician do you most admire and why?
- What was a high moment in your political life so far and a low moment?
- Which speech, TV programme/film or piece of writing has influenced you most politically so far, good or bad?

The second go-round was a 'popcorn' one where each participant speaks once but pops whenever they are ready to talk. Normally, this open question was asked: 'How optimistic or pessimistic are you about the present situation of the peace process?' It sought to hear the energy and frustration levels of participants early on in the weekend. It also gave everyone a flavour of what was on people's minds, what they had been through and what was becoming important for them. Because it was late in

The relational journey that each must make toward hearing the story of the other

the night, we allowed some relaxation of the 'only speak once' rule provided everyone was heard. For the facilitators, this gave us a heads up on what topics were going to come up over the next two days. Often this session went on until midnight followed by informal social time which could go on for another two hours - Irish style!

At the Agenda-Setting session first thing on Saturday morning, each party was invited to suggest themes, topics or issues they wish to discuss: 'Are there some questions that one party particularly wants to ask or explore with the other?' Time was allowed for some intra-party caucus if large numbers of their group were present. The facilitator then pulled together the list of issues on the flip chart and organised them into 3 or 4 broad topics. This session was important in affirming the working principle that participants set their own agenda and it was not determined by Glencree. By remaining neutral, Glencree built political credibility for the workshops as a democratic space where participants negotiated between them the issues they wanted to work on. This was balanced by the understanding that the facilitator managed the dialogue process and the logistical arrangements.

At this point, everyone was ready to start into open-ended and interactive dialogue sessions that continue into Sunday morning until about 11.30am to explore each of the agreed topics and develop understanding around particular issues and problem areas where blockage is occurring within the peace process. [See the second half of this article for a more detailed exploration of the role of the facilitator in these open exchange sessions.]

The informal conversations over meals, around the coffee breaks and the personal chats in the corners in the evenings contributed significantly to both interpersonal and intergroup understanding. Add to that the opportunities for the walks together outside and the fun sessions at night and into the morning. The fact that participants had to share bedroom space (twin bedrooms) at Glencree, created more possibilities for people from very different narratives to talk privately and get to know how the other is thinking.

The closing go-round session on Sunday morning was scheduled an hour or more before lunch. This was a another 'popcorn' go-round where each participant was invited to let the group know what new political insights or understandings they had gained from the workshop and what they will bring back to their party about the constraints under which other parties were operating at present. When the workshops first started, this tended to be a short session but as the learning deepened more reflective comments were offered by those participants returning a number of times.

Inclusive participation

Initially in 1994-95, Glencree focused on the younger members of the political parties in Northern Ireland and the Republic, namely, Ulster Unionists, PUP, Alliance Party, Sinn Féin, SDLP, Workers Party (NI), Fianna Fail, Fine Gael, Labour and the Progressive Democrats. By 1998 many of these younger politicians had moved up the political ladder to become 'sub-leaders and influentials' (Kelman, 1990) within their party with considerable analysis and experience of being able to connect with the senior party leadership. Some of them wrote speeches for their party leader and were involved in policy making. The majority of those attending the workshops were male - especially those from the unionist tradition. In the years that followed, almost every political party in Ireland and Britain sent second-track politicians to the workshops.

From time to time, British politicians came from the Conservative, Labour and Liberal Democrat parties both from England and Scotland, as well as the Scottish Nationalist Party and Plaid Cymru in Wales. This principle of inclusivity was important to Glencree, based on the learning from South Africa that, if parties are not included in the process, then they are more likely to become spoilers. Stedman (2002) defined 'spoilers' as stakeholders who have an interest in undermining the principal parties' abilities to reach and implement an agreement. Their power comes from mobilising internal constituencies within a party or outside it.

During the politically frustrating years from 1999 through to 2003 with the non-resolution of the decommissioning issue between the Ulster Unionists led by David Trimble and Sinn Féin led by Gerry Adams and Martin McGuinness was a difficult time for this work. This impasse prevented the full implementation of the Good Friday

Agreement and stopped the power-sharing Executive from taking office. Glencree reached out to the anti-Agreement groups within the unionist community to come into dialogue with the other parties.

Between 2004 and 2006, the period may have been our most important in contributing to the peace process. Senior officials in the Democratic Unionist Party (DUP) together with researchers and a number of elected Assembly members agreed to participate in dialogue workshops with elected members of the Dail, a development that had not happened before. This meant the workshops moved up a gear from second track closer to official power, known as one and a half track. The workshops helped to change DUP perceptions of southern Ireland and supported the new political momentum orchestrated by the British and Irish governments that eventually led to the St. Andrews Agreement and the restoration of the Executive at Stormont in 2007.

Preparation: Recruitment and Connection

The changing context, the calling of elections and the flow of political events always affected the decision as to when to hold a workshop. It is not fully appreciated the amount of preparatory work that the convening organisation has to do before any workshop begins and to create credibility in the dialogue process. The spotlight always goes on the workshop itself and not on all the invisible, quiet and discreet work of building relationships with potential participants and enemy protagonists to encourage them to attend. As Ropers (2004) reminds us:

> *'The real challenge for dialogue projects may lie not in the mastery of effective facilitative methods to support communication during the encounters, but in the organisational arrangements of financing and preparing the sessions.'*

There is a huge time commitment involved in keeping up the currency of contacts with all the political parties both in Belfast and Dublin and keeping open the lines of official and unofficial communication. Here the work of Ian White was crucial. The official route is to write to the parties and extend an invitation to nominate two to three party members, but in the end it relies on cultivating informal relationships with committed individuals who are prepared to invest the time in coming away for a whole weekend, despite family and party commitments. One of the parties held control over representation and appointed a liaison person through whom all official contact was made.

Is it best to split the role of the person doing the preparatory work from the role of the facilitator? Or should they be done by the same person? We tried each approach at different times depending on resources. The disadvantage of the facilitator not being involved in the inviting and contacting before each workshop is the loss of connection and not being in the loop of what is going on politically at that time. On the other hand, this is a demanding role right up to the event because you might never know who is coming until the last minute. You can arrive tired and stressed to the event, which does not allow you time to prepare yourself inside for being calm within the dialogue proceedings. Teamwork is essential between these two roles of 'web maker' and facilitator.

The term 'web maker' comes from the writings of John Paul Lederach (2005) who has examined this relationship-building role more closely and very much speaks to the Glencree experience. The web maker is like a spider at work who gets to know peacemakers on the front line or higher up in groups and then connects them up into a peacemaking web. They tend to be individuals in risky situations who move up or down the vertical line within the peacemaking pyramid [see diagram 1] or who move horizontally across the conflict lines so as to create processes that link people together. They open up a line of communication (Pruitt, 2003) to the extremes that have been put at arm's length. They hold the web relationships in place over long periods and don't allow violence to disrupt them. As this line becomes more stable, then the web can link them to others more politically distant. The added advantage is when such people are supported by a hub, such as Glencree, where they can be brought together at a safe, private location.

For example, more Glencree legwork was required after the 1998 Good Friday

Agreement to stay connected with the various parties because of the political uncertainty around and the fear that the political process might collapse. One of the lessons of the NI peace process is that everyone [politicians, diplomats, church people, peacemakers] redouble their efforts when things go off the rails. More preparation was needed to get the 'right people' at the appropriate level and 'right' time to the workshops. Sometimes different members of the Glencree team handled the contact with parties on one side while another team member worked the other side because of changing perceptions/suspicions held by them towards Glencree.

Role of Facilitators at each Layer of the Dialogue Process

Once the workshop starts into discussion of each topic from Saturday morning onwards, open exchange of views is encouraged as opposed to using go-rounds. The role of the facilitator is to maintain a productive free flowing conversation where the space remains safe, respectful and non-threatening for parties to come in and out of the talk as they wish. At a minimum, you act as a traffic cop when more than one participant wants to speak at the same time by acknowledging the hand signals of those queuing up to get into the discussion. You also need to ensure that two or three participants do not dominate the dialogue in their efforts to make their point known. However, the work of the facilitator is more than that. Much depends on where the group is at in terms of getting clarity on the issues and arriving at shared meaning. There is huge wisdom embedded in the North American Indian saying:

'You talk and talk and then the talk begins'

This suggests three layers of dialogic talking: conversational talk, talking it out and talking it through. It takes time and patience to get to the third layer and it comes after the hot venting of emotion, the competitive clash of thoughts and the human expression of vulnerability. That's when the breakthrough normally comes – when participants really engage with each other to hear and understand what is important to the other. This creates the platform for humanization to emerge in a further and fourth layer.

Diagram 3 sets out four layers of an interactive dialogue process to provide a map for the facilitator to make judgement calls on when and where to intervene and for what purpose. It cannot be a predetermined route map or a scientific guide because you have to use your own gut instinct and intuition on whether to intervene or not, whether to control the discussion tightly or to let it go loose, whether to work on the task/issue at hand or to process the emotional/relational tension in the room. When the talk becomes unproductive, you need to step in to manage the process by summarising the positive bits and reframing the unproductive bits, while at the same time holding the hope and balancing the power.

At layer one, you create the safe interactive space right from the start where each point of view can be heard and respected. This does not necessarily mean going around the whole circle to ensure every voice gets heard but certainly to get first thoughts from as many parties as possible. You do not need to intervene much but you will want to acknowledge non-verbally whatever issue, question or comment surfaces at this early stage in order to create a listening culture. Opening contributions tend to be polite but someone is bound to come straight off the starting blocks to sound off on a recent event or ask some direct questions.

Layer one gives way to layer two when participants move from surface issues to go deeper into their own party analysis of the topic under discussion. A crucial process issue arises here of 'Which comes first?' – for a party to understand the other or to be understood? Resist the temptation of trying to get one party to understand the other's point of view too early on in the storytelling process. It is much harder for one party to reach out cognitively and emotionally to understand the other before they have been understood themselves. The point at which they are ready to give recognition to the other is when they have been fully heard and understood by the circle with support from the facilitator.

Parties need to feel that their sincerely-held political goals and collective fears are being acknowledged before being encouraged to translate these into future focused interests. Sometimes it is difficult for parties to put words on it and to be exact on what they mean so you need to make the understanding explicit through accurate reflective feedback. This includes separating out what seems to be really important for that party from the rhetoric, to make sense of the experience they have been through and to clarify the meaning behind their words. It is as if to say: 'Is that it?'

Diagram 3: four layers of interactive political dialogue

Layer 1
Hearing first thoughts and opening concerns/issues of what is important for each party in the circle

Layer 2
Supporting each party to identify key symbolic issues, group fears, future focused interests and constraints

Layer 3
Productive dialogue – supporting each party to face and engage with the realities of other to each other's satisfaction, given political constraints of their constituency

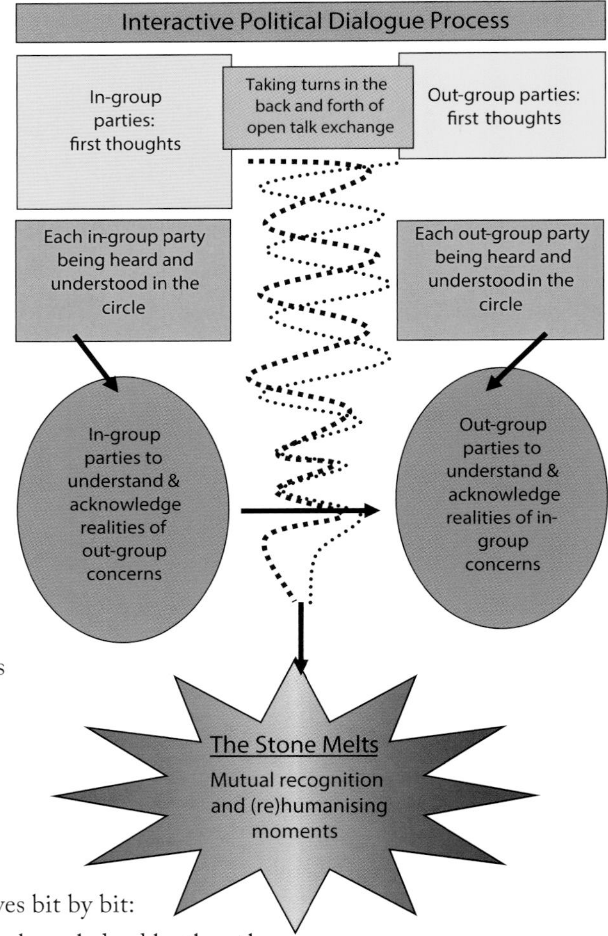

Layer 4
Inter-group hostility dissolves bit by bit:

- as each feels heard and acknowledged by the other
- as new understandings and insights emerge about the complexities of the conflicted issues
- from which a new inter-group relationship of trust gets built

A common platform of shared understandings gets formed for co-creating mutual solutions and unexpected outcomes on the journey

But a word of warning: the facilitator only goes deep when the participants are ready and want to go there. Non-verbal cues are important here as you maintain eye contact around the circle to see how connected participants are to what is being said verbally and what their body language is saying. Remember the body often gives clues in advance of the verbal. Then a probing question might open up some hidden meanings or assumptions that have not yet been uncovered.

Layer two is very much the storytelling phase of dialogue and requires several aspects to be worked on at the same time as parties listen concurrently to strong party perspectives. First, a contribution will probably be framed in positional language and peppered with enemy perceptions and blame against the other. Narrative theorists call it the 'saturated story' (Winslade and Monk, 2008) where feelings, issues and assumptions are compacted together in an obsessive collective narrative. If the elements of the perspective are in sequence, it has the elements of a rehearsed and polished story that draws on their own party's narrative of the Troubles. It will have been told again and again about their group's political experience over the years and held in the group emotional memory (Volkan, 2006). PUP party leader, David Ervine, often wondered why he hated people he did not know. He came to the realisation that he was the subject of a 'taught' narrative and needed to move on to a 'thought' narrative. Party statements are probably not the whole truth but embedded in them are the grains of truth waiting to be elicited, acknowledged and re-configured. Dismissing such stories as pure spin is disrespectful and undermines the building of understanding and trust. Facilitators may have to intervene to acknowledge the meaning of the story for that party, the context from which they come and the journey they have made. This goes some way towards the circle understanding and analysing how the basic needs of each party are being met through its own saturated story.

Secondly, account needs to be taken of the barriers to dialogue. Back in 1994 before the ceasefires, it must be remembered that many politicians didn't meet across party lines and the 'politics of the latest atrocity' kept the polarisation intact over the thirty years of the Troubles. Political violence created fear in each community of the other, driving people into the hands of those who protected them. When the state did not come to fill the void, a community was left to its own young men to protect them through paramilitary groups.

Diagram 4: Polarisation dynamics

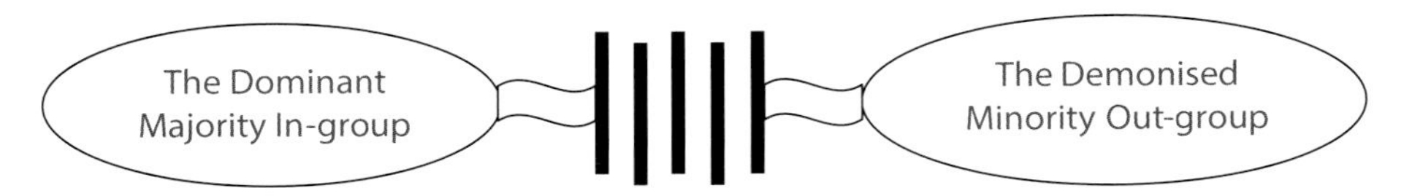

Psychological and relational barriers

The workshops held immediately after the ceasefires made it possible for protagonists to sit in the room together and to work through many emotional and relational barriers that get in the way of renewing direct communication. Some of the participants would have lived through the trauma of Bloody Sunday (Derry) and Bloody Friday (Belfast) in 1972, the worst year of the violence. Others would have marched with the Civil Rights movement 1968-72, taken part in Orange parades, done time in prison for shootings, or done service with the British Army or the RUC. Participants from the dominant unionist majority came in fear of the demon they were about to meet; some could not control their anger at what the other had done to their people; while others grappled silently with their perceptions of the threat that the others still posed to their community. Those coming from the minority nationalist outgroup came with feelings of humiliation of being treated as second class citizens, of their ethnic Irish identity not being recognised and a sense of indignity when moral/religious judgements are made about them which effectively excludes them from being at home in Northern Ireland. In effect, both sides have experienced dehumanization and demonization at the hands of the other either personally or collectively.

These tensions would at times surface in the room. Nearly all the Northern Ireland participants had suffered from their own trauma of losing family members or were affected by secondary victimisation. In the interactive storytelling that unfolded, you could hear the personal pain breaking through, both within and outside the sessions.

Thirdly, it is essential to listen to the 'personal' in the story being told and to support a party to speak from their personal experience. Politicians will resist this shift initially, but it is amazing when someone has the courage to speak personally, how it opens up the space for others. The power of recognising and acknowledging the efforts made by each party in telling their story and their willingness to talk about their own experience, cannot be underestimated. We forget about the internal dialogue that must be going on inside a person's lived experience and the struggle for the unspoken voice to find a way to express itself in words.

Emotion is embedded in and attached to the personal story. By drawing the hot emotion, frustration, annoyance and anger to yourself as facilitator through reflective listening, you can ensure the attack does not land on the other party. This party-to-facilitator dialogue is crucial for de-escalation. Parties want to tell the circle what they experienced, what it was like to have been there and how it affected them. By clarifying and reframing concerns and fears behind statements that could be perceived as an attack or blame on another party, you prevent escalation in the room and a potential political standoff or a walkout.

When a party says the same thing a second or third time, the instinctive reaction of the facilitator is to wish they would stop repeating themselves. However, this is actually a cue telling you that is the bit they want to have heard. Once it is heard and acknowledged, the person is likely to move on.

The breakthrough into layer three comes as party-to-party dialogue gets off the ground and one party reaches out to engage the other; when one party is ready to make a shift in their perspective by being able to take on or consider the perspective of the other.

You can see it coming when one party actually shifts in their seat and turns their body to hear the other, asks them a question or responds reflectively to a point already made. Weingarten (2003) identifies it as the point when one party is able to listen carefully to the other without defensiveness. For Bush and Folger (2005) 'the hallmark of a recognition shift is letting go - however briefly or partially - of one's focus on self and becoming interested in the perspective of the other party as such, concerned about the situation of the other as a fellow human being, not as an instrument for fulfilling one's own needs.'

When moments like this arise, you will need to hold back others, who are waiting in the queue to voice their point of view, to connect those two or three participants in sustained dialogue for some moments. This may require you to support one party to understand what the other is saying. Rogers (1977) calls it the bi-lateral check. Here are some questions which are useful to consolidate party-to-party understanding:

- What do you think Sinn Féin does not yet fully understand about your situation?
- Which bit does the Unionist party [name of person] not yet fully appreciate?
- What do you now understand about what the British Government has said here in the room that you did not appreciate before?
- In what way has your question/concern been answered by the Irish Government [name of person] in what you have just heard?
- Is there anything you want to ask SDLP that you still have a question about?
- What is it that you do not yet understand about what the Alliance Party did last week?
- Could you turn to British Labour [name of person] and put that concern you have just raised directly to them?

Layer three gives the parties the possibility to work with the difficult questions they want to ask of the other that have been going around in their mind for some time or have come up for them in the circle. The challenge for each party person who asks such a question is whether they are ready to listen respectfully, take the answer on board and revise the assumption they have made for some time. This is the difference between layer two, where the question is being used to get at the other and to score a political point, and layer three where the pace is much slower, perhaps some silence, and the listening party gives themselves thinking time before attempting to respond. They have reached the point where each can speak more honestly about the situation they are in and think aloud in the circle about the challenge being presented to their previously frozen political assumptions.

Through the process of being heard and acknowledged at layer two, and now being able to understand what is important for the other at layer three, former protagonists realise that the conflict has multiple truths and not as fixed as once perceived. Each party can no longer claim exclusive rights to the truth. The process changes their perceptions of the other. Each side begins to see their opponent in a new way as they hear the other's story and the human struggle they have been through. 'I no longer have to defend my position as an Orangeman/Shinner and am able to tell you about all the Orange/Provo views.' What seemed demonic or weird now appears heroic and reasonable when seen in the other person's context. This is called the transformation moment – that micro-moment when something changes for a person and they frame the situation differently, something that seemed impossible before.

It is unclear what makes up the chemistry of these change moments and whether the relational change comes about by the cognitive or the affective. Does a person's thinking change by affective empathy when they have been touched by the emotion in the other's story: 'I am feeling what it must have been like for you.' Or does a person feel warmer towards another when they have heard in some new way [through cognitive empathy] what the other is saying: 'I can understand better why you had to take that course of action.' Maybe it is contingent on personal style and whether a person is mainly a left brain logical thinker or has a right brain approach who learns relationally through their experience with others. If the circle supports both affective and cognitive empathy, then hopefully the change fires on twin engines and has a Gemini rocket effect.

The process changes their perceptions of the other

In the interactions of the workshops, there was a powerful sequential link between new information and new understandings by one party about the other and the emergence of new insights, often called the 'Aha! Moment' - the 'Eureka moment' - when the light bulb switches on for people. Melchin and Picard (2009) believe that 'insights, once achieved, reshape the way we experience the sensory data the next time around'. It is a profoundly experiential moment which changes feelings and thought. Affective insights change feelings about the other when they hear what matters to them in ways they were unable to before. Cognitive insights are moments of discovery and clarity following periods of confusion allowing a party to accept the necessity for change.

Once we reach this synergistic point of new understandings and new insights, we are on the threshold of layer four. It is a sort of magical humanising moment that just happens. New insights give new meaning, allowing the person to have a breakthrough experience. It enables a 'softening of the heart' or the 'melting of the stone' of old assumptions which, in turn, allows people to reach out to each other. It unlocks the door in the wall to the other side. The hardened collective fear is dissolving and respect for the other is building. The stone may not melt all in one go but dissolves over a period of time as parties re-engage with each other through a number of workshops.

It is hard to trace the moments when relational change happens through the I-You humanising encounter, whether it takes place in the circle or during the informal time. It is a relational transaction that progressively builds through the mutual acknowledgement experience of what each other side is actually thinking as opposed to previously held perceptions. But it is more than that. By one out-group person feeling acknowledged and understood by an in-group person, and vice versa, 'you are seeing the person behind the Unionist/Nationalist label...the meaning behind the rhetoric'. By one side reclaiming their loss of dignity and humanity, it freed the other to regain their self-respect. 'We are now meeting each other at an equal level.'

A commitment grows with each other to keep going with the dialogue because 'we are all inextricably caught up in this together.' Increasing trust between members of the group - and trust in the process itself - leads to the expression of the sorts of thoughts and feelings that are usually kept hidden. Parties no longer 'have to put one another in a difficult position and watching each other's back.' Some found it hard to realise how far they had come. They could remember at an earlier stage working with the question: 'Are we going to talk to each other?' and 'Will the peace process leave the station?' Now, having made the journey together on the peace process train, it was all about 'how things are going to work.'

Between the workshops

At the end of each workshop, a list of names and emails/addresses/phone numbers of people who attended were circulated so that participants could keep in contact with each other. This proved to be very valuable in a conflict situation where politicians would change their mobile numbers frequently for security reasons. Sometimes, learning points and outcomes were distilled in a synopsis after the workshop to enable ideas to be fed back by the participants to their respective parties and policy-making meetings.

Many participants followed up the contacts and used each other as lines of communication between the parties in the lead up to the negotiations at Stormont. Their friendships have endured over the years and they have worked together on the problems arising from the non-implementation of the Good Friday/Belfast agreement and on interface projects on the ground such as the safe conduct of parades.

Primacy of dialogue

Political dialogue reaffirms the primacy of politics and breathes new political oxygen into the body politic of a protracted identity conflict like that in Northern Ireland, enabling the birth of a peace process, even though it may start from very small fragile beginnings. It struggles to find such a space given the dominance of hard military/militant power and the revengeful grip of hawkish thinking. But when it takes hold in second track political activists, it can make inroads into the top political leadership or bide its time for the ripe moment when military/militant approaches have over-extended themselves and forced the people to re-think (Zartman, 2003).

After many hours of engagement, participants in the Glencree workshops were surprised that their original fears of the other had dissolved and the demonic horns on their protagonists have melted considerably. The workshops supported participants to connect with the other, to hear what it is like for each other and to shift into an equal power relationship. Their ability to humanise the political relationship created the basis for many more political things to happen which would come to fruition in the post-conflict phase and showing leadership on how to work together.

The political dialogue workshops confirmed the strategic role they play in building analytical capacity. Over the course of the workshops both southern and northern political activists were able to fine tune their political thinking and to do some considerable rethinking of their respective national and unionist narratives. We saw the mindsets of politicians shifting to meet the new realities of the times. This could not have happened in public space because of the political climate. Private off-site space gives the freedom to explore and discuss issues and to see the humanity of the other. Participants come away with a clearer understanding of their own real interests

New insights give new meaning, allowing the person to have a breakthrough experience

as well as those of their protagonists, particularly in how they can be resolved at the negotiating table.

However, the workshops also build motivational capacity similar to the original T-groups initiated by Kurt Lewin in the late 1940s (Johnson & Johnson, 1975). Participants become more self aware of their own identity after being able to tell their story and voice their concerns. They left with greater hope in themselves, overcoming personal despair and doubts that the peace process might stall. After all, it is a political process greater than any one party. Perhaps this was the most important outcome. Participants went away re-energised with a new sense of what is possible. This proved to be infectious within their own party, particularly at times when their own political community was disenchanted.

The danger is that dialogue workshops are discounted as the 'the talk-a-lot' project. Of course, dialogue is not enough; people want to see tangible negotiated outcomes and value for money in peacemaking projects. What they tend not to see because they are under the radar is that long lasting political relationships come slowly in protracted failed situations.

References

Bush R.A.B and Folger J.P. *The Promise of Mediation: The Transformative Approach to Conflict,* Jossey-Bass (2005), p77.

Corry, G. *'Impact of Steel Shutter Film on the Beginnings of Glencree Centre',* in C.Murphy and L. Adair (ed.), *A Place for Peace: Glencree Centre for Reconciliation 1974-2004,* Liffey Press (2004).

Corry, G. *'Political Dialogue Workshops: Deepening the Peace Process in Northern Ireland',* Conflict Resolution Quarterly, 30/1 (2004), 53-80.

Johnson, D W & Johnson, F P. *Joining Together: Group Theory and Group Skills, Prentice-Hall* (1975), p15.

EU concept paper, *'Dialogue and Mediation as European Union Tools to Address and Prevent Conflict',* Folke Bernardotte Academy (2009).

Kelman, H. C. *'Interactive Problem Solving: A social-psychological approach to conflict resolution',* in John Burton and Frank Dukes, *Conflict: Readings in Management and Resolution,* Macmillan (1990).

Kelman, H. C. *'Experiences from 30 Years of Action research on the Israeli-Palestinian Conflict',* Paper presented to the Harvard PON (2003).

Lederach, J. P. *The Moral Imagination, The Art and Soul of Building Peace,* Oxford, 2005.

Melchin, K.R and Picard, Cheryl. *Transforming Conflict through Insight, University of Toronto Press* (2009), p58. Pruitt, D. G. *Communication Chains in negotiation between Organisations,* Occasional

Paper 3, *Program on International Conflict Resolution,* Sabanci University, Turkey, 2003. www.sabanciuniv.edu/ssbf/conf/eng/docs/

Rogers, C. *On Personal Power: Inner Strength and its Revolutionary Impact,* Delacorte Press, 1977, pp129-133.

Ropers, N. *'From Resolution to Transformation: The role of Dialogue Projects',* Berghof Center for Constructive Conflict Management. www.berghof-handbook.net

Stedman, S. *'Reflections on Implementing Peace Agreements in Civil Wars'*, Paper presented to Glencree Summer School 2001.

Volkan, V. D. *Killing in the Name of Identity: A Study of Bloody Conflicts,* Pitchstone Publishing, 2006.

Winslade, J & Monk, G. *Practicing Narrative Mediation: A New Approach to Conflict Resolution,* Jossey-Bass (2008).

Weingarten, Kaethe. *Common Shock: Witnessing Violence Every Day: How we are harmed, How we can heal,* Dutton (2003), p133.

Zartman, W. *'The Timing of Peace Initiatives: Hurting Stalemates and Ripe Moments',* in Chapter 2 of John Darby & Roger MacGinty, eds, *Contemporary Peacemaking: Conflict, Violence, and Peace Processes.* Palgrave Macmillan (2003).

Through the dialogue they learnt over time to see the humanity in one another

LIVE: Let's Involve the Victim's Experience

Jacinta De Paor

Background

I grew up in a house which I often said embodied the peace process. My mother was from Coleraine, the daughter of an RIC[1] police officer. My father was from Waterford, in turn, his mother was a Barry from Cork. Both families lived through the turbulent 1920s in Ireland. There was always a lot of good political discussion in the house and I grew up with an interest in politics and a strong awareness of the challenges posed by difference and diversity. A career in psychology led me to work both in Ireland and the US with a variety of people who struggled to 'fit in': young offenders; people with schizophrenia; adults and children who had experienced sexual abuse and trauma. Labeling people inevitably leads to sweeping generalisations and stereotyping, a breeding ground for prejudice often built on fear of the 'other'. Once that barrier of fear is removed people are more easily able to see their shared common humanity. So in 1998, when a position became available for someone to work with victim/survivors in the Glencree Centre for Peace and Reconciliation, I felt it was made for me.

[1] The Royal Irish Constabulary (RIC) was an all island police force from the nineteenth century to the establishment of the Free State in 1922.

The LIVE programme (Let's Involve the Victim's Experience)

The LIVE programme, an acronym for 'Let's Involve the Victim's Experience' was the brainchild of Ian White, then director of Glencree. Through his involvement in the Glencree Political Dialogue Programme he saw the need for victim/survivor voices to be heard. Following the Good Friday Agreement in 1998, victim/survivors struggled to get their needs met. The stress of living in areas where tensions flared regularly took a strong emotional, physical and psychological toll on people in terms of fear, loss and trauma.

During my first year there, I worked alongside the Programme Coordinator, Jan de Vries. When he left for the US at the end of that year I took over the organisation and delivery of LIVE. At that time I remember victims saying to me that they felt that they were being seen as an embarrassment to the Peace Process and were being told, *'Get on with life, don't be looking back into the past we need to move forward'*. There was a very limited real understanding of how people had suffered as a result of the conflict.

Bringing Victim/Survivors Together

The main purpose of LIVE was to bring together victim/survivors from 'all communities' on these islands, to share their experiences and also to foster dialogue between them and ex combatants in order to support reconciliation at grassroots level. A unique feature of the programme was that it included all three strands of the Peace Process partners, Northern Ireland, Britain and the Republic of Ireland. It was also the first time that such an inclusive group of victims/survivors had been brought together on these islands.

Participants were provided with the opportunity to talk about what they had experienced and to share those experiences, when they were ready, with other victim/survivors in a group setting. Talking about traumatic memories presented an opportunity for detailed processing of those memories and for many it was the first time they had done anything like this. The empathic support that participants created relationally within the group ensured that often, people instinctively understood each other without having to express it verbally. Sometimes just listening and being witness to the stories told was powerful enough in and of itself.

Quilt in Glencree Armoury Café

We were very clear with those who came, that the LIVE Programme was not a therapy programme. As a psychologist I was experienced enough to keep those boundaries and helped our facilitators to do the same. However, the outcomes of the programme were often therapeutic due to the sharing and support that was available in a supportive environment away from the pressure of their own streets and neighbourhoods.

The LIVE Way

The methodology became known as the LIVE way. The work was mostly done in a residential setting at Glencree over a series of weekends. The main advantage to the residential aspect of the work was that participants got away from their families, neighbourhoods and responsibilities which allowed for a greater length and depth of interactions. Glencree itself was remote, deep in the Dublin Mountains, the only distraction being birdsong or the odd rabbit or deer that disturbed the peace.

From my previous experience and trainings, I devised a series of carefully crafted workshops designed to facilitate discussion with the minimum of trauma. At the end of nine years we ended up with a comprehensive programme for dialogue. Facilitators came from the North and the South of Ireland with some from the US, France and Canada. The most important attributes being their training, skill and their neutrality regarding the conflict. They worked hard to provide a supportive and empathic environment to help people share their stories with each other in a spirit of trust.

As part of the process, we provided the facilitation and built in a flexible agenda. This ensured that participants had a strong input into the direction of the programme. As well as the structured settings, we had workshops and presentations on issues identified by the participants as important to them; we also had interactive theatre; exercises in coping with stress and social events. The nature of the programme was such that we often changed direction half way through the weekend when I could see something of greater significance and importance was emerging from within the participant discussions.

Outside the formal sessions, we had walks and music evenings where a lot of very significant serious exchanges took place as well as lots of good humoured fun. I remember one fancy dress party, where Scarlett O'Hara from the film Gone with the Wind arrived in an outfit, hoops and all.

Glencree was a very busy centre and in addition to ours there were other programmes running and interesting visitors coming to the Centre. When these visits coincided with our programme events I capitalised shamelessly on this and would often link them with our participants. This was to broaden the participant's experience of Glencree and for them to experience a little of life beyond these shores and see the common links between persons in conflict. Colm O'Regan brought a group of Australian Aboriginal people to visit and I asked if our two groups could meet. The experience was one of deep learning for both parties. Young people came in from the Glencree Youth Programme; people from the Glencree Churches Programme; politicians from the Political Programme and many others which added a depth and richness to the discussions at the weekends. LIVE participants were very touched by the young people, often seeing in them the embodiment of why they had come to Glencree, to make a better future. The members of the Glencree International Volunteer Programme, who lived at Glencree and supported the programmes, brought insights from other worlds in conflict, from Afghanistan, Palestine, Bosnia, South Africa and Nepal, Haiti, to name but a few places.

'Never again'

Most of the participants attended LIVE as part of their efforts to come to terms with the trauma, grief, anger, survivor guilt and stress experienced during the conflict. Many had lost loved ones, through violence, some had survived killings and others lived with the continuous threat of violence. Parents of British soldiers who were killed serving in Northern Ireland came; people came from most of the major incidents in NI; people came from the south who had survived isolated violent incidents in the Republic, for instance: bombings; people whose businesses had been targeted; a relative of a customer shot in an IRA bank raid; someone whose relative had disappeared. Over and over again I was to hear a common theme echoed by the parent of a soldier in tears over their son being shot dead, 'I don't want any other parent to have to go through what I'm going through'.

They certainly didn't come to Glencree for physical comfort. In that large imposing barracks building sometimes the heating would fail, the water was brown, it would rain continuously and an ex-combatant described the beds as worse than those in prison. But people came, making long journeys from Britain or down on the bus from Derry starting out in the early hours of the morning and arriving at six o'clock in the evening, tired and often in pain as a result of their conflict injuries. They came because they wanted their loss and suffering to mean something.

Tree commemorating
Tim Parry

Gathering participants

The LIVE project was publicised in newspapers, on the radio, through newsletters. We went north and met small and larger victim/survivor groups and told them about the programme. We often had to convince them that Glencree was safe because at that time it was unusual to have somewhere safe and secure to go to. Many had never been south of the border before and nothing prepared some of them for the remoteness and the beauty of Glencree when they did come.

'They all came into the room that first year' (1998)

So they all came into the room in that first year, victims/survivors and combatants, people who were geographically spread and ideologically different were welcomed. We had relatives of a young lad killed by British soldiers with a rubber bullet. We had people whose sons were killed as British soldiers and those who were injured in bombings who were serving in the Irish army along the border. We had people who had served as police; victims of bombings in Britain in places like Warrington and Canary Wharf. We had people whose relatives had been in the IRA and had been killed. We didn't distinguish between participants, as far as we were concerned it was anyone who considered themselves to be a victim or survivor be they Catholic, Protestant, unionist or nationalist, whether they had served in the police or the armed forces, legitimate or not, there were no judgments at LIVE.

The Sessions

The sessions started on Friday evening with dinner. Facilitators welcomed everybody, the ground rules were simple and people were asked to listen to each person's story as if it was their own, without interrupting. Respect for each other's opinion and maintaining confidentiality were important and we asked that people should only share what they wanted to or felt comfortable with and that listening was as important as talking. In the after dinner session on Friday evening, people got an opportunity to share what was uppermost on their mind at the time. The sessions were often opened up with questions; I learned very quickly the importance of good open questions that would deepen understanding and elicit curiosity, as opposed to closing down dialogue. Training acquired through Public Conversations Project that I attended in the United States was very helpful in this regard.

On Saturday morning, issues raised on Friday evening could be explored further within a more structured programme and the Saturday sessions were often followed by walks outside, a bus trip to Powerscourt or Glendalough or a walk to a nearby lake. I constantly watched carefully to see who might or might not be talking to whom and it was wonderful to witness people becoming more relaxed and chatting to each other as the days progressed.

We valued each person's story equally, despite often having many high profile victim/survivors at the sessions. At that time, there was much debate about who was and was not an authentic victim of the conflict and we worked to challenge the notion of the existence of a hierarchy of victims.

Participants valued those opportunities afforded to them by LIVE. English people often said that they learnt about Irish history for the first time. Working class Protestants were shocked to learn that they were often as poor as their Catholic counterparts and that their upbringing was remarkably similar to theirs. People talked to 'the other' who may have lived a few streets away from them but because of sectarianism, had had no previous contact. Many from the South who lived at a distance from the cauldron of the conflict, met and learned about the impact of the violence on entire communities in Northern Ireland. While the formal sessions ran in the morning and afternoon and early evening, much of the deep discussion happened into the late evening or night. There, with the benefit of the quiet in Glencree and the odd drink or two, people shared deep personal hurts and suffering with honesty and a sense of relief.

I insisted on a high ratio of facilitators to participants which was often challenged by funders, but I persisted. The facilitation team worked intensely, in small groups, with people who did not feel able to speak in the large group. Sometimes this even necessitated working on a one to one basis if we noticed that a victim needed special attention. The team met continuously throughout the weekend to assess how people were doing. While there was no pressure on people to speak, we also reassured them that being a witness to another's loss and trauma was also powerful. We took small steps, recognising that not everybody was prepared to either encounter themselves or 'the other'. When they had departed, having first made sure that they had support when they went home, our facilitators debriefed again and usually crept home shattered. Then work started for the next session.

Jacinta de Paor and Eamon Rafter at Glencree workshop

While there were often people, from outside, who requested to sit in the sessions, we were cautious about the impact this could have on the group and always consulted participants in advance. We tried to discourage voyeurism by stressing that, regardless of reasons or status, all who attended were expected to share their story. This often included television crews and media people who wanted to record the process. The work we did was always attractive to researchers who frequently asked to interview participants and we were reticent about that, fearing that the participants could be used only as research subjects. While we recognised the importance of research, our programme's primary purpose was about establishing avenues for sustainable peace, not the betterment of people's careers.

Challenges and Lessons Learnt

In my view, the first couple of years of the LIVE Programme achieved its aims. At the behest of the participants, both victim/survivors and ex-combatants met together in a sensitively controlled environment and benefited from the cross fertilisation of people and ideas.

After year three, we adopted what was called the H model. This involved separate ex-combatant and victim/survivor sessions and the idea was that the horizontal bar in the H would provide the bridge to bring both victims and ex combatants together. While there was some interaction between the two groupings, it was very intermittent and there was never enough to establish a foundation for real transformation. By having two parts of the same programme operate in parallel isolation, we were never going to realise our programme aims. With hindsight, by having the two programme coordinators jointly facilitate sessions, across both parts of the programme, we would have assured that the perspectives of both victim/survivor and former combatant were represented at all sessions thus leading to a richness and greater depth of interaction between the two groups. This was something that was done and which achieved success in the last six months of the LIVE programme. It greatly assisted in the process of transformation and saw participants actively seeking solutions to a peaceful future for their children. Creative innovations that began there continue, even today, beyond the life of the LIVE programme.

Bringing people together with different ideologies and trying to facilitate a dialogue where some victim/survivors saw themselves as being more worthy of being called a victim than another was challenging. However, the LIVE process heightened participant's awareness of themselves and others; encouraging them to take responsibility for their own participation; to withdraw and take time out if they did not feel capable of proceeding. Meetings between victims/survivors and ex-combatants required intense, careful preparation for both parties before any face to face or group meetings could take place.

While it was clear that victim/survivors often had difficulty hearing each other's perspectives, despite living side by side or on the next street, through the dialogue they learned over time to see the humanity in one another. While there were many who had difficulty travelling down together, they were often observed travelling home together after the weekend. People developed and maintained friendships through coming to Glencree during those weekends and even the occasional romance blossomed.

Despite preparation there were many examples of incidents that happened which told us to be prepared for the unexpected. We had a challenging group of nationalist and unionists in the room one weekend. The discussion was animated and heated; one of the nationalists made a gesture with a pointed finger which a unionist interpreted as that of a pointed gun. It emerged that he had been a victim of republican violence. It took time and patient dialogue over a number of meetings to help each understand where 'the other' was coming from.

On the financial front, there were horrendous reporting requirements for the funding and after the first year, the funding seemed to be increasingly connected to numbers or 'bums on seats' rather than the quality and depth of the work. This clampdown was as a result of some groups in border areas running cross border bus trips or offering computer courses across the border that often had limited reconciliation potential or content. This caused problems for those of us who were encouraging deep thinking and reflection in the dialogue sessions which had many positive ripple effects in their families and communities.

The political environment or an increase in violence had implications for attendance. It often led to last minute cancellations of people coming across the border which resulted in limited perspectives in group discussions. For the first number of years of the LIVE programme, both the Catholic/nationalist community and the Protestant/ unionist community were equally represented. However, mid-way through the nine year programme unionists stopped coming down. This was as a direct result of remarks made by a public figure in the Republic which were misinterpreted. Despite efforts to repair the damage, it meant us having to engage unionists on an individual basis in Northern Ireland.

More Lessons Learnt

Internationally, the LIVE programme was represented when I spoke in the U.S. to The Association for Conflict Resolution's Conferences in Florida, Philadelphia and Minnesota. I also presented at Quinnipiac University, Connecticut and at Process Psychotherapy trainings in Portland Oregon. I represented the programme at Leuven University's international project on Victims of Terrorism and was a consultant to the Victim's Unit of the Basque Government in Spain amongst many others. This latter was as a direct result of a BBC Radio 4 interview given by a British LIVE participant, the father of a soldier killed in Derry, being heard by the London Correspondent for El País and thus began the LIVE connection with the Basque Government and Spanish victims of violence. When I went abroad, I often found that people talked about Northern Ireland and the Troubles, in a voyeuristic way. I wanted them to hear a different story; I wanted them to hear real people talking, about their lives, hopes and aspirations, rather than being talked about. At all these events people were constantly asking me whether I had a 'how to' manual of the methodologies that I had developed. It is one of my great regrets that I never had time to compile one. I was always 'doing the work' but never had time to write up what I was creating and developing, in the detail needed for publication.

With the benefit of hindsight, we should have developed an exit strategy for victims/survivors to move on more quickly but the context in which people were living was still difficult and the deep effect of trauma and post-traumatic stress disorder (PTSD) was only something that was beginning to be understood by professionals in the field. We were moving from a place where support constituted a young police constable being handed a bottle of whiskey by their superior officer when in hospital recovering from a serious bomb explosion, to a place where support was victim/survivor led. In 2008, we were in the process of instituting a mentoring programme, where participants would bring new people to LIVE and support them back at home when the programme funding finished.

Amazing Encounters

There were some amazing engagements I remember. One evening when we were in a group session one woman whose husband was killed said, *'I don't know why I came this weekend, it's a bad weekend for me to come down, there's an anniversary coming up. I don't know why I'm down here'.* As the conversation developed, a man who was a former paramilitary spoke to her. He asked to address her directly. So now we had a dialogue spontaneously happening between the two. I asked her *'Is that alright with you'?* And she said, *'yes'.* So, he said: *'I want to say something. Your husband was killed in very traumatic circumstances, I won't go into it now but the day he was killed, I was a prisoner in Long Kesh and I heard the news'.* Then he said, *'In that moment, I decided to renounce violence'.* Then she said; *'Now I know why I came this weekend'!* After that, those two worked and continue to work together in communities to build peace, not in any public high profile way, but they do what they can to bring grassroots communities to peace.

I remember the visit of Prince Charles to Glencree in February 2002. One event took place in the Canada Room. All the programme staff and representatives of programme participants were there including his own staff, politicians and other dignitaries. Things were proceeding as planned, with inputs from participants. And then something remarkable happened. A participant from the LIVE programme, a former paratrooper started to speak. I heard him tell Prince Charles that his mother was killed in Aldershot in retaliation for Bloody Sunday; he went on to say that he joined the army as soon as he could and hated all things Irish. Coming to Glencree and engaging in the LIVE Programme made him aware of the complexities of Irish history and furthered his own journey towards forgiveness and reconciliation. Prince Charles was listening avidly but, as he was on a tight schedule his staff were signing to him that he had to leave. He ignored them and he went on to talk about his own personal journey towards forgiveness for those who had killed his uncle, Lord Mountbatten, in the seventies at the height of the conflict. This was LIVE in action.

Jo Berry[2] and Pat Magee[3] of the Building Bridges Project[4], have spoken publicly about being members of the LIVE programme and have gone on to bring their reconciliation work across the globe. Their initial meetings happened through the work of another member, Anne Gallagher[5] (sadly deceased last year) from the Seeds of Hope Project. Various dignitaries came in acknowledgement of the work we were doing and joined in our workshops such as: Baroness Nuala O'Loan, former NI Police Ombudsman; Sir Kenneth Bloomfield former head of NI Civil Service and NI Victim's Commissioner; Kadar Asmal, Minister for Education in South Africa, to name but some. They all shared their stories and experiences of conflict and trauma with the group.

One of the most significant and memorable events I organised was in Long Kesh (the main prison at the height of the Troubles). The prison had long been shut down and I got permission to hold a private workshop there for LIVE participants on the weekend of our Annual Conference. They came in buses from Derry, Belfast, in cars from all over the Republic and some even flew in to Belfast from Britain. The significance of the event was those who came: former INLA, PIRA, loyalists, politicians, British parents of soldiers killed in Northern Ireland, some from Republic of Ireland who had lost family members, former police and even a former prison guard at Long Kesh.

[2] Sir Anthony Berry MP was killed in the IRA Brighton Bombing during the 1984 Tory Party Conference, his daughter Jo was thrown into a conflict she knew very little about. In November 2000 Jo Berry met Pat Magee, the man responsible for her father's death and today, they work together towards building peace.

[3] Belfast-born Pat Magee, former IRA activist, was given multiple life sentences for the Brighton Bombing. Released under the Good Friday Agreement in 1999, he has since been actively involved in peace work.

[4] Jo Berry and Pat Magee now run an organisation promoting peace and conflict resolution throughout the world. You can find out more at buildingbridgesforpeace.org

[5] Anne Gallagher founded Seeds of Hope, an organisation that facilitates storytelling, based on the Troubles, through music, art, drama, writing and sport. Her family was very strongly impacted by the conflict in Northern Ireland.

It was incredible to witness a frank discussion between a former prison guard and a man who had been a prisoner and to hear them talk together in one of the guards towers with such respect and good humour.

Although the programme finished in 2008, due to lack of funding, the work of LIVE is recognised and still talked about when the subject of reconciliation arises. At the recent Sarajevo Peace Event held in June 2014, both LIVE and Glencree were referenced in a positive way.

I am still in contact with past participants and facilitators of the LIVE programme, as are they with me, through a wide set of networks and social media. I often marvel at the former members of the Glencree International Volunteers Programme, who live all over the world, as they still connect with each other, at times in languages that I don't even recognise. The common thread is that they all spent time at Glencree and developed a deep connection to the programme and its participants. They are remembered fondly by those same participants who ask me about them, even today.

I wish that Glencree continues to prosper and that more outreach work is done. I also wish that both International and Irish students gain a unique, on site, opportunity to have an authentic experience of the incredible work accomplished there. To this end the publication of a workshop series for difficult dialogues needs to happen, as well as training in Glencree methodologies and mentoring for those that request it. But more that this, I wish that more can experience the deep and abiding philosophy of peace that pervades there.

Finally, I must pay tribute to those brave and wonderful people, the participants, who despite the awful traumas they were still living with, made the journey to the programme and who continued that journey with us over the nine years of LIVE: the one year programme that kept on growing.

A core value guiding the work of Glencree is inclusivity

Working with Former Combatants & the Sustainable Peace Network

Wilhelm Verwoerd

A Brief History of the Former Combatants Programme

The work with former combatants[1] grew out of the 'LIVE' programme. Within this programme there were sporadic opportunities for dialogue between members of the LIVE programme and former politically motivated prisoners. These encounters highlighted the need for a parallel programme involving non-state and state combatant groupings, and providing more regular 'survivor-combatant' interactions.

At the beginning of 2002 the basic 'H' vision for a new Glencree 'Survivors and Former Combatants Programme' was to have one programme with two strands - accommodating the needs of victims/survivors and former combatants while providing more structured, cross-cutting opportunities for engagement. However, while the 'H' vision provided a useful guiding framework, the practical implementation proved to be even more tricky than expected. Thus we ended up with two, more loosely connected programmes – the LIVE Programme and the Former Combatants Programme –

[1] The language of 'combatants' remained contested throughout this programme, but we used it as a relatively inclusive, non-judgemental term, following the Geneva Conventions, to refer to 'all armed parties to the conflict' (in this case the conflict in and about Northern Ireland).

which reflected the deep tensions in this sector of peace work.

'My son admired the Irish; we thought there were just a few bad people and that if the baddies could be sorted out everything would be fine. I hated the killers; the worst for me was the tit for tat killings...I could not understand why people were killing each other. I was all bitter when I went to Glencree 8 years ago... listening to stories of other victims I realized that they felt the same.

I used to think of 'goodies' and 'baddies' and then realized I wanted to kill the people who killed my son... then gradually I began to see that you ex-prisoners are just normal human beings...horrible, violent things are in all of us.'

During an extensive consultative process in 2002 to encourage a shared sense of ownership of the new programme, it became clear that especially politically motivated former prisoners did not want to be part of a programme where they would be required or expected to meet with people who saw themselves as 'victims'.

They were happy to be part of something where they could explore their issues and where they could talk about ways in which they had also suffered and their families had suffered, but they were not comfortable with the label of 'victim' to describe themselves.

'At the beginning of this journey I would rather have taken a physical beating, like those we got in prison, than sitting in the room with a victim.' Thus the focus of the Former Combatants programme for the first couple of years was formulated as follows: *'To help consolidate the peace process by providing an inclusive forum within which current and former military and paramilitary participants can meet, exchange views, build relationships and address issues.'*

The language of 'combatants' remained contested throughout this programme, but we used it as a relatively inclusive, non-judgemental term, following the Geneva Conventions, to refer to 'all armed parties to the conflict' (in this case the conflict in and about Northern Ireland).

During 2002 and 2003 regular, bi-monthly residential opportunities were created for former members of state security forces and former politically motivated prisoners, from republican and loyalist backgrounds, to meet at a human level. Many participants also expressed their appreciation for these rare opportunities to talk, formally and informally, again and again, within the relatively secluded setting provided by Glencree. The central issue emerging from the workshops was the on-going challenge of social inclusion or re-integration of politically motivated ex-prisoners. This issue highlighted the need for this former combatants forum to also include members of wider society. From 2003 onwards the Glencree residentials, therefore, also included participants from church, business, political, youth work backgrounds. During the latter half of 2004 a range of participants questioned whether the format of bi-monthly inclusive/multilateral 'ex-combatant' workshops at Glencree should be continued. These discussions underscored progress made within the peace process at that time. It was argued that participants from political ex-prisoners organisations in particular were starting to meet regularly and freely in NI/the North. It was accepted, however, that if there was a specific theme that could be best addressed at Glencree, for example an exploration of the role of the South/RoI in the peace process, that this should be pursued.

It had also become clear that to significantly increase the number of participants from police and/or military backgrounds, as well as from under represented groupings such as the UDA, more 'single identity' work in NI/the North and Britain needed to be done. A key focus for the Former Combatants Programme thus became the facilitation of 'single identity' and 'bilateral' activities. These included:

- A series of bilateral engagements between republican ex-prisoners and influential members of southern Irish society, which addressed some of the misunderstandings between southern nationalists and northern republicans and also focussed on the practical needs of politically motivated ex-prisoners south of the border;

- A focused bilateral engagement between senior retired UDR officers and representatives of republican ex-prisoners;

- Single identity capacity building work for participants from UDR and UDA backgrounds.

These activities highlighted the on-going need for 'bringing the southern voice' into the peace process, and in particular the strong need for ex-combatants to meet with representatives of wider society (business, churches, youth) from the South.

The Sustainable Peace Network project - Towards Inclusive Journeying through Conflict

During 2004 another important development began to take formal shape, with the emergence of what became known as the 'Sustainable Peace Network' (SPN). This ground-breaking project made significant progress towards the original 'H' vision, by bringing former combatants and survivors (and members of wider society) together. It also encouraged these carefully selected and influential participants to move beyond dialogue, towards on-going co-operative action.

The initial impetus for this project came from a chance encounter in August 2001 between Alistair Little and Wilhelm Verwoerd at a Glencree Summer School. Drawing on personal experiences of political conflict in Northern Ireland and South

Africa, respectively, and sharing a sense of the restorative and healing potential of nature, a vision began to take shape of bringing former enemies together with the help of nature based activities, such as a wilderness trail in South Africa.

This encounter coincided with Glencree's expansion of its work with victims/survivors and former combatants and led to a visit to South Africa in November 2001. This visit included Alistair and a republican ex-prisoner and involved meetings with South Africans from different racial backgrounds, exposure to poverty in townships and a wilderness trail in northern KwaZulu Natal. Encouraging feedback from this 2001 pilot visit resulted in two further visits to South Africa (in 2002 and 2004). These visits included (potential) participants within the LIVE and Former Combatants programmes.

'I believed the problems in Northern Ireland did not appear out of nothing, they appeared out of an all-Ireland situation. In my experience a lot of southerners did not care a damn...they buried their heads in the sand, almost like the middle and upper classes in Northern Ireland. Unless people were directly affected they just don't care...also in England...and through this disinterest they almost colluded by thus allowing the conflict to continue.

I gradually moved from a strong anti-IRA position – believing that nothing could justify the spilling of one drop of blood – to a position where I accepted that the then Stormont government would not have relented without the IRA taking up arms. Through contacts with in- laws who were heavily involved I got an insight into what motivated them, into the minds of paramilitaries.'

Out of these visits emerged the following goal and objectives of the SPN:

Overall goal

To cultivate a growing network of leaders in sustainable peace work, within and between the United Kingdom and Ireland.

Specific aims

1. *Provide opportunities for personal growth for 100 (potential) leaders, by 2010;*
2. *Promote sustainable relationships between victims/survivors, ex-combatants and members of the broader society on the islands of Ireland and Britain;*
3. *Enhance appreciation for the roles of wilderness or nature-based activities in peace cultivation.*

Between 2005 and 2010 annual groups of 12-15 diverse participants were carefully selected, with the help of nominations from previous participants. Each group consisted roughly of one third of participants from wider society and two thirds of survivors and former combatants, with participants drawn from different regions in Northern Ireland, the Republic of Ireland and Great Britain.

'For me, as I say, a lot of my thinking changed, a lot of my attitudes changed. OK, I've been dealing and working with loyalist ex-combatants, but I had never ever spoken with victims...

They never insulted me the whole time I was there in South Africa. You were sitting debating with someone whose two mates were shot dead and who was shot, himself, or with someone else who was wounded. We were going out, when we were in South Africa, sitting socially and having a drink together...

You were coming around saying to yourself 'these people here, they should be hating me, they should be clawing out my eyes!'

Each new group of participants was taken on what became known as the Journey through Conflict process – a careful weaving of 'Life Histories', 'Deep Dialogue' and 'Wild Nature' strands of activities into a facilitated journey of (re)humanisation and deepened understanding.[2] Within the emerging SPN this process included two journeys into wild nature, supplemented by preparation and follow-up events, which also encouraged the growth of enduring relationships. The first journey involved a

[2] For more detail on this process, see Alistair Little and Wilhelm Verwoerd, *Journey through Conflict Trail Guide.*

Working closely with people who have been at the coal face of deep often violent political conflict... has been deeply humbling and rewarding

four-day event in the Scottish Highlands (2005-7, 2010) or the Wicklow mountains (2008-9). The second was a two-week journey to South Africa, which included a five-day wilderness trail in northern KwaZulu Natal.

Participants who completed the initial cycle of activities in Ireland, Northern Ireland, Scotland and South Africa also helped with additional fundraising to make the South African leg of future group journeys possible. By 2010, the project aim of 100 participants in the SPN project was reached, with encouraging further evidence of a significant 'ripple effect' spreading out from these participants to reach thousands more people.[3] Amongst many examples of this ripple effect was a Catholic participant, whose two brothers were murdered by the UVF, who invited Alistair and a participant from a republican ex-prisoner background to join him on a panel at a public event in Poleglass (a strongly republican part of West Belfast). This remarkable event was also covered by a number of local newspapers.

Andersonstown News | www.belfastmedia.com | 1st March 2010 — NEWS | 5

Orangeman shares platform with ex-IRA man, ex-UVF man and victim

Four different stories told at Cloona House discussion

BY CIARA QUINN
c.quinn@belfastmediagroup.com

THEY say that many issues can be resolved if people just sit down and get around the table.

On a cold and grey Thursday evening last week, Cloona House opened its doors to a former republican and loyalist prisoner, an Orangeman and a community worker who lost two brothers to the conflict.

In a question and answer session, potential ways forward for the local and wider communities were discussed, as each person told their story and how the journey from conflict to reconciliation can be achieved through dialogue and discussion.

The panel included republican ex-prisoner and Sinn Féin member Seán Lennon who served time for his part in the killing of two British corporals during the funeral of IRA volunteer Caoimhín Ó Brádaigh in 1988; former UVF member Alistair Little, who joined the paramilitary organisation at age 14; Orange Order member John McSkea; and Director of Cloona House Gerry McR[illegible]

IT'S GOOD TO TALK: Barry McFarlane, whose two brothers were shot dead by the UVF in Mount Vernon in 1975; Alistair Little, former UVF prisoner; John McSkea, an Orangeman, and Seán Lennon, former republican prisoner [illegible]

[3] See Domecka research (2012) and section on "Ripples" within the *Journey through Conflict Trail Guide*, pp.94-121.

The promotion of 'sustainable relations' between participants within each year group and between the growing number of year groups was supported by the ongoing development of a loosely structured 'Sustainable Peace Network'.

The network activity included regular meetings of a steering group with representatives from each year group, social events, fundraising and outreach events, and a 'capturing of learning' working group that sought to document the learning from the project.[4]

Key challenges and learnings

In the course of co-ordinating, developing and facilitating the Former Combatants programme and the SPN project many challenges were faced and a lot of lessons learnt. These challenges and learnings include the following:

Difficulty of finding appropriate language

> *'[W]ords are a mysterious, ambiguous, ambivalent phenomenon.*
> *They are capable of being rays of light in a realm of darkness.*
> *They are equally capable of being lethal arrows.*
> *Worst of all at times they can be the one and the other. And even both at once.'*
>
> Vaclav Havel

Throughout the years we struggled to find appropriate language, even to describe the 'LIVE', 'former combatants', 'survivors and ex-combatants' activities. We recognised that, at least for funding purposes, the naming of these programmes and the identification of 'target groups' were necessary. However, we also realised that by doing so we might unintentionally be contributing to problematic labelling and separation between 'victims' and 'combatants' ('perpetrators').[5] An awareness of the dangers of simplistic and exclusionary distinctions contributed to the language of 'sustainable peace' being used.[6]

Another language related challenge was the need to balance a sensitivity to the power of language and the need to avoid potentially offensive language with encouraging honest, real conversation, even if words to describe, for example, a former enemy might not always be 'politically correct'.[7]

[4] This working group was led by prof. Brandon Hamber, current Director of INCORE (University of Ulster) and a member of the facilitation team within the Former Combatants programme and the SPN project.

[5] See article by Govier and Verwoerd on *'How not to polarize 'victim' and 'perpetrators'*, 2004.

[6] See also the Glencree Working Paper by Wilhelm Verwoerd on *'Can peace be 'built'? Metaphors for Peace Practice'.*

[7] See *'Beyond 'us' and 'them': towards the art of appropriate language'* (2006), workshop material developed by Wilhelm Verwoerd.

Towards Inclusivity

A core value guiding the work of Glencree is inclusivity. The work with former combatants, victims/survivors and wider society highlighted how important but also how challenging this commitment to inclusivity is. For example, during the early stages of the Former Combatants programme, it was difficult to find participants from state force backgrounds (ex-police, ex-army) who were willing to talk to ex-prisoners from loyalist and/or republican backgrounds. There were some participants in the LIVE programme, such as an injured former British police person, who were willing to become involved in the Former Combatants programme. However, the consultative process highlighted that this would only be possible if they were willing to participate in their role as a former combatant and not in the first place as a victim. Other potential participants from Irish or British army or police backgrounds questioned the legitimacy of describing former prisoners as 'combatants'. From a facilitation point of view we had to stand firm on the principle that we were trying to create a relatively inclusive, non-judgemental space, within which participants were given opportunities to explore their opposing views.

A related difficulty was the need to balance inclusivity with (physical and emotional) safety. At the early stages some ex-prisoner groupings, for example, were not clearly committed to the suspension/renunciation of political violence. It took a number of years before members of these organisations could be included in the multilateral workshops. During this period they were included, however, in the overall programme through single identity capacity building activities. The balancing act between inclusivity and (enough) safety was especially challenging when those directly involved in and affected by political violence were brought together.

Promoting dialogue between victims/survivors and former combatants

While we ensured that the participation in this type of engagement took place on a voluntary basis, we learnt the hard way that once-off events with an emphasis on 'victim' and 'perpetrator' roles are particularly risky and have limited potential to truly deepen mutual understanding. We also came to understand that large scale events, involving more than around 20 people at a time, typically do not allow for in depth, really meaningful interactions.

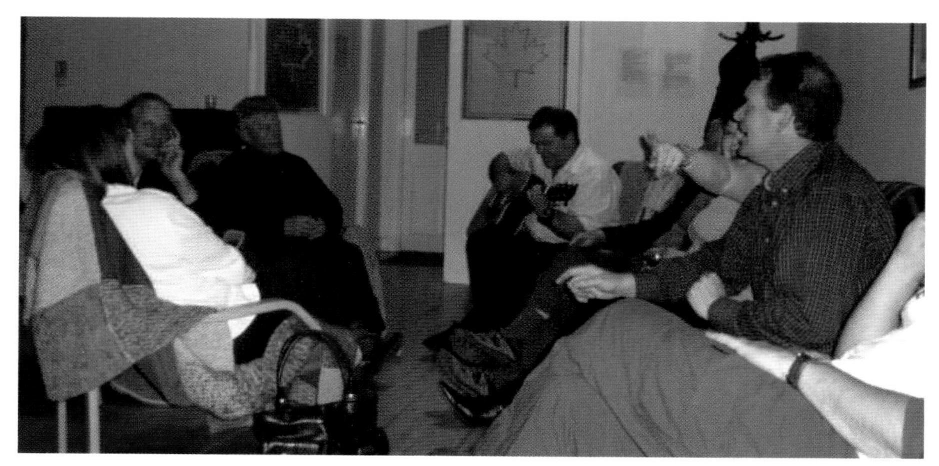

What we found to be more promising were a series of events involving the same people from these groupings, with separate preparation and follow-up events and linked with local support. Particularly promising were the inclusive, non-judgemental spaces provided by the skilled facilitation of Journey through Conflict type sharing of Life Histories. This 'storytelling' process includes individualised preparation and follow up as well as opportunities for further exploration of difficult issues. The selection of appropriate residential venues - with access to nature, with relatively few distractions, and allowing opportunities for informal interaction – were also critical to progress made.

It also proved to be very valuable to include a wider range of conflict roles (bystanders, beneficiaries, supporters, community members) beyond those with direct experience of armed conflict. In the process we avoided the pitfall of participants with the most visible conflict roles (former combatants and victims/survivors) in effect being expected to carry too much responsibility for past conflict and for future peace. On the other hand, members of wider society often struggled to find their place within a group that included survivors and former combatants. Those with a more indirect experience of violent conflict often felt, initially, that their story was not as important. However, over time they usually realised that their experience is a vital part of the wider story of political, inter-community conflict, and they deepened their understanding of their shared responsibility to cultivate *sustainable* peace.

'What stood out for me is that where you were born - not how you are as a person, what you believed in etc - could determine to what extent you were affected by the Troubles. Those who, I think the group would agree, told the most painful stories were from working class backgrounds. That's something that the North, in demonising so called 'terrorists', still ignores. Last night showed the extent to which the Troubles has really torn up society.' (wider society participant)

The SPN project can be seen as an attempt to address the above challenges. In the process a number of further hills had to be climbed:

Conflicts within groups

Given the diversity of backgrounds in each SPN group it was not surprising that we often had to deal with personality tensions and deep political divisions. Our response included stressing the importance of *working* on the group agreement, and taking 'time-out' when tempers flare, with the team of facilitators ready to calm individuals before returning to the group process, guided by working agreement. We have also been careful not to put pressure on people to 'become friends', understanding and explaining 'reconciliation' in terms of a willingness to humanize relationships and to co-operate for the sake of peace, rather than expecting, even implicitly, everyone to become good friends.

Naming 'elephants' from the past, without losing sight of common ground and a vision for the future

Unresolved conflicts in some of the earliest groups led to an emphasis on the theme of *sustainability* and peace. This emphasis on sustainability in the sense of 'sustere' – literally 'holding from below' – was part of an attempt to provide a broad vision, a 'containing' or 'holding' space within which division and difference could be faced. However, in the process insufficient naming of the 'elephants in the room' tended to take place. Realising that we might in effect be colluding with a widespread culture of politeness ('whatever you say, say nothing'), the pendulum swung towards addressing thorny issues from the start within each group, making more and more time to discuss these issues. However, this emphasis often resulted in insufficient time available to address the overarching theme/challenge of sustainable peace.

Cultivating the SPN

From 2004-2007 Glencree employed the limited financial and human resources within the SPN strand of the Survivors and Former Combatants programme mainly to develop and deliver the growing cycle of activities for each new SPN year group.

This meant that some of the potential of the network between different year groups remained unfulfilled. We also underestimated the need for separate group processes to cultivate deep connections between the year groups.

The fact that each year group shared 'wild nature' experiences provided a good starting point for people to connect, but more needed to be done to cultivate the network. From 2008-2011 more emphasis was placed on activities across the year groups and a more effective SPN steering group was in place comprising representatives from different year groups. Still, administrative and network management resources remained inadequate, given the huge challenge of cultivating a dynamic network between busy, geographically dispersed participants, from very different political and social backgrounds, most of whom would not naturally be inclined to be and stay connected.

Critical 'yeast'

While it proved to be difficult to fully utilise the potential of the SPN, we still believe that the underlying 'critical yeast'[8] approach is worth pursuing. Rather than a more quantitative focus on 'critical mass' the SPN project highlights the more promising potential of an intensive focus on the growth of individual participants as well as the painstaking cultivation of relationships between small groups of participants in influential roles or with leadership potential. Recent longitudinal research confirms that this approach is more likely to have a more *enduring* impact on *larger numbers* of people than bowing to the seductive pressure of ticking monitoring boxes by getting as many 'bums on seats' as quickly as possible. This brings us to another big challenge, namely the gathering or capturing of learning.

Capturing Learning

It has proved to be extremely difficult to combine programme co-ordination and facilitation with regular gathering of learning. Some participants and students with the necessary skills have helped over the years, and we did arrange a number of workshops with a reflective emphasis, such as the 'Roots of Reconciliation'.[9] In addition to the already mentioned *Journey through Conflict Trail Guide* there is also a forthcoming article which focuses specifically on the promise of weaving nature-based activities into a process such as *Journey through Conflict.*[10] It is worth looking a bit more closely at an encouraging recent piece of longitudinal research:

'The Meaning and Impact of the Sustainable Peace Network project'[11]

During 2011 a contracted researcher carried out fifteen in-depth, individual interviews with SPN participants from the 2007 and 2008 year groups. These interviews provide a longitudinal perspective on evidence collected via written questionnaires before and after each of the Journey through Conflict cycle of workshops. An initial qualitative analysis of the 2007 questionnaires, plus video interviews during the process, was done during 2008, using NVivo software.[12] Promising evidence of positive 'impact' emerged. However, the big question remained: would the positive changes referred to endure over time; would the change be sustained?

[8] See John Paul Lederach, *The Moral Imagination,* pp. 90-1, 181.

[9] See the writings of Halperin (2004, 2006), Dunne (2012).

[10] See Verwoerd, Little and Hamber (forthcoming) on *'Nature-based peace cultivation'.*

[11] See Domecka (2012).

[12] See Fox et al (2008).

With funding from Irish Peace Centres detailed follow up research was done. The 2011 interviews used a narrative methodology, allowing each participant to give a personal account of the meaning and impact of the SPN project.

Summary of findings

The above capturing of learning process provides encouraging evidence of significant progress with regards to the three stated aims of the SPN project - providing opportunities for personal growth; promoting enduring relationships, with a positive ripple effect; and enhancing nature-based peace cultivation.

- Personal growth/development

  The 2011 individual interviews and the 2012 reflective workshop confirmed an enduring, positive contribution to the personal development of participants, initially highlighted by the qualitative analysis of the 2007 questionnaires and interviews. Consistent patterns of personal growth include the reduction of a range of fears, greater self-awareness and increased self-confidence.

'The first significant change experienced was a reduction or removal of their initial fears, whether those were about meeting and talking to other participants, about the wilderness or their physical and emotional limits, being afraid they would not be able to make a significant contribution to the group.' (Domecka, 2012)

'It's painful as an individual doing this type of work because it takes you to places where you think you don't want to go, but you need to go there. I feel that I needed to go there, to come out the other side and learn from it, but it is really not easy.' (Participant, 2012)

'Obviously when my son was killed I didn't understand how you felt at that time. Where I once was to where I am now, I've come a hell of a long way. I don't hate anybody anymore.' (Participant, 2012)

'The second major change that was referred to by participants is the shift to being less judgmental and more open… to see an individual with his or her particular features rather than a stereotypical representative of a certain group. A great majority of participants expressed their appreciation for the opportunity to meet and form relationships with others they would not have met/interacted with otherwise.' (Domecka, 2012)

'I've never had the chance of being in that kind of mixed company from all different backgrounds in life…I know it was good for me to be there and has helped me a lot in understanding the types of things that people have done and the reasons why they've done it. When I've seen people's emotions and people crying and everything else, it was just so real and you could understand everybody's pain and their whole life, what they've been through – between jail and between committing murder and sons or whoever being murdered. It doesn't mean that the pain goes away… (and) of course there are things that I still can't understand, but time for that will come hopefully.

It's hard to believe that it is almost 4 years – it seems like yesterday. I wasn't afraid to say what I said, even though people got angry at it, and I might have got angry too at other people's stories. But I think that was all part of the process and it definitely helped. I told you about the fear I had at the beginning going away (two brothers lured away and murdered during the 1970s). I have no fear now. I actually look forward to meeting you (former member of an organisation responsible for the brothers' murders) and everybody else. I think that is a big change.' (Participant, 2012)

- Relationship cultivation

  A large majority of participants consistently referred to positive changes in their relationships with participants from different/opposing backgrounds. These changes include attitudinal shifts, such as moving beyond stereotypes and conflict labels, deepened understanding of motivations and life experiences of the 'other', and the establishment/growth of relationships across conflict divides

- Positive ripples

  The longitudinal capturing of learning process also helped to highlight the positive impact of participation in the SPN and Journey through Conflict within many participants' personal (family, friends) and work (community, organisational) spheres of influence.[13]

'All agree the project had a great impact on their personal development helping them to see their lives and the problems of post-Troubles Northern Ireland from a different perspective. The change of perspective accompanied by a feeling of 'receiving a lot' and a need to 'give something back' became a trigger for action and further changes in different spheres of private and professional life.' (Domecka, 2012)

'What I've learnt is a sense of not being afraid to do the (peace) work that I'm doing and to continue on. Even if you are not making a big, massive difference you are giving other people confidence as well to go on to meet and greet and share and live each other's experiences and show how we have things in common and use them to try and bring peoples together.' (Participant, 2012)

Concluding remarks

Working closely with people who have been at the coal face of deep, often violent political conflict and who are making significant progress in transforming the painful legacy of this kind of conflict has been deeply humbling and rewarding. Reflecting on the Former Combatants programme and the Sustainable Peace Network project is also encouraging. For this mostly behind-the-scenes, patient , often messy work highlights the fact that a relatively remote residential space such as Glencree - guided by values of inclusivity and non- judgementalism, as part of a carefully facilitated process of deepening understanding and cultivating humanising connections - has a real and ongoing contribution to make towards enduring peace on the island of Ireland.

I would like to acknowledge the important contributions of colleagues - at the Glencree Centre, the Wilderness Foundation (UK) and Wilderness Leadership School (SA),

[13]For a fuller discussion of the challenges and constraints of this ripple effect (the 'returning home' stage of *Journey through Conflict*), see the *Trail Guide*.

INCORE (UU), the Sustainability Institute (SA) - as well as co-facilitators and many participants within this programme. In particular I want to pay tribute to Alistair Little for the vast experience and hardwon practical wisdom he brought to this programme and the Sustainable Peace Network project; for his invaluable roles as behind-the-scenes coach, co-facilitator and developer of the *Journey through Conflict* process.

Bibliography

Domecka, Markieta, 2012, *'The Meaning and Significance of the Sustainable Peace Network Project'*, Irish Peace Centres Experiential Learning Paper, Glencree Centre for Peace and Reconciliation.

Dunne, Sarah, 2012, *'Navigating the Labyrinth: Journey through Conflict as a process of Recognition'*,

M.Phil in *Conflict Resolution and Reconciliation,* Trinity College, Dublin, unpublished essay.

Fox, Adam et al, 2008, *'Preliminary Qualitative Analysis of the Sustainable Peace Network Induction programme 2007'*, unpublished paper, available on request.

Govier, Trudy & Verwoerd, Wilhelm, 2004. *'How not to polarize 'victims' and 'perpetrators''*, *Peace Review,* 16 (3), pp.371-377.

Halperin, Richard, 2005, *''Tell my story': Approaches used at the Glencree Centre for Peace and Reconciliation'*, unpublished paper, available on request.

Halperin, Richard, 2006, *'Reflections on 'Roots of Reconciliation: Humanising Enemies"*, unpublished paper, available on request.

Lederach, John Paul, 2005, *The Moral Imagination: The Art and Soul of Building Peace,* Oxford University Press. Little, Alistair & Verwoerd, Wilhelm, 2013, *Journey through Conflict Trail Guide: Introduction,* Trafford Publishing.

Verwoerd, Wilhelm, 2004, *'Troubled Scatterlings in a South African Wilderness', A Place for Peace: Glencree Centre for Reconciliation,* 1974-2004, Dublin: The Liffey Press, pp.166-175.

Verwoerd, Wilhelm, 2006, *'Towards Inclusive Remembrance after the 'Troubles': A philosophical perspective from within the South African Truth and Reconciliation Commission',* in D. Tombs & J. Liechty (editors), *Explorations in Reconciliation,* Aldershot: Ashgate.

Verwoerd, Wilhelm, 2006, *'Beyond 'us' and 'them': towards the art of appropriate language',* unpublished workshop material, available on request.

Verwoerd, Wilhelm & Little, Alistair, 2008, *'Towards Truth and Shared Responsibility after the Troubles',* in L. O'Hagan (ed), *Stories in Conflict, Towards Understanding and Healing.*

Verwoerd, Wilhelm, 2008, *'Can peace be 'built'? Metaphors for Peace Practice',* Glencree Working Paper, Glencree Centre for Peace and Reconciliation.

Verwoerd, Wilhelm, Little, Alistair and Hamber, Brandon, 2013, *'Nature-based Peace Cultivation',* (forthcoming).

If religion is the problem – or an element of it - it can also be part of the solution

Peacebuilding Possibilities for People of Faith

Colin Murphy

Introduction

Glencree has been working with Christian faith communities in Ireland/Northern Ireland since its foundation in 1974. This reflective piece on the programme covers the period 1997-2012. The intention is to review the programme work and draw some conclusions about what we learnt. The varied elements of this work within the programme are:

- The Believers Enquiry, 1997/1998
- Cross-Border Parish Exchanges
- 1998/2001 Jerusalem Holy Sites
- Research 2003/2005
- Glencree Churches Programme (EU Peace I, II Programmes), 2002/2010

It also focuses on Civil Society Leaders 'Breathing Spaces' Programme 2008/2011 which was funded through EU Peace III Programme. Each aspect will be covered in turn and the overall piece aims to give a sense of what areas we worked in and how the work developed throughout that period. I will also include comments and reflections by participants and facilitators on different aspects of the programme in order to draw together some key learning points

Programme background and context

Glencree, as a civil society non-governmental organisation, has a broad sense of the role of people of faith play in nurturing peace: 'If religion is the problem – or an element of it - it can also be part of the solution'. This reflection acknowledges that expressions of Christianity in Ireland/Northern Ireland, including sectarianism, have served to divide our people, created widespread alienation and even been used to justify violence. Consequently, peacebuilding work in faith communities remains necessary and urgent.

A current definition of sectarianism states:

> *'Sectarianism should be considered as a form of racism specific to the Irish context. Sectarianism is the diversity of prejudicial and discriminatory attitudes, behaviours and practices between members of the two majority communities in and about Northern Ireland, who may be defined as Catholic or Protestant; Irish or British; Nationalist or Unionist; or combinations thereof'.*
>
> 'Defining Sectarianism and Hate Crime' Neil Jarman 2012

The Believers Enquiry

At the end of the first decade of The Troubles, some Glencree members and staff felt that the organisation could usefully engage with Christian leadership groups on the issue of faith violence and peace. This endeavour, which became The Believers Enquiry, sought to examine the peacebuilding role of Christian believers in Ireland. The project involved church leadership groups in a process that included a preliminary workshop, written submission, oral hearing, response and conclusions.

The key question put to participating groups was; '*How can your group assist the process of peace-building in Ireland and between Ireland and Britain, and what ideas to you have as to how other groups could work with you in this endeavour?*'

Participating groups were:

- Church of Ireland
- Conference of Religious in Ireland
- ECONI (Evangelical Contribution to Northern Ireland (now Contemporary Christianity)
- Methodist Church in Ireland
- National Conference of Priests in Ireland
- Presbyterian Church in Ireland
- Religious Society of Friends (Quakers)

Glencree noted with regret that the following groups declined the invitation to participate:

- Baptist Union of Ireland
- Free Presbyterian Church in Ireland
- The Irish Commission for Justice and Peace

Glencree Council mandated a group to conduct the Enquiry and prepare a report. Members were: Dr. Colum Kenny (Believers Enquiry researcher and author), Maeve Shiels, Sally Shiells, John Shiels, Máirín Colleary, Colin Murphy and Ian White (Glencree Director). The report was launched by the President of Ireland, Mrs. Mary McAleese in February 1999.

The project report: 'Imprisoned Within Structures?' offers a unique insight into the thinking and possible future actions of a broad spectrum of traditional, centrist and evangelical Christians as revealed through written responses and discussions.

Key findings of the Believers Enquiry are summarised as follows:

'The process of building peace is helped when we first confess our imperfections and acknowledge the pain we have caused. Disputes between believers are a scandal.

There is an urgent need for churches throughout Ireland to address the issues, which divide believers. Churches should resource their members to come together to build peace and to understand each other's history, customs and beliefs'

'There is a place in the process of reconciliation of believers for a Truth Commission. Educators can help create the conditions for peace.

Those believers who work in schools and other organisations must strive to overcome prejudice and to ensure that their children are not only educated for mutual understanding but are also brought together from different traditions both to work and play. The language we use can be a sly form of violence. We must watch our tongues'

Cross-border parish exchanges

Funded by Cooperation North, this Glencree initiative worked to create cross-community, cross-border local faith community pairings, (e.g. Enniskerry, Co. Wicklow: Lurgan, Co. Armagh and Holywood, Co Down). The initiative enabled the groups to meet, hear others' stories, reflect on the recommendations of the Believers Enquiry, ask questions, confront difficult issues, e.g. inter-church marriage (Ne Temere Decree) and have social time together. There were also opportunities for joint worship, if a particular group requested it. As with other Glencree initiatives, the exchanges provided participants with the opportunity to travel to the other part of Ireland and meet people at community level - often for the first time.

Inter-faith work on the Holy Sites issue in Jerusalem

Glencree noted that one of the elements of the Israel/Palestine Road Map addressed the possibility of a consensus agreement on future management of the contested holy sites in Jerusalem. Given the contemporary nature of disputes around religious space in Northern Ireland, Glencree decided to enquire if any transfer of lessons learnt and positive actions would be possible. A series of visits to Israel/Palestine created contacts with Islamic/Hebrew and Christian leaders in Jerusalem, Tel Aviv and Ramallah over the period 2004-2007. It was clear from these exchanges that some faith leaders in Israel/Palestine would value opportunities to meet with their counterparts in Northern Ireland.

Glencree Churches Programme

The basic premise of Glencree Churches Programme:

Cold, sectarian relationships and conflicts could be transformed positively and creative activity supported and enhanced

This initiative, funded by EU Peace Programmes I and II, was undertaken to encourage religious believers in Republic of Ireland and Northern Ireland and the border region opportunities to become positive role model and promoters of peace.

Making contact with other church forums is a positive learning experience

The project objectives were to:

- Build the capacity of local church-based communities to cope with conflict and to build peace with their neighbours
- Equip and support participants to face up to the legacies of the conflict and to find ways to promote peace-building and reconciliation
- Develop further the horizontal and vertical peace-building partnerships

Local workshops and residential weekends were held at Glencree and elsewhere. The Programme was administered by Glencree and supervised on a part-time contract basis by a Churches Programme organiser and three field workers who were based in the Border region. The Churches Programme reached an estimated three hundred participants.

Reflections on learning

As I write the narrative of the Churches Programme, it occurs to me now that I am discussing a historical phenomenon. The need for people of faith to be involved in the work of peacebuilding and reconciliation on this island seems self-evident, and yet, Glencree has not been so directly involved in this of late. The learning throughout the programme has been significant and suggests that there is still a need to engage in this work. Here are some key themes which have emerged:

- People of different faiths often say similar things about faith representatives. One of these is that they have been hard to engage with in relation to issues of sectarianism and that they often seem to lack the will to move outside their safe zones using their non action on these matters as a form of control
- People continued to attend churches at the same time as they were expressing reservations and even hatred about the people of other faiths and were failing to ask questions of their churches in relation to their part in reconciliation

- Forgiveness was often talked about as a religious issue but needs to be acted on in a more substantial way if there is to be increased understanding and common action among people of different faiths

- There is a need within faith communities for people to move beyond their comfort zones, to cross the border, build relationships and challenge some of the myths that are still prevalent where sectarian narratives still prevent communities engaging with one another

- If the different churches in Ireland are to remain relevant, church leaders need to listen with real intent and respect to their members and structures need to change to be more open to a real dialogue process

- Inter-faith dialogue can provide important opportunities for people to voice concerns, not just to stay safe. Offence should never be intended, but there is a key role in facilitation to support honesty and ask the hard questions

- Glencree Churches Programme events have provided vital opportunities for small steps to be taken, often quite locally. Though this is not easy for many, it has provided a process to question the aggressive presentation of identity through sectarian narratives

It is important for us, therefore, to be reminded of how participants voiced their concerns in programme events in order to make use of this learning. The following is a sample of these comments and the contaxt they emerged from.

'This work identifies how important sectarianism is in dividing our communities, we need to do more in understanding each other's cultures'

'I enjoy meeting up with the group, especially coming from another culture'

'Every (community understanding) step you take is like walking on an ice-floe'

Riverbrook Cross-Border Initiative Churches event, Customs House, Belcoo, Co. Fermanagh

'North Belfast is like patchwork quilt – all separate areas marked out by peace walls, murals and curb stones; people know where they are going. They do not go to the nearest bus stop; they go to the bus stop where they feel safe. They will take a bus to the city centre that does not go into an area where they don't feel safe, rather than take the shortest route'

WISP (Women in Search of Peace) (West Belfast, East Belfast, Fermanagh, Cavan).

The project forged an alliance between members of women's groups in each area, who travelled and met together to ask questions about identity, loyalties, family histories etc.

The Macartan Project: Cross-community work with clergy in border region

'Communities and individuals who live in the border counties (in this case Monaghan/ Tyrone) often have difficulty speaking to each other because of their sectarian or traumatic histories. The Macartan query is 'What questions are people asking in the churches today?'

Response; 'People are not asking questions in the church today. They go to other agencies for their answers. The church has a diminished authority'.

'Wednesday the fourth of July. I received a call from a senior clergyman, postponing yet again my meeting with him. I am noting this for a number of reasons. First that (his C of I) bishop said that the incumbent would be helpful to the project and me. Second that he would introduce me to other Church of Ireland of clergy. Third, that by September, it will have taken me four months to get the requested half-hour meeting. Fourth, he gave reasons that the postponement was due to the marching season and a summer youth club.

My feeling is one of annoyance of the power exerted through non-action, which is a form of control'.

The Macartan Project

In early 2006, the Glencree Churches Programme identified the cross-border region known as the Clogher Valley, as a community area that may have appreciated support from Glencree. The Centre sought to enable individuals or groups to meet informally in order to have 'a new conversation' on matters that concerned them in their area. I was brought in to facilitate this piece of work, which was known as the Macartan Project. St Macartan, whose 1,500th Anniversary was in 2006, was one of St. Patrick's colleagues and also the bishop of Clogher. People of various religious persuasions - and also those with no particular religious beliefs - were contacted in the area and invited to take part in a process, which began from a single question; 'What question(s) are people asking the church today?' The responses were collated under the headings of Church/Clergy/Laity/Young people/Politics and Community. Over the next three years, participants met a number of times to have conversations about their responses.

Many of the responses asked 'what can we do about...?' The assumption being made was that going to church was worth it - a premise that wasn't generally addressed. The main concern revealed through the process was that Church structures militate against listening. These structures are learned and imposed from childhood, from the seating arrangements in a church building, which expect people not to meet each other, to the notion that those leading the service or the Church are the ones who 'know'. Another form of structure is found within the language that different people and churches use about what is important.

The overriding sentiment was that if the Church is to begin to breathe afresh, all members need to listen with respect and without fear to the heads and the hearts of people. It also needs to create space to meet authentically with anyone who has a view about Church - those both inside and outside its institutions.

John Harding, Facilitator

Cookstown Churches Forum:
'The main learning points at the Glencree residential included: The togetherness created trust, open group discussions – things emerged that hadn't been shared before. Need to go across the border and break down myths and barriers'. 'We don't have the opportunity to have a lot of discussion in our own forum meetings in Cookstown. Ideally, we would like to meet four or five groups'.

South Tyrone Spring School:
'Around 14/15 years of age I loved history; loved politics. I found an old book on Che Guevara belonging to my father and read it from cover to cover. Che was talking about revolution; his whole thing was that armed struggle should be the smallest part of it. That was my motivation- politics was the way forward'.

'Flags along the border, flags are used differently in the North. They awakened sadness in me. We moved out of our comfort zone'. 'The Republic of Ireland is a comfort zone. I'm disappointed and disillusioned at the lack of progress in Northern Ireland. There are flags in the North used for intimidation, are people intimidated by holy statutes in the South?'

'Marching? We encountered a roadblock outside Tempo (County Fermanagh), a group going to the Apprentice Boys March in Derry. I found it a little off-putting. Why do people need to declare their identity in such an in-your-face manner?'

Other voices:

'There is no great future without forgiveness. How many people are coming into our churches filled with hatred? We need to have generosity and forgiveness in ourselves in order to forgive other

'You cannot just make 'safe' statements in a 'safe' space. You shouldn't feel like you can't speak out. Please don't make it too safe'

'I am responsible for my own actions. Please let me know if I have offended you. I am sorry if what I said offended you but I am not sorry for saying it'

'Making contact with other church forums is a positive learning experience'

'People in Northern Ireland have a fear that it is the wish of the South to gobble them up. This halts their chance to make a contribution to the Island of Ireland'

'I fear that there will be no development beyond this meeting. I want to meet people who don't think the way I do. There is a need to be 'brutally honest' and to ask real questions.'

'My fear is that we are just creating a greater comfort zone, instead of moving outside it. I hope we can discuss our enthusiasm to move outside the group?'

'Everybody whose lives we touch is affected because of our meeting' 'Accept reality. Accept the other and bond'

'Glencree is an affirming place and we greatly appreciate it'

'There is a sense of friendliness, welcoming. The atmosphere is safe but challenging. It's not just a 'Yes' shop'

The Churches Programme was an inspired approach to give clergy and people affiliated with churches the opportunity to meet together and talk about the role of churches in delivering peace in Northern Ireland and the six Border Counties.

Colin Murphy outside Jerusalem

The Churches Programme set about to work with faith believers
With clergy, people of the lay and other faith receivers
We quickly found that sects abound
Divides on fundamental ground
So mounted our twelve county plan as Peace lII grant achievers.

The team was small, but keen, extant, and met outwith Glencree
We roamed through sundered boundaries to find, to meet, to be
With those who tried to understand
The over and the underhand
Religious cant and dogma mixed with words of charity.

Wide-ranging treatments were applied, one-off to residential
And some were small in darkened hall and some were influential
Civil leaders (Breathing Spaces, Peace III)
Advisory team from far flung places
Church and clergy fora met in talks experiential.

'What was achieved?' I hear you cry and 'Really, did it matter?'
'It must have been an infernal din amidst the raucous chatter'
And yet, old hates can be supplanted
Weary hearts, restored, enchanted
Seeds of change that grow so soft and neither break nor shatter.

What is left of all this work and is there a legacy?
The Programme is disbanded now, the team no longer 'we'
And still we find sectarian modes
Propounded in religious codes
But people changed, made peace and friends - that's good enough for me.

Katie Rutledge, Facilitator

Breathing Spaces

The objective of the *Breathing Spaces* element of the Glencree Churches Programme was to give civil society leaders, primarily in the 12 northern counties of Ireland/ Northern Ireland, opportunities to take time out for dialogue about values and ideas of common interest and pressing concern, including the current and projected economic situation. The project aimed especially to engage with faith community leaders.

The *Breathing Spaces* process recognised that civil society, especially workplaces, has too often become a place of relational contention where the lowest common denominator often boils down to meeting targets and making sure the correct procedures are followed. This can be a difficult place for creative leadership, especially in times of austerity. Workplaces that are governed by manuals and procedures that lose sight of shared responsibility, can be uncreative arenas for leaders and managers who find themselves at the centre of a pressured vortex.

The *Breathing Spaces* process asked if the old values of hope, trust, reconciliation, respect, integrity, and self-control are valid and if so, how can they be articulated? Participants were given opportunities to hear views from specialist speakers and to talk with other leaders and community activists about how austerity is impinging on their work and finding positive ways to move forward.

Colin Murphy and Archbishop Diarmuid Martin
at 'Breathing Spaces' conference Dromartin, September, 2011

Issues included:

- How can leaders, including those in faith communities, find ways to come into the public space with words of encouragement and hope that make sense for everybody?

- How can the corrosive effects of sectarianism that have blighted the lives of people in Northern Ireland/Ireland be 'owned' and transformed?

- How can the South face up to its responsibilities for our conflicts and to finding ways forward?

- How can meetings with the 'other' be facilitated in creative and non-threatening ways?

- What are the gender and ageism issues that contribute to our conflicts? How can the 'power in the room' be recognised and facilitated?

- How can the specific possibilities and challenges be faced by leaders?

- What is peace?

- What do the old texts have to say about violence, scapegoating, blame, moralising etc. that make sense today?

Young Irish Christian Leaders Meet Archbishop Diarmuid Martin at The Corrymeela Community in North Antrim:

'We sat in a circle, allowing our eyes to rest, in turn, on his slow-moving hands, on other young faces, and on the seagulls circling Rathlin Island under low, leaden skies. He spoke carefully, yet with an earnestness, which was, I gathered, both for him and us, a breath of fresh air. Diarmuid Martin received us, and our words, graciously. Carefully, constructively, a space had been crafted for 30 young people from all corners of Ireland and from many Christian traditions to engage in genuine dialogue with the Archbishop of Dublin.

Considered preparation and skilled facilitation fostered a 'breathing space' where we could all speak authentically, a 'breathing space' in which young people and church leaders could air personal disquiets in an open and honest way. The opportunity to witness the possibility of such a space in Ireland was heartening. That a leader of a Christian tradition would willingly give of his time, not only to listen to the thoughts of ecumenically-minded young people, but to converse with them as equals, gave us a profound insight into the challenges faced by such people. The fact that the dialogue was not simply a once-off session, but rather an element in an ongoing series of Glencree-inspired encounters at different locations around Ireland, provided breathing space between the 'breathing spaces'.

This time provided for contemplation and discernment. Furthermore, it led to richer and more fruitful discussions which have served as a source of reassurance and encouragement for the young people present as they grapple with the often suffocating realities of what it means to be active in church life today in an increasingly secular society. The discussion continued at a follow up supper in Archbishop's House, Dublin'.

John Delap, Student Christian Movement, Dublin

Learning Outcomes

In the period 2009/2011, three residential, Breathing Spaces 24-hour events were organised in the border region for approximate ninety people. Participants were drawn from many areas of civil society including business, the professions, faith, education, health, the arts and others. In addition, two events were held for young Christian leaders, especially those from immigrant communities. Issues discussed are expressed by these edited comments by speakers and other participants and these comments need to be referenced as an essential part of this learning process:

'Our individualistic society has created a culture based on reward. Instead of this, the question asked by faith communities should simply be, 'do you want a better earth?'

'We are a people traumatised by failure. Surveying the wreckage that is the Republic of Ireland today, where so many of our major institutions have been exposed as corrupt at worst, inept at best, we know that as we head into a decade of centenaries we have much to contemplate'

'Our politicians have failed us by presiding over a spectacular bust in the economy, members of all parties who now blame Departments of Finance for supplying them with the figures on which they based their expansionist policies of the last general election campaign'

'Certainly we in the Republic could be forgiven for asking now, as Yeats did in his poem 'September 1913' as the Dublin lockout was underway:

Was it for this the Wild Geese spread The grey wing upon every tide;
For this that all that blood was shed, For this Edward Fitzgerald died,
And Robert Emmet and Wolfe Tone, All that delirium of the brave?'

(W.B. Yeats)

'Ireland today is multi-cultural, multi-denominational and multi-faith in its make-up. Breathing Spaces plays an important role in challenging the churches to work together in building peace in Northern Ireland. I am delighted that together our faith communities are challenging civil society to look in a more focused way to the future of Ireland, North and South. Who better to listen to on that theme than young Church leaders?'

'You might say that both parts of the island comprise what have been both failed political and economic systems which are increasingly dependent on outside larger political and economic entities – the EU where the Republic is concerned and the UK and EU where Northern Ireland is concerned. We should be glad that this is so and that all of us on this island are beginning to wake up from the delusions of our history and the nightmare that was our 20th century, as we seek new ways forward in tandem with one another'.

Afterword

The words *'hope'*, *'forgiveness'* and *'trust'* must not be seen merely as 'old' words - if they are not seen as relevant and new in terms of peacebuilding, then we are lost. The faith-based work of Glencree has often been talked about as a historical moment - something that happened in the past, even though this work has been revisited in more recent times. Many of the comments here reflect our experience and suggest that sectarianism is still a reality. We need to process the learning made throughout the programme and face up to this challenge:

How can civil society face the twin phenomena of religious extremism and rampant secularism in ways that avoid religion being used as a justification for violence?

It is clear that the corrosive effects of sectarianism haven't gone away in Ireland/ Northern Ireland and that religion is part of the problem in many conflict regions:

Sri Lanka, the wider Middle East, sub-Saharan Africa and Afghanistan, to name a few examples. Having reached this conclusion, surely the next step is to ensure that each relevant peace process addresses the faith element of its problem (which, strangely enough, none of those mentioned above actually does). Though we may live in a much-changed context today, religion still constitutes the backdrop for much of the understandings we have about the world we live in. I am reluctant to define this society as 'secular' and therefore not accommodating of people who express a religious identity. It therefore seems important that we continue to engage with conflict issues that are impacted by religious belief. There is no better civil society organisation than Glencree to grab the nettle of religion-based conflict in ways that enable people of faith to find practical and unexpected ways to peace.

'Breathing Spaces' Conference, Dromartin September, 2011

When the relationships are built, then the issues causing the divides can be addressed

Sharing Lessons from Ireland in International Contexts

Ian White

Introduction and Background

After more than ten years of working in international contexts, we are in the process of reflecting on the lessons we have learnt. However, as a prelude to this, it is important to define which of the many lessons from the Irish context resonate most, so that we are clear about what we have to offer. This preliminary reflection will explore how the Glencree International Programme (GIP) has been informed by key lessons from the Irish Peace Process and how we began to apply these lessons in a range of different countries. It is essential to be clear about what we bring, if we are to help others find a way through intractable conflict, as it is ultimately up to them to find a way forward. I will also draw out some of the broad lessons we have learnt from international work, which we intend to define in more specific detail as we move forward.

When describing the peacebuilding activity of the Glencree Centre for Peace and Reconciliation (Glencree), it is common to describe it as two main strands, one having

Workshop with women in Afghanistan

a domestic Irish/British focus and the other having an international focus. While this represents the most accessible description of the work of the organisation over the last twenty years, it is also important to appreciate that these are not two stand-alone programme areas and that they are, in fact, connected and interact with each other. The interplay between these two dynamic dimensions of the organisation's work creates a new dynamic, which allows both the domestic and international work to feed off each other in a mutually-reinforcing way. This complementary interface between activities allows the International Programme to benefit from the inputs and perspectives of other stakeholders in the Irish conflict and peace process, rather than solely rely on the experience and knowledge accumulated by Glencree itself. On the other hand, the GIP serves as an ongoing outreach activity through which Glencree maintains and builds its web of relationships within Ireland, north and south and Britain.

The Glencree International Programme (GIP) developed gradually and organically as a natural extension of the domestic work in which the organisation was engaged between 1991 and the year 2000. (Details of the Glencree domestic programme are given in other sections of this publication). While the work of the GIP was not formalised until around 2004 and remained somewhat ad hoc until then, the organisation had begun to establish an international profile much earlier. In the late 1990s and early 2000s Glencree hosted a number of significant international guests, which connected the organisation to the rich South African experience of transitioning out of violence. These guests were invited by Glencree to undertake specific tasks including, capacity-building with former combatants, addressing and sharing experience with gatherings of Irish and Northern Irish political leaders and activists, or addressing summer schools where diverse groups of political and civil society actors engaged in peacebuilding would gather. These guests included former South Africa President F.W. De Klerk, Rev. Alex Borraine, the Vice Chair of the South African Truth and Reconciliation Commission and Roelf Meyer, the former Chief Negotiator with the National Party and Minister for Defense. At a time when South Africa was emerging from its own protracted violent conflict, these key informants shared their experience with civil society actors and politicians who were in positions of influence and wished to explore new possibilities in peacebuilding.

Concerned at the lack of pace in political progress being made in Ireland in the mid 1990s, Glencree invited and hosted another important cross party South African Delegation in partnership with AWEPA (Association of European Parliamentarians with Africa). The delegation comprised members of leaderships from the main parties in South Africa: Mac Maharaj (ANC), Constand Viljoen (Freedom Front) and Leon Wessells (National Party). The specific task of this delegation was to address party political audiences and elected politicians at particular venues in Belfast and in Glencree in an attempt to inform, assure and inspire. A special seminar was organised for members of the Irish Forum for Peace and Reconciliation.

In addition to the partnerships with highly-experienced South African actors, Glencree started to connect with the rich source of well-trained and experienced mediation and ADR practitioners in Canada in 1998. A small team of Canadians offered capacity-building opportunities to some three hundred political and civil society stakeholders in the Irish Peace process. Many former combatants and political actors from Ireland, north and south received training from the expert Canadian team. General John De Chastelaine was also a frequent visitor to Glencree throughout the late 1990s and early 2000s, as strategies were developed by the organisation to complement his efforts to remove weapons and violence from politics. To this day, Glencree maintains a special relationship with Canada, having hosted two Canadian Prime Ministers and many other supportive Canadians.

The GIP grew from three International requests for support received by Glencree between 2000 and 2003. A request to engage in community capacity-building in Colombia; a request to engage with Israeli and Palestinian Members of Parliament and a request to build the capacity of the Liberation Tigers of Tamil Eelam (LTTE) police service of Sri Lanka. These were the founding projects upon which the GIP was built and Glencree were very happy to accept a role in all three of these contexts. The GIP learned much from these three projects which informed its own understanding of the world of peacebuilding in international contexts and the role that it could play within it.

Since its commencement, there have been many other unique, specifically-designed short and long-term missions undertaken by the GIP. These missions have been a mixture of short-term projects, which usually form one part of a larger initiative, where the lead role is played by a Glencree partner organisation. For example, PACTA *('Pacta sent servanda – agreements must be kept')* Glencree's Finnish partner organisation, which has made a significant contribution through its concerted efforts to stabilise relations and reduce violence related to the Malay separatist groups in Southern Thailand. As part of its ongoing work, GIP has offered and delivered short-term capacity-building experiences to a range of political and civil society stakeholder groups from Thailand, while PACTA retains responsibility for the overall intervention.

The GIP has also been proactive and has made a number of long-term commitments to specific countries in conflict. This longer term engagement is informed by the realisation from the Irish Peace Process that protracted violent conflicts cannot be resolved overnight. To quote former Irish President Mary McAleese, 'The period of healing required is at least equal to the time spent in violent conflict'. Therefore, it becomes important for GIP to adopt a long-term view of its work in particular countries. Glencree has engaged in such long-term work programmes in Afghanistan (2006-2013) and in Haiti (2004-2013).

The International Impact and Perception of the Good Friday Agreement (GFA)

The signing of the GFA was perceived as a major achievement - not only by the majority of people in Ireland north and south - but also, by many others internationally who found themselves engaged in their own continuous cycles of protracted violent conflict. While the international community may not have fully appreciated the amount of effort required after the signing of the GFA to ensure its full and successful implementation, many were able to draw hope from the ability of stakeholders in the Irish conflict to use creative strategies to at least manage, if not resolve, a conflict which, heretofore, was often referred to as 'intractable'.

The learning from the Irish experience of peacebuilding comprises not just the formal negotiations, which resulted in the signing of the Good Friday Agreement, but also

They left with greater hope in themselves

includes the pre-negotiation phase and post-agreement phase. For International Programme participants, it is important that they have a holistic experience of our peacebuilding process, rather than assume that the Good Friday Agreement was negotiated without the stage being set. Additionally, it is essential that participants understand that the implementation of the GFA has not been without its challenges, and that some people in Ireland may have felt more pain arising from the implementation phase rather than the negotiation phase.

The Glencree experience of peacebuilding activity in Ireland north and south and between Ireland and Britain, significantly pre-dates the negotiation phase of the Irish Peace Process. Glencree in the pre-negotiation phase of the Peace Process focused on building the improbable relationships required for a formal Track I process to develop. In the words of one political participant: 'Glencree helped to create the oxygen which allowed the Track I process to take place'.

During, and in the immediate aftermath of, the negotiation phase of the GFA, Glencree continued to complement the efforts of the governmental and all political actors engaged in the process by sensitising the wider public about issues that had to be addressed. In our description of the process, we emphasise that negotiations did not finish with the signing of the Agreement on Good Friday 1998. In fact, while the St. Andrews Agreement post-dates the Good Friday Agreement and was necessitated by the entry of the DUP into the Executive and the emergence of Sinn Fein as the largest nationalist voice in Northern Ireland, negotiations between parties on finer issues continue to take place. Actions were taken by Glencree such as hosting Prince Charles on a state visit; or hosting political activities which allowed the DUP, in particular, to engage directly with the Irish political establishment. This included facilitating the DUP's membership of the British/Irish inter-parliamentary body (now the British Irish Inter-parliamentary Assembly), a public event which did much to reframe political relationships between the islands and parties. Likewise, the hosting of Dessie O'Hare upon his release from prison after twenty years, enabled the Irish government to honour its commitment to the GFA in terms of prisoner releases.

In this post-Agreement phase of our peace process, there is still much to do. Perhaps you could say we now need to work on issues that have been difficult, such as how do we ensure that former political prisoners can assume their role as full and equal citizens? How do we heal the wounds caused by the turbulent past so that we cannot slide back into the dark days? From the pre/during/post negotiation phases of our peace process it is very clear that:

- Just because Ireland has a peace process that has resulted in a reduction of violence and new hope for a shared future, we, as civil society actors in this process do not have a blueprint for other violent contexts; all conflicts are different and in any case our process is not complete

- The implementation of an agreement is as important and often just as difficult as the negotiations leading to an agreement

- The scene needs to be set and actors need the capacity to deliver on a negotiation process

- Leadership, even if flawed, while moving in the right direction towards a settlement, must be supported

- While official and unofficial third party efforts need to be inclusive, it is desirable to have independent bi-lateral relationships with all stakeholder groups. Particular parties will be challenged by different things during the negotiation and implementation phases and organisations such as Glencree have responded with appropriate support

- Negotiations, even when they reach a formal agreement, continue and rather than being seen as renegotiations should be understood as extensions to the original negotiations

- Exposure to the learnings of one phase or aspect of our peace process alone is dangerous and interconnections between the three phases need to be understood

The Complexity of Dynamics in a Peace Process

Informed by more than twenty years of its own experience working in cooperation with both Irish and British Governments, in the political arena, with former prisoners, victims and a plethora of other key institutions and groups in Ireland, north and south and in Britain, Glencree was well-positioned to understand the changing dynamics of a peace process. Glencree has developed a full appreciation from its experience that peace processes are not linear and often defy logic.

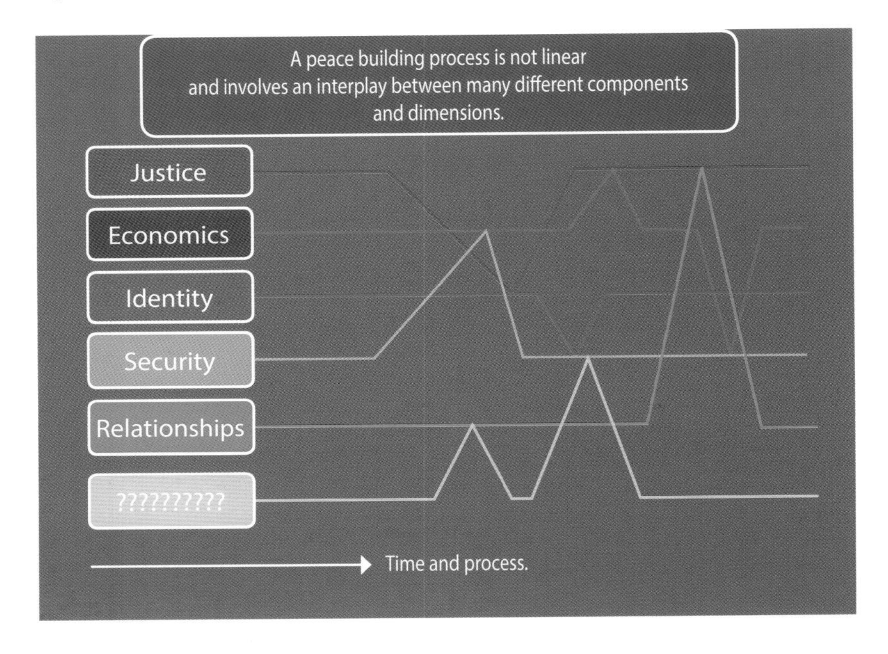

This graphic was created to help peacebuilding practitioners in Haiti to appreciate the full and complex nature of a peace process

John Paul Lederach offers the following definition of reconciliation which sums up the GIP understanding of the concept:

> *'Reconciliation is a wandering in the desert – that is, it consists less of a linear, formulaic progression, and more of a fitful, long series of steps forward and backward and forward anew'*

Among the offerings that Glencree brings to stakeholders in other violent conflicts, is a deep awareness of the uniqueness and complexity of protracted violent conflicts. Each conflict has many interconnected dimensions and components including: justice, healing the past, power differentials, security sector reform, economic development and identity. Work on one dimension inevitably impacts on other dimensions and the management of the interplay between these dimensions creates a dynamic process. In many ways, this is the first lesson from the Irish process - that peacebuilding is a dynamic process, not a project.

The Irish Peace Process predates the ceasefires of 1994 and many of us who have worked on it - either as political or civil society stakeholders - often take our own knowledge and experience for granted. Approaches to peacebuilding, concepts of peacebuilding and specific interventions which have been applied and tested in Ireland over three decades, are very familiar and even considered basic or 'old-hat' by many peacebuilding practitioners in Ireland. Yet, these very same phenomena are considered enlightening in many other contexts.

A good example of this lies in the term 'process' - a term with which we have become very familiar. One lesson which we have found resonates with stakeholders in

Peace Committee Training in Haiti, 2008

protracted social conflict in many contexts, is in relation to the term 'process' itself. The notion of peace as a process rather than a product or project, appears to have released many participants in the GIP from a constant pursuit of a final solution. If a conflict is proving intractable in a certain context, then a process approach changes the context and creates new possibilities for resolution or at least management of the core conflict. When parties to a conflict can only see their own end game objective, there is a need to help them 'think outside-the-box' which often allows them to look at the positions, interests and needs of the other group.

For many years, specialist conflict resolution practitioners 'parachuted' into Northern Ireland offering solutions (often simplistic) to our violent conflict. Out of these well-meaning encounters came an awakening that only those involved in the conflict can manage it; outsiders can support the indigenous actors, but cannot take ownership of the solution, which must lie with the indigenous actors. Inclusive ownership of, and stakeholder 'buy-in' to the peace process, was a key to success in Ireland. Even though this common ownership continues to present challenges, it is an important lesson that Glencree transports to others internationally. GIP sees peace processes as journeys that involve the management of conflict, which over time, transforms relationships between protagonists, which allows new possibilities to surface. The lesson that peace is a complex and dynamic process rather than a product, is well received by others in political and civil society internationally. GIP, therefore, does not 'parachute' into conflicts, but it does offer ongoing accompaniment and support as stakeholders in the conflicts seek to engage in process-based work.

Identifying Lessons to Share

Glencree has been equipped to play its role in international peace building by twenty years experience of active and relevant programming in the Irish context. While this is still the case, as the GIP becomes active in other contexts, the source of learning is no longer just the Irish Peace Process, but now includes the processes in which it engages internationally. The GIP therefore, shares lessons from its international experience as well as from its experience in the Irish context.

In addition to lessons we can draw from our experience about the design and out-workings of the Irish peace process, the many years of peacebuilding activity has also left a highly-skilled cohort of peacebuilding practitioners. Many of these highly-skilled practitioners have engaged in a wide variety of peacebuilding programmes and interventions. In particular, Glencree developed skills in a number of areas, including: facilitation of intergroup and political dialogue, mediation, capacity-building, supporting positive leadership and - more strategically - around the integration of former combatants and the transition from victim to survivor. The International Programme therefore, has a capacity not just to share experiences and lessons, but also its skills. Dialogue and training, for example, are two key tools in the Glencree tool bag, and facilitators in different international contexts are assisted not just to understand these dynamic tools and their value, but they are also equipped with the skills to use the tools. What follows is a short description of the main lessons about peacebuilding and peace processes in Ireland that participants in the Glencree International Programme find resonate with the needs and possibilities in their context.

Neutrality

There is no such thing as neutral. Everyone born into, and who has lived in a context of a protracted violent conflict is carrying his or her own baggage and prejudices which have been formed by their interactions with the conflict and other stakeholders. This reality obviously applies to stakeholders in the conflict, but it also applies to third party mediators, peacebuilders and facilitators. While indigenous third parties often declare themselves as neutral, it has become clear to the GIP that they limit their own potential to assist in peacebuilding, unless they acknowledge and declare their true relationship to the conflict. Peacebuilders who are in denial about their own prejudices run the danger of escalating – or, at least, hindering the peacebuilding process rather than being part of the solution. Such individuals and organisations tend to oversimplify the conflict being addressed and are constantly in pursuit of simplistic results rather than a meaningful process of engagement which addresses the key issues.

Peacebuilders who recognise their own prejudices and can still be objective are the ones that will assist stakeholders develop some degree of confidence in each other and help them think 'out of the box' and move forward. This requires a high degree of transparency with the stakeholders. When Glencree commenced its political dialogue programme, the key facilitators met every political party in Ireland to extend the invitation to participate. Part of this invitation was a clear explanation of the religious and political backgrounds and leanings of the main facilitators.

Re-humanising of Relationships - a Heart-and-Head Approach

In deep-rooted violent conflicts where communities become polarised, it is common for not just a discrediting but also a de-humanising of the other. This is not restricted to leaders of opposing groups, but permeates through all stakeholder groups. In order to make progress in a peace process, this dynamic of demonisation needs not only to cease, but, in fact, opportunities must be created for it to be reversed. In many ways, the Glencree political programme is a model of re-humanisation. Through inclusive dialogue workshops, adversaries were enabled to see and explore their differences in such a way that increasingly, they recognised the humanity in the other. This involved working at an emotional level, without neglecting the very real and difficult political differences that had to be acknowledged, in order for progress to be made. The International Programme continues to apply a heart-and-head approach to its work.

State and non-state armed groups engaged in protracted social conflict as is experienced frequently by Glencree in its International Programme, are often well-organised and they usually have the ability to be strategic and tactical. However, that is only a partial description of the characteristics of armed groups. Other characteristics relate to the unconscious and emotional passion that is often displayed by armed actors. A holistic approach to peacebuilding has to take both dimensions into consideration and even understand that there is an interplay between the pragmatism of the head and the emotions and feelings that accompany that.

Humility

Before we can build improbable relationships between parties in conflict, we must, as a third party, establish a relationship between us and the stakeholders. Stakeholders in protracted violent conflicts become wary of the peacebuilder that offers solutions. In order to build the relationships with stakeholders that are required in order to move a peace process forward, there is a constant need to exercise and demonstrate a high degree of humility and non-judgement. The only objective of the peacebuilder is to assist disputing parties to reach their own solutions. Because of the noble practice in which the peacebuilder engages, it is easy for the third party to assume superiority and expect stakeholders to come to their level. An effective peacebuilder will assess the capacity of the stakeholders and move towards them, rather than wait for them to move to the level of the facilitator.

It is essential that the peacebuilder's expectations are realistic and that he/she doesn't commit to things that cannot be achieved. The peacebuilder must make clear that he/she is not coming with answers or solutions but with opportunities and possibilities. To think you have the answers not only damages the prospects for building a little peace, but also damages the credibility of the third party, as stakeholders may perceive them as being arrogant and condescending.

Colette Nkunda in Bamako, Mali at World Aids Day event 2014

The people with the closest relationship to, and responsibility for the conflict are the ones engaged in it. While they may have difficulty processing their understanding of the conflict - or in other words, difficulty seeing 'the wood for the trees' - their knowledge is much greater than any outsider or, for that matter, well-intended insiders who are in denial of their relationship to it. At the outset of work with international groups who come from a different cultural, religious or national background, Glencree has developed an introductory comment which helps create confidence among the participants in relation to the role to be played by Glencree. Any practitioner using this needs to not just understand the full implications of it, but needs to believe it. This is where peacebuilding becomes much more complex than simple professional or academic practice:

'If what I say challenges you, then I am satisfied. If, however, something I say offends or insults you, please do not forgive me. Tell me and I will seek the forgiveness from you.'

Inclusivity

While there is no definition of 'inclusivity' in any dictionary, Glencree has coined this term as being the pro-active alternative to inclusiveness. It is simply not sufficient for a third-party to make a generic invitation to stakeholders to participate in a process. Inclusivity is the act of assessing who finds that they can't participate and working to remove the obstacles to their participation. This requires a working knowledge of - and empathy with - the needs of the various stakeholder groups.

Inclusivity is often misconstrued as solely referring to the inclusion of the stakeholders in the conflict while, in fact, it must go beyond that definition if it is to address all of the important relationships which influence a conflict. It is likely, as experienced by Glencree, that in a political process which involves adversaries sharing physical space and engaging with each other directly, at times, groups will absent themselves from the process. Perhaps they will absent themselves because of the need for internal retrospection or strategic planning, or perhaps because of expulsion and/or manipulative behavior of another stakeholder.

Either way, the task of including all of the stakeholders in an interactive process and keeping them in it, is often a major challenge and it must remain as an aspiration for the peacebuilding actor rather than ignored as being too much trouble. Using exclusion as a sanction against one of the parties to the conflict is a short-sighted and simplistic mechanism to try to force progress within and among the stakeholder groups. This is a high-risk strategy and can result in an escalation of violent conflict as groups feel excluded and not represented again.

Physical spaces for meetings are important as we seek to create inclusive environments, conducive to positive outcomes from our work. What may seem to be a safe 'neutral' meeting space to one party may be totally unacceptable to another. Glencree itself has been such a safe meeting space where everyone could either feel equally welcome and comfortable or, as was the reality at times, equally uncomfortable. In the slums of Haiti, any kind of meeting space is difficult to find - never mind mutually acceptable space. An important part of our work in St. Martin has been to provide small, safe spaces where all members of the community are welcome and where local, inclusive peace committees can engage with each other to plan peacebuilding activities aimed at addressing the causes and effects of violent conflict in their community.

Broad Lessons from International Contexts

In addition to learning more about how Glencree itself can improve its practice based on reflecting on its role in the Irish context, there are broad lessons that appear to resonate with stakeholders in other international contexts in which we work. The sharing of broad lessons from the peace process tends to provoke more specific enquiries from the stakeholder groups with whom we work. More focused and specific technical support - and even mentoring needs - are often identified by sharing the broad lessons with international actors. This approach, which starts with broad or general lessons, points the way to specific lessons, which are appropriate to share in any specific context.

Exclusion and Marginalisation - the Other Side of the Inclusion Coin

In 2005, together with Concern, Glencree pioneered a new approach to gang- (Baz) related violence in the slums of St. Martin, in Port-au-Prince, Haiti. The analysis of the conflict pointed to the fact that many of the Baz felt marginalised or excluded from mainstream society and had developed a complex - and perhaps even schizoid - relationship to the community to which they belonged and lived. The powerlessness to make a change in their own circumstances contributed to a high level of frustration, which frequently gave rise to violence. The Baz were often guilty of abusing members of their own community and yet, when there was a threat from external actors, either state (Haitian National Police or UN) or non-state (Baz from outside the community), the indigenous Baz from that community became defenders of the community, fulfilling a vigilante-type role. When there was no threat from outside, the Baz ruled the slum with a heavy hand, leaving many victims too frightened or powerless to take any action - in a state where the justice system is weak and inaccessible for many.

In an effort to repair some of the torn social fabric of the community and reframe the relationship between the Baz and the community to which they belong, Glencree delivered a series of capacity-building trainings to a variety of groups in the community - including the Baz. This training prepared them for an inclusive community dialogue, which engaged the Baz together with a cross section of their community, including some of those who had suffered as a result of the actions of the Baz. This community dialogue process allowed the Baz chiefs to transform their relationship to their own community. Through capacity-building in the area of leadership, which included formal training as well as ongoing support and mentoring, the Chiefs were able to lead their members in a more positive direction; the result was a rapid reduction in violence. The Baz leaders were motivated to move towards non-violence by the possibility of a more connected, resilient and respectful relationship with their community.

When a group is marginalised or excluded from mainstream society, it has no reason to abide by the rules of that society and a reckless sense of 'nothing to lose' can give rise to violent activity, particularly in a context where even the Baz leaders are not sure how they will feed their children tomorrow. This is not an attempt to justify the behaviour of the Baz, but understanding their reality helps us understand their behaviour.

The challenge currently being faced by Glencree in this Haitian context is how to sustain a significantly lower level of violence. We know that change in the economic capacity of the community will remove the poverty, which creates the context for the violence to thrive. However, Glencree is not a development organisation and therefore, its core skillset is not poverty alleviation. The changing of the economic reality at local community level has pushed Glencree into partnership with international agencies with development expertise who can provide development activity, which complements the peacebuilding work of Glencree and makes violence reduction more sustainable.

Locating the Power to Create Change - the Need for a Multi-Level Approach

A recurring fact emerging from the work of Glencree in Northern Ireland, Haiti, Israel, Liberia, Palestine and Afghanistan points to the need to redress real and perceived power imbalances as part of a peacebuilding process. One response to this from Glencree is to adopt a multi-level approach to its work, and this, again, contributes to sustainability of reduced levels of violence. The Glencree multi-level approach recognises that:

- The power to change the reality and circumstances of a group or community does not lie solely within the group or community and there are always outside actors who have substantial influence (either enabling or obstructive) that need to be engaged

- Power differentials are a reality around the world. The powerful may have been given the power by their constituency, they may have taken the power by force or they may have inherited the power. Each of those different scenarios require a different type of approach but all approaches have the same objective which is to build improbable relationships between the different levels of influence in society. Through ongoing engagement the new relationships and new ways of using power which benefit all stakeholders are explored

- Connections and relationships not only between divided groups at each level need to be rebuilt but also relationships between the levels need to be strong in order to create inclusive and equitable society

This diagram outlines the multi-level approach applied by Glencree. This approach also recognises that the edges between these levels are blurred with some people having allegiance to more than one level.

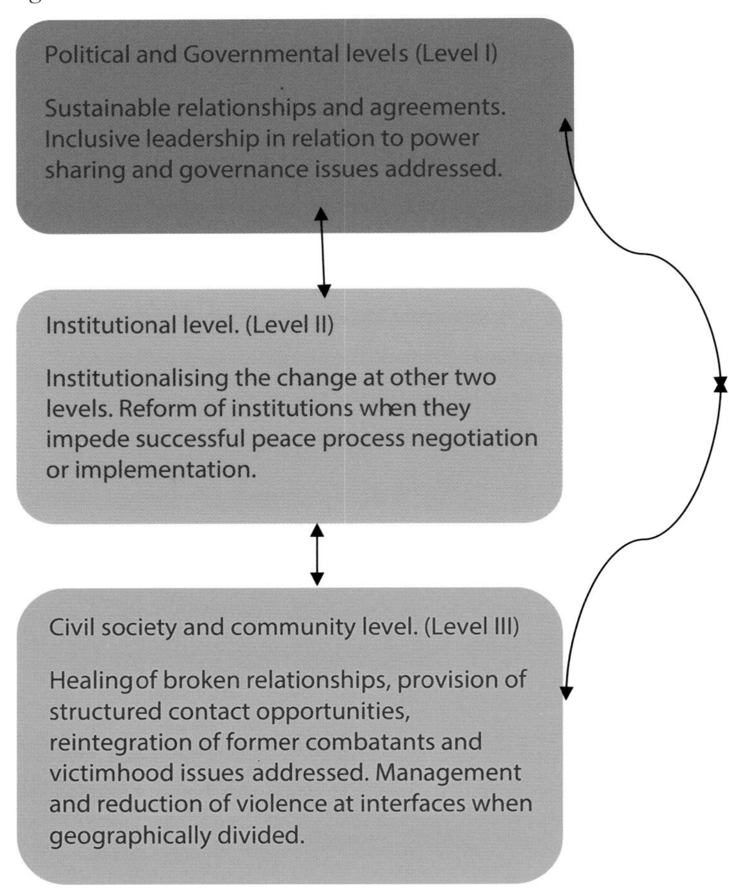

Glencree has applied this basic model in Haiti where the divisions between those with power and those without, is not only stark, but which directly contributes to the ongoing Baz-related violence. Lakou Lape is a Haitian-owned and governed peacebuilding initiative, which was born out of the dialogue and training process delivered between 2005 and 2012 by Glencree in partnership with Concern. Glencree worked firstly within each level to provide training and build the capacity of key stakeholders to engage in dialogue with each other. Then, through a series of bi- and multilateral dialogues and trainings, where one of the main principles to which participants are asked to agree, focuses on the issue of equality of participation and an acceptance by them that everyone - regardless of status outside the process - has an equally-important contribution to make within the process.

This approach has resulted in a re-humanisation of the relationships between the main stakeholders, which again serves to sustain reduced levels of violence in their community. While the dialogue within and between the levels was an essential ingredient in the process, allowing new and more accurate perceptions of each other to emerge, dialogue needs a practical focus after a while, so that the renewed relationships have a reason to sustain. In this example, the post dialogue, inclusive practical action manifested itself through the creation of a new inclusive institution called Lakou Lape ('peace community' in Creole). Lakou Lape is supported by Glencree and other international actors, and has an inclusive governance system bringing together actors from all three levels - including former Baz leaders and leaders in industry and business.

Peace Dividend

Glencree has placed much of its international focus on developing contexts where poverty and violence feed off each other in a cyclical type of relationship. The context created by poverty provides an environment conducive to the escalation of violence. At the same time, with high levels of violence, it is difficult to achieve any kind of real economic development and so the cycle repeats itself.

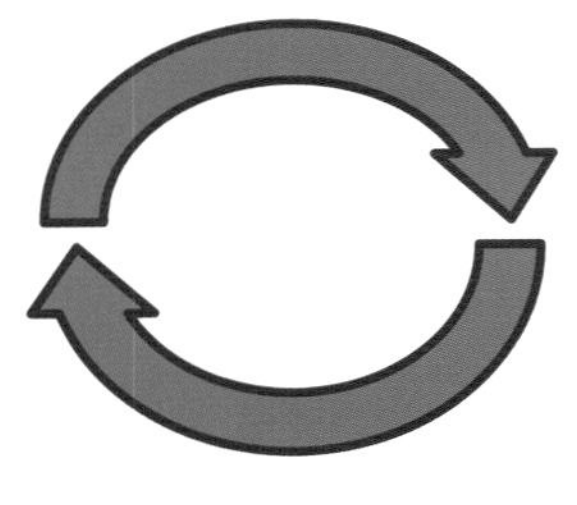

This dynamic connection between violence and poverty helps us understand how most non-state armed actors (and also state-armed actors) come from socio-economically-disadvantaged backgrounds where they do not have equal opportunities to wealth, work, education and other basic rights. Therefore, in order to make a reduction of violence sustainable, we also need to look at economic wellbeing, at the same time as we work on building those improbable relationships across the cleavages in conflicted societies and communities. When the relationships are built, then the issues causing the divides can be addressed. In Haiti, it is a constant challenge for Glencree as a peacebuilding organisation to, first of all, create economic and community development activity in those communities engaged with the programme. Secondly, it is essential to ensure that any peace dividend impacts on the entire community rather than being seen to reward bad behaviour by focusing only on armed groups. There have been criticisms of the DDR (Disarmament, Demobilisation and Reinsertion) approach, which is seen by some as a 'one-size–fits-all' approach by the United Nations and governments, globally. Some critics argue that the DDR model prioritises former fighters and the benefits are not felt strongly enough by the wider community. This criticism of DDR is accompanied by the other main criticism that quite often the former combatants engage in the two 'D's and rarely get the 'R' in return.

Identity

Many of the protracted violent conflicts in which Glencree engages have many drivers and inter-related components. Identity issues tend to surface at some point in the work being conducted. In Afghanistan, for example, tribal and/or ethnic identity often sets a person apart from other groups. While on a day-to-day basis, the members of

Ian White presenting certificates in Haiti

Afghan ethnic groups can work together and extend some level of respect to each other, at times of heightened tension between ethnic groups, through the fear of loss of identity, their ethnicity takes on a new importance and becomes another driver of the conflict. This learning is drawn directly from Northern Ireland where we often experience a need for expression to be given to people's identity through parades, art, murals etc. Again, even in Northern Ireland, while identity is important, it is not until you perceive it to be under threat that it contributes to violence.

Post Violent Conflict or Post Conflict Violence - A Case for Inclusive and Equal Access to Justice?

Northern Ireland, since the signing of the Good Friday Agreement, has become known as a 'post conflict environment'. In fact, this definition of the current condition of Northern Ireland is quite wrong in the opinion of the author of this piece. In reality, Northern Ireland has a peace process, but conflict remains high and the fluctuating trust between stakeholders is sometimes at a remarkably low level.

Setting aside the threat from Republican dissidents, one of the reasons that the durability of the process is tested by outbursts of violence is because of what some marginalised communities perceive as the lack of access to justice. When it is perceived that members of other groups or communities are getting justice and you are not (which is a common dynamic in protracted conflicts) and where stakeholders have a sense of being marginalised, then frustration at what appears to be a discriminatory justice system, can easily erupt into violence. Furthermore, as is often experienced by Glencree in Afghanistan and more recently in Liberia, when an individual does not - or feels that they do not have - access to justice, then revenge is something quite similar.

Conclusion

The following table is intended to provide a synopsis of the areas of GIP work over the past fifteen years, starting from small beginnings and tentative steps. Most of this work has not been referenced in this piece and still needs to be documented in greater detail. In all of these cases we have felt that the Irish experience has something to offer. This preliminary reflection has tried to clarify how our own learning from Northern Ireland feeds into this work and offers different possibilities in different contexts. We will continue to draw out specific learning from the projects in which we have been involved, so that the lessons from Ireland can be made more effective in making a difference elsewhere.

It should be clear that the range of the work alluded to, is broad. Even though the engagement in some of these cases has not been long term, there are key perspectives from our experience that contribute something of value. Working in partnership can bring results that help people to see opportunities and possible alternative approaches where they may not have been able to previously. Through our own reflection process we can be more strategic about what we have to offer and where we feel we can add this value.

Synopsis of areas of work of Glencree International Programme since 2000	
Country/ Region	**Nature of work**
Sri Lanka	Partnering with An Garda Siochana to provide Human Rights-based Police Training to the LTTE Police Service Hosting two meetings of the LTTE political wing as they considered responses to the proposals made by the Government of Sri Lanka. (2000 - 2004)
Colombia	Partnering with Trocaire to provide capacity-building programmes to strengthen the ability of civil society groups to manage or resolve local level conflicts. (1999-2002)
Israel Palestine	Partnering with the Van Leer Institute primarily to establish linkages between joint Israeli and Palestinian civil society groups and Irish civil society groups with the objective of facilitating a sharing of experience The hosting of six joint visits involving Members of the Knesset and Members of the Palestinian Legislative Council The chairing and facilitation of fourworkshops in the region and in Ireland to give consideration to issuesarising out of the planned withdrawal of Israeli Settlements from Gaza. This process also involved representatives from all four members of the quartet Facilitation of a former prisoners workshop in Gaza catering for the leaderships of Alaqsa Martyrs, Hamas, Islamic Jihad and PFLP and with the purpose of sharing Ireland's experience of peacebuilding and making a contribution to Palestinian Unity 2002-ongoing
Liberia	Capacity-building with the Liberian Truth and Reconciliation Commission includingthe development of a working definition for Reconciliation Work with Liberian Members of Parliament to link them more clearly to the work of the TRC and prepare them for the TRC report and what will be required of them when the report is produced. 2005-2006
Haiti	In partnership with Concern Worldwide, delivered an inclusive and comprehensive violence reduction programme in two slums in Port au Prince Established a Haitian-owned practical peacebuilding NGO called Lakou Lape and continue to provide a local resource for the management of intergroup violence - in particular, in the slums of Haiti. 2004-2012 With limited support for Lakou Lape continuing.
Afghanistan	Provided peacebuilding training to seven Afghan NGOs with active peacebuilding programmes and built an informal network of peacebuilders out of this training. The development of a conflict-sensitivity tool to "conflict-proof" the development activities of Norwegian Church Aid. The development together with Norwegian Church Aid (NCA) of a concept and applicationto the Norwegian Embassy, Kabul,which integrated peacebuilding and development into the same process. The delivery of a twelve-week peace studies programme by Islamic Scholars in six Afghan Universities. Each programme catered for inclusive groups of forty students each 2006-2012

Nepal	Hosting of two delegations of civil society and political actors as well as government officials who had engagement with the Nepali Peace Process and wanted to learn from some aspects of the ŀish Peace Process 2009-Ongoing
Thailand	In partnership with PACTA a Finnish peacebuilding NGO, Glencree facilitated a small delegation of Unionist and Republican politicians and activists to share experience with Thai Government Officials, Politicians, peacebuilding institutes, and civil society actors fromSouthern Provinces in Thailand Hosting of a group of Thai Officials and academics with a specific interest in the role of the military in a peace process. Hosting of a group of members of the Southern Border Provinces Advisory Committee to a fact-finding visit to Ireland North and South. 2008-Ongoing
The Kurdish Conflict	In partnership with the Democratic Progress Institute, Glencree hosted two groups of key stakeholders from Turkey who are directlyengaged with the Kurdish conflict. After a number of single identity events, it is envisaged that a fully-inclusive event will be hosted where all stakeholder groups will be represented. 2011-Ongoing.
Moldova and Transnistria	Hosting and support for representatives of stakeholder groups from Moldova and Transdnistria as part of the contribution of Ireland during its Presidency of the OSCE. 2010 – ongoing
General	International Programme staff are regularly invited to address audiences both in Ireland, North and South and also internationally. These events are too numerous to list but are important opportunities to strengthen the work of our partners in the field and create enabling opportunities to advance our work.

The Role of International Volunteers

Eamon Rafter & Sorcha Tormey

The principle of voluntarism was an essential part of the early development of Glencree. Programme participants were voluntary and this made their participation more meaningful. In the same way people from the North and the South and many different countries gave their time and skills to help make the site a place where the work could be done. The contribution of literally hundreds of people over many years was vital to the spirit of the work and means that the values and mission of the organisation remain alive in many diverse locations.

International Volunteers Reunion August 2009

By the time the organisation was running focused programmes to support reconciliation on the island of Ireland in the eighties and early nineties, an International Volunteer Programme had become central to the way the work was done. The programme brought a diverse group of individuals of different ages and backgrounds from many different countries to live on 'the mountain' and make a real contribution to the work. These volunteers lived on-site in the Wicklow Wing and brought a sense of community and vibrancy to the Centre. They made an essential contribution to the programme work by looking after visitors and creating an atmosphere which was so valuable in supporting the work.

Many of them came from countries such as Israel, Palestine, Afghanistan, Haiti and the Balkans, where conflict was a reality and they could share their own firsthand experience. When programme participants came to stay, they got to know the Glencree volunteers and often formed lasting friendships with them. Glencree tried to offer a learning dimension to the programme, but there was so much work to be done on-site to support the running of the Centre that it was hard to provide the right balance. However, the experience was life-changing for many who have subsequently

Glencree Centre for Peace and Reconciliation values the principle and practice of volunteerism at all levels of our work. The teamwork of salaried staff and volunteers allows us to offer our visitors and programme participants the best services possible. Volunteers contribute their time, unique talents, skills and knowledge. They provide support for salaried staff to concentrate on their own areas of responsibility within the organisation.

Volunteers add value to the work of the organisation through their commitment and by virtue of the fact that they are resident in Glencree. They provide a welcoming atmosphere that is so important to the work we do.

As volunteers at Glencree come from all over the world, they bring their own cultural perspectives and experience. This allows for a diverse and intercultural atmosphere, which is important in reconciliation work. Programme participants welcome the volunteers' contribution and find great value in the social time they spend with them.

Glencree statement on volunteering 2006

returned to visit and meet the friends they had made and got to know during their time at Glencree. The residential programme work could not have been done without the volunteers. Without them, Glencree would have seemed less diverse, vibrant and colourful and we will be forever indebted to their generosity and spirit.

Volunteer Reunion Lunch

Sorcha Tormey was an international volunteer at Glencree who came from Australia and went on to work as a member of the Peace Education Team. She describes the experience:

'My time at Glencree began with the drive up the winding road from Enniskerry, Co. Wicklow. I was nervous and excited on that Sunday evening in early September 2005. I had no idea what was in store and what it would mean to be part of the International Volunteer Programme and part of this community nestled away in the Wicklow Mountains. The imposing sight of the Barracks building was a flash of grey as the car turned another corner and my mind raced with thoughts about the people

I was about to meet, the work we would be doing and all that this experience at Glencree would bring.

I had decided to apply to be part of the international volunteer programme after completing a master's degree in peace and conflict studies at the University of Queensland, Australia. Originally from Ireland, I had moved to Brisbane as a child with my family. As a first venture into the work of peace and conflict transformation, it made sense to go back to Ireland to learn about the conflict there and try to understand how it impacted the place where I was from. When I began researching peace centres and organisations on the island of Ireland, I was excited to find a centre in Wicklow as I had grown up in Bray, just down the road. I was drawn to Glencree because the people working there were undertaking peacebuilding programmes within and between different communities. From the little research I had done it seemed to be quite rare to find an organisation directly and actively engaged in the work of peace and conflict transformation.

International volunteers usually lived and worked at Glencree for twelve months (although some stayed for both longer and shorter periods) and so I moved into the Wicklow Wing, the volunteer accommodation, with fourteen other volunteers from Palestine, India, Germany, Hungary, the United States, Canada, China, the Philippines, South Africa and New Zealand. Because there were so many of us, we were sharing rooms and generally living on top of each other. I had assumed that this would be a big adjustment and one of the more challenging aspects of volunteer life but surprisingly it worked well and we quickly settled into life on the mountain.

The International Volunteer Programme was divided into two streams. Most volunteers worked for the Centre in a general capacity and undertook a number of different duties that directly supported all programme staff and groups that visited. This may have involved assisting with hosting and facilitating groups and visitors, working in the kitchen, housekeeping, maintaining the Centre grounds, helping out with transportation, as well as anything else that might have been needed. The variety of programmes and the sensitivity of the work that the groups were involved in meant that the international volunteer team became very adept at responding to different circumstances and situations as they arose. This was especially true with groups that stayed overnight when most of the centre staff had gone home for the day, and it was up to programme staff and the volunteers to ensure that participants had all that they needed. In this way, the International Volunteer Programme was integral not only to the day-to-day running of the organisation, but in creating and developing a strong sense of community and enabling the centre to be a place of welcome and safety for all who stayed there.

The second stream of the International Volunteer Programme was made up of a small number of volunteers working mainly as interns supporting specific programmes within the centre. I had applied and been accepted to work as an intern for the Peace Education Programme along with Meenu Raghunathan, a volunteer from India, Nneka Madu who had come from the United States and Elaine Adair-Smith who had arrived from Canada. We had been brought into the programme to work with Conn Mulvenna and Claudia Bradshaw, two people who were passionately committed to the vision of Glencree and, particularly, the work of the Peace Education Programme. The work of the programme involved either short programmes with individual schools and youth groups from north or south of the border, or longer programmes working on a cross-border or cross-community basis with cluster groups. We also had opportunities to work with young people from different countries who were either coming from a context of violent, political conflict or were interested in learning about the conflict and subsequent peace process on the island of Ireland.

At that time, there were over 2000 young people participating in the Peace Education programme at Glencree each year and bringing with them a lot of energy, excitement and interest in the work of the Centre. The programmes facilitated with these young people were interactive, participant-focused and were designed to enable them to reflect on situations of conflict, to draw out their ideas about how to work with those situations and recognise and develop the skills they have to enact peaceful change in their own lives and the lives of those around them. Depending on the needs of the groups, the workshops focused on specific themes such as working with conflict, leadership, citizenship, group work and team-building.

Glencree Staff and Volunteers at Belfast Marathon 2007

In order to meet the demands of the programme and accommodate the large number of young people participating in it, a facilitator panel was created made up of fifteen people from a variety of backgrounds who would come to the Centre on a sessional basis to work with the groups. This was a wonderful addition to the Peace Education Programme team - not only because of the quality of the work being delivered by the facilitators, but because of the support they gave to the programme and the Centre as a whole. The panel was extra special because a handful of those facilitators had previously been participants in the Peace Education Programme as members of a youth group and were now coming back to continue the work of the programme, in particular Shane O'Connor, Riona Judge McCormack, Eimear Friel and Alan Hayes. As an intern on the programme, it was an invaluable experience to have the opportunity to work with all of the facilitators and learn about tailoring peace education to the needs and interests of the young people we were working with.

Living on the mountain was a very rewarding experiences but, of course, there were challenges, especially for volunteers living so far away from their family and friends back home. We were so fortunate to have the support of members of the Glencree community who went to great lengths to help us out. In particular, Rosy Wilson, one of the longest-serving local volunteers at Glencree, who gave so much time and effort to the Centre in so many ways and who in particular supported the international volunteer programme with regular ESL classes. We also would have been lost without the assistance and friendship of resident Centre caretaker Pat Fleming and there was many a volunteer who struggled to say goodbye to him when their time at Glencree came to an end. Many of us were very fortunate to spend time with our neighbour down the road, Brendan Crowley, who was wonderful company with his famous repertoire of proverbs usually delivered 'as gaeilge'. The last piece of advice he gave me, which I will never forget was, 'Sorcha, never sell a hen on a wet day'. Centre staff were also a vital support, in particular, Eamon Rafter who worked closely with a number of international volunteer teams before the programme came to an end in 2011.

Six months after I started volunteering at Glencree, I was appointed full-time as Peace Education Programme Officer, following in the footsteps of Claudia after her resignation. For the next two years I worked closely with Conn, Eamon, the International Volunteer team and the panel of facilitators to deliver the Peace Education Programme. Towards the end of my time as a full-time staff member I also had the opportunity to work with Sean O'Boyle and Ian White on the International Programme and travel to Afghanistan. Afterwards, I continued to work as a sessional facilitator with Phil Killeen on the Women's Programme, working particularly on a cross-border, cross-community basis with women from north and south of the border. During my time at the Centre, I also had the opportunity to connect in with the work of Wilhelm Verwoerd, Jacinta De Paor and Colin Murphy, which I appreciated immensely.

Little did I know on that first drive up the mountain to Glencree that I was going to meet an incredible group of people and learn so much about the joys and challenges of community and peacebuilding work. The untimely death of Conn Mulvenna in 2012 was not only a great loss to the world and those working so hard for peace and justice, but it was also a stark reminder of how special Glencree is as a place of peace and reconciliation and how important it is that the work continues. As a volunteer and staff member, I feel so fortunate to have had the opportunity to learn from the people who work there.

My hope is that Glencree, as both a community and a peacebuilding organisation, is supported so that it can continue to be of benefit to people experiencing violent conflict and promote peace and justice within and between communities on the island of Ireland and around the world.'

Sorcha Tormey, Brisbane, Australia, 2013

Key lessons for the future

The International Volunteer Programme was suspended in 2011 with the closure of the residential facilities because of the ongoing financial challenge. This was the first time in approximately twenty years that Glencree was no longer a residential community with volunteers living on site. We are not clear whether there will be international volunteers on-site in the future, but it is important to reflect on what we have learnt and bear this in mind in the event of the programme being renewed. The following are some of the key things that emerged over a period of time in relation to hosting and working with international volunteers.

- A good recruitment process is essential to attract the right people and it is important that there is enough information about the work they will be doing. Willingness to spend time in a remote location is a requirement and they may not have had this type of experience before.

- The duration of the period spent at Glencree was normally one year, but this was not possible for many people. A shorter duration of six months should also be considered.

- The living conditions of the volunteers would need to be improved as the current facilities would not be adequate. Single rooms that afford some privacy and better cooking and leisure facilities would be desirable.

- Clarity about the expectations of Glencree with regard to the abilities of volunteers is important. A good supervision structure and some mentoring support is also needed for the process to be rewarding for the volunteer.

- The option of having local volunteers and some from Northern Ireland allows for better diversity in the volunteer team and provides support for those coming from very different cultural backgrounds

- Some clear policy on bringing volunteers from developing countries who need to feel that they can get the most out of the opportunity and go home with additional skills, knowledge and experience

- A clear learning path and links to programme work should be defined as some volunteers were disappointed that they could not access the peacebuilding opportunities for which they had come to Glencree in the first place.

- Glencree should be sure that it can offer an opportunity to volunteers and only restart the programme if this is the case. The needs of the organisation are not reason enough to do so.

These are some of the key points that would inform a future volunteer programme at Glencree. The contribution of volunteers to the work of Glencree has been huge and we feel that the experience has also offered a lot to those who have come here. It is essential that such a programme is well managed and that the right supports are available for people living in a fairly remote area. We hope that we have not seen the end of Glencree as a residential community, although for now, we have to accept that we no longer have this rich asset to help our work.

'If you want to make peace with your enemy, you have to work with your enemy. Then he becomes your partner.'
Nelson Mandela

Author Biographies

William Devas is CEO of the Glencree Centre for Peace and Reconciliation. He is a trained mediator and dialogue and storytelling facilitator and has been working in peacebuilding since 2010. Following a few years in hotel management, tourism and large event management William spent eight years working in International Humanitarian Aid and Development, travelling widely in Africa, Asia and Latin America. He was brought up in England, studied in Scotland and lives in Dublin.

Roelf Meyer is an independent consultant on peace processes who has worked in Northern Ireland, Sri Lanka, Rwanda, Burundi, Kosovo and Bolivia. He was chief negotiator for the National Party (NP) government in the negotiations on the settlement of the South African conflict and after the elections he continued in the portfolio of Constitutional Affairs in the cabinet of former President Nelson Mandela.

Geoffrey Corry is a family and workplace mediator, trainer, and conflict management specialist who has worked for the past twenty-five years in Ireland. He has been active in peacemaking since 1974 through the Glencree Centre for Peace and Reconciliation, where he served as chairperson (1982–1987), lead facilitator for the Political Dialogue Programme, and director for fourteen Glencree summer schools (1994–2007)

Eamon Rafter is Learning Co-ordinator at Glencree where he has worked since 2005. He is a peace educator and facilitator with responsibility for education and training programmes with schools, youth, universities, adult and community groups. He has worked on peacebuilding programmes in Ireland north and south, Israel & Palestine, South Africa, Afghanistan and in several European countries. His role also involves documenting and sharing the learning of the organisation and in this capacity he has compiled and edited this publication.

Phil Killeen is Coordinator of the Women's Programme at the Glencree Centre for Peace and Reconciliation working with women north and south. She is an experienced senior manager and human resource professional and worked in the service industry with clients in the public, private and semi-state sector. She is a business and training consultant, holds a BA in Industrial Relations & Personnel Management, is a Chartered Member of the CIPD and a Licensed Master Practitioner of NLP.

Ian White is originally from Newtonards in Northern Ireland, but moved to Dublin in 1983 and worked for a number of peacebuilding organisations before becoming Excecutive Director of Glencree in 1994. He held this post for a decade developing initiatives with politicians, victims, former combatants, religious, young leaders and women before establishing his own peacebuilding consultancy. Between 2010 and 2014 he returned to Glencree to formally establish and manage the International Programme with work in Haiti, Afghanistan, Israel, Palestine, Liberia and Thailand. Ian now works as a private consultant with a number of state and non-state clients in different countries.

Jacinta De Paor is psychologist, process therapy practitioner and owner of 'Next Phases: Conflict Exploration, Facilitation & Training' and she currently serves on the management committee of 'Facing Forward'. From 1999 to 2008 she was Director of Glencree's LIVE Programme for Dialogue between Combatants and Victims. She has also worked with Young Offenders, as a counsellor to students with disabilities, as supervisor to Adult Ed Staff with VEC Newbridge and in the US at the Psych Dept., John Hopkins University, Baltimore, US, working on a project on schizophrenia. Jacinta has developed a number of programmes and advised on conflict & trauma with the Basque Government and with Geneva and Leuven Universities. She has presented her work at the US Association for Conflict Resolution (ACR), at the European Conference on Trauma & at Quinnipiac University, USA.

Wilhelm Verwoerd is a former researcher on the South African Truth and Reconciliation Commission and lecturer in Philosophy at University of Stellenbosch, South Africa. He was programme co-ordinator of the Survivors and Former Combatants Programme at Glencree, from 2002. He then co-founded the Glencree Sustainable Peace Network and was a co-ordinator and facilitator until 2011. Wilhelm is author of 'My Winds of Change' (1996) and in 2008 his PhD thesis 'Equity, Mercy, Forgiveness: Interpreting Amnesty within the South African Truth and Reconciliation Commission', was published. He returned to South Africa in 2012 to help develop the work of a new organisation 'Beyond Walls'.

Colin Murphy lived in Belfast until 1975 and then moved south. He got involved with Glencree in the early eighties and later, as CEO, was instrumental in the re-opening of the organisation in 1992. He then worked as the Programme Manager of the Glencree Churches Programme, an inclusive cross-border initiative that examined the role of the churches in the conflict. In this programme individuals were offered the opportunity to explore ways that different churches can combat sectarianism and facilitate peace.

Sorcha Tormey was born in Ireland and grew up in Australia. She came back to Ireland and to Glencree in 2005 as an International volunteer and later joined the Peace Education team working as an administrator and facilitator in the programme. She also worked as a facilitator on the Women's Programme. Sorcha is currently completing her PhD at the University of Queensland in Brisbane, Australia.

CW00661063

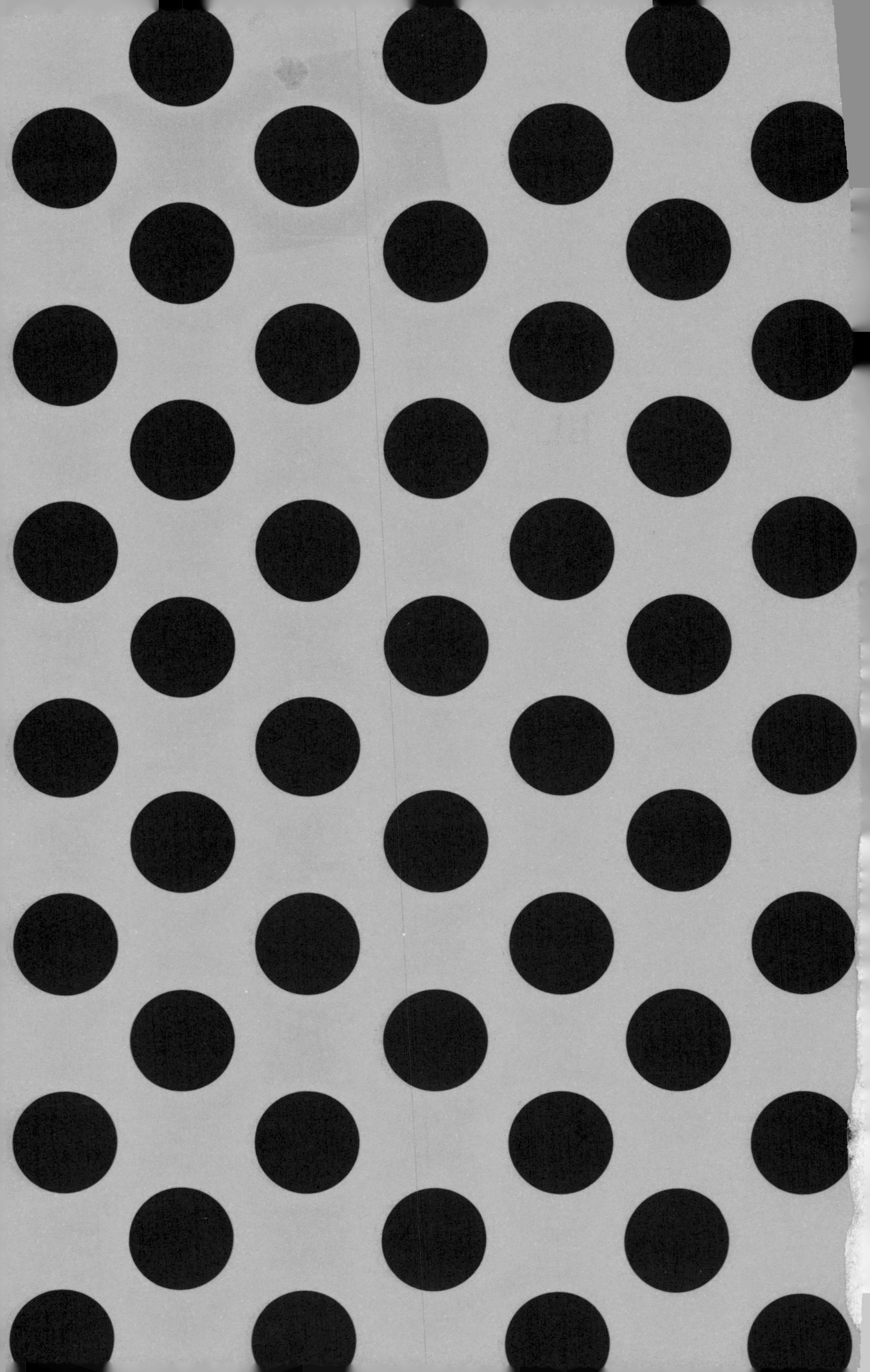

BLACK CAVIAR

Bronwen Healy Photography

BLACK CAVIAR

The Horse of a Lifetime

GERARD WHATELEY

The ABC 'Wave' device is a trademark of the Australian Broadcasting Corporation and is used under licence by HarperCollins*Publishers* Australia.

First published in Australia in 2012
by HarperCollins*Publishers* Australia Pty Limited
ABN 36 009 913 517
harpercollins.com.au

HarperCollins*Publishers*
Level 13, 201 Elizabeth Street, Sydney NSW 2000, Australia
31 View Road, Glenfield, Auckland 0627, New Zealand
A 53, Sector 57, Noida, UP, India
77–85 Fulham Palace Road, London W6 8JB, United Kingdom
2 Bloor Street East, 20th floor, Toronto, Ontario M4W 1A8, Canada
10 East 53rd Street, New York NY 10022, USA

National Library of Australia Cataloguing-in-Publication entry:

Whateley, Gerard
Black Caviar: the horse of a lifetime / Gerard Whateley.
ISBN 978 0 7333 3136 7 (hbk.)
Includes bibliographical references and index.
Black Caviar (Race horse)
Race horses – Australia – Biography.
Horse-racing – Australia.
798.400929

Cover design by Matt Stanton, HarperCollins Design Studio
Cover images by Bronwen Healy Photography
Picture research by Linda Brainwood
Typeset in 12/17pt Bembo by Kirby Jones
Printed and bound in Australia by Griffin Press
The papers used by HarperCollins in the manufacture of this book
are a natural, recyclable product made from wood grown in sustainable
plantation forests. The fibre source and manufacturing processes meet
recognised international environmental standards, and carry certification.

5 4 3 2 1 12 13 14 15

For my Dad
who taught me to look for sporting greatness.

And Black Caviar
who embodied it like no other.

Newspix / Peter Wallis

Black Caviar being led by owners Jannene and Colin Madden and Pam Hawkes after winning the BTC Cup at Doomben, 14 May 2011.

A Word from the Owners

The phenomenon that is Black Caviar is something that has evolved out of many parts. The impact she has had on a nation, individuals, and the racing industry as a whole is extraordinary. Hers is a story that demands to be recorded for historic purpose, for retelling now and as a resource for review and analysis at a later time. And Gerard Whateley has succeeded in capturing her story in a way few others could do.

As for ourselves, this remarkable horse has had an impact far beyond anything any of us could have contemplated. She has brought together our respective families, providing excitement and pleasure, nervous nights and heart palpitations, and the full gamut of human emotions. She has also brought our families together at racetracks around Australia and now extending to Royal Ascot.

Through Black Caviar we have met the most remarkable of people whose common theme has been the love and fascination of a most remarkable horse. They extend from schoolchildren to the Queen, from emotional grandparents holding aloft grandchildren to enable them to see Black Caviar, to racing club committee members overwhelmed at what she has been able to do for them and their clubs.

She has taken us out of our anonymous comfort zones, to be confronted by all manner of media and activities never contemplated as an outcome of buying into a horse with a few friends. She has been truly a life-changing experience for us all.

We read her story with pride, awe and emotion.

Well done, Gerard.

Well done, Black Caviar.

Colin and Jannene Madden,
on behalf of co-owners Lena Attebo and Neil Werrett,
Pam and Barry Hawkes, Jill and David Taylor, and
Kerrin and Gary Wilkie

Contents

	A Word from the Owners	vii
	A Word from the Trainer	1
	Prelude	5
1	The Back of Bourke	11
2	Moody Racing	25
3	I've Found the Horse for You	45
4	An Excuse to Have Lunch	57
5	The Untried Yearling	65
6	The Pain Barrier	77
7	Racing Purgatory	83
8	Inherit the Earth	93
9	The Fastest Horse in the World	105
10	Nelly	117
11	Perfect Ten	127
12	Like Nothing Before	147
13	Northern Exposure	159
14	State of Origin	175
15	Spring Parade	191
16	The Black Caviar Effect	205
17	Unanimous Support	217
18	Friday Night Delights	229
19	Faster Stronger Longer	245
20	Lightning Strikes Twice	263
21	Dynasty	279
22	A State of Gratitude	285
23	Now Go See the World	301
24	Land of Pomp and Glory	307
25	A Quarter of an Inch	321
	Epilogue	341
	Race Statistics	344
	Notes and Acknowledgments	357
	Index	382

Trainer Peter Moody at home with Black Caviar.

A Word from the Trainer

I didn't realise just how much it had been brewing up inside me until I got back from Royal Ascot. For twelve months we had planned for the fastest horse in the world to win the biggest sprint race in Europe at the most famous racecourse on the planet. Expectations were enormous. I'd been driven mad by media on both sides of the world. While behind the scenes we were trying to either hold the mare together or patch her up to make it possible.

I've always said there's no pressure on me, I'm copping this easy. I don't worry about myself much as long as there's bread and butter on the table and a beer in the fridge. I'm a pretty easy-going sort of bloke. Funny thing is, when I got back from England I'd never slept so good for years. I was going to bed at 7.30 p.m. and not twitching a muscle. I wasn't tired during the day and I was so much more relaxed. I thought it wasn't worrying me. But obviously it was.

I've been around horses all my life and never known one better than Black Caviar. I find judging her place in the history of racing hard. I'm so close to her. That's why I've always deferred to other people's opinions. What I know is, Black Caviar is the finest horse I've ever seen or worked with – until I saw Frankel win on that Tuesday at Royal Ascot. But knowing what she's gone through to produce those performances, people would appreciate how great she is. Some people far removed would not realise the adversity she's gone through to do that. To me, she's an out and out freak to carry the issues she has through her career and be undefeated. Horses are not machines, but every time I asked her to, she went out and got the job done.

The last time I had her completely right going to the races was when she had her second start. After that there were always issues. Never a bowed tendon or a big hole in a suspensory ligament or massive lameness that would've ended it all. But muscle tears and ligament damage and sore feet that required constant treatment. I haven't driven the owners mad with it. I speak to them when I've got a bigger issue, but the day-to-day general maintenance, I'd have had them totally sleepless if I'd told them the issues she's gone through.

I've got a great theory: happy horses run well. Horses aren't happy when they're sore. But then you run into horses that have a great pain threshold and they'll go through it. She's one of those. She obviously has an unbelievable pain threshold and was able to carry a lot of things other horses wouldn't, like a champion footballer or cricketer. They carry themselves through where a lesser player will lay down and have three weeks' rest. The champion will strap himself up and go out and get the job done. I had to judge whether to give her the chance to achieve, and she always carried me, proving what a magnificent equine athlete she is.

She's got so much ability she's been able to overcome my mistakes. Self-praise is worth nothing, but a lot of people have commended me on the patience I've shown with her. They suggest that other people wouldn't have been as patient, they would've raced her more here and there, and we wouldn't still have her. I puff my chest out over that a bit.

It's hard not to be sentimental about her. From a training perspective I was probably lucky I've had a gradual climb to her. I had Typhoon Tracy, who was a great mare, a multiple Group 1 winner, a Horse of the Year. I've been climbing the ladder. She didn't just drop into my lap as a Johnny-come-lately, which would have been a hell of a scary experience. But I'd gradually learnt how to handle people, how to handle the press and how to handle the pressures of preparing a horse like her. And the fact that her build-up has been gradual too. It didn't all happen in one season with her.

If there was a disappointment for me it was that the people at Ascot didn't get to appreciate her greatness. But I think those who genuinely appreciate fine horses would realise what a mammoth program she'd had. They'd appreciate that she was out on her feet. They'd appreciate what a herculean effort it was to be there and win.

The racing over there gets very little coverage. But here's this horse from the other side of the world, the British horseracing public were so appreciative that we took her there because they'd never had so much publicity ever. Frankel, the best horse in the world – you ask the average person in London who Frankel was and they wouldn't know. But ask them who Black Caviar was and they'd say that's the mare that wears the colours that taxi went past was painted in. They'd know.

That's what has been amazing. Not just non-racing people, but non-sports people love her. I've done interviews with women's magazines and with the *Financial Review,* which doesn't have a sport section. I met folk from the length and breadth of Australia. I signed racebooks, photographs, flags and cigarette papers.

The purest sight of all, though, was to see her gallop. You've never seen a horse going so fast, and then she'll drop six inches closer to the ground, lengthen her stride and go faster again. People tell me it raises their spirits to see this mare race, to see her win. That's how incredible she is for our sport.

This much I know. I won't live to see another horse like Black Caviar.

Peter Moody

Bronwen Healy Photography

The flying Black Caviar in full stride.

Prelude

There is a stillness to racing's crowded hour. A quiet calm amplified by the darkness. For its participants, dragged from bed to the track by a tradition of ungodly starts, it is too early for conversation. It keeps things simple, as the only words spoken are instructions. In the ritual of trackwork the imperative is to watch and learn.

Before dawn, a horse will be heard before it is seen. The sharp snort of air expelled from the nostrils. The touch of hooves on the sandy track. Each to their own rhythm. The thud of a heavy gallop. The clip of a light canter.

Here you have to know what you are looking for. The shadows of those sent forth from the surrounding gated communities are indistinguishable. Not even the names spoken match those in any form guide.

But all are not equal in the equine population. One among them had become Australia's greatest racehorse.

She was powerful rather than beautiful. An athlete, not a model. She had started out highly strung and over-eager, her hulking frame working against her developing muscles. Under a masterful and patient touch, she had learnt to harness her energy and unleash the full extent of her ability.

Her presence in a race encapsulated the purpose of competition, for she proved herself the fastest of them all. But her record grew to defy the very nature of sport, for invincibility was long thought to be fleeting, perfection unattainable.

Her gift was to make victory appear certain, uncomplicated, assured. Her spell was to convert audiences from hard-bitten punters to racing agnostics, giving all an emotional stake whenever she ran.

Her legacy was to return a faded caper to its glory days more than half a century past. She drew crowds to racetracks in such numbers that officials dusted off the house-full sign, or even threw the gates open for fear of a stampede.

The major football code of the day made way for her. And her name became the most recognised sporting moniker in a nation obsessed by such matters.

What began as a racing story came to transcend sport. By the time Black Caviar departed our shores to take on the world, she was a national icon.

But for all that had been shared, the secret of Black Caviar lay in that hour before dawn. Those who lived the story knew the best gallops of her career were not attained in the unprecedented run of crushing victories before the adoring crowds. They were, instead, made in the dark at Caulfield Racecourse.

Peter Moody had worked with horses for longer than he could remember. He learnt the ways of racing in outback Queensland, where the quality of the stock might have differed from the urban big-time, but the rhythms and routines were as recognisable as in any metropolitan centre.

He was a self-made man in a world where empires are inherited. When the horse of a lifetime came along, he had the insight to recognise her, the skills to mould her and the ambition to create a legend.

Moody had deciphered early on that to have his mare in peak

condition on a Saturday, he needed to gallop her at full speed on the preceding Tuesday. For this task, race jockey Luke Nolen was summoned. At those times, the full extent of her powers was displayed. And her annihilating stride would flow unrestrained.

While a typical thoroughbred will quicken its stride to reach maximum velocity, Black Caviar lengthened hers. It was the physical anomaly that gave rise to her freakish capability. She would expend less energy, covering more ground. In a race it would allow her to ever so gracefully ease away from her frantically chasing rivals. She would cruelly break them with barely a hint of exertion.

Alone on the training track, the beauty of her motion moved even the most unsentimental observer. For a heavy mare, Black Caviar was light on her feet. Her power came from her large hindquarters that would plant, coil and propel her forward with frightening force. By comparison, her front legs would brush the ground, blithely touching for balance as she lifted into the air.

Jeff O'Connor, Moody's racing manager, had witnessed first hand all of Black Caviar's racetrack triumphs. For him, that catalogue of illustrious victories did not compare with what took place at Caulfield before dawn.

'You see a horse galloping in one pure motion and you know this is better than a race performance. Luke hardly moves and the horse is just poetry. It is unbelievable.'

Rival trainers in the observation tower at Caulfield cottoned on quickly. They would abandon their own endeavours to click their stopwatches in unison with Moody to quantify for themselves the wonder before them. To a man, they knew they would never see another horse move like this. Yet they rarely felt the need to speak of it, for this was a private indulgence.

Black Caviar ran time in private and won races in public. She reminded the current generation of the stirring pride their grandparents would have felt in the days of Phar Lap. In a sport common to every civilised society, she redefined the notion of perfection.

She was the dream of every breeder who studied the pedigrees, mixed the bloodlines and attended the birth of a foal. She was the wish of every owner who ever raised a hand at a yearling sale. She was the promise for every trainer who let a thoroughbred tear through the wind at full gallop. She was the lure of every jockey searching for the horse to carry their name into the record books.

It is what fuels an industry to ignite before dawn in a silence that can only exist before the rest of the world wakes up. The horse that could not be beaten. The quest for Black Caviar.

Newspix / Colleen Petch

First out of the Moody Stables before dawn, Luke Nolen was summoned when Black Caviar would gallop at full power.

Courtesy Peter Moody

15-year-old Peter Moody with trainer Frank Cavanough, jockey Tom Johnstone and Coming Country at Roma in 1984.

1

The Back of Bourke

Our best stories, our foundation stories, both fantastic and far-fetched, have their origins out the back of Bourke. In the case of Peter Gordon Moody's story, this is not so much figuratively as literally true.

Wyandra is the desolate, dusty outback of Queensland, 840 kilometres west of Brisbane on the Matilda Highway. Halfway between the larger centres of Charleville and Cunnamulla, its existence is owed to the doomed explorer Edmund Kennedy, a Guernsey-born surveyor, who in 1847 set his expedition's camp near the banks of the Warrego River. That imprint became a fixture on the great inland railway link by the booming 1890s, the settlement became vital to the movement of passengers, freight and mail to local properties.

John and Charlotte Moody had been among the pioneers of the Wyandra district before the turn of the twentieth century. John was a grazier who bought large parcels of property and wielded significant influence as one of the founders of Queensland Primary Producers' Ltd. John and Charlotte had twelve children, all of whom settled in the surrounding Paroo Shire. The family property was Alpha, a 40,000-hectare sheep and cattle station. Two generations on, it was the home of Garth and Jan Moody. Their son Peter was born on 31 July 1969 and took his place at Alpha with his three older sisters.

Wyandra was remote and its people were resourceful. The shearing shed was on the main street and the General Store doubled as the Post Office. The lone pub was the faded weatherboard Gladstone Hotel. On the dusty tracks that deputised as roads, if you did not ride, you had to walk. In 1969 the town itself was still not connected to the state electricity grid, relying instead on the Power House. It was isolated and rough. You might have said this outpost was the land that time forgot, if you could be certain time had ever known the place existed at all.

The district was rich horse country. Horses were the pulse of the place, by necessity as well as for fun. Children learned to ride as they were learning to walk. Be they rodeo riders, boundary riders, jackaroos or sheepherders, they were taught from the start that whatever they did with their horse, from breaking them in to shoeing and grooming, they did it themselves.

Wyandra staged gymkhanas and polocrosse competitions, and the Moodys raced thoroughbreds on the local amateur circuit. It connected them to the wider racing world at a time when folk, regardless of locale, marvelled at the deeds of Rain Lover lumping the top weight to complete his quest of back-to-back Melbourne Cups, a tale soured by the cruelty of the brazen nobbling of Cup favourite Big Philou in the lead-up to the race. The horse lovers of western Queensland did not have to look south much longer for inspiration and gratification. Out of the border town of Goondiwindi emerged Gunsynd to rule the turf in the years that a young lad was taking his inaugural strides in a formative passion.

Peter's first steed was an old stock horse named Doubtful. Then, at the age of three he was given his own pony. He showed such a natural aptitude at the Neimenmulla Pony Club, held at nearby Rosevale Station, that they nicknamed him George

Moore. It was the grandest accolade as Moore was the much-loved prodigy of Mackay, on Queensland's north coast, who dominated the riding ranks in Australia like no other in a history-making partnership with trainer T.J. Smith. His record of 119 Group 1 winners remained out of reach more than forty years after his retirement. Smith had christened Moore 'Cotton Fingers' for his gossamer touch on the back of such powerful beasts.

Moody was six years the junior of his youngest sister so he learnt early to fend for himself. His toys were a .303 shotgun with the bolt removed and a blue heeler-dingo cross. 'You got kicked out of the house in the morning and you wouldn't be expected back until you heard the dinner bell of a night. Inevitably you'd end up down in the cattle yards or the horse yards doing something you shouldn't have been.' As a child he was pulled from the bottom of a dam at the climax of such a misadventure, his life saved by a local ringer.

There was no pretence of privacy in Wyandra. The telephone resembled a party line with half a dozen properties sharing the same number. Distinctive ring tones identified the intended recipient but it was commonplace to have third parties eavesdropping on the conversation. The click of lifted receivers was the shameless giveaway. Everyone knew each other's business, at least in part because many of them were related. When Peter started school, the student body numbered twenty-five, mostly from outlying stations. 'Fifteen or sixteen of them would have been Moodys.' In fact the Wyandra State School was located on Moody Street.

Peter was a child of the bush. There was no advantage and little comfort to his upbringing. His father was a regular at the Gladstone where he imbibed to a fearsome extent. Given the gruelling nature of extensive farming and the secluded life on the land, few would condemn the practice or diagnose the problem. As the decades passed without variation, many a man was worn down by that life. But it did reverberate at home. When Peter was eight, his parents separated. Garth Moody drank relentlessly, smoked addictively, lived hard and was dead by the age of sixty.

'I used to cop a boot in the arse and a smack in the ear probably no more than I deserved but I still had a great upbringing. Dad used to take us to pony clubs and horse shows. I grew up with three older sisters so I was always protected from things. But you probably look back on it and if it weren't for him I wouldn't be where I am today. So you have your disappointments but you make the most of what's afforded you.'

After the split, Peter's mother Jan moved the children to Charleville, ninety-seven kilometres away. Had that not occurred, Peter expected he would never have escaped the Moody inheritance, left to chase sheep and cattle on the station forever more. Instead, he took his first step into a larger world.

The domineering quality of Charleville was resilience, for it was the proverbial land of drought or flooding rain. One often following the other with unrelenting force. It was a busy pastoral town on archetypal grazing country that retained elements of its heritage as a railway centre.

On the edge of the Charleville Showgrounds, carved out of the brigalow and the mulga, stood the racecourse. On the red dirt track, which puffed into clouds in the dry and spat mud in the wet, a boy would come to recognise the answers to all his future questions.

The community thrived on the half a dozen occasions each year the Central Warrego Race Club staged its meetings. Those days bound the community together. It was both a shared passion and a responsibility. The race meeting was the touchstone to raise critical funds for local projects such as its school and hospital. Socially, those days were vital to the fabric of Charleville. The harsh climate dictated that the racing season commenced in May and concluded with the annual highlight, the Charleville Cup on the first Tuesday of November.

The racing itself was unusually competitive. There was little money in western Queensland racing. The typical winner's purse stretched to only a couple of thousand dollars, barely enough to cover the cost of having a horse in work. It was, instead, a matter of pride. Trevor Miller from Cunnamulla, Kenny Waller from Roma and Charlie Prow from Blackall were the district's dominant trainers. But whether it was a hobby or a profession, many of the locals paid for the upkeep of a racing prospect. It ensured the betting ring was the hub of activity. Bookmakers were plentiful and they pitted their wits against the punters and owners. Each race operated on a charged fusion of the desire and the necessity to win.

When the Charleville card of five races was completed and accounts settled, the bookies joined the punters, and the trainers came with the jockeys to the Cattle Camp Hotel Motel. Over the years the TAB became its mecca and the late meeting from Toowoomba the focus of attention. There the racing folk would remain late into the night swapping tales of fortune and misfortune, until many retired to the motel, leaving the return journey for the following day.

Moody was instantly drawn into the heart of the local racing culture. He found the outlet he had sought beyond pony clubs and exhibitions. He was exhilarated by the Saturday races and intrigued by the preparatory work between meetings. By the time Gurners Lane ran down the mighty Kingston Town to win the 1982 Melbourne Cup, Moody dreamt of Flemington via the circuitous route of Charleville.

Peter took up with a couple of local trainers, mucking out stables and marking out his destiny. 'Some people love dogs, some people love cats, some people love horses. For me they've always been a great mate.'

Tony Facey was one trainer happy to have a kid of such dedication around. Facey had forsaken a well-educated and close-knit family in Victoria, lured by the wide-open spaces of outback Queensland. As a teenager he had taken a job at Wyandra's

Glaverton Station and went on to work contract mustering and horse dealing in the surrounding area. He found notoriety through his passion for rodeo riding and aged twenty-four was crowned Australian Champion Bulldogger. As time passed, Facey drifted to Charleville running wild brumbies or putting together a mob of goats. In his forties he discovered a knack for training racehorses. Moody watched Facey rise to the rank of the Shire's leading trainer in 1983 with such victories as the Charleville Newmarket Cup before his premature death three years later aged fifty-one. His mark is still measured with the annual running of the Tony Facey Memorial Plate at Charleville's October meeting.

Facey had fatefully introduced Peter to another local trainer. Frank Cavanough was an old horseman who had survived for years on rat cunning and know-how. In him, Moody found a kindred spirit. And Frank taught him everything he knew from a lifetime in racing.

Cavanough trained exclusively for and on the private property of local bookmaker David Power. The owner regarded his trainer as 'a big, rough old bastard. Very tough, hard man. But he was a good horseman'. While that was true enough, Cavanough proved a generous soul who took the time to educate young guys about horses and about life. What they learnt quickly was that he ruled with an iron fist. The first time he told them to do something, they got told. The second time they would get a backhander. There was no mucking about with Cavanough.

Peter began arriving at the stables before first light with an exercise book under his arm. Cavanough inquired what he thought he was doing with it. 'I'm going to write down everything you do.' Rather than doing the expected school homework, Peter would sit at the kitchen table each night, transcribing notes about every horse he had observed in the stable.

Such habits serve him well to this day. 'I don't have a great concentration span. When I'm relating to my horses and recording all of my information, I like to hand write it because I find that I then reflect on what's happened. Quite often I might take something away from it that I mightn't have remembered. It probably adds an hour to my workload each day but I find it very important that I reflect on the day's events to plan for the future with the horses.'

A huge lump of a lad as a teenager, Moody was driving the race-day float, with Cavanough sleeping by his side, to every far-flung dirt and dust track in western Queensland in pursuit of winners. The white-haired trainer and his eager apprentice two generations his junior, were regarded with affection and curiosity throughout the district. Power recalled years later: 'The way Pete has gone through the racing industry comes from his days in Charleville. Frank was an ex-pug and he'd also been a foreman on a road gang, and they clicked.'

The association with Cavanough is captured in a photograph from Roma Racecourse in 1984: the fifteen-year-old strapper planted commandingly alongside Coming Country after victory in the Purse Handicap. As if to show all the elements were already assembled, there stands Peter Moody under the classic bush Akubra.

With not only a view of, but also a place in the adult world, Moody was impatient to see more. The independence he had fashioned brought with it maturity. He mixed naturally with veterans and comfortably instructed those who, by age alone, were his seniors. He had a reputation as a big, tough bugger who would get stuck into other strappers and make sure they were doing their job.

Moody had a voracious appetite to learn but no tolerance for academia. Having completed Year 10, he surprised no one by formalising the view school was no longer for him. 'I wasn't a bad scholar. I wasn't the worst. On the days that I went.'

Soon after, his horizons broadened. Frank's grandson Brett Cavanough had also left school as a fifteen-year-old to begin the family induction. He had worked in a couple of Queensland stables while learning the delicate craft of horse breaking. Brett had an association with the country's leading stable, Tulloch Lodge in Sydney, the kingdom of trainer Tommy Smith. His brother and right-hand man, Ernie Smith, had the job of replenishing the staff of an expansive operation. Admiring the stock Brett was from, Ernie asked: 'Can you get me some of those real good country boys to come down here and work?' Brett immediately thought of Peter and his cousin Alf. 'There's a couple of them here working in the shearing sheds.'

That recommendation was all it took. Peter rolled up his swag, jumped on a bus and set off. Beyond leaving his mother, he never hesitated, comprehending the opportunity he had been given. 'You can learn a lot if you kept your mouth shut and your eyes open.'

With his eyes wide open, he saw for the first time a grass racetrack. The splendour of Randwick.

T.J. Smith was the greatest trainer the country had known. He rose from obscure battler, armed only with a brumby and the winnings from a two-up game, to become the world's best in his craft. The magnitude of his rule is illustrated by the thirty-three consecutive training premierships in Sydney and the 279 Group 1 wins he amassed. His stable was a champion's production line from Tulloch to Gunsynd to Kingston Town.

His story entranced Peter Moody. Tommy was the product of the small town of Goolgowi in the Riverina district of New South Wales. He had learnt the ways of horses from his father as they drove bullock teams and ran a breaking-in business together. He started with little more than his wits and the rogue galloper Bragger. But he took on and conquered the most competitive of racing havens. Peter had known the story better than any childhood fairy tale and cherished the fable contained within. He was a disciple long before he met the man.

That was in 1984. The Tulloch Lodge star of the day was the three-year-old Red Anchor, the chestnut who bounded away with that year's Cox Plate and a week later claimed the Victoria Derby. It was a most instructive time not only for the equine endeavours. Tommy Smith had his legacy project well in tow. He was preparing his daughter, Gai, entrusting her with the tools and secrets to ensure she would succeed him in the years ahead and boldly expand an already rich inheritance.

Smith's moniker of the Little General was well earned. As legendary as he was for his success, he was famously hard on his staff. Smith had retained the tough edge of his upbringing. He was demanding and a stickler for detail. He had an uncanny ability to identify the quality of a horse before his rivals did. The rest was built on a strong work ethic. Just like his people, he worked his horses fearsomely. The trademark look of the T.J. Smith galloper was bone and muscle.

The environment suited Moody perfectly. His dedication saw him rise to a level of responsibility. From strapping one horse, he took over the supervision of many. Soon he was orchestrating the work for a team of horses numbering more than a hundred.

In his three years with the stable, he soaked up the wealth of experience and knowledge possessed by veteran horsemen connected with Smith. Tom Barker served at Tulloch Lodge for forty years. He had a way with horses demonstrated by his time as the strapper of Kingston Town, the grand black galloper etched in folklore as the only winner of the Cox Plate, Australia's championship race, on three successive occasions. Barker's worth, though, seemed even greater with people. The man, nicknamed 'Spider', took new arrivals under his wing. Decades later, those who worked under him fondly remembered the profound influence he had on budding careers.

Stable foreman Terry Catip gave Moody a connection to Queensland. Hailing from Warwick, 130 kilometres south-west of Brisbane, he was responsible for enacting Smith's instructions. Catip would later take the skills he mastered at Tulloch Lodge back to Warwick to train for decades in his own right.

Moody's experience proved formative for both method and understanding and also shaped his competitive instincts. 'I felt such fierce loyalty to T.J. Smith that I'd fight over it. I'd have a blue with someone at the pub if they said a bad word against him. People aligned with other trainers were the opposition and you treated them as such. You'd walk past someone who strapped a horse for Brian Mayfield-Smith, who in that year had just beaten T.J. for the premiership, and you'd nearly spit at them.'

Brett Cavanough took a sabbatical from horse racing to become a champion shearer but when he found his way back, he graduated to the title of leading country trainer in New South Wales. To this day he breaks in nearly every horse that passes through the gates of Moody Racing and credits both his and Moody's success to the learnings of Tulloch Lodge. 'We're all educated in the mould of T.J. The systems Pete and I use when we're breaking in and training, it all stems from there.'

To expand his education, Moody enlisted for a stint at Lindsay Park, the centrepiece of Colin Hayes' empire. He was another who had risen from nothing. His story began with a steeplechaser named Surefoot. Hayes purchased the nag for £9 and rode him in Oakbank's famed Great Eastern Steeplechase. He bet his honeymoon money each way at odds of 60/1 and when Surefoot ran third, used the profits to stake his training career.

The gentleman South Australian revolutionised training in Australia when he abandoned the bustle of a metropolitan stable to establish a private complex in the Barossa Valley. Sceptics regarded such a move with suspicion. Believing it to be folly, prominent clients removed talented horses from Hayes upon commencement in 1970. From that 800-hectare property C.S. Hayes forged his Hall of Fame career that stretched to 5333 winners.

Against the tranquil surrounds of Lindsay Park, Moody saw that Hayes ran a military-style operation without the need to compete for time and space with rival trainers or the restrictions imposed at training centres based at city racetracks. And like Smith had been, Hayes was also training the next generation, grooming son David to inherit the earth.

Moody rounded out his apprenticeship back at Randwick under Bart Cummings. The world had never known a better trainer of stayers. The Australian turf had a triumvirate of iconic horsemen. The canny teenager put himself as close as possible to each of them in turn. David Power could not help but admire the pluck and commitment of the stablehand he had grown to like. 'He wanted to learn. That's why he went with the best.'

Moody fell victim to his youth only once. At the age of eighteen, he decided he knew it all. He headed back to Charleville intent on training from home. He divided his attention between playing front row for the rugby league team, chasing girls and preparing horses. 'I thought I was a genius. But soon I was eating paint off the walls. I realised I couldn't make a living in the bush and if I wanted to be a horse trainer I had to go back to the seaboard.'

Randwick had a hold on him. On the first day of December 1988, Moody returned to begin a decade-long partnership with trainer Bill Mitchell, first as foreman in Sydney, then as assistant trainer in Brisbane.

Mitchell was a child of the racing fraternity, the third son of Major James Mitchell. The patriarch had purchased Yarraman Park Stud from former jockey George Moore in the late '60s when the legendary figure set off to train in France, a venture that later came to full fruition with a decade of dominance in Hong Kong. From that property in the Hunter Valley of New South Wales, Major Mitchell ran horses and raised his family in the ways of racing. When he emerged in the late '80s as a fresh, young face on the landscape, Bill Mitchell assembled an army and immediately became a major player, producing top-level performers that ranged from the warhorse Stylish Century to the abundantly gifted Dignity Dancer.

Moody's timing was immaculate and his influence tangible. Mitchell recognised from the outset a young man with a firm grasp of training. The rough edges just needed to be smoothed. The relationship between trainer and foreman is one of implicit trust and understanding. For Moody it was not so much learning what to do but what not to do with horses and clients alike. Mitchell nurtured the raw materials and the result was a most rewarding relationship. 'He hasn't changed much really, and I think that people appreciate that he calls a spade a shovel.'

Moody craved a return to his home state but was not quite ready to branch out alone. Mitchell identified the opportunity to assist him and strengthen his operation in the process. A Brisbane stable was established under Moody's command. There he glimpsed and guided greatness for the first time. By pure chance.

Breeder Rod Ashdown went to see a trainer about a chestnut colt by Nediym. It had already been a litany of woe. Emanating from his Glengarry Stud, the yearling was a commodity of much promise. He was sent to Queensland's premier yearling sale, the 1996 Magic Millions, with a hefty reserve price attached. But his prospects were sabotaged when the horse became cast in his box and took an ugly chunk out of his leg. Ashdown pragmatically removed the reserve and watched under a pall of disappointment as the colt was knocked down in the auction ring for a measly $20,000. The new owner ordered a further vet check in the immediate aftermath and, unsatisfied with the findings, returned the colt to its breeder.

Ashdown had little alternative but to race the horse himself. He was left to door-knock for a trainer. His intended inquiry went unanswered. On the return trip, he drove past Bill Mitchell's place and spied Moody mowing the lawns in forty-degree heat. He stopped and the pair chatted. At the end of the conversation, General Nediym was part of Moody's life.

It proved to be his break-out assignment. Dating back to his first job with Frank Cavanough, Moody was obliged to follow the instructions of established trainers. While he formed his own opinions and expressed them without reserve, he was bound by his employers to operate within someone else's system. In Mitchell's Brisbane stable, Moody was autonomous. Day to day, his task was to shape General Nediym. Both their reputations would be moulded by the outcome.

In sixteen starts, the General posted twelve wins. His domination of the Magic Millions Classic, one of the most prestigious two-year-old races on the calendar, remains the most scintillating win in that Gold Coast event. General Nediym was blessed with frightening speed confirmed when, as a three-year-old, he defeated the older horses down the Flemington straight course to claim both the Lightning Stakes and Newmarket Handicap, the mark of sprinting grandeur. Equal in importance to the results, was the kudos they gave Moody. It put him in the right circles with breeders and influential owners. These were the relationships he needed to help underpin his desire to do all this in his own right.

Moody was learning the ways of training. He blended what was innate with what he had observed and put it into service. Like all the great trainers, he focused on deciphering the ways of the horse. 'Probably the art of being a good racehorse trainer is trying to read their minds. You hear this adage "horse whisperer" and it's probably not that far from the truth. You've got to read the individual and try to get some sort of feel for what they're telling you. Knowing where you can take them, how far you can push them, then trying to work within those boundaries and exploiting their good points. The similarities between people and horses, I find, are great. They're not a dumb animal, they're a smart animal and they create and develop a lot of similar habits to humans.'

Ten years to the day after he set up with Mitchell, having drawn all he could from racing's pool of wisdom and experience, P.G. Moody steeled himself and struck out alone.

Newspix / Nicole Garmston

Peter Moody and Luke Nolen found each other by accident. Sharing a relaxed rural Queensland disposition, they proved the perfect combination for temperament and complementary talents.

2

Moody Racing

The great trainers come to be defined by their champions. The horses every trainer is searching for. The names that resonate beyond premierships and statistics. The banner act to advertise the business and the stable. A champion tests a trainer's acumen and verifies whether they can handle the pressure at the highest level of racing. While waiting for such an opportunity to present itself, a trainer first has to cajole the modest and the sluggish to achieve beyond their station.

Peter Moody began the quest in the last month of 1998. It was a move both natural and bold. Those who had grown to know him guessed he would succeed. The man himself did not lack for confidence but, as with any start-up venture, he did lack for stock. Reassurance came early, in the form of Ebony Way.

The two-year-old son of American sire River of Life was given a tune-up trial in the outer Brisbane suburb of Deagon six days ahead of his racetrack debut. In the first race on the 28 December Eagle Farm program, Ebony Way met with some late specking in the betting ring but remained an $11 outsider in the field of seven. Under accomplished jockey Jimmy Byrne, the gelding was immediately prominent in the run. By the 400-metre mark,

Ebony Way had taken the lead and was travelling strongly. He was unchallenged in the run to the post, commandingly protecting a two-length margin. Moody Racing had its first winner.

So impressed was Moody that he took Ebony Way to the Gold Coast for the Magic Millions Classic on the second Saturday of January. Three years after claiming the spoils in the million-dollar race with General Nediym for Bill Mitchell, Moody was back for himself. Ebony Way was far from disgraced, finishing midfield behind future star Testa Rossa. The gelding won once more at Eagle Farm as a two-year-old before his career was curtailed by injury after just five starts. It might have been a brief run for Ebony Way but it was significant for Moody in the surge to get things moving from scratch, and he had shown he would never shy from putting his horses in the best company.

While it was his name in the race book, his operation was a partnership from the outset. Moody's wife, Sarah, shared the same rural and equine sensibility as her husband, having grown up in country New Zealand with a mother devoted to horses. Sarah had dabbled in various aspects of racing. She had been a jumps jockey and as a teenager represented New Zealand in a world series. She had broken in ponies in France and England for tycoon Kerry Packer. Her husband knew from the start she was a keeper. 'She's a bloody good horsewoman. Better than I could ever be.'

He had met Sarah Belcham at Randwick and brought her back to Brisbane, where they married in 1994 in the mounting enclosure of Eagle Farm Racecourse. In the formative years of Moody Racing, Sarah rode trackwork and Peter backed her judgment. Punting on the right stable horses helped the couple to purchase their first house. 'Best track rider I ever had. Then I got her pregnant.'

Cara was the first born, followed soon after by twins Breann and Celine. Moody was now a young father as well as an aspiring horse trainer. The family relied on his capacity to turn fifty horses of varying levels of ability into a flourishing, financially secure stable. He called in his mum to help. Having run the Commonwealth Employment Service office in Charleville, Jan stepped in to handle the business while Sarah raised the girls and Peter trained the horses. 'Those early days were the days that really told. You'd come home and you weren't sure which cheques you could sign or what bills you could pay. I certainly couldn't have got there on my own. But good luck is made by hard work. We were fortunate enough to find some of the right clients and the right horses.'

Within two years, Moody had the Brisbane arm of the operation balanced and it was an ambitious eye towards Melbourne that set his endeavour soaring. At thirty-two, Moody had access to eight boxes in a corner across the road and down an alleyway from Caulfield Racecourse. He knew first impressions in racing's most competitive hub would be long-lasting, so he handpicked the horses he brought south and studied carefully the assignments he prescribed them. Within seven months he had trained more than a dozen winners from that satellite stable.

Among them was a colt by first-season sire Carnegie, a modest $130,000 purchase from the Karaka sale in New Zealand. Wealthy businessman Ron Wanless sent most of his high-price purchases to Gerald Ryan, Brisbane's premier trainer. The crumbs, as it were, ended up with blokes like Moody. They were speculative bets by Wanless to test horses and humans alike.

At Karaka, Moody had been the under bidder to Wanless on a Straight Strike filly that raced as More Diamonds. 'I had never met Ron and I asked him if I could train her. At the end of the sales he gave me that filly to train and he also gave me his other purchase.' More Diamonds could do little better than a Maiden win at Ipswich. The Carnegie colt revealed himself as a speck of gold the first time he trialled at Eagle Farm. Against the expectations of his breeding, the colt won over a half mile. Cheekily his trainer rang the owner and declared: 'We'll win a Derby with this horse.'

Amalfi was a handsome enough brown colt, but in April 2001 he drew little attention as a 20/1 shot on debut over 1200 metres at Eagle Farm. In what was to become a signature of the Moody method, he won straight off. The plan was set for an assault on the oldest classic on the racing calendar: the Victoria Derby.

Predating the Melbourne Cup, the Derby had a lineage that told the story of Australian racing. Phar Lap was adjudged the greatest winner of the race on an honour roll shared by Poseidon, Comic Court, Tulloch, Tobin Bronze, Red Anchor and Dulcify. In the accumulation of a staggering thirty-five Derbies nationwide, T.J. Smith had won the Victoria Derby five times. His daughter, Gai Waterhouse, had announced her arrival as a succeeding force when Nothin' Leica Dane, part owned by Tommy, emerged victorious in 1995. The enduring image of that day hangs in the Flemington Press Room: Gai and T.J. beaming and embraced, three years before his death.

To win the Derby was the fast-track to prominence. That was as true for a trainer as it was for a horse. Amalfi came to Melbourne boosted by a subsequent win at Doomben in August. He placed in a pair of quality races over unsuitably shorter distances at Moonee Valley, before he was catapulted into calculations with a resounding victory in the traditional lead-up race, the Norman Robinson Stakes, on Caulfield Cup Day. It was a win of such authority that it promoted Amalfi to near favouritism for the Derby and vaulted Moody onto the radar for racing's biggest week.

The Melbourne Cup Carnival thrived on the story of the little guy as much as the iconic names of the turf. That was the egalitarian nature of Australian racing. Moody's story had that sprinkling of fairy dust. The trainer from the middle of Woop Woop trying to upstage the establishment. If this were to be Peter Moody's entrée to racing's big show, it would be some entrance.

Amalfi was pitted against the nobly bred Ustinov, son of the 1991 Melbourne Cup-winning mare Let's Elope. Just as his dam had been, Ustinov was trained by Bart Cummings. Moody knew first hand what a combination this was. Then there was the aristocratic Sydneysider Viscount, owned by the billionaire Ingham brothers and prepared by their trainer John Hawkes. Viscount had beaten Amalfi previously at Moonee Valley. Then, as a three-year-old in the championship weight-for-age race the Cox Plate, Viscount had been sandwiched between star gallopers Northerly and Sunline in a tight and controversial finish that had plenty wondering if Viscount would have caused a staggering upset if not for the severe interference he suffered.

On the first day of the Cup carnival, the 2001 Victoria Derby was a race laced with intriguing storylines. Over the searching test of 2500 metres for the first time, Amalfi settled with only two runners behind him in the twelve-horse field. Moody's anxiety eased as Amalfi steadily picked up ground under jockey Damien Oliver. He surged from the 400-metre mark, wrested the lead and at the moment of decision, Amalfi was striving to hold off the finishing surge of rank outsider Zarek. The margin diminished with every stride. Ustinov was too far astern and Viscount had not figured. It was a race in two. As Amalfi and Zarek went to the line, the call rang out: 'Photo. Maybe Amalfi in a desperately tight go.' So it was.

Moody had captured the mainstream. 'I won the Derby as a nobody. I remember I caught the train three days later on Cup Day to Flemington where I had one runner and about 300 people came up and shook my hand. It made me feel about ten-foot tall and bulletproof. I decided I would grab this opportunity with both hands and run off the back of it.'

Amalfi's Derby was no one-off Cinderella story. Moody took up occupation of the fabled stables of the late Hall of Fame trainer Angus Armanasco. For half a century, Armanasco had been one of racing's most fondly regarded figures. From that Caulfield headquarters he had guided the careers of numerous brilliant gallopers who had gone on to become industry-shaping sires, the quality of Star Kingdom, Biscay, Bletchingly and Zeditave. Moody could breathe in the history and hear the ghosts of past success.

Melbourne Cup week was repeatedly bountiful for him. The profile that came with such Group 1 wins reinforced Moody's status as an emerging talent in the training ranks. He prepared Ancient Song to win the Salinger Stakes in 2003. Twelve months after, Sky Cuddle poked through the middle of a muddle to snare the Emirates Stakes. Only a heavy track and race day scratchings had granted the mare a place in the field, promoted from first emergency. Plans were hastily altered. Young jockey Jason Benbow began his Saturday duties at the Victorian provincial meeting in Geelong before being summoned by Moody to headquarters where he pinched the main event aboard Sky Cuddle. Punters did not welcome the striking chestnut, as a 60/1 chance edging out the favourite Lad of the Manor in a crowded photo finish. But Moody treasured it as reward for his circle of loyalty. Stuart and Trish Ramsey from Turangga Farm in New South Wales owned the mare. They had been among his clients from the outset.

Critically, those Group 1 victories were complemented by a mass of winners in every corner of Victoria. Moody would saddle up anywhere and everywhere. He believed there was a race for every horse and it was his personal crusade to seek it out. His propensity to travel made him both a novelty and a revolutionary. For the man himself it was just a way of life. 'I used to have to travel 300 kilometres for a feed of Kentucky Fried Chicken when I lived in outback Queensland, so a trip to a Victorian country track was never going to be a problem.'

He rapidly became the state's leading provincial trainer; 111 winners nationwide became 121 the next season and then 169. In his second full season in Victoria he was runner-up to Lee Freedman in the trainers' premiership. His lethal strike rate became his calling card.

It was at a nondescript midweek Caulfield meeting in May 2004 that a pressman prone to bold statements declared Moody 'the best trainer in Australia'.

'How do you judge that?' was the quick rebuke of a colleague.

'Ah dunno. Just reckon he is. Plenty of winners lately.'

This exchange was documented in the *Herald Sun*. It was ahead of its time but spoke of the reputation being forged.

It was said Moody horses were rarely pretty, just lean, and as fit and keen as outback cattle dogs. They invariably raced forward, just as Tommy Smith had reckoned. The philosophy mandated that if a horse was positioned in the first four, the variables were reduced and the role of luck nullified. Under such a formula, the winners came rolling in.

As momentum built, Batman found his Robin. Quite by accident.

Moody booked a jockey named Nolen for two rides at Sale on 3 May 2003. Shaun Nolen had been an apprentice jockey at the Toowoomba stable of Mick Nolan, who Moody had used on occasion in Queensland. He assumed he was renewing an old acquaintance. What Moody did not know was that Shaun had an older brother, Luke. 'I didn't even realise there were two of them.'

Luke and Shaun Nolen had spent a good chunk of their adolescence in country Queensland. They were forever around horses long before the chance to make a profession out of them presented itself. Luke saw a gift in his younger brother. 'He could ride anything. He could get bad horses going. Shaun was touted as the jockey when we were younger. Everyone told me he was more natural on a horse.'

Undeterred, Luke pioneered the path. He took to it so well he claimed the title of champion apprentice jockey in Melbourne and was dux of his year at riding school. However, as graduation into the senior riding ranks loomed, his motivation waned. Waterskiing, snowboarding and speedboating held greater appeal than the discipline of chasing mounts. He planned his riding commitments around his social calendar and gave up all the advantages gained through a stellar initiation.

Nolen had reached a crossroads. Serendipitously, Moody was the welcome stranger. The three-year-old Umagold won the fillies' maiden race at Sale under L. Nolen for P.G. Moody and it was written in the stars.

Where it had given others pause, Moody was drawn to Nolen's disposition. 'He was this laid-back, laconic, bush sort of bloke. He suited me down to a tee. It's his attitude and mannerism – I wouldn't say work ethic, you've got to give him a kick to get him moving – but we clicked from day one.'

Moody wanted a stable jockey at a time when every hoop sought the liberation of freelancing. He was hardly offering the plum job of the industry. His team of horses rarely topped twenty and by the necessity of possessing only limited ability, they were racing at Bairnsdale, Donald and Echuca. Previously, when Moody brought a horse to the city, he had success with leading jockeys Damien Oliver and Kerrin McEvoy. What he needed, though, was continuity.

'We had bad horses but we had great clients. Because we were able to win races with those moderate horses we taught them to be six-foot tall and bulletproof. They came to town and won races they shouldn't have. Luke was able to go to those places with me and then come to town and do the job with me. Rather than replace him like I used to do, I saw this bloke had the ability to be getting the job done. As much as a lot of clients in the early days didn't want to know Luke Nolen, I stuck solid because he was solid with me.'

Together the partnership and the operation thrived. But fortune takes as well as gives. As the winners mounted, Group 1 success cruelly eluded them as a pairing. Nolen could not make the weight on Sky Cuddle. The jockey had finished second nine times at the elite level, mostly for Moody, before registering his breakthrough win in the big time aboard Wonderful World for Bart Cummings in the 2006 Caulfield Guineas. A year later he ran down that very horse, when riding El Segundo to victory in the Cox Plate.

As Moody and Nolen were finally poised at Brisbane's winter carnival in 2008, luck delivered a wretched blow. Nolen was dislodged from the Cummings galloper Antidotes as they sought to take a winning split in a feature Doomben sprint. The jockey was propelled over the horse's shoulder. He looked set to escape injury but was churned under Antidotes' hind legs. It left him with bruising to the brain and seven fractures in the face requiring a series of metal plates. A week later, Riva San, the filly Moody had prepared for a tilt at the Queensland Oaks, duly claimed the Group 1 prize. Nolen was forced to watch from his hospital bed. His recovery was slow and frustrating.

It wasn't until the Blue Diamond Stakes in February 2009, almost six years after they came together, that the Moody/Nolen partnership was fully consummated. Reward for Effort blitzed the Group 1 field of two-year-olds and the horse's name seemed particularly apt to both jockey and trainer.

In the autumn of 2011, when Master Harry broke clear in a Listed sprint at Flemington, the pairing reached the milestone of 500 winners together, prompting comparisons to other historic combinations of the turf: Bart Cummings and Roy Higgins; Jim Moloney and Pat Hyland; Colin Hayes and Jim Courtney; and the greatest of all, T.J. Smith and George Moore.

Together they rose to claim riding and training premierships, each dependent on the other's success. Moody's achievement in the season of 2009–10 was to break a thirty-three-year duopoly in Melbourne racing. Either the Freedman brothers, under the stewardship of trainer Lee, or the Hayes clan, variously directed by father Colin, sons David and Peter or trusted lieutenant

Tony McEvoy, had won every training title since 1976. Moody had conquered what he had studied. His tally that season reached eighty-three metropolitan winners. Five at Group 1 level. Add a further ninety-nine provincial winners and it was a prize money bonanza of $8.4 million accumulated by his horses with a strike rate of one winner for every four runners.

A farm boy from a desolate outback land staged the rebellion. A man who came from nothing had risen to the top in a decade. 'I started at the bottom rung of the ladder and there's been plenty of hard work and plenty of cold shitty mornings that I wished I was home in bed and not out doing what I was doing. But at the end of the day it's the only thing I know how to do.'

The racing community felt no jealousy or resentment toward him. Instead there was a note of admiration for his achievements. Caulfield Cup-winning trainer Jim Mason observed Moody at close quarters as a co-tenant in the trainers' tower. 'He's like a champion horse. Occasionally something comes along that's just better than everything else. That's Pete.' Prolific and influential owner David Moodie, added Moody to his roster of trainers, based on character as much as accomplishment. 'People like him, he's never burned anyone.'

Like everybody else, Nolen knows where he stands with Moody. 'He works me hard and expects me to do my best. He sticks. You look around the place, there is a lot of old furniture there and I am talking about employees. If it is a good fit, they seem to stay forever.'

The constants in Moody's life are family and friends; inevitably they are also part of the team. If loyalty has become a quaint notion of gentler times, here is a man who stands as the last bastion of ancient ways.

Tony Haydon is an industry lifer. He took up with Moody when he was the assistant trainer for Mitchell, first as an apprentice jockey then as his right-hand man. They share the disposition of country Queenslanders and a firm friendship, as well as a professional reliance. As the assistant trainer, Haydon lives at the stables and shares the workload of the large team. Of a morning he loads the production line, despatching the horses from the yard out to Moody on the track to administer the work. They debate the best strategies for problem solving and achieving success every day. Each challenging, and ultimately improving, the methods they apply. Outside of Sarah, Haydon is closer to his burly boss than anyone.

'He was always going to be a trainer. He's one of those people that is striding forward all the time, he's always switched on. It's like he's got ADD. He's a perfectionist. He's good with the horses and he's good with his staff as well. He's a good all-round sort of bloke. A spade's a spade, that sort of thing. He wears his heart on his sleeve. If there's a dust-up, it's all over in five minutes and we laugh about it later on over a beer.'

While Moody sought horizons beyond Charleville, the characteristics of the place reside in his soul. As soon as he was afloat in Melbourne, he bought 'thirty acres of heaven' in Belgrave South on which to live. When his business is done for the day and Moody turns the car into the driveway, he knows he is home physically as well as spiritually. Here, his wife and three daughters are a family. It is simple and uncluttered. Any drama resides beyond the front gate. As he learnt to do growing up, he butchers his own meat and does much of his own farming. It is the independence he always craved and will never give up. 'I could be back at Charleville, except the grass is greener here.'

Both he and Sarah wanted to share their experience of a rural upbringing with their children, but without the burden of isolation, being only a half-hour drive from the heart of Melbourne. They run a few head of cattle, some sheep, a couple of dogs and ride horses. For recreation there is a showjumping yard set up with knee-high fences. Dad and Mum's favourite moments are when the girls are up cantering and jumping.

Moody makes no secret of his vow to walk away from horse training once his daughters have finished their education, as his one resentment is the time the profession costs him with his girls. 'The most challenging thing for me has probably been the mental aspect. I sit back and think what I've put my family through by the career that I've chosen. There's nothing worse than the girls asking Dad, "We've got a swimming carnival on, are you going to pop out?" You just know you can't be there. It's moments like that when you walk outside and light up a cigarette and think, "Shit, is this worth it?"'

Having learnt from those with racing as their lifetime vocation, it is this dedication to family that will keep him from following down that path. His stated ambition at the time he reached the top of the profession was to one day become a relief trainer – a man stable heads could call in to hold the reins while they took the holiday long promised to their family. It is an altruistic notion to solve what he sees as the curse of the industry. When there is no need for his services, he will pursue an intense interest in Australia's war history.

Big Pete is a victim of the gaspers and afflicted with sleep apnoea that he controls by sleeping with an oxygen mask. 'Sarah quite often jokes that I'm always worried about the diet and the wellbeing of the horses and I abuse my own body through my habits of not eating as good as I should, smoking cigarettes, love a cold beer. Very, very mindful of the fact that alcoholism is close up in my family and I only allow myself to drink beer, but I do love it. I probably average five hours' sleep a night. It's a fair bit of bodily abuse there I suppose. I have this little theory in life; if I live 'til my mid fifties or sixties, I'm probably going to see more daylight hours than a normal person that's lived to eighty or ninety. Anyhow, is that some sort of a trade-off? Maybe that makes me feel better, I don't know. It is a funny one, you work hard for the health and fitness and wellbeing of your horses and abuse your own body. It doesn't make a lot of sense. But listen, I've got a couple of little bad habits, surely I'm allowed a couple.'

Moody has a work ethic unsurpassed. Every employer since his childhood had been struck by it. While he now answers to no one, that discipline remains undiminished. The alarm sounds at 3.05 every morning. 'I refuse to get up at three o'clock.'

He is a man who values actions rather than words. That said, he has an undeniable way with the language. Natural. Straightforward. Without false airs or apology. If there is an outback sensibility then Moody embodies it. He will lose his train of thought and simply end the sentence with 'shit'. 'They don't let me talk to school children because I swear too much.' He finishes the aside with a smile breaking across his face, chortling and rolling his head back on his thick neck. Among his most endearing qualities is his tendency to launch into a rant. The sort of diatribe that would prompt the listener to burst out laughing but for fear of the ramifications of doing so. It is as heartfelt as it is harmless. It makes him who he is. He sees the world in black and white. If you are the type that needs a bit of coddling, that is not his go.

And by his own admission you do not have to be old to be grumpy – as perfectly captured once in print: 'Young people these days, there's been a change of values. I see it in my own kids: if I ask them to mow the lawn, they look at me as if I've got three heads. When I was a kid, if you didn't move when you were asked, you'd get a smack in the ear and a kick up the backside. You took pride in everything you did, not only in your work, but in your appearance. Now, you're trying to have a beer and a feed in a pub and there'll be three twenty-year-old blokes with their jeans so low that their bum cheeks are hanging out, and flies from their cracks are flying into your face. You feel like knocking them out with a piece of wood. I'm a bit backward in terms of knowing about this so-called Y generation and metrosexuals and so forth, and I'm only thirty-nine, yet I feel like I'm 109 when I look at these bastards.'

He would argue he is better with horses than he is with people.

The portfolio of Group 1 winners from his redbrick Caulfield barn has burgeoned to include Wanted, Set for Fame, Anacheeva, Headway, Magnus, Testifiable, Cinque Cento and Markus Maximus. The most talented of these would have succeeded under most competent trainers. But that is not true of all. The 2009 West Australian Derby win of Markus Maximus was the product of broad thinking and intuitive training. Here was a gelding that took some convincing to win and never subsequently managed to do so again.

While the Caulfield and Melbourne Cups remain in the future, amid all the success Moody completed a lesser-known but deeply felt Cups double. It was a personal indulgence, so he drew no one else in.

Astro Gains was a plain bay gelding of enough potential to tease but never quite blossom. In his first year of racing he racked up half a dozen minor placings to sit alongside a lone win. Moody had him pegged as a grinding stayer and sent him out in the South Australian Derby of 2009. While he was no match for runaway winner Rebel Raider, it was enough to make Moody consider a Cups campaign. When injury intervened, keeping Astro Gains away from the track for more than a year, the plan was put on hold.

Returning in the spring of 2010, Astro Gains did not recapture the early promise, a realisation confirmed by an inglorious display on Geelong Cup Day. Without a hint of disappointment, Moody changed tack. As the demands of Melbourne Cup week loomed, he loaded the five-year-old into his float and took off alone one night for Cobar in central New South Wales. There he entrusted the gelding into the care of bush trainer Shane Iverson to complete the odyssey west. The goal was the Charleville Cup. Moody gave only one piece of advice, along with his good wishes: add blinkers to help the moody galloper keep up in the early stages of the race.

In front of 800 spectators on the first Tuesday in November, Astro Gains romped away with the Charleville Cup. In the betting ring, bookmaker David Power laughed out loud and cheered. Power had been the owner when a boy, not yet a teenager, found his way to his private stables and an apprenticeship under a rugged old trainer. Frank Cavanough had long since passed away, but this day Power and Moody shared the ownership of a motley gelding named Astro Gains who fulfilled an unspoken destiny. Moody grinned broadly when informed of the result 1500 kilometres away, as the bustle of Americain's Melbourne Cup win faded at Flemington.

A couple of weeks later, Moody received a modest cheque from the Central Warrego Race Club for his portion of the $9750 winner's purse and the trophy he recognised from a youth well spent. He placed it in his office alongside the Wyandra Cup that his parents had won in the 1970s. Proof that a man of quality never forgot where he came from.

As Moody fulfilled dreams he had never thought to cast, he unearthed the jewel for which every trainer fossicked. A champion.

Typhoon Tracy was tall and lean when Gold Coast breeder and shoe retailer John Hutchins delivered her to Moody. The daughter of Red Ransom was athletic rather than powerful. It gave her an air of elegance. As a filly she would cruise around Caulfield, never bothering to win a practice gallop. But the trainer recognised faultless motion in her effortless style. The best way he could describe it was 'she is all horse' in the way he might have described Marilyn Monroe as 'all woman'.

He took his time with Typhoon Tracy, bringing her along without haste. Moody brought her into the stable for a solid grounding and education, but opted against sending her to a race as a two-year-old. Instead, he let her grow and strengthen, holding her back until September 2008. As was his wont, he taught her to win on debut. Typhoon Tracy started at $6 and won by almost six lengths. Emerging star Whobegotyou took the feature Bill Stutt Stakes on that program, but he was not alone in departing with a burgeoning reputation.

Moody waited until the new year before launching the winning spree. Tracy loved to bounce and run. And there was no getting past her. She did so in a sequence of races at Caulfield, Moonee Valley and Flemington to such a convincing extent that she was boldly entered as a three-year-old against the older mares in the pinnacle Group 1 race for females, the Coolmore Classic on Golden Slipper Day. She drew the outside barrier in a field of sixteen and was hunted out of the gate by jockey Glen Boss. Together they careered across the front of the field and landed against the rail. Promptly the inexperienced filly dropped her head to her chest, pricked her ears and came back within herself, conserving her energy for the true test at the end. It made an impression on her veteran jockey who had partnered many a champion lady, including the incomparable Makybe Diva and Doncaster Handicap winner Private Steer.

Typhoon Tracy rounded the corner on the wrong leg, leaving her unbalanced and vulnerable. She was headed by rival Culminate. Once Boss corrected the error, she roared back along the inside and decisively claimed the prize. The endorsement of 'top class' was bestowed on the filly, who had accumulated five wins from five starts, including a prestigious Group 1. As the possibilities were laid out before an excited Moody, he caught himself: 'I have never had a horse with this record before so you get a bit protective and be careful where you run them and not do the wrong thing.'

Moody was cautious rather than opportunistic. He backed out of further taxing runs in Sydney with a horse that was still young and inexperienced. Typhoon Tracy's 2009 spring campaign misfired early and she tasted defeat at her debut at weight-for-age level, the racing conditions that most accurately measured class. Expectations were recalibrated and Moody targeted races against her own sex. That canny call saw her become the girl who stole Derby Day.

Blessed with brilliant speed complemented by her crucial ability to relax in a race, the four-year-old stalked a hot pace in the Group 1 Myer Classic. When Luke Nolen presented her to the leaders early in the Flemington straight, she dashed up and thrillingly shot away to post the most dazzling of five-length victories. Earlier that day Moody's horse Headway had narrowly won the first of the features, the Coolmore Stud Stakes. He was positively giddy after the deeds of Typhoon Tracy: 'Without a doubt this is my biggest day. Flemington has been terrific to me during Cup week and I've won the majority of my Group 1s here, but to win two on one day with my wife and mother here with me is terrific.'

Upon her resumption in the autumn, it was clear Typhoon Tracy was the best horse in the land. She reeled off wins in the weight-for-age C.F. Orr and Futurity Stakes double, downing local and international male contenders, before claiming the Queen of the Turf in Sydney. She left such an impression, it was suggested she had a touch of Sunline about her. The sensational New Zealand mare had set the benchmark for all Australasian females past and present in a glittering career at the turn of the twenty-first century. Of her twenty-five wins, thirteen were achieved in Group 1 races, and she always led throughout. Although Typhoon Tracy failed to win the country's premier mile race, the Doncaster Handicap, she was the standout choice for Horse of the Year. Nolen shared that season with Tracy and knew her to be the best miler he had ridden. 'Great temperament, great attitude and a great will to win.'

Hutchins had confided in Moody that he had always wanted a horse good enough to run in a Cox Plate and compete overseas. The trainer entertained the possibilities but flinched at both. He might have taken Typhoon Tracy to the Hong Kong Mile and attempted to emulate Sunline's heroic victory a decade before, but his restraint won the argument. Moody mapped out a Cox Plate preparation but could not convince himself she would see out the 2040 metres of the iconic race. Later, the decision left him encumbered with lament: 'That's one of my biggest regrets in racing – not giving her a chance at a Cox Plate.'

But ultimately Moody was both proud and grateful. 'Typhoon Tracy was instrumental in developing our stable from being a good handy stable that turned out probably 150 winners a year which were half bush horses, half city horses, to being a major metropolitan stable and competitive at the highest level throughout the year. She did a tremendous job for us; she's certainly one that will always be in the back of my mind. She was the first top class galloper that I had the opportunity to work with under my own banner.'

It was that sense of loyalty that brought the journey to an end. After a winless spring where she had previously been dominant, came Typhoon Tracy's swansong. The mare summoned all her courage to bow out a winner in a thrilling 2011 C.F. Orr Stakes.

At her best, Tracy would have broken clear after claiming Danzylum halfway down the straight. Instead she was in a struggle, never quite getting away from Ortensia and suddenly at the mercy of a charging Heart of Dreams. It seemed she would be swamped, but she refused to resign herself to that fate. Under desperate riding from Nolen, she found just enough. The last of what she had. The margin was slight but it was there. It was also historic. Only Lord, Manikato and Vo Rogue had won the race on multiple and consecutive occasions.

Reality mixed in with the celebrations. A year prior, in the same circumstances, Heart of Dreams had taken no ground in those last 100 metres. This time he ran Typhoon Tracy to a heartbeat. One of the owners thought Moody would announce her retirement on the spot. He waited until the following Monday, and in the ultimate mark of respect decided: that'll do girl, that'll do.

Moody handled Typhoon Tracy masterfully. He took full toll when she was in her prime, nursed her back when the brilliance faded and ensured there would be no unnecessary strain in a mercenary grab for the dregs. A trainer cannot do more for his horse. Through it he had recognised his own cautionary traits and vowed not to be restrained by them again. Typhoon Tracy had vaulted him to the top echelon and given him invaluable experience he would put into practice immediately. For Typhoon Tracy's successor was already on the runway.

Bronwen Healy Photography

Black Caviar most striking aspect is not beauty, it is power. She is an elite athlete not a super model.

3

I've Found the Horse for You

Racing is addictive. Just a casual association can draw you in. The beauty of the horse. The adrenaline of the race. The vibrancy of the event. Repeated exposure can prove irresistibly habit-forming.

Rick Jamieson knew the build-up to the Caulfield and Melbourne Cups from the mid-1980s like few others. He was Harry the Hirer, the owner of the company with the contract to erect marquees and fit out the racecourses before the arrival of the beautiful people. It left him susceptible. Slowly, slowly it lured him in. Not to the punt. Nor to the alcohol. But to the mystery of the horse itself. He wanted to understand the origins of the great horses. The idea lodged itself deep in his consciousness and there it took root. From such fascination, theories grow. Once conceived, those notions demand to be put into practice, and Jamieson entered the breeding business. He called it a hobby but knew it was closer to compulsion.

'I got interested in breeding. The more I looked at it the more it intrigued me, the deeper I would look. I started to plot pedigrees and particularly pedigrees of champion racehorses. I started to formulate my own ideas on breeding and then I started to purchase a few mares and to experiment a little bit.'

The ideas seemed impenetrable to the outsider. It was a study of genetics. How to blend speed and stamina. Which sires left their stamp? Which mares controlled the hereditary pool? Jamieson learnt in the first decade of application that it was not a strict science. It was a blend of research, knowledge, hunch – and patience. What you bred today, you would have the final verdict on in five years.

While the learning of a craft necessitated rookie mistakes, Jamieson insured where he could against failure. He purchased an old cattle farm in Nagambie and set about transforming it into a majestic stud, christened Gilgai Farm. The idyllic environ of Victoria's Goulburn River, an hour and a half out of Melbourne, is rich horse country. Lush, manicured paddocks with vintage homesteads and adjoining stables. A horse could not help but be happy on such a landscape.

As Jamieson built his project, he sought out and purchased broodmares. Accompanied by friend and bloodstock agent Peter Ford, he travelled to the 2005 Inglis Australian Broodmare Sale in Sydney but found the pickings were not to his liking. On the brink of declaring the trip a failure, Ford found what they had been looking for in the supplementary sale. He rang Jamieson and stated: 'I'm buying you a horse.'

By Desert Sun out of the Group 2-winning mare Scandinavia, the filly had been the agonising failure of the training co-operative Aquinita Racing. She had been a sought-after $305,000 purchase at the 2003 Magic Millions sales, but before she had even been fully syndicated had gone amiss at the breakers. Her physical frailties put her career on indefinite hold. As such, money was refunded and the rising two-year-old was left without owners, let alone a name.

She was allowed time to recuperate and nursed to full health. With a renewed sense of hopefulness, the filly commenced training. Whenever she reached a gallop at trackwork, she would sizzle. But the strain that caused on her body drew fault in muscles, joints and bones. Her raw talent was undeniable, but her constitution did not match her propensity for speed. Eventually the battle was conceded. She would never see race day. All that could be done was to salvage a portion of the investment by selling her as a breeding proposition.

Jamieson heard in Ford's voice that he had found the jewel they had hoped to uncover. His initial examination of the pedigree page was more than agreeable. The physical inspection was better still. 'What we found was a beautiful strong mare, beautiful walker, everything about her was just perfect really. Peter did a terrific job in picking her out. So we set about buying her.' The cost was $115,000.

The breeder applied his wits to the forensic study of his purchase's bloodlines while delegating the task of naming the horse to the farm manager. It was a name that would only ever be relevant on paper and exist in theory, never to echo from the public address across a racetrack. Under those circumstances perhaps it was thought better not to waste a clever name that could be put to better use. Or maybe it was a casual sense of humour at play. When the papers returned to Jamieson's desk, they came stamped with the name Like Billio. 'I couldn't believe it. I rang him and said, "What do you think this is? A goat?" We changed the name to Helsinge, being a town in Scandinavia.'

At the heart of Jamieson's thinking, in the search for the right pairing, was to reinforce Helsinge's pedigree. Feeling compelled to get it right the first time around with a mare lacking either racetrack credentials or condemnations, it caused him a good deal of consternation. However, he ran the possibilities and he kept coming back to a stallion fresh on the scene: Bel Esprit.

Nothing in racing is quite so fraught as the two-year-old circuit. Large, ungainly specimens with only a beginner's sense of what they are doing, it is a blend of blistering speed and unrefined instincts. At once thrilling and hair-raising.

On Cox Plate Day 2001, boutique trainer John Symons produced an unraced Royal Academy colt named Bel Esprit in the opening race and watched as he bolted in by four lengths. To prove it was no fluke he repeated the feat a fortnight later at Flemington in the Maribyrnong Plate, always a key marker for the feature juvenile events ahead.

Bel Esprit was immediately adopted as a racing favourite due mainly to the involvement of legendary AFL coach Kevin Sheedy in his ownership. Affectionately regarded as the nutty professor in the nation's coaching ranks, Sheedy had led Essendon for a generation, proving himself both a survivor and chameleon. He could regularly be found in the TAB of the Bombers' training base at Windy Hill indulging his passion for the races. The logical extension was to try his luck as an owner. Here he had hit pay dirt.

The Blue Diamond Series offer the first serious test of the country's fresh crop of two-year-olds. Bel Esprit swept the preliminaries, winning the Preview and the Prelude. He was installed as even money favourite for the main event. The richest race for two-year-olds in Victoria coincided with a pre-season AFL fixture in which Sheedy was to coach. Timings were synchronised to ensure he could watch the race during the half-time break. Channel Nine agreed to embed the race in the football coverage. Racing tapped a new level of exposure. The footy public was given a vested interest whether they cared for the sport or not.

Bel Esprit delayed the start with his fractious antics behind the barrier stalls. By the time he was loaded into the gates, Sheedy was compelled to be in the coach's box at Colonial Stadium and in full view as he watched the race unfold on the stadium's big screen.

Veteran bush jockey Wayne Treloar allowed Bel Esprit to scorch through the middle section of the 1200-metre scamper. The colt's turn of foot left his rivals three lengths astern coming to the home corner. It represented a risky strategy. Basic physics meant he had to tire in the concluding stages. It set up a heart-stopping finale. Bel Esprit shortened stride. The filly Brief Embrace hurtled from the pack. The eyes of those at Caulfield and those at the footy darted back and forth, calculating the distance to the finishing post; the crowds held their collective breath. Treloar shook Bel Esprit vigorously and he lasted to win by a neck.

His two-year-old exploits brought to mind previous youngsters who graduated to dominate the sprinting scene. The likes of Rancher and Zeditave. The heightened expectation, combined with the Sheedy connection, ensured Bel Esprit was always in the headlines. Post the Blue Diamond, he was banned from racing pending an improvement in manners. He had to satisfy stewards that his rogue tendencies could be controlled before being given clearance to run in the world's premier two-year-old race, the Golden Slipper. The application of a bull chain prior to a barrier trial at Bendigo quietened the colt and he was permitted to start at Rosehill in the Slipper. He finished fifth as Queensland filly Calaway Gal broke the race record.

Rather than targeting pure sprinting events, Symons experimented with the colt's stamina by extending Bel Esprit in distance. As a three-year-old, he ran second to Helenus in the 1600-metre Caulfield Guineas before beating only one runner home in Northerly's second Cox Plate. It left him an unfulfilled talent. His run of outs stretched to nine and his worth waned as he had proved himself neither one thing nor the other.

It placed an ever-increasing bounty on a second Group 1 victory to recommend him as a breeding prospect. Symons got it at the 2003 Brisbane winter carnival in the Doomben 10,000, when Bel Esprit turned in a stunning all-the-way victory, defying top-flight mares Private Steer and Spinning Hill. It was the win that fulfilled his precocious talent. Eliza Park Stud had a controlling interest in Bel Esprit and his attraction as a stallion was assured.

Jamieson could see the fault lines in his plan. As every prospective bloodstock agent, owner and trainer would. An unraced mare and an untested stallion. There was no way of knowing what the resulting foal would possess. If his choice proved a poor one it might not be a tough sell so much as impossible. But a man has to trust his instincts and back his judgment. If every action in racing is a gamble, Jamieson took his biggest punt. Helsinge would go to Bel Esprit in the spring.

It was in the bitingly cold pre-dawn hours on 18 August 2006 when that eagerly awaited foal came into the world. With no more than ten births a year, each was a momentous event at Gilgai Farm. This had also been a struggle.

Meaghan Strickland-Wood was another whose soul racing had captured. She had worked with horses all her life but never with thoroughbreds, until she took the equine management position with Jamieson. She was in the paddock at the heart of the property for what was proving a tight foaling. With the necessary assistance, Helsinge dropped her foal at 5.20 a.m. Typical of a maiden dam, she was a little shocked by what had transpired and her filly was initially quite unsure. At a quarter to six, though, it was noted that the foal wobbled on her newborn legs and stood for the first time. Soon she was moving around the paddock. For Strickland-Wood, the filly would hold a place in her mind for what was required next. 'I had to give her a bottle when we first started with her because she had trouble latching onto the mare's teats. Sometimes with the maidens their teats aren't very long and well stretched from lots of foals, so the foals can have a little trouble. So she started off life with a bottle.'

Of the three fillies born at Gilgai that year, Helsinge's foal was the standout. As she grew, Jamieson was struck by her size and strength. There was beauty to her movement. So utterly natural and powerful for such a young horse. Equally, he was drawn to her relaxed temperament. To him it seemed she always had her head down eating. The filly played on his mind to the extent that he was wavering on one of his foundation principles. His was a breeding and selling operation. Not a racing enterprise. To fall in love with one foal, and sacrifice the income from the sale, was to become the newsagent who kept buying Tatts tickets just in case the next one would prove to be the winner.

For all the promise he could see, there was one legitimate concern that nagged at the edge of his mind. The filly was offset in the front legs. Her knees were not quite aligned. On any juvenile, let alone a large one, such a flaw presented a risk. If her legs could not carry her powerful frame, she would suffer the same fate as her mother and never see the starting gates.

Jamieson resolved to stick to the plan and sell her. It was a quick decision. He could not afford the luxury of second guessing for fear of changing his mind. The Bel Esprit yearling was sent to Swettenham Stud to be prepared for the 2008 Inglis Melbourne Premier Sale. It was done.

If it is the breeder who conjures the riddle, then it is the trainer who is left to unravel it. The worth of these men and women resides not only in their capacity to educate and prepare a galloper but in their ability to choose it in the first place. The ability to decipher the potential of the bloodlines, to see the traits of a family and then study the physical form in search of confirmation. Success grows from selection as surely as any football team springs from the draft.

There is nothing precise about yearling sales. Many a million-dollar flop stands as testimony to that. It is an examination of instinct. Good breeding is good breeding. The top lot at any sale is virtually assured from the outset. It becomes only a question of how high the final price will climb. If that was all there was, every trainer and owner in the world would bid for the same handful of horses and pass in the rest.

Peter Moody had built his operation on his own judgment. The stable's accomplishments were owed largely to his choice of horses. He preferred to buy them and place them with owners, rather than the other way around. It left him free to select those he felt would thrive under the education and grooming of his system.

He craved the challenge to scour the catalogues for the gems; to apply all his experience to find the fleck of recognition. He always made the time to run an educated eye over the horseflesh and reach a verdict. The competitor in him liked the charade of masking his enthusiasm so as not to alert the entire sale ring. The object of his interest had to come at a reasonable price or the exercise was a failure. From there it could go either way. For those he might boast about, there were plenty of slow ones for which he had made the casting bid.

When the catalogue for the Melbourne Premier Sale arrived, Moody scanned it for familiar breeds. He could not have missed Lot 520 and the presence of Scandinavia in the second generation of the filly offered. That dam had produced his talented sprinter Magnus. Dead honest, he was a breath away from being a superstar. It left Magnus saddled with the compliment of gallant. He won four races, including the Group 1 Galaxy at Warwick Farm in 2007. But he ran eleven other placings. He chased home a litany of Australian greats. Takeover Target, Miss Andretti, Apache Cat and Weekend Hussler had all denied him major victories. He became the measure through which the deeds of each could be compared.

Moody warded off the temptation to become downhearted and instead kept fronting up. He thought enough of Magnus to take him to England twice, his first expedition to Royal Ascot. Magnus' best result was a third in the King's Stand Stakes behind Miss Andretti. He finished runner-up at Kranji in Singapore's premier sprint race, completing an all-Australian quinella with Takeover Target.

Magnus was the sort of horse you built a stable around. Consistent in the best company. It was a trait that sat well with Moody. Days ahead of the sale, he headed to the Swettenham parade to inspect the closely related filly.

The trainer's decisive and definitive nature unsurprisingly stretched to first impressions. His philosophy was simple enough and applied to horses just as it did people. He either liked you or he did not: 'You sit down with a person at lunch and you know it's going to be good or bad within thirty seconds. This person is going to annoy the hell out of me or this is going to be a pretty crazy day. You know it straight away. You get that feeling. It's the same with horses. A horse walks out of the box in front of me, I pretty much like it or I don't. If it grabs me then I go looking to try and eliminate the risks associated. But first and foremost I've got to like the horse that walks out in front of me.'

As the Bel Esprit filly came into his sight there was a lot resting on that moment.

When Moody says he 'fell in love with her from day one', he knows the shadow hindsight casts. Of course he would say that. But he has the markings to prove the bona fides of the statement. Over the years he had developed his own shorthand to register his thoughts. He scribbled the markings on the catalogue page: CE for correct enough; OK for good size and body; and Q for quality – the rarest compliment he bestowed.

It had been almost a year since he had last recorded a Q on a yearling page. That was a Redoute's Choice filly at the Sydney sales. She had fetched $1.5 million in the ring and went on to become VRC Oaks winner Samantha Miss. It was too rich for Moody's blood but had reinforced the feeling that he knew what he was looking at.

Moody was awestruck by the Helsigne filly: 'She was just a magnificent individual, she had a presence about her, an action about her. Every time she took a stride every part of her body moved. It's like walking down the beach and seeing certain parts of someone's anatomy wiggle. You just can't help yourself, you have to turn around and have a look. Both males and females. And that was her. She just had it all.'

The critical assessments then followed. Moody might be brutally decisive, but he was governed by an optimistic nature. He did not obsess over imperfections or deformities looking to strike off horses, but rather pursued the reasons to proceed. This played well for the filly before him.

He noted the slight offset in front that had tormented Jamieson. She was a little back on one knee. Moody engaged the conversation with himself: 'Right now is she athletic enough to overcome that? The way she moves, yes, I believe she is. A lot of people look at that and say, "Big heavy horse, offset knee, it's going to break down. It won't race." But I'll back her athletic ability to be able to overcome that.'

Jamieson was present as Moody got his initial glimpse of his filly. From a distance, he was watching the watcher. 'In the parade at Swettenham he was drilling down fairly hard, which made me smile, because he's a bloody good trainer. For a fellow like Peter Moody to be having a look at our horse as seriously as he was, that made us feel fairly good.' The breeder had attached a $100,000 reserve to the lot. It had seemed like a reach to set the bar that high. But as he observed one of Melbourne's leading trainers in full inspection mode, he felt a sense of reassurance.

By the time he left, Moody was all in. He would not only bid, he would buy her. He calculated the top end. It might take a bid of $150,000 to make the hammer fall. He rang a few prospective clients to share his enthusiasm and the financial equation. To one in particular, an order he had looked to fill for some time, he said: 'I think I've found the horse for you.'

Newspix / Nicole Garmston

The owners of Black Caviar at the Australian Race Horse of the Year, 2011 (left to right): Lena Attebo, Neil Werrett, Jill Taylor, David Taylor, Pam Hawkes, Barry Hawkes, Colin Madden, Kerrin Wilkie and Gary Wilkie. Jannene Madden is absent.

4

An Excuse to Have Lunch

Anyone might have owned Black Caviar. In a way, anyone did. Where the owners of iconic gallopers of the past had been vaulted into the public consciousness, individually the custodians of this mare remained relatively anonymous.

Phar Lap's owner, David Davis, had been famously cantankerous. Tulloch's E.A. Haley sensationally overruled trainer Tommy Smith and deprived his three-year-old of the chance to win the Melbourne Cup.

The deeds of Makybe Diva became inextricably linked with the story of a Port Lincoln tuna fisherman. Audiences came to love the extroverted celebrations of Tony Santic and his family, complete with custom-made masquerade masks in the mare's racing colours that mingled the Australian and Croatian flags, a design that told of their cultural heritage.

Octagonal championed the cerise of the Chicken Kings. Jack and Bob Ingham won their way into Australian hearts high-fiving the rank and file at Rosehill on a day when pink-iced donuts were handed out in honour of the Big O.

At the height of his jubilation, Nick Moraitis held up the gleaming silver Cox Plate before the punters lining the Moonee

Valley straight as if he were invoking a benediction. His fearless frontrunner Might and Power was one of the most beloved gallopers of his generation, and the man they dubbed the 'greengrocer' was a face beamed to every corner of the nation.

Elderly Singaporean businessman Dato Tan Chin Nam might never have raised a glimmer of recognition bar for gallopers like Saintly and So You Think and a man named Bart. Instead, one of Moonee Valley Racing Club's most famous races adopted his name to honour his litany of champion horses and his partnership with Cummings.

But at the peak of her fame, it was doubtful anyone other than close friends and specialist racing journalists could have recited the names of Black Caviar's owners. You would have heard them on radio and seen them on breakfast television. You could read about them in everything from the local paper to the national broadsheet as they tried to share the sense of good fortune and privilege. They were fêted at functions and paraded at race meetings. Yet they remained, quite deliberately, secondary to the glow of the horse. 'G.J. & Mrs K.J. Wilkie, Werrett Bloodstock P L Synd (Mgr: N. Werrett), C. & Mrs J. Madden, Mrs P. Hawkes & D.M. & Mrs J. Taylor.' Early on they handed custody of their mare over to the people and the country took them at their word.

How that collective came to be was endearing for how unremarkable the story was. It was not the million-to-one, luck-defying, rags-to-riches tale you could marvel at but never quite relate to. Nor was it the production line of an international breeding operation or an oil-rich sheikh with an obsession for global racing dominance. It can instead be explained by the bonds of decades-old friendships forged through family, school and business. It was entrenched in the norms of suburban and rural life. The additional kickers were a shared passion for waterskiing and more than a passing interest in horses.

* * *

On the gentle waters of the Murray River, a houseboat launched from the border town of Echuca carries a group of friends including the Maddens, the Wilkies and Neil Werrett on their annual summer retreat, drifting towards a state of relaxation. It is not hard to imagine the conversation as the red wine eased the pressures of the outside world. What they should do was buy a racehorse. A connection to ensure more regular opportunities to catch up. The odd day at the races. Road trips to provincial tracks. A bit of fun. At various times and to differing levels, they each had involvements with racehorses. Whereas joining a commercial syndicate was pot luck with a group of strangers, buying a horse together, as Gary Wilkie put it, 'would give us an excuse to have lunch'.

This was hardly the first time such a conversation had transpired in that forum. Jannene Madden knew it well enough. Her husband Colin had previously taken shares in horses with Werrett. The link between Jannene, Pam and the Werretts stretched back so far their grandparents had been friends when Melbourne's south-east was still farmland. Madden had searched for a mutual endeavour for him and his friend after the death of Werrett's wife. He took the leap to join Werrett in the racing game: 'Sometimes in life you get together and have a laugh. Sometimes there are sad moments. Neil had been through some sad times. It was so we could have something to laugh about rather than cry about. To share something that was really good.'

Colin Madden, a solicitor of more than thirty years, was utterly pragmatic. He figured whatever money he spent on horses he would not see again. Instead, one of those initial ventures turned up a potentially smart sprinting filly named Bel Mer. She was sired by Bel Esprit and was about to launch her career under the guidance of Caulfield trainer Mick Price. Bel Mer's career culminated in a Group 1 win in Adelaide and, much to Madden's amazement and amusement, 'we got our money back'.

Despite scant knowledge of breeding, Madden was particularly drawn to Bel Esprit. His great sporting passion was AFL club Essendon. The Kevin Sheedy link was irresistible. 'I know bugger all about horses but I'll jump on anything involved with Essendon.' If the chance arose to do it again, he was keen.

The casual recounting of the Echuca plan tended to enhance the idea of a novice fluke – but that would be an injustice to Werrett. He had been racing horses for the best part of three decades with increasing success. His first horse, Kotiko, gave him the taste of victory in a metropolitan race in Adelaide. The Sydney businessman had come to be regarded as a prolific owner with a multitude of stables. Madden proved to be his good luck charm. Bel Mer's Robert Sangster Stakes win in March 2009 was his first at the top level.

On the cruise of 2007, Werrett had insisted that this group of friends 'get organised' on the topic they had long contemplated. The consensus was they would back his knowledge and experience and commit a serious wad of money to enhance their chances of a horse worthy of the ambition. Then they called it a night. If there is a reflection that best sums up the tone of that discussion, and whether the participants would remember the pledge made once the glow of the wine subsided, it came from Werrett: 'After the weekend away we had to make sure on the Tuesday and Wednesday that everyone was serious about it.'

Still it took until another cruise the following year for the formal commitments to be made and the specifications agreed upon. The majority demanded the horse be trained in Melbourne. Grateful to have consensus at last, Werrett acquiesced and placed the docket with Peter Moody. He was on the lookout for a filly.

When Moody called, it left an immediate impression on Werrett. 'He was really upbeat about a yearling by Bel Esprit that was being offered at the Melbourne sales. I could tell from Peter's voice that he was pretty keen on this filly.'

Werrett did not require further prompting than the tone of the call. Of the trainer's contacts, he was the keenest and quickest to reply. En route to the races at Flemington, Werrett stopped by the Oaklands Junction precinct and had a look at the filly. Werrett phoned Moody: 'Gee, she's a pretty big horse.' It was an observation that contained its own note of concern. Moody replied: 'That's the way I like them.' It was a statement that contained its own soothing reassurance.

It was not that Werrett left so starstruck that he resolved he must have her. It was his faith in Moody. 'If you ask an expert to give you an opinion you don't second-guess the expert.' The trainer interpreted the instructions 'that if I liked her as much as I suggested, to go ahead and purchase her. He didn't put a ceiling on what I could spend but I knew realistically what he was looking at'.

The price would depend on the competition.

Troy Corstens was the general manager of Team Corstens Racing. A future trainer himself, he had an astute eye for a yearling. His role was to recruit a racing team for his father Leon, who had long served as a foreman for Bart Cummings and orchestrated the success of Let's Elope. Corstens transferred that knowledge to his own training career, highlighted by the Victoria Derby win of Helenus. Troy thought the Helsinge filly to be the standout of the sale and recommended her to Melbourne businessman and horse enthusiast Peter Carrick. He was the principal of Grange Thoroughbreds, a breeding and racing operation based on a 280-acre property near Nagambie. Carrick was focused on the purchase of fillies to serve the dual ambitions of winning races and producing foals.

Corstens saw in the filly what he regarded as the whole package. 'She was basically just like a colt. She was big and strong, and she had an awesome presence about her. We were very keen to get a hold of her.'

When the appropriate time came, the filly was brought into the auditorium and paraded before potential suitors. Inglis director and auctioneer Peter Heagney made the pitch. 'We offer to you a filly by Bel Esprit out of Helsinge by Desert Sun, first foal of a half sister to that wonderful sprinter in Magnus. Didn't he run a great race in the Oakleigh Plate the other day? Lovely family, continues to improve. This is just one of those Black Type families that just keep producing stakes winner after stakes winner.'

Heagney sought an opening bid of $100,000. That proposition fell on a motionless auditorium. As did the next two descending increments. The bidding started at a modest $30,000. It gave Moody false optimism. From a slow start, the pace picked up. It paired down to a duel with Corstens who held the bid at $200,000. He watched as Moody came over the top, his hand raised at $210,000. 'Peter looked at me, and I looked at him and thought, "Well, that's just about enough for a Bel Esprit filly," because he hadn't set the world on fire at the time, and that was probably the stupidest thing to ever come out of it.'

Moody had carried the day on a purchase of passion. 'You get a rush of blood and every now and again you go overboard. She was one I just wanted rain, hail or shine. I don't know how much further I would've gone but I reckon I would've gone further.'

Werrett's initial budget had in fact been $100,000. He was prepared to stretch that by another 40 per cent. The underbidders made an immediate approach to buy a portion of the yearling. Werrett had options to split the purchase or tell his friends they were in for double what had been proposed. The owner held his nerve and redoubled his faith in his trainer. He retained half the filly himself and carved up four shares for his friends at $35,000 apiece, a sum that included a year of training fees.

From the houseboat, the Maddens and Wilkies stumped up. Not everybody who had been present maintained the same level of enthusiasm. For David Taylor, that was the way in. 'One of the chaps on the houseboat excursion decided not to go ahead. I was fortunate enough to be invited in.' Gary Wilkie had known Taylor, a real estate agent, for some twenty-five years. They had long vowed to race a horse together.

Taylor's separate forays had been streakily successful. A horse named Man Irish was his introduction to horse ownership, a passion that can torture its devotees for the best part of a lifetime. The first time he saw that horse at Flemington, he won by fifteen lengths. His second horse, Ivan's Pride, won his first five races.

Drunk with such good fortune, Taylor barely hesitated at Wilkie's proposal. His wife Jill, busy with twin girls in the early years of primary school, was less enamoured with the idea, complete with its hefty price tag. Whatever embarrassment she felt in hindsight over her reluctance passed to the extent she could tell the story against herself quite delightfully. 'I'm not transferring money for a stupid bloody horse,' was her decree when the time came to pay up. David did it himself. 'When the bank statement came I wrote on it "Bloody Horse". I don't think I even knew what her name was when she raced the first time.'

Jannene Madden invited her sister Pam Hawkes into the horse. Pam, Jannene and Neil went as far back as Sunday school together in Keysborough. They had all started out from farming backgrounds, but only Pam remained on a potato farm on the Mornington Peninsula. While there were spuds, beetroots and onions, there were always horses on the property. Old horses in Hawkes' care that might only have been alive because of her devotion to them.

When the chance to race a horse presented itself, Pam needed no convincing. Although, given what she had surrounded herself with, she had her own stipulation: 'I only want a fast one.'

Newspix / Russel Tindale

Baby-faced Jarrad Noske aboard Black Caviar at her first race start.

5

The Untried Yearling

Flemington, Cromwell Handicap, 18 April 2009
Caulfield, Blue Sapphire Stakes, 2 May 2009

No one ever gave up while there was an untried yearling in the paddock. For the monotony and the repetition, the rigid discipline and inescapable groundwork, there is one moment of purity and clarity for a racehorse trainer. It can be fleeting or lasting but it cannot be rushed, for nothing can be learnt prematurely. As familiarity with a horse grows, suspicions are harboured and opinions formed. But nothing is truly known until that horse gallops for the first time. Uninhibited. Flat out. When they stretch their neck, prick their ears and tear through the breeze. In that moment, anything is possible. After it, a trainer knows what he has.

Pam Hawkes was typical of the owners who had bought their ticket in the Bel Esprit–Helsinge lottery. They were as wide-eyed as doting parents. Hawkes was in Ireland when the sales were staged. At the first opportunity after her return, she bundled off to Cloverdale, an agistment property at Pakenham South to view their pride and joy.

'We went out to the actual paddock and I remember it was G1 on that paddock. Gary had always referred to the horse as G1 standing for Group 1 and we all laughed. That was the very first time we saw her, at Kaz Morphett's place, and she was beautiful. She was very quiet. She was in a paddock with a chestnut mare and she was only very young. There was a group of us in there hanging around, hanging all over her and looking at her and she was very quiet right from the start.'

As the months went by, the fun task of naming the horse was undertaken. Each owner was allotted five choices to be emailed to Gary Wilkie. A shortlist would be compiled and votes cast thereafter. Typically, owners will scour the breeding of horses and look for trigger points through the generations from which to extrapolate a fresh name. Hawkes was drawn to Scandinavia, the broodmare that might have been Like Billio. It came from her love of geography and a penchant for looking at maps. She recognised immediately the link Rick Jamieson had created with Helsinge and the idea germinated. 'Caviar, the luxury food, came from the waters around the Scandinavian countries. Helsinge was a town in Denmark, north of Copenhagen, and so we put in Black Caviar.' While not unanimous, the vote fell her way. It became the subject of considerable mirth and some relief that the list of unsuccessful nominations contained the rather less exotic suggestion Fish Eggs.

With the name registered, they decided to create their own set of racing colours. It was a mark of how wholehearted the group was. Most owners will tend to race in the silks of the stable trainer. Black Caviar was to be a special case from the outset. Shannon Wilkie, the daughter of Gary and his wife Kerrin, seized on the components in the name. While it was initially mistaken as either orange or pink, the silks were salmon and the black dots were the fish eggs.

Many an overenthusiastic owner would have reached this point before reality took hold. Pessimistic reports from the trainer.

Setbacks leading to prolonged periods in the paddock. Modest entries in provincial maiden races. Disappointment at the track. The fun, high-priced though it might be, tends to be derived from the creation and the anticipation. It is what makes those early days so heady.

Not that they necessarily knew it, but statements of temperance were at various times in the balance. The filly's size was proving a problem and Moody's skills were being thoroughly tested. Assistant trainer Tony Haydon had watched Black Caviar carefully as she came through the Caulfield stables at regular intervals. He was struck that when she lined up for a gallop or jump out with young horses at the same stage of development and learning, she was noticeably more professional and possessed considerably more natural ability. 'There was a style about her. She just stood out that little bit when she was working.'

Haydon was thinking Black Caviar would be the perfect horse for the Blue Diamond Stakes, and the chance to emulate her sire. But they could not keep her on the track long enough to mount such an assault. 'Every time she'd step up to faster work, she would tear a chest muscle. Usually it's shin soreness with two-year-olds. But not her. She was such a good galloper, the hard thing was to get her to relax. Everything else she picked up really quickly as most of the good horses do, but trying to get her not to try so hard, that was the hard thing. At one stage it looked like she probably wouldn't even make it to the races. But Moods did a great job with her. Maintaining her and trying to look after her. I think if we had pushed her she wouldn't have got too far.'

After a year of waiting, Moody sent word that Black Caviar's first public outing would be the official trials at Cranbourne on 30 March 2009. There was no curbing the enthusiasm. The Wilkies were in attendance. Hawkes and Jannene Madden travelled together. They headed for the bustle of the concrete saddling area prior to the trial for a peek at the filly. It was a full-blown dress rehearsal of what they all hoped lay ahead. Moody exchanged a quiet word of encouragement with Hawkes: 'I think we've got a nice filly here. You're going to have a bit of fun with her.' The nerves from the trip were replaced with quiet expectation on the trainer's say-so. Pam Hawkes skipped back to the car and headed around to a vantage point near the finishing post.

Moody had been in the game long enough to have a strong sense of what stood before him. The filly was a natural runner who had the makings of a very good horse. This was the morning to test that opinion. This was an experiment. A week or two premature perhaps, but Moody had to know. He had called it an 'educational gallop', but he did not specify whether that was for the benefit of horse or human. He wanted Luke Nolen aboard and, whatever he felt, he was careful to underplay when he gave his jockey the brief: 'This is a big, raw filly with ability. Have a soft burn around and we will learn a bit more when you come back.'

Nolen wore the stable colours, white with white and blue striped sleeves, easily picked as Black Caviar jumped from the inside barrier in what can be helter-skelter affairs filled with rookie gallopers and undisclosed rogues. She was a touch slow away, but the horse on her outside blundered the first step badly. No sooner had she balanced up than Black Caviar mustered commendable speed on the rail and after 200 metres had established a comfortable lead. Hawkes could not see the early part of the trial, but she heard the race caller state that Black Caviar was in front coming to the turn, a fact confirmed as the filly rounded into view. That initial shot of adrenaline intensified as the filly broke clear, opening the margin with every stride. Nolen had decided to 'let her rip' and was taken aback with the reaction. She simply ran away from her pursuers in what the jockey regarded as a particularly soft win. As she reached the line, caller Adam Olszanski offered the endorsement: 'She looks pretty smart.'

Hawkes was beaming. Then a peculiar thought occurred to her. It was the affliction of the racing game. You were never quite satisfied, always thinking about what came next. 'There go the odds!'

Gary Wilkie to that point had not met Moody in person, but, given the small number of people in attendance at Cranbourne, he had wound up half a step away from his trainer as the trial unfolded. After watching your horse turn in such a rousing gallop there would never be a better time to say hello. Wilkie introduced himself as one of the owners at the very moment Moody was trying to process what he had just seen.

Wilkie embarked on a conversation: 'How was that?'

Moody answered: 'Very good.'

The hopeful owner probed a little deeper. He got an affirmative to the proposition 'Can she run?' and followed up with 'How fast and how far?'

'Don't know and don't know,' came the reply. Wilkie accepted this as checkmate and let Moody be on his way.

The truth in Moody's head and the turmoil in his stomach were too delicate, he judged, to be shared. As carefully as trainers guide their horses, so must the expectations of the associated humans be moderated. Moody had just had the apparition that tantalises all participants in the racing game.

'Every time you take a young, inexperienced, green, immature horse out onto the training track for its first bit of serious work, you always wonder is this the one that's going to let down and be the next superstar? You'd be lying if you said that each time that new one came along and had its first bit of fast work that you weren't looking for something brilliant to excite you.' Some people think in grand schemes and vaulting ambition. Moody was too grounded for that. His measure could be understood by any person alive who stirred to the click of an alarm clock. 'Is this the one that's going to make it easier to get out of bed for the next twelve months?'

As Black Caviar stopped the clock in trial number four in what would prove to be the fastest time of the morning, eclipsing anything subsequently posted by seasoned and talented gallopers, Moody thought only this: 'Holy hell.' Here was a total newcomer, comparatively uneducated and a long way from peak fitness. If he was completely honest, this was unlike anything he had seen before. She was low flying. If he could hold this robust filly together, anything was possible. As those thoughts took hold, he cautioned himself. In the dark of the trainers' tower at trackwork, these gallops were referred to as morning glories. Horses that would give you an atlas – they would show you the world. But those 'glories' were never replicated when anyone else was watching.

Moody is a man not easily fooled. 'When you see raw brilliance, you're still not sure where that's going to lead to. It's a bit like a young footballer, or cricketer, or swimmer – they can look great in the junior ranks but it's when they step out into the big time some climb to the occasion and others melt.' Whatever it was to be it was time to find out.

Fundamental to the Moody method of training was teaching his horses to win. It was nothing more than basic logic. Horses learnt how to be winners. And horses learnt how to be losers. If it were a habit, as he believed, best it be the former. Moody would obsess over debut runs. Finding a level that was within a thoroughbred's capability regardless of locale. He sought soft kills to build confidence.

Black Caviar had something of a twin through that inauguration period. Moody had bought a second filly from the same Melbourne sale. By Reset, she was in the mould for size and style, just a shade lighter in colour. She became Set For Fame and also won a trial on that morning at Cranbourne. The girls would debut on the same day. Set For Fame was entered for a maiden at Hamilton. Moody's judgment was endorsed when she romped home by seven lengths. In the case of Black Caviar, though, he felt no need to be inventive. For a fast filly, the straight at Flemington was ideal. For a big filly, the absence of a turn was a clear bonus. A 1000-metre scamper for two-year-olds was the task.

There was no disguising what had happened at Cranbourne. One experienced watcher not only tipped Black Caviar to win first up but declared her the best bet of the day. Moody did his best to downplay what was about to be unleashed. He warned that it was not possible to know precisely the capability his filly possessed. Privately, though, Rick Jamieson had got word. He had heard about the trial and was on the brink of deciding to which sire Helsinge should go next. Through a mutual friend, he had made contact with Moody seeking a clearer picture of her strengths and possible shortcomings. 'I remember he said to me, "You probably won't breed a better one than this."'

The butterflies Jannene Madden felt were uncontrollable as she and Colin headed to Flemington early on 18 April. It was a mix of anxiety and excitement like she had rarely known. Ahead of the second race, the Cromwell Handicap, bookies opened Black Caviar at the tight quote of $2.40. There would be no release on favouritism.

As Black Caviar patrolled the mounting yard, again it was her size that differentiated her from her angly, immature rivals. Sixteen-year-old Perth jockey Jarrad Noske had the honour of donning the salmon silks for the first time. Apprenticed to his mother Jodie, he was in the first week of a three-month loan to test his skills in Victoria. Moody was impressed with both the weight of winners, more than a hundred in the west, and his attitude. He did not hesitate to entrust the youngster with the ride.

That was not quite true for all. As Moody legged him aboard, Pam Hawkes was struck by the discrepancy in size between man and beast. 'When he was getting up onto the horse he looked like a Grade 6 boy, very smooth face and quite tiny. I thought, "This massive powerful horse, I hope this boy can hold it." He was a touch overwhelmed also I think, he was a bit unsure of himself. But Peter had told him not to win by too much, to hold her until he felt ready to go.'

That exchange had caused Hawkes a slight double-take. She knew as well as anyone how good the trial had been, but as a student of form she had been following a horse named Kwassa Kwassa. In her best judgment, he was ideally suited in a race such as this. He had been an early two-year-old who had won at Moonee Valley on debut in November and franked that with a follow-up win down the Flemington straight. When the field was declared, she had thought: 'Gee, either Peter thinks this horse is pretty good or we are going to get done.'

Noske excelled in what proved a simple enough task. Black Caviar jumped a little awkwardly from the gates, her head up leaning right then ducking back left. Noske gave her a little squeeze and she was straight on the bridle. Black Caviar glided up alongside the leader and when she took the front at the 300, there was no need to push. Three or four big strides opened the lovely expanse of daylight between their filly and the competition, answering every question expressed and imagined. Race caller Greg Miles commended Black Caviar as 'living up to the very good trial' as the winning margin officially registered at five lengths. Kwassa Kwassa filled second.

An impressed Moody told waiting reporters: 'This might have been the start of two good careers.' Of the jockey he added: 'He seems a real nice kid and on top of that he seems to have a hell of a lot of talent.' Of the horse he said: 'She's a smashing type of filly.'

The season's key two-year-old races had already been determined. Moody's Reward For Effort had led all the way to claim the Blue Diamond. Queenslander Phelan Ready took the eye with a barnstorming win at long odds in the Magic Millions Classic on the Gold Coast. He emphasised the quality of that run by scooting away with the Golden Slipper on a bog track in April.

Such was the commanding nature of Black Caviar's late-season win, combined with the extremely slick time of 56.63 seconds, that it prompted some good judges to aver that she was the pick of the young crop.

Hawkes was delighted. She figured it would be a flash in the pan and was going to maximise the enjoyment of the moment. In the days after that debut win she ordered for herself a set of number plates: BLK CVR. She would never travel in anonymity again.

Not everyone was on hand for the first giant leap. Jill Taylor still had not reconciled the 'bloody horse' with her busy life. Despite husband David's best efforts to convince her to come to Flemington, Jill was overwhelmed with the weekend commitments of children. As she dropped the twins at a party, a couple of the dads from school told her they were headed to the TAB as a mark of solidarity. She coolly replied she would not even know what the horse's name was. 'When they came back they said, "She was amazing. She didn't just win, it was the distance that she won by." David rang from the track and they were all happy and laughing. I said, "Okay, whatever."'

It was a facade. She could not help but thaw given the excitement that was being relayed. She relented and said she would be there next time to see what all the fuss was about.

That day came a fortnight later at Caulfield. It was a step up to black-type level in the Listed Blue Sapphire Stakes. Black Caviar's reputation was booming. Sometimes that lasts just a start or two. Affirmation was required and this would be a telling day. Tony Vasil had a good opinion of his colt Carrara. He had been a debut winner on protest in a Seymour maiden that included more than one good-class horse. Peter Snowden had the well-regarded Lonhro colt Demerit in his first race. He would subsequently win the Caulfield Guineas Prelude in the spring.

Black Caviar was tardy at the start in the Blue Sapphire and found herself in the ruck after only a few strides. It was an awkward position for Noske to find himself on the $1.50 favourite. The hint in the air was that the showy debut winner was about to learn about the rough and tumble of racing. Noske thought about riding her back in the field, but quickly assessed she was going only half pace.

Moody and Nolen were at the Adelaide races, where they would soon produce Astro Gains to run second in the South Australian Derby. They watched on television as events transpired at Caulfield. Jockey and horse plotted a wide, searching course forward. Veteran hoop Danny Brereton was aboard Carrara as he strode to the front and travelled sweetly down the railway side. Brereton was startled to look over and see Black Caviar go past him. But he assessed it would come at a cost. As they cornered, he expected to be pegging back a tiring filly having expelled all her energy in that mid-race move. If he was initially startled, he was then flat-out gobsmacked as Black Caviar got further and further away. Only Noske knew how risk-free his strategy had felt. 'She just ambled up there. She was the winner a long way out.'

From the neighbouring state, Nolen knew what Brereton must have been thinking as he went through precisely the same chain of emotions. 'It seemed like she made a run for half a mile. Her class enabled her to do that. But when she kicked again on straightening it was an unbelievable effort. The ease at which she went about it and the tough run she had, it was quite extraordinary. We thought we had something special to start with but it was starting to sink in that she could be a little bit better than we even anticipated.' Nolen started counting the days before he could get himself a piece of it.

When Brereton shared his impressions with Moody at trackwork the following Tuesday morning, it confirmed to the trainer that he had a Spring Carnival contender. He had flirted with the idea of floating Black Caviar to Brisbane for a crack at the Group 1 Sires Produce Stakes and cashing in before the season was out. Instead, he decided cotton wool was preferable, with an eye to the riches of Melbourne.

Newspix / Darren Mcnamara

An injured Black Caviar beats Wanted in the Danehill Stakes at Flemington.

6

The Pain Barrier

Moonee Valley, William Crockett Stakes, 22 August 2009
Flemington, Danehill Stakes, 5 September 2009

As much as anything in horse racing can be predictable, Black Caviar's racetrack return was entirely so. It was late August, when the spring participants shake out the cobwebs and shed their winter coats. The feature races roll from September and most trainers like the security of a warm-up run. Moody had a swag of Group 1 choices from which to choose. Publicly he picked out the Thousand Guineas for fillies over 1600 metres in the middle of Caulfield's three-day carnival as the primary goal, but would not rule out changing tack to either tackle the males in the Caulfield Guineas or even the older horses in a race like the Manikato Stakes. He spoke in despatches of the filly possessing a 'special X factor'.

Moonee Valley is a tight circuit nestled in the hum of Melbourne's northern suburbs. One turn begets the next and the next on a layout shaped like a saucer. Big striding horses are typically best suited to the wide-open spaces afforded by the grand expanse of Flemington. Tractability is not an issue when there is no turning to be done. But it is the single greatest determining factor when you are spinning like a merry-go-round.

This was part of what Black Caviar needed to learn, for Moonee Valley hosted a couple of the most suitable and prestigious sprints the future might hold. Some years prior, the track had been relayed to introduce a camber around the home bend in the fashion of a velodrome. The track became a speciality. Fields of Omagh ran in five Cox Plates, winning two. There was never a horse that could run into the bend and use the natural angle of the track to propel itself out of it for the short finishing burst, better than that durable gelding.

Black Caviar loved it. She was not a filly to be held up for one parting shot in a race. She liked to ratchet up the pressure and thus could be at full bore as she came to slingshot for the homeward run. Over the 1200 metres she cornered like a Formula One car.

Nolen got the feel for the filly under race conditions in the William Crockett Stakes. 'She bombed the start a little again. We thought we'd eradicated that problem but we hadn't obviously. She travelled outside the leader. I gave her a shake-up and she won as she liked. I was a bit kind to her late but she still gapped them.' In time he would come to understand exactly what it was and how to convey that to the layman. What he did know immediately was that not many horses won by such margins with so little need for effort. He estimated he only got halfway through second gear. 'It's a good thing to be on her and not competing against her.'

Together they beat the moderately performed Miraculous Miss by three and three-quarter lengths. He could probably have chosen an exact margin if he had been asked. Moody did not shy away from the gathering spruik. 'In terms of raw ability the only one I've been involved with showing similar ability was General Nediym.'

She was not the finished product, as was evidenced by her inability to get out of the barriers cleanly. At precisely the wrong moment she was prone to taking half a step backwards. It was interpreted that she had bad barrier manners. Moody had an alternative theory that concerned him more than the length head start she was conceding. Black Caviar was the proverbial bull at the literal gate. Sensing what a physical specimen she was, Black Caviar tried to do everything at a million miles an hour. So attuned to the task of racing had she become and so eager to get going, she would try to anticipate the start.

Moody's equation was this: 'You've got 550 kilograms on four little legs coming out of a square box six-foot by two-and-a-half foot wide from a standing start. If it tries to propel itself too quickly, quite often they fall over or stumble or run along on their nose and knees for a while. That was a habit that we had to slowly try and curtail with her.' More than any other aspect of her education this was where Moody put the effort. Having not yet mastered the art at training, she would have to keep learning on the job.

It should have ended at start number four. There never should have been a streak, just a handy hat-trick that in racing was barely worthy of note. Mistakes in short races foretell defeat. There is no time to recover lost ground. The errors Black Caviar had made previously left her vulnerable, but they had not been catastrophic.

That came as the gates sprang back to start the Group 2 Danehill Stakes at Flemington. Black Caviar was stepping up in grade but again was a long odds-on favourite. She reacted precisely as the steel structure creaked to life. In the first heartbeat, Nolen thought she had finally stepped on cue. In the next, he realised she was coming out too quickly. She stumbled and for the first couple of strides was down on her nose. On the course broadcast, Greg Miles captured it with a gasp: 'Oooh, Black Caviar really knuckled. She began terribly down in gate two today.' She veered wickedly inwards. Nolen braced. Instinct and bitter experience told him he was about to hit the track. Moody did not breathe. If he had he might have prayed. Black Caviar cannoned into the Patinack Farm gelding Point Pain, the only thing that stood between her and the inside rail. His career would pass largely undistinguished, registering only a couple of moderate wins on the Gold Coast and Sunshine Coast. But without him the story would have ended there. For Moody knew: 'If it wasn't for the horse drawn on the inside I've got no doubt in the world she would've fallen over.'

In the stands, Pam Hawkes watched the big screen aghast. 'It was just the most awful moment.' Under Nolen, Black Caviar scrambled on all fours in a panic-stricken effort to get upright. He could not interfere, as to haul the reins would guarantee she would tip over. With all manner of physical force working unnaturally, the muscles in her chest strained and tore off the bone. But it was not in vain as she retrieved herself to be erect. And galloping. Even in that mad scramble she had moved with surprising speed and once the fear of falling had passed, it was apparent she had lost little ground. Nolen sat tight to make an instant assessment as to whether she was good to race on. Black Caviar answered that for him as she took up the lead.

Nolen could feel the strain as she struggled to build her customary momentum. But this was a race and it was no longer enough to be grateful that she might complete it. The task had returned to winning it. Even before the thunder of hooves threatened from behind, Nolen knew he would have to be vigorous. In that realisation alone lived the evidence that all was not well. From behind, the stablemate Wanted was eating into the lead. Six months from then, with the fury of a once-in-a-century storm about to unleash on Flemington, Wanted would win the Group 1 Newmarket Handicap. His challenge was a worthy one. Black Caviar strained for Nolen. This was the courage he had known in a warhorse like his Cox Plate winner El Segundo. 'She was there to be beaten and she really stuck her head out and fought like a caged lion. Her resilience to win shone through. It was a great quality to see in her.'

The margin of defiance was three-quarters of a length. Moody was racked by conflicting emotions. He knotted with worry. He did not need the diagnosis of the vets some hours later to know what the problem was. He had treated her for soft tissue damage in the chest previously. This was the injury he feared. But as he calculated the cost of victory, he also swelled with pride. He saw in Black Caviar the great willingness to win.

'Like all good athletes she was able to run through the pain barrier. I think any great sportsperson who has had to carry injuries during their career, it shows their courage and their willingness to get on with the job. Fortunately she's no different.'

The celebration among the owners was muted despite the level of the achievement. There was no talk of the spoils. Jannene Madden wondered if the ride that promised so much had been prematurely and permanently derailed. 'We were all adamant that we wanted to give Black Caviar the best possible chance of recovery. We knew that Peter had the very best people working with her and we were hoping that she was going to get well and go on to race again. But no one really knew.'

Moody resolved himself to the uncertainty that lay ahead. 'We knew we had a hell of a good racehorse, but from that point onwards we've always just been worried whether she'd stay in one piece.'

Bronwen Healy Photography

Peter Clarke called her 'the princess'. At Willowood Equicentre he applied the therapy of good kindness and firmness to Black Caviar.

7

Racing Purgatory

Moonee Valley, Australia Stakes, 22 January 2010

It was always the fast ones that got injured. From trainer to stablehand, everyone at racing's coalface would tell you the same thing. Luke Nolen liked to think the slow ones could run down a major arterial like Dandenong Road in peak-hour traffic and not get hit. The talented ones would get hurt on a lazy summer's afternoon alone in a paddock.

Peter Moody tortured himself during Black Caviar's enforced lay-off. He brought her to the family property, Carbrecel Park, and allowed her to recuperate in the paddock nearest the house.

Once vets established the extent of Black Caviar's muscle damage, Moody turned to long-time confidant and chiropractor Michael Bryant. Affectionately known by the staff as the 'muscle man', he prescribed a lengthy break. The muscle had to be given time to knit and heal. The complication with Black Caviar was her bulk. If they tried anything too soon, she might suffer an immediate relapse or, worse still, tear the same muscle in a different place. To assist with muscle repair, an egg went into her feed twice a day.

Numerous times, day and night, Moody would stray to the back door and stand vigil. Staring and longing. Wishing and hoping. 'Here was what I thought to be the best horse I'd ever worked with standing in the paddock eating grass instead of galloping in front of the crowds earning money. It was unbelievably frustrating.'

He would inhale deeply on a cigarette and attempt what he imagined was a state of Zen. He would convince himself that this period would teach him patience. He would see the benefits of this purgatory when Black Caviar grew to full size with bones like reinforced steel. Previously he had not been patient enough. Bone chips and spurs were the price of his eagerness to race his stock. He would accept this as his mandatory sentence. When the time came for Black Caviar to return to the track, he would inherit the earth.

Moody recalled an old Queensland saying that the cheapest vets were Dr Green and Dr Time. Grass and plenty of time off. When he had satisfied himself and the experts he trusted that time enough had passed, the trainer knew he would have to be clever. He needed a path other than exposing Black Caviar to the strain of the preparatory galloping program at Caulfield. He needed non-conventional therapy for her. There was a method he had helped pioneer and someone he had learnt to trust.

It was back to the Goulburn Valley for Black Caviar, not far from her place of birth. She was taken to Murchison and admitted into the care of former trainer Peter Clarke. Like any good advocate for alternative remedies, Clarke might have been regarded as mildly eccentric. When he had trained his own gallopers he did so at the beach, working his horses into the current to build and hone muscle. His brainchild was to create his own beach, in conditions he could control and manipulate. That concept became his water walker, the centrepiece of the equine equivalent of a country spa.

Willowood Equicentre boasted the capacity to bring a horse to the brink of peak racing fitness without having to put a saddle on its back. It was not only perfect for the unsound horse, but often the only way to get them back to the races. That was only the physical aspect. Clarke believed in an holistic approach. So much rested on a horse's mental state. His sanctuary included thirty beautifully manicured paddocks for a horse to 'keep free and be happy'.

Black Caviar came to be known as 'the Princess' on this property. At first, though, Clarke thought her to be more of a madam: 'Had a mind of her own. The Bel Esprits are renowned for this; it's the reason why a lot of them actually don't become good horses, because they don't turn the corner. But she's responded very well to the therapy of good kindness and firmness.' While he harboured a reservation or two, Clarke had never seen a physical specimen like her. 'The first day I met this horse and I put my hands on her, you can just feel the power. I'm not joking. You can feel the power. She was so strong, so strong and she's very, very strong-willed.'

Her daily program began with a feed. Then into the water walker for thirty minutes pacing against the current, in a three-kilometre workout. It was back to the paddock for a lunchtime massage. The afternoon concluded with another three kilometres on the treadmill, walking up an incline.

Like Moody, Clarke kept Black Caviar in the paddock he could see from the veranda. She was not, however, the sole occupant. Andy was the twenty-seven-year-old pony who had been the companion of many a good thoroughbred. And there was a young goat, which, of course, was named Billy. An old trainer's tale states goats keep disease out and that was enough of a premise for Billy to be granted permanent residency. When the trio first came together there was duelling. After a stirring battle of wills in this horse, goat and pony show, Black Caviar had her way. Clarke passively observed it unfold. 'It's all the balance of nature.'

Through trial and error, Moody and Clarke had tightened the regime to deliver racetrack winners. The understanding had become so firm that Moody barely worried about instructions and Clarke sent only cursory text messages of reassurance. Moody knew the benefits and had the results as testimony. 'To get the best out of a horse, it needs to be pain free. If you told someone twenty years ago you were going to train a horse on a walking machine full of water, they would have looked at you like you had three heads. Peter is the grandfather of that and it has been revolutionary. I find it a massive aid for injured horses, and older horses who have been out of form, and after time at Murchison, suddenly recapture it all.'

Black Caviar flourished and was delivered back to Caulfield without a hint of the previous discomfort. She had returned stronger, if that was possible, nearing 570 kilograms. She thrived on the work and Moody just needed one gallop to assure himself she was ready. That transpired, much to his satisfaction, on a Monday morning on the steeple grass. He was set to reap the rewards for his patience.

The 2010 Festival of Racing, the recast Autumn Carnival that never quite reached the season that bore its name, would be Black Caviar's showcase. The trainer had two choices for her stepping-off point. He could send her straight to the Lightning Stakes at Flemington and win her inaugural Group 1 race, a prize he was surely entitled to. Or he could continue to play the long game, preparing for a future payoff. The latter option was the Australia Stakes under lights at Moonee Valley, the ideal pipe opener for the weight-for-age Group 1 William Reid Stakes, three weeks hence. Moody had waited this long; he would take the conservative route.

Twenty weeks after the dramas of Flemington, Black Caviar stood at the 1200-metre start at the Valley, a three-year-old filly squaring off for the first time against older horses. Among her four rivals was the highly talented but erratic Here de Angels. The Mark Kavanagh-trained gelding was the testing material. On

Boxing Day he had romped away with the Christmas Stakes. Later in the preparation he would be beaten by a nose in the Oakleigh Plate by Starspangledbanner. He was fast and liked to lead. He was also notoriously cranky. When not on his game, he could miss the start hopelessly or hamper other runners. Moody thought him a good, tough old handicapper. On any day this would be a test. Punters agreed. When betting agencies first posted markets, Here de Angels was crunched. At barrier fly he had been backed from $5 into $2.90. The note of caution surrounding Black Caviar had her drift from an unrealistic $1.30 to $1.70.

They had drawn side by side which, on this occasion, was not worthy of note. The pair jumped in virtual unison and tested each other's motors along the back straight. Having got a taste of what Here de Angels had, Nolen took partial hold of Black Caviar and allowed the older galloper the lead. She sat comfortably at his girth. Both Michael Rodd, aboard Here de Angels, and Nolen kept the tempo steady. No sense carving each other up and presenting the race, through sheer negligence, to a swooper. In the artificial light, Black Caviar rolled into her work coming to the bend. Just as she had rehearsed previously, she sprinted into the corner and rocketed out of it. Like those before him, Here de Angels had no reply. She left him standing two and a quarter lengths astern. It was a thrashing.

Moody was attuned to feeling relief in victory before any other emotion. In the winner's stall he breathed heavily. 'We thought she was going terrific but until you get them back on track you aren't a hundred per cent sure.'

Eight days on, the David Hayes-trained Nicconi bloused Wanted to claim the Lightning Stakes. Moody felt two shots of disappointment. His colt was desperately close to a big race win. Wanted was proving eerily similar to Magnus, the perennial bridesmaid in the major sprint races. The greater source of angst for Moody was that he knew for a stone cold fact Black Caviar would have won that race. Wanted was a game second stringer but he was lengths inferior to the mare. He had pulled the wrong rein. He did not dwell on it, though. Her turn was about to come.

Having always vowed the horse would be a good excuse to have lunch together, Gary Wilkie made the booking for sixty in a Moonee Valley dining room for William Reid Stakes Day. The race club printed the menus in salmon and black and revelled in the prospect of playing host to the filly's first win of absolute significance. Outfits were chosen and hats purchased as the owners primed themselves for graduation to Group 1 company. Races had long been divided into grades of which the sixty-four Group 1 races dotted throughout the season were the most coveted, as they measured excellence and assigned prestige and value. Trainers and jockeys made their reputations in such races and owners aspired to have a horse simply worthy of competing in them.

With a field of nine declared, including Nicconi and Wanted, Black Caviar had been installed, as always, as odds-on favourite despite drawing the outside barrier. In fact, she was considered a shoo-in. While there were battle-hardened horses with notionally better credentials, there was not a galloper in sight who could match the dynamism Black Caviar possessed. It was thought she would start the shortest price of any horse in Melbourne for the past thirty years.

While her comeback could not have gone better, Moody still felt a near permanent sense of anxiety with Black Caviar. Whenever she galloped with the throttle open, she held nothing back. Because of her size and shape, the work to offset a raging appetite was constant and demanding. Moody was only half joking when he observed: 'She eats nearly as well as her trainer.' At the peak of these gallops, Moody would involuntarily close his eyes. The glorious sight of a freak horse in full motion he found gut wrenching, for it brought forward the question: will she come back in one piece? 'Because she puts everything into it, you're terrified she's going to hurt herself every time she goes out to do something.'

Nolen had rounded off her preparation with a last serious gallop on the Tuesday before the William Reid. He relayed that she could not have been better placed for her biggest moment: 'Fantastic. She'd made really nice improvement off the back of that first-up run. We were bullish about her chances.' Thursday was a restrained gallop, nothing more. Moody never thought to close his eyes during something so sedate. Precisely where the damage was done would remain a mystery. Some time after cooling down from her work, Black Caviar was in pain. Moody was alerted and immediate scans ordered. The results were devastating. It was officially reported as an injury to a branch of the off-fore suspensory ligament. She had torn a little bit of bone, the size of a pinhead, from her ankle. That involved the rupture of ligaments and attachments at the back of her leg.

The injury hit Moody hard. 'That was probably one of the most heartbreaking moments of my life. Thinking I've got such a great horse with so much ability, undefeated. We're now second time on the sidelines with injury. Are we ever going to see this horse fulfil her true potential?'

For Nolen it came without warning. Moody's words were: 'We've lost that mare this morning. She's gone amiss.' It left the jockey numb. 'It was shattering because we thought we had a mortgage on the race. We were left to ponder this mare, whether she was going to crack it for a Group 1. It's like a Ferrari in the garage and it's done an axle so you can't drive it. It's this magnificent car that you can't go and have a spin in. She was a bit the same.'

Wrought though he was, Moody had to tell her owners who he knew were geared up for the main event. Pam Hawkes recalled:

'It must have been a dreadful phone call for Peter to make to tell us that Black Caviar had hurt her leg and that we were scratching. We were just devastated really that something had happened again.'

Against type, Moody in these moments had the sensitivity of a doctor. He was reassuring. He buried his own disappointment. This was not life-threatening nor would it shorten her career. In the scheme of ailments, this was minor. They would start the recuperation process afresh. There would be no jabbing or prodding. Black Caviar would spell until all physical trace of the injury had cleared. Then it would be back to Murchison. They would still have their day.

Nolen had come to admire Moody in adversity. 'He's always been very forthcoming with information to owners. Anything they need to hear, Pete has a wonderful way of explaining it in simple, layman's terms. Because of the way he handled things, it galvanised the owners and Pete. They went out for tea that week and they coped with it really well. Everyone knew what we had, we just had to wait for it a bit longer.'

The news broke publicly as a sensation. Early reports suggested Black Caviar was out for twelve months. Moody calmed the raging speculation. He would get her back for the spring.

Gary Wilkie suggested his friends find solace in each other's company at the races. They kept their lunch booking at Moonee Valley. The relaxed air that came with being spectators rather than participants eased the bitter disappointment. They watched Turffontein for Anthony Cummings cause a boil-over, nutting the increasingly luckless Wanted in the William Reid. It was a fate Moody did not deserve. He would have felt the world was conspiring against him.

When it was done, Moody took Black Caviar home. Nolen told the story with the cheeky tone associated with a tale that ended well: 'I think she spelled about twenty metres from Peter's bedroom window. He always kept a very close eye on her up at his mansion there on Millionaire's Hill at Belgrave South.'

Moody resumed his vigil, his private malaise deepened by regret. Could he get her back to win the Group 1 he had just passed up?

Newspix / Darren Mcnamara

Black Caviar returns a winner in the 2010 Schillaci Stakes at Caulfield.

8

Inherit the Earth

Caulfield, Schillaci Stakes, 9 October 2010
Moonee Valley, Schweppes Stakes, 23 October 2010

To look at Black Caviar was to know she was fast. Less obvious was the notion she was fragile. When the now four-year-old mare returned home to Caulfield to begin the campaign that would make or break her career, the overwhelming conclusion was that Black Caviar had grown into her body. No longer a hulking torso on spindly legs, she had filled out into a powerful, co-ordinated, fluent racehorse. Potential is the great tease of sport. Peter Moody was set to convert that commodity into something tangible.

The vibe around Black Caviar had been created off Broadway. She had commenced under the veil of the national football codes and the second dip coincided with the run to finals action. The lone venture in January was masked by the Australian Open tennis. Racing folk well knew what the possibilities might be, but sports fans generally were a virgin audience. An audience that turned to matters of the turf in spring.

Horse racing had lost the prominence it had held on the Australian sporting landscape half a century before. A time when

VFL broadcasts and the like would be interrupted to carry the calls of each race from the metropolitan meeting of the day. And when racing news routinely carried the back page of *The Sun News Pictorial* in addition to numerous specialist publications in mainstream demand.

Against that decline, carnival time in Melbourne has never been more popular. It is a designated party marked on the calendar by people who, for the remainder of the year, would not glance at a form guide. Carnival days are about dresses, shoes and hats; hospitality and fashion parades; marquees and dining rooms. The horses can seem incidental. Some attendees made it a popular boast to have not seen a horse all day despite their proximity to the track. The racing industry has come to stake its reputation and livelihood on these days. Whether that serves the actual sport well is a matter of debate.

Do great horses draw crowds? Or is it the Hollywood heiress, actor and reality TV star? As they depart, shoes slung over their shoulder, do they give a fig about racing? Would they come again when the Birdcage is not open and pass the afternoon having a bet with friends? Did the drunks who fought on the train platform discourage racing's true believers from even attending when the sport is at its finest? Crowds did not fluctuate on the quality of the fields, more likely on the weather and whim of the social set.

Still, the Melbourne Spring Carnival was the window through which racing could shine and the season of 2010 was brimming with possibilities.

Bart Cummings' last great champion, So You Think, had established himself as the best horse in the country. He was on a mission to defend his Cox Plate and then attempt an assault on the Melbourne Cup as his master sought a thirteenth trophy. It was the story that spoke all languages.

Gai Waterhouse added colour to the traditional starch of racing. Her army was headed by More Joyous. The three-year-old had proven herself the dominant filly in Sydney and had graduated to open company in the new season. More Joyous carried a seven-race winning streak south to the Carnival and looked the logical challenger to So You Think.

Much excitement surrounded the new star in the sprinting ranks, Hay List. In the calendar year of 2009, the Statue of Liberty gelding had won his first eight starts in Perth, switching between Ascot and Belmont Park. His first defeat came at his initial attempt in a Group race. The West Australian owners wanted him tested on the eastern seaboard, so he was relocated into the care of Gosford trainer John McNair. After a taste of Sydney racing in June, he bolted in at Eagle Farm against a handy field and was set for the early pickings in Melbourne.

On debut at Moonee Valley, Hay List eased away from the capable Catapulted and Moody's Blue Diamond winner Reward for Effort to win the Group 3 McEwen Stakes. He followed that by unveiling the full artillery, emphatically leading all the way to win the opening Group 1 of the season, the Manikato Stakes. He was a specimen to behold, weighing more than 600 kilograms. McNair gave the tale of the tape: 'He's got the size, he's got the strength, he's got the attitude. He's got a massive cruising speed and an incredibly instant turn of foot. All of those things, you put them together, it's almost the complete racehorse.'

An ABC News report measured opinion surrounding him with the line: 'Those in the know say Hay List could be the best sprinter in the world.'

The AFL's drawn Grand Final between Collingwood and St Kilda had forced the replay on to NRL Grand Final weekend, so football monopolised the headlines for a week longer than scheduled. Flemington's Cup Carnival Preview Day was shunted to Sunday, with popular warhorse Zipping knocking out Melbourne Cup winner Shocking in the feature Turnbull Stakes. Hay List had what was regarded as a tune-up gallop on that program, softly winning down the straight, furthering his credentials as a spring dynamo. As he was doing so, tens of thousands of Collingwood supporters celebrated the end of a twenty-year premiership drought, and racing had to bide its time for the limelight until Caulfield.

Putting his usual caution aside, Moody had felt no need to be anything other than optimistic with Black Caviar. She had the fitness grounding from the water walker and relished her reintegration into stable life. Moody's prudence was evident in the scarcity of fast work he ordered for her. When she had returned to his care, Black Caviar was nudging 580 kilograms, well above her ideal racing weight. Moody had done his sums weeks in advance. She would not be ready to race any earlier than the beginning of October, Caulfield Guineas Day.

It was the Cranbourne trials that would again serve as Moody's key gauge. Labelled the 'glamour mare' in the press, Black Caviar commanded full attention in the first heat of the morning. Despite the heavy track, she cruised around seemingly in second gear, dominating the fourteen-horse trial. She had almost a length to spare on the line over city galloper Emjay Hussey. Moody called it a canter. She handled the gallop well within herself and that was Moody's one note of surprise. It was only the second serious piece of work he had exposed her to. He thought Black Caviar would be blowing with the exertion. She was not. So far so good.

The exercise was repeated a couple of weeks later, if less officially, at Caulfield, and Moody put his plans into action. She was still big, but only racing would now get her fitter. Black Caviar would resume in the Group 2 Schillaci Stakes. Her return was classified as 'much anticipated', with punters curious to see if she could emerge as a worthy challenger to Hay List.

It felt like day one over again, complete with all the insecurities and nagging doubts. If they could get through this first run swift and sound, they could pick up the thread of an interrupted journey. If things went awry, the promise of a prosperous day would be empty.

Arriving at Caulfield, Jannene Madden and Pam Hawkes compared notes on a night's broken sleep. They were grateful to have the race scheduled early so they would soon know one way or the other. Hawkes recalled: 'I don't think I ate or drank anything after we arrived at the track. All I was interested in was the race and to make sure that she was well again and that she was ready to run.'

In the eight-horse field was the fading Mic Mac, who once would have seemed ideally suited. By the same sire as Hay List, Mic Mac had started in a blaze of glory, with five victories, his career peaking with a Group 2 win over Whobegotyou at Caulfield, the spring before. His lustre had faded. Lee Freedman's First Command was coming off a brave Open Handicap win with top weight at the same track a fortnight earlier. Of great interest was Blue Diamond winner Star Witness, who had a hint of the miraculous about him when he had come from the clouds to capture that two-year-old prize. Black Caviar was sent out $1.80 favourite, but there were not hordes of punters prepared to take the leap of faith required of the cramped price.

Luke Nolen had kept close tabs on Black Caviar from the moment he had heard she was back from Murchison. He could sense the anticipation around the stable and knew Moody was happy with the suspect leg. 'Everything seemed to be heading in the right direction for once.' As Black Caviar sprang from the barriers for the 1000 metres of the Schillaci Stakes, that optimism was to be put to the test.

The pace came from out deep on the track in the form of Winter King and Mic Mac. Black Caviar slid through on the rails from her inside draw to ensure she did not get crossed and boxed in. It was a race full of pace as Tully Dreamer flashed forward well off the track down the railway side. There was pressure upon pressure rushing to the corner. As it seemed certain Tully Dreamer would turn in front, Nolen gave Black Caviar a squeeze to keep her in the race. He was taken aback by the response: 'She went whoosh.' It was captured in the race call:

> Into the straight Black Caviar left them standing
> She opened up a two or three length break on Winter King
> Mic Mac, First Command, General Truce and Star Witness
> But Black Caviar, she has scorched clear
> And does it in a walk-up start
> That was the run of an out-and-out superstar

Her performance was astonishing. Particularly as Nolen shut her right down over the concluding stages and she was still only seven-tenths of a second outside the track record. The jockey noted: 'She wasn't here to have a gut-buster. We were here to win and get through the run safely. She feels a bit bigger and fatter than last time. I think she'll take a lot of benefit out of that. I just hope I wasn't too kind on her late.'

In the stands, Black Caviar's owners hardly saw that last fifty metres. They were too busy jumping up and down and hugging each other. Hawkes barely contained her emotions. 'Once that was over the relief, it was like after your child's born I think, the relief of knowing that everything was okay and she was back where she had left off. It had been such a long time. You like to think that what they say is right but to actually see her run down that straight and with such strength out in front, it was marvellous.'

At the presentation, Neil Werrett noted it was nine months to the day since she had broken down. Those gathered behind him realised they had felt every day of it. The anguish was at last behind them as they retreated to a marquee to enjoy the remainder of the afternoon.

Black Caviar's win began one of the finest sequence of races a Melbourne Spring Carnival had witnessed. Forty minutes later, So You Think gleamed like an oil painting in the bright sunshine and mocked his opposition to lead all the way in the Yalumba Stakes.

Just as the Cox Plate was being declared a formality, More Joyous broke the weight-carrying record for a mare in the time-honoured Toorak Handicap. Under 58 kilograms, she burst from the ruck to debunk history. So You Think would still have to beat More Joyous at Moonee Valley.

Then Moody and Nolen stamped Caulfield as their own. Nolen rode a perfectly judged race aboard Anacheeva from the inside gate in the feature Caulfield Guineas. He tucked in directly behind the leader, eased off the rail in the straight and went around only that lead horse, Run For Levi, to salute. Moody had enacted a faultless campaign with surprisingly little fanfare. The colt had won at 1200, 1400 and now the 1600 metres of the Guineas. Anacheeva was rightly acclaimed the best three-year-old colt in the land to that time.

To cap the day, Moody and Nolen produced the game mare Avenue to win the program closer. A treble on the opening day of the Spring. Well they should have celebrated.

The Black Caviar crew was too exhausted to hit the town. They had enjoyed the spoils of the afternoon but the build-up had taken its toll. For Pam Hawkes, that might have been just as well. 'We'd had a big group celebrating during the day. I remember I was breath-tested because I had to drive the little van home. I showed the policeman the cup we'd been presented and I think he thought, "I've got a live one here. She'll be over the limit." But I hadn't had a drink; I seriously hadn't had a drink all day. It was just relief.'

Moody and Nolen dominated the sports pages of the Sunday papers. The Guineas win demonstrated beautifully their rise to dominance in Victorian racing. Moody's armoury of gallopers ran deep as he attacked the carnival. Nolen was the jockey who did not make mistakes. He was not noted for producing miracle rides because he played the percentages. In his best moments he made perfection seem boring.

The pair never spoke the morning after a feature race day. There was no need. The work had been done. But Nolen could not help himself. It was not to bask in the satisfaction or fish for a compliment. It was a health check. On Black Caviar. 'When she got through that first run it was the only time I think I've ever rung Pete to see how everyone's pulled up. I just wanted to make sure she had four legs and none of them were swelled up and they were all cool and everything was under control. Yeah, she'd stayed in one piece. It was great to get that chance to go more than two runs deep into her preparation and get to show the Victorian racing public just how good this mare was.'

Anticipation was immediately set to Black Caviar's first clash with powerhouse Hay List. Moody was a promoter's dream. 'He's an outstanding horse but I've never been one to run and hide so it's going to happen.' They were slated to meet twice, first at the Cox Plate meeting then in the main event, the Group 1 Patinack Farm Classic on Final Day at Flemington. The initial date, though, was scuppered when Hay List came down with an elevated temperature and did not accept for the Schweppes Stakes.

Black Caviar would face a worthy test regardless. Hot Danish was the darling of Sydney racing. A wonderfully honest mare who had cracked her Group 1 maiden in the All Aged Stakes at the conclusion of the Autumn carnival at Randwick. She had reversed the placings on Melito from the T.J. Smith Stakes a fortnight prior. Both Hot Danish and Melito brought the best of the Sydney sprinting form to Moonee Valley.

In the mounting yard tucked behind the grandstands, Nolen shared with Moody a theory he had been developing. 'I think the faster she goes, the better she feels.' The trainer liked the sound of that. As he legged the jockey aboard he added: 'I just keep getting scared something's going to fly off.'

Black Caviar was not as spritely away this time. The salmon and black was visibly out of formation in the line of silks. She needed to muster with Hot Danish, who had drawn the inside, and True Persuasion, who was condemned to burn petrol to find the lead from out wide. Having made True Persuasion work to cross down to the rail, Black Caviar rather cruelly marched up on his outside coming to the school. Melito was on her back, having put Hot Danish in a pocket on the fence. The fluster shown by the jockeys of those two mares gave the game away. Black Caviar was cranking to a pace they had no chance of matching.

> Black Caviar at the 300 on the bend went up and went straight past True Persuasion
> She put two lengths on him in a stride
> Black Caviar turns well clear of True Persuasion
> Hot Danish, Melito and Stanzout
> But this is a galloping exhibition
> Inside the hundred, Black Caviar opens right up
> And the streak goes on

The amped-up Cox Plate crowd had expected Black Caviar to win. The $1.40 starting price evidenced that. But the five-and-a-half-length margin was pure exhilaration. To beat top-class horses in such a contemptuous manner spoke of the rarest quality. The educated crowd on such a pure day's racing recognised the brilliance before it. Moody turned from his vantage point on the fence and said to no one in particular and everyone at once: 'She's pretty special, isn't she?'

Les Bridge had seen plenty in his training days. He had won a Melbourne Cup and a Golden Slipper to prove he knew his way around. He felt as fondly of Hot Danish as any horse he had strapped the saddle on. But he was dumbfounded by what he had witnessed. He had the blank expression of a disaster victim. 'I don't know what to make of it. It was all over too quickly.' While the rationale eluded him, the conclusion did not. 'No use chasing a horse like that around.'

Trainer Gerald Ryan watched as Melito made no impression. 'I don't think there would have been a sprinter in the world beat Black Caviar. She was awesome.'

Nolen was effusive in his praise: 'She is just head and shoulders above anything I've ridden. She just did that so easily.'

Moody was ready to issue the highest of all compliments: 'The only guide I've got is General Nediym, he's the only great sprinter I've worked with. And she's better than him. It's just scintillating what she does.' At the presentation, Moody had worked his pre-race banter with Nolen to a post-race conclusion: 'She scares the hell out of me.'

While Black Caviar's status was building, she was still the undercard to the championship race of the Australian turf. At his tenth career start, So You Think was out to claim his second Cox Plate. The previous year, as a three-year-old, he had been a surprise victor, testimony to the wizardry of his trainer. Now he was the bona fide champ. More Joyous had her admirers. As did sluggers like Zipping, Whobegotyou and Shoot Out.

So You Think never gave them a chance. He bounded from the gates and took the soft run outside More Joyous who was forced to lead. Down the side of the track heading for the home corner, the doomsday scenario unfolded for Gai's mare. She was staring eyeball to eyeball with an equine predator. Full throttle, So You Think dropped her and strode off into history. Bart's health left him frail as he lifted the Cox Plate and cast his eye towards the Melbourne Cup. By the time his horse ran a week later, he would be watching from a hospital bed.

They were the story. Black Caviar would dutifully wait her turn.

Bronwen Healy Photography

The tools of the trade. Luke Nolen's skull cap, goggles and saddle laid aside in victory.

Newspix / Darren Tindale

Ben Melham's polite victory salute in the 2010 Patinack Farm Classic.

9

The Fastest Horse in the World

Flemington, Patinack Farm Classic, 6 November 2010

It had not always been the case, but finally Black Caviar's timing was perfect. By the time she sauntered into the Flemington mounting yard near the conclusion of a gruelling week, racing needed another hero.

The Melbourne Cup Carnival is a test of stamina at the best of times. Four days comprising thirty-seven races complete with unusually early starts. The mass of humanity, the crawling traffic and the gallons of alcohol makes demands of participant and spectator alike. Commencing with Derby Day, the weather forecast for 2010 was threatening. But not nearly as mean as the black clouds that amassed at lunchtime.

Back in March, the Victoria Racing Club's Super Saturday had abruptly halted under one of the most ferocious hailstorms Melbourne had ever seen. It struck in the immediate aftermath of the Newmarket Handicap, the first of three scheduled Group 1 races. It cut power to the course and left it blanketed with ice.

Trains were halted and cars left dimpled like golf balls by the storm. It ended the meeting on the spot. Eight months on, the scene at Flemington turned murky and nasty as Star Witness won the opening Group 1, the Coolmore Stud Stakes. If you were superstitious, you might have felt as though the gods were frowning upon the decadence of drinking and punting.

So You Think had a greater battle with the elements than he did with his rivals. He dominated the Mackinnon Stakes as rain spat in his face and mud flicked from his powerful hooves. His trademark mane was matted but his ability shone through. Bart Cummings was in hospital with pneumonia. Given what those present at Flemington were subjected to, it might have been a blessing he was not there.

By the time the Derby field galloped to the far reaches of the course, they were ghosts in the mist. Visibility was gone. Patience was being severely tested. Lion Hunter streeted his rivals in the classic. It was the sort of result you get when one horse proves a mudlark against a bunch of paddlers.

On the lawn in front of the Hill Stand, punters had laid out a tarpaulin and they queued for runs down the makeshift slip and slide. In their suits. A few women could not resist either. Racing's day of days had degenerated long before it concluded.

The 150th running of the Melbourne Cup was one for the ages. The yearning for So You Think to win was akin to the craving for Damien Oliver aboard Media Puzzle in the immediate aftermath of his brother's death. And the collective wish for the completion of Makybe Diva's hat trick in 2005. Bart made it to the track. He seemed a little smaller now. His grand horse swept to the front in the straight but, as the hope was given full voice, the French bull Americain stormed through and the Cup was his.

In a bitter postscript, So You Think was sold from under Bart's nose to the Irish stud Coolmore for tens of millions of dollars. The trainer swore angrily at the betrayal. The Australian public lost its idol within days of truly discovering him. A dozen dazzling runs and he was gone.

The void had opened for Black Caviar.

The sprinting duel of the spring was on. What had started as a search for a challenger to Hay List had flipped. The proposition now was whether Hay List could make any sort of impression on the untouchable mare. When the futures market opened in October on the Patinack Classic, Hay List had been a $1.50 favourite with Black Caviar, unsighted for nine months, quoted at $5. The world had turned.

Hay List had recovered from the temperature that kept him away from Moonee Valley but was becoming either eerily unlucky or downright jinxed. As proof that horses will do the darnedest things, the five-year-old had jumped into his water trough in a paddock accident the Thursday prior to Cup week. He had peeled back the skin on his shinbone and was taken to Werribee Vet Clinic where stitches were inserted into the wound. Trainer John McNair was left to wait and hope for an adequate recovery. Hay List would need to convince Racing Victoria vets he was capable of running. McNair had the greater task of assessing whether he was capable of winning.

Moody was not one to find comfort in other trainer's misfortune. He was on edge. The seven-race streak was lovely but the only thing that mattered was finally winning this Group 1 race. He had allowed that quest to become an albatross by not getting it done sooner. He felt that burden and that pressure. He wanted a smooth run to get Black Caviar to the barriers and then she could take care of her own fate. He did not get it.

On Derby Day, Luke Nolen aboard Moody's filly Curtana had caused interference as they unsuccessfully strived to hold off Star Witness in the Coolmore. The jockey knew enough to understand he was staring at a suspension. Events move quickly in Cup week as the circumstances demand speedy solutions. As Nolen walked to the Stewards' Room after the last race to learn his fate, a three-meeting suspension would render him banned from riding Black Caviar. He guessed that with a guilty plea, he was looking at five or six meetings on the sidelines.

In the ten steps across the carpet from the Jockeys' Room to judgment, he was intercepted by John Hawkes. The Hall of Fame trainer had dramatically added to the complexion of Tuesday's Melbourne Cup when Maluckyday had rocketed into calculations with a brilliant win in that morning's Lexus Stakes. The lightly raced son of Zabeel appeared the ideal featherweight wildcard. Furthering the mystique, Maluckyday was owned by Nick Moraitis and carried the colours of Might and Power, the 1997 Cup winner. Comparisons were sought and duly flowed as Might and Power's regular jockey Jim Cassidy had steered Maluckyday into Tuesday's field. Cassidy, however, was already committed to Gai Waterhouse's mare Once Were Wild. The prize ride was vacant. Hawkes wanted Nolen to fill it.

The automatic answer was yes. A jockey spends his career seeking live chances in a Melbourne Cup, opportunities that he might one day convert into the greatest win of all. But that was not what Nolen was thinking about. He said yes all right, and felt he had lucked into a stack of chips to play before the judiciary.

'I'm not noted as a very good talker in the Stewards' Room by any stretch but I thought I'd bamboozle them with legal jargon. I tried to barter my ride in the Melbourne Cup. I would forgo Maluckyday, a genuinely good ride, to be able to ride Black Caviar. I thought I put a remarkable case myself. But they weren't thinking laterally like I was.'

Nolen walked out with a nine-meeting suspension. He would ride Maluckyday to finish second in the Cup, but he had to tell Moody he did not have a jockey for their most important day so far.

Moody was a trainer who stayed with what he knew. If he trusted you on a small job he would give you a big one without flinching. Ben Melham had a hunch this would be the case. He had been riding for Moody since he was an apprentice, both at trackwork and in races. His reputation at twenty-two was that of an underrated jockey. He did not have a Group 1 win to his credit to overturn such a perception. Just to be sure Moody knew he was up to the task, Melham made a point of telling him he was available. And he was able.

Moody did not hesitate: 'I try to afford them loyalty and I think I get it back in spades. The opportunity has been there to use bigger name jockeys or out-there jockeys who could promote the stable, but it's repaid me tenfold being loyal to my own.' Melham had the booking. His heart leapt and his brain cautioned: 'Do not be the jockey to get Black Caviar beaten.'

The sun smiled on Flemington for Emirates Stakes Day for the only time that week. For the bedraggled army of workers and spectators, it was a blessed relief. Hay List got to the track, but in what sort of shape was still to be revealed. Moody barely made it. He was suffering with a heavy cold and blamed the atrocities of the Derby Day weather. On a lesser occasion, he would have been an absentee.

Black Caviar's six rivals were either all Group 1 winners to that time or would subsequently become so. It was a small but select gathering. She ran $1.90, with Hay List out to $3.50 and Star Witness a $7 chance.

As the moment of reckoning approached, Melham stood Black Caviar steady in the gates. He felt his career flash before his eyes. The pressure of the build-up had been intense, as was the reality that this was his one chance with this remarkable horse and his best hope to claim a top-level win. He pushed any negative thoughts aside, safe in the knowledge of the horse beneath him. To acquaint himself with her, he had ridden her at trackwork a couple of days before. That was enough to know. She would carry him as long he as did not make any mistakes.

Black Caviar led from the outset as if she were determined not to provide a single moment of doubt. She galloped freely near the outer grandstand rail. Some way inside of her, Eagle Falls kept up for nearly half the race. Hay List settled between them and clicked off the first 600 metres within reach. Star Witness swung off Black Caviar's tail. It was at that point that the promotion demanded the battle commence. Hay List moved up as Eagle Falls dropped away. No sooner had the bell been rung than the knockout blow was struck.

He's got a really good hold on Black Caviar
And Schofield is now at work on Hay List
Star Witness presents
He hasn't released the brakes yet on Black Caviar
She's cruising at the 250
He's riding the ears off Star Witness
Forget about Hay List
Black Caviar down at the clock tower
She's out by three
She's a Group 1 winning mare now
She's the fastest in the world
Black Caviar by four lengths

It was done with such a smooth move. Black Caviar reached her top cruising speed and Hay List folded. He was not fit and healthy after all. Not for such a searing test in the fires of Flemington. James Winks had ridden Star Witness cleverly. When he eased off Black Caviar's heels he had enjoyed the cheap run in the slipstream. But as he launched the chase, the lure was suddenly gone, dangled too far in the distance. Melham moved only slightly and Black Caviar had taken her cue. For as long as she had waited to prove herself a Group 1 horse, the last 100 metres looked like a victory lap. She burnt her rivals off going three-quarter pace.

Even though he could barely croak with his failing voice, Moody was ecstatic. He spoke of the hairs on the back of his neck standing erect: 'Winning that first Group 1 was a big weight off my shoulders. I erred in the autumn of that year by not running her in the Lightning. Hindsight tells us she would have won it and won it quite comfortably. I would've kicked myself forever if she hadn't won a Group 1. If something had happened and she had gone amiss. That was a big relief.'

Trainer Lee Freedman was steeped in the history of racing and knew precisely what he had just witnessed: 'I saw Vain in the late 1960s and he was awesome. She is as good as I've seen anywhere in the world. Simply sensational.'

The people associated with Black Caviar would each come to have their favourite chapter. For Jill Taylor she had hers. That bloody horse had just shown her how good racing could be. 'I remember speaking to the others come Wednesday or Thursday of the following week. We still hadn't come down from that height. It was just amazing, absolutely amazing. That's when it really hit home.'

At home it hit Nolen hard. He watched from the couch and felt the inner conflict. He felt the joy for Black Caviar and Moody. He was full of admiration for Melham and how he had handled the task. 'But it's hard to watch any horse win that you've been riding, especially when you're fit and well. It was really disappointing.'

Moody had instructed Melham that there were to be no overt celebrations until he got back to scale and dismounted. Such was the trainer's paranoia for Black Caviar's physical wellbeing, he forbade any action that might unbalance her. Melham was obedient to a fault, politely raising his left hand as they passed the post in the most subdued victory salute imaginable. He had his prize. He did not need histrionics to accompany it. Certainly, Black Caviar had not indulged in extravagances. Melham felt in complete control. He also knew he had never got anywhere near the bottom of what she was capable of.

'It's an incredible feeling. The roar of the crowd was sensational. It was the greatest high that I've experienced and probably will ever experience. Obviously I was a little bit nervous; I hadn't ridden a Group 1 winner. She was a very short price favourite and a lot of people came to watch her win her first Group 1. It was a bit of pressure but I felt as though I handled it okay. It's easy to handle when you're riding a superstar like that.'

Black Caviar seemed to inspire Melham with the boldness to achieve. He missed doubling his Group 1 tally in the very next race, when his mount Chasm was beaten in a three-way photo in the Emirates Stakes. The race after, he won the feature mares event. His brush with Black Caviar became the day he would never forget.

When the hubbub settled and the search for meaning began, people wondered about winning streaks in racing. Specifically, about horses that had never met with defeat. Black Caviar had just reached eight wins. The comparable Australian record was nine. One of the joint holders of that mark was the remarkable Grand Flaneur. In his three-year-old season the colt had won the 1880 AJC and Victoria Derbies and the Melbourne Cup. After three more wins in 1881, he was retired to stud unbeaten. In recent assessments of the merit of each Melbourne Cup winner, Grand Flaneur was the enigma. His body of work not quite enough to measure against Carbine and Phar Lap, yet his place in history undeniable.

World racing was undertaking the same examinations. On the Saturday that Black Caviar moved into the Australian turf's royal family, the United States was braced for a coronation. Moody was up early on Sunday morning to watch the final chapter of an incredible story.

Sports Illustrated avowed that if Zenyatta could win America's richest race, the Breeders' Cup Classic, for a second time, finalising her career at twenty wins from twenty starts, she would cement her legacy as the greatest female thoroughbred ever. *60 Minutes* recounted that she would be the first American athlete to retire unbeaten since boxer Rocky Marciano bowed out of the ring more than half a century earlier.

All of America was invested in the quest for perfection Zenyatta was undertaking. The six-year-old mare, housed in Hollywood, had restored US racing to a grandeur lost decades before. She was a filly who had been given time to grow and mature, before being exposed to the rigours of racing. She was a powerful animal, standing taller than her male rivals. And Zenyatta was a creature of theatre. She would dance and prance in the mounting yard, a goose step that became her trademark, the stuff of folklore.

For all that, it was her deeds on the track that had captured the imagination. Zenyatta would sit last in her races and face the prospect of circling the entire field to win, a task she had successfully completed on nineteen occasions. She had stood rivals improbable, and near-impossible starts, but she had always wound them in. Trainer John Shirreffs had been left to fatefully wonder: 'I just don't know how far somebody would have to be in front for her not to catch them. I just don't know.'

Perfect careers are to be treasured. The life-size statue of Hungarian racehorse Kincsem stood in Budapest as testament to that. In a career beginning in 1876, she won fifty-four races and became a national icon en route to retiring unbeaten. Kincsem's major wins included the Hungarian Oaks and Austrian Derby. She travelled to England to win the Goodwood Cup. Those events were so difficult to fathom and so long in the past as to be set aside as a record that could never be challenged.

In modern times, the mark for the perfect career stood at nineteen. Peppers Pride was a filly that raced only in her birth state of New Mexico, always against New Mexico-bred horses. She won twelve times at Stakes level and was hailed as the little New Mexico-bred filly that could. She was widely admired, but no one made a serious case for her to be considered among the greats.

Zenyatta was on the verge of precisely that. The viewer was schooled to expect to see her last. But after 200 metres of the Breeders' Cup Classic, it seemed there had been an awful mistake or horrible accident. She was so far from the second-last horse, it was impossible to believe this was in the script. In the back stretch Zenyatta began to pick up interest and ground. As they turned for home, whether you were at Churchill Downs or watching half a world away at Belgrave South, you were compelled to stand: Zenyatta was flying. That was such a wonderful description of a horse finishing so powerfully as to take your breath away. Kiwi was flying at the end of the 1983 Melbourne Cup, coming from last so late that he only entered the call in the final seconds. This was something else. Zenyatta might actually have been flying. As the post approached so she reached Blame. It would come to the last lunge. They would hit the line for a photo. A photo everyone knew she had been beaten in. Zenyatta had this time been too late. American hearts broke. This was Babe Ruth striking out in his last at bat. Only so much worse.

Marcus Armytage captured the moment for the British newspaper *The Telegraph*: 'In terms of endings it was less Disney, more disaster movie as, in one of the most dramatic races you will see, Zenyatta, at one stage tailed off and more than 20 lengths off the pace, failed by a head in her quest for perfection; 20 wins from 20 starts. Instead Blame took the Classic and Zenyatta's jockey,

Mike Smith, tearfully took the blame. In defeat Zenyatta lost nothing and yet everything.'

Moody took it all in. The parallel to his own universe was striking. From time to time he would talk of Zenyatta. It was difficult to tell whether he viewed it as a cautionary tale or the ultimate challenge. But it was planted in his mind. The magic number in modern world racing was twenty.

Newspix / Colleen Petch

The rhythm of stable life with strapper Donna Fisher.

10

Nelly

You know Fortune and Razor and Roje and Nicky. Oscar and Matty and Buck and Pussy. But can you recall the most famous racehorse of all? Nelly.

You would never have heard the name Black Caviar around the Caulfield stables of Moody Racing. In fact, if you were surreptitiously trying to gather information from Melbourne's leading yard to use against bookmakers for financial gain, you would have needed a decoding device. Dating from a time when trainers jealously protected information to launch their own punting largesse, it was a quaint racing tradition that every horse had a stable name. Like all good nicknames, some were obvious: Typhoon Tracy was Cyclone. Some would draw from character traits: you would find Slick, Smart and Shock. No one could quite recollect how Black Caviar came to be Nelly. The best Tony Haydon could offer was 'it suits her attitude'. Moody thought, 'She looks like a bit of a Nelly.' So Nelly it was.

Every stable searched endlessly for a headline act. Turnover was high. Judgments made summarily. Moody was particularly ruthless. He would not waste his time or the money of his owners on horses who could not fulfil the task of winning. They were out the back door. When the quest uncovered that most precious commodity, contrarily, it could not become a stable star. Moody would never allow that. It was not for fear of turning Nelly into a prima donna in the general population. Rather, each horse, regardless of status, had to fit into a system in which the numbers stretched to seventy or eighty on any given morning. To treat one as special was to risk neglecting not only the rest of the team but the owners, who in good faith paid the bills. Even more pressing, Moody reasoned the best horse did not need as much help to win a race as the worst horse in the barn. 'You've actually got to spend more time and effort on the horses with lesser ability to try and get them to win a race. Lee Freedman is one of our great trainers. He said the best thing about a good horse is it makes it easier for us trainers to hide our mistakes because they've got the ability to overcome it. There's no truer statement ever made.'

While Moody was clear that not one extra minute was to be spent on Nelly, there was a buzz whenever she was in residence. The whiteboard at the stable entrance would specify to insiders which horses were currently in session. When the first column noted Nelly, Haydon could sense the uplift in vibe around the place. He was a better judge on that front than any, as he lived at the stables. He knew it to be true because he felt it intensely himself. 'I've been doing this all my working life. Just to get to be with her basically every day when she's in work, it makes you get out of bed. It helps you enjoy your job a little bit more on those cold frosty mornings. You go out and you see her and you carry on. She's put a spring in my step. She's made me want to stay a lot longer.'

Trackwork on a metropolitan racetrack begins under a blanket of silence that can only exist before the rest of the world wakes up. Behind the gated community in the redbrick buildings, first light would spill from each box at 3.30 a.m. Nelly would stand in the corner of the number one cubicle with a rug fastened down the length of her neck and tucked under the heavy cover flanking her frame. She looked like a girl snuggled under the doona, clinging to the last moments of sleep before answering a wake-up call.

The initial sound would be the squeal of the stable's heavy metal gate and the clang of a rake mucking out the box and dumping the dirty straw and waste into the wheelie bin outside. Through the grate along the interior wall, a horse could see her neighbour, but it was too early for any form of exchange.

Nelly would soon be greeted by her strapper, Donna Fisher, the surest sign her day was underway. A senior member of the Moody Racing staff, Fisher returned from holidays about the same time as Black Caviar returned from that first injury. With Nelly's original strapper enrolling at university, Fisher was assigned to fill the vacancy.

For any groom, the task is to build a relationship with a horse: learn the animal's quirks and win its trust. The affection between human and beast is evidenced through the tenderness of touch and tone of voice. As part of that bond, the strapper must establish a level of authority. For each was bound to follow the instructions of the boss.

Nelly quickly learnt the sound of Donna's voice. Donna learnt to pat her on the neck or the cheeks but never on the front of her head. Do that and she would throw her head around and just as likely take a nip at you. 'She thinks that you're trying to hold her there and she just doesn't seem to cope with feeling trapped.' Nelly learnt the rhythms of stable life and threw herself into them wholeheartedly. But when the work was done, she liked to be left alone. No fussing or primping after a 4 p.m. curfew or you would risk a sour response. 'She's a typical female, she hates being annoyed.'

What Donna unlocked in Nelly was that she loved to walk. Endlessly, it seemed. She would not do it at any great pace or with any specific purpose. It was more a dawdle. Together they would set off on laps of Caulfield's sandy paths. They were a canny match. From behind, the strapper nestled neatly under Nelly's shoulder leaving the mare to tower over her, enhancing the appearance of her powerful hindquarters. 'She feels very tall next to me but I am actually quite short compared to a lot of people around here.'

They would trek through the cluster of stable complexes, along the seemingly endless fencing and past the pool. When Nelly would reach a cutting that opened up a view of the track itself, Monash University directly opposite and the hub of Caulfield railway station, she would stop. Nelly would plant her hooves, raise her neck to full extension and turn her head elegantly to the right. As the breeze tickled her mane, Nelly was entranced. At first Donna found the behaviour perplexing and a little irksome. Moody would never approve. Smack her on the arse and get her moving. But it had come to be her favourite part of the day. Donna wondered what Nelly would be contemplating: the lights of the university building before it filled with students, the echo of the public address informing commuters of the next train to depart. They would stay perfectly still for two or three minutes. Then, without fuss, Nelly would lower her head, tug the lead and off they would go.

'It's a very unusual thing for a horse to do. I've only known one other. Typhoon Tracy used to do exactly the same thing on the same area. Other than those two, I haven't seen any other horse do it every lap that they walk around. Some might stop every now and then, but her and Cyclone used to do it every lap. It's the only time Nelly will stand still when she's not in her box.'

The rest of their time together involved the necessities. Twice a day Donna would take Nelly for a swim. There would be a roll in the sand and the subsequent hose-down. Then the morning dressing: brushing her mane and tail, cleaning her hooves. There was an important distinction in how the grooming was conducted. The strapper was careful to treat the horse like an elite athlete rather than a supermodel.

The other constant presence for Nelly was track rider Patrick Bell. When the weight battle got the better of the New Zealand jockey, he came across the Tasman to ride in the dark rather than the glare of race day. Haydon brought Bell into the team because he was strong in style but quiet in nature. The perfect blend for mares, in particular. When he was enlisted to ride Black Caviar every morning, he too earned a nickname: the Golden Child.

Bell would call on Nelly before 4 a.m. and begin fitting her up with a towel, padding and the saddle. With the strappings set to the right tension, he would clean out the dirt caught around her shoes, leg up and leave the box. They were first out each morning; the melodious click on the concrete to the stable gate the only alert that work was about to commence.

It is hard to get an adequate answer from racing people as to why it is necessary to work horses at such an unnatural hour. But given this remains the convention, the rationale for Black Caviar being first off the rank was easier to grasp. The track was at its truest, without the markings and dents of the hundreds of workers that would soon take their turn. Also it was quieter, before the equine traffic and the human observers peaked.

Bell described Nelly as beautiful. 'She does everything you ask plus more. You walk her and she walks along happy on a long rein. You ask her to trot and she trots along happy. The hardest part is probably galloping her. She gets a little bit keen in her galloping because she's got all this speed and she just wants to use it.'

Together they used the guide of the white railing to navigate towards the floodlighting of the tunnel linking the stables to the infield. It was a stark contrast to the dark at the ends of the tunnel: cavernous curving concrete with strip fluorescent lights along the walls and square panels overhead. They would emerge under the trainers' tower, where the silhouette of Peter Moody could be distinguished by the red sniper's spot of his lit cigarette.

When Moody spoke of the hours of solitude in the profession, these were the stretches to which he referred. 'People see you in a race-day context, done up in a suit and tie and parading in front of the crowd with your horses, and I suppose to the outside world it can appear quite glamorous. But the early mornings, the cold and the wet and the damp that we get used to in Melbourne for half the year, it certainly takes the glamour off things I can assure you, at three and four and five o'clock in the morning. There's been plenty of ugly mornings we've been standing out here shivering and freezing. The layman probably doesn't realise how much behind-the-scenes work goes on. Not so much by me but by my staff. What they've got to go through and trudge through at half-past three in the morning. The menial tasks that are involved with catering for a five- or six-hundred kilo animal that doesn't have good toiletry habits and has to be maintained as a supreme athlete. That's what we're trying to develop here, so you know there's certainly a down and dirty side to the business.'

Moody's morning tools are his binoculars, stopwatch and a walkie-talkie to communicate with Haydon in the yard. On the desk is a cup of coffee. He calls the shots from the handwritten work sheet prepared the previous day. 'Two halves the lead. Three and one the sand.' A television mounted overhead shows yesterday's race replays. These hours are about the next winner rather than the previous one, so the TV is largely ignored, and serves mainly to cast more light in the elevated enclave. Voices echo here. And the language can be colourful. 'That colt pulls like a ten-year-old schoolboy.' 'He needs to be gelded. He's just not going to do it while he's got his pride and joys there.'

Bell and Nelly picked up their orders as they passed underneath the tower and headed into the distance. It would give the rider the sense of being alone with one of the most sought-after females in the land. 'When I'm out there on my own with her in the dark you hear only the wind, the birds and her feet hitting the ground with such caress. For a big animal she's so light on her feet. It's just amazing. It makes me so happy sometimes I even start singing to her to keep her as happy as I can.'

While few could hear, all could see. They were watched at nearly every step, passing beneath the lights and back into the shadows. Moody would click his watch at designated markers. The results scribed in his book. As the phenomenon began to grow, so too did the attention, even in this haven. Nelly was known the length and breadth of the Caulfield establishment. Bell started to notice it: 'You're walking up to the track and sometimes you get people that trot up just to be next to her; to see her and say they walked out onto the track with Black Caviar.'

Haydon found the goodwill a reaffirmation of the racing game. You did not puff your chest out in victory or drag your backside in defeat. You did not gloat or mope. In his experience, racing people stuck together and rejoiced in each other's successes without jealously or spite because 'it's either the shithouse or the penthouse and it's only a fine line between them'.

There was a collective thrill around Black Caviar and a reflected glory for all the participants of the sport. From time to time, Haydon paused long enough to take in the Caviar Effect. 'When Nelly leaves the stable and goes out to work people have got one eye on their horse and one eye on her. They notice. They know when she comes out, they watch her work and see what she's doing. They keep an interest all the time, so people are always asking how she's going.'

With her exercise done, Nelly and Bell would retrace their steps back to the stable. Moody would inspect her as she passed back through to reassure himself all was well. When he liked what he saw, he would lean out of the tower and chirp 'Sweet' or 'Thanks, mate'. Once she had slipped from sight, Moody had disciplined himself not to give her another thought. 'It's a bit like a football coach. You can have the star player but you've got to make sure there's someone ready to step into his shoes, and if you neglect them they're not going to be ready.'

The serious work of the morning would come from the main barn, somewhere between thirty-five and forty-two horses in full racing mode. The supplementary tasks could include jump-outs. A rusty set of barrier gates was stationed on one of the grass tracks and used in the teaching of young horses in particular to make a clean getaway at the start of a race. Moody and Haydon would assist in the loading of three or four horses at a time. Moody would come around to the front of the gates and man the lever for the manual release. 'Off in 3. 1, 2, 3,' he would announce without hesitation and cast his eye over how each horse leapt, making mental notes on what specific improvements would need to be made.

Back at the stable, Moody would head to the office and fill in the whiteboard, marking the specifics of what each horse required. Those who were to be sent for a spell would be wiped off. Instructions were issued for those heading to the races that day. Moody's reputation as a hands-on trainer was evident as he bent before any horse that caught his eye and ran the palm of his hand over its shin, searching for signs of soundness or soreness. Half a dozen hours after he had driven out of Belgrave South, the first part of the workload was complete. There were still races to be planned, notes to be re-recorded, owners to be informed, tomorrow's plans to be made. Then there were the races themselves, where he would go to learn if all the work would pay dividends. While Moody had learnt to delegate, he still felt the thrill of being on hand to see his horses compete. If it was a Friday in summer, the last at the Moonee Valley night meeting might not run until 10.15 p.m. If you did not mark it out carefully, one day could run into the next and the next and your compass could become completely skewed.

This routine was the lot of the racehorse trainer. If he were asked to take stock of his time, he would have concluded, without a word of complaint, that he was short on minutes and deprived of sleep. Having a good horse tended to exacerbate those shortcomings.

Moody had a premonition about what had been unleashed with Black Caviar and how it would soon escalate. There were two choices. He could hide her away and become the reclusive trainer that, in his heart, he might have wished to be. Or he could leap headlong into a phenomenon.

He reasoned that the sport of racing had given him everything, from his livelihood to his reputation. Before he was born he knew it had entranced his father just as it did him. Everyone who had passed on their experience and offered guidance through the years had dreamt of being in this position. Few ever found it. He formed a determination that he would repay them all by creating the story of a generation. He would showcase Black Caviar for the front and back page of the newspapers, for the television news. He would agree to photo shoots he previously would have viewed with disdain. He would open his life up in intimate interviews. He would welcome every interested soul and see if he could convert a few beyond that. To do so he would sacrifice whatever spare minutes he had. But he could not do it alone.

Moody called together Black Caviar's owners before her quest resumed. 'I said this is going to get big and I can't handle it. You're all business people and I've got a business to run. The easiest part was going to be racing her. The hype, the media and the commerce surrounding her were about to become unprecedented. If we attempted to do it we couldn't. We wouldn't have the time and we'd lose focus on our jobs.'

With that Moody broke his own rule. Black Caviar was special all right. She became the first horse to have a manager to handle her off-track affairs.

Newspix / Darren Tindale

Peter Moody and Luke Nolen sign photographs of Black Caviar's Newmarket Handicap win.

11

Perfect Ten

Flemington, Lightning Stakes, 19 February 2011
Flemington, Newmarket Handicap, 12 March 2011

History is made by those who show up. The task was as old as racing itself. When a horse had beaten the best so comprehensively as to reduce races to processions, all that remained was to beat the handicapper.

The Newmarket Handicap of 2011 had all the elements of great racing theatre: the fastest horse in the world, an unbeatable galloper out to establish an unprecedented streak the likes of which might never be seen again. But this time she would be laden with the lead bars that had stopped many an equine locomotive down the generations. And it would happen in the grandest of all Australian sprint races. When the forefathers conceived such a race, it was precisely with such circumstances in mind.

Every sports fan with even a casual regard for horse racing rode with Black Caviar as Super Saturday broke over Flemington.

Luke Nolen woke early as both habit and race day demanded. As consciousness took hold, he ran through the checklist of what lay in store. Trackwork at Caulfield. A session in the sauna to reach his riding weight and study the form guide. Drive to Flemington for a full book of rides. Try not to be consumed by all things Black Caviar. That last item seemed less achievable than the rest. He was about to roll out of bed when his wife Alicia stirred enough to wish him happy birthday. Without her, it might not even have occurred to him.

The week had been intense. Black Caviar's tilt at history not only dominated the papers and evening news bulletins but had spilled over into programs stretching from *Sunrise* to *6.30 with George Negus*. Nolen liked to joke that Peter Moody smoked for Australia. Things had reached such a pressurised state that the jockey was convinced the trainer was on personal best pace. Each stick seemed to be gone in three tremendous drags. Nolen could not escape it either. The magnitude of what they were attempting was lost on no one. This was the day he had always hoped for. It seemed fitting that it coincided with a personal milestone.

From the time he was a kid on the family farm at Manangatang, in north-western Victoria, Nolen loved horses. Growing up, his bedroom had been a shrine to the great gallopers of the mid-1990s: Octagonal, Saintly and Mahogany. The family moved to country Queensland when he was ten, first to live at Jandowae on the western Darling Downs, where his parents ran the newsagency. Then to nearby Dalby. It was something of a nomadic existence. Luke would say of his father that it was hard to grow roots when you have got wings.

Wherever they resided there were always horses. Luke and his younger brother Shaun would work from sunup to sundown during the school holidays. Their specialty was breaking in the troublesome ponies of local children.

In the middle years of high school, Luke was working at the Dalby stables of trainer Des Burns. They were thirty-hour weeks, split before and after school. Burns was one of the last, old-fashioned trainers of country Queensland. He knew how to handle a good horse, as evidenced by his wonder sprinter Sleep Walk, a winner of thirty-four races from seventy-eight starts. He knew how to orchestrate, unload and carry off a successful betting plunge on his gallopers. He routinely put the frighteners up bookmakers. It was on the other side of Toowoomba, two and a half hours from Dalby along the Warrego Highway, that he forged his reputation with a multitude of winners across three decades at Ipswich. The Turf Club had jockeys wear black armbands the week he died of a heart attack in 2006.

Nolen got the taste from the canny trainer, enough to give up on his idea of being a graphic artist and direct all his energies towards becoming a jockey. At seventeen, he seized the future and returned to Victoria, indentured as an apprentice to trainer Gerald Egan on his property at Mansfield.

Egan was a horseman of great renown. He would ride through the high country for days on end in the tradition of the Man from Snowy River, under his Akubra with stockwhip in hand. He dominated the local Mansfield racing scene as a trainer and launched raids to other parts of the state, including successful incursions into Melbourne. But it was thought his great gift was educating young men. When the son of Melbourne Cup-winning jockey Greg Hall was ready to enter the racing game, his father insisted his education begin under Egan.

Nolen was quiet and desperately shy, but his relaxed attitude made him a natural on the back of a racehorse. Egan learnt quickly that his young ward would rather pick up a snake than a broom, so he let him ride all day and left the mucking-out to others.

His tutelage was diverse. The apprentice joined his master at showjumping events, gymkhanas and rodeos. Nolen earned the nickname Trumby, after the Queensland ringer made famous by country music icon Slim Dusty, from a bull-riding champion after a successful cowhide drag. Trumby could ride and fight. He could not read or write. Nolen liked it so much he had the name inscribed on custom-made numberplates.

Nolen did not appear manically motivated, but Egan never mistook his casual demeanour for a lack of determination. 'When he got on a horse he rode to win.' The winning began at Albury in October 1998 aboard seven-year-old Price Hike. It was his sixth ride on the gelding. Seven days after that breakthrough, the pair combined to win the Berrigan Cup.

Nolen's dreams would not have differed from many of his contemporaries'. He hoped to one day win a big race and perhaps be associated with a top-line horse the calibre of those he had pinned up pictures of on the wall.

'As jockeys go, some search their whole career and don't find one like this, a superstar like Black Caviar. I'm very fortunate I've been on a once-in-a-lifetime horse at the age of thirty-one. A lot has got to do with luck, a bit of mistaken identity and probably work ethic. All those things combined for me to find Black Caviar.'

He likened it not so much to winning the lottery, as knowing what the Lotto numbers would be and then using them however you chose. In that same thought, it occurred to Nolen he would never get another one. 'I'll get to reflect on this stuff late in my riding career when I'm not attracting the same amount of attention that I am now and think, "Jeez, wouldn't it be great if another Black Caviar came along." But I'm a realist; she might be the only one I ever find. I'm still pretty young, I've still got a lot of my career in front of me I hope, but I don't think I'll ever find another one like her. For me she's probably a one in ten million horse.'

Three weeks prior to the Newmarket Handicap, Black Caviar had trounced eight rivals, including the rehabilitated Hay List, in the Lightning Stakes. Nolen tasted Group 1 success aboard her at last.

Long before its elevation to the top bracket of Australian races, the Lightning had become an essential catch for the great sprinters.

Run over 1000 metres and under weight-for-age conditions, it favoured the class horses and boasted Todman, Wenona Girl, Placid Ark and Shaftesbury Avenue among its winners.

The race's importance had grown once it was instated as the first leg of the annual Global Sprint Challenge. As international racing sought to expand its theoretical method of comparing horses, a collection of sprint races was congregated into a series to pit the fastest horses on the planet against each other. The Lightning had become the gateway to races in Japan, Singapore, the United Kingdom and Hong Kong.

The Australian pioneer was Choisir. The big chestnut colt won the Lightning of 2003 as a three-year-old in startling fashion. Jockey Glen Boss piloted a lone course down the inside rail while his twelve rivals took their mounts to the opposite side of the Flemington straight. The free-wheeling Choisir carved out time and turned Boss from a fool to a genius in a tick more than fifty-six seconds by leading all the way. Boss reflected: 'I haven't seen it before or since, where someone has gone it alone down the straight in a Group 1 race and won.'

The win confirmed Choisir as a speed demon, and Newcastle trainer Paul Perry accepted the invitation and challenge to attend Royal Ascot. A curious English audience was astounded. In Tuesday's King's Stand Stakes, Choisir ran the locals off their feet, setting a fast tempo and then surging clear in the final furlong. Perry backed up his colt on the Saturday in the Golden Jubilee Stakes, an unusual thing to do by conservative English standards, and had precisely the same result.

The impact was twofold. Choisir was guaranteed a lucrative life as a dual-hemisphere sire. And Australian trainers realised their sprinters were superior to their Old Dart cousins. The frontiers of adventure were open. Takeover Target, Miss Andretti and Scenic Blast all took their Lightning win to the international bank and hit the jackpot at Royal Ascot.

Early in 2011, Black Caviar had been named the Champion Sprinter of the World in the World Thoroughbred Rankings. The Patinack Farm Classic victory rated the best of any short-course win for the previous twelve months. As she stood ready for action in her first start of the new year, a golden ticket awaited at the finish line.

Black Caviar jumped well enough in the Lightning and positioned right up on the speed. Hay List was handed a watching brief, sitting handsomely three-quarters of a length away on her outside. Moody's desire was that Nolen allow the mare to travel within herself for as long as possible and hope when the whips were cracking he would not need to ask too much of her. He had kept Black Caviar a bit soft in condition, allowing for substantial improvement in a lengthy, taxing preparation. To a trainer's eye she was burly. It occurred to more than one that maybe she was even vulnerable. At halfway, Glyn Schofield meant to find out. He asked Hay List to creep alongside Black Caviar. In his peripheral vision, Nolen saw the gelding coming and it sparked the race.

> They join the course proper in the Lightning
> Black Caviar under a firm hold
> Hay List is asked to go with her
> He can't keep up for the moment
> Warm Love and True Persuasion
> It's a canter again at the 200
> Black Caviar dashed clear of them and the crowd starts to
> offer its appreciation
> She's got four lengths on Hay List
> Black Caviar, baby she's getting better

The way she toyed with Hay List was even more contemptuous than before. Without the alibi of injury or interruption, the gelding could not counter the lethal acceleration of Black Caviar.

Hopeless though it was, Schofield was vigorous with Hay List and still he lost ground with every stride.

Nolen was struck by how effortless Black Caviar made it seem against proven Group 1 horses: 'It feels like you're cantering beside them and she's got endless reserves to call upon. The jockeys beside you are starting to feel for their horses and I'm still in the relaxed seat well in control of my mount. When you push the button, she puts the race beyond doubt so quickly. She's a bit deceiving that way. You feel like you're going three-quarter pace but you're going quicker than that. It feels like you're almost moving in slow motion compared to the horses around her. That giant, flowing stride she's got enables her to do it. You've really got to witness her beside another horse to get a great appreciation of it. They look like they're going up and down in the one spot. She looks like she's out in the meadows having a canter around.'

Pressman Adrian Dunn raved: 'Black Caviar's second Group 1 was locked away with ridiculous ease and with more than half the Lightning Stakes to be run. Nolen let the mare slip for a couple of hundred metres then put the handbrake on.'

Moody stamped it awesome. 'When they got to the clock tower here and he hadn't asked and the others were off the bridle, it was pretty exciting stuff to watch, wasn't it.' Vanquished trainer John McNair did not sugar-coat Hay List's defeat. 'She just brained us.'

Post-race, Moody was pressed as to whether he would follow the established path to Royal Ascot. There was great hope in the question for an affirmative answer. Everyone who had witnessed it knew, given the history, she would be an invincible force in Europe. And who does not love a world-beater? To that end Moody disappointed, but at least he entertained. 'They've got televisions in the rest of the world and there's plenty of planes that come this way. So, if any of them want to jump on one and come and have a crack, I'm sure they'll find a slot for them in a Group 1 race in Australia.'

That ninth successive win put Black Caviar alongside Grand Flaneur, Mollison, Eye Liner and Rancher for the greatest winning streaks from career inception in the history of Australian racing. Victory in the Newmarket would establish a fresh mark.

The Newmarket Handicap is the premier sprint race on the Australian turf, first run in 1874 over a distance of six furlongs. Like the Melbourne Cup, it was a handicap event with the capacity for twenty-four runners. As is the case with the Cup, it was an international oddity. Every major sprint race in the Northern Hemisphere was run under the set weight conditions of the weight-for-age scale. It was a formula established in the 1860s by Admiral Rous, the English Jockey Club handicapper, that prescribed weights according to a horse's age and maturity rather than ability. It promoted quality by refusing to penalise the better horses. The finest races in the world were run employing those parameters, including each leg of the Global Sprint Challenge. The fathers of the Melbourne Cup and Newmarket Handicap craved equality. Champions would be placed at the mercy of the handicapper, who would subjectively prescribe a weight that made the best horse beatable.

In its earliest days the Newmarket formed stronger links with the Melbourne Cup than would have been predicted given the extremes of the races' lengths, at 1200 and 3200 metres, respectively. One was a flat-out dash, the other an extreme test of stamina. All the stars of the colony's fledgling racing scene were drawn to the Victoria Racing Club's glamour sprint. Malua won the 1884 Newmarket Handicap and completed the unique double when he took the Melbourne Cup later that same year. Carbine ran favourite in the 1889 Newmarket, finishing third en route to winning the Melbourne Cup the following year. Comedy King travelled from England and ran highly fancied into fifth in the sprint, then won the two-miler nine months later.

The Newmarket's most famous winner was Bernborough, who unleashed his trademark finishing burst, despite the burden of 63 kilograms, to prevail in the 1946 photo finish. Other Hall of Fame gallopers, Heroic and Ajax, graced the winner's list. Its reputation held through the modern era as Schillaci, General Nediym, Exceed and Excel, Alinghi and Weekend Hussler proved their mettle in victory.

Moody had begun subtle negotiations with Racing Victoria's chief handicapper Greg Carpenter in the spring as to what weight Black Caviar could be expected to carry and which historical impediments would need to be overcome. The spirit of handicapping in Australia had altered slightly to find the line where a champion would be at their most vulnerable but not impose a weight that made it either impossible to win or unreasonable to even make an attempt.

The previous decade had endorsed the handicapping methods, with a series of flooding finishes. Only one of the previous ten editions of the Newmarket had been determined by a margin exceeding one length. That was when the filly Alinghi defeated colt Fastnet Rock by a length and a quarter. The most thrilling Newmarket finish of all came in 2002, when eight horses crossed the line within a length of the winner Rubitano. Barely a neck separated the first six in a claustrophobic photo.

Carpenter had in mind a benchmark figure of 57.5 kilograms for Black Caviar, but the destruction in the Lightning meant there was little choice but to allot what he regarded as the maximum of 58 kilograms. Moody's concern was not so much the actual weight Black Caviar would receive, but how much she would be asked to concede to her rivals. When weights were released, Hay List had 56.5 kilograms representing a swing of 3.5 kilograms in his favour from their previous meeting.

Carpenter categorised it as a formidable challenge for Black Caviar. On what he knew of weights and measures – and that was a lot – it would take a super effort to pull it off.

In 137 stagings of the Newmarket Handicap, the top weight had been successful only twelve times. In the past fifty years, twenty-one horses had been asked to carry 58 kilograms or more and only Shaftesbury Avenue had prevailed. Some fine horses had failed, including Baguette, Century, Razor Sharp, Hareeba and Mahogany. The weight-carrying record for a mare since the introduction of metrics was Maybe Mahal, who was a five-time Group 1 winner when assigned 56.5 kilograms. She got there in 1978 with barely a neck to spare. The only mare to win the race with more of an impost was Pendant, who as a seven-year-old carried 60.5 kilograms to victory in 1906.

Moody had been schooled on the facts and was cool in his initial response: 'She's only won two Group 1s. I just want to let everyone know who is thinking of backing her that she's no better than 50–50 to go around.' The alternative to running in the Newmarket was filling up the float and driving Black Caviar four hours up the Hume Highway to a barrier trial at Albury in preparation for her first clockwise run in Sydney.

Despite the underwhelming response, Carpenter was quietly hopeful he had hooked his fish. 'The victory of Black Caviar in the Lightning Stakes stunned even the most hardened and seasoned racegoer. Those that saw it understand they witnessed a moment of rare greatness. They will find it difficult to believe Hay List, even with a swing in the weights, can mount a challenge. They will return to Flemington with a spring in their step and a sense of expectation that was, until a few weeks ago, a sense seemingly assigned to a time long past.'

Moody wrestled an inner torment he had not faced before with his treasure. He was a student of history, believing it repeated itself more often than it was defied. Public sentiment demanded he run Black Caviar. West Australian trainer Fred Kersley had resisted such a public and media push in 2002 when Northerly had unlocked the possibility of replicating the almighty feat of Rising

Fast by winning the Caulfield Cup and Cox Plate in consecutive weeks. Rising Fast became the only horse to complete the iconic treble in the Melbourne Cup of 1954. No horse had been to the precipice since. Kersley would not be swayed into an attempt on the summit, believing it was unfair to ask Northerly to shoulder 60 kilograms in the most gruelling race of all. He regretted it almost immediately and has forever more.

Moody was gripped by the idea that he did not need to run Black Caviar in the Newmarket. He questioned his own motives. Would it be an act of vanity, wanting to prove what his charge was capable of? 'That was the one race I thought, "Shit, am I doing the right thing? Do you need to be doing this?"'

Even as those doubts germinated, he knew Black Caviar did need to run. Legend is measured by accomplishment rather than style. To be considered worthy of the lofty company the trainer felt she might one day join, this sort of win was essential: the day she was there to be beaten by measures quantifiable and implied. As surely as Phar Lap had to win the Melbourne Cup of 1930, so Black Caviar needed the Newmarket Handicap of 2011. That was the anxiety that fuelled the tension around Caulfield in the build-up and had Moody sucking hard on the cigarettes.

Among the owners there was a sense of nervous anticipation. Pam Hawkes' daughter had flown in from Ireland specifically for the race. She had not seen Black Caviar before and feared she might jinx the whole exercise. 'What if she loses? It'll be my fault.'

A venue had been booked for a party that evening. Hopefully, a celebration. The morning ensured, regardless of events at the track, it would be for the Maddens. As Colin and Jannene were readying themselves, their daughter Ainslie and son-in-law Gus, who had arrived from Townsville, shared the news that they were going to have a baby.

On course, strapper Donna Fisher caught the elevated atmosphere as soon as she walked Nelly off the float. The mare had her hooves taped and bell boots on to ensure she did not dislodge a shoe on the trip. As those accoutrements were cast off, people started to gather in front of stall ninety-four. Never one to be tied up in the designated box, Nelly, led by Donna, commenced the first of countless laps of the saddling enclosure in the countdown to 2.35 p.m.

Nolen could not get close to a winner on the undercard. He trailed with a sense of frustration as Moody stablemate Panipique beat his mount Kulgrinda in the second race. Each time he emerged from the Jockeys' Room, Nolen summoned his best attempt at a calm exterior. He was shooting for steely resolve. Inside, though, he was churning: 'You try to shut it out as much as you can but you can't help but think about the race, about this record and what she's trying to do.'

Once Moody had saddled Black Caviar, Fisher led her to the mouth of the tunnel linking the paddock to the mounting yard. As they completed their journey up the incline and into the amphitheatre ahead, all they could see were people. Everywhere. Fisher could not spy a space between the mob of humanity on the four sides of the yard. They held salmon and black flags printed with 'Black Caviar' on one side and a pre-emptive '10/10' on the other. As she gazed out, every pair of eyes fixed on them.

Dressed in the salmon and black silks, Nolen walked over to the owners for a cursory chat. Such dialogue rarely touched on the race itself. Rather, polite banter about plans for the evening and assurances that all was well. Then he paired off with Moody. There was not a lot said. Too much depth to a discussion now might spark the simmering nerves each was feeling. Moody asked Nolen to be as kind as he could for as long as he could. There was no need to be three lengths in front at the furlong. Half an inch on the line would be enough. Together they walked towards their horse.

Nolen had come to treasure much about Black Caviar in their time together, but nothing more than the calm she exuded when tensions were peaking. The sight of her, as he was about to be legged aboard, calmed him better than any tranquilliser. 'On race day she's like the pony at home. You could canter her over a few cavaletti, put her around a few witches' hats and take her over a couple of logs she's so relaxed. She's just plain old Nelly. She's like an old gelding who's been there and done it a hundred times, not ten. It's a remarkable quality for a sprinter in particular to have.'

Pam Hawkes would not take her eyes off Black Caviar once she entered the mounting yard. She would fondly admire the horse she had visited while spelling at Murchison. In those surrounds she could be any old mare. 'Tapped the tin on the gate and she just looked up and wandered over, just like anything that I've got at home.' Hawkes' favourite moment was not the picture perfect shot of Black Caviar at the finishing post alone; it was the transformation she saw when jockey and horse came together. 'Black Caviar when she's in the mounting yard is a different horse to the one that we see on the racetrack. She's very relaxed and very slow, in fact she holds up the traffic because she ambles along. So she's just Nelly in the mounting yard. As soon as Peter bunks Luke on she immediately changes, she seems to grow. She knows why she's there. She changes into Black Caviar, and look out.'

On the final lap around the yard, Nolen leant down and told Fisher to lap up the attention around them. 'It's probably a pretty short career in the grand scheme of things and there aren't many times you get to enjoy and reflect. All these people cheering this great mare, it's a great thing to be a part of.'

At the top of the majestic straight course running the length of Flemington, the Newmarket field assembled. Hay List was a race-eve scratching with soreness in his off-side shoulder. It robbed the race of the most likely challenger but hardly cast a pall. Hay List was testing the patience of even his most hardened backers. Present and correct for the iconic sprint were the previous season's Golden Slipper winner Crystal Lily and Blue Diamond victor Star Witness who, in the spring, had doubled up at Group 1 level with the Coolmore Stakes; the Oakleigh Plate winner Eagle Falls; Group 1 winning mares Response and Beaded; Lightning and Newmarket placegetter Grand Duels; along with King Pulse, Hinchinbrook and Chasm, who had all filled minor placings in Group 1 events. There was not a duffer in sight.

Regardless of what was about to unfold, Black Caviar had already broken one fabled record. She was to start the shortest-priced favourite in the history of the race at $1.18, making Bernborough's $1.44 quote look a luxury.

Before the barriers crashed back, a hush descended on Flemington as all attention was honed. Black Caviar began nicely from her draw of seven, although she sprang from gate number eighteen with the field ushered to the middle of the track. Crystal Lily made the early running as Nolen gave his mount time to find her tempo. Grand Duels was nuisance value immediately on her outside. Nolen felt a sense of annoyance as Danny Nikolic put unnecessary pressure on. It brought them into formation, three in line, from the 800-metre pole. Craig Newitt had camped Beaded directly behind Black Caviar's hindquarters. Other than Grand Duels, who got the stitch quickly having been set an unrealistic task, it was Newitt's urgency at the 600 that gave insight into what was taking place. At the halfway mark of a short race, he was struggling to keep pace. Nolen could sense the panic behind him. He had the pursuers off the bit and was determined not to relinquish that advantage.

Crystal Lily was the last line of resistance. She was receiving an eight-kilo allowance from the mare beginning to take the monstrous strides. Nolen had no intention of being cute with Black Caviar, given the conditions. He went full bore. He would expend the reserves he had previously marvelled at. He would empty the tank. As he readied for the fight, Crystal Lily's jockey Stephen Baster saw just how well his rival was travelling and realised resistance was useless.

At the 400 she starts to ease way from them Black Caviar
and there's that sense of trepidation and anticipation on
the course
She broke away from Crystal Lily
Oh they're cheering already. She's home again at the clock
tower
This is a moment of equine perfection
Black Caviar broke away with fifty-eight
She's into racing folklore
She's the fastest horse you ever saw

Black Caviar blasted past Crystal Lily. She made a mockery of the weight designated to anchor her. She was set free by Nolen. It was exquisite to behold a creature in perfect harmony with nature.

Nolen felt the emotion surge. He had seen Damien Oliver salute the heavens in a tribute to his dead brother after winning the Melbourne Cup on Media Puzzle. He could recall Glen Boss theatrically shaking his head from side to side in sheer disbelief when Makybe Diva did it for the third time. Together they passed the post three lengths clear, space enough to absorb the accomplishment. L. Nolen and Black Caviar would forever be linked by this conquest. He felt fortune, honour and a tremendous sense of gratitude towards the horse beneath him.

As they idled down and Nolen threatened to get carried away, Baster caught up to him again. 'That was just rude, mate. That was just rude.' Crystal Lily had run second ahead of Beaded. Both were gallant. Both were no competition.

There was so much to take in. Black Caviar had not only carried the weight, she had stopped the clock in 1 minute 7.36 seconds. The fastest Newmarket ever. Had Nolen not backed off in the last thirty metres she might well have broken the track record of 1 minute 7.16 seconds. It had stood for a decade, set by

Iglesia on a flint-hard track with a howling tailwind. Today was nothing of the kind.

Moody stood to watch the race beside Sarah and their teenage daughters. He vowed to forever remember this afternoon. He was grateful the girls were old enough to appreciate and enjoy it; to share the moment with him. Moody thought over his suggestion to Nolen that there was no need to be three lengths in front at the furlong. By that mark she was four lengths clear. He could not have been happier. Under his white panama hat a smile stretched across his face as the certainty of victory set in.

At instants of such grandeur or tumult, observers and participants create different memories. They either weave together in a complete tapestry or radically contradict. As Black Caviar took flight, what witnesses remembered was the wall of sound that followed her to the finish.

Matt Stewart documented it for the *Herald Sun*: 'They began applauding 300 metres from home, just as Nolen stopped kidding and released the brakes in what has become a familiar tease. As this happened, Peter Moody's stable foreman, Tony Haydon, stood under the stewards tower at the 100m and clasped his hands together and appeared to pray.'

There was no need for requests, Haydon was giving thanks to the heavens. 'People basically stopped talking and there was just clapping. That was probably one of the greatest days I've ever seen. It put the hair up on the back of your neck.'

Hawkes had given up holding her breath earlier than usual. It was the din of the crowd, how early it started and what a powerful force it built to that touched her heart. 'They were cheering from about the 300. That's when the crowd and the horse decided that it was time for her to go. As they cheered, the horse just put lengths on the next horse.' Hawkes did not so much lose her head as her blue hat when she scampered down from the grandstand in the post-race euphoria.

People surged towards the famed walk of the roses, the alleyway parallel to the track leading back to the mounting yard, to greet their hero's return. On the public side of the mounting yard fence was the staff from Gilgai Farm. Meaghan Strickland-Wood stood with her mother, cousin and a couple of close friends having just watched the foal she had helped into the world become its conquering force. She started talking to the people around her, people she had never met, unable to stop herself from sharing her small role in the story. 'You're just so thrilled to be there and be part of it. They were really surprised and started asking questions about her. It's nice that you can share it with other people.'

Rick Jamieson had been invited to the coronation to witness the fruitfulness of his theory. He had not known a race day like it. With every corner turned, he would pick up a shard of conversation relating to Black Caviar. He had taken in the scene pre-race with people lined ten deep around the fence and children waving their flags. His heart was uplifted as the race reached its conclusion. 'I don't think I've ever seen it before. To watch people start to clap 200 metres from the winning post, as she passes the winning post, they continued to clap until she came back into the mounting yard and they still continued to clap. It was an unbelievable scene and it was an unbelievable thing for me. I sat in the background there and I had goose bumps all afternoon.'

The papers told of seventy-three-year-old May White: 'This is like the old days when everyone in Melbourne would come to the races. That's what good horses can do.' Paul Milton came from Warragul to be part of it: 'My dad and I got up at six o'clock this morning so we could get here early and get a good spot. I just wanted to get a good photo.' And one of a pair of shearers who travelled more than two hours for such an event said: 'We all like champions. No matter who it is, we like to see 'em. Horses, cricket players, whatever.'

Gary and Kerrin Wilkie had the distinction of leading their horse under the archway at the re-entry to the mounting yard and triumphantly back to the winner's stall. The applause rained down from the surrounding grandstands. Be they chairman or punter, all stood for the reception. As Gary absorbed the scene he wished for everyone, once in their lives, to experience something such as this. 'We're just a group of people who bought a racehorse and this is how it's turned out', he said. 'It's too much to sometimes comprehend,' added Kerrin.

Fisher greeted Black Caviar as she always did, with a pat and a 'Good girl'. They pushed their way past the battery of cameras and resumed walking. As they did, Donna noticed the change in Nelly that suggested she knew precisely the pandemonium she was responsible for. 'After a race she would usually go full pelt back to the stalls, like she does at trackwork.' Instead, despite the pumping adrenaline, Nelly seemed relaxed. If Donna was not mistaken, the mare was in fact posing for the assembled photographers.

Moody composed himself for the analysis. 'I breathed a big sigh of relief. She carried me again. It's the highlight of my career thus far. I'd like to think there might be more highlights but it'd be hard to outdo this one. Typhoon Tracy will always be the darling in my heart but this one's got that extra special X factor, doesn't she. This creates a bit of resurgence for racing. We're getting into footy season. We've got cricket world cups. You know, if she doesn't headline the bloody sports news tonight I might nought whatever station doesn't have her there.'

It was said on ABC Radio and was a reference to his frustration with the 7 p.m. ABC TV News. For the past three weeks, that bulletin had failed to include the Festival's feature race result. Moody saw it as the final barrier obstructing the completion of his promotional crusade: the conversion of racing's most heathen. Had he been at home that night, he would have noted with great satisfaction that there was no further omission.

But his duties were about to extend beyond what he had envisaged or could possibly have imagined. The VRC had ordered the immediate printing of commemorative postcards, with a photo of Black Caviar crossing the line, to be distributed to the crowd. It replicated an idea after Makybe Diva won her third Melbourne Cup. That afternoon friends signed the back of each other's cards so as to always recall with whom they had shared the memory. This time Moody and Nolen had been asked to sit for a ten-minute autograph session after the last race. 'I thought it was a bit of a wank to be honest,' Moody confided. 'Who would want us to sign these photos? Here's two blokes who were battling to write their name when they left school.'

After an hour and a quarter, they had not put a dent in an ever-replenishing line. It seemed to Moody as though every one of the 24,583 people at Flemington was in the queue. 'People from all walks of life. I think half the Collingwood football team was there to get an autograph from Luke Nolen and Peter Moody. People had come down from the Committee Room to get the signatures. The opportunity to take in what appreciation people had of this horse and how they spoke of her in such reverent terms, it was very overwhelming. I stood back in amazement and awe and watched Makybe Diva win a third Melbourne Cup and saw what it meant to the Freedmans. I've watched Fred Kersley with Northerly and the McKees with Sunline and thought, "Wow, wouldn't it be exciting to be part of that." This has even surpassed that. For me to be the person standing next to her and taking it in is an unbelievable experience.'

History was made and so many had shown up to share it.

Newspix / Nicole Garmston

The best racehorse in the world wins again at Moonee Valley in the William Reid Stakes.

12

Like Nothing Before

Moonee Valley, William Reid Stakes, 25 March 2011

When faced with the rare sight of perfection in sport, the mind can be drawn in a couple of directions: to accept it for the beauty and wonder it represents, or to attempt to rationalise, quantify and classify. Both are perfectly legitimate reflexes, revealing much about the respondent's disposition.

Author John Harms is a man who finds truth and romance in sport. In Black Caviar he saw a figure that made him believe the irresistible force of chance, that governed all matters from life to death, could be resisted. He wrote in Brisbane's *Courier Mail*: 'We're drawn to the possibility that chance can be defied. The human condition has stacked the odds against us and we cling to any hope. We need to believe it's still worth planting; still worth joining up; still worth building communities. As she tallies the victories, Black Caviar, trained by a knockabout bloke from Charleville, will attract a bigger and bigger following. She's beautiful to watch. She can lift the spirit. And she is coming to mean so much to us.'

The hard-headed sought remedy and reason in facts and figures. Here they found a veritable gold mine. In addition to being a game of hunches and theories, racing is a business based on numbers. Percentages determine odds. Weights are calculated by the worth of performances. There is the attempt to define and classify the intangible nature of winning, to make it more palpable.

There were systems both public and private. That which carries the greatest gravitas is set down by the International Federation of Horseracing Authorities. A committee comprising representation from thirteen countries bestowed the World Thoroughbred Rankings (WTR). The heads of handicapping from England, France, Ireland, Germany, Italy, Hong Kong, New Zealand, Singapore, South Africa, United Arab Emirates, Canada, the United States and Australia held a vote. A numerical system had been devised to achieve the same end as tennis and golf rankings. It was complicated by the fact that the horses it set to rank competed over varying distances, under differing conditions and rarely in the same event. While formulated, there was a necessary edge of subjectivity attached to decisions.

Greg Carpenter had the honour and the burden of being the local man on the committee. Australian racing had become an easier sell as its sprinters spread their wings in the Northern Hemisphere and as invading forces from Asia and Europe loosened the local grip on the Caulfield and Melbourne Cups. While no longer foreign ground to the overseas members of the committee, their respect for Australian horses was sometimes grudging.

Carpenter knew how remarkable a performance Black Caviar had turned in at Flemington. It was his duty to bring the rest of the world along. If he did his job well, Australia would have a world champion on its hands. A horse from these parts had never been hailed the best on the planet since the WTR expanded from a European operation to the global realm in 2002.

Under consideration was the six-month period that contained such iconic races as the Breeder's Cup, Prix l'Arc de Triomphe and the Japan Cup as well as the premier meetings of Hong Kong and Dubai. As the rankings were debated, Black Caviar found herself pitched in competition with Blame, the horse who had so famously ended the run of Zenyatta at Churchill Downs. The Epsom Derby winner Workforce proved his worth by claiming the Arc in Paris. Japanese star Victoire Pisa was a stirring winner of the Dubai World Cup.

Carpenter was certain Black Caviar's Newmarket Handicap was superior. He marked out his territory at a rating of 132. It was a number never previously awarded to either a sprinter or mare. The Australian handicapper was prepared to mount the pressure publicly ahead of the congress to ratify the rankings. 'At the moment two of us have her at 132, another two rate her at 130, there are four of them with altitude sickness and the other four are scared of heights. It is uncharted territory and a rating like that would give her the accolade she deserves.'

When the first round of World Thoroughbred Ratings for 2011 was released in Paris, Black Caviar was graded at 130, officially the highest rated horse in the world. Carpenter would later have his day, but even that provisional measure was astounding.

It exceeded Zenyatta's peak career figure of 128 from the Breeder's Cup Classic in 2009. French mare Goldikova was the only other female to previously warrant 130 for her six-length win in the Jacques Le Marois at Deauville in August 2009. In the time Australian horses had been examined under the scheme, none had achieved such a mark. Makybe Diva was awarded a 124 rating for her third Melbourne Cup, while So You Think's rampage the previous spring had drawn a pair of 126s.

Of her international contemporaries, Black Caviar was graded eight points above Rocket Man, the Australian-bred, Singapore-based sprinter who had won the Golden Shaheen in Dubai, and JJ The Jet Plane, who had previously beaten him in the Hong Kong Sprint. That equated to a differential of three lengths at level weights. In the assessment of industry experts worldwide, Black Caviar, with the standard two-kilogram sex allowance for a mare, would have beaten that pair by four and a half lengths in any given race.

Carpenter explained the intricacies of the system to a broad audience that had never previously paid much attention. 'An International Rating measures a peak performance and is not a reflection of an accumulation of Group 1 wins. I have been asked if winning the William Reid, and indeed if she continues on her winning ways in Sydney and Brisbane, will get her to a higher rating. The answer is almost certainly no.'

A further set of rankings provided by Timeform was equally unequivocal. Timeform was founded in England in 1948 by pioneering punter-analyst Phil Bull. It had grown to be regarded as the single most informative and precise record of the merits of the best racehorses in the world.

Black Caviar was not only the best horse in the world but her rating of 135 meant that since the system began measuring Australian racing in 1960, the only horses to rate higher than her were Tulloch (138), Kingston Town (137) and Manikato (136).

You had to go back a generation to find the female parallels for Black Caviar. Only the French filly Allez France in the early 1970s and the flying British-trained Habibti in the early 1980s had ever registered better than the Australian. Those mares rated at 136.

Gary Crispe, the official compiler of the Australian Timeform ratings, described the Newmarket as a 'brutal display of superior equine ability'. The analysis compared Black Caviar's win against the previous five editions of the race, factored in the opposition and then, finally and most decisively, the clock. 'Black Caviar's overall race time of 67.36 seconds was just under two seconds inside standard for the 1200m at Flemington while her last 600m of 32.69 seconds was one and a half seconds inside standard.'

One of Sydney's first and most respected independent ratings scholars, Michael McHugh, assessed that performance as equal to the peak figure produced by Kingston Town, the benchmark since he had been applying his method. While McHugh marvelled at the consistency of Manikato, who had won twenty-nine races across six seasons, the Man never managed a rating as high as Black Caviar's Newmarket.

The UK *Racing Post* Ratings completed Black Caviar's beautiful set of numbers. Its assessment of 133 was outright the best figure ever recorded for a filly or mare. By the end of the calendar year, Black Caviar had created further records: six times posting ratings of 130 and above for individual races; and registering 129 or better for ten consecutive races.

Beyond the statistics, the sheer thrill of the Newmarket bubbled in sporting circles for days afterwards. As superlatives were bestowed, the debate over the merits of comparing Black Caviar with Vain, long hailed as the yardstick for any sprinting star in these parts, appeared also to have been settled.

Vain was the freakish chestnut sprinter of the late 1960s who won twelve of his fourteen starts by walloping big margins. At the Melbourne Cup Carnival of '69, he won a hat trick of Group 1 races: the Craven A Stakes (1200 metres) by twelve lengths, the Linlithgow Stakes (1400 metres) by six, and then carried a record ten pounds over weight for age to win the George Adams Handicap (1600 metres) on Final Day.

As an opposing jockey, Roy Higgins had witnessed the deeds of Vain firsthand, and jealously guarded his legacy. On the eve of the Newmarket he had set the terms for Black Caviar: 'Vain under handicap conditions, he carried huge weights against all classes. He would've beaten this class of horse by about four lengths. If she goes out and beats them by three or four lengths well, yeah, we do have another Vain on our hands.'

Euroa stud-master Tim Johnson had been consulted for a unique perspective. His grandfather, Walter, had bred Vain and raced him with other family members. Tim had been twelve when Vain scorched the turf. 'The way she races is very much the way

Vain did, high cruising speed and then the ability to quicken. She's certainly right up there in the ability to demolish her opponents. In racing we don't see that all that often. So we go back to horses like Vain for comparison and it's a worthy comparison.'

Johnson also unlocked a secret of what Rick Jamieson had cast in Black Caviar. She was inbred to Vain, being her great-grandfather on one side and great-great-grandfather on the other. As a breeding specification, this made the mare a three by four cross of Vain. Those who had seen both horses knew that she carried more in common than the genes alone.

While her status was richly examined, her worth was established by those who coveted the prize of Australia. Moody described as astronomical the offers touted by the world's billionaire stables. In Europe these establishments, either racing operations or the global studs, made it a matter of pride that there was not a horse they could not buy. The answer on Black Caviar was a stern no. Even when a Hong Kong-based venture put $5 million on the table.

Black Caviar had an encore performance in store for Melbourne and an old score to settle. She had been denied the William Reid Stakes by ill-timed injury twelve months before. Peter Moody had no intention of missing out again. It was low-hanging fruit, given the field would be inferior to the Newmarket and with its weight-for-age status, her competitors would be at a hellish disadvantage.

The William Reid Stakes was the race made famous by Manikato, who won it on five consecutive occasions between 1979 and 1983. That astounding feat had been given some recent context by Zipping. The marvellous warhorse of leviathan owner Lloyd Williams racked up four successive victories in the Sandown Classics. It was the last feature of the Melbourne spring, run eleven days after the Melbourne Cup. In three of Zipping's four wins, he was backing up after highly commendable runs in the punishing two-miler. When he won the Classic for a fourth time in 2010, caller Greg Miles declared him, 'You're a Quaddie Beauty.' As a mark of admiration, on his retirement the race was renamed the Zipping Classic. By comparison with Manikato's dominance of the William Reid, it was not only one fewer but a grade down, at Group 2 level.

Black Caviar's engagement was a huge bonus for the William Reid. Following the global trend of staging major sporting events at night, the Moonee Valley Racing Club had rescheduled its feature autumn sprint under lights. It had also placed the race at the conclusion of the Festival calendar rather than in its midst. It dearly needed star power to justify the risk, as it coincided with the first Friday night of the AFL season. Black Caviar was again Moonee Valley's charm, booked for one night only.

More than 9600 patrons were drawn to her on the final night-racing date of the season, ten times the size of the typical gathering. The club sold out its 2500 dining packages. Some 500 racegoers caught the chartered buses from regional Victoria on a $30 deal. The traffic congestion swelled to make horses and jockeys alike late to arrive. There was even a woman brought to the track in her hospital bed to view the great mare. Neil Werrett ensured the owners took the time to meet her and share the thrill: 'When you see something like that you really start to know how special she is to the public.'

Moody and Luke Nolen had additional motivation. Amid a series of clever initiatives to garner industry support and bolster night racing, a trainer who surpassed the $1 million earnings barrier with his or her runners on the evening circuit would drive away in a $134,000 Mercedes-Benz GL350. A jockey achieving the same became the proud owner of a $33,500 television. If Black Caviar claimed the winner's cheque on offer, the price was right and the showcase was theirs.

Nolen knew the rhythms of Moonee Valley with Black Caviar well enough, but the reaction this night brought in to sharp focus the changed circumstances surrounding them. The parade ring is an amphitheatre in its own right, surrounded by a three-tier viewing terrace and enclosed by the rear of the grandstand from which patrons watched through the towering windows of the bars. It seemed every punter on the course was clamouring for a view. Maybe more even than for the parade preceding a Cox Plate. On the bottom concrete landing were two girls who might more easily have been pictured at the airport awaiting the arrival of Justin Bieber. Instead, they were dressed in replica jackets of the salmon and black silks holding aloft a beautifully stitched homemade sign: *Blink and You'll Miss Her.*

As jockey and horse escaped that enclosure and emerged from the tunnel to the track, spontaneous applause erupted. Before the race. Nolen found it charming and unnerving. 'I've never seen it before, never witnessed it before myself in racing. Cheering a champion out on to the track. Normally that's the response coming back.'

The crowd was there for one reason only. He had better win. This was his new and permanent reality.

Black Caviar had six rivals, including the eternally game but overmatched Crystal Lily. The three-year-old had received an eight-kilo concession in the Newmarket at the handicapper's discretion. Tonight it was reduced to 2.5kg under the mandatory conditions of weight for age. Moody had propped up the field with Hinchinbrook, a galloper he was thinking of taking to England, and Master Harry, a talented lower grade sprinter who was on trial at the top level.

In an effort to ensure a field, racing authorities had taken the precaution to provide prize money of $10,000 through to eighth place. This led Anthony Sharwood to observe on *The Punch* website: 'Even then, only seven showed up. Which presumably means you could have run around at Moonee Valley yourself, or walked, albeit with a jockey on your back and the occasional utterance of "neigh", and collected $10,000. And to think, I wasted the weekend at home being a father and husband.'

The moment of great anticipation had been delayed the best part of half an hour by an earlier protest. Geelong and St Kilda were locked in a tight, dour battle in the last quarter at the MCG. In a throwback to nearly half a century ago, ABC Radio interrupted its national broadcast of the AFL to take the William Reid Stakes live. In the eighty seconds listeners were away, Jimmy Bartel kicked the goal of the night and the Cats wrestled the lead. The ABC, which has some of the keenest letter writers in the county among its loyal audience, along with listeners who have the talkback number on speed dial, took only one complaint against a flood of endorsements for the editorial decision.

Black Caviar was lackadaisical out of the barriers, even by her standards. Because she had drawn the outside gate, this was more problematic than usual. She settled with only two runners behind and was condemned to a three-wide posting on the crescent run from barrier to post. It was an unusual sight. Not since her second run had she been in the back half of a field. Striding up on the pace, unafraid of leading if necessary, had become her modus operandi. Getting caught three wide was a sure recipe for defeat in racing. On a circuit, a horse would literally be required to run further than a rival hugging the inside rail. It also denied a galloper the benefit of cover, the slipstream behind other runners.

Deep outside Master Harry, Nolen tried to improve Black Caviar's predicament from the 800. Crystal Lily and True Persuasion came into sight. At the redbrick school down the side, Nolen pushed hard on Black Caviar, a vigour unseen since win number four when all stops were pulled out to win.

The urgency caused a ripple in the crowd, a rise in the caller's voice and a heart flutter for Moody. All the work the trainer had put into the mare after the Newmarket had been geared towards her Sydney debut. In its own way, this win had been taken for granted. Perhaps as a result, she didn't seem quite as tractable as usual around the Valley. The zip seemed a little flattened.

As those thoughts and conclusions percolated, they were suddenly quashed. For no sooner had Nolen started pushing than he suddenly backed off. Black Caviar had responded so quickly to his touch that she had hurtled to the leaders and past them before the turn. The race was won by the 200. Crystal Lily never relented in the face of crushing defeat and Nolen was particularly kind to his mare knowing the tasks that lay ahead. In fact, Moody's instruction had been only: 'Do not hit her.' The margin was two lengths. And still it constituted a donkey licking.

Damien Oliver had watched it unfold aboard Master Harry. He had seen Black Caviar go from his mount's girth, take up the chase and dash away. He looked into the stands at the delight that greeted her as she headed back to the winner's circle. He would remark to journalist Rod Nicholson as he passed by: 'What a treat it was for so many people to be here to see such a champion. Unfortunately for jockeys, we only see her backside.'

Moody could afford to giggle about the momentary anxieties of the race. 'He just had to wake her up a little bit on the night. It's a bit late, she should be at home having a camp.'

Nolen could not quite grasp the fuss. 'She put them away and sat up for the photo. When I went, there's not many horses that are going to go with her at weight-for-age for that distance. You ride to your strengths and that's what we did tonight. All the people are here to see one horse, and I'm glad she didn't let anyone down.'

The story carried around the nation. In Adelaide's *Sunday Mail* the fervour surrounding the streak was given its place among historic record runs: 'When Joe DiMaggio died, his 56-game streak was hailed as "perhaps the most enduring record in sports". 'Yet 70 years after DiMaggio raised the spirits of wartime America, on the other side of the world a racehorse has been doing exactly that – hitting home runs with every attempt.'

Her achievement was bracketed with the Australian cricket team's winning run of sixteen Test matches. And the Brisbane

Lions' three AFL premierships. But as always came with the qualifier, she had never been beaten.

Astute racing observer Steve Moran unapologetically declared: 'Black Caviar is the best horse I have seen.'

At a lunch prior to the William Reid, Steve had asked Moody about the future and the prospect of a clash with Gai Waterhouse's More Joyous. '"Flemington 1200 metres would be a no-brainer for this mare," he [Moody] said.

'"What about 1350 metres around Doomben?" I asked. Still Black Caviar, he insisted.

'"Rosehill 1500 metres?" I pressed.

'"Starting to get interesting," he conceded.'

Moran mused over how Black Caviar could ever be seriously challenged. He could make a case only for the star of Singapore, Rocket Man. Trained by Patrick Shaw, he was a speed merchant who demoralised rivals.

'His relentless on-speed style would make a clash with Black Caviar interesting. Nothing, I fancy, would ever come from behind to beat her in her distance range but a horse with Rocket Man's sustained speed might see Luke Nolen having to let her go for once. Even so, I suspect it would be no contest.'

Soon after, Rocket Man took his career-defining victory in Singapore's feature Group 1 KrisFlyer Sprint. He stormed to a four-and-three-quarter-length win, leaving Shaw bullish about a date with Black Caviar. 'He'll beat her, I've always thought he's clearly the better horse. I've been wanting it. We'll take her on any time.'

Except he never did.

Sydney-bound, the discourse pondered whether Black Caviar would ever find herself under challenge in a race again.

Bronwen Healy Photography

Black Caviar at full gallop to win the T.J. Smith Stakes at Randwick in Sydney.

13

Northern Exposure

Randwick, T.J. Smith Stakes, 9 April 2011

It was in the dystopian novel *1984* that George Orwell proposed the terrifying concept of Room 101, which contained nothing more than a person's most primal fear. For the humans engaged with Black Caviar, that dread was defeat. As desperately as they wished to keep it at bay, each would find themselves contemplating how it might happen, what it would look like and how they would react. For it still seemed inevitable.

Ever the pragmatist, Peter Moody was sure he could take defeat in his hefty stride. He worried about everybody else. 'At the end of the day she's a racehorse. She's there to race. The chances of her being beaten are probably quite great. She's susceptible to injury through her bulk and the way she goes about things in a race. There'll be no one sadder than I if she ever gets beaten but I think there'll be a lot of people more disappointed than I when she does. It'll hurt if it ever happens but I've probably steeled myself through getting beat too often to worry about it.'

Tony Haydon imagined Black Caviar herself would be mightily peeved if the worst were to happen. For his part, he figured he would drop his lip for a few days. 'No one wants to see a champ get beat and especially when they're so close to you. I don't want to see her get beat. I'd probably have a tear in my eye or something like that because I'm quite soft. Hopefully that day doesn't come but it'll happen. Everyone gets beat, every champ gets beat.'

Patrick Bell, more often than not, watched Black Caviar's races on television. He never felt overly worked up, as he was a man of great faith. He too had been around racing long enough to know the probabilities. 'I've always thought in the back of my head that she's got to get beat one day, I hope today's not the day. But eventually everyone gets beat, it's just a matter of time.'

When Donna Fisher unclipped the lead strap and sent Nelly on her way, she found her nerves were racked. 'It's very exciting but then very scary because of the fact that she actually hasn't been beaten. You get the nervous thing of "Oh, is today the day that maybe something might happen, one of the horses might be too good for her?" If she's beaten and she's been beaten fair and square, there's nothing you can do about that. All she can do is give her best.'

The Taylors had morbidly joked about it. Jill: 'I've never considered her losing; it's just never entered my mind. That's what you do. You go to the racetrack, she races, you win, you have champagne in the winner's bar and then you go and celebrate all night. That's just how it is.' David: 'She's going to need counselling when it loses.'

Luke Nolen would cut off the question as soon as he sensed it edging towards the consideration of defeat. 'I haven't. I won't. I can't. I think I'd have to go see a psychiatrist to get me back to normal. I don't want to ever think about it. Chances are it probably will too. But until that day happens I'm not going to pre-empt any of it. There aren't any certainties. Especially in our game.'

Whatever the theorising, they all came to stare defeat squarely in the eye atop the famous Randwick rise. There, every heart skipped a beat.

* * *

If sales can be viewed as competition and prevailing in an auction regarded as winning, then the owners of Black Caviar had already lost in Sydney. The Inglis Australian Easter Yearling Sales boast of selling the best horseflesh of the year. In Lot 277 of the 2011 sales, they had precisely that. Helsinge had dropped a colt by stallion Casino Prince, the first offspring to come to market since the greatness of Black Caviar had been revealed.

Rick Jamieson had offered a full brother at the 2009 Melbourne Premier Sale. The Bel Esprit colt was not the size of his sister and, with no evidence to support the breeder's pairing to that stage, probably disappointed, selling for a modest $75,000. The buyers were legendary jockey Roy Higgins and his syndication partner Wylie Dalziel from Chefs on the Run. Six weeks after purchase, Black Caviar began her career and they sat back and watched their investment boom.

The colt came to be named Moshe and was sent to Team Hawkes under the tutelage of John Hawkes and sons Michael and Wayne. Moshe won on debut at Bendigo and twice at Moonee Valley, but he did not measure up in his attempts at Stakes races. He was retired to stud after just five starts. Modest, yes. Valuable still. Now any foal of Helsinge was the hottest property on turf.

Neil Werrett gathered the band together. They were ready to reinvest. Invest being the operative term. There were no concerns about the money ventured being money lost this time. A colt opened not only the possibilities of racing but breeding. Owning stallions was where the real money was made. They wanted Black Caviar's half-brother, the Casino Prince colt.

So did mining magnate Nathan Tinkler, the richest person in Australia under the age of forty. Tinkler had used a portion of his fortune to establish the wildly ambitious Patinack Farm racing and stud speculation. He had spent tens of millions of dollars on horseflesh across Australia to get the venture established. His sporting tastes extended beyond racing and, in his home town of Newcastle, he bought the NRL club the Knights and the A-League franchise the Jets.

Tinkler had raced the sire Casino Prince, a talented colt whose career was highlighted by victory over Tuesday Joy in the 2008 Group 1 Chipping Norton Stakes. It was the win that shored up his stud prospects. Trained by Anthony Cummings, Casino Prince was unlucky not to boast a more impressive résumé. He placed in a series of high-calibre races including the Cadbury Guineas, Australian Cup and Doncaster Handicap. Tinkler raced his horses to establish them as stallions. Now he wanted the second generation to fortify his project.

Gary Wilkie had a business connection with Jamieson that dated back many years. The inside word was that the breeder had budgeted for $600,000 for the Casino Prince–Helsinge colt and he had deliberately chosen the elite Sydney sale rather than Melbourne to maximise his returns. Accordingly, the Black Caviar camp set their limit at that mark. But Jamieson had an inkling that with the right interest, he would do better.

The bidding duel that ensued stopped the most seasoned sales veteran. It escalated into essential viewing. Werrett stood with Moody, but this time it was the owner calling the shots. In the opposing camp, trainer John Hawkes kept upping the ante. Werrett and Moody followed an established path; they left their maximum far behind. Werrett pushed the bidding through the million-dollar barrier. This time he would have to expand the syndicate if the sale fell his way. Each bid caused a recalculation. Eventually, though, a man has to accept his limitations.

Tinkler had set no limit. He was buying. The last bid of thirty-three ended the battle, a call of $1,025,000. Hawkes remained initially coy about the identity of his benefactor. Werrett abided by no such niceties: 'Nathan Tinkler has a lot more money than we have and he wasn't going to stop. It would have been nice to have another member of the family.' It was supposed Tinkler would have bid double what he paid if necessary for the horse with the breeding to fulfil Patinack Farm's ambitions.

If Jamieson did not know it beforehand, he did in the aftermath. He had been sitting on the proverbial gold mine: 'I'm thrilled to bits.' The frantic auction topped the sale. The yearling fetched the highest price of any sold in Australia in 2011. It was glorious fodder for the press and they set the scene for the highlight of the Sydney Autumn Carnival, Black Caviar.

Werrett did not dwell on the disappointment. He had the real thing coming to his patch in Sydney for the first time. By majority demand, he had done all the commuting thus far. While there was a caravan of sixty heading north from Melbourne, he would finally enjoy his mare in his backyard without the need to fly for the privilege.

The Black Caviar Roadshow rolled into Sydney at 4 a.m., completing the overnight drive from Caulfield. Darkness was no cover. The mare's arrival had been scheduled and anticipated, as eagerly scrutinised as Air Force One touching the tarmac. The media at Randwick saw more of her than they bargained for. Moody was summoned to the airwaves and took the hint that every detail needed to be shared. 'She came off the truck in good shape, had a good drink and a leak and a mouthful of tucker. Her temperature was good so we threw a saddle on her and she went out for a trot and had a good look around.'

It was Friday morning prior to the T.J. Smith Stakes, the highlight of AJC Derby Day, usurping even the 150th running of the three-year-old classic. While her deeds preceded her, this visit was a litmus test, as it would show how Black Caviar was perceived elsewhere in Australia. There was never a better case study than a Melbourne horse setting foot on Sydney turf.

The divide between Sydney and Melbourne is greater than a mere border. There is intense competition between the racing communities of Australia's two key states, an unease that breeds rank parochialism. At each carnival, tallies are kept so a measure of superiority can be asserted at the close. Many a great horse from one district had been derided in the other. Tie The Knot was a 'Sydney champion' who never quite measured up in the Melbourne majors. Northerly went winless in a trio of Sydney starts after proving himself the ultimate force in Melbourne.

Success, and the accompanying embrace, were hardly guaranteed for Black Caviar. Sydney racing stalwart Max Presnell set the terms in the *Sydney Morning Herald*: 'Now Black Caviar comes to Sydney for Saturday's T.J. Smith at Randwick. Can she produce the same dazzle in the reverse direction? Black Caviar has worked attractively our way at Caulfield but a gallop isn't a race. Many Melbourne horses, broken in using the Sydney direction and working smoothly on that leg down south, have come here for a race and been out of sync.'

The greatest peculiarity of Australian racing grew from the origins of the sport. In Sydney the founders chose to race in the clockwise direction, while in Melbourne they instituted anti-clockwise racing. And never the twain did meet.

The change of direction had left many a gifted horse to lead with its wrong leg and lose its action entirely as it tried to recover equilibrium while turning the opposite way. To fast-track her education, Moody had insisted every gallop Black Caviar undertook after the Newmarket was the right-hand way of going. That work was set to be tested under the full pressure of Group 1 racing.

The horse had been seen, now the trainer had to be heard. A press conference was scheduled in the Newmarket Room at the Inglis Bloodstock sales complex. It was a media engagement not only attended by the rank-and-file racing writers but feature writers and news hounds as well. It was demanded of Moody that he recount the tale so far, and his recollections would colour all corners of the following day's papers.

The quote that most tickled the Sydney scribes was Bart Cummings' description of Black Caviar as having 'the neck of a Duchess and the arse of a cook'. Moody was portrayed as a horseman to the soles of his boots.

With a high demand for any insights into future plans, Moody extolled the virtues of Hong Kong as staging the fairest test of the world's sprinters while tacitly underplaying Royal Ascot for its lesser quality of opposition and blatant lack of prize money. While he acknowledged the desire that Black Caviar head abroad, he openly stated he wanted to take her further, believing she would prove herself the best miler in the world also when he deigned to run her in longer events.

Keeping to his regular refrain, he championed the status of Australian racing, careful that the message was not skewed to imply that the sport was more worthy or exciting elsewhere. 'We've got the best racing product in the world. Where else in the world can a taxidriver train a champion? Where else can Billy Bloggs, the brickie's labourer, own a share in Makybe Diva or Black Caviar? That doesn't happen anywhere else in the world. You've got to be a lord, a lady or a Russian oil baron and a Texan mogul to be involved in racing.'

There was one moment when Moody did risk upsetting the Sydney establishment. He bluntly stated that Black Caviar would not be left alone at any stage while at Randwick. At the previous year's carnival his horses had become sick and it undermined the performances of gallopers including Typhoon Tracy, Set For Fame and Willow Creek. Moody let it hang in the air that it might not have been natural bad luck and furthered the point when asked if his previous experience was linked to his demand for abnormally tight security. 'Most definitely. We don't want anything going wrong.'

But the message that resonated most strongly from this lengthy media call related to Black Caviar's task the following day. 'No disrespect to her rivals but facts and figures tells you the opposition cannot beat her, plain and simple.' It was said without a hint of arrogance.

There were eight rivals to deal with. Hay List was among them. Having missed the Newmarket Handicap, he had arrived in Sydney first and narrowly won the Group 2 Challenge Stakes. It had not been the emphatic win befitting his previous standards, thus his reputation had not yet been fully restored. On the New South Wales tote he was out beyond $15, the fourth pick in the market. The 2008 Doncaster Handicap winner Triple Honour was resuming from a spell. As was talented mare Alverta, who had enhanced her Group 1 Coolmore Classic form racing in Europe. Her best result was a commendable third behind former crack Australian colt Starspangledbanner in the July Cup at Newmarket.

In Saturday's *Daily Telegraph*, Tony Thomas pleaded with Sydney-siders to put aside ancient grudges and join the jamboree: 'No matter what you are passionate about, somewhere there lives someone who is simply the best at it. Well, that's Black Caviar. I'm not that keen on the opera but I'd want to see Pavarotti. I've never been to the ballet but I reckon I'd turn up to see Darcey Bussell dance one more time.

'It's about the best. It's about watching them, admiring them for their God-given talents, marvelling at the sheer precision and grace unlike anything you've ever seen. That's why you should get to Randwick today.'

That was precisely the tone that permeated the 25,368 crowd who accepted the Royal Randwick invitation. Sydney was geed up. One fan had posted a home-recorded song on YouTube to the tune of *Cat's in the Cradle.*

She's black and tough and really fast
And now I'm going to meet her at last
She's finally up here at last.

History would tell you that Phar Lap inspired poetry from the common folk. It does not record whether any of it was good.

Sydney's premier racetrack is a roomy course with sweeping bends. The straight measures 401 metres, the early section of which is uphill. Professional punters would say a horse must wait until it had topped the rise before making its final run to the finishing post. It was senseless to reach full acceleration working against an incline.

As they reached the high ground with 300 metres left to run in the T.J. Smith Stakes, Black Caviar was giving Hay List a five-length head start. She had not broken her rivals with punishing midrace sectionals. She had not put paid to them on the turn with one savage hammer blow. Black Caviar was under serious threat in a race, just when most had given up on that very eventuality. For a heartbeat, the heaving crowd in the decrepit stands and on the lush lawn wondered if she was about to be beaten. Even Moody, who had orchestrated the scenario, felt dread momentarily.

Nolen and Moody would stand together in the mounting yard before a race hundreds of times a year at venues from splendid to dismal, assessing the chances of champions and duds. Like a married couple, their conversations had developed a familiar routine. 'Bounce, squeeze and travel.' Nolen knew what Moody was going to say before he moved his lips. The trainer liked his horses out of the gates and up in the race. 'That's Peter Moody's instructions for nearly every racehorse we have. Pete has long thought that jockeys are very simple thinkers and doesn't like to confuse us with many instructions. Yeah, bounce, squeeze and travel, that's what he says.'

Not this day. Moody had learnt the idiosyncrasies of Randwick as a teenager. He needed Nolen to have his wits about him and, on this occasion, help the mare. 'It was the only real instructions he'd given me in the times I'd ridden her. He said, "Nurse her around the corner, don't drag her round. And wait until you top the rise before you go for her."'

Nobody else was privy to that conversation. Not the throng of media. Not the swag of jockeys who poured out of the Jockeys' Room to get a glimpse at the best horse in the world. And not the owners. Had they heard Moody's words, they might have been braced.

Black Caviar jumped off-balance again. Hay List raced without hesitation out of the gates and to the lead. Black Caviar paired up with Crystal Lily behind him. She got pushed a little wide by the filly she had been terrorising in Melbourne, so Nolen eased back a touch further to a clear third. True to Moody's word, Nolen did not stoke the mare down the side of the track. He sat conservatively and held her close coming to the home bend. For all he tried to assist, Black Caviar still lugged around that corner. She wobbled out like a drunk. Then she took another stride sideways, hanging further still like a rickety shopping trolley. While Black Caviar drifted, Hay List travelled like an arrow. Glyn Schofield's years of riding had taught him that when you travelled so well at such a point you did not get beaten. Black Caviar had conceded ground at precisely the moment she would usually surge for victory. The deficit was alarming.

It struck Moody like a blow to the chest. 'I'd be lying if I said my heart didn't miss a beat. It was quite a shock to see him shoot away from her over the famous Randwick rise. He was a long way in front.' Moody was powerless to do anything other than grimace.

Nolen took a firm grip of the reins and balanced Black Caviar. He felt no panic, as there was time enough to retrieve what had been lost. Once she was settled beneath him, Nolen stoked her with his urgings. Then he released her. Black Caviar sprang like a coil. 'I saw Hay List was so far in front and said to her, "Let's go, love," and off she went.'

Black Caviar descended with frightening magnificence. At full velocity she was a captivating sight. Neck lowered with menacing intent. Stride long and languid, her front hooves brushing the ground at impact before rising again. Her rear planted firmly with each bound, propelling her forward. She went from a query at the 200 to a certainty at the 100. Schofield atop Hay List went from optimistic to fatalistic: 'I could hear her coming. Then she hit overdrive and I could see her going.'

She spectacularly raced away from Hay List. While you could not take your eyes off Black Caviar, it was essential to view the back play. Hay List was still getting away from his trailing rivals despite being passed as if he were nailed to the fence.

The Sydney punters were euphoric. The ovation was largely in response to the horse. But a small portion of it owed to the crowd's good fortune – to have been present for the finest race of Black Caviar's career.

Claire Bird sat propped on a pony beyond the finish line poised to conduct the post-race interview with the winning jockey. She had been Sunline's strapper when that mare ruled the world. The New Zealand mare won thirty-two races in three countries including two brilliant barrier-to-post Cox Plate victories. Bird had been a key character in the affection generated towards her horse. She could never forget the Doncaster Handicap of 2002 there at Randwick. Sunline, loaded with 58 kilograms, held off the powerful finishing burst of the outstanding Shogun Lodge in a win that encapsulated her champion qualities. Bird felt protective of Sunline's record as the swell towards Black Caviar grew. But as the noise reached her in the late afternoon sun, it brought a lump to her throat and a tear to her eye. She knew racing greatness. And this was the impact it had.

Andrew Eddy would capture the prevailing sentiment for *The Age* when he returned to his laptop in the Press Room, where verse had been penned for nearly every champion the turf had known: 'In almost every sense, this was her greatest victory. She'd run quicker times and won by greater margins, but yesterday at Randwick the world's champion racehorse Black Caviar had a good, long look at the possibility of defeat and decided it was not for her.'

It had a physical impact on observers. Moody was reeling but he was immediately required to put the effort into words: 'Lucky I'm young and I have got a good heart,' he managed. Gary Wilkie commented: 'That was absolutely extraordinary,' then his voice cracked mid-interview and he had to excuse himself as the emotion became overwhelming.

Beyond the finish, where Alison Road borders the track, cars had pulled over, their occupants alighting to hang on the cyclone fence. Nolen would normally be alone with his thoughts in the thirty seconds after passing the line. Instead, he found himself conversing with the folk beyond the racecourse who had heard the race on their radios and had to catch a glimpse to commit it permanently to memory.

Donna Fisher took in that scene and saw further proof that Black Caviar understood the stir she had caused. 'She's getting better with the way she's reacting to things and slowly starting to play to the crowd a bit. In Sydney cars stopped on the side of the road and Luke actually plays to the crowd too. Luke took her over to the fence and she just trotted along looking at them.'

As he waited for the mare to return, Moody thought of T.J. Smith, his first mentor in big-time racing, and the honour of winning the race that carried his name. 'This is a really special win for me personally. I spent my first three years here with the Little General and it was like coming home. So many memories and now I've got one more, a pretty good one too. I had a sizeable bet that I wouldn't cry,' Moody said with a briefly faltering voice. 'There was a fair bit of money on the line, but, sorry boys, it's not going to happen. Nearly, but not quite.'

In matters of judging horses on the Sydney turf, guru Ken Callander gave verdicts like a Roman emperor with a twitching thumb. In this case, he could not help but approve: 'When I was a kid and Tulloch was in his prime, the old-timers only wanted to talk about Phar Lap, then when Kingston Town hit town they wanted to talk about Tulloch. Forget yesterday and enjoy Black Caviar. I have been going to Randwick for fifty years and I haven't seen any faster or more brilliant racehorse.'

In an age where every theory and performance must be scrutinised and quantified, the mowing-down of Hay List by Black Caviar gave grounds for further research. It led to the rise of the cult of the long stride.

Tom Waterhouse is a racing blueblood, the son of trainer Gai. His paternal grandfather is legendary bookmaker Bill Waterhouse, a maverick who wielded tremendous influence in the racing scene for decades. His maternal grandfather was Tommy Smith.

It was family lore that the great horses covered more ground with each stride than did their rivals. A long stride led to an efficient use of energy and a physical advantage.

'My grandfather, Bill Waterhouse, he always talks about the champion Bernborough and how he had the longest stride of any horse he'd ever seen. My other grandfather, T.J. Smith, always told my mum when looking at the sale ring to always try and find those horses that stride out because the really great horses have a longer stride than other horses.'

Tom Waterhouse undertook to determine the length of Black Caviar's stride and found what he espoused to be her secret.

'If you look in the last 100 or 200 metres of the T.J. Smith at Randwick, Hay List actually strode a few more times than Black

Caviar, yet Black Caviar absolutely blitzed Hay List. It's a sign of a great horse that it only takes thirteen strides for Black Caviar yet it's fifteen strides for Hay List, and Black Caviar wins by such a margin, it's incredible. It's amazing when you watch her; you actually think that she's going easy or that she won't make up the ground. I thought, "Oh Hay List has got it for sure." As a bookie you're so excited because you think maybe you're going to get a good result here. But she's just so efficient and covers so much ground that she doesn't look like she's exerting much energy or going that hard. Yet she's just going at such a pace and covering so much distance, it's phenomenal.'

Sydney was converted. Moody had paid homage to Tommy Smith, a man to whom he felt he owed so much. He had triumphed at Randwick, the course that had so captured his imagination at first sight. There was one more stop, though, with more riding on it still. Moody was homeward bound, and like a father ready to present his newborn babe.

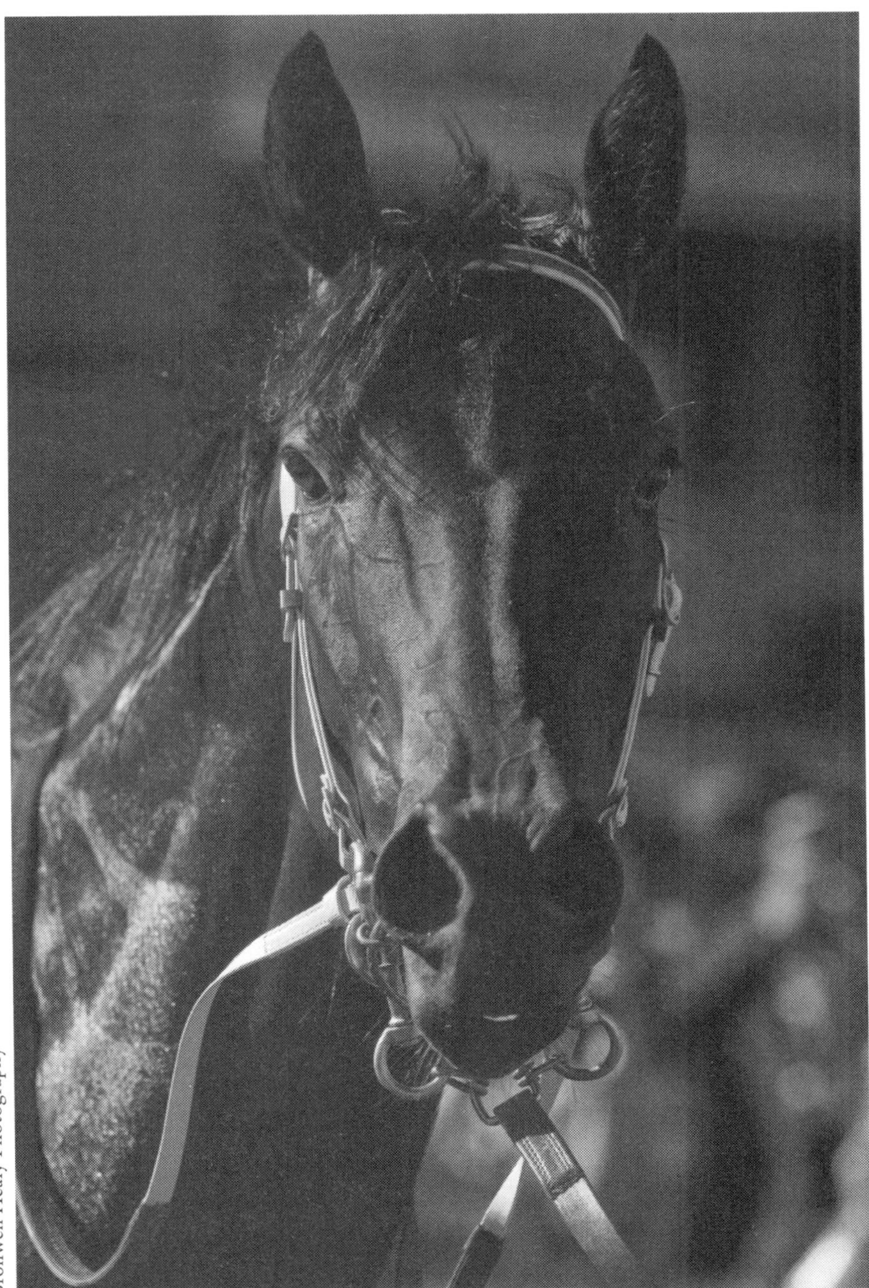

Bronwen Healy Photography

Black Caviar stared at defeat in the T.J. Smith Stakes at Randwick and decided it was not for her.

Newspix / Peter Wallis

Luke Nolen hails Black Caviar number one on the post in the BTC Cup at Doomben.

14

State of Origin

Doomben, BTC Cup, 14 May 2011

Peter Moody was a man who met his debts. He felt obligation deeply. It was a trait that spoke directly to his heritage. In his state of origin they took great pride in him, the bush kid from Wyandra and Charleville who went to Melbourne, became a top trainer and ended up with the best horse in the world. It married precisely with the way he viewed himself.

'For me personally, going home to Queensland where I was born and bred; it was great to showcase racing. That's where I basically learnt my craft and kicked off. So it was a bit of repayment, a thank you for giving me my start in life to take her back there.'

The Brisbane Winter Carnival had suitable races for Black Caviar, but had it not, Luke Nolen was fairly certain Moody would have ensured it was on her itinerary regardless. 'If Peter hadn't showcased the best horse he's ever had in Queensland, they probably would have taken his Queensland passport off him.'

Moody had imagined a day laced with a bit of sentiment mixed with some genuine excitement. He still underestimated the phenomenon that had him in its grip.

In 2011, Queensland had been subjected to the brunt of nature's fury. Terrifying floods had left three-quarters of the Sunshine State a designated disaster area. Barely a life had been untouched, with spirits weighed down as if by sandbags under the magnitude of their misfortune.

Whether you view sport as escapism, a metaphor for the human condition, or life's dessert cart, it was as if the representatives of the state took it upon themselves to do the only thing they could to revive a battered consciousness – win.

A-League club Brisbane Roar claimed the championship with a preposterous last-gasp grand final revival. Delirium gripped 50,000-plus spectators decked out in the team's orange, as Ange Postecoglou's men grabbed two goals in the last three minutes of extra time and then prevailed in a penalty shootout. They did it inside a stadium that, at the peak of the deluge, had been under water and aflame.

The netball team, Queensland Firebirds, produced a perfect season in the Australia and New Zealand Netball League. The Reds would muscle their way from laughing stock to champions in the Super 15 Rugby Union. And the Maroons vanquished New South Wales, as favourite son Darren Lockyer drew time on his decorated rugby league career.

Sport in the northern state had never known such a period of dominance. They called Brisbane 'Title Town'. Each victory was celebrated with a suitable perspective and an additional sense of gratitude.

The prospect of Black Caviar gracing the Brisbane turf had sparked a manic sense of expectation. Racing officials had some sense of it, if not the full grasp. An advertising campaign was built around Muhammad Ali's catchcry 'The champ is here', mixed with a pulsating drumbeat and clips from her dozen victories. It was cleverly conceived, outstandingly orchestrated and became particularly distinctive as a racing promotion built entirely on a horse rather than a party. It drummed up interest. Brisbane Racing Club chief executive Stephen Ferguson told the press: 'Brisbane's been through a very tough time of late and Black Caviar provides us all with a ray of sunshine. Instead of people just being attracted to an event, they're attracted to a racehorse, which we think's fantastic.'

The mare was to have been flown to Brisbane to acclimatise for future international ventures. But problems with the airline, caused by procedural changes, scuppered the plan. Instead, Moody loaded her onto the float with a two-day trip in prospect. Dubbo was nominated as halfway.

Moody's transport driver, Peter Courtney, was entrusted with the journey and given the challenge of keeping his cargo secret. He indulged in a bit of cloak-and-dagger to satisfy his inner spy but was prepared to let his guard drop as he refuelled. An elderly gentleman got out of his caravan and quietly approached to ask if the famous horse was inside. 'I thought he looked harmless, so I told him yes, she was at the back, and he asked if he could just touch the outside of the truck where she was so he could tell people he got that close to Black Caviar.'

Brisbane Racing Club's track manager, Bill Shuck, was enlisted by Moody as a co-conspirator. Black Caviar would not only arrive anonymously but incognito.

A stable complex, which would ultimately house a dozen horses, had been constructed on the infield of Eagle Farm Racecourse. It would start off with a sole occupant. Security was in place when the Moody Racing float pulled up on a Sunday and unloaded its freight. Those present were told it was Set For Fame, the filly that had been Black Caviar's near twin in the early days together at the stables. She had gone on to become a three-time Group 2 winner, not quite graduating to the elite. The cover story was that Set For Fame was the forward scout to test accommodation and arrangements before Black Caviar's arrival the following Thursday.

The Brisbane carnival was leveraged entirely on her presence and once it became known there was movement in the stables, Shuck began fielding questions from nervous administrators. He lied to both the chief executive and chairman pressing his decoy story. He would not even tell his girlfriend the truth.

Shuck lived in the house 400 metres from the stables. Once again, Black Caviar was under the care of a guardian who could see her from his bedroom window.

The cone of silence held for two days. By then there were photographers stalking in the trees and a positive identification was made. The jig was up. Crucially, the ruse had lasted long enough to give Nelly the necessary peace to recover from the road trip.

In a quirk that is hard to imagine being replicated anywhere else in the world, Brisbane's two racetracks, Eagle Farm and Doomben, are literally across the road from one another. Black Caviar would make the shuttle from Eagle Farm to run in the BTC Cup at Doomben. She was given a dress rehearsal a week prior to the race. Galloping alone on the Doomben track at 6.15 a.m., she drew a healthy group of spectators along with four television cameras to capture her every stride.

Moody was on hand to make his assessment, but Nolen was left to race-day duties in Melbourne. It put Pat Bell in the saddle with instructions to stoke his regular partner to full speed at the climax of an 800-metre stride-out. The jockey, who had the keys most every day with a brief to cruise the back streets, had finally been given clearance to get on the freeway and open the throttle. He was going all the way. As Bell galloped Nelly, he understood the prevailing theories as absolute truth.

'It was pretty scary when she hit top gear. I've never felt like that in my life. I've heard Pete say once before her rear end is like a V8 engine and that's where all the power comes from. She's got such a big hindquarters she can just stride so far and when you ride her you notice it unbelievably. When you ask her to quicken, a lot of horses will quicken their whole stride and their action, where she just starts getting a bigger stride and covers so much more ground.'

Moody left Doomben for Melbourne content that Black Caviar was thriving under the demands of her campaign. With five weeks between engagements, he had sent her briefly to Murchison after leaving Sydney to freshen her body and mind. The time off had paid handsome dividends. So relaxed was Moody that he remained at Caulfield while Nolen was dispatched to handle the final preparatory gallop and the corresponding media demands.

A battalion greeted jockey and horse. Not only the scribes, reporters and camera operators but the trainers, strappers and assorted workers from other stables who refused to miss their brush with fame. Nolen felt in the gathering an edge of frenzy beyond what was typical.

Black Caviar worked stylishly. Nolen, too, was a tad surprised at how sharp she felt. He had come to think of these gallops as his nervous Nelly days. Race days were so within the horse's control that the jockey had learnt to entrust the responsibility to her. For these gallops, the burden sat squarely on him. The work had to be assigned and carried out precisely. The sectionals governing the pace and exertion in the work needed to be right to tune the athlete for competition. But he needed to return her sound. No ripping around corners at a reckless speed, as she might if left to her own devices. Once that was achieved, he would be glad to be getting out of Brisbane.

Local trainer Robert Heathcote was one observer. He intended saddling up two-time Group 2 winner Buffering against her. 'If that was just a familiarisation gallop then we're in serious trouble.' With that he turned from adversary to fan. 'It's quite exciting. I'm going to race against her on Saturday and the reality is if she runs her best, I simply can't beat her. She's the best sprinter

I've ever seen in my lifetime of racing. I'd be happy for Buffering to get within six lengths.'

Demand was insatiable. Morning tea was put on later in the week for a celebrity viewing as Black Caviar walked a handful of laps around the Eagle Farm enclosure. She picked her way through the infield, across the track, around the stabling area and into the sunbathed mounting yard. All rippling muscle and glistening coat. While she did nothing more than stride the catwalk, the hyperbole it prompted knew no bounds. Phil Lutton wrote for the *Brisbane Times*: 'She's Michael Jordan dunking from the free-throw line. She's Flo-Jo in full flight. She's an army tank driving through a brick wall. She's girl power in a saddlecloth.'

The day before the race, sixty-three people attended the formal press conference, a gathering Moody drily noted was greater than you would see at a midweek race meeting. It was then off to the Breakfast Creek Hotel on the banks of the Brisbane River, to fulfil an engagement as the guest speaker.

It was Black Caviar's connection to the public that continued to startle Moody. 'A lady saw this car and float driving down the highway. She recognised myself from the previous night's television news, that I was associated with this great racehorse. This woman drove about twenty mile out of her way to follow me to Nudgee Beach just on the off-chance that Black Caviar may have been on this float. And there she was, standing in water up to her waist in her underwear so she could pat this horse. She was a horse lover but had no affiliation with racing at all. For someone to do that I thought that was quite unbelievable.'

There was a delightful innocence to that anecdote. If you had witnessed the entire escapade you might have thought it tended towards the ludicrous. As Black Caviar took the few strides from the float to the beach, jittery racing officials formed a human shield across the road. Shuck quipped: 'We made sure that we would get run over before she would get run over. The lights were on but we were not taking any chances.'

Staring at each other from either side of the highway snaking from the airport to the city centre, Brisbane's two racetracks stand as monuments to a bygone era. Relics of a time when twin venues serviced the pre-eminent sport and entertainment in town. As the traffic choked Nudgee Road and the first of 20,134 people squeezed their way into Doomben Racecourse for BTC Cup Day, it might have been 2011 but it felt like half a century earlier.

Living memory could recall the June day in 1961 when a record 31,000 people came to Eagle Farm to see Tulloch crown his golden career with victory in the Brisbane Cup. Old-timers would still regale those who asked with tales of that day.

For Doomben, the greatest day in its history was the best part of four decades in the past – the Labour Day public holiday set aside to honour the freshly retired Gunsynd. While Kingston Town had subsequently won a Derby, and Might and Power thundered away with the Doomben Cup, it was that day in 1973 that Queensland racing folk kept harking back to for an occasion of similar significance.

Hailing from Goondiwindi, Gunsynd had started his career in Brisbane and built a cult following. He was a gent, remembered as fondly for his penchant to play to a crowd as his dominance in Australia's finest mile races. He had a willing accomplice in jockey Roy Higgins and, on his farewell day, what was planned to be a simple canter down the home straight became a royal greeting. Gunsynd was allowed to stop every few strides and stand regally before his subjects. Officially the crowd was declared at 18,000 but such was the chaos around the track that the police ordered the Flat gates opened to let further people and cars in. The true number was a matter of conjecture.

Much as he had courted the public's affection for Black Caviar, Moody could feel the noose tightening like the pink tie around his neck. Here was the whole of his home state entranced, almost betrothed to his horse on the promise, his promise, that she would win. From the sanctuary of his hotel room with his wife, with the broiling world he had helped conjure outside, the prospect was overwhelming. While the sense of frustration left him feeling ungrateful, he could no longer deny it was there.

He turned to Sarah and gave in. 'Crikey. I'd probably be the only person in Australia today who wouldn't be disappointed if she got beaten once, because then she becomes another horse.'

Whether it was the look on his wife's face or the betrayal that stabbed at his heart, he knew immediately it was the stupidest thing he had ever come up with. 'To suggest that, I needed to smack myself after I even thought it, let alone said it.'

Even with that resolution, it didn't ease his anxiety. He had often joked that it was just as well the horse did not fret like the owners on race day. At Doomben, he was the chief offender. With the meeting underway and the commotion taking shape, the time arrived for the staff to head over the road and bring Black Caviar in. Moody hijacked the operation as a method of escape. Over at the stables he attacked his cigarettes, desperate to find a state of calm. When one vice failed, he moved to the next, chugging cans of XXXX – parochial to a fault – before putting the headline act in harness.

From the moment Black Caviar stepped on course she was a magnet for fans. She was filmed on camera phones coming off the float, and word spread. Soon it seemed to the trainer there were more people in the saddling area than watching the undercard from the grandstands.

The next sighting of Moody was in the float car park, his latest attempt at finding refuge, under a distinctive white bucket hat. It

Meaghan Strickland-Wood

Black Caviar at the foot of her dam Helsinge. Of the foals born at Gilgai Farm in 2006, she was the standout.

Newspix / Mark Calleja

Peter Moody with Black Caviar at Nudgee Beach. The trainer took his filly to Queensland as a thank you to the state that gave him his start.

Newspix / David Geraghty

Winning the Victoria Derby with Amalfi was the fast-track to prominence. The young trainer from the middle of Woop Woop upstaged the establishment at his first attempt in 2001.

Two of his favourite girls. Daughter Breann among the many admirers on Lightning Stakes Day at Flemington in 2011.

Newspix / Jay Town

Batman found his Robin quite by accident. Jockey Luke Nolen always knows precisely where he stands with Peter Moody.

Newspix / Nicole Garmston

Bronwen Healy Photography

Bound for greatness. Broodmare Helsinge in April 2012 with her colt by leading sire Redoute's Choice.

Newspix / Darrin Braybrook

Raw speed and power, Black Caviar's sire Bel Esprit dominated the fraught two-year-old circuit in 2001.

Newspix / Nicole Garmstona

The horses that captured Peter Moody's heart: his first champion Typhoon Tracy (left) with his horse of a lifetime Black Caviar (right).

Newspix / Nicole Garmston

The horse, goat and pony show. Black Caviar with her unlikely troupe on retreat at Murchison.

Bronwen Healy Photography

Drawn in by the allure of horse racing, breeder Rick Jamieson has created a racing dynasty with the progeny of unraced mare Helsinge.

Bronwen Healy Photography

Easing the strain. Black Caviar thrives on the alternative remedy of Peter Clarke's water walker at Willowood Equicentre.

Newspix / Colleen Petch

Plain old Nelly. The vibe at the Caulfield stables always lifted when Black Caviar was in residence.

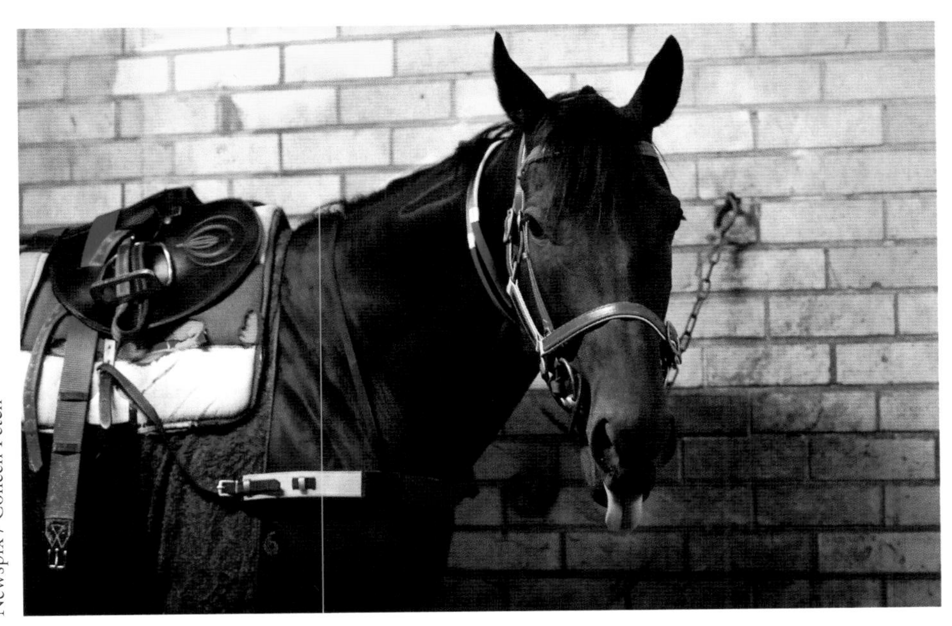

Newspix / Colleen Petch

Stable life starts before the rest of the world wakes up. Nelly was always first out of the box and onto the track.

Newspix / George Salpigtidis

A horseman to the soles of his boots, Peter Moody conquered the Melbourne scene inside a decade.

Racing's version of *Where's Wally*. The record crowd of 85,112 on the 2011 Emirates Stakes Day unanimously supported Black Caviar.

Bronwen Healy Photography

Hair blowing in the wind. Black Caviar's long, low stride was the source of such elegant destruction.

Bronwen Healy Photography

Faster than any horse in history. Black Caviar ran the first sub-10 second 200-metre sectional under challenge from Hay List in the 2012 Lightning Stakes.

Newspix / Peter Wallis

Newspix / Ellen Smith

A bid to build a dream on. Inglis Bloodstock opened the Black Caviar Bar at Oaklands Junction in honour of the most famous horse it ever sold.

Newspix / Nicole Garmston

Racing needed another hero by the close of the 2010 Spring Carnival. Jockey Ben Melham helped Black Caviar fill that void as they posted their first Group 1 victories together.

Newspix / Wayne Ludbey

Hear the barrackers shouting. South Australian racing had rarely known a day to match Black Caviar's record-breaking twentieth victory.

Newspix / Peter Wallis

The cynosure of all eyes. Black Caviar greeted by Peter Moody and owner Neil Werrett after victory in the 2011 BTC Cup at Doomben.

AAP Image/Racing Victoria, Gary Wild

Black Caviar boards her flight for London. The Airstable labelled by ground staff with a poster of its famous cargo.

Sarah Ebbett Photograph

The run to history. Black Caviar summoned all her courage to win the 2012 Diamond Jubilee Stakes at Royal Ascot.

Charlie Forgham-Bailey/Colorsport/Corbis

'Geez jock, that was a bit close wasn't it?' Luke Nolen eases the post-race tension by planting a kiss on Peter Moody.

The Picture Library Ltd / Alan Davidson

The Royal seal of approval. The Queen of the Turf bows before the Queen of England as Black Caviar received the ultimate commendation for gallantry.

Bronwen Healy Photography

hardly matched his dark suit but was a sentimental gesture of the headgear he had sported so often in his Brisbane days.

Race caller Alan Thomas had been coming to Doomben all his life. But as he looked down from his perch in the broadcast box he had frequented since 1994, he knew he had never seen the course quite like this. On his way in, he had stopped briefly to chat to a grandmother who had brought her three grandchildren to share in the day. He had pondered what it was that made Black Caviar special, how she had come so quickly to touch the generations like no other horse in recent times. He decided it was best that it remain undefined, a glorious intangible, proven to exist only by the presence of so many admirers.

Mixed with the eagerness was a slight sense of nervousness. Thomas had called many topflight sports apart from racing. But this was a day that might top them all. 'The selfish part of the day for me was I'm only going to get one crack at this champion. I thought, "Oh don't get beaten on my watch please." I don't want to be the race caller that brought Black Caviar down.'

While the odds ran heavily with Black Caviar, that was a risk. Hay List had enrolled for another crack. A fortnight after winning plaudits in the T.J. Smith, the gelding took his turn in the Group 1 All Aged Stakes at Randwick. Nothing was ever uneventful for John McNair and his horse. Jockey Glyn Schofield was involved in a fall from the top-weight Hawk Island in the Sydney Cup, the race prior. When he should have been donning the white, green and red silks, he was in an ambulance heading for St Vincent's Hospital with a broken collarbone.

With less than forty minutes to post time, McNair was scrambling for a replacement. His good fortune was the availability of the nation's big-race specialist, Glen Boss. His decision was a simple one for an important task. Hay List was stretching out to 1400 metres and Randwick was as wet as can be, rated a Heavy 10. There was huge investment in him and not just in the fact that he ran a warm favourite. Hay List had won the crowd at Randwick with his gallantry behind Black Caviar. Justice demanded this be his race. More than that, he could further define the magnitude of what the Australian turf was witnessing in Black Caviar. The enduring definition of a champion is a horse that beats other good horses by big margins. Hay List could enhance his status and in doing so boost that of his greatest rival.

So he did. Hay List jumped straight to the front where Boss allowed him to cruise unchallenged. He had the race on his terms long before the corner. Just as he had done two weeks earlier, Hay List bounded clear coming up the rise. In the absence of the freakish one, the gap was never challenged. It held at three-and-a-half lengths. To great applause, Boss stood high in the irons three bounds from the post and shook his head in admiration. He then leant forward and gave the horse an endearing pat.

Rarely one to contain his emotions, Boss felt a touch guilty. 'This is bittersweet for me. He is Schoie's horse and it was a privilege for me to ride him for ten minutes. He's as good a sprinter as I've ridden.' As he said it, he wondered what it must be like aboard Black Caviar.

McNair gave Hay List a further barrier trial before leaving Sydney for Brisbane, ensuring he still had plenty left to give. That was a demolition. The Central Coast trainer finally had his hulking sprinter in perfect order. 'We are planning to throw a spanner in the works. It is going to be a hell of a race.' With Schofield sidelined, Boss would again be in the saddle.

In Thomas' mind, the BTC Cup was a fair-dinkum race: 'Once they said we're going to bring Hay List to Brisbane, we're going to take Black Caviar on, I knew she'd have to race him and I knew that if she wasn't on her game and he was, that there was a very good chance that he could beat her on that day.'

Such was the stranglehold these two horses exercised over the discussion previewing the BTC Cup that Group 1 winners like Black Piranha and Sniper's Bullet and future Emirates Stakes winner Albert The Fat didn't even register in the commentary.

A wave of people moved across the racecourse tracking Black Caviar's every move. Finally, she was in the mounting yard and the human traffic stuttered under heavy congestion. Nolen likened the atmosphere to a Cox Plate crowd. Doomben and Moonee Valley shared distinctive characteristics. They were intimate settings. The audience was close to the stage and the principals. The parade ring was behind the grandstand, making for a theatrical entrance onto the track. Safely on the back of Black Caviar, Nolen began the walk and each section of the crowd he reached burst into applause. 'It was like the boys coming out of the rooms and running down the race for a footy game. They cheered her all the way. It was great.'

The number of spectators presented Pam Hawkes and Jannene Madden with a considerable problem. Having watched the goings-on in the mounting yard, they could not break through the crowd to get to their designated vantage point to see the race. Jannene had been in Townsville with her daughter in the days before and had been amazed by the build-up even that far away. It was a Queensland event, not only for the capital. She had bought her outfit and hat in the town 1300 kilometres north of Brisbane and been treated like a celebrity. Here she was, all dressed up with nowhere to go. 'We were very concerned we weren't going to see the race for a while, there were just so many people to get through. It was such a big day for Doomben they actually had to close the gates, they had so many people wanting to go into the track and watch her.'

Hawkes felt this was a reception elevated further from what they had previously experienced. 'Brisbane I think was recovering after the equine flu, racing in Queensland had gone through a very rough patch and suddenly there was a good horse up here and we're going to come out and see it. And come out they did in their droves.'

All made their marks aided by the delay created when Albert The Fat threw jockey Damien Browne out the back of the barriers at the first attempt at a start. Pre-race musings had centred on whether Black Caviar would lead Hay List, as she had in the Patinack Farm and the Lightning Stakes, or whether Nolen would ease again and take up the chase as had occurred in Sydney. Against the general consensus, it was immediately apparent he would do the latter. The decision probably rested in the way they left the structure: Hay List pinged, Black Caviar dwelt. There was a length between them by the time you had identified their colours. She took no harm from it. Hay List led with Buffering pressuring. Black Caviar lobbed behind them in third without any crowding. She was in the box seat. Nolen eased out three deep past the landmark Glenlogan Park sign, a few strides before the 600.

She closed rapidly on the lead pair, but again, as they made the right-hand bend, Black Caviar wobbled out and Hay List steered with the perfect combination of speed and agility. Briefly, he held a three-length advantage. Boss had cribbed a couple of cheap sectionals midrace so there was plenty left when he let Hay List go. His rational mind thought there was not a horse in the world that could go with him. He feared, though, that there might be one.

Nolen sat utterly unconcerned. They had enjoyed a lovely run, bar the mild scramble around the turn. Black Caviar balanced up much more quickly than in Sydney and pinged after Hay List. In a lethal burst, she had him. It might not have been as dramatic, but it was every bit as emphatic. With that low, unpitying action in full motion, Black Caviar left him two lengths astern. Again Hay List had put five lengths on the rest of the field. As they reached the line, Nolen released his left hand from the reins and extended his index finger to the crowd. She was the undisputed number one.

When Boss caught up to Nolen past the post, he clasped his hand in tribute to what the two had just experienced. A man has to know when he is beaten. It was impossible to feel bitter in such a moment of splendour. Larry Cassidy had put Buffering directly in the line of fire. He wanted to learn what these two beasts were capable of. 'I looked outside me and Black Caviar was trotting and they just left me. I went from going well to gone in a stride. They are the best two sprinters I have ever seen.'

McNair could comfort himself with the thought that at least they were getting closer.

On the lawns under the red sponsors' umbrellas, on the balconies and in the grandstands proper, people leapt with the unrestrained elation of children. They roared in outright satisfaction. Watching with Sarah and his three girls, Moody felt the relief like never before. 'Here was an old Queensland boy in front of a crowd like this.'

Neil Werrett was determined that this one was for Moody. They pushed him out from the glare of the television cameras to lead Black Caviar in. Werrett watched in near-tranquillity. 'It is just so good that she keeps winning. I had my day when she won the T.J. Smith in Sydney. This is Pete's day. It is his home town. We set a plan at Christmas to showcase her to the country and let everyone see her, and it is great that the people love her so much.'

The late afternoon Queensland sun spilt a different light on the sea of salmon. Black Caviar seemed a little darker than usual. The silks on Nolen had a luminous quality as he paraded the conquering hero for all to adore. Jockey and horse cast a beautiful shadow on the grass before the teeming masses. Moody had lost his hat as he held the lead rein to guide her back. He posed with Black Caviar once the winner's rug had been draped over her. He looked with great tenderness at his mare who was agitated enough to raise the hair of her mane upright down the length of her neck.

Thomas noted scenes he felt certain he would never again behold. 'After the race, the emotion, the applause just kept going. She was the cynosure of all eyes. Wherever she went, everyone just watched. Luke Nolen took her down the top of the straight and I could see the panoramic view. Just to watch the crowd, just watch how they took it all in, lapped it up, enjoyed the moment. Go back and tell your kids and your grandkids, I was at Doomben the day Black Caviar came to town. I say to people who are still here, "What was it like when Tulloch won the Brisbane Cup?" And those who were there say, "Oh it was unbelievable." So years down the track the people who were here, someone's going to ask, "What was it like?" It was amazing.'

There was no formal autograph-signing scheduled, but Moody and Nolen were thrust all manner of paraphernalia over the mounting yard fence to scribble on. Race books, caps, shirts custom-made in the salmon and black. Moody's favourite was the fellow who asked him to sign a cigarette paper. 'Anything they could get their hands on for us to sign, to have some commemorative part of racing history. It was phenomenal. I've never seen the likes of it in racing.'

Among the tributes paid was a poem commissioned by Quest Newspapers and *City North News* from noted Queensland poet Rupert McCall. It concluded:

> I ventured to the racecourse just to see her in the flesh
> Expectation, history and inspiration mesh
> And they culminate in something that reverberates with pride
> In the undulating beauty of her mesmerising stride
> For beyond the sacred stopwatch that defines her special place
> The telling of the story lives on every person's face
> And the day will overwhelm me when I cast my memory back
> Just to say I saw the Caviar, the Caviar in Black

It had been intended that Black Caviar would race again a fortnight later and conclude her season with one last clash against Hay List in the Doomben 10,000, intriguingly, over the longer trip of 1350 metres. Neither would make it.

Moody inspected Black Caviar on the Thursday after the BTC Cup and sensed she had done enough. He assured the owners it was better to send her for a break one run early than being left with an exhausted horse. The campaign had been arduous but fruitful, clipping off five Group 1 races. Anything more, especially something so challenging, was not only risky but could jeopardise the spring. Moody pulled stumps. Like many a good Victorian, Black Caviar wintered in Queensland.

A raging favourite, Hay List was scratched on the eve of the 10,000 when McNair discovered soreness in the gelding's off-hind fetlock. It would develop into a serious leg infection, compounded further by the onset of a bout of colic. Hay List was plunged into a fight for his life.

McNair ordered an around-the-clock vigil. 'We had some luck and picked up the colic early. If it had presented at 6.30 at night when I'd left the stable instead of 9.30 a.m., I might have arrived the next morning to find a dead horse.'

When the colic struck, Hay List had to be removed from the course of antibiotics fighting the infection. What had been a manageable situation deteriorated dramatically. The leg infection revealed itself to be similar to the affliction that claimed the life of the popular mare Hot Danish only a couple of months earlier. 'It was almost an identical circumstance. His illness not only could have ended his race career, it nearly ended his life. If it had not been for the colic attack he would have been over it in very quick time and we might never have had to deal with what we were dealt. The infection was the biggest challenge and biggest worry.'

When Black Caviar was readying herself to resume hostilities, Hay List was recuperating at Muskoka Farm on New South Wales' Hawkesbury River. He had survived a hellish few months but faced a long road back to racing.

Newspix / Colleen Petch

The centre of attention and affection at the Caulfield Carnival in the Spring of 2011.

15

Spring Parade

Caulfield, Schillaci Stakes, 8 October 2011

What is sport without tension? A contest deprived the uncertainty of outcome and the unpredictability that fuels the narrative. Sport relies on the twist that demands adversity be conquered. The contest flavoured by the tantalising possibility of upset or the terrifying prospect of defeat.

The spring of 2011 offered no such thing. These were the days of miracle and wonder. Certainty of success like few had ever experienced. How would it endure in the minds of spectators?

Cricket faced these questions during the years of Australian domination under Steve Waugh and Ricky Ponting. There were moments of admiration, yet the national team as often tended towards tedium as adoration. The Test team visited ruthless destruction on ill-equipped opponents. Their confrontational methods left them open to the charge of behaving like brutes and bullies.

Tennis and golf under the champions Roger Federer and Tiger Woods knew such periods of assured results. Their winning streaks were disproportionate to nearly any other phase of history.

Bereft of adequate rivals, they were, curiously, pitted against each other by commentators as an artificial means of comparison. Their major victories were viewed through their respective quests to run down the records of Pete Sampras and Jack Nicklaus.

Golf wrestled with the Tiger phenomenon because the success or otherwise of tournaments was determined by the release of the man's annual schedule. It was definitively determined that golf was better when Woods was winning. When he was absent, it battled for relevance.

Cautious though he was, Peter Moody had come to believe Black Caviar was invincible and he was prepared to put it on the public record. 'It's got to the stage that I have so much belief in her ability that the only way I believe she can get beat is if something untoward happens. She injures herself. Not even getting blocked by some other horses can really stop her because she's got so much bulk and strength she can force a passage. If she comes back in one piece she will have won the race.' Moody could have been guilty of hubris, except for the fact that he was merely echoing what everyone else thought to be true.

Black Caviar's accomplishments of the previous season saw her crowned as the Australian Racehorse of the Year at a gala dinner in Melbourne. It gave Moody back-to-back victories following Typhoon Tracy's acclamation the year before. On stage to accept the award, the trainer was asked how Black Caviar had returned from her spell in preparation for the new season. He replied that she was better than she had ever been. At his table, Neil Werrett did a double take. 'I looked at Peter and thought how is that possible?'

Not only was Black Caviar in fine form, there was a tragic depletion in natural rivals. Hay List was in the ranks of the long-term injured. Hot Danish was dead.

Most shockingly, Crystal Lily had collapsed and died during trackwork at Flemington in the early days of spring. She was participating in a trial down the straight when she suffered a heart attack. Glen Boss had his shoulder smashed in the subsequent fall, an injury that sidelined him for the next four months and went within a whisker of ending his career.

On describing the incident, Crystal Lily's co-trainer Simon Zahra's tone was disbelief: 'She was probably halfway through the trial and started to drop out suddenly and then collapsed to the ground. She's never had any issues in her whole life, from day one.' The fatality prompted a wave of sadness. Crystal Lily had proven her brilliance, defying the late challengers to win the Golden Slipper despite dramatically veering towards the outside rail. But she had won more admirers in defeat, through her unflinching chasing of Black Caviar. Her death served to emphasise how fleeting the careers of the best racehorses could be.

The selection of Black Caviar's spring season carried state-of-the-nation gravitas and gave rise to ferocious lobbying. She would reorder the conventional highlights of a carnival. A sprinter rather than a stayer, Black Caviar would never run in the iconic races of the turf like the Cox Plate and Melbourne Cup, just as an Olympic sprinter would never attempt the marathon. Instead, she recast her races from support events to the main event.

The Australian Turf Club concocted a half-baked scheme for a Sydney match race, Black Caviar against Hay List and More Joyous, which was ludicrously touted to compete with the final day of the Flemington carnival. That possibility arose during a squabble over prize money. The Victoria Racing Club had proactively thrown out the lure of a $600,000 bonus for an international competitor to take their chances against Black Caviar. It was a carrot specifically aimed at Rocket Man's South African owner, Fred Crabbia. But the original terms left Black Caviar's owners ineligible to claim the bounty. That potential mutiny was resolved when conditions were altered to pay the bonus if Black Caviar won a leg of the Global Sprint Challenge abroad.

Another plan was under consideration. Privately, Moody contemplated an experimental campaign, one that would test not only his horse but also his training nous. His instincts had always told him that Black Caviar would be better still if she were allowed to escape the narrow confines of pure sprinting. His blueprint would have her starting with the Group 1 Manikato Stakes – on the eve of the AFL Grand Final – extend her to 1400 metres for the first time at Caulfield and culminate in the Myer Classic over a mile on Derby Day.

Perhaps if Moody had been left to his own devices, this would have happened. Instead, convention won the day, and he settled for a rerun of the previous spring. Democratically, Caulfield, Moonee Valley and Flemington would each take their turn. With that declaration, the truth was out there. Black Caviar could not be beaten in her nominated assignments. If the circumstances did not change, then neither would the outcome.

Repetition did nothing to undermine the raging expectation and unadulterated excitement surrounding her reappearance. Quite the opposite. In her absence from the racetrack, Black Caviar's fame had grown exponentially. Her name had stretched beyond the sporting landscape and into the mainstream consciousness. The tale of Black Caviar was told on the ABC's *Australian Story*. In doing so, she became the first animal to be afforded such a status in the long-running history of the acclaimed documentary series. *Paint the Town Black* prepared the landscape for win number fourteen, a streak that would equal the longest winning sequence in the career of Phar Lap.

The shadow cast by the legend of the Red Terror knows no bounds. The iconic horse of the Depression years holds a holy place in the lexicon of Australian sport. He lived fast, died young and left a beautiful corpse for the generations to worship at the Melbourne Museum. Phar Lap peeled off those fourteen wins in his four-year-old season of 1930–31. The streak consisted of five wins in Sydney and nine in Melbourne, and ranged in distance from seven furlongs to two miles (1400 to 3200 metres) and took in four Group 1 victories, including the Cox Plate and Melbourne Cup. It formed the backbone of his imperious record.

Black Caviar had no prospect of replicating the diversity of Phar Laps' feats but the benchmark became so widely accepted that it was interpreted and referred to as some form of record. While it was no such thing, each chapter in Black Caviar's career needed relevance and context beyond the mere act of winning. None could be as enticing or more readily comprehensible as that which would put her on a standing with Phar Lap.

The first public sighting of Black Caviar in a fresh preparation came in a Caulfield jump-out over 800 metres on the last Tuesday in September. Word-of-mouth reports spread quickly. The mare ambled out of the gates a clear last, then picked up and scooted through in one hell of a hurry to be many lengths clear. Even though her race-day deeds were well known, the story was recounted with a sense of awe. By midmorning, that trial had become an internet sensation, the clip bearing out the tale.

It was Nolen's first sit on the mare since Brisbane. He wore a red jacket and black cap, as if to prove difficult to pick from a line-up. That was an exercise in futility. Black Caviar rolled in from the jump, enhancing the illusion of being left behind. But the stunning acceleration was unmistakable. She purred through to round up her rivals and open an ever-widening margin. By the home corner, the designated finish, her lead was conservatively estimated at six lengths.

With quasi-organised trials, horses of varyingly ability grouped together by the local trainers rather than official fields convened by authority, the quality of opposition can be anything from unknown to dubious. That gallop, for instance, included the poorly performed Moody horse Paranoia, the sort of mount that

Black Caviar would beat by a minute in a fifty-six-second race. But it emerged that one of her rivals was Sydney three-year-old Smart Missile, highly fancied for the Caulfield Guineas. The currency of the gallop soared.

Moody might have steered clear of the hype. But perhaps he thought, 'Why bother downplaying what was perfectly obvious?' Everything was precisely in place. His first two words upon being asked for an assessment seemed enough: 'Super. Super.'

The moment the AFL season was completed and Geelong shared the spoils of its third premiership in five years with its grateful public, Black Caviar was saddled with the sporting agenda. She presented racing with the opportunity to bound into the Spring Carnival on the front and back pages. The previous year, she had started racing's prime time as the understudy to So You Think. This time around, Black Caviar would *be* racing.

There was no peace for Moody, be it 4 a.m. in the Caulfield trainers' tower or in the evening at home if the phone was on. Every media outlet in Australia, whether they understood the intricacies of the story or not, craved a taste of Black Caviar.

To the outsider, racing can be intimidating, complete with its distinct dialect and peculiar rituals. Some use this as an excuse to avoid the responsibility of trying to understand. One reporter asked Moody for an interview before 'Black Caviar raced Phar Lap in the Caulfield Cup'. 'The word "ridiculous" comes to mind for some of the questions we've been asked this week,' Moody chided publicly. 'We welcome all inquiries, but please, do your homework a little bit.'

As he had forecast, preparing Black Caviar had become the easy part. Moody determined that training the best racehorse in the world was 'a dead-set pain in the arse'. One morning before dawn he launched into one of his exasperated but humorous tirades to Dave Lewis from *The Australian*: 'You know what I'd love to do? I'd like to win the lotto, buy a 5 per cent share in a racehorse and drive the trainer mad by ringing up every night to see how it's going. I'd be doing that while lying on a beach in far north Queensland eating prawns and drinking beer. I'd have my fourth wife, a 21-year-old six-foot blonde stroking my overgrown stomach and I'd stay up there until I died from a massive heart attack with a cigarette in my mouth.'

The interview concluded with the trademark rider: 'Not that I'm complaining.'

Amid the maelstrom a strange sensation was building. The pressure was magnifying. Werrett sensed that as Black Caviar was getting set to do what came so naturally, the humans were finding the ordeal almost extrasensory. 'The expectations on her seemed to get bigger with every win. I think it was because she had five months off, it was a long break, and during that period there was so much publicity about her. There was the *Australian Story* on the ABC, other TV programs about her, newspaper articles, the build-up to that race was amazing.'

Moody and Nolen were drawn into hypothetical contemplations of who would be held primarily culpable if Black Caviar did get beaten. Moody concluded: 'I know, as every football coach and manager out there knows, that as soon as things go downhill the first bloke to get kicked is the coach.' Nolen thought he was on the front line: 'They're going to be barking mad if she gets beat, and the fall bloke is the jockey usually and unfortunately.' Nolen hoped that they would at least string trainer and jockey up together.

Caulfield Guineas Day, 8 October 2011, dawned heavy with cloud and anticipation. Despite three feature races and a burgeoning reputation for quality surpassed only by Victoria Derby Day, the spring stepping-off point was leveraged entirely around the 1.20 p.m. running of the Schillaci Stakes.

Where the previous year's staging had given a startling indication of what was brewing, this time it was viewed as a formality. The topflight sprinters had contested the Manikato Stakes eight nights prior. In a sparkling performance, the three-year-old Golden Slipper-winner Sepoy missed the start, then worked furiously to attain the lead, before leaving his rivals standing. In his wake came Gai Waterhouse's bonny mare More Joyous.

Having passed on that race in preference to the Group 2 Schillaci, Moody had forfeited the attempt to stretch Black Caviar's consecutive wins at the elite level to seven – a record owned by the mighty Bernborough. In the lower-tier race, Black Caviar's seven rivals might have been best assessed as aspirational gallopers rather than bona fide challengers.

Karuta Queen had proven herself speedy enough to contest Sepoy's Golden Slipper but was consigned to the second half of the field after an injury-interrupted lead-up. She had returned to racing well. Over the 1100-metre course at Rosehill three weeks before, Karuta Queen had scorched in a manner that allowed young jockey Tommy Berry to cheekily blow a kiss to the crowd before his filly crossed the finish line. He was fined $200 for the gesture.

Karuta Queen's Queanbeyan-based trainer Neville Layt declared his intention to take on Black Caviar, reasoning his flyer would have a huge weight advantage around the slick Caulfield circuit. 'Black Caviar is the best horse in the world. More than likely she is going to beat us, but when you run those times over 1000 metres, only Black Caviar can pass her.' Layt was cast in the necessary role of cockeyed optimist.

Against the typical pattern of these feature spring days in Melbourne, the crowd arrived early. A salmon and black army was handed flags and masks as they entered the course. With the stands full and most every vantage point taken, Black Caviar stood ready in the gates. Course broadcaster Greg Miles mused on the public address, 'This is it,' a proclamation usually reserved for Cups but unequivocally appropriate in the circumstances.

Werrett had never seen Moody so nervous. The increased exposure meant even the little rituals within the camp were exposed. The trainer stood rolling a dollar coin between his fingers. Colin Madden had observed this habit in Moody during one of Black Caviar's early victories. While both men staunchly advocated that they were not in the least superstitious, Madden would hand Moody the same gold coin before each of Black Caviar's races. Even if you do not believe in them, why tempt the fates?

Black Caviar neither dawdled nor pinged from the gates. Those more acutely tuned and anxiety-ridden bounced before her, but there was no start conceded. The running order forecast was dutifully adhered to. Karuta Queen knew no other way than to run free. Black Caviar sat fourth, off the fence. Time and space were hers. She moved fluently without apparent exertion. Once she was in rhythm and distinctly under her own steam, Black Caviar moved ahead from the flank of Morgan Dollar to the girth of Platinum Skye. On the turning circle of the corner, Black Caviar advanced her position again. Nolen remained perfectly compact. He lived the cliché to sit and steer.

With the straight revealing itself, two jockeys had the same thought. For Nolen's part, and it was without a hint of supposition, he knew he would win. Black Caviar travelled effortlessly. At a given moment he would encourage her and that would be that. Just ahead, twenty-year-old Tommy Berry made his calculations. For all the days he had partnered Karuta Queen, including nine races for five wins, they had never travelled quite so well. Unchallenged in front, they had chosen the tempo. Not an ounce of energy had been wasted or frittered away. As Berry set up to charge clear and give the field something to chase, he felt the presence of a monster. Only briefly. For it was with him and away from him with frightening speed. Karuta Queen had done nothing wrong. Berry had been helpless to do anything at all. But their fate was instantly and completely sealed.

Berry could not disguise the thrill he felt in his own demise. 'I didn't get much of a look at her as she went that quick. She just cantered past. I might never experience something like that again.'

Nolen barely moved until the lead was his. He sat as quietly and balanced as ever. To be sure and to ensure there was an element of exertion in the gallop: Nolen wriggled the reins and allowed the mare to sprint for 100 metres. Then he scrunched back down to enjoy the win.

Karuta Queen leads but Black Caviar's got her immediately
She's out to chase the ghost of Phar Lap for this magical win
number fourteen
Black Caviar has assumed the front and burst away
Karuta Queen, Stirling Grove and Kulgrinda
But it's all Black Caviar
The Queen is in session for the spring
She bolts in by four lengths

The crowd of 32,126, a third more than usual for Guineas Day, did what they came to do. Applaud a champion. The ovation was not raucous; the win had happened so quickly and met with no resistance. Instead, it was marked by appreciation. Again, the overwhelming reaction was awe at the ease of the destruction.

Karuta Queen defied the rest of the field just as Berry sensed she would. Despite the 5.5-kilogram advantage she held, the margin of defeat was four-and-a-quarter lengths. Connections sought out photographers for an image of their filly in the honourable wake of a champion. It was a moment they never intended to forget. Equally, it was a moment they never intended to repeat.

In a sign to perfectly encapsulate the times, a banner was unfurled as Black Caviar returned to the mounting yard. It read: *BC OMG*.

New Zealand trainer Steve McKee had seen amazing feats in his time as the co-trainer of the mighty mare Sunline. But he had never seen anything quite so brutal as this: 'She's unbelievable. The power she gets from behind is great, staggering. It might be a funny thing to say but it's probably not until she gets beaten – and she probably never will – that we will know how good she is because she's simply too good for anything in these parts.'

Moody stood satisfied. As was usual for him, he would have settled for victory by a fingernail, but knew it would never have come to that. His observation was to share that Black Caviar loved what she did.

In the tunnel connecting the Jockeys' Room to the mounting yard, Nolen artfully skirted around arrogance where his mount had just exemplified it. He confirmed what was widely suspected. It was a mere track gallop. She was, perhaps, eighty-five per cent fit. Such an assessment belied the clock: 56.73 seconds, just three-quarters of a second outside the track record. As a study of how Black Caviar won the race, the sectional times plotting her speed were instructive. Out of the barriers for the 1000–800 split she ran 13.18 seconds; 800–600 10.42; 600–400 10.77; 400–200 10.81; and 200–finish 11.55 seconds as she was being eased down. The numbers revealed the pattern. She had broken her opponents by the halfway mark.

With Phar Lap foremost in every mind, it was not surprising that Black Caviar should be compared to another cherished Australian icon: Don Bradman. Pondering his Monday column for *The Australian,* Patrick Smith conceived that a straight recount of Black Caviar's deeds could never be enough. It was just a charcoal outline. 'Just as Bradman's average of 99.94 denotes the freakish, it does not in any way describe it. Like Bradman, Black Caviar's story is told in the seeing and not the jotting.'

Few have contributed more than Les Carlyon to the modern narrative of racing. He ventured that Black Caviar transcended the sport. 'They make it look bigger and better and grander, nicer, if you like, than it really is and people are attracted to that. There's a terribly nasty, seedy, brutish side to boxing, but Muhammad Ali made it attractive to a lot of people. Bradman probably inspired a lot of people who didn't care much for cricket.'

In the midst of the adulation, Moody insisted on perspective. On the subject of the immortal deeds of Australia's greatest racehorse, he stated: 'Phar Lap kept the nation on its feet during the Depression. Nothing will equal him.'

Later in the afternoon, once Black Caviar had retreated from sight back to her home stables a short walk from the heaving crowd, the tempo of a typical feature race day returned.

The Caulfield Guineas had an impressive strike rate for producing a sparkling spectacle. Lonhro, Weekend Hussler, Starspangledbanner and Whobegotyou all confirmed their star status with compelling victories in the classic, en route to brilliant careers. As heart-pounding, knuckle-clenching duels go, there had been few better than Redoute's Choice's stirring fightback to down Testa Rossa in 1999. God's Own was knocked out of the race on multiple occasions before casting aside such wretched luck and lumps to overhaul Paratroopers in the final bound of 2005.

The 2011 instalment immediately took its place with the best in class. The Darley-owned colt Helmet had finally got his head straight and given a glimpse of his wealth of ability in the Guineas Prelude a fortnight prior. He ran both heavily backed and short-priced. But from the barrier fly he was in a battle with fellow Sydney colt Manawanui.

Together they roared up the incline from the 1600-metre start, a suicide mission for many a hardened equine, let alone precocious three-year-olds. To the eye they were going too fast. Once they belatedly settled, Helmet was three lengths clear of Manawanui, who held a decent margin on the rest of the field. They were sitting ducks for the backmarkers.

Coming into the straight, jockey Kerrin McEvoy poured even more pressure into the pace Helmet was carving out and, as Manawanui grimly held on, it was apparent against all intuition that they had dropped the rest. As Manawanui gripped and clawed and closed, Helmet kept his head at full extension stretching for the finishing post. That head was the margin when they split the line. A surge of exhilaration pulsed through the crowd. It was racing at its best.

Helmet was declared a star and installed as the Cox Plate favourite. Manawanui was granted a stranglehold on the Victoria Derby. It was the sort of race that demanded retelling and reliving. It captured the very essence of competition and tension. Yet by the time the program closed, the conversation had returned to the exploits of Black Caviar.

Roy Beardsworth/Colorsport/Corbis

English colt Frankel wins acclaim at Royal Ascot.

16

The Black Caviar Effect

Moonee Valley, Schweppes Stakes, 22 October 2011

The 'Black Caviar effect' fully revealed itself a week later. The Melbourne Racing Club's thunderously good Guineas Day crowd left a comparatively lacklustre gathering for the Caulfield Cup. Rather than attending multiple race days, plenty of people simply adjusted their itinerary in accordance with the drawcard.

Cup Day had to settle for the understudies. Both Sepoy and More Joyous fulfilled their roles. Sepoy, trained by Peter Snowden, eased to victory in the Group 2 Caulfield Sprint from a pair of Moody gallopers, Curtana and Mid Summer Music. The win was meritorious for the weight-carrying record established for a three-year-old in the race and advanced Sepoy's record to nine wins from ten starts. But in the immediate aftermath, Snowden declared that his colt would not confront Black Caviar under any circumstances, and thus the last pretence of true spring competition was laid to rest.

More Joyous was gallant, but hardly spectacular, wearing down Sister Madly in the Group 2 Tristarc Stakes. Jockey Nash Rawiller gently assessed that the mare was not the conquering force she had once been. The time when she may have threatened Black Caviar was deemed passed.

Southern Speed won the Caulfield Cup under superb steerage from Craig Williams, who was seeing two and three moves ahead during the race. It did not constitute a complete boilover, though. The shock came as raging favourite December Draw was eased out of the race on the home bend with what would later be revealed as a fractured leg. In prospect and in reality, the Cup was hardly a vintage edition.

The Melbourne Racing Club did not fade from view immediately when its carnival closed, however. It had a plan – a wisp of imagination that no racing administration in Victoria had shown before. Chairman Mike Symons proposed a match race between Black Caviar and the hitherto unbeaten English three-year-old Frankel, the horse that had taken the mantle of the world's best racehorse from Black Caviar in the winter. It would be an autumn extravaganza over 1400 metres, either harnessing the history of the Futurity Stakes or inventing a race specifically for the task.

The pitch came after Frankel's ninth career victory. That had been in the 1600-metre Queen Elizabeth II Stakes at Ascot. The parallels with the deeds of Black Caviar were set out in *The Guardian* newspaper: 'From halfway it quickly became apparent that Frankel's unbeaten record was in no doubt. Queally shook the reins to send him to the front over a furlong out, and although old rival Excelebration tried his best to stay with the winner, he had no answer to such a brutal turn of foot.'

Frankel's jockey, Tom Queally, surmised: 'It looks like he'll never be beaten.'

The Telegraph documented the magnetism of British racing's idol: 'It was the indecorous rush of normally respectable race-goers, Ascot members who don't normally break into a trot, jostling and pushing their way from the grandstand to the winner's enclosure to get the best vantage point that was the give-away. It is what they had come to see. Frankel, the best horse in a generation had just strengthened the argument that he should be lauded among the best ever by imperiously romping home, barely coming off the bridle.'

Given the reluctance of owner Prince Khalid Abdullah and trainer Sir Henry Cecil for their horses to travel, a trip across the globe with such a valuable commodity was never truly likely. But the enthusiasm with which the tender was greeted in the Australian press spoke of two factors: desperation for a fresh angle in the Black Caviar story and acknowledgment of what was, at its core, a good idea.

In its visionary document *Racing to 2020*, released in November 2008, Racing Victoria Limited had committed to a concept called 'Super Match Racing'. In an initiative to liven up the sport, it recommended Australian stars meet in match races, with two competitors going head-to-head. Further, it suggested that Australian champions face the world's best to provide 'major promotional opportunity for Victorian Racing'. It had never subsequently found the willingness to stake its own ambition.

Match races in Australia had never been a priority. The most fondly recalled was not a two-horse duel by design, but rather a race that evolved when Rain Lover and Big Philou were the only two acceptors for the 1970 Queen Elizabeth Stakes at Flemington. It is as well recalled for the broadcast of Bert Bryant, who weaved all manner of story-telling through the race. In the delightfully close finish, Bryant plumped, correctly, for Big Philou by a nose. He concluded the broadcast with a note of relief: 'If you got it wrong in a two-horse race, you'd have to give it up forever.'

The most recent match race had been the TAB Challenge on Thousand Guineas Day at Caulfield in 1992, pitting Better Loosen Up against Let's Elope. Rain had played havoc with the Cox Plate preparations of the pair and Better Loosen Up, in particular, was in desperate need of a serious gallop. Necessity became the mother of invention and, as a result, aficionados adjudged this a lacklustre exercise, merely high-pressure trackwork. Perhaps that was a misunderstanding made by untrained eyes. With white whips flailing, Mick Dittman lifted Let's Elope, the Melbourne Cup-winning mare, past Michael Clarke and the former Japan Cup champion Better Loosen Up. Hindsight suggests this was better than it appeared. Rather than two fading greats whose best belonged to bygone days, Let's Elope crossed the line second in the Cox Plate having flattened Better Loosen Up, likely denying him a second win in the race.

Regardless, there had been no two-horse race on these shores in the class of the fabled Seabiscuit–War Admiral clash of 1938 at Pimlico Racecourse in the United States. The 'Match of the Century' came to underpin a Hollywood movie.

Had racing an eye for promotion similar to that of Don King, Black Caviar and Sepoy would have been lured into a spring date. The established champion against the number-one contender. Sepoy had done what only the very best two-year-olds through Australian history could manage, sweeping the Blue Diamond/ Golden Slipper double. The feat had not been achieved for more than twenty years, and he put his name alongside Courtza, Manikato, Bounding Away and John's Hope. More impressive, though, was the contemptuous manner in which the wins were achieved. The Diamond was a one-act affair, won by four-and-a-half lengths. He made off with the Slipper by two lengths ahead of Mosheen, who went on to prove herself outstanding. In half a dozen two-year-old starts, Sepoy was beaten only once – on a paddling-wet track at Rosehill. He returned at three to further his credentials. His assets were his speed and strength to sustain. What made him dangerous was his capacity to lead Black Caviar. In the ownership of Darley, Australia's largest stable with its headquarters in Dubai, it was only a matter of time before the colt was exported to enhance his stud value. The opportunity to line Black Caviar and Sepoy up against each other was small but distinct.

Victoria Racing Club might have paid a $100,000 retainer to each camp for a straight track showdown an hour before the Melbourne Cup, with a million-dollar winner-take-all purse. In the moment when all of Australia peered into horse racing, the sport might have put its standard bearers on display. But the nay-sayers would carry the day. The short-sighted would argue that Melbourne Cup Day did not need Black Caviar. The narks surmised that defeat for Sepoy would somehow diminish his prospects as a sire. The thirst for competition went unquenched. Racing missed the moment of a lifetime.

Instead the bold, if fanciful, notion of Black Caviar versus Frankel grabbed the agenda. Opinions were cast, mainly along nationalist lines. Trainer David Hayes observed: 'Black Caviar is the best racehorse I've seen and Frankel is something else, although I've never seen anything dominate like she does.'

European visitors cited the international ratings, in which Frankel held sway. English journalist and UK television's *At the Races* commentator Matt Chapman was in Australia for Cox Plate Day and his first glimpse of Black Caviar.

'Look, Frankel–Black Caviar, Black Caviar–Frankel. In a way it's a ridiculous argument. They're two different horses running over completely different distances. She's supreme, elegant and beautiful at her distance. Frankel is in a world of his own over a mile. Realistically they're never going to meet but we have two absolute champions that we can savour. If you're a fan of horse racing just think that on opposite sides of the world you've got two magnificent specimens of an equine athlete. One's a sprinter and she's the best sprinter. One's a colt and he's the best miler. We don't need to compare them. Frankel is officially the better horse but those official rankings are pointless because they are two different disciplines. Just enjoy two brilliant horses.'

But Chapman made the point that Black Caviar needed to voyage from Australia to ultimately prove her worth. Why Frankel would not be required to do so might have been a matter of imperial smugness. It did not go unnoticed.

When Cox Plate Day is at its best, the A.J. Moir Stakes, now known as the Schweppes Stakes, works in perfect harmony with the weight-for-age championship. Kingston Town's third Cox Plate lives in the annals, alongside the Moir victory of the mighty sprinter Manikato, a win that took him beyond the million-dollar stakes earning barrier. The King and the Man.

Apache Cat created such a stir in the Schweppes of 2009 that it threatened to overshadow the main event. In the twilight of a brilliant career, the popular gelding, with a distinctive splash of white marking half his face, like the signature mask from *The Phantom of the Opera,* surged on an inside run to narrowly claim the day and send the crowd into raptures. Two hours later, Bart Cummings sent the three-year-old So You Think on his path to greatness. That was an afternoon for the racing purist.

When acceptances were taken for the 2011 Schweppes Stakes, though, only four opponents were revealed for Black Caviar and an air of anticlimax settled on the proposition. Matt Stewart supposed in the *Herald Sun* of Black Caviar's Cox Plate Day commitment: 'She is a famous guest of honour, rather than a competitor, a queen waving briefly from a balcony.'

Among her rivals was Scenic Blast, whose exploits earned him an early place on a few of the honour rolls now boasting the name of Black Caviar. The Western Australian sprinter was awarded the 2008–09 Horse of the Year title on the back of his Lightning Stakes/Newmarket Handicap double. And he had already been to Royal Ascot to claim the King's Stand Stakes. Trainer Daniel Morton subsequently campaigned the gelding unsuccessfully in Japan and Hong Kong, which had the unfortunate consequence of inducing a bleeding attack. In Australia that carried a mandatory three-month ban with a reoccurrence incurring a lifetime prohibition. United States equine drug laws provide a haven for bleeders, and Scenic Blast was relocated. He raced in the US five times for three placings, the last of those at Hollywood Park some eleven months before Cox Plate Day. Now he had been returned to sender and was seen for the first time at Breakfast with the Best on the Tuesday morning of Cox Plate week. Morton entertained no illusions, though. Rejuvenating Scenic Blast was a long-term project.

It was an old rival that was the source of consternation in the lead-up. Here de Angels had left the care of Mark Kavanagh and been taken up by Goulburn trainer Wendy Roche. What had not changed was the horse's roguish tendencies at the barriers. The talented sprinter had been banned from racing in Victoria at the end of 2010 and, although that had been lifted, New South Wales stewards had been moved to issue a warning after the horse badly blundered the start in Sydney a week before.

Here de Angels had drawn the outside barrier in the five-horse field. His neighbour was Black Caviar. Moody was typically blunt: 'When you draw next to a horse with any perceived barrier habits, you obviously hold your breath. You wouldn't live with yourself if he wanted to climb in the stalls and hurt her, particularly when he played up and missed the kick six lengths in a stakes race six days ago and didn't cop any sort of ban from it.' The trainer denied he threatened to scratch Black Caviar from the race but conceded it was a consideration the owners would need to make.

Curiously, stewards made an unprecedented and, arguably, unnecessary ruling. It was determined a vacant barrier would be left between the two gallopers. Regardless of your view of the wisdom or otherwise of the decision, it was special treatment meted out for a star. It provoked a divisive discussion that lasted two days but was settled in a matter of seconds.

The crowd at Moonee Valley gathered as heavy rain fell. It would abate for just enough of the meeting itself. Encouragingly, Karuta Queen scooted around the 1200-metre circuit to win the Group 3 Red Anchor Stakes, proving her worth and showing no ill effects, physical or psychological, from being beaten by Black Caviar.

By the time they loaded for the Schweppes, there were only four contestants after the scratching that morning of Balavan. Suitably scolded, Here de Angels demonstrated no histrionics, and was better behaved at the barriers than in any race of his life. Without delay the Moonee Valley bell rang out and the starter sent them on their way. Not wishing to tempt fate any longer than was necessary, Black Caviar jumped promptly in line with the rest of the field.

If there was a demonstration of the new reality of Black Caviar's races, this was it. It had become a checklist. A formula for risk aversion. How did she get away? Where was she positioned? Was anything getting in her way? Has she got a clear run at where she needs to go?

These questions ticked over in the mind of Colin Madden. 'That's all I was watching. She got away cleanly. And where she positioned herself one out, that was okay. She loves motoring around the corner here at the Valley.'

The Moody-trained Doubtful Jack was assigned the task of leading. Black Caviar lobbed into second. Nolen diligently executed his duty to keep the mare safe. There was no need for crowding and the associated risks in such a small field. There would be no clipping of heels or being galloped on from behind. In formation they exited the back straight and idled for the school at the 600-metre pole. Here de Angels made the first move from the rear, cheekily tacking onto the hind of Black Caviar with a mind to challenge prior to the bend.

From the Legends Balcony before the tight turn in, the patrons saw it happen. The end pronounced so swiftly, like the lowering of a guillotine. Ruthless and merciful all at once. It was done on the camber of the bend like an Olympic cyclist on the slick boards of the velodrome. For a brief moment Black Caviar moved to stride side by side with Doubtful Jack. And then she was gone as the cheering set in.

> Doubtful Jack held together in front
> Black Caviar stalks her way into the race
> She goes up to eyeball her stablemate and went straight past him
> Black Caviar opened up on the corner
> Her magnificence stretches out into the straight with a four-length advantage
> Doubtful Jack, Here de Angels, Scenic Blast
> But at the hundred Cox Plate Day gets its brush with greatness again
> Black Caviar sprinted away and won by five lengths

It was, in all likelihood, the easiest win yet.

Madden pondered, a little whimsically: 'She cruised today yet I was still anxious. Why is this? I'm fifty-seven years of age and I'm just as excited as I was as a kid.'

Yes, it was the equivalent of the Royal wave, and that very week in Melbourne thousands of people of all ages had lined the streets to exchange precisely that with Queen Elizabeth II. All left satisfied.

To accommodate the demands from the scrum of journalists, Moody was ushered out on the turf of the course proper. There he was dealing, for the first time, with a sense best described as underwhelmed. While Black Caviar had won by six lengths, there was a unanimous suspicion from the press gallery that she could have won by ten. Was there ever a thought of opening the throttle, allowing a win that would be mythologised? The trainer calmly countered the complaints. 'Why?' In a race, winning is the object. Having an athlete, be it human or animal, at full capacity exponentially increased the chance of injury. In a risk-versus-reward equation, the opportunity to show off did not warrant the chance of breaking down.

This was Moody's moment to enter the argument of the week, the insistence that Black Caviar go and face the world. He channelled the Queensland bushie part of his character to make his case. 'We want to enjoy her in Australia. I'm as keen as anyone to see her overseas and put all these nay-sayers and doubters that say we have to travel overseas to prove herself the best, I think it's a heap of bullshit to be honest. Let's enjoy her in Australia. Have a look what she's doing for racing. Why should we supplement every other bastard's racing around the rest of the world? Let's supplement our own. Let's enjoy her in Australia for as long as we can.'

Doubtless the Englishman Chapman wore some of that. 'She had a nice little canter didn't she. It was good fun. Good way to earn a bit of prize money. Give the crowd a boost. Did we learn anything new about Black Caviar today? Well I did because I saw her in the flesh for the first time and she's got a tasty backside on her. But that's all I learnt about her today.' Careful not to appear churlish he quickly added: 'Enjoy her. Caress her like you would your missus. Black Caviar is very special.'

It was the win that took Black Caviar's record past Phar Lap's streak and equal to the fifteen-straight race wins of Bernborough and Carbine. Those who were affronted by Black Caviar's lack of opposition were either suffering from a convenient memory lapse, or a distinct lack of research. In nine of fourteen consecutive wins, Phar Lap had raced against four or fewer rivals. In the 1930 Randwick Plate and the VRC Fisher Plate there were only three runners including Phar Lap. Bookmakers refused to offer odds, so there was no on-course betting as the iconic galloper romped to victory. Besides, not all Don Bradman's centuries were equal either. While the worth of Black Caviar's latest win was questioned, there was no denying the reaction it drew.

Ninety minutes after the race finished, reigning Melbourne Cup champion Americain would provide the adrenaline-charged thrill in the Moonee Valley Cup. In his first Australian race since marching into folklore the previous November, Americain was under pressure approaching the turn. But the French stallion muscled clear of congestion and rounded up his rivals to dash to victory and clear favouritism to defend his title in the great two-miler.

The main event lacked its usual cachet and was open to a surprise. The 2011 Cox Plate would go down as a race won by the daring and guile of Craig Williams. The jockey took the mare Pinker Pinker through needle-eye openings on the fence, the last of which resembled slipping a 500-kilogram beast through a closing lift door.

A storm broke in the immediate aftermath and, as the thunder rumbled and lightning lit the darkening sky, the masses were washed away. Black Caviar carried the front pages the next morning.

Newspix / Nicole Garmston

The record crowd at Flemington to see Black Caviar in the 2011 Patinack Farm Classic.

17

Unanimous Support

Flemington, Patinack Farm Classic, 5 November 2011

Loyalty in racing is as transferable as currency. Punters are not barrackers, and therein lay a fundamental difference between racing and other sports. In football, affiliations are established at birth. They endure in good times and in bad. On a racetrack, allegiances last as long as it takes a bookmaker to change the odds. Racing dances a fine line between gambling and sport. The very nature of the punt leads enthusiasts to cheer through their pockets. Unanimous support in the Sport of Kings simply does not occur.

Phar Lap proverbially carried the nation in the 1930 Melbourne Cup, yet on race eve as punters laid their bets at the traditional Call of the Card there was spirited backing for other horses. When a nation famously roared for its hero, Makybe Diva, as she swept to her third successive Cup in 2005 she was nothing like an odds-on favourite, let alone an undisputed choice. But on the final day of the 2011 Melbourne Cup Carnival, that line was breeched like never before.

An hour before the Patinack Farm Classic, bookmaker Alan Eskander stood at his stand on the famed Flemington Rails and thought that he would not lay a bet on any one of Black Caviar's six opponents. This was awful for business. But he could not help but admire the oddity of it all. Seemingly, not a single punter in the record crowd of 85,112 wanted to invest against her. It would have been a shameful act even to think about it. Furthermore, it would disqualify that person from the very purpose of the day: to cheer.

Eskander also realised that despite the prohibitive quote of $1.04 offered on the mare, plenty of punters wanted to invest their small amount to enlist financial as well as emotional support. Those odds made her the shortest-priced favourite in a Group 1 race in Australia since Valerius started at 1/33 in the 1961 Chipping Norton Stakes. A $10 wager on Black Caviar would return a profit of 40 cents. Some 'bought' a betting ticket as a keepsake of the occasion, with no intention of handing it back. It had been joked that the only way to make money on Black Caviar was to get a betting ticket signed by Peter Moody and Luke Nolen and auction it on eBay.

The other method of assessing Black Caviar was a literal examination of the odds. The $1.04 translated to a likelihood that she would be beaten in the Patinack once in twenty-five runnings. That did not compute. She would win this race 100 times out of 100. That was just as well, because by this stage those involved needed the respite offered by certainty.

Victoria's leading trainer and jockey combination had endured a wretched week. Peter Moody had officiated at the launch of the Melbourne Cup Carnival, capturing the spirit of the competition and its consequences. 'This is our World Series. It's our Championship and I think it's quickly becoming a part of world racing folklore.'

Moody and Nolen were consistently on the back foot thereafter. In the opening race of thirty-seven that week at

Flemington, honest three-year-old Highly Recommended was gunned down in the last stride by Galah in the Carbine Club. They backed that up when Macedonian was condemned to second in the Lexus Stakes, leaving the pair without a Melbourne Cup runner. Be they outright favourite or moderately fancied, they all went under alike. Unthinkably, as they previewed Stakes Day, neither Moody nor Nolen had a Flemington winner to their credit.

'It's been a long week,' Nolen wryly smiled at the Friday press conference. 'Thank God I'm riding Black Caviar and there's something to look forward to.'

Neil Werrett, on the other hand, had been a major player for the past month. He had shares in Caulfield winner Foreteller and Cup Day victor Combat Kitty. Each, though, was a small morsel compared to his black flash. He was finding that his experience as an owner had changed with his expectations. 'Now I find when a trainer rings up and says, "You have a nice horse," you go and watch it trial then it runs a nice third. You say to yourself that it's okay, but you're probably a little disappointed because you're so used to Black Caviar winning trials and races with her head on her chest.'

The entire owners' syndicate was coming to grips with that reality. They had, a year and half ago, combined to buy a second horse, a filly by the boom new sire Fastnet Rock. The $300,000 purchase was again put into Moody's care. On the Thursday before the Cox Plate, the filly, Secret Indulgence, had made an inauspicious debut, finishing midfield in a Ballarat maiden. She was entered again the Monday after Cup week, where she would run fourth at Mornington. Secret Indulgence was a journey back to racing reality for the luckiest people alive. Pam Hawkes did not mind one bit. 'Anticipation is usually the best bit you get with a horse, whether it be a foal or something you buy at the yearling sales. I'll be quite happy to go back to Moe, back to Swan Hill, back to Bairnsdale and enjoy it just the same as I did before. This is a once-in-a-lifetime ride that we're all getting and we're thoroughly enjoying it.'

The Flemington Carnival basked in a magnificent Melbourne Cup, dominated as expected by the Europeans. The invasion presented as an epic race as the visitors surged from the clock tower. Where to look? First Luca Cumani's Manighar, then the German import Lucas Cranach swept up. Godolphin's Lost in the Moment emerged from the slowest part of the track only to be swallowed up just as quickly in the inferior ground. As you scanned frantically, the answer came out wide. The English chestnut Red Cadeaux finished with the burst that claims Melbourne Cups. Michael Rodd, on Red Cadeaux, felt a surge of realisation that the Cup was his in the very moment the French galloper Dunaden came poking through on his inside.

Craig Williams was sentenced to miss the ride through suspension, a verdict upheld at appeal after the close of business on Cup eve. He had guided Dunaden to his warm-up win in the Geelong Cup and knew in his heart the Cup was at his mercy. As his belief promised to come to fruition, Williams was hiding in a cinema with his family, trying to avoid the trauma of lost opportunity. His replacement, Christophe Lemaire, executed the perfect ride in his first race at Flemington. He had exercised patience where other fingers were itchy. He had saved ground rather than driving off the track on the corner, as compatriot Americain had done. Lemaire had what every jockey craved in the final desperate moments of an endurance event – the last crack. Together, Dunaden and Red Cadeaux levelled up and stayed in sync. As they hit the line, the judge atop the grandstand called dead heat. Technology would find a margin for the French. It was thought to be a pixel rather than a nose. There had never been a tighter verdict in a Melbourne Cup.

Such a great contest quelled any sense of misery or foreboding over the locals' absence from the moment of decision. Australia's capacity and desire to produce stayers for its iconic race was weak. The industry treasured speed. And it had never had a better specimen than Black Caviar to prove the point. With a nod to *Back to the Future,* Nolen made the lovely observation that 'if she went any faster she'd travel back in time'.

Moody stacked the Patinack with three other runners, some guessed that he wanted to guarantee the race was run. However, it had already been confirmed that a Group 1 race would not be cancelled even in the event that Black Caviar was one day the lone acceptor. More likely, Moody was keen to chase the juicy prize money on offer at the minor end. It placed the trainer in a curious bind. He mused over Black Caviar's liking for the straight course at Flemington: 'She's just so dominant when she doesn't have to turn. That's scary for the opposition I would suppose.' He was that opposition. At once the architect of destruction and its primary victim.

Black Caviar was entrenched in the national discourse, even to the point of finding a place on Melbourne talkback radio station 3AW's daily *Rumour File*. 'Caviar Vindaloo' was put to air to recount his tale: 'It comes to my attention that security may have been breached at the stables of a well-known horse trainer on Melbourne Cup Day. Allegedly, during a game of cricket involving a family of persons of Indian descent, the batsman at the time hit the ball over the fence into the adjacent property, of yes you guessed it, the aforementioned trainer. Two eager fieldsmen jumped the fence to retrieve the pill, only to discover a horse looking on with affable interest at this little adventure. They were immediately confronted by a person who not only inquired of their athletic ability in the pole vault, but as to what the Donald Duck they were doing there in the first place. The Indians' reply: "We are fetching the cricket ball which got hit over the fence sir. Hey, who is that horse, sir?" Minder's reply: "That's Black Caviar." One of our Indian friends immediately produced a phone cam and fired off a series of photos. After that they were told to do the Fosbury Flop back over the fence, Kookaburra in hand.'

It had been noted that, by the superficial measure of beauty, Black Caviar would not turn heads in the parade. For her, that sort of attention had to be earned through deed and reputation. And on this day it seemed that the quest of the many was to catch their own snapshot of racing's deity. Crowds thronged around the mounting yard and, with each circuit Black Caviar travelled, produced a Mexican wave of rising camera phones. Despite a ban on such devices in the yard itself, plenty flagrantly broke that rule to capture a personal memory. Long-time racing journalist Stephen Howell thought with all the hype the only thing missing was a bikini-clad girl holding up Black Caviar's number three. As he uttered the sentence out loud, a leggy blonde in a replica of the salmon and black racing silks strode by. She was handing out flags. 'The next generation of racegoers lapped this up,' Howell wrote later.

When Nolen was bunked aboard and set down the walk of the roses, Black Caviar was again cheered all the way out onto the track. It had become a ritual. In fact, it was a pageant. Nolen fantasised that perhaps he could immediately turn around and take her back to the winner's stall, sparing himself the anguish of the race itself. There was an assumption that this was easy. He was careful to remember it was not. 'It's not like you're a pop star at a concert and everyone's there to watch you. Everyone's coming here to see you win. They can probably belt out a bad tune every second song and the people would still walk away happy most of the time. But if you run second I don't know if they'd walk away as happy.'

The expanse of Flemington has an intriguing sense of enclosure in November. Peering into the distance to the top of the straight 1200 metres away, you can take in the full landscape. The heat of the day gave the view a shimmer. Apart from those on the balcony of the VRC offices above, there was relative quiet as Black Caviar jumped. Her barrier manners had improved to such an extent that it was barely noted that she came out in unison with the field. The first 400 metres were raced in isolation from the crowd. But the build-up began at the marquees of the Birdcage. Nolen had guided his mount two steps inwards immediately to establish the bubble he liked her to race in now. They allowed Buffering the lead but it was only ever slight. Heading to the course proper and the public lawns, near the statues of Makybe Diva and Bart, they assumed the running.

Nash Rawiller shook and hustled Buffering to keep up, and Nolen sat without movement. Rawiller was not instantly dropped and in his mind this was a commendation. He had made a race of it. At least for longer than any other horse this spring. No other horse was ever part of the race.

The wave of applause began from the decaying Members' Stand, where previous generations had done the same for Phar Lap and Tulloch. It enveloped the track once the infield marquee sprang up, capturing the noise from the New Members' and the Hill Stands. Nolen kept everything perfectly balanced. Subtly, he lengthened the reins and twice slapped them down Black Caviar's shoulder. She obeyed the prompt and was promptly four lengths clear.

The jockey had lamented his inability to provide a sexy answer when asked if he could hear the crowd at previous wins. He could not. Between the wind rushing by and the concentration required to fulfil his end of the bargain, it was not within earshot. Today was the exception. The noise was joyful. It was exultant. It will live in the memories of those who were there. For it came from every soul on the racetrack.

Nolen coming to the course proper he sits quietly but she's
about to go Black Caviar
She runs up to Buffering, Scenic Blast on her back
They're starting to be ridden along behind her and she's on
the brink of breaking them
Nolen hasn't moved at the 200 and it's race over
Black Caviar opened up by four and every man, woman and
child at Flemington sends the adulation down
Black Caviar, the jockey never moved. She won by three
lengths untouched

From the inside of the track, *Herald Sun* photographer Colleen Petch captured the sense of jubilation as Black Caviar rushed by. The picture was racing's version of *Where's Wally*? Some waved their flags. Others had their arms raised in triumph. Children were frozen in the shouting of her name. There was an abundance of cameras. If you were to sum up the mood you would focus in on the smiles. Contented, beaming smiles.

Take any punter there that day. Whoever you might have stood next to trackside, in the bookies queue, at the bar. Casual racegoer Michael West was on a buck's day that was of far less interest than finally seeing Black Caviar in the flesh. He had felt the amazement she could conjure watching on television and listening to the radio, but he understood this was a delicacy to be sampled first hand. He stood in the public congestion near the 200 and craned his neck to watch the big screen first and then turn to his left and wait for her to appear. 'Then we saw the salmon and wondered where the rest of them were.' West was a devoted sports fan who would traipse the fairways to study Tiger Woods and sit in the Melbourne Cricket Club to view Sachin Tendulkar. He could recognise the best when he saw it, without the need for embellishment or explanation. 'We just stood there and marvelled at how good this racehorse was.'

She was different to anything he had ever seen before: the effortless motion, the ears pricked, ever alert. The capacity to grind her rivals into the dust.

In the mounting yard was former ABC Sydney race caller David Morrow. He had been the lone broadcaster to correctly nominate Octagonal victorious in the thrilling and deceiving Mercedes Classic of 1997, when the Big O beat Arkady by an eyelash with one last monumental lunge. Morrow had described Usain Bolt's audacious 100-metre world record run in Beijing. He pronounced Black Caviar the equal of anything he had witnessed.

The milestones accumulated with the win. The Patinack Farm Classic of 2010 had been her first Group 1 win. The repeat took that tally to seven, equalling the deeds of Makybe Diva and Emancipation. For mares, the only name that stood above them was Sunline with thirteen. First prize out of the million-dollar pot took Black Caviar's earnings beyond $4 million.

Black Caviar remained the only winner for Nolen and Moody at the carnival. Their mare King's Rose was hailed all over a winner in the next and final Group 1, the Emirates Stakes, before Albert The Fat stormed home to edge her out in a photo finish.

At the Patinack presentation it was David Taylor's turn to make the acceptance speech. He was the odd one out among the owners. He no longer felt any anxiety watching Black Caviar race. He knew she would win. 'I'm looking forward to next year when we go out to a longer distance and we're racing against other horses to put, frankly, excitement back into it for me.'

Sports broadcaster Bruce McAvaney touched on the conflict within many. 'Probably the most excited I could be on a racecourse now would be to walk in not knowing whether she was going to win. Look, it's been a long time since we've gone there expecting her to be challenged. It's still fun to watch her – I haven't seen anything like her – but how adventurous can Peter Moody be? He's in a situation where no one wants the horse to lose; we'd all be devastated. Yet at the same time we want her to be challenged. We want the best of both worlds, don't we?'

Expatriot English journalist Michael Lynch reasoned in *The Sunday Age* of Black Caviar: 'Hundreds of years ago when kings and queens wanted to impress their majesty upon their populations, they embarked on what was known as a royal progress around their kingdoms. It was a way for rulers such as Queen Elizabeth I to establish their sovereignty and reinforce their subject's loyalty.

'Black Caviar is perhaps the closest thing contemporary Australia has to royalty, albeit of the equine variety. Throughout the year she too has embarked on what amounts to a regal progression round the land.'

Among her subjects were Perth Racing officials who were to be blessed with the next stop of the caravan. Chief executive Michael Heath and general manager of racing and vision, Marty Young, had spent the week in the Flemington inner sanctum in a state of anticipation. There were two plans for Perth's reinvented Super Saturday program a fortnight hence, featuring the Railway and Winterbottom Stakes. If Black Caviar boarded the flight across the Nullarbor, WA was staring at the biggest race meeting ever staged in the state. With Black Caviar, free-to-air television stations were eager to secure broadcasting rights for the Group 1 events. National media attention of an unprecedented level was assured. Without Black Caviar, Super Saturday was reduced to a fine local event.

What would differentiate Perth from the Melbourne Spring was the determination of the locals to race their horses against the great one. Trainers with inferior beasts would not shirk the challenge. There were those who thought the wild west might serve up something akin to combat rather than racing. That seemed an unkind interpretation. If Perth were staging the ball of a lifetime why wouldn't you want a ticket to the dance?

Nursing a mild hangover on Sunday morning, Moody remained committed to the trip west. But twenty-four hours later the die was cast. The trouble with winning in the manner Black Caviar had patented was that it all looked so easy. At the closest quarters that was not the reality. You could not run such times without making a supreme effort. On Perth radio, talking to a disconsolate public, Moody gave an intimate insight into his galloper: 'It takes as much out of her as any normal horse and even though it might look easy, I can assure you she shows the effects of racing. If we brought her over there you wouldn't get to see the best of her and we would risk injury and risk defeat and we're not prepared to do that.'

Whether this was overly circumspect or a sensible precaution was a matter of opinion. Regardless of the reason, the impact was palpable. It was as if the sport itself went into recess.

Bronwen Healy Photography

The huge Friday night crowd at Moonee Valley as Black Caviar begins her 2012 campaign.

18

Friday Night Delights

Moonee Valley , Australia Stakes, 27 January 2012

To a fault, Peter Moody had been fastidiously patient with Black Caviar. Whenever the choice presented, he had opted for caution over valour. This was both masterful and necessary for a horse that had been physically on the edge. It did, however, leave him open to the accusation of being over-protective – hand-picking fights his pug could not lose.

The exalted figure of Muhammad Ali had recognised the consequence such easy victories could unintentionally create. 'I started believing I couldn't be whipped. After losing to Joe Frazier, I'd won a lot of easy fights against Blue Lewis, Henry Cooper, Buster Mathis, Jurgen Blin and Jerry Quarry. I didn't have to train hard and discipline myself in order to win. I learned that too many easy victories can ruin a fighter just like a long line of defeats. You start thinking your name alone will win.'

His critics would say Moody had a world champion that he would not race against the world. Had the soft kills continued, the underground mumblings might have taken a serious hold. Was Black Caviar a cream puff champion? Nothing made Moody seethe quite so much. Not for himself, but for his mare. It smacked of a lack of respect. It was downright ungrateful. It was ignorant. Moody was transported back to his teenage days. So angry he could spit at the detractors.

While he rejected the notion outright, it still sparked in him a competitive edge. He was contemplating Black Caviar's legacy. Winning would always remain the objective. But winning the right races now weighed more heavily. There was no shortage of advice and there were myriad options but the end game, by unanimous decree, was Royal Ascot. Every time the owners were polled, the answer came back the same. They came to view it as racing's Olympic Games, dripping with history and prestige. There was no escaping the romantic notion of racing in front of the Queen. In his heart, the trainer was wedded to that climax also.

On Boxing Day, while new Australian Test cricket opener Ed Cowan was staging an occupation of the crease at the Melbourne Cricket Ground, Moody was testing his stock of stayers at the traditional Caulfield race meeting.

On Christmas Eve he had prepared a double at Sandown. In a post-Christmas rush he backed that up with three more. Moody's satisfaction was tempered only by his impatience to head back to his stables at the opposite end of the track once the message arrived that Nelly had been delivered back into his care.

The sight of her crystallised the thought that had been rattling around in his head. It was time to let the horse race. She looked mighty. Moody had ideas to be bold and unorthodox. Careful of the early crow – the racing proclamation made prematurely that invites unforseen catastrophe or jinx – he was reticent to declare his hand. He had led people to assume the program began at 1200 metres with the Australia Stakes at Moonee Valley. Then it was to 1400 metres for the first time in the C.F. Orr Stakes and again in the Futurity Stakes, both Group 1 races at Caulfield.

Inspecting Black Caviar caused a secondary reflex beyond that sense of awe he recalled so well from their first meeting. She also looked heavy. Barely three weeks in the paddock had added bulk and driven her beyond 600 kilograms. Moody had four weeks to return her to a fighting weight to commence her defining campaign.

If Moody had sported any illusions about the intensity of the media's glare, they were quashed with the release of the year-ending World Thoroughbred Rankings in London. Australian handicapper Greg Carpenter had won the debate at the December conference of the International Federation of Horseracing Authorities in Hong Kong. The interim rating of 130 for Black Caviar's Newmarket Handicap win was lifted to 132, confirming her as the highest-rated female racehorse in history. Carpenter's lobbying saw Australian racing held in a higher regard than ever before.

While Frankel remained at the head of the overall ranking, Black Caviar was Carpenter's *pièce de résistance*. 'It is absolutely extraordinary. I hope people here in Australia realise that Black Caviar is no longer just an Australian champion; she is embraced by the world. Racing fans all over the globe understand and follow Black Caviar's career very closely. We've had conversations before about the need for sprinters to get their due recognition against the world's best. So it's been terrific for me advocating on behalf of Australian horses and Black Caviar that there has been this recognition of just how great this mare is.'

Moody accepted the obligation that came with the accolade. He serviced the acclaim locally, then was 'driven mad from overseas'. The racing media in England was sussing out and setting up Royal Ascot. Moody was humble in regards to Black Caviar's favourable assessment ahead of other great mares of the era, openly pondering the difficulty of comparing horses from other parts of the world. Moody had seen firsthand the deeds of French mare Goldikova in Europe. She won fourteen Group 1 races, the majority in open company. She had been named European Horse of the Year in 2010 and twice American Champion Female Turf Horse. Her career was crowned with a hat trick of victories in the Breeders' Cup Mile. Moody easily recounted her record with unwavering admiration. 'To be rated above her is quite unbelievable. But as great as it is, it doesn't put bread and butter on the table.'

During an interview on Channel Four's *At the Races* in the UK, he fixed his sights on the American wonder mare Zenyatta, the horse he watched fall so agonisingly short of the perfect career when attempting win number twenty in the Breeders' Cup Classic: 'She's three wins away from equalling Zenyatta's modern day record and we kick off in about two weeks' time to chase that. We're going into uncharted territory for the first time this preparation. She'll step up to seven furlongs. My feeling is she needs to run a very strong seven furlongs on our flat tracks here in Australia to be coming up there and running six furlongs in the Golden Jubilee and the July Cup. I'd want to see her very strong at the end of those races for me to want to go up there and compete in those races because I know how testing they are on your undulating tracks.'

Moody had always been reticent to create high levels of expectation, whether it was in the stable, with his owners or on the public record. In his international interviews, he tempered the prevailing view that 'you ain't seen nothing yet'.

'Her performances and the demolition of her opposition seem to be with relative ease. But there's no doubt in the world that any trainer of any good horse will tell you that when they're running the times that she runs and carrying the weights, it's certainly no easy task. It may look easy but it certainly is taxing on the horses themselves. To think she could go faster, I'm not so sure. She's running fantastic times comfortably and easily but it's a bit hard to imagine she could go faster.'

In Australia, however, Moody's rhetoric was bolder, in the vein of the best is yet to come. 'I really think we're going to see one hell of a horse at seven furlongs and I think I'll be regretting that there's not a mile race at the end of her two runs at seven, because she's in unbelievable order. For two years I've thought that she'll be better again at seven or even a mile. She's such a relaxed horse with a brilliant turn of foot and she doesn't over-race.'

His bullish attitude was based on Black Caviar's physical condition. For the first time she was without niggling complaint. She presented not only robust, but sturdy. The routine inspections of veterinary and chiropractic practitioners revealed none of the concerns of the past. The trainer felt her wellbeing was obvious from appearance. She positively beamed. Her deep brown coat glistened in the summer light. Moody felt he could finally stow the cotton wool and hang up the kid gloves.

It was there for all to see on a Tuesday morning in January 2012. Black Caviar needed the shadow-boxing of a jump-out to have her ready for racing. Moody could not have kept her presence a secret even had he wanted to. He was more than happy, though, to take the wraps off.

A nasty northerly wind blew like a furnace, whipping the dirt off the labyrinth of dusty pathways around Caulfield. Such conditions were prone to upset the flighty disposition of a fragile thoroughbred. At the commencement of the morning jump-outs, one of Moody's two-year-olds thrashed about in the barrier stalls, flipped itself over and landed on apprentice jockey Daniel Stackhouse. It left him with a fractured pelvis. The vital activity of a busy morning ground to a halt as the young rider was treated by ambulance officers and ferried to the Alfred Hospital.

The sombre mood combined with the steadily increasing intensity of a blazing sun to magnify the frazzling effect on those left to wait. Luke Nolen in particular was suffering. The previous afternoon his wife, Alicia, had given birth to their second child, a daughter, Kailey. Much like Caulfield, Nolen described his condition as 'dusty'. 'I had a few drinks for her. You've got to wet the head and I really wet it.'

At his sharpest, the jockey had an uncomplicated way with language. He articulated precisely what occurred to him without much need for refinement. With the edge slightly dulled, his thoughts flowed in an even more uninhibited fashion. In a lovely interview with TVN host Bruce Clark, he described Alicia as being 'a bit sore last night' and shared his surreal sense of events.

'I was a bit surprised when a girl popped out. Dane was a bit disappointed too. He really wanted a little brother but he's got a little sister so he can look after her and protect her. That'll be my sire's fees, my service fees finished. I think she's going to put me up on blocks and retire me.'

Clark proffered that Kailey would now be his favourite girl regardless of what Black Caviar did during the next six months. It was the sort of sentiment that required instant affirmation. From Nolen there was a telltale pause, so wonderfully innocent it made you laugh out loud. He rallied and somewhat belatedly wagered: 'Yeah, I'd say so at this stage.'

Nolen shook off his sense of vague bewilderment when he sat astride Nelly, poised in those familiar gates. The trial consisted of a motley collection of seven runners. Black Caviar began slowly out of the inside barrier, picked up swiftly and ambled along beneath a speedy chestnut who, by comparison, was made to look as if he was careering along. At the moment of Nolen's choosing, he signalled to Black Caviar with his customary squeeze, that it was time to get to work. She took that younger galloper and breezed into the daylight on her own. The sight was as impressive as ever. Various glances at stopwatches confirmed what was plain to see. It was fast and it was enough to have her ready for a first-up run at 1200 metres.

The one source of frustration for onlookers was the inability to identify other horses participating in the dash. That riddle was partly solved nine days later. Craig Newitt had ridden a three-year-old for trainer Mick Price. The colt Instinction, a Flemington winner in Melbourne Cup week, was on trial for a crack at the Festival of Racing classics. On Australia Day, the grey colt surprisingly upstaged a quality field in the Listed Zeditave Stakes. Newitt gave the game up post-race: 'He stood her up fifteen lengths and got beat five or six. There's no better guide than Black Caviar, is there? He's had a few problems but he's come back really good.' Instinction ran a 20/1 outsider. Had the facts been known, he would not have been half that quote.

By this stage, it was difficult to imagine that the popularity of Black Caviar could have been underestimated. But in the Friday dusk, as the queues stretched back from the turnstiles in the centre of Moonee Valley Racecourse, it was clear the multitudes were well beyond those anticipated. With the race meeting well underway, programs sold out and catering wagons under siege, officials were staring down major embarrassment. The only decision available was enacted. The gates were thrown open and the human tide flowed freely through.

Moonee Valley Night Racing had launched to great fanfare on 26 January 1998. It was the first metropolitan meeting in this country staged under lights. With bars converted into quasi-nightclubs, singer Paul Kelly in concert and the then Group 1 Australia Stakes on the program, more than 30,000 people attended, making for a raging success. While night racing remained crucial to the identity of Moonee Valley and a valuable fixture on the racing calendar, it had receded to a niche event with a hardcore following, which expanded only for Christmas functions and the like. The Club had made a concerted push to reinvigorate and broaden the appeal of the concept, particularly through the summer months. Success had been modest. Until this night.

As the endless stream of cars emerged from beneath the back straight and into the centre of the course, the scene was a throwback to the Cox Plates of the '70s. It was a time prior to marquees and corporatisation. As Dulcify and Surround ran the circumference of the track, thousands of vehicles packed the infield, providing the backdrop. This Friday night in 2012 was something to behold. The car park had not needed a 'Full' sign for decades. Soon enough there was no room to get in.

From his lofty perch in the judge's box, situated on the steel roof of the steep grandstand, the surging lines of human traffic transfixed Simon Petch. 'You can usually hear a pin drop at these Friday night meetings. Have a look at the people coming in.' Petch was well versed in the ways of Black Caviar. For each of her Melbourne runs he had been either the judge, charged with confirming her victories and measuring the expanse of the margin, or working on the scales, ensuring prescribed weights were allocated and returned correctly. 'I wish I'd kept the race books from all of them as souvenirs.'

That would have proved difficult on Australia Stakes night, for there was none to be had by the time the bell rang out to start the first race. Moonee Valley had worked on a guesstimate of 8000 people. Only once since the inauguration of night racing had the crowd risen near the 10,000 mark. That was when Black Caviar had won the William Reid Stakes in March 2011. That was in the afterglow of the Newmarket euphoria and her ascension to the mantle as the best horse in the world. Now, with the Australian Open tennis tournament commanding the agenda, it was reasoned as overly optimistic to expect that same crowd again.

Moonee Valley Racing Club's chief executive, Michael Browell, was torn between a smile and a grimace as it became clear the delays were too long and staffing levels were groaning under the surge in demand. An hour before race time, he ordered the turnstiles stop collecting, further gate receipts forfeited and punters allowed on track for free. A backlash would be felt on talkback radio in the coming days. It took forty-five minutes to get a beer and food was out of the question. Browell watched as vantage points on the lawn and in the stands were taken up and protected half an hour before Black Caviar was due.

'To see the line eight wide all the way back to the harness track, from what I'm told it's never happened here for night racing before. The atmosphere is electric. You don't see this for night racing. And everyone knows what's going to happen. The script's already written. She wins. But people want to be here to see the mighty mare.'

The intimacy of Moonee Valley allowed the fans close-quarter access to their idol. Security stood outside Black Caviar's allotted corner stall, number fifty-four, but the sign bearing her name was the only evidence of her.

Nelly was walking laps in the small oval enclosure behind the grandstand at the turn out of the home straight. Neck sloped downwards and fringe hanging to her eyes, she might have passed anonymously if not for the cameras pointed in her direction. You could hear the amazement of those seeing her for the first time. The initial impression was to mistakenly think her nondescript. The second was to shamelessly admire her ample backside. 'You can see where the power comes from.'

One punter, who claimed to have the inside word, was eager to impart his knowledge. He had a conspiracy theory. Moody should be asked about the fragile nature of Black Caviar's tendons. He was to rush her through to twenty wins, then retire her before she fell apart completely. 'She'll never go overseas,' he opined.

On one side of the yard were a couple of girls wearing faded pink summer dresses with black polka dots. On another side were a pair of blokes, stubbies in hand, wearing salmon and black masquerade masks.

Three generations of the Brettell family stood in near reverential silence, interrupted only for the imparting of a word of knowledge or a phrase of admiration. Paul had served as chief executive of Moonee Valley and held that post at the birth of night racing. The Life Member's badge clipped to his suit jacket spoke of services rendered. Son Peter shared his father's passion for the sport and his professional duties had also seen him once working for the Club. His son Jasper completed the picture. There would never be a better time to understand the ways of his elders.

Colin Madden came to stand inconspicuously amid the admirers and the curious. He nodded to Donna and once satisfied by the appearance of his horse, quietly departed, returning to the dining room catering for the eighty-strong entourage of connections.

In search of ideas to expand and enrich the experience, Racing Victoria initiated the Black Caviar Cheer Squad. It was launched through Facebook with a limited seventy-two-hour period in which to register. A squadron in excess of 350 nominated for the fun. Formalised or contrived groups of barrackers tend to have a mixed level of acceptance in sport. Footy cheer squads have been an integral part of club support since the days of floggers and duffel coats. English cricket's Barmy Army is thought to add vibrancy and witticism to a summer of cricket. But Australia's corresponding Fanatics are derided as puerile and irksome, with their intrusive chants and inane ditties.

T-shirts had been ordered to clothe the Black Caviar Cheer Squad. 'I [Heart] BC' was a simple enough motto. Two versions had been requisitioned. Black with salmon lettering and the inverse. Those had come from the manufacturers as raging orange and it was thought best they were left in the box. The cheer squad marched from the top of the Moonee Valley straight with banners raised. *The Best Thing Since Phar Lap* was the lead claim. The formation tended towards union rally. Nestled in the front row of the grandstand, they went through their routine:

> 1, 2, 3, 4. Who's the speed queen we adore?
> 5, 6, 7, 8. Who's Australia's sprinting great?
> Blaaaack Caviar
> Caviar, Caviar, Caviar. Oi, Oi, Oi.

It was naff, but harmless enough.

Channel Seven had deemed the Australia Stakes worthy of inclusion in the evening's telecast of the Australian Open Tennis. It was the second of the men's semi-finals, between world number one Novak Djokovic and British aspirant Andy Murray. At 3–2 in the first set, Moonee Valley appeared in the Mega Wall, a screen split into eight locations to which the director might at any moment relocate the audience. Not since her sire Bel Esprit was granted the right of interruption in that AFL pre-season match a decade before, had racing muscled into a mainstream sporting broadcast.

Bruce McAvaney gave a quick rundown for the uninitiated, including the expert commentator by his side, US tennis great Jim Courier. 'The most popular horse in Australia for over eighty years. Probably the closest thing we've ever had to the immortal Phar Lap. She's never lost a race.'

There was no prospect of defeat in this race either. This was a sure thing. But that seemed to add to the attraction rather than undermine it. A meeting that might ordinarily have attracted a thousand people and specialist coverage on racing television and radio, had an estimated 15,300 spectators at the course and was beamed into one of the peak events of the year on free-to-air television and broadcast on ABC Radio.

Black Caviar sprang from the inside barrier, the equal of Zedi Knight and Doubtful Jack. Nolen felt no compunction to lead. He immediately eased to allow the two speedy conveyances to set the pace ahead. Out of the back straight she was closer to the trailing trio than the lead pair.

Like a local who knows the traffic patterns and the precise moment when to manoeuvre, Black Caviar towed up to the hindquarters of Doubtful Jack passing the school. Ears pricked, she again did all that was necessary heading into the bend.

> Black Caviar's bounding on their backs and she's out three wide about to go to them around the turn
> She strides into the camber, rushes up around the bend, takes the lead and Black Caviar turns with a two-length advantage
> Zedi Knight, Doubtful Jack and Rock Classic
> Black Caviar races down past the cheer squad four lengths clear
> Seventeen in a row, now it gets serious

Nolen's hands were not demanding but encouraging. He clicked her up only once she had taken the lead, with the race safely in her keeping. The jockey knew not to be too soft on her and, where he had closed down in the past, he let the mare run through the line. This was not a night for complacency, given what lay in store. Had Nolen pushed, Black Caviar would have clipped a further tenth of a second from her time and broken the track record of Miss Andretti.

As Channel Seven departed, McAvaney felt the euphoria that had gripped the Valley. 'I could talk for two hours about that. But we're not going to do that. She's awesome.'

Moody had stood back a fraction further than usual to watch the race. He puffed away at the mouth of the tunnel, where he had an unimpeded view of the big screen. From there he adjudged Black Caviar's action to be every bit as a good as her attitude.

It was, as always, characterised by its effortless nature. But Moody did not allow the conversation to go down this familiar path. 'It's easy to say not extended, but how much faster do they go?' To an inquiry as to how he felt about the imminent increase in distance to 1400 metres: 'Do you want to back one of those to run her down in an extra 200 metres?'

As Nolen took Black Caviar on a victory parade down the straight, he clapped the patrons as they applauded the mare. In a touching moment, the clerk of the course leaned over and ruffled Black Caviar's forelock.

Nolen chuckled back at the winner's circle that he and Moody should get a percentage of the gate. 'A percentage of nothing's nothing, isn't it?' He straightened himself for a serious thought: 'It's a wonderful privilege to be on top of Black Caviar. I thank God every day.'

A commemorative rug was bestowed on Black Caviar; salmon embroidered with the map of Australia and signed by members of the Black Caviar Cheer Squad.

When the night was done, Gary Wilkie headed home to experience it all over again. He watched the recording of the television coverage to sample what he had not taken in at first hand. 'It's a wonderful, humbling feeling to go to the races and have all of these people support your racehorse.' He saw Jill Taylor share the ever-present sense of nerves in the build-up and Neil Werrett describe it as daunting once the winning was done.

Wilkie listened to the words spoken about his mare and savoured every image. His favourite ritual in the solitude of home was to view the race itself over and over again. He did it for the buzz and to ensure it was not taken for granted. Black Caviar never disappointed him. 'I liked it when she's just cruising to catch up to the others and as soon as she gets there it's just an amazing feeling to watch, that let down and just go past them. She was in a hurry then, too, at that stage.'

Before he conceded to sleep soon after 2 a.m., his mind was occupied, like many others, with what came next. The C.F. Orr Stakes was booked for two Saturdays hence. Beyond that, Moody remained cryptic. Either he did not know or he was not telling. 'The old adage of Kevin Sheedy, one match at a time. Good on ya, Sheeds! There's a race for her every Saturday on the eastern seaboard of Australia and most parts of the world for the next six months. We're going to sit down and have a meeting on Friday with the owners. That'll tell us a bit more and get everyone's gut feel.'

The possibilities seemed endless.

Bronwen Healy Photography

Tony Haydon and Peter Moody examine the signatures of the Black Caviar Cheer Squad on a specially bestowed rug.

Newspix / Michael Dodge

Black Caviar leaves her rivals behind in the C.F. Orr Stakes at Caulfield over 1400 metres.

19

Faster Stronger Longer

Caulfield, C.F. Orr Stakes, 11 February 2012

The limitations of a horse can never be known until they are declared. By then it is too late. There are genetic markers to indicate proficiency on wet tracks or capacity to run additional distance. They are guidelines rather than laws.

From the earliest days, when he set her on a path to the 1600-metre Caulfield Guineas, Peter Moody believed Black Caviar would thrive at distances beyond the sprinting range. In seventeen starts she had never been beyond 1200 metres. Moody would finally have the proof to his hunch in the C.F. Orr Stakes. 'I'll either be a genius or a mug.' Because if Black Caviar could not stretch to 1400 metres, she would lose. That was a physiological certainty.

The Australian Racing Hall of Fame is littered with cautionary tales. Todman, Vain, Manikato: dominant sprinters who could demolish rivals over the short course but got the stitch the first time they were required to pace themselves and see out an additional 200 metres. The graveyard race for the three sprint kings was the AJC Sires Produce Stakes. The mitigating circumstance was that they were all two-year-olds. After speeding exhibitions to win the Golden Slipper, each suffered humbling defeat when rated certainties to prevail. The unbeaten Todman was considered invincible in the 1957 Sires at odds of 1/6, but future champion Tulloch ran him down. Vain was a near-identical case twelve years later, suffering a more stunning upset when overhauled by moderately performed outsider Beau Babylon. Manikato did not boast a perfect record, but had tremendously impressed, taking the Blue Diamond/Golden Slipper double. He led into the Randwick straight in 1978 but tired badly to finish fifth.

More recent history had highlighted the folly of making assumptions. As a three-year-old, Weekend Hussler was the darling of the turf. From his commanding arrival in the big time, his powerful runaway victory in the Caulfield Guineas, he won six Group 1 races in the season of 2007–08. He belittled his own age group and thrashed the older brigade in the Oakleigh Plate and Newmarket Handicap. At the height of Weekend Hussler's deeds, his craggy-faced trainer Ross McDonald would demonstrate his level of confidence prior to a race by suggesting punters should bet their house on his horse. The joke soon ran to multiple houses with the upgrade to mansions, Monopoly-style.

As McDonald contemplated fresh challenges, he outlined the most ambitious plan. Believing there were no confines to his horse's burgeoning ability, he announced the intent to emulate the legendary Rising Fast and win the Caulfield Cup, Cox Plate and Melbourne Cup in the same spring.

While the Hussonet gelding was electrifying in his sprinting wins, he was equally dominant out to a mile. Anything beyond that was the unknown. At his first test, over 1800 metres in the Underwood Stakes at Caulfield, he simply ran away from seasoned stayers Pompeii Ruler, Littorio and Maldivian. Punters and bookmakers concurred that the first leg, the Caulfield Cup, was at his mercy. Had you turned on racing television station TVN at any time in the next two weeks, you might have been convinced it was a mere formality that Weekend Hussler would rampage through the two Cups and a Plate.

The trouble was, he could not go one step beyond those 1800 metres. In his final preparatory gallop, the Turnbull Stakes at Flemington, he ran odds-on favourite but turned in the worst run of his career, tailing into eighth at the end of 2000 metres. All manner of excuses were made on his behalf, mostly by those usually charged with the duties of independent analysis: seasoned commentators, form students and professional punters. Weekend Hussler was still highly fancied over 2400 metres in the Caulfield Cup. Despite the most perfect ride from Brad Rawiller, the balloon pricked entering the straight. Weekend Hussler could not stay and no amount of wishing, hoping, thinking or praying could make it otherwise.

For those who demanded some uncertainty and risk in the Black Caviar story, this rise to 1400 metres was it. Yet in the days leading up to the race, the media penned lines about her eighteenth win as if she had already taken the prize. It was commendable to believe, but that did not make it fact. The pundits had embraced the role of cheerleading.

Not by all, though. An astute student of breeding, racing writer Andrew Garvey laid out in *The Age* the limitations in the Black Caviar pedigree: 'Horses don't read pedigrees but in the countdown to Black Caviar's first attempt at a distance further than 1200 metres, her family tree makes interesting reading for people looking for a reason why she will not win her 18th consecutive race.'

Garvey had traced the origins of the female family back four generations. Owner–breeder David Hains, whose trademark yellow and red colours were carried to fame by Kingston Town and Kingston Rule, had imported the Danish Oaks winner Love Song. While there was no immediate success, her descendants did create a worthwhile impression. Love Song was the granddam of Song of Norway and her best foal was Scandinavia. She won the Group 2 QTC Cup and placed in the Newmarket and Lightning Stakes. In seventeen starts she did not race beyond 1200 metres. Scandinavia's best foals, Magnus and Wilander, were also never tested beyond that threshold under the training of Moody and Lee Freedman in a combined thirty-seven starts. Helsinge was the half-sister to those colts and never raced.

While Garvey had read and deciphered many a successful pedigree, he had also learnt to trust what he saw for himself: 'A case could be made on pedigree that Black Caviar might be a risk at the trip, but 17 race replays would indicate otherwise.'

The questions surrounding Black Caviar were not whether she would win, but when she would race. A week on from the Australia Stakes, Moody took a lunch date with the owners at South Melbourne's Emerald Hotel. He knew the up-market pub so well, he could order the calamari without any need to glance at other options. Conversely, the menu for discussion that afternoon was lengthy and took far more consideration.

Major racing clubs around the world had made it known they wanted Black Caviar to grace their turf or dirt. Beyond the questions at home, Moody was fielding intense interest from England, France and Ireland, along with the United States, Singapore, Japan and Hong Kong. The most immediate interest, though, was from Dubai.

The Dubai World Cup night in March hosted two suitable sprints, the richest of which was the Golden Shaheen. Moody had casually thrown in nominations for Black Caviar that were initially greeted as speculative. Now he had a serious possibility. The Dubai Racing Club's international manager, Martin Talty, was quick to lobby. 'What racecourse wouldn't want Black Caviar? We are over the moon that she has been entered. We know she is going to have three runs in Australia but there is the option of a $2 million race or a $1 million race on the way to Ascot. Everyone in Australia was desperately looking forward to her taking on Sepoy and if she runs in the Golden Shaheen then she would.'

He was, however, quick to quash talk of an appearance fee to entice the mare. The world's richest race meeting, held at the purpose-built Meydan track, drew horses from around the globe, particularly the headliners from international stables Godolphin and Darley, both of which had been created by the sheikhs of Dubai's ruling Al Maktoum family. Racing authorities dictated that Black Caviar would be drawn by the prestige, not an inducement. That said, the prize was the biggest cheque she would ever race for.

Moody saw the benefits of breaking up the arduous trip to England with a month's stopover in the Gulf State. As he outlined the Dubai option, he had the Black Caviar collective intrigued. He almost talked himself into it, but he chose the moment to share a more audacious idea still. He had the notion to run Black Caviar on three consecutive Saturdays. It would require gymnastics he had never previously contemplated with his most valuable asset. If all went to plan in the Orr (1400 metres), he would attempt the highly unorthodox strategy of returning Black Caviar to the pure speed distance of 1000 metres in the Lightning Stakes, before pushing back to the 1400 metres of the Futurity Stakes.

Embedded in this strategy was the major milestone of Black Caviar's twentieth win on home soil. The extra run, while high risk, was the best means to that end.

Moody sought two resolutions from the owners. First, an affirmation of their trust and second, confirmation that, above all else, Royal Ascot remained the priority. Both were forthcoming. Gary Wilkie gave voice to the collective faith they had in their trainer: 'Let's face it, he bought the horse, he knows the horse, he's got seventeen wins, so we're going to be very much guided by what he says. We haven't been in this position before and Peter has. Our preferred option is to head to Royal Ascot. That'd be just absolutely special. But if he says no there's something wrong, we'd pull the pin on that idea and look at another option. Or if indeed she has had enough, I suppose at the end of the day we might have to retire her. But it's not something we want to think about now.'

Despite the eagerness of the media, which awaited word from the Emerald luncheon like a puff of smoke from the Vatican, their decisions were not made known. But Moody had his mandate.

He kept his own counsel until the morning of the Orr. He artfully deflected the futures debate until the business at hand was concluded. He did so in all bar one interview. That was with US racing network TVG. There he confirmed that Black Caviar would run in a Saturday trilogy.

The C.F. Orr Stakes had a history of gathering one of the highest quality fields of the season. Instituted in 1925, it was first run at the now defunct Williamstown Racecourse and had subsequently been staged at all four surviving metropolitan tracks in Melbourne. Its distance of 1400 metres and scheduling, at the start of the summer/autumn features, made it a highly versatile race serving multiple purposes. The short break between the November spring climax and February's reignition meant class horses found their peak condition and best form much sooner than returning from winter hibernation.

The Orr tested sprinters. Manikato won it on three successive occasions. Milers were well suited. Typhoon Tracy's double was the recent evidence of that. The charm of the race lay in its suitability for the country's best weight-for-age horses. Cox Plate winners including Flight, Tobin Bronze and Surround had prevailed. In 2009, the previously one-dimensional Maldivian rose above imposed limitations when he galloped brilliantly to victory returning from his 2008 Cox Plate triumph. Champion Queensland frontrunner Vo Rogue and the majestic Lonhro graced the honour roll.

What made the Orr so egalitarian, though, was the string of Melbourne Cup winners who returned the following year and captured the imagination. This had been true for generations. Bart Cummings' father, Jim, produced Comic Court to win the 1951 Orr three months after he started a family tradition in the big two-miler. Rising Fast had done it. Saintly, Let's Elope and At Talaq were among those who had scored scorching victories in triumphant graduation from the rank of stayers to stars.

Jockey Wayne Harris had partnered the muscular chestnut Jeune to victory in the 1994 Melbourne Cup. The stallion had shown promise early in his career in England and was identified by owner Sheikh Hamdan bin Rashid Al Maktoum as an ideal candidate for export to the antipodes. It followed the highly successful program pioneered when At Talaq won the Cup eight years earlier for trainer Colin Hayes. The famed blue silks with the white epaulettes of Sheikh Hamdan became a dominating force in Australian racing in concert with the Hayes clan: Fraar won a Caulfield Cup, Almaraad a Cox Plate. By 1990, son David Hayes had inherited the family business and on a murky, wet Flemington afternoon Jeune powered to victory on the Tuesday with the nation stopped. His influence was not restricted to his racing days. Jeune became a prolific sire until his death in 2006. His most famous son was Caulfield Cup winner Mummify.

In Harris's view, Jeune's crowning achievement was his stupendous win in the 1995 Orr Stakes, where he came from last to mow down sprinters the calibre of Blue Diamond winner Hurricane Sky and grand campaigner Schillaci. While waiting to see Black Caviar contest the latest renewal of the race, Harris imparted: 'All things aside, I reckon his best win was when he came back and won the Orr Stakes. He showed what a good horse he was on that occasion. If they can show their greatness, they can win this race.'

Such history was ignored in the lead-up to Black Caviar's Orr tilt when Sydney's *Daily Telegraph* proposed the notion: 'Usain Bolt racing a field of Kenyan long-distance runners over 400m is a perfect way to describe Black Caviar's attempt to win 18 straight races in Saturday's C.F. Orr Stakes at Caulfield.'

The line might have seemed clever, but the view could only be tolerated if you knew nothing about racing. Unfortunately, it played strongly to those in precisely that camp.

Caulfield Cup winner Southern Speed fitted the historic profile perfectly. The South Australian mare had shown her ability from the earliest days. Her career, which began with two accomplished wins in Adelaide, got a boost at her first Flemington appearance when she trounced some handy fillies, including Moody's Do Ra Mi, in the Group 3 Vanity in February 2011. Her spring campaign as a four-year-old progressed methodically but without victory until trainer Leon Macdonald produced her perfectly tuned for the Caulfield Cup. Southern Speed had resumed on Australia Day under the burden of 60 kilograms in a Listed 1400-metre race and burst from the pack to swamp her rivals under jockey Craig Williams. It put her on a natural course to the Orr.

From the Melbourne Cup were Bart Cummings' pair Illo and Precedence. A previous Cup winner, Efficient, entering the dim twilight of his career, was also present. The best credentialled apart from Southern Speed was Perth's premier galloper Playing God. In the summer carnival he had taken out the Group 1 Kingston Town Stakes after a reasonable eastern states campaign that ended in an average Cox Plate run.

Black Caviar was meeting a style of horse she had never previously encountered – mature, seasoned racers with an ability to settle and unleash a run at the climax of the journey, rather than scolded scamperers from beginning to end.

* * *

The Melbourne Racing Club had learnt from the debacle at Moonee Valley. It was decreed that Festival Family Day would be free entry. Charging patrons at the gate to enter a racecourse on all bar the half-dozen weeks of the Spring Carnival was an anachronism. Demanding a fee from those under eighteen, who could neither bet nor drink legally, was plainly ludicrous. The lifeblood of racing clubs is not gate receipts, it is betting turnover and catering facilities. The $20 saved by a punter at the gate would be spent inside. Racing authorities had their own research to prove it to be true. Yet they failed to roll out such a strategy.

The wisdom of those at Caulfield was immediately apparent. While heavy grey clouds threatened storms in the morning, Melbourne's weather found a compromise, offering as much faith as you could ever draw that the rain would hold off in the main. The vibe on the course was transplanted from the spring. Such *joie de vivre* seemed to have been quarantined to that designated period. And it was purer than racing in the party season. As the course filled, it was apparent people had not come for nine races but for one horse.

It was throwback to the days of Bernborough, probably the biggest drawcard racing in Australia ever had. In the immediate aftermath of the Second World War, the giant Queensland galloper was fixed as a national icon. Caulfield Cup Day 1946 saw 108,000 pour through the gates, over half of whom were attending the races for the first time. That was ten per cent of Melbourne's population drawn in at the climax of Bernborough's farewell season. While he had defied the heavy weights allotted by handicappers on so many occasions, lugging ten stone ten pounds was beyond him that day.

Sixty-six years on, an unseasonally large gathering of 20,427 graced the same track. It seemed like so many more than that.

Grandparents patiently lined the jumping castle and teapot carousel while their youngsters bounced and spun delightedly. When the designated time came, those children indulged Pop as he pointed out the big brown horse they had come to admire. On the course was a woman from Chicago on a fleeting twenty-four-hour visit specifically to see the mare for herself. She shared the scene with a lady from the northern New South Wales town of Grafton, who sought spiritual refuge from the misery of her flood-stricken home.

On the public lawn were two men, old enough to know better, sporting jodhpurs to complement the specially made salmon and black silks. Not far off were babes in arms, too young to have any choice, dressed in the same.

The hordes descended on the mounting yard twenty minutes before her scheduled arrival to ensure positions, whether a prized view or partial. The old wooden grandstand on the turn out of the straight had survived the suspicious fire of 1922 that had levelled the Members' Stand and the accidental blaze five years later that lay ruin to the Guineas Stand. Nowadays, it filled perhaps twice a year. Today it brimmed beyond capacity.

Beneath the crowd's gaze, the object of all affection came wandering by. With Moody at a jogtrot behind, binoculars slung over his wrist, Black Caviar took a sustained look to her left over the low hedge and straight into the camera sights of those who lined her route. The conclusion of all who captured the moment was that she well knew they were gathered for a glimpse of her.

Moody had been making this walk, to and fro from the saddling stalls to the mounting yard, all afternoon. Never at a great pace. The official race book had been printed with a special fold-out poster of Black Caviar complete with an autograph page on the reverse side. The trainer could not go ten steps without obliging a request to scribble his name. When word reached him that Nelly was on the track, he quipped: 'She can share the annoyance with me.' Still, he refused to disappoint anyone.

For those in need of a reminder that Moody Racing was more than one horse, the trainer had already seen to that. Into his care had come the European stayer Manighar. The gelding had competed in the past two Caulfield and Melbourne Cups for world-renowned Italian trainer Luca Cumani. Manighar had proved to be an endurance stayer who lacked the necessary dash to win Australia's most treasured races. His fifth and seventh in the Cups of 2010 had improved to a commendable fourth and fifth in 2011, but they defined him as the classic English one-pacer.

Manighar was now a permanent resident and provided Moody the sort of fascinating challenge he craved. The six-year-old had never started in a race shorter than 2400 metres. His new trainer had him first up at a mile in the T.S. Carlyon Cup. Over the preceding month, Moody had prescribed in his handwritten notes short, sharp gallops for Manighar in the morning darkness at Caulfield. Without meaning to be derogatory to the European methods, he viewed Manighar as a 4000-metre hurdler. He was testing to see if he could inject speed into legs that had been accustomed to marathons. Moody had tinkered sufficiently to put his progress to the test.

He had told connections, including former Australian cricketer and prominent racehorse owner Simon O'Donnell, that the horse had something better than a silly chance. O'Donnell watched from the Channel Nine broadcast hut as the race went live to air. His surprise and delight was captured for all to share. Manighar bounced up on the pace and travelled so convincingly, he had the race won at the halfway mark. When Nolen let him free in the straight, the speed Moody had conjured was startling.

The trainer was self-effacing after the race: 'It's just a change of routine for an old horse like him and he's enjoyed it. He's come from one of the greatest trainers in the world so don't kid yourself that I've improved him.' He could deny that charge all he wanted, but that was precisely what he was guilty of. In Moody's list of accomplishments, this was one of his best. And he was only just getting started with Manighar.

Satisfaction would have to wait, as Black Caviar's hour was at hand. Moody stood with Nolen on the centre lawn of the mounting yard while Black Caviar trod circuits of the redbrick circumference. With each lap, she sagged that little bit further behind the number seven horse, Illo. Each circuit seemed to exaggerate her mannerisms. She kept her neck low and dropped pace with every passing. It caused a ripple of mirth from those looking on. That playfulness ended as Nolen was legged aboard. Black Caviar drew herself up and tensed for action.

The view of the public lawn was identical to its appearance as the runners take their place for the Caulfield Cup each year. Jam-packed. Hardly a blade of grass to be seen through the pressing bodies. Heaving with anticipation.

Black Caviar knew the 1400-metre start well, as it put her close to her home stables. She also knew that she never usually came this way on race day. Instead of jogging from the left-hand turn out of the yard up to the 1200-metre chute, Nolen had brought her back down the straight, past the grandstands for the preliminary canter and around the back of the course to the waiting barriers. She noted the departure from routine and Nolen observed an edge in her demeanour.

It led her to ping the gates better than in any previous attempt. Whatever tinges of anxiety Black Caviar felt travelled through the reins to Nolen's hands. She did not drop immediately into her fully relaxed stride. The jockey knew he was riding this time, rather than fulfilling his customary role as passenger. 'She travelled stronger than she usually does. I just had to manage her.'

Danzylum strode to the front but was soon restrained by Nick Hall. It was an unusual tactic. He was a horse best served allowed to bowl along freely and set an even tempo. He was being asked to stack his rivals up on a slow pace and try to sprint away. The legs of an eight-year-old veteran of seventy-five starts were manifestly unsuited to the task. Midas Touch lobbed second, with Steven King showing no desire to increase either tempo or pressure. Once a placegetter in the English St Leger, before being imported for unrealised Melbourne Cup duties, he was hardly going to surge away on a lightning move.

Those tactics led more than one observer to ponder if the jockeys had become so caught up in events and their role as extras as to preclude either initiative or dare. Inhibition born of fear of becoming the mug who ruined a race involving Black Caviar on some hairbrained escapade. To have tested Black Caviar's stamina required a horse and jockey willing to run at breakneck speed and string the field out in the hope that the thundering pursuers would never arrive. The effect could have been twofold: to dull the acceleration in the legs of the mare, and give the middle-distance horses a chance to get momentum rolling on a late withering burst. Resigned perhaps to the futility of the task, no one tried. The walk, trot and canter played straight into Nolen's hands.

Black Caviar settled fourth around stablemate Doubtful Jack. Down the railway side, approaching the 600-metre marker, a sense of familiarity returned to Black Caviar. On those mornings when he partnered her in fast work, this was the trigger for Nolen to slip Nelly a bit of rein. He repeated the exercise under race conditions and felt the surge from Black Caviar. She understood precisely. Nolen smiled to himself. 'She thought it was game on.'

Black Caviar loomed three deep on the corner, rounded up the leaders with ease and ended their hopes of slipping to an unanticipated lead. Nolen had not needed to expend energy to head the speedier leaders of the past. He had the proverbial lap full of horse. 'She had the race in her keeping a long way out.'

Black Caviar cruised up to them approaching the 200, the
200 that matters
She sprinted clear
She dashed four away from Southern Speed and Playing
God
Black Caviar, the crowd salutes her
She salutes the judge for the eighteenth time

The roar exploded at the 200-metre mark. The question had been posed and answered in the same stride. The acceleration was not only undiminished, it might even have been enhanced. There was a pang of emotion felt by trainer and spectator alike.

In a hard-bitten TAB, 100 men gave voice to a mighty cheer and a sustained standing ovation for a horse not one of them had backed. In lounge rooms, as the viewer numbers doubled for the race itself, the sight united generations with a spontaneous tear.

Those watching under the old semaphore board at the end of the straight saw the field racing directly towards them. For fifty metres, Nolen gave Black Caviar a shake to make a good thing of it and then began to throttle down. Together they cruised.

The blasé reaction was to describe it as ridiculously easy. You had to look a little further than Nolen and Black Caviar to see the devastating effect. Behind them, jockeys flailed hopelessly. Urgency peaked as prospects faded. Williams gave Southern Speed two good thumps on the rump with the whip to gear her to full velocity. Still she was giving ground. Steven Parnham wrestled with Playing God in the forlorn attempt to drag him along. Others hauled the steerage this way and that, to no avail.

It was a command performance that touched those intimately involved. Moody had stood on the back step of the viewing area under the enclosed grandstand. He trembled with emotion. 'It's mind-boggling. I know people doubt the opposition but they're good horses. There's a Caulfield Cup winner that looked outstanding three weeks ago and what she does to good horses is beyond belief.'

As they pulled up in the distance, Nolen slowed Black Caviar to a standstill. Largely unobserved, he unselfconsciously leant forward, put his arms down around her and kissed the back of her neck. It occurred to him that this journey was closer to its conclusion than its beginning. He, for one, would cherish every minute of it. That was why he had ensured that his mum had made the two-hour trip along the Hume Freeway from Benalla to witness for herself the highlight of her son's professional life. 'My mum, she won't come to the city unless it's a baptism or a child's birthday. She's very set in her ways back home. It was great to see her. She had a wonderful time.'

Neil Werrett felt like he had not breathed for twenty minutes but was exultant as he entered the mounting yard. 'Today was one of her most outstanding efforts. The 1400 Peter's been saying for a long time would be right up her alley. To run a strong 1400 gives us a lot of confidence for the Diamond Jubilee when she goes to Ascot. I'm pretty excited about that.'

The variance in reaction from the media was instructive. *Sydney Morning Herald* sports writer at large, Richard Hinds, had set himself the assignment of measuring not what racing could do for Black Caviar but what Black Caviar could do for racing: 'It probably did not help that Saturday's performance was not spine tingling, but mechanical. Long before Black Caviar loped clear and strode effortlessly to the line, she had removed any dramatic plot twists from the script. Her appearance at the 200 metre mark, in front of the kids' playground, was hailed heartily. But not from the bottom of the lungs like you cheer a champion in a tight struggle.

'But she is racing's incredible freak show. The crowds flock to see a horse, not a horse race. When the next great freak appears the same people will rush to a golf tournament, a cricket match or a pushbike race. You won't see them at the track.'

Channel Nine had made a feature of 'the critics' throughout the telecast. It led Simon O'Donnell to speak for those who imagined a borderline persecution complex on Black Caviar's behalf: 'In my mind, no doubt, this is the greatest thing we've seen go round on a racecourse. Critics should go to an asylum and check themselves in. We get into some bad habits in this country. Because she is what she is, some people sit back and can't wait for something to go wrong. We've got to embrace what we've got here. This is the greatest horse any Australian has ever seen in their lifetime. Yet people still are trying to pick holes in what she's doing. Let's look at the positive things. There's enough things going on in the world that give us bad news every day. Let's for God sake soak up the great news and that's exactly what this mare is all about.'

Soon after the presentation was completed, a dirty rain shower swept over Caulfield. In the ensuing gloom, veteran sprinter Eagle Falls ran home to win the Group 3 Rubiton Stakes. His trainer David Hayes, a man with an infectious smile, arrived at the winner's stall sporting the official salmon and black tie of Black Caviar. Hayes was born into racing. He lived and breathed the profession, having been raised in it by his father, a gentle man with a pioneering spirit. At the outset of his career, David had trained Better Loosen Up to win a Cox Plate and the ultimate thrill of a Japan Cup under the Australian flag. He had conquered the ultracompetitive cauldron of Hong Kong racing, becoming the colony's champion trainer. The sight of Black Caviar, though, touched the horse lover, the fan, the child in him. He referred to her as the Great One. 'She's the best I've ever seen. Someone gave me the tie so I thought why not join the party.'

That was the innocent spirit that marked the day and pushed it further away from what the opinion makers had witnessed.

After Black Caviar had been hosed down and the adrenaline of competition settled, Donna Fisher resumed walking Nelly.

As she passed by the front of the stalls, a group of children on the other side of the fence ran alongside cheering excitedly. For the next twenty minutes, strapper and horse churned out laps of the exercise yard with a couple of hundred people, at least half of whom were kids, leaning over to pat the great mare. Donna indulged them all.

Long-time racegoer Philip Tyndall was among those at the intimate gathering. 'What amazed me was how calm and relaxed Black Caviar was through the whole thing. To me, this just demonstrated the wonderful temperament that she obviously has, and it confirmed what I've known for years, and what the racing authorities never seem to promote; that by going to the races there are these great moments and it's not only on the track. This was amongst the most memorable times I've ever had at the races, and most people there weren't even aware of it.'

Underneath the grandstand, on the thoroughfare to the train station, a giant salmon board had been erect. It started with only *THANK YOU Black Caviar* printed at the top. With black permanent markers, those in attendance inscribed their salutations and documented their presence. Alan and Fiona from Launceston captured the spirit of the task best: 'Rapt to be invited to Nelly's 18th.'

As at the end of any such party, people stood and read the messages diligently and curiously before adding their own. There were love hearts and 'Happy Valentine's Day' wishes. A multitude of 'Go You Good Thing', the catchcry of the casual punter. There were dedications to 'The horse of the century' and the Maori nod 'Kia Kaha (Be Brave)'. Many a wag resorted to variations of the timeless English jibe: 'Give the Poms something to whinge about.'

And for posterity, there was SR: 'Flew here all the way from Chicago USA just to see you!! Let's go 18!'

Newspix / Alex Coppel

The epic Lightning Stakes clash between Hay List and Black Caviar.

20

Lightning Strikes Twice

Flemington, Lightning Stakes, 18 February 2012

Nothing in sport is quite so treasured as rivalry. For in the matching of champions, greatness is accentuated and ultimately judged.

Any enduring fable requires a foil. To air the true loathing that existed between them, Muhammad Ali had Joe Frazier. For the Cold War metaphor to resonate, Bobby Fischer needed Boris Spassky. There was never a pairing so perfectly contrasted for talent and temperament as Bjorn Borg and John McEnroe.

The search for worthy opposition had become fruitless for Black Caviar. That void bordered on being detrimental to her reputation. She sought the competitor that could threaten her on merit, rather than profit from mishap. The rival that would draw from her everything she was capable of.

In the aftermath of the Orr demolition, Moody finally snapped when the phrase 'limited opposition' was put to him: 'That annoys me as much as anything. She's beaten Melbourne Cup winners, Caulfield Cup winners, Slipper winners, All Aged winners, every Group 1 in Australia. She's beaten them all and the amazing thing is she's made them look second rate. She's belittled them. When are we going to stop kidding ourselves that she's beating nothing? When she's not there everyone's getting in raptures about them in their given grades and races. But all of a sudden when she beats them, they're not much good. That's the one thing that really pisses me off.'

As the Global Sprint Challenge for 2012 was launched, the racing manager of the series, Leigh Jordan, fielded an inquiry as to whether there was a galloper on the planet capable of taking it to Black Caviar. 'Currently with the sprinters I've seen around the world, no. She's just so far superior.'

The re-emergence of Hay List was timely. But no one kidded themselves that his presence was a clear and present danger. Part-owner Peter Davenport was met with little short of scorn when he took the conch and proclaimed the terms of the fresh preparation. 'It's my prerogative as owner to say silly things. I will end up either with egg on my face or a slap on the back. But Hay List has never been on his game when he has taken on Black Caviar. Never. When the moon and the stars are in alignment, he'll be the horse to beat her. I guarantee it.'

Such grandiose assessments had seemed fantasy to trainer John McNair. Veterinary advice had suggested Hay List would never make it back to the track. The once powerful horse was a stricken figure in the aftermath of an aggressive leg infection. McNair's wife, Sue, dedicated herself to the six-year-old with the tender affection of a nurse. The gelding, possessed of a kind nature, was receptive to such a touch. McNair marvelled at the connection formed. 'She has fallen in love with the horse and he has bonded with her like nothing I have ever seen. With horses that are as pleasant and well natured like this guy, you can't help but become attached to him.'

When Hay List returned to the public gaze for his tune-up trial in Sydney, Ray Thomas in *The Daily Telegraph* commented that he was 620 kilograms of muscle and raw power. Importantly, his speed proved undiminished. McNair was praised for his horsemanship, and the trainer's gentle speculations were optimistic: 'When he was very ill, was I sure of him making a successful comeback? No, I wasn't. But I suspect now he might have returned a better horse than ever. I wouldn't be expecting a judgment on that straight away but if I'm right, I believe he could be a couple of lengths better than he was last year. Only time will tell.'

Hay List was to resume his career running in the Lightning Stakes at Flemington. Without a breath of arrogance, McNair wanted a win to reassure his galloper. The weight-for-age conditions were ideal. The horse to beat would be Sydney three-year-old Foxwedge, the colt who had run Sepoy to a narrow margin in the spring. When those calculations were made, Black Caviar was not in the picture for the 1000-metre sprint. Peter Moody was about to change all that.

Black Caviar had never come through a race better than the way she recovered from the Orr Stakes. Chiropractor Michael Bryant, who knew the muscule issues of the past intimately, had right of veto. Moody wanted an unconditional physical clearance for the mare. Bryant was unequivocal: 'I was completely happy with her the way she pulled up.'

The trainer would embrace risk. He reasoned she would not be quite as sharp over the reduced distance but took comfort in what he saw as home-turf advantage. Black Caviar had never looked vulnerable down the Flemington straight. With no corner to navigate, Moody regarded her as bombproof.

The trick was in the distance. Randwick clocker Craig Thompson researched the success rate of horses dropping back from 1400 metres to 1000 metres in seven days. He dated his search to the commencement of the 2008 racing season, finding 120 horses who had attempted the feat. Only one had been successful. That was on the backwater circuit at Kangaroo Island.

'Look, there are exceptions, and Black Caviar is an exception, but the stat does reveal something about how difficult it is to come back so sharply in trip and win, especially in seven days.'

Bookmakers were finally accepting bets on her rivals, as the unsentimental assessors identified the gamble. By his own admission, Luke Nolen was a glass half-empty man. But he quietly admired Moody's boldness. 'Peter's never run and hid from anything in his life and he's been a little bit unorthodox with a couple of things he's done in his career.' Moody accepted ultimate responsibility for the venture and Matt Stewart published the trainer's blunt assessment in the *Herald Sun*: 'If she gets beat, everyone will be wanting to kick the shit out of me. Hell, I'll probably want to kick the shit out of myself.'

In terms of Black Caviar's career, it was a delicate time for Moody to introduce variables. Black Caviar had drawn level with Ajax, the wonderful chestnut colt of the late 1930s, who won eighteen consecutive races before being beaten as the shortest-priced favourite in history at the incomprehensible odds of 1/40. His streak commenced on 4 November 1937 in the VRC Linlithgow Stakes and lasted through to 11 March 1939 in the VRC C.M. Lloyd Stakes. Included in those victories was success in the Newmarket Handicap as a three-year-old, before graduating to sweep the weight-for-age circuit, culminating in the Cox Plate. Cruelly, in a career distinguished by thirty-six wins, it was his defeat in the 1939 Rawson Stakes, downed by Spear Chief in a three-horse race, for which he is most readily remembered.

Black Caviar needed this nineteenth win not only to equal Zenyatta, but to have a share of the Australasian record for the most consecutive victories. The record was held jointly by Desert Gold, who set the mark in 1916, and Gloaming, who drew alongside in 1921.

While Black Caviar's attraction was now, surely, more than just her winning streak, her magic was still conjured by her perfection. No less an authority than Bruce McAvaney expressed a widely held view in *The Australian*: 'If she is beaten – and I hope we never see the day – her currency is diminished dramatically because that air of invincibility is gone and you never get it back.'

Defeat, though, could not have erased what had been done, the passion that had grown around her or the emotion that was released. It could not be undone. How could you attempt to deny what had been witnessed?

Yet that prevailing wisdom rang true even to David Taylor as he contemplated the protection of her unblemished record ahead of the Lightning. 'I'd say personally that's the biggest thing of the lot. To win twenty and beat the record of nineteen set by Zenyatta. To me, and I'm sure it's the feeling behind Peter and the rest of us, that's what we'd really love to do.'

The Victoria Racing Club had written the handbook on staging major meetings, given the growing success of the Melbourne Cup Carnival. By comparison, Lightning Stakes Day had shaped as a doddle. That was until senior management was called together on the Friday afternoon prior to the Orr Stakes for a confidential briefing from VRC chief executive Dale Monteith that would change the entire logistical exercise of the week ahead. Moody had given the VRC the heads-up of the deviation in Black Caviar's schedule. It was as if the Queen had passed word of an unscheduled Royal visit. Everything from the train timetable to the allocation of picnic blankets would be boosted or revamped once Black Caviar's presence was confirmed. Staffing levels would be reinforced, from catering facilities to totalisators. The gates would open earlier for a crowd that was expected to be double the previous estimate.

Monteith had dedicated decades of service to the racing industry, having held the chief executive position first at the Victoria Amateur Turf Club before ascending to the role at the VRC. The phenomenon of this one horse, he adjudged, was unprecedented in his experience. 'It's been a whole different mindset with Black Caviar than I've experienced in my time in racing to any other champion racehorse. I think she's a horse of two generations. She transcends racing. She's captured the imagination of non-racing people as well as racing people. It's just amazing the impact she's having.'

So the swarms headed for Flemington. Whatever they were expecting, they got more than they bargained for.

By delightful coincidence, Black Caviar's million-dollar half-brother, bought by Nathan Tinkler in that spirited bidding duel, would make his debut in the opening race on the card. The highest-priced yearling sold in Australia the previous year, the Casino Prince colt had, rather oddly, been christened All Too Hard. Housed at the Flemington stables of John, Wayne and Michael Hawkes, he had displayed the family trait for early speed.

All Too Hard was a light shade of bay to his sister's deep brown, but as with Black Caviar, a throng of curious observers was initially struck by the size of the colt. Inquiries about his immediate prospects had been deferred with the judgment that he would make a nice three-year-old. As he strode around the mounting yard, he already looked like one.

Privately, trainer Wayne Hawkes expected All Too Hard to win first up, just as older brother Moshe had done for the stable. That debut performance had been at the provincial circuit of Bendigo. The lofty opinion of All Too Hard was reflected in his entry in a Listed event, the Talindert Stakes.

Thirteen years earlier it had been the race that launched the brilliant career of Redoute's Choice. Trained by Rick Hore-Lacy, the colt had proved so dominant at Flemington that a week later he contested the Blue Diamond Stakes and promptly won. At the conclusion of his racing days, Redoute's Choice became a modern sensation as a sire. His impact on the Australian racing scene ran deep. So the challenging two-year-old event to which All Too Hard was assigned for his debut performance had a rich pedigree.

All Too Hard jumped a tad awkwardly but jockey Dwayne Dunn gave him time to find his stride. He sat contentedly midfield behind a steady pace until they reached the course proper, where he strode purposefully within reach of the leaders.

Peter Moody's colt Liberty Rock, a winner on debut at Kyneton, broke for the post under Luke Nolen and momentarily had Dunn scrambling. The irony was lost on no one. Had the hammer fallen differently and Black Caviar's owners succeeded in that auction ten months before, Moody and Nolen would have been in control of the colt winding up on the outside. Instead, they were conspiring to hold him off. Once Dunn produced the whip, though, All Too Hard accelerated superbly, rounded up the lure and ran away for a comfortable victory.

Dunn knew a good two-year-old when he let one loose. He had four consecutive Blue Diamond wins in his CV to prove that. He did not think twice when asked to assess the quality of the steed he had just piloted: 'He's up there with the best. I don't know which direction Team Hawkes will go with him, but I'm happy to go anywhere to ride him. He's a lovely horse. To do that was very good.'

The win created the perfect tone for an anticipated afternoon of high-class equine entertainment. That note, though, would prove fleeting as expectations ran aground. While it made little logical sense, as each race was an individual and unrelated exercise in chance and probability, punters had long ago learnt that when hot favourites start toppling, it could become contagious.

Race Four was a Group 3 event for fillies, The Vanity. VRC Oaks winner Mosheen had been backed as if unbeatable and started at the prohibitive quote of $1.45. She loomed up in the straight for Danny Nikolic to hit the front but never stole the promised break. In a driving three-way finish, she was caught in the last hop by Shopaholic.

If that was unnerving, the abject failure of Caulfield Guineas-winner Helmet in the next race was positively alarming. He was sent out at $1.65 in the C.S. Hayes Stakes and lobbed just behind the pace. The colt found nothing when Kerrin McEvoy began urging and was left lamenting in fifth.

Racing is governed by omens and hunches. They are what had Pam Hawkes scurrying through her local shops early on Saturday morning when she should have been preparing for the races. 'My husband is quite a superstitious man. Apparently he has a lucky hanky. The previous week I'd taken his new blue suit to the dry cleaners. When he discovered the hanky wasn't in his pocket I had to go back to the dry cleaners but it was gone. So I spent the morning looking for a hanky that was a bit similar, couldn't find one and had to own up and tell him that it really didn't matter. His hanky was not that important.'

Pam claimed not to be in the least bit superstitious. It was just that she always wore her lucky golden frog on a necklace and custom-designed Black Caviar earrings for each race.

Neil Werrett sensed the prevailing unease and grimaced when asked about the sequence of beaten favourites. 'I saw them. Maybe the third favourite can win. Luckily she doesn't know about it. I think that's probably the key. She was walking around beautifully in the parade ring before. Not even a sweat. She's acting normally. I think all the owners are sweating up more than she is.'

Acclaimed Fairfax sports columnist Greg Baum concurred with Werrett's assessment. He penned, without, he claims, one word of journalistic licence, that Black Caviar was lolloping around the sun-drenched parade ring pausing every now and then to sniff the roses.

But Moody was on edge and he wanted Nolen in the same frame of mind. As they stood together in the mounting yard he told his long-term companion: 'I feel a bit sorry for you and her today. It's the first time I've ever placed either of you under pressure.'

Watching the exchange was fellow Caulfield trainer Mick Price. Even by the standards of the close-knit racing fraternity, he and Moody were tight friends. Price had been a constant presence in the training tower from the day Moody set up in Melbourne. The connection was closer still as their young families were neighbours in Belgrave South. Together they were quick with a joke or to light up your smoke. 'I used to introduce him as the second best trainer in Victoria but I've had to pull up on that one. Now he introduces me like that.'

Price had spent part of the preceding week with Moody in a helicopter, hopping from property to property inspecting yearlings. He had an intimate view of the anxieties at play. 'He's an outstanding horse trainer, a great bloke and a great mate of mine. The way he's managed this mare, I don't think another trainer would be able to do as good a job. I think last week, first time at 1400, was her easiest race that she's ever done. I think Pete exposes himself to her toughest test coming back against 1000-metre horses that are specifically prepared. But she is a champion and I still think she can win.'

As Price offered that endorsement, Hay List marched by. He had never looked better. He was indeed everything that had been reported. A hulking beast to physically shade even Black Caviar. He was suited for battle. White blinkers adorned his face as he trotted down the rose-lined laneway to the track, mimicking the hood of the boxer ready for the fight.

Black Caviar and Hay List were separated in the barriers by only one horse. They sprang forth, propelled by the force of their hind legs. Before they had taken twenty strides, and once sufficiently clear of Lone Rock between them, Glyn Schofield subtly angled Hay List left to race in close proximity to Black Caviar. The jockey wanted their adversaries to feel Hay List's giant presence. Inside of them was Buffering, racing for the first time since finishing second to Black Caviar in the Patinack Classic on

Stakes Day. Trainer Robert Heathcote had offered jockey Michael Rodd the most basic instructions: 'Go as fast as you can for as long as you can.' To keep up, they were going like the proverbial clappers.

Hay List briefly shaded Black Caviar, but Nolen too had his directions. Pre-race talk had centred on Black Caviar's rivals ensuring a fast-run race, with the notion of hurtling along early and dulling her sting in the drive to the line. On this front, Moody had been explicit. Don't let Hay List get too far away. Nolen was not to be dictated to. He had the best horse; he was to take the fight to him.

Nolen obliged the order and let Black Caviar have her head. Before halfway she pushed through in the middle to reclaim a slender advantage. The pressure was immense. The small field was strung out under the intense tempo. Rodd was feeling for the whip on Buffering before the 400. Foxwedge and Temple of Boom could not maintain contact.

Schofield sensed these two gallopers were going as fast as horses could run. Nolen had become accustomed to the illusion of travelling in slow motion aboard his giant striding mare. That was not the sensation as the 300-metre pole loomed. They were tearing along. Together the jockeys went from standing in the irons, biding their time, to pushing furiously with all the force their upper bodies allowed.

Hay List responded immediately to Schofield's urgency. In three strides he rejoined Black Caviar. The force was with him. He had her this time. It drew a gasp from the crowd. And then a roar. Finally, Black Caviar needed the desperate urgings of her public.

Nolen gritted his teeth and called on the strength he knew her to possess. Having waltzed through her recent races like Cinderella, now she needed the instincts of Xena. The Warrior Princess summoned the fight. The jockey had wondered when this moment would come. 'These horses that have it soft for such a period of time, you wonder the day she's pressured is she still going to perform to her best or is she going to fold up? For those couple of strides I was worried.'

> Up to the course proper, nearly a line of three
> Hay List the outside, Black Caviar the middle, Buffering's
> already under the whip
> Foxwedge is three lengths away, he's being ridden along
> They come away Black Caviar and Hay List to the 200
> Hay List tries grimly to hold on
> Black Caviar stretching out
> She found a length
> Black Caviar gets away from Hay List
> She's going to come away and win
> Black Caviar strikes for a second time in the Lightning
> She beats Hay List
> He was a supremely good run

It was as honest as racing can be. When Nolen asked, Black Caviar found. She lowered her head and took three seismic strides of her own. She expelled the reserves of energy previously untapped. In the surge she swished her tail at the effort. Schofield saw it happen. He snatched for the whip but it was already too late. Just as he expected to pounce, Hay List had lost touch. Suddenly it was as if he was running up the escalator.

Nolen, too, produced his whip. He waved it wide of Black Caviar's bounteous rear end. He would not touch her with it unless Hay List threatened again. But he was poised in case of emergency. With each stride, Black Caviar carved out a margin. At full force, she appeared flawless. Head stretched. Ears pricked. Neck drenched with sweat and adrenaline coursing through her. Metronomic with each bound. At the very edge of exertion, she remained so perfectly controlled.

Hay List faltered in the desperation scramble. Lungs bursting, his stride shortened. He leant inwards under the strain and crabbed at the ground below. His challenge was repelled.

Nolen eased only in the last couple of strides. On days previous he had felt the weight of history, or gratitude for his good fortune, or humility at his privilege as he flashed past the post. Today he felt profound admiration. 'I've got to take my hat off to that mare. She's bloody wonderful. She really toughed it out. She touched me today. The chips were down and she showed a lot of courage.'

The race was an instant classic. In the Members' Stand they rose to applaud the moment Black Caviar beat Hay List to the line. The standing ovation was for both horses. That was immediately obvious. Observers in the mounting yard were swept up in the exhilaration. Drew Morphett had broadcast the best of sport for more than forty years. His voice quivered as he put words to the scene: 'I've got tears in my eyes, I was shouting that much. It was absolutely phenomenal. Again I thought Hay List had really put it to her and she had a fight on her hands. But she ended up winning comfortably. It was absolutely fantastic.'

Melbourne's leading form analyst Deane Lester sat barely a couple of steps away. 'Hay List amazed me because he'd been to hell and back with injuries. We see horses struggle to come back at a lower level, but he was at the elite level and ran right to his best. What a race it was. To see them go toe to toe like that, it was a prize fight and the champ prevailed again.'

Implicit in every plaudit was a commendation for Hay List.

Peter Moody stood deeply sated. 'She was pushed by a great horse but she's just a champion. All due respect, he's a great horse, isn't he? But he's just unfortunate in an era when he's run into an equine freak. He's the only horse that's ever made her fight.'

Usually reticent to join the public discourse, Sarah Moody positively bubbled with delight. 'That's just amazing. You know what really is exciting is Hay List brought his A game. He was here a hundred per cent and it was fantastic to see him run so well. And she put him away. That's how special she is. She had to work today. She had to dig deep. I think she's had it easy for a little while and all of a sudden it's "Holy crap I've got to actually have a go here". It was terrific, tremendous, fantastic. I'm pleased I'm here. I'm pleased I'm a part of it.'

David Taylor had craved a return to competition and the accompanying jangling of nerves. The apprehension that gripped him as the pair had roared by, locked in mortal combat, reminded him to be careful what you wished for. The sight, though, had made him feel alive. 'That's just simply amazing. What a great race by Hay List. Our horse, she is amazing, isn't she? To come back after last week and do that. She really had to dig in, didn't she? What a wonderful race that was, it truly was.'

Pam Hawkes felt wrung out like a participant rather than a spectator. 'Normally I sit and watch the race possibly holding my breath. But the extra roar that you heard was me. Because for a change I had to join in and encourage her.'

In the sanctuary of the Jockeys' Room, Schofield needed confirmation for his own peace of mind. Some acknowledgment that what he had felt was real and not imagined. He posed the question to Nolen: 'Did I have you worried?'

The reply came: 'You did for a couple of strides.'

That was enough for the former South African. He laughed. 'I couldn't be more proud of this horse and the way he ran today. She was flat to the boards from the 500 to the 200 chasing me, trying to keep up with me. We've come mighty close. We've stretched her all the way from the start and she's only just got the better of us. Fantastic effort from my horse. He's a champion in his own right.'

Nolen did not kid in the exchange. He felt the pang of regret for the Hay List camp. 'He loves his horse as much as I love mine. And it's hard, obviously the Davenports, John McNair, they all wear their hearts on their sleeves a bit when talking about Hay List. You've got to feel for them.'

The feeling around Flemington was one of satisfaction. The temptation to pity Hay List was offset by a tremendous sense of pride. Under his dare, Black Caviar had revealed what she was capable of. She stopped the clock at 55.53 seconds, 0.03 outside the track record of Special, set in 1988. Hundredths of seconds were not measured at that time. It was briefly a matter of dispute as to whether Black Caviar's time should be registered as the fastest on the reconstructed Flemington track.

It was in the sectional times that the truly astounding information resided. In the 200 metres between the 600- and 400-metre mark, Black Caviar clocked 9.98 seconds. A sub ten-second split in a horse race was unheard of. No evidence would subsequently be produced of this having ever occurred before. Few in racing circles before this day believed it was even physically possible.

When it was necessary, when she faced an adversary blessed with speed, power and determination in her own image, Black Caviar ran faster than any horse in history.

Newspix / Ron Wells

Those present at Flemington for the 2012 Lightning Stakes got more than they bargained for.

Newspix / Mark Evans

Black Caviar's half sister sells for $2.6 million at the Easter Inglis Yearling Sale in Sydney.

21

Dynasty

Absence made the mare grow grander.

Doubtless Black Caviar would have won the Futurity Stakes, given the way it mimicked the sit-and-sprint pattern of the Orr. It probably would have garnered the enthusiasm and plaudits of a rerun. Peter Moody abandoned the third leg of the trilogy. His announcement ran front and back page of the *Herald Sun*. His initial instincts told him the Lightning had required such supreme effort that it was unreasonable to expect Black Caviar to front up seven days on. The mare's recuperative abilities shocked him. By the Sunday morning stable visit, she was ready to go another fifteen rounds.

But Moody had done his sums on Royal Ascot. He could not afford to flatten her in this campaign, as anything more than a fleeting break was outside the timetable. 'There's nothing wrong with her. To the contrary, she's at the top of her game. I had to look at the bigger picture. What would I have had left? If she heads to the paddock in that condition it's only going to enhance her prospects for her next campaign. It's all geared around having her at her peak when she flies across to England for the Diamond Jubilee Stakes. Everything is being tailored like a Savile Row suit to have her cherry ripe for that race on June 23.'

What happened in the ensuing weeks did more to vault Black Caviar's reputation than anything she might have done herself.

Sepoy, the flashy colt once considered Black Caviar's most worthy opponent, shouldered 58 kilograms in the Oakleigh Plate, the same weight Black Caviar had made light of in the previous year's Newmarket. The chestnut led the frantic field of seventeen into the straight before faltering under the impost into fifth. His aura dimmed, Sepoy headed to Dubai for the Golden Shaheen. There, he turned in a career-worst performance, beating only two runners home. His star had faded.

Hay List shirked nothing. Even when he was entitled to. Trainer John McNair cut up rough after his horse was allotted 58.5 kilograms for the Newmarket Handicap. He felt Melbourne ungrateful and unworthy. 'To my mind I wouldn't only not run, I wouldn't go back to Melbourne this year if it was my decision. They only care about one horse down there. With that weight, they obviously don't want us there.' Defeat, however gallant, had got the better of McNair. He misinterpreted sentiment towards his horse.

Fortuitously, the owners overruled him. The Davenport family believed the gelding had earned the chance of his own tilt at history. Not since 1959 had a galloper successfully lugged such a weight to victory in the grand sprint. The task had the capacity to frank Hay List's greatness independent of the Black shadow.

Moody was in the mounting yard ahead of the Newmarket with his middle-distance hope King's Rose. He was well aware of the angst that gripped McNair. As the field headed for the track he sidled over to chat with his rival, hoping it might ease the tension. Just before barrier fly, Moody confided with a note of unmistakable affection: 'Black Caviar's old nemesis Hay List is here and he looks absolutely fantastic. I think he's nearly the best of good things.' The endorsement contained an implied wish.

The Super Saturday crowd held the same hopeful outlook. The bookmakers, though, sided against Hay List. Alan Eskander reasoned that you were unworthy of your place on the rails if you were not prepared to risk Hay List, given the historical impediments to victory. His brethren took on the punters. The bookies stood the top weight for the proverbial fortune.

In the final surge, the rank and file were at Hay List's back. Up the middle of the track, which had proved the inferior ground that afternoon, Hay List levelled with Buffering. The optical illusion, caused by two horses so wide apart on the straight run, was that Buffering held sway and Hay List was bursting to overhaul him. That was not the reality. Hay List had loomed up on his quarry with ample time to overtake. But just as the prize appeared at his mercy, the lead weights threw an anchor. Glyn Schofield felt it grimly. The big horse wobbled under the ultimate strain. The jockey's urgings moved from encouraging to desperate. Hay List railed with all his strength. Still he was head and head with Buffering. As they hit the line, a margin was imperceptible. Only a suspicion lingered that Hay List had landed a late giant stride. Every eye awaited a glimpse of the photo finish. From the fair-minded to the misty-eyed sentimentalist, all implored that the judge find a margin for Hay List. The fates surely owed him that. So it was. His bravery would this day be rewarded.

McNair declined to be interviewed. He knew the name Black Caviar would be uttered and he did not have the heart for it. This was Hay List's day. He would keep his swelling pride to himself. Schofield, though, had sense of humour enough for both: 'I felt halfway down going to the barriers he was looking around, "Where is she?" He couldn't find her. There were a lot of horses to look through and he couldn't find her. Jokes aside, we're so happy with the win. I'm just grateful this fella has got his name up in the winner's stall.'

The first three runners home in the Newmarket Handicap – Hay List, Buffering and Foxwedge – were the next three across the line-up behind Black Caviar in the Lightning Stakes. Those who sought to question the mare's opposition were fast running short of safe harbour.

They were smoked out entirely within a fortnight. Under lights at Moonee Valley in the William Reid Stakes, the precocious colt Foxwedge turned the tables on Hay List, with Buffering again completing the trifecta. That result completed a set for Black Caviar that would forever guard against the cynics. There are fifteen Group 1 sprint races contested in an Australian racing season. Black Caviar had defeated winners of each and every one of them. She had raced the best sprinters of her generation, not the moribund leftovers, and routinely thrashed them.

While her competitors shored up her legacy, her little brother created the dynasty.

After his impressive first-up success, All Too Hard fronted earlier on Super Saturday in the Group 2 Sires Produce Stakes. He decimated the field. Dwayne Dunn brought him with a withering run from the top of the straight and he cleared out well before the post. It sent a thrill through the entire racing industry. The bloodlines of Black Caviar would course through the progeny of a sire.

Trainer Wayne Hawkes guessed that a stallion's box at Patinack Farm was being painted in the name of All Too Hard even as he returned to scale. 'Breeding sometimes doesn't count for a lot but I reckon it has here. I don't want to compare him to her. He's a colt, she's a filly. He's probably worth more than her now. It's a crazy thing, isn't it? She's the freak and she's the best and this bloke arguably is worth more money than her. He's all but done his job. He can only go one better and that would be to win a Group 1. If he makes it to that level, gee whiz. He's not a natural two-year-old. He's doing this on raw ability alone. He's going to be a serious three-year-old.'

With impeccable timing, the immediate beneficiary of the frenzy would be Rick Jamieson. The Helsinge filly by leading sire Redoute's Choice was bound for the Inglis Easter Yearling Sale in Sydney. The breeder had strongly hinted this would be the last filly out of the broodmare to come to the open market. It was as if the Earth's final diamond was up for grabs.

In a highly charged auditorium, with the nation's media poised, ambition held sway over economics. The opening bid on Lot 200 answered to a million dollars. It immediately jumped half a million higher. Most with intent, including Moody, were out before they could even get involved. Still the bids came unabated. Leading Japanese owner and breeder Katsumi Yoshida sparred with BC3 Thoroughbreds chief executive Bill Vlahos and trainer Danny O'Brien as the price soared to a staggering $2.6 million. The Australians had their way, paying the equal greatest sum to any filly previously purchased in this country.

Jamieson soaked in the sense of accomplishment that went well beyond the financial pay-off. 'I think it's gone mad but you know we're starting to see an emergence of something very special. I might be talking too soon, and perhaps in another year or two we'll see, but I have a feeling that we're starting to see the emergence of a dynasty. If that's correct the value of that entire family will just continue to rise. It will be very important in Australian racing.'

O'Brien felt both privilege and responsibility. 'We're not going to be able to buy Black Caviar and we certainly can't buy All Too Hard, so this was the last opportunity. Everyone who has looked at her has been very positive and we certainly could not fault her. The closer you got to it the more you realised that it was going to be closer to $3 million. It is a lot of money, but as I said of Black Caviar herself, what price would you put on her?'

While that was true of Black Caviar the racing commodity, it held just as firmly in her guise as star attraction.

Newspix / Simon Cross

Dedicated Black Caviar fan Paul Friend congratulates Peter Moody at Morphettville after Black Caviar's 20th win.

22

A State of Gratitude

Morphettville, Robert Sangster Stakes, 28 April 2012

If there was a state that most dramatically demonstrated the degradation of racing from its glory days, it was South Australia. The origins of the Turf Club dated back to 1838 and for generations metropolitan meetings were shared between Morphettville, Victoria Park and Cheltenham. Great trainers had emerged from the province, from Bart Cummings and Colin Hayes through to John Hawkes. More recent were David Hall, who had begun the career of Makybe Diva, taking her to a first Cup before accepting a highly successful posting in Hong Kong, and Mark Kavanagh, the former jumps jockey who had roared through the ranks with a string of top-line horses culminating in the 2009 Melbourne Cup win of Shocking.

But decay had long since set in. The South Australian Jockey Club embarked on a phase of rationalisation that saw Cheltenham Park Racecourse sold to housing developers for $85 million. Those funds were to have been used to restore Victoria Park, before the shotgun decision to close that track also. As of February 2009, Morphettville had operated alone. With prize-money levels sinking and the monotony of racing at the same venue week after week, South Australia had become a racing backwater.

The South Australian situation weighed in Moody's contemplations of the path to Ascot. Brisbane pleaded for a return appearance, even casting favourite sporting identities in an invitational video sent to the owners. But the trainer was bound to disappoint his home state just this once. Adelaide was preferred for suitability and convenience. 'It's a state that's got an unbelievable history of racing. And it's probably a little bit in the doldrums, I don't think anyone would deny that. So it gives them a great opportunity to showcase South Australian racing not only on a national level but on an international level.'

The deal was sweeter still as Moody prescribed two runs, a fortnight apart, both at Group 1 level. Brenton Wilkinson had taken on the chief executive's posting at the SAJC in its darkest hour. Three years into the job, he saw in Black Caviar salvation. 'When I told my wife the big news, she said I was bright red in the face. I'm just so thrilled that the state will get to see the greatest horse of our time.' Under the direction of Premier Jay Weatherill, a Cabinet committee was formed to assist with preparations that would include the provision of free public transport to the track.

The greatest days of South Australian racing could be traced through the life of broadcaster Alf Gard. As an eight-year-old he had come to Morphettville with his father to see Phar Lap win the SAJC Elder Stakes in May 1931. It was a two-horse race against only Fruition. The Red Terror won by five lengths. A week later, again at Morphettville, the then three-year-old carried nine stone five pounds against the older horses to win the King's Cup under handicap conditions. There was tote betting only on the six-horse field with Phar Lap returning £1 1s for a £1 stake. Over eighty years later, the vision of Australia's equine hero still lived strongly in Gard's mind.

His passion for sport had led him to the ABC and, when ill health interrupted the career of colleague Tom Habey, Gard was encouraged to take up the art of race calling. By 1954 he was sharing duties with Habey when the newly crowned Queen Elizabeth II attended Morphettville for the Queen's Cup. Her young husband, the Duke of Edinburgh, and 32,000 racegoers accompanied the monarch.

When Tulloch was lured to South Australia for the S.J. Pullman Stakes in the autumn of 1961, Gard was the course broadcaster. Enterprising racing officials inflated the winner's purse to more than £2500, enough to lift the six-year-old beyond £100,000 in prize money. Tulloch was in the twilight of his career and the temptation to become the first horse through that threshold was irresistible for trainer T.J. Smith. Together, horse and trainer were fêted like movie stars. On the crowded Cheltenham track, 35,000 listened as Gard provided the description. 'Tulloch is the best horse I've called. It was a small field but he was a mighty, mighty galloper. When the Queen came out that was a wonderful day. There was a big crowd there that day. There was a big crowd for Phar Lap. There was a big crowd for Tulloch. And now Black Caviar has brought the crowd back again. You have to have a champion in all sports.'

While Adelaide might have been ridiculed by other states for its parochial heart, what South Australians did at least as well, and probably better than most, was patronise its major events. Be it the Australian Formula 1 Grand Prix – before Melbourne stole it – or the Adelaide Festival. Bruce McAvaney had always remained a local resident while fulfilling his brief covering the great sporting events of the country and the world. 'We do get behind our big events. We don't get a lot of cracks at things like this. I think it's the fact we feel like we are seeing the best in the world. Look at Lance Armstrong when he came here. We went ape over that in those Tours Down Under. I'd put Black Caviar in that category.'

So Morphettville was sold out long before race day dawned, 30,000 tickets fully subscribed for a meeting that had attracted barely 3200 the year before. Because of her presence, the Robert Sangster Stakes eclipsed the South Australian Oaks as the feature race. For only the second time in her career, Black Caviar would compete in a race restricted to fillies and mares. At stake was the Australasian record of twenty consecutive wins and an international landmark that dated back to the 1800s.

As a measure of Black Caviar's domination of the local media, Saturday's front page of *The Advertiser* carried her image under the headline 'Race that Will Stop a Nation'. A souvenir edition was emblazoned 'Race of Our Lives'. Relegated to the back page was the build-up to the AFL showdown, the derby between local teams Adelaide and Port Adelaide. In thirty-one previous stagings, no sporting event had ever rivalled a Crows–Power clash. Priorities had distinctly altered. Channel Seven had again chosen to interrupt its regular programming to televise Black Caviar's race. With Channel Nine already showing the Sydney Cup meeting from Randwick, television history was made. Never before had two free-to-air stations broadcast live racing in direct competition.

The traffic snaked along Anzac Highway to the track. Trams fed patrons to the gates and the railway crossing chimed at frequent intervals. Passing through the turnstile, visitors were handed two free passes to a future race meeting at Morphettville as the Club tried to convert inquisitiveness and enthusiasm into future dedication. Along with the tickets was thrust a Black Caviar flag. The merchandise stand was raided in the manner of a rock concert for T-shirts, caps, ties and stubby holders. It was apparent that this was a crowd that had come to barrack not observe. The atmosphere was marked by a sense of gratitude at having been chosen.

Journeys had been made from near and far. Cheree had driven twelve hours from San Remo, the gateway to Phillip Island in southern Victoria, to ensure she was trackside to see Black

Caviar for the eighteenth time in twenty races. Trav was coming the 400 kilometres from the regional centre of Whyalla, on the east coast of the Eyre Peninsula, to see her for the first time. A family trekked 700 kilometres from Marree, population seventy, north of Adelaide at the junction of the Oodnadatta and Birdsville Tracks. Kate's childhood home had been a twenty-minute walk from Morphettville Racecourse. 'It has taken me nearly forty-nine years to get to my first ever horse race today. Is that taking a long enough route?'

One semi-regular track watcher said there was an amateur Aussie Rules club that played at a ground across the road. On a typical winter Saturday, low-level football outdrew the race meeting.

Jockey Glen Boss wheeled his suitcase and carried his saddle from the car park to the mounting yard. The scene and the vibe took him back to his history-making partnership with Makybe Diva: 'You can have all the fanfare and ambassadors and have the celebrities come to the races to try and attract people, but nothing brings people to the races like great horses. Her ability has generated so much interest throughout Australia and around the world.

'The style and the manner that she goes about her business has really captivated people who are not involved in racing: the general public. She's on mainstream television. In the papers, she's not in the sport, she's in the general pages. She gets full-page spreads. She's created amazing interest. Without Peter Moody really being on the front foot and giving her to the public, being available to everyone, to all the press, this probably wouldn't be as big as it is.'

Boss was booked to ride against Black Caviar in the main event. He was not asked about his prospects. He did not mind in the slightest.

Luke Nolen found the universal goodwill of rivals stopped at the door of the Jockeys' Room. 'A couple of the local boys threw in, "Zenyatta got beat at her twentieth, you know." I thought, "This is nice of you boys."'

Among those gathered was the mouthy English commentator from *At the Races*, Matt Chapman, who had created a stir in Cox Plate week. He was cast as the provocateur in Melbourne. He returned to Adelaide a convert. 'I wouldn't miss it for anything. This is history. People saw Phar Lap, I never saw Phar Lap. I've watched the movie a hundred times. I did see Makybe Diva. I was lucky enough to be at her third Melbourne Cup. That was a day I will never ever forget. I want to see Black Caviar break this record.'

Twenty-four hours on a plane for this whistle stop had given Chapman a lot of time to ponder his lines. Perhaps too much. Not since Bart Cummings had coined 'the neck of a Duchess and the arse of a cook' had there been such a lurid depiction of the mare. 'She looks like Mike Tyson, she's all muscle but she flows when she's racing like Beyoncé. She's like Ginger Rogers from the old days the way she moves. She's sexy. She's what you want to find late at night in an Adelaide bar, that's what she is. She'll give you a good night but she'll also look like a female.'

It was not the only time Black Caviar's appearance was the centre of discussion. Moody had warned that she was 'a little bit hairy', hardly a look that was in vogue for a girls' day at the races. The trainer noted the weather had turned for the worse in Melbourne, meaning she was not as bright in the coat as she had been previously. It was the climate, he insisted, rather than her wellbeing.

And *The Advertiser* had published a curious column under the by-line of Black Caviar herself: 'I'm a simple soul at heart, sensitive even, which is why I wish they wouldn't keep harping on about my weight. And especially my "legendary" rear end. Can't say I've seen it myself but comparisons with Jennifer Lopez and Beyoncé are not as flattering as some might think.

'I'm not denying that I'm a big girl but I work out regularly and you won't find a fitter one. I love the spotlight – but not when it's on my rear.'

Black Caviar's overnight journey to Adelaide had not been made without incident. 3AW Breakfast host Ross Stevenson would report on the Rumour File an occurrence outside Stawell, 240 kilometres from Melbourne. 'Something happened that has never happened in the history of horse racing on Friday. Black Caviar was charged with speeding. The float transporting Black Caviar to Adelaide was stopped by a policeman who asked the driver for an explanation of why he was speeding and what was in the back. He said, "I've got Black Caviar", which was absolutely true. And the copper said, "No worries mate but you're still getting a ticket."'

For all the fuss and the slight misadventure, Black Caviar was, as always, utterly unfazed. On a pleasingly warm afternoon, she patrolled the parade ring on the periphery of the mania. Cannily, the SAJC had created a no-go zone at the far end of the stabling enclosure. The public could still glimpse Nelly at a forty-five-degree angle, but the immediate surrounds of the yard were left uncluttered.

Morphettville retained an old-world charm here. An ornate ceramic fountain bubbled in the middle of the circuit lined by red roses and enclosed by a pretty white railing. Into this haven came each of the owners of Black Caviar, at their own pace, to admire their mare.

Under a tree stood Neil Werrett and his lifelong friend Bruce McMahon. Their fathers had gone to school together and they had been riding around the same farms in Keysborough and Tatong since they were boys. McMahon could tell a story or three about the typically reserved Werrett. 'He was the maddest man on a horse you've ever seen. People don't realise how well he can ride. I've seen him catch a kangaroo at full gallop and actually bring it to hand.' Other escapades, they laughed, might be frowned upon.

Werrett had shared the ownership of his first horse, Kotiko, with McMahon. The fond recollections came in shorthand notes as each was prompted by the other's memory. Bred by McMahon's father-in-law, Kotiko raced with early distinction on the outer provincial circuit, registering wins at Berrigan, Wangaratta and Wodonga. The mare showed sufficient potential to warrant a move to the South Australian stable of Bart Cummings, under the care of foreman Leon Corstens. She blossomed. They had their first metropolitan success in April 1985 at Victoria Park, when Kotiko won the 1000-metre event under jockey John Letts, one of Adelaide's favourite sons. A month later at Morphettville, Kotiko won the Cornish Festival Plate. McMahon recalled: 'They wouldn't let us on the plane with the trophy. It was too big.'

That preliminary success in the racing world coincided with Werrett's professional relocation to Sydney. He could place the flight the day after a party at his sister's to celebrate one of Kotiko's Adelaide victories. While he and McMahon had combined in only one other horse through the years – 'a bad one' – Werrett's interests had burgeoned.

Three weeks before the Adelaide foray, he had been at Rosehill for the Golden Slipper Stakes. His filly Snitzerland had burst away, entering the straight in the $3.5 million feature for two-year-olds, and Werrett seemed destined for his biggest win yet. 'Believe it or not, we thought we'd win it even though she was 20/1. When she kicked clear at the 300, I thought we had won it.' Gai Waterhouse's power-packed colt Pierro came off Snitzerland's heels and mowed her down in the last fifty metres. 'It was the funniest feeling because it was fantastic to run second but so disappointing because you thought you had it. Where did that bastard come from?' It was the edge between the agony and ecstasy of it all that he had been spared with Black Caviar.

While Werrett reminisced and Nelly marked time, Moody and Nolen plundered the undercard. The trainer had sent three companions across with Black Caviar to devilish effect. They won the first race with the gelding Cosmic Causeway and achieved a patiently awaited breakthrough with the New Zealand import So Pristine in the Group 2 Queen of the South Stakes. The pronouncement of that victory over the public address drew a spontaneous cheer out the back of the grandstand. It was interpreted by the course broadcaster that the 'pressure is building' as the stablemates came in. But there was no sense of that in the crowd. Things were unfolding precisely as they should.

Vantage points had long been claimed when the number one saddlecloth was draped on Black Caviar's back. The concrete steps running up the back of the grandstand were gridlocked by those taking photos of the parade below. There was not a seat to be had looking out at the track. The marquees brimmed. The public lawn was crammed. In the betting ring, one bookmaker 'sold' souvenir betting tickets for $1: 'I was there when Black Caviar broke the world record winning her 20th consecutive race. I placed my bet with E. Curly Seal.' Finally, a bagman had worked an angle to make money from the horse that could not lose.

As 3.53 p.m. approached, the sense of enthusiasm was distinct in its innocence. The mere act of Luke Nolen being legged aboard Black Caviar prompted a cheer. In addition to those inside Morphettville, dozens gathered against the cyclone wire fence on adjoining Park Terrace, peering into the track at the 800-metre mark. Moody had concluded a breakfast radio interview during the week expressing the sentiment: 'If you get the opportunity make sure you take it up because this is one of our few world champions in Australia, and Adelaide has got a great opportunity to see her in action.' And so they had.

Of the various fields she had met en route to this record tilt, none had been quite so anonymous as this. Barely the name of a rival had been spoken. In the assemblage of nine was Robert Smerdon's mare Lone Rock. Wet tracks in Sydney had sent her to Adelaide, thwarting her attempts to avoid Black Caviar. At the Adelaide carnival the previous year, Lone Rock had marched off with the Group 1 Goodwood Handicap. Beyond her, they were lining up for the honour of being beaten by Black Caviar in a race that would long be remembered.

As the gates flew open, the crowd erupted. Black Caviar beat all bar the Strathalbyn mare Just Sybil out of the gates. Nolen guided her in a dead straight line from barrier three, keeping space between his mount and the rail. Spurcific scorched for Glen Boss from the outside gate and momentarily they formed a line of three. Nolen let this unfold through the first 400 metres, then decisively eased Black Caviar behind the pace and angled her to the outside of the duo ahead. He sought to avoid the inconvenience of becoming boxed in and the catastrophe that might court. Nolen defused such risks in one elegant manoeuvre.

Free to run, he powered Black Caviar into the home turn and returned to the lead prior to straightening. The West Australian Power Princess grabbed hold of Black Caviar's rump and tried to keep up. Lone Rock had drifted back near the rear and was conceding an ill-judged start.

A little over-stimulated and absolutely wired, the crowd went particularly early. The roar would have to sustain nearly 400 metres. That was hardly going to be a problem.

> Nolen let Black Caviar go for the run for history as they turn for home at Morphettville
> She applied her trademark finisher
> She put three lengths on her rivals Sistine Angel and Power Princess
> But away she goes Black Caviar
> This Australian record
> This international landmark
> Adelaide behold the legendary Black Caviar

Four lengths clear at the 100-metre mark, Nolen showed uncustomary vigour. He did not sense the comfortable margin he held and produced the whip, one of the rare times he had done so on Black Caviar. Sistine Angel, Power Princess and Lone Rock were fighting out the minor end of the prize but there was no imminent threat. Moody had kept the mare quite burley, marking his time towards peak fitness in late June. Because of her heavier coat, she sweated noticeably, not nearly the sleek racing machine of the previous sighting. From the jockey's reaction, she did not go quite as smoothly either.

The margin as she passed the post to the surrounding rapture was four and a half lengths. The reflex reaction was that she had needed the run. Nolen confirmed the sentiment. 'She has definitely been more impressive. It was a bit tradesman-like and that's because she was so big in condition. That'll get the juices flowing and that'll bring her right on for the next tilt here in a fortnight.'

The reviews were moderate. Black Caviar was being graded on a curve. The overwhelming assessments left Moody nonplussed. 'The only thing that maybe made it look a bit, I don't know, plain, was that Luke gave her a little crack with the whip. I asked him why he did it and he said he couldn't quite see the big screen, to see what was behind him. Fair enough. She was fine and she will improve a lot off that. She's got a way to go.'

Such arguments were mere semantics for the thousands in attendance. Thoroughbreds had come to Australia on the *Lady Penrhyn* as part of the First Fleet. Race meetings were commonplace before officers of Governor Macquarie's 73rd Regiment staged the first officially recognised program at Sydney's Hyde Park in October 1810. The lineage of Australian champions traced from Carbine to Phar Lap, Bernborough, Tulloch, Kingston Town, Makybe Diva and now Black Caviar. Never before in mainstream racing had a horse produced a streak to number twenty. Globally, it was the win that had so cruelly eluded Zenyatta. It elevated Black Caviar past the little New Mexico filly-that-could, Peppers Pride. It stood rivalled only by Kincsem, a tale from the nineteenth century, evidenced only by the bronze statue in Budapest.

History was promised and history was made. Adelaide turned on a hero's reception that delayed the last race indefinitely. Nolen repeated what he had done in Brisbane, walking Black Caviar down the full length of the straight for all to admire and venerate. A touch out of character, she did not seem as amenable to do so as in the past. Still, the curtain call lasted substantially longer than the race.

Wilkinson took the time for a sustained look at what had been done and saw that it was good. 'I was standing in the mounting yard when the race was about to start and I just turned and looked at the grandstand and looked down the Derby lawn and saw this sea of faces with their Black Caviar flags waving. The cheer when Luke Nolen was legged up on her was spine-tingling. Even my chairman David Peacock, he had tears in his eyes when they jumped. It was a very emotional day. A couple of older members of the Jockey Club, who I don't think talk to each other, even shook hands and embraced at the end of the race to say what a magnificent event for Morphettville.'

McAvaney had been coming to the track for as long as he could remember. He too had been there to see Tulloch and while he could recall the day, he had been too young to have a lasting judgment of the horse. 'I feel like we're in the presence of perhaps the greatest horse we've ever seen. These are the things that great sport lives on. This is about as big as it will ever get in South Australian racing.'

When it was done and the trophies presented, the crowd joined in a rousing three cheers and all were free to go on their way. Nelly retreated out the back. Once she had been to the swabbing barn, those permitted into the enclosure were given a chance to pat their turf idol. Two brothers, the sons of a local trainer, flanked her left and right. 'I've patted her twice now,' one declared as he raced off. Security guards who had stood sternly rebuking encroachers throughout the afternoon melted, as they lined each other up for photographs. To see her close up was to recognise the run had taken a toll.

Moody was scampering to the airport for a flight back to Melbourne. He did not have time to watch the delayed last race in which his charge Kulgrinda briefly hit the front. He listened in the car as she was run down, having to settle for second, leaving Moody with a treble rather than a clean sweep. As he had dashed from the course with owner David Moodie by his side, he was hailed one last time to sign an autograph. Moody faultlessly stopped, smiled, scribbled and chatted for longer than he could afford.

The bonhomie in the Chairman's Room an hour after the race was infectious. Hanging alongside the well-stocked bar was a lithograph of the South Australian-bred and owned Tobin Bronze. He was the middle-distance champion of the late 1960s who dominated weight-for-age racing in addition to wins in the Caulfield Cup and Doncaster Handicap. He had been sold to America and, while not quite as successful there, won the 1968 Azucar Purse at Hollywood Park. His induction into Australian Racing's Hall of Fame merely confirmed him as Adelaide's finest equine. In the opposite corner of the plush dining room was the less likely sight of an ice-cream machine, employed for the day to delight the children, but it proved to be equally magnetic for the adults.

On the table in the middle of the room sat the gold cups that had been bestowed in victory: the large centrepiece for the owners, accompanied by miniatures for trainer and jockey. Colin Madden knew this trophy well. A replica of the Robert Sangster Stakes trophy sat on his desk, proof of his first Group 1 win.

Neither Madden nor Werrett had been at Morphettville for Bel Mer's 2009 victory in the race. But the memory was vivid and lasting. As they watched on television Werrett promised his son, who had just turned seventeen: 'If this wins, I'll buy you a car.' The old man came good. 'I'd got 15/1!'

To mark the most delightful case of beginner's luck in horse ownership, Madden had had a $200 knock-off of the trophy struck, which he regarded most fondly. This time, though, he vowed to pay full price for the replica.

As the old friends laughed at their own good fortune, they swapped notes about the race itself. Werrett was glad to have the record tilt behind them. Madden had been toey as he pondered how Nolen would avoid becoming cluttered up. They were both struck and touched by the pure delight of the crowd.

It was not long before their familiar pattern of conversation drifted to another shared passion: AFL. Werrett had the bragging rights. His Magpies had defeated Madden's Bombers earlier in the week on Anzac Day. The victor ribbed and chided. Right then came the flash of recollection. Among the Collingwood players who had queued for autographs after the Newmarket Handicap more than a year ago, had been Dale Thomas and Heath Shaw. Werrett and fellow owner David Taylor, who shared the same affliction of passion for the Magpies, invited them to join the celebrations. Late in the night, the extroverted Thomas vowed if Black Caviar could turn ten out of ten into twenty out of twenty, he would get an image of the horse tattooed on his backside. As Werrett recounted the tale he imagined only that he would tease Thomas should they ever cross paths again.

Instead, a month later, the footballer nicknamed Daisy shocked teammates and dismayed his coach, when he dropped his shorts to reveal he had made good on the bet. It was a full-colour tattoo of the mare in full stride, complete with Nolen brandishing the whip in the salmon and black silks. The image, once posted on social media, went viral, proof enough that Black Caviar had left a permanent mark on the AFL scene.

Bronwen Healy Photography

Moprhettville sold out twice in three weeks as the people of Adelaide embraced Black Caviar.

Newspix / Calum Robertson

It's a Happy 21st for Black Caviar in Adelaide.

23

Now Go See the World

Morphettville, The Goodwood, 12 May 2012

The AFL commands the sporting landscape along the country's southern coast. It might be Australia's winter game but it has come to dominate the sport cycle year round. The sense of a city's emotional investment could be gauged when the mood of the people directly reflected the fortunes of a club. This was true of Adelaide and its Crows.

It was the club chairman Rob Chapman who first suggested Adelaide's Round 7 encounter with the reigning premiers Geelong be rescheduled half an hour earlier to pave the way for sports fans to trek from AAMI Stadium to Morphettville to take in the best of both worlds. 'Our first thought was around cannibalising the crowd. Everyone will want to go and see Black Caviar and that's a sell-out. 30,000 people. We're hopeful of 40,000 people here. Perhaps a good percentage of this crowd would like to, if not get to the track, then get to a pub or get home and watch the great mare on TV.' Chapman neglected to mention he owned a horse he hoped would line up against Black Caviar.

He got an immediately favourable hearing from the AFL's chief executive Andrew Demetriou, a man notorious for his love of horse racing. 'It's getting very, very strong preferential treatment this one. If there's a way that it works with our broadcasters and the schedule and it allows people to share in the joy of seeing Black Caviar run then why not.'

It came to pass that the footy deferred to the horse. By the time the runners for the Goodwood headed to the barriers, you could spy the red, blue and yellow guernseys in the crowd. The home team had belted the Cats, a win that spoke of promise and ambition. Rather than bask in the club song and post-siren reflections, plenty scooted for the car park, heading for the second leg of a unique daily double. Among them was Chapman, who watched with local trainer Mark Minervini as their three-year-old gelding, with the very football name, Go The Knuckle, went out onto the track.

Having been out of step during the formative stages of her career, Black Caviar had developed an art for immaculate timing. On this day she was a balm for the aching hearts of horse lovers. By tragic coincidence the week had seen the deaths of grand campaigners Vo Rogue and Northerly.

In the late '80s, Vo Rogue was the bold Queensland front-runner who defied mediocre breeding and unconventional training to thrill racegoers. He would dare to establish breathtaking mid-race leads and defy fellow greats such as Super Impose and Better Loosen Up to run him down. Vo Rogue had been bought out of a paddock for $5000 and worked on bitumen without shoes, and Les Carlyon saw the horse and his trainer Vic Rail as the very incarnation of the sport in those parts. 'The great thing about racing in Australia is that it is rotten with democracy. Vic Rail, hefting an old Syd Hill saddle and wearing jeans with airconditioning vents, steals the Melbourne autumn and is seen heading off for drinks with baronets and premiers.'

Northerly was the West Australian champion christened the Fighting Tiger by broadcaster Greg Miles. To beat the gelding you had to sneak up on him right at the post. For if he saw you coming, he would repel the challenge. His form carried him to two Cox Plates, a Caulfield Cup with the top weight of 58 kilograms and two Australian Cups. His greatness was enshrined in his three meetings with the mighty mare Sunline. Each time, he beat her.

Their deaths barely a day apart had led to a flood of tributes as sports fans took time to reminisce about their favourite thoroughbreds. The sight of Black Caviar was a reassurance that the majesty of the racetrack endured.

Nelly lolloped around the parade ring now familiar to her. She certainly looked fitter and brighter, but above all, she seemed profoundly relaxed. In the pleasant sunshine, she regularly halted and gave the impression that, if not nudged along, she might nod off. Whenever she paused, a flurry of activity ensued, as bystanders positioned themselves for photographs with the mare in the background. She elegantly obliged for minutes at a time.

The same was true of her trainer. Moody had a light day, needing only to see stable runners on television from interstate venues. When he stood still, well-wishers seeking autographs and photographs swarmed around him. He accepted a handwritten placard of thanks, bordered by home-grown roses. From time to time the trainer peeped at his watch. 'I've got to go and get the saddle,' he said as much as a reminder to himself as a reason to break away.

The Goodwood had for 121 years been South Australia's premier sprint race. In recent times it had drawn a delighted public to witness what would prove Takeover Target's final career win. He was the rags-to-riches nag trained by the Queanbeyan taxidriver Joe Janiak who conquered the world. Takeover Target had needed every ounce of character to win at Morphettville in 2007, the surest sign age was wearying his gallantry. He beat the modestly performed I Am Invincible by just a length. There was not a quibble to be heard.

The assemblage of nine for the 2012 Goodwood was the smallest in the race's history. The best credentialled rival was Mark Kavanagh's We're Gonna Rock. He was a frustratingly talented gelding who would pick and choose when to apply himself. His infuriating inconsistency had seen him run sixth as a hot favourite in Adelaide a fortnight earlier. His career peak was a narrow second to More Joyous in the Group 1 Toorak Handicap.

For a short-course scamper, the collection of runners was notable for the odd lack of early speed. Once the reality confirmed what his study had suggested, Nolen had no hesitation in leading. Black Caviar cruised to the turn and kidded thereafter. There was a school of thought that said she would be given a full test, delivering her to peak fitness ahead of the flight to London. In the straight, that was shown to be ill-founded. The jockey was as inanimate as he had ever been. Nolen did not even click her up to establish a decisive margin before gearing down.

> Black Caviar well clear, three lengths on We're Gonna Rock
> He issues some sort of challenge and he won't be dropped
> But Black Caviar, she's two lengths clear
> Happy twenty-first, girl
> Now go see the world

It had to be seen live to be recognised, as it did not quite reveal itself in the replay, but there was a fleeting moment of consternation. We're Gonna Rock emerged from the pack, resolute in his chase. As he reached full momentum under Michael Rodd, he was eating into the gap between himself and Black Caviar. At this very instant, you wondered if Nolen was paying absolute attention to the safety of the situation. The poker player in him never flinched as the length between them was protected to the post.

Neil Werrett had wondered too if she was going too easy. He posed that question to Moody. That was when the trainer revealed the pre-race instructions to his jockey: 'I told him if he hit her with that whip, I'd be hitting him with it after.' True or not, it drew a laugh with every retelling.

The ease of the win partially calmed the undertone of anxiety that had existed privately after Sangster.

Nolen was particularly self-deprecating about his role: 'I just sat there on Saturday. I keep her out of trouble, keep her happy like I do my lovely wife and we get on very good.'

At the presentation he captured the prevailing mood perfectly: 'What a day it's been in Adelaide. The Crows beat the Cats and Black Caviar wins at Morphettville. The sun won't come up tomorrow.'

The crowd offered four cheers for the encore performance. Three did not seem enough. The keys to the City of Marion were presented. And Moody laughed that this was the best twenty-first he had been to. Apart, perhaps, from his own, which he recalled with a giveaway chuckle.

The last word spoke to the challenge of the future. David Taylor sent it echoing around the track at the conclusion of the formalities: 'We'll show the Poms what a real racehorse looks like.'

Newspix / Michael Klein

The racy body suit worn by Black Caviar for her trip to London.

24

Land of Pomp and Glory

The Moody Racing float rattled into the freight yard at Melbourne Airport on a bitingly cold winter's night. Driver Peter Courtney had shuttled Black Caviar to racecourses around the country throughout her career. That very morning he had paid the speeding fine issued on the trip to Adelaide. Tonight he delivered Nelly to a departure point rather than a destination.

In the garish yellow glow of the sodium lights, the back of the truck was lowered for assistant trainer Tony Haydon to climb in. He settled the mare, clipped on the lead and offered a word of reassurance given the unusual environment.

Black Caviar strode forth clad in her custom-made 'bat suit'. Unveiled the day before, the figure-hugging compression garment became an instant sensation. Variously described as sexy and racy, it was assessed on national radio as 'the biggest sporting fashion statement since Cathy Freeman wore her hooded bodysuit to win gold at the Sydney Olympics'.

The black spandex suit mimicked the compression clothing routinely worn by human athletes in and between competition.

Peter Moody figured if it was good enough for Olympic hurdler Sally Pearson, recently dubbed Blonde Caviar, to wear on a flight to London, then he wanted it for the fastest Australian on four legs.

It had seemed unlikely that Black Caviar's departure could match the romance of Phar Lap leaving these shores. Yet here was an image to forever represent the most significant equine expedition in eighty years, as easily called to mind as the Red Terror being winched in a wooden crate aboard the steamer *Ulimaroa*. That iconic, grainy newsreel flickers in the permanent exhibition at Melbourne Museum. The narration captures the sentiment of the day. 'Now you can all say goodbye to the conqueror. Like Christopher Columbus he's going to discover America. Let's hope he's as successful as Chris was. Good luck Phar Lap. Australia is with you. I'll say we are. Goodbye old man.'

Phar Lap's voyage was a three-parter spanning almost two months. Black Caviar had in store a thirty-hour flight from wheels-up in Melbourne with stopovers in Singapore and Sharjah during which she could not leave the plane.

The Airstable stood ready to accept its cargo. The container – 2.4 metres wide and high and a third longer – could snuggly transport three thoroughbreds. That was considered economy travel. The walls could ease to accommodate two in business class. Black Caviar travelled alone. First class.

These transport containers are typically a nondescript white. Not, though, in this case. Peter, a Qantas worker, had seen to that. He had sourced two posters of Black Caviar in the full flight of racetrack victory and pasted them to the exterior, like rock concert flyers on the underside of a bridge.

There were a dozen people present in fluorescent safety vests under the watch of Dave. He had worked security at this yard for ten years. Heavy-set, he walked a fine line between downright mean and merely menacing. Tonight he was a big softy. 'I couldn't tell you the name of any horse to have won a Melbourne Cup in the past ten years. But I know this horse.'

Black Caviar paced, pausing to look at the mountainous stacks of shipping containers in the distance. Her boarding call came informally, a shout from the tarmac on the other side of the cyclone wire fence. She was marched up the ramp of the Airstable, prompting applause from those present.

Shut in and gone from view, she gave a decent kick, perhaps to protest the confines, perhaps to test the sturdiness of the structure as it was towed to the hulking cargo plane. A hydraulic platform lifted the box to the open nose for loading. Four workers guided it in and established her place next to a giant A380 engine bound for scheduled maintenance.

Dozens of Qantas staff had requested the late shift on Wednesday night knowing who was due. Regulations were such that only the rostered workers could look on. The plane was closed for departure and, as it taxied away, those who spend their days tending aircraft, watching them routinely come and go, were moved to raise their phones to take a photo of this particular plane as a keepsake.

As flight SQ7297 headed for the top of the runway, Colin Madden watched intently. He had seen off a daughter on an international adventure before. 'I've done that. I teared up.' He had not intended to be here. The formal goodbyes had been said at the stable the previous afternoon. But as he and wife Jannene sat down to dinner, they knew they had to wave goodbye.

At 23.13, the heavy mechanical drone of the 747-400 filled the air. Defying its size, it roared by and heaved into the black sky. Black Caviar was away. Madden said to himself and to the heavens at once: 'Good luck girl.'

Taking on the world – and never accepting the limitations of geography and population – is an intrinsic part of the Australian character. Domestic success is commendable, but world titles and gold medals are the stuff of sporting folklore.

Of the rivalries Australia fosters, none resonates as strongly as contest with the mother country. England and its former penal colony wage sporting warfare like few other countries. Cricket's Ashes are the constant, but the fervour can take hold wherever an Australian and an Englishman swing a racquet, pedal a bike, or kick a ball.

There was natural antagonism imbedded in the idea of Black Caviar venturing to Royal Ascot. Moody had felt it since Frankel supplanted his mare at the top of the world rankings. He regarded the English notion of superiority as 'stuck up' and was happy to be the antipodean antagonist.

'I really ridicule the fact we've got to go to England to prove ourselves to be as good as we know we are. You've never seen anything like this horse before. So it would be an absolute tragedy if she went there and got beat by your B-grade sprinters for half the prize money, three quarters of the way around the world.'

But he did not shirk the challenge. 'We are really happy to get up there and smack a bit of European arse.'

Moody was on a war footing long before Black Caviar stepped on the plane. He soon found a very different mood operating among the Brits.

The English fawned over Black Caviar from the moment she first trod the Heathrow tarmac. As J.A. McGrath wrote in *The Telegraph:* 'Not since the days when the Francois Boutin-trained Arazi drew crowds of reporters from both sides of the Atlantic, embarking on his three-year-old campaign at Saint-Cloud in 1992, has there been such media interest in a foreign horse.'

The British media flocked to Abington Place, at Newmarket, where an Australian flag hung over the archway leading to the private courtyard where Black Caviar was in residence. They came with a sense of fascination. They found Moody's barbs about

English racing endearing rather than cutting. Totally absent was any sense of rivalry. The Brits wanted to see the wonder of Black Caviar for themselves.

From the cabbie who painted his taxi pink with black polka dots in her honour to Prince Charles and his wife Camilla, who requested an audience with the owners at Royal Ascot, British racing felt positively giddy.

The countdown to the Diamond Jubilee Stakes was billed as the most powerful build-up to a race in the rich history of Royal Ascot and the biggest gamble ever undertaken by a foreign horse at the meeting.

It is the grandeur of Royal Ascot that makes the greatest impression on the first-timer. At its heart is a blend of the old world with the new. The men come in top hats and morning suits; the women wear the latest in elegant fashion. The observance of such dress codes links the wearers to the racegoers of centuries past.

Queen Anne instituted racing on the royal grounds of Berkshire in 1711. The natural characteristics of the track have barely altered since then. The majesty of the new grandstand, a fine feat of architecture using glass to striking effect, adds a thoroughly modern aspect. The charm of the course is captured in the Parade Ring, with its perfectly manicured turf, nestled at the rear of the grandstand.

Each day commences at 2 p.m. with the Royal Procession down the majestic Straight Mile. The Garden Gates at the top of the course open for Her Majesty the Queen, members of the royal family and guests in horse-drawn landaus. Barely requiring announcement, the procession focuses the attention. As the formation reaches the winning post, 'God Save the Queen' fills the air, followed by a three hearty cheers.

This made it all seem real to Pam Hawkes. 'I love horses and I love pomp and ceremony. The carriage turned almost directly under where we were sitting and that was just superb. I thought we're actually here, isn't this good.'

The procession might have opened proceedings, but it was the destruction brought by Frankel that set the carnival alight.

Curiously, the horse rated the best in the world was in the very first race of the week. Frankel was cast as the warm-up act. It added to a growing impression that he was playing second fiddle to Black Caviar. Trainer Sir Henry Cecil and jockey Tom Queally could barely have missed the undertone.

Racegoers had been offered a cardboard paddle produced in Frankel's pale green and pink colours inscribed with the words, 'Go Frankel'. Only a few accepted the gift. But the sight of the unbeaten son of Galileo walking onto the track prompted spontaneous applause.

Released from the furthest point of the Straight Mile on the Royal Hunt Cup Course, Frankel took his place in the slipstream of his stablemate Bullet Train, who led the field. On his outer was Helmet, the expat Australian who ran favourite in the 2011 Cox Plate.

On the far side was Frankel's regular marksman, Excelebration, the horse thought to be the second best miler on the planet. The official program listed Excelebration's role as a theatre program might: '... vain pursuit of Frankel looks the likeliest scenario once again'.

They held the order below the three-furlong pole when Queally subtly angled Frankel off heels and thrillingly surged by. Excelebration tried desperately to cling to such a definitive move. At the two-furlong mark his jockey, Joseph O'Brien, had the whip out in forlorn pursuit. Queally vigorously shook the reigns and Frankel accelerated in a manner rarely seen. It was monstrous. The expanse opened with every stride. There was no easing up. Cecil meant the world to understand the awesome force before it.

Frankel's win was the sort of event that is difficult to immediately do justice to. It needed a period of digestion. Group 1 races are not often won by a margin of eleven lengths. As Frankel returned to the Parade Ring, BBC host Clare Balding made the formal announcement to the lords and ladies: 'The best racehorse we have ever seen. The fabulous and frighteningly phenomenal Frankel.' There was no quibbling over the hyperbole.

Peter Moody had been among those from the other side of the world who wondered if Frankel was overrated. Such doubts had been totally blown apart. 'Seeing is believing. That was the greatest performance I've ever seen on a racecourse and he's the best horse I've ever seen.'

Greg Wood captured it for *The Guardian*: 'It is not just that no horse in the world could have lived with Frankel yesterday. It is unlikely that any horse ever foaled would have beaten him either.'

Frankel had shown all of what he could do on the track, but the aftermath revealed what he had not been able to achieve. The florid reports of arguably the greatest gallop of all time were carried ten pages into the sports section of the major British newspapers. While the front pages hailed footballer Wayne Rooney's goal that advanced England to the knockout stage of Euro 2012, Frankel could not break out of the racing pages.

Day two was a pilgrimage to see an old friend in a foreign land. So You Think's departure from Australia had been tinged with sadness but countered by a great sense of hope that he would soar. Instead the world had wearied him a little.

Coolmore had bought the horse Bart Cummings regarded as the best he had ever trained. Like common thieves with no appreciation for the rare jewel they had stolen, they never understood So You Think. The proof was in the simplest action. They cut his trademark forelock on arrival in the Northern Hemisphere. Les Carlyon observed it as an act of vandalism. Then

O'Brien removed the physical attribute that set So You Think above his contemporaries – his brilliant turn of foot. Under the Ballydoyle regime, the stallion was trained too long, too often and too hard. They had made him a grinder.

Though he had won four Group 1 races in Europe, audiences never saw the horse that might have been. He was depicted in *Racing Post* as a cautionary tale 'that not everything that comes from the other side of the world is quite as good as it looks. For every Kylie there is a Dannii'.

It could only be settled in one way. So You Think would have to win the 150th anniversary running of the Prince of Wales's Stakes. And he would have to do so in the guise of a villain, denying the Queen her first Group 1 triumph as an owner since 1977.

So You Think remained the most instantly recognisable of horses. Not for his supreme physical shape and dark coat but for his fringe which hangs over his eyes like a rebellious teenager's. O'Brien noted: 'I have never known a horse to have a mane and tail grow so quickly.' The boarding school mentality had eased and he was allowed to wear it long.

So You Think headed onto the track flanked by his pacemaker Robin Hood. In this race last year the team tactics had gone awry and he was beaten in a duel to the line by Rewilding. This time would be different. Jockey Joseph O'Brien sat with a cushion in third as Robin Hood carved out the pace. Entering the straight, So You Think swept for the lead. From behind, Carlton House in the royal silks levelled up on the far side. It prompted a surge in sentiment from the partisan crowd. The two horses paired off to fight it out.

Just as the struggle seemed inevitable, So You Think quickened. His dash had been restored. Head held high, So You Think charged to victory. For the Australians in the crowd, emotions peaked and pride swelled. As much as anything in sport can be, this victory was deserved.

O'Brien felt it too. He copped to his crimes. 'I'd like to say to the Australian people I'm sorry I've made a muck up of training this horse for so long. I made a right dog's dinner of it. I knew that Bart Cummings had done a better job than me. That was the reality. He [So You Think] had turned into a fantasy horse over there and, when so many people think you're getting it wrong, they can't all be wrong. In the final furlong, it was time to get it right.'

It would prove to be So You Think's final run and the one to ease anxieties about his true potential. He bowed out of racing the winner of ten Group 1 races – five in each hemisphere. The most successful Australian equine export of all.

Ascot Gold Cup day was lashed by rain, softening the ground considerably. Out of the gloom came the renaissance of the most famous jockey of modern times, Frankie Dettori.

His detractors were edging the Italian maestro towards retirement. Perhaps a worse fate would have been replacement. For almost two decades, the forty-one-year-old had been the number-one jockey for racing's most powerful operation, Godolphin. But his hold on the job was loosening. In a bid to keep the veteran on his toes and inject a little competition, the firm had hired Mickael Barzalona, a young Frenchman who harboured an unashamed desire to ascend the throne. He had been preferred for a number of high-profile rides, triggering in Dettori an unusual level of self-doubt.

Ascot had always been kind to Dettori, most memorably on a September afternoon in 1996 when he produced his 'Magnificent Seven' to ride the card – all seven wins of the day. Today, he needed to recapture the old magic. For Dettori might well have gambled his job by deciding to switch mounts in the prestigious Gold Cup. He sought release from Opinion Poll, the more favoured of Godolphin's pair, to ride the grey Colour Vision. A jockey's judgment is paramount, both on the track and off. Sheikh Mohammed, the ruler of Dubai and founder of the global stable, had never been scared of changing company policy and personnel.

In the marathon run of 4000 metres, Dettori positioned his mount perfectly, close behind the pace. Upon turning into the straight he drove Colour Vision to the lead, only for Barzalona to loom large on his outside with Opinion Poll. The royal blue of Godolphin was assured of the prize, but Dettori had to get the win. The final furlong was suddenly a referendum for the top job and momentarily Barzalona held the momentum.

Dettori made the snap decision to switch the whip to his right hand in an attempt to galvanise Colour Vision for the last surge. It brought an immediate response, including the unintended consequence of the horse veering out sharply to twice bump Opinion Poll. A resolute Colour Vision proved his superior stamina and reasserted a margin to come home the winner. Dettori, never one to contain his emotions, stood in the irons and thrashed the air. He closed his eyes, clenched his fist, and roared his relief and excitement.

When he returned to the winner's enclosure Dettori was embraced by Sheikh Mohammed. The warmth of the gesture was more telling than any words.

By Friday, when the women's high heels were sinking into the yielding turf, all the royal meeting required was the royal seal. In the year of Her Majesty's Diamond Jubilee, a winner in her own back yard was demanded.

So You Think had thwarted the Queen on Wednesday. But the filly Estimate carried the royal silks to a runaway victory in the Queen's Vase. There is no pretence to the Queen's affection for racing. It is her chosen recreation and passion. Her whole-hearted smile was proof enough as the reality of victory became clear. It prompted a wave of hats-off hurrahs.

If that was not feel-good enough, the Duke of Edinburgh was on duty for the presentation. To sustained and affectionate applause, the Queen stepped forward to receive the trophy from her husband. Alastair Down summed up the prevailing sentiment in *Racing Post:* 'They have been private allies of deep and abiding longevity and it was there for all to see that they both enjoyed every second of this hugely lighthearted public moment.'

Even ahead of the climax it was convincingly argued Royal Ascot had never known a finer carnival.

Saturday was Australia Day. The first hint of what lay ahead came at Waterloo Station in London. Half a dozen men huddled in their grey morning suits, complete with waistcoat and matching top hat. What distinguished them was the salmon and black spotted tie each was wearing.

On the train, a woman from Brisbane told the local patron by her side that she had never been further than Dubai in her fifty years, but felt compelled to make the journey to share this day. Mark wore his replica silk cap rather than a top hat. By day's end he had been offered a hundred quid for it on numerous occasions, but politely declined. He and girlfriend Gemma had planned a European holiday around Diamond Jubilee Stakes Day.

On the walk from the station through Ascot Wood, past the touts who were buying and selling spare tickets, it became apparent that Black Caviar ties were the national dress of the afternoon. And even the women wore salmon.

Racing Post had declared it 'G'day Five of Royal Ascot' with the invitation emblazoned on the front page: 'Great Britain welcomes Aussie Phenomenon Black Caviar – Now Dazzle Us Baby'. All the major papers carried stories of the Wonder from Down Under with feature articles dedicated to Peter Moody and Luke Nolen.

At the gates, patrons were offered Black Caviar paddles, and the take-up was significantly greater than for Frankel on Tuesday.

Bookmaking firm William Hill had staff dispensing small jars of black lumpfish caviar.

Australians came together in the toffee-nosed Royal Enclosure, on the front lawn and in the grandstand. The convicts moved the picnic furniture to improve their view. Park benches were draped with Australian flags. The scale of the invasion went beyond even the most generous of predictions.

Hosts for the on-course broadcast rejoiced at the devotion and the sheer number of those who had come to support Black Caviar. In Melbourne's Federation Square, the dedication was mirrored as more than 2000 fans braved freezing conditions after midnight, proof that sport is an experience best shared. Waving their Black Caviar flags, their presence was felt on the television screens at Royal Ascot. The reaffirming atmosphere bound people together on both sides of the world.

Almost all were oblivious to the circumstances that had the mission on the brink of collapse.

Newspix / Mitch Bear

In the dead of night, thousands packed Melbourne's Federation Square to cheer Black Caviar to victory at Royal Ascot.

Sarah Ebbett Photography

Moment of destiny. Black Caviar led out onto the most famous racetrack of all by Tony Haydon (left) and Paddy Bell (right).

25

A Quarter of an Inch

Royal Ascot, Diamond Jubilee Stakes, 23 June 2012

The Ascot car park is not quite the formalised social venue of the corresponding precinct at Flemington. In the meadow across the road from the Sovereign's Gate, small groups congregate around open car boots to share a post-race ale in a manner more accustomed to the rustic Warrnambool Racing Carnival. It had become tradition on the Tuesday night for the Australian contingent to gather for a catered barbecue organised by Inglis Bloodstock. The invitation seemed no more formal than to look for the Australian flag. In the years since Choisir had first conquered the meeting, numbers had swelled at this gathering from dozens to hundreds.

The camaraderie was warm and the conversation vibrant. Frankel was the talk of the party. It was interpreted that his astounding gallop had been the throwing down of the gauntlet, challenging Black Caviar to do something similar in the Diamond Jubilee Stakes to bookend the week. Certainly Peter Moody's phone had been buzzing with messages encouraging him to 'let her rip' in reply.

He already knew he did not have the horse to oblige.

That morning at Newmarket, Moody had enlisted Nolen for the mare's only gallop between the flight and race day. It was a breeze up as much for the trainer's benefit to assess her action. It was not the searching gallop Moody would have prescribed ahead of a Group 1 event at home. By design, Black Caviar was as fit as Moody could get her before boarding the plane and 20 kilograms lighter than her usual racing weight. He wanted her to rest rather than work after the arduous trip given that she had been in training for most of the past 12 months.

Racing Post track watcher David Milnes was on hand for the first glimpse of what was under the bonnet. 'Finally allowed to let rip on the Limekilns, Black Caviar showed a Frankelesque acceleration between the two and the six-furlong pole in a solo exercise that will long live in the memory.'

While that might have been overstating the case, Nolen was reassured. Working well within herself, Black Caviar felt strong striding up a hill steeper than what she would encounter in the concluding stages on Saturday. Moody thought it was sharp but tradesman-like. She did not have her natural bounce and he could not ignore the deterioration in her coat. Acclimatisation was proving difficult. Her long winter coat had come through at the early onset of the Southern hemisphere winter. While the local horses were getting their summer coats, Black Caviar was a horse caught between seasons. Moody saw her lustre was gone.

'You can shampoo and brush them as much as you like but the wellness comes from the inside. They can have a long coat but they can still look well and healthy, but with her it was more like a wire brush than a silk purse. And that told me she was a fair way off her top.'

With the barbecue in full swing, Moody quietly rounded up the five couples that owned Black Caviar and drew them aside, undetected. He tempered any sense of alarm by assuring them there was not a problem. But Moody did not sugar coat the message. To his eye Black Caviar had one good gallop left in her and only just that. They would not see a replica of Frankel. If they won on Saturday the job was done and she would not be capable of an encore performance.

The owners had made their bookings to stay on for the July Cup at Newmarket three weeks after Royal Ascot. It had always been mooted that she would run in both. But the group understood what was being conveyed. Black Caviar would be back in Australia by the time that race was run.

There was a sense of reality rather than foreboding as the gathering broke to re-join the surrounding festivities. But they all agreed to tell no one.

Moody was about to realise just how close to the truth he was.

The maintenance of Black Caviar was constant. She was always a patch-up job. That was not unusual for a mare of her bulk and ability, size and speed. Her longevity was a credit to her support team. Moody acknowledged she had not been fully sound going to the races since her second start. 'Now many trainers will tell you most of their good horses have been the same. But there haven't been too many horses as good as her.'

Moody had learnt to make his assessments of what she could overcome, and monitor closely the fluctuations in her physical and mental condition. This is an essential skill in the arsenal of any trainer. Horses are forever presenting with fresh and challenging problems. Moody understood that Black Caviar had the pain threshold of an elite athlete. Rather than apply the limitations he would for an average galloper, he trusted her and challenged her. She pushed the boundaries and every time she came back a winner.

Rather than topping her off for the race of her life, the track gallop at Newmarket had flattened Black Caviar. Nolen would come to observe: 'Essentially what she's done is left her work for Saturday there on the Tuesday. It wasn't hard work but it must have been hard enough that she hasn't brought her A-game to the races. It's such a tough journey; they might only be good for one gallop. You don't really know until you get them there under race pressure.'

Worse, it had exacerbated the niggling complaints both old and new. In the space of one morning she had gone from relatively sound to troubled.

The core problem had always been the suspensory ligament she first injured as a three-year-old after her fifth win. It had been active on and off for the past two years. The career of many a horse ended when a suspensory ligament tore. When Moody spoke of his preparedness that any of her past half dozen runs could have been her last, this was the affliction to which he obliquely referred. Moody had known when to stop and when to push, and the suspensory had held together. There was heat in the ligament after trackwork. She was bumping it when she exercised. That was out of character. Tony Haydon had a special boot made to try to offer her protection. But it was nasty. It was like having a sprained ankle and constantly banging it.

Soft tissue problems were a regular nuisance for Black Caviar, but the latest was new. At her previous win in Adelaide she had torn the equivalent of a quadriceps muscle. The tensor fasciae latae was a highly unusual injury in a horse, and while not instantly career threatening had the potential to curtail a horse's racing days. Typhoon Tracy's career had been ended by a persistent hamstring injury that eventually would not satisfactorily repair.

Black Caviar had become the veteran competitor that adjusted to protect old ailments and, in doing so, suffered new injuries. Her regular chiropractor, Mick Bryant, found the four-centimetre tear and put her through highly sophisticated laser treatment. To avoid stress on the pelvic limb, Nelly was not allowed to swim for almost three weeks. She was given the all clear only a couple of days before leaving for England. Her first gallop had revealed it was still a sore spot.

And her near front foot had been troublesome for the entire campaign. In her last week at Caulfield she had pulled the shoe off three times in four days.

Behind the secure gate of Abington Place, Moody feared Black Caviar was coming apart. Haydon was tending to her morning and afternoon. He strapped the suspensory, lasered the quad and had her feet and legs in buckets of ice water. Few horses would have tolerated such a regimen.

Moody's diagnosis was more than the sum of the parts. 'She was just dead set rooted. You could see it in her. She was down and out.'

He had seen her like this a year beforehand and it had caused him to abandon plans to run in the Doomben 10,000. But here they were on the other side of the world preparing for the culmination of her career. 'In an ideal world maybe I should've pulled the plug before we went but I didn't do that. We were there. The old Aussie have-a-go attitude probably came out in me.'

Keeping to his established pattern, he did not trouble the owners with the mounting woes. Until he had something definitive, he could worry enough for all of them.

Hour by hour Haydon monitored Nelly. 'I don't think I had any true concerns that she would make it to the races. My concern was that she mightn't have been at her best. Any other horse you'd probably scratch. But she's different. She's hard. She's tough. She's competitive. I knew if we got her there, even if she's only 50 per cent, she'll do the rest.'

Driving rain fell through Black Caviar's final press appearance keeping it brief and alleviating any need to remove her body suit. Moody masked the concern he felt with well placed and crowd pleasing humour. And he tried to rein in expectations. 'If we wanted to let her rip we'd do it at home. A quarter of an inch will do us. Quarter of an inch will do us.' He might have repeated it for his own benefit.

On race eve, over dinner at Frankie Dettori's Bar and Grill restaurant in Chelsea, word swept the Australian patrons that Black Caviar would be scratched the following morning. Theories abounded. She had worked too hard on Tuesday morning and lost weight alarmingly in the aftermath. The diagnosis and the timing were slightly off, but the sentiment had substance.

In fact the Friday had provided Moody his lone day of comfort. 'For 24 hours I thought she'd really bounced back. But on the Saturday morning I saw her and thought, "oh shit". I wouldn't have asked any other horse that I've trained to carry the culmination of things she took into the race particularly given the expectation.'

Moody had Black Caviar trotted up under Paddy Bell to observe her action. That was the best guide to her precarious soundness. When a horse is cool it will feel the aches and pains. When the blood starts flowing those complaints will not be an inhibitor.

Bryant was on hand at the stable. Moody would claim to be unsentimental but he had seen through the years how the trainer loved his horses. 'If at any stage he thought she was going to get beat he would have stopped. But we had seen her run through the pain barrier before. I've got no doubt she is the toughest horse mentally that I've ever seen and I've been doing this for 41 years. That certainly affected our thinking. If any horse could do it, this horse could do it.'

The decision rested with Moody. It was pointless being squeamish or else a trainer would scratch his horses more often than he ran. This had to be objective and instinctive. 'Every time for the past ten starts I've thought, "am I doing the right thing?"' But never had he faced that question with Black Caviar when the stakes were so high.

He was happy enough with her under saddle. The rest was an estimation of what she could overcome when the adrenalin of race day kicked in. The risk was not to her wellbeing. The risk was defeat. Having proven herself to him repeatedly like no horse he had ever worked with, she was entitled to the chance to do it again. Moody decided Black Caviar would run. 'Any less a horse and you wouldn't have run her. It was the biggest task I've asked of her. I backed her to carry my judgment and I backed for nothing to break down or fly off.'

Luke Nolen knew none of this. For three days he had tried not to think about the race. He had pretended to be a tourist complete with his wife, two children and his mum, who was travelling overseas for the first time. Worry is like a rocking chair, he would say: it gives you something to do but gets you nowhere. Even as he paced along the Ascot track with Moody by his side before Saturday's Royal Procession, they spoke of events back home rather than the task at hand.

Moody would never sow the seed of doubt in his jockey's mind. 'Pete, he's a great coach like that. He won't ever talk about that sort of stuff pre-race, whether they're a bit sore, because if you go out there thinking like that, it's already in your head. It's funny what creeps into the subconscious when you should be focused on one thing only and that's winning the race.'

The trainer had once told Nolen that if he ever got to the barriers and Black Caviar did not feel right, regardless of whether God himself was there to see her run, he had the authority to dismount and have her withdrawn. Moody did not dare repeat those instructions. 'If I had legged him up at Ascot and said "hey I'm not happy, if you're not happy pull her out" and then if she goes out and gets beat, all of a sudden it's on him. I never would put that race day pressure on him.'

Nolen would be left to put the pieces together that night, building the case in retrospect from impressions and memory. At first glance she looked a little plain. She was a bit funny in the yard, not her usual relaxed self. She was a bit rough in her action heading out on to the track.

Looking on at the parade was former jockey Simon Marshall. He knew Black Caviar to be the greatest horse he had seen and, in his guise as a television commentator, had marvelled over her appearance on numerous occasions. Just as Moody had been struck that morning, what Marshall observed with an experienced eye created a dull sense of dread.

'It was the worst I've seen the mare presented in the mounting yard. She walked past loping along with her head down. She looked dull in the coat. She looked tucked up, a little light in the flank, through the barrel, for her. And she was agitated, kicking out at the security men that got too close to her hindquarters. Those are idiosyncrasies and mannerisms as a past rider that you look for. You like to see a horse happy on the day. Quite clearly she wasn't at home.'

Black Caviar passed under the grandstand and emerged on to the track to a mighty ovation. Out of the usual routine, Moody walked alongside and held her back for just a brief moment. He fondly slapped her down the neck to send her on her way. 'You've done us proud old girl, now come back in one piece.'

Anticipation before the start of the Diamond Jubilee Stakes built like a wave as Black Caviar made her way to the gates in front of almost 80,000 spectators. There had been nothing in this brilliant week to match the suspense that built as the 14 competitors milled in front of the barrier stalls. It gave pause to contemplate the challenge. No mare had won this race for 27 years. While Choisir had triumphed, all our subsequent sprinters, including Takeover Target and Miss Andretti who had won the King's Stand Stakes on the Tuesday, had met defeat over the testing 1200-metre course. But Black Caviar's backers seemed impervious to doubt as they sent her out at odds of 1/6. Such faith echoed in lounge rooms, pubs and public venues all over Australia, as a nation stirred in the dead of night and, completely out of season, stopped for a horse race.

There was an eruption as the field was sent on its way. Black Caviar strode from the outside gate immediately onto a downhill run dictated by the gradient of the track. Nolen allowed her time to find her stride. Inside of them the former Australian Soul, now in the Godolphin blue for Frankie Dettori, set the early pace. Between them was Bogart. Even as they reached the plateau before the straight course links to the course proper, Nolen had his concerns. Black Caviar was not up on the bridle, neck arched, ears pricked. Typically she was eager and strong once the rhythm of the run was established. She would set about breaking up the field on her own. When the jockey expected to be restraining the power – 'not yet, not yet, not yet' – he was asking her to chase. 'She'll travel keenly down the straight, she always has. Almost bull at a gate. Very keen to take me where I need to go. At Ascot she was not like that.'

From the infield, Moody could see what Nolen felt. 'She never charges but Luke is usually high in the saddle sitting against her. I thought a long way out you'll need to be every bit as good as I know you are to do this.'

At the halfway mark, Black Caviar looked as though she would slip by Soul. In his career for Peter Snowden, the handy sprinter had never proved good enough to compete in Group 1 races let alone challenge the best of all. But here he was serving it up to the champ. Black Caviar did not reach him until Nolen was firmly urging. Haydon was typically the most emotional during her races. 'I noticed that she came off the bridle earlier than she usually does. I was a little bit concerned then. I actually started cheering her on. And I never do that.' The anticipated margin did not open. Nolen was as busy as Dettori at the two-furlong mark.

While Nolen was necessarily occupied with the immediate surrounds, French jockey Thierry Jarnet was cunningly moving into position. The filly Moonlight Cloud had drawn over on the far side of the track in barrier five and from the moment the field jumped, Jarnet had let her drift across the expanse of Ascot. He did not force her into openings nor wedge her into pockets. He did not rush her progress. He was prepared to concede a length to compatriot Restiadargent to navigate the desired course all the way to the grandstand side. When Black Caviar was knuckling down to tackle Soul, Moonlight Cloud was tacking up behind her and Nolen had no prospect of knowing she was there.

Renowned trainer Freddy Head had been deferential toward Black Caviar throughout the build-up. But he was bullish about Moonlight Cloud's chances of causing an upset. Head would confess that fact to Moody the following Monday as they shared a cup of tea at his Chantilly stables.

Black Caviar toiled to find a break. She was flat out. Nolen had shaken the reins and pulled the whip to beat off Soul. Moody could see her doing it hard. 'It was only ever a length. When he went for her, he gave her a squeeze and then a backhander, and she's only a length in front I thought, "Oh, the tank's empty."'

She had responded to Nolen's vigour and urgency not emphatically but sufficiently. He stowed the whip and continued to push at her neck for the next few strides. Nowhere near her best, she had done enough. 'I could feel that she was at her top and had done her job. All I was going to do was continue to annoy her if I kept riding her to the line. She's been a special, special horse to me; I've never wanted to annoy her. And that's all it was, just trying to be kind to her late.'

Nolen held his hands still at the base of her neck and Black Caviar understood that her work was done. She was hurting. In the run she had re-torn the quadricep muscle. With each stride, as her hip flexed and her leg extended, it would have screamed with pain. Bryant would find the tear to be twice as long as the original injury. If a footballer had torn that muscle he would have stopped on the spot, limped from the field and not played for the next month. Nolen dropped his hands. Black Caviar gave into the pain and she stopped.

It happened too suddenly. Nolen had expected her to cruise, as they had done numerous times before. Instead she shut down. He could see the mowed strip on the grass indicating the finishing line. It was half a dozen strides away. Observers would find the image incongruous, almost absurd. Nolen sitting perfectly still on his mare while Jarnet flailed his whip extravagantly narrowing an ever-diminishing gap. It was a scene from a pantomime. Behind you!

Finally Nolen saw Moonlight Cloud for the first time out of corner of his eye. It was startling. He had not expected a challenger on this angle of attack. 'I was surprised when they came on the outside because that horse had drawn inside. I was a little surprised there. I thought the post was coming quick enough but it wasn't and they were coming quicker than I anticipated due to the fact she had stopped.'

Nolen had only one course of action. A reflex he had been taught as an apprentice. He had to get Black Caviar to flatten and stretch for the line. Such was the ingrained connection between them, as soon as he twitched his mare responded. 'When I felt them coming I gave her that last little rub. She hasn't really lengthened again, she didn't actually pick up because she was completely spent, but she put that graceful head right out. That's all that was required and that's what she did for me, thank God.'

Black Caviar she dares the Europeans to keep up
She's got about a length on Soul
She hasn't quite broken away yet
Moonlight Cloud finishes on
It's Black Caviar by a length
Moonlight Cloud coming out of the pack with Restiadargent

Black Caviar's a length in front
She's hanging on
Moonlight Cloud with a late dash at her
Black Caviar by a nose
She's crowned her career at Royal Ascot

As the cheers turned to gasps, Black Caviar lowered her neck and lunged for the post. Nolen knew they had made it. Only one thought flashed through his head: 'oh shit, they got close.'

Quickly Dettori was again by his side.

'Lukey, what are you doing? You should know you must ride them out here at Ascot. Must. Must. She win? She win?'

'Yes she held on Frankie, she held on.'

Dettori leant over and gave Black Caviar a pat. 'She's magnificent.'

Moody felt numb. Behind his sunglasses and under his top hat, his face was expressionless. He saw that she had won on the post, although those around him rather unnervingly had doubts. 'It wasn't the adulation, jumping up and down, cheering for joy that I've been through before. It was phew. She carried me. She carried Luke. She carried us.'

He did not realise the enormity of where Nolen had stopped riding until the bombardment of questions began. 'I had people at me straight away. I was wanting to grab them and throttle them. It's won. Here I was having to defend my horse and then defend my jockey. One bloke said to me: "Is his job in any jeopardy over that?" I just felt like reaching over and punching him. The fastest horse in the world has just won a Group 1 and you want to talk about the jockey.'

Nolen had about 90 seconds to make sense of it. He knew his mistake and how it would be depicted. He felt bitter disappointment. He feared it would overshadow the bravery of the horse beneath him. He never considered any alternative to falling on his sword. 'I was just so critical of myself that I let them back in the race. When you're your own worst critic you're always going to be honest in your assessment of the race.'

There was anguish on his face as he returned to Moody waiting on the track.

'Geez jock, that was a bit close wasn't it?'

Nolen opted for actions rather than words. 'Pete's given her a pat and I've just grabbed him and put one on his cheek. He said, "Oh get away." Then I grabbed a bit harder and gave him a kiss.'

Those who knew Black Caviar best could see she was hurt and exhausted. The clerk of the course though was insistent with Nolen. 'Take her down the straight and show her off. They're all here to see her. Show her off.' The applause was rapturous but neither of their hearts was truly in it. As they left the track, Nolen had the sense his trial was about to begin.

He was grateful for a couple of friendly faces. 'Colin Madden, he kept grabbing me saying, "Don't you worry about it we still won, we still won the bloody thing. Don't beat yourself up. I still love ya. We still won." And Pam Hawkes, they were the two that sought me out immediately. Pam gave me a high five coming back in.'

Nolen could have scripted the first question. What happened in the closing stages? For all that had happened this is what he would have liked to take back. 'The thing I erred on was calling it a brain fade and I probably shouldn't have. It all seemed to play on from there.'

As the British press does best, by the following morning Nolen was 'Flukey Lukey' the 'Blunder From Down Under' who survived the 'Moment Of Strewth'.

Under the barrage Nolen never flinched. But had Black Caviar been beaten, Moody would have intervened and accepted the blame. 'When she came into the Parade and Luke got off her, I looked her in the eye and she was just fucked. Even if she had've got beat under Luke's ride, I'm not a jockey lover by any means, but I would've stood up and defended him for the fact that the horse was running on empty. I knew that. Tony, my right-hand man, knew that. Paddy, who rides her work, knew that. We knew. But we got it right.'

Bryant was awash with admiration for Moody. 'He made a massive call if she was to go to the races. He had that much confidence in the horse and he made the right call. It was a great training performance. Everyone worked behind the scenes frantically.'

No one had worked harder than Haydon. It was his honour to stretch the Royal Ascot victory rug over Black Caviar's visibly heaving body. 'It was chaos in the enclosure. With all those people it felt like they were sucking all the air out. I've never seen her that buggered after a run.'

But it was not the spectacle that had been envisioned. The mood in victory teetered on disappointment. Aidan O'Brien sensed the underwhelming cloud hovering and made it known to the Australian contingent that this victory was not to be underestimated. Here was a big powerful filly, on a sticky foreign track, summoning all her courage to win Europe's premier sprint race. Time would see it regarded more fondly than in the immediate aftermath.

On the day when it had all gone wrong, Black Caviar had still prevailed.

Nolen and Moody were pulled from press conference to television interview. The trainer's anxiety over Black Caviar's wellbeing stretched his tolerance to breaking point. Asked if the victory had sunk in, he snapped: 'I haven't had time because no bastard will let me go and see my horse.' An hour after the race, the jockey was still in the racing silks confessing to his sins. The most memorable of all summations being: 'The big engine shut down and I shit myself duly.'

Once the Queen had presented the gold trophy to Pam Hawkes, who held it aloft as if she were at Wimbledon, the owners were guided to a private bar beside the Parade Ring. There was an air of shell shock in the room as each tried to comprehend what had taken place.

Neil Werrett hoped the first taste of champagne would halt the spinning sensation that had him disoriented. 'From where I was, it was a difficult angle, but I thought we'd lost. I honestly did. I stopped breathing. When Luke dropped the reins she just pulled up pretty quickly. Luckily she bobbed when she did otherwise we would've been gone. I'm relieved to say that at least we've won but not as excited as I should be.'

Madden had the same sense of bewilderment. 'Pretty spooky stuff wasn't it. I thought we lost. I thought it's happened, it's actually happened. No one else around me would say anything.' When Black Caviar's name flashed up the winner, he did not feel the elation he might have imagined. 'It was relief, it wasn't joy. It was a funny emotion. She's done a great job and she needs some sort of break right now. I feel like somehow we fell in, rather than grasped it.'

Gary Wilkie liked to think he was the optimist to Werrett's pessimist, but he honestly could not recall whether he thought Black Caviar had won on the post or wished it.

Hawkes retained her whimsical nature in the most anxiety-riddled moment she had experienced in racing. 'I thought we'd won and then the French horse swooped and I thought, "oh that's close". I couldn't pick it from where I was standing. I wasn't even upset. I go out there every time prepared that we might get beaten and today I thought it's a big ask to bring a horse this distance. If we lose then something better has beaten her. So I thought, "oh well, she's lost" and then, "oh good, she's won". And I think the "oh good, she's won" was better.'

The Taylors were the only members of the group certain that Black Caviar had prevailed. For Jill, the disconcerting moment was when the photo was called for. 'I thought that she had won and when I heard "photo finish" I went into a bit of a spin and thought, "did I see it wrong?"' David's guilty pleasure was to revel in the rush the circumstances provided. 'I've never known an inch to be worth a mile, but it was today. I found it exciting, I really did. It was fantastic to have that thrill of "are we or are we not?" which is what most horse racing is generally about. I love that part of it.'

Moody did not break free of the demands and obligations until the last race of the program was set to run. He headed for the saddling enclosure full of trepidation. 'I got down there just before they were going to load the truck and I was amazed. I went from thinking I was going to find her lying in the corner of the box and instead here's this horse standing with her ears pricked, whinnying, watching the other horses walk in and out. This is the thing about this horse, she has unbelievable recuperative powers.'

Unburdened by the sight, Moody headed to the car park to join Mick Bryant and Brett Cavanough. They had hired a car and a driver to provide the flexibility to either head into London for the official party or return to Newmarket for pizza and beers. Their choices were thwarted when the car refused to start. For the next four hours, as he celebrated the peak achievement of his professional life with two of his closest friends, Moody relied on the kindness of strangers sharing food and drink from the boot of their cars. 'We had a ball.'

Nolen knew he would be all right once the ribbing commenced. Fellow jockey Luke Currie had been the best man at his wedding and shared the biggest moments of his career including making this trip to Royal Ascot. Currie walked by well within earshot as Nolen was concluding an interview and heckled: 'Got to keep riding them to the line, jock.' Nolen broke into a smile and eased up on the torture. 'He knew that I'd be disappointed in myself. He knew, because he's been there and done it. He said, "Don't worry about it mate. She won. Just enjoy it."'

As the night wore on in the company of family and friends, the stresses of the last 50 yards of the race and torment of the margin began to recede.

While the controversy swirled, steadily the admiration of Black Caviar began to flow. Simon Marshall told his tour group given what they had seen and what they would learn about the mare, that they had witnessed one of the greatest moments in Australian sport. 'I've ridden plenty of champions in my time that have not been 100 per cent, but their will to win, their heart and their desire gets them over the line under the adrenalin of the day. Her will and her greatness, her ticker to compete, combined for what was, in my opinion, her greatest win.'

At Home House in West London the owners' celebrations were a touch subdued. The dramatic flourish and upheaval of the race would take a few days to grasp. But there was one moment each recalled with clarity and fondness.

In the crowded confines post race, they had all clambered in for a photograph around their treasured mare. They were mindful not to make her pose for long. As the huddle broke, Black Caviar was led away, only to loop around into another group of admirers. Central among them was the Queen. Horse and monarch stood barely two paces apart, each seeming to regard the other. Every observer would recount the story precisely. The gentle giant of a horse stepped forward and lowered her head. The Queen reached out with her gloved right hand and patted Black Caviar tenderly on the nose. At the end of a grueling odyssey here was her commendation for gallantry. Longtime Ascot observers and Royal watchers could not recall an encounter like it.

The soft glow of the scene belied its nature. Like everything else that had transpired, only Moody knew how precarious it was.

'We walked her up in front of the Queen, Paddy on one side, I was on the other. I asked, "Would you like to give her a pat ma'am?" She was quite keen to. Black Caviar was standing there stuffed, saying, "I don't know whether I've got another step in me." The Queen is standing back wondering if she should give her a pat. Paddy and I coaxed the mare to take one more step and she nearly collapsed. I thought she was going to lay down, she was that tired, and put her head in the Queen's lap.'

It was drizzling with rain when Black Caviar arrived back at Newmarket. Haydon let her mosey around a field picking at the grass, pushing him wherever she chose to go. Her stable companion, the English gelding Saloon, was brought to join them. Haydon joked that Nelly had fallen in love on her first overseas trip. The pair had been inseparable.

When she was done, Haydon led her back to the box and patched her up with bandages and ice. Too battle weary to object, she nuzzled in close to Haydon while he tidied her up. 'She's a sweetie. You have to be with her to understand. She's nearly human sometimes, the way she is with her eye. She's just different.'

Haydon gave her a couple of carrots and let her be.

Bronwen Healy Photography

Newspix / Nicole Garmston

A tender moment with the horse Luke Nolen will always remember.

Epilogue

Away from the maddening crowds, relieved of the pressure he had at first found unbearable before coming to thrive on it, Luke Nolen knew what he would remember. When he closed his eyes he was there, on the back of Black Caviar at full stride. It was the simple thrill of riding her.

'That's wonderful. That's absolutely wonderful. If you could bottle that feeling I'd probably be able to give up riding because I'd make a fortune selling it, I wouldn't have to worry about anything else.'

On the wooden deck at his local pub, Nolen wondered if he had done so for the last time. Were that to be the case, he would be disappointed but content.

'Very few jockeys know what I know about sharing a kinship with a special horse that's been as big as racing itself. They're littered through the past, these great horses and the jockeys who rode them. When she does retire, I'll become one of those stories. And it's a wonderful privilege.'

The day after victory in the Diamond Jubilee Stakes, Peter Moody had boarded a train for France. On the journey he rang Neil Werrett. 'Listen, prepare yourself for the worst, my feeling will be retirement.'

The following Saturday, the owners of Black Caviar went to the races together, as good friends do. By the Irish Derby meeting at The Curragh, the shock had passed. It was replaced by the warm embrace of accomplishment, which Werrett tempered with reality. 'I'm happy for her to retire. She's fulfilled all our dreams. If she's had enough physically we'll look forward to the breeding season and having a little foal on the ground in 12 months. She's been too good a horse to all of us.'

From time to time, while Tony Haydon tended to her injuries, he would put his head on Black Caviar's rib cage and just listen. Here he could feel her essence. 'That's why I get out of bed every day.' Whether it was now or whether it was soon, he was bracing himself for the day when the name 'Nelly' would no longer appear on the stable whiteboard. 'She'll leave a bloody big hole mate. She's a champ.'

Jeff O'Connor thought there would be relief tinged with sadness when the day came. Only then would they have time to reflect on what had been lived through. And the purest of all gallops would be consigned to memory. Or maybe not.

'I've never ridden Caviar. I'd love to jump on her, no fear, and gallop her around the paddock just to feel what it is like. One day there'll be a massive barbecue at Moods' farm and we'll all take turns. I reckon Pete has already been on her.'

Moody laughs uproariously at the accusation. 'You'll have to leave that as one of the great unknown mysteries.'

Each had been granted the promise of racing. They had found the horse that could not be beaten. They had held perfection. Its speed and its heart. But they had come to know that this alone was not her gift. Beyond the victories and above the adulation lay the truth. All who came to know her name and those who gathered to share her deeds felt it. And the memory would forever endure. Black Caviar had touched their souls.

Bronwen Healy Photography

A girl has to relax. Black Caviar was a morning regular at Melbourne's Mordialloc Beach.

Race Statistics

The highest class of thoroughbred racing in Australia is Group and listed level or Black Type racing. There are a variety of races that take place every day around Australia but those that carry the greatest status are designated by the Australian Racing Board as Black Type races. In the late 1970s Group races were further divided into four categories beginning with Listed races and ascending through Group 3, Group 2 and to the top echelon of Group 1. A Group 1 race must carry at least $350,000 prizemoney. In the 2012-13 racing season there will be 68 Group 1 races spread across the major carnivals in Melbourne, Sydney, Brisbane, Adelaide and Perth.

RACE 1

18 April 2009, Flemington

Cromwell Handicap 2yo Open $75,000 • 1000 metres • Dead 4

Placing	No.	Horse	Weight (kg)	Jockey	Trainer	Starting price
1st	11	Black Caviar	51.5	Jarrad Noske (10) (–1.5)	Peter Moody	$3
2nd	1	Kwassa Kwassa	57	Logan Mc Gill (11) (–2.0)	Shane Stockdale	$5
3rd	2	Take The Rap	53	Brenton Avdulla (3) (–3.0)	Danny O'Brien	$6
4th	3	Amaethon	55	Chris Symons (6)	Mathew Ellerton	$7
5th	6	Khas Kura	55	Ben Melham (5)	Peter Snowden	$13
6th	8	Commonage Close	54	Peter Mertens (8)	Robbie Laing	$51
7th	12	Phar Too Fast	53	Mark Pegus (1)	Jason Coyle	$11
8th	5	Promising Pete	55	Dale Smith (2)	Peter Snowden	$31
9th	9	Miss Papier	53	Matthew Pumpa (7)	Tom Hughes (Jnr)	$41
10th	10	White Pegasus	51	Ibrahim Gundogdu (12) (–2.0)	John White	$81
11th	7	Rockaloft	55	Ms Robyn Freeman-Key (4)	Karl Rhodes	$61
12th	4	Bensky	55	Matthew Allen (9)	Colin & Cindy Alderson	$12

All started • Margins: 5 lengths, neck • Time: 0:56.63 (Last 600m 32.76)

RACE 2

2 May 2009, Caulfield

Blue Sapphire Stakes 2yo Listed $100,500 • 1200 metres • Good 3

Placing	No.	Horse	Weight (kg)	Jockey	Trainer	Starting price
1st	2	Black Caviar	57.5	Jarrad Noske (7)	Peter Moody	$1.50
2nd	4	Demerit	57	Chris Symons (2)	Peter Snowden	$11
3rd	3	Carrara	57.5	Danny Brereton (8)	Tony Vasil	$15
4th	1	Take The Rap	58	Mark Flaherty (9)	Danny O'Brien	$17
5th	7	Quietzer	56.5	Matthew Pumpa (10)	David Hayes	$11
6th	6	Point Pain	57	Nicholas Hall (3)	Mick Price	$31
7th	5	Star Prosperity	57	Dwayne Dunn (6)	Lee Freedman	$13
8th	9	Connemara Bay	55.5	Peter Mertens (1)	Barry Barnes	$21
9th	10	Blackgold	55	Ibrahim Gundogdu (5)	Rick Hore-Lacy	$31
10th	8	Radon	56	Michael McDonald (4)	Colin Davies	$101

All started • Margins: 6 lengths, ½ neck • Time: 1:09.76 (Last 600m 35.10)

RACE 3

22 August 2009, Moonee Valley

William Crockett Stakes 3yo Fillies Listed $101,000 • 1200 metres • Good 3

Placing	No.	Horse	Weight (kg)	Jockey	Trainer	Starting price
1st	1	Black Caviar	56.5	Luke Nolen (3)	Peter Moody	$1.20
2nd	6	Miraculous Miss	55	Steven King (2)	Mark Kavanagh	$31
3rd	4	Orbiting Belle	55	Dale Smith (5)	Mick Price	$17
4th	5	Absolute Faith	55	Craig Newitt (4)	John McArdle	$26
5th	2	Noesis	56.5	Stephen Baster (1)	Leon Corstens	$8

Scratched: Maka Ena • Margins: 3¾ lengths, ½ head
• Time: 1:11.15 (Last 600m 34.41)

RACE 4

5 September 2009, Flemington

Danehill Stakes 3yo Group 2 $251,500 • 1200 metres • Good 3

Placing	No.	Horse	Weight (kg)	Jockey	Trainer	Starting price
1st	10	Black Caviar	54	Luke Nolen (2)	Peter Moody	$1.45
2nd	3	Wanted	55.5	Brad Rawiller (3)	Peter Moody	$31
3rd	4	Rarefied	55.5	Mark Zahra (5)	Peter Snowden	$10
4th	2	Delago Bolt	57	Steve Arnold (9)	Gary Portelli	$16
5th	7	Tollesprit	55	Mark Pegus (6)	Shane Fliedner	$15
6th	11	Corsaire	54	Craig Newitt (4)	Mick Price	$21
7th	5	Extra Zero	55.5	Craig Williams (8)	David Hayes	$21
8th	9	Point Pain	55	Nicholas Hall (1)	Mick Price	$101
9th	8	Grand Harmony	55	Damien Oliver (7)	Mark Kavanagh	$13

Scratched: Manhattan Rain, Rostova • Margins: ¾ length, ½ length • Time: 1:09.96 (Last 600m 33.63)

RACE 5

22 January 2010, Moonee Valley

Essendon Mazda Australia Stakes 3yo+ WFA Group 2 $202,500 • 1200 metres • Dead 4

Placing	No.	Horse	Weight (kg)	Jockey	Trainer	Starting price
1st	6	Black Caviar	53	Luke Nolen (4)	Peter Moody	$1.70
2nd	3	Here de Angels	58.5	Michael Rodd (3)	Mark Kavanagh	$2.90
3rd	4	La Rocket	58.5	Stephen Baster (1)	Dale Sutton	$51
4th	2	Royal Ida	58.5	Damien Oliver (5)	Luke Oliver	$13
5th	5	Ferocia	58.5	Craig Williams (2)	Damien Williams	$201

Scratched: Heart Of Dreams • Margins: 2¼ lengths, 1¾ lengths • Time: 1:10.18 (Last 600m 34.08)

RACE 6

9 October 2010, Caulfield

PFD Food Services Schillaci Stakes 3yo+ WFA Group 2 $201,000
• 1000 metres • Good 3

Placing	No.	Horse	Weight (kg)	Jockey	Trainer	Starting price
1st	6	Black Caviar	56.5	Luke Nolen (2)	Peter Moody	$1.80
2nd	4	Winter King	58.5	Nash Rawiller (6)	David Payne	$26
3rd	8	General Truce	53	Dean Yendall (4)	Ricky Maund	$31
4th	7	Star Witness	53	James Winks (1)	Danny O'Brien	$8
5th	1	Mic Mac	58.5	Blake Shinn (7)	Paul Messara	$8
6th	3	First Command	58.5	Steve Arnold (8)	Lee Freedman	$10
7th	2	Good Control	58.5	Glen Boss (3)	Patrick Lee	$81
8th	5	Tully Dreamer	58.5	Damien Oliver (5)	Matthew Hyland	$151

Scratched: Pellizotti • Margins: 1¼ lengths, 2¼ lengths
• Time: 0:56.68 (Last 600m 32.76)

RACE 7

23 October 2010, Moonee Valley

Schweppes Stakes WFA Group 2 $305,000 • 1200 metres • Dead 4

Placing	No.	Horse	Weight (kg)	Jockey	Trainer	Starting price
1st	6	Black Caviar	56.5	Luke Nolen (2)	Peter Moody	$1.40
2nd	4	Hot Danish	56.5	Tim Clark (1)	Les Bridge	$6
3rd	3	True Persuasion	58.5	Craig Newitt (6)	Mick Price	$31
4th	1	Eagle Falls	58.5	Damien Oliver (3)	David Hayes	$16
5th	5	Melito	56.5	Corey Brown (4)	Gerald Ryan	$12
6th	2	Stanzout	58.5	Craig Williams (5)	Colin Davies	$51

All started • Margins: 5½ lengths, ¾ lengths
• Time: 1:11.01 (Last 600m 35.26)

RACE 8

6 November 2010, Flemington

Patinack Farm Classic WFA Group 1 $752,500 • 1200 metres • Dead 4

Placing	No.	Horse	Weight (kg)	Jockey	Trainer	Starting price
1st	6	Black Caviar	56.5	Ben Melham (6)	Peter Moody	$1.90
2nd	7	Star Witness	53.5	James Winks (5)	Danny O'Brien	$7
3rd	5	Ortensia	56.5	Craig Williams (7)	Tony Noonan	$26
4th	1	All Silent	58.5	Dwayne Dunn (4)	Grahame Begg	$31
5th	4	Melito	56.5	Corey Brown (3)	Gerald Ryan	$41
6th	2	Hay List	58.5	Glyn Schofield (2)	John McNair	$3.50
7th	3	Eagle Falls	58.5	Nash Rawiller (1)	David Hayes	$67

All started • Margins: 4 lengths, 2¼ lengths
• Time: 1:07.96 (Last 600m 33.36)

RACE 9

19 February 2011, Flemington

Coolmore Lightning Stakes WFA Group 1 $752,500 • 1000 metres • Dead 4

Placing	No.	Horse	Weight (kg)	Jockey	Trainer	Starting price
1st	7	Black Caviar	56.5	Luke Nolen (6)	Peter Moody	$1.28
2nd	1	Hay List	58.5	Glyn Schofield (9)	John McNair	$5.50
3rd	10	Warm Love	53.5	Ben Melham (5)	David Brideoake	$81
4th	2	Grand Duels	58.5	Steve Arnold (4)	Byron Cozamanis	$31
5th	9	Crystal Lily	53.5	Damien Oliver (3)	Mathew Ellerton & Simon Zahra	$17
6th	3	True Persuasion	58.5	Craig Newitt (7)	Mick Price	$81
7th	6	King Pulse	58.5	Mark Zahra (2)	Michael Moroney	$31
8th	4	Leapfrog	58.5	Paul Hammersley (1)	Bruce W. Hill	$201
9th	5	Tollesprit	58.5	James Winks (8)	Shane Fliedner	$101

Scratched: Stirling Grove • Margins: 3¼ lengths, 1¾ lengths
• Time: 0:57.20 (Last 600m 32.95)

RACE 10

12 March 2011, Flemington

Lexus Newmarket Handicap Group 1 $1,005,000 • 1200 metres • Good 3

Placing	No.	Horse	Weight (kg)	Jockey	Trainer	Starting price
1st	1	Black Caviar	58	Luke Nolen (7)	Peter Moody	$1.18
2nd	11	Crystal Lily	50	Stephen Baster (1)	Mathew Ellerton & Simon Zahra	$67
3rd	6	Beaded	52.5	Craig Newitt (6)	Peter Snowden	$21
4th	9	Response	52	Craig Williams (9)	Mathew Ellerton & Simon Zahra	$31
5th	8	King Pulse	52.5	Corey Brown (5) (+0.5)	Michael Moroney	$101
6th	12	Hinchinbrook	50	Jason Maskiell (4)	Peter Moody	$26
7th	5	Star Witness	53	Ben Melham (2)	Danny O'Brien	$16
8th	7	Chasm	52	Jason Benbow (8)	Heath Conners	$101
9th	3	Eagle Falls	55	Damien Oliver (11)	David Hayes	$31
10th	10	Snapparazi	52	Dean Yendall (3)	Barbara Marshman	$301
11th	4	Grand Duels	54	Danny Nikolic (10)	Byron Cozamanis	$101

Scratched: Hay List • Margins: 3 lengths, ¾ lengths
• Time: 1:07.36 (race record) (Last 600m 32.69)

RACE 11

25 March 2011, Moonee Valley

Pulse Pharmacy William Reid Stakes WFA Group 1 $510,000 • 1200 metres • Good 3

Placing	No.	Horse	Weight (kg)	Jockey	Trainer	Starting price
1st	4	Black Caviar	56.5	Luke Nolen (6)	Peter Moody	$1.09
2nd	8	Crystal Lily	54	Stephen Baster (7)	Mathew Ellerton & Simon Zahra	$15
3rd	6	Hinchinbrook	56	Brad Rawiller (5)	Peter Moody	$31
4th	3	Perturbo	58.5	Ben Melham (2)	Colin & Cindy Alderson	$101
5th	1	True Persuasion	58.5	Craig Newitt (4)	Mick Price	$41
6th	7	Master Harry	56	Damien Oliver (3)	Peter Moody	$61
7th	5	Das Machen	56.5	Dale Smith (1)	Mick Price	$61

Scratched: King Pulse, Panipique • Margins: 1¾ lengths, 1¼ lengths
• Time: 1:10.00 (Last 600m 34.47)

RACE 12

9 April 2011, Randwick

Darley T.J. Smith Stakes WFA Group 1 $1,003,300 • 1200 metres • Dead 4

Placing	No.	Horse	Weight (kg)	Jockey	Trainer	Starting price
1st	7	Black Caviar	56.5	Luke Nolen (5)	Peter Moody	$1.14
2nd	1	Hay List	58.5	Glyn Schofield (10)	John McNair	$21
3rd	4	Triple Honour	58.5	Jim Cassidy (9)	Chris Waller	$151
4th	8	Alverta	56.5	Hugh Bowman (8)	Paul Messara	$101
5th	10	Hinchinbrook	56.5	Brad Rawiller (4)	Peter Moody	$51
6th	9	Response	56.5	Dwayne Dunn (7)	Mathew Ellerton & Simon Zahra	$67
7th	11	Crystal Lily	54.5	Stephen Baster (3)	Mathew Ellerton & Simon Zahra	$21
8th	3	All Silent	58.5	Brenton Avdulla (11)	Grahame Begg	$101
9th	2	Shoot Out	58.5	Corey Brown (2)	John Wallace	$21
10th	5	Shellscrape	58.5	Nash Rawiller (6)	Chris Waller	$81
11th	6	Demerit	58.5	Kerrin McEvoy (1)	Peter Snowden	$67

All started • Margins: 2¾ lengths, 5 lengths
• Time: 1:08.71 (race record) (Last 600m 34.77)

RACE 13

14 May 2011, Doomben

Bundaberg Distilling BTC Cup WFA Group 1 $405,500 • 1200 metres • Dead 4

Placing	No.	Horse	Weight (kg)	Jockey	Trainer	Starting price
1st	6	Black Caviar	56.5	Luke Nolen (4)	Peter Moody	$1.14
2nd	3	Hay List	58.5	Glen Boss (6)	John McNair	$5.50
3rd	5	Buffering	57	Larry Cassidy (7)	Robert Heathcote	$31
4th	8	No Evidence Needed	56.5	Dwayne Dunn (8)	John P. Thompson	$201
5th	2	Black Piranha	58.5	Matthew Palmer (3)	Con Karakatsanis	$61
6th	4	Albert The Fat	58.5	Damien Browne (1)	Paul Messara	$41
7th	7	Melito	56.5	Glen Colless (2)	Gerald Ryan	$26
8th	1	Sniper's Bullet	58.5	Chris Munce (5)	Tracey Bartley	$101

All started • Margins: 2 lengths, 4¾ lengths
• Time: 1:08.85 (Last 600m 32.87)

RACE 14

8 October 2011, Caulfield

Schweppes Schillaci Stakes 3yo+ WFA Group 2 $201,000 • 1000 metres • Dead 4

Placing	No.	Horse	Weight (kg)	Jockey	Trainer	Starting price
1st	6	Black Caviar	56.5	Luke Nolen (5)	Peter Moody	$1.07
2nd	9	Karuta Queen	51	Tommy Berry (8)	Neville Layt	$13
3rd	2	Stirling Grove	58.5	Damien Oliver (2)	Richard Jolly	$31
4th	8	Platinum Skye	56.5	Nash Rawiller (7)	Gary Portelli	$151
5th	1	Morgan Dollar	58.5	Chris Symons (3)	Stuart Gower	$151
6th	7	Kulgrinda	56.5	Craig Newitt (6)	Peter Moody	$17
7th	4	Tasos	58.5	Dwayne Dunn (4)	Brett Partelle	$151
8th	5	Ra Ikane	58.5	Brad Rawiller (1)	Michael Kent	$67

Scratched: Eight Bills • Margins: 4¼ lengths, long neck
• Time: 0:56.73 (Last 600m 33.46)

RACE 15

22 October 2011, Moonee Valley

Schweppes Stakes WFA Group 2 $302,500 • 1200 metres • Dead 4

Placing	No.	Horse	Weight (kg)	Jockey	Trainer	Starting price
1st	5	Black Caviar	56.5	Luke Nolen (3)	Peter Moody	$1.05
2nd	3	Doubtful Jack	58.5	Dwayne Dunn (1)	Peter Moody	$31
3rd	2	Here de Angels	58.5	Clare Lindop (4)	Wendy Roche	$61
4th	1	Scenic Blast	58.5	Steve Arnold (2)	Dan Morton	$21

Scratched: Balavan • Margins: 6 lengths, 1¼ lengths
• Time: 1:10.13 (Last 600m 33.73)

RACE 16

5 November 2011, Flemington

Patinack Farm Classic WFA Group 1 $1,002,500 • 1200 metres • Good 3

Placing	No.	Horse	Weight (kg)	Jockey	Trainer	Starting price
1st	3	Black Caviar	56.5	Luke Nolen (4)	Peter Moody	$1.05
2nd	2	Buffering	58.5	Nash Rawiller (5)	Robert Heathcote	$41
3rd	5	Mid Summer Music	56.5	Ben Melham (2)	Peter Moody	$31
4th	6	Curtana	56.5	Darren Beadman (3)	Peter Moody	$81
5th	1	Scenic Blast	58.5	Steve Arnold (1)	Dan Morton	$51
6th	4	Response	56.5	Dwayne Dunn (6)	Mathew Ellerton & Simon Zahra	$51
7th	7	Panipique	56.5	Michael Walker (7)	Peter Moody	$201

All started • Margins: 2¾ lengths, length • Time: 1:08.32 (Last 600m 32.78)

RACE 17

27 January 2012, Moonee Valley

Australia Stakes 3yo+ WFA Group 2 $201,000 • 1200 metres • Good 3

Placing	No.	Horse	Weight (kg)	Jockey	Trainer	Starting price
1st	6	Black Caviar	56.5	Luke Nolen (1)	Peter Moody	$1.05
2nd	3	Zedi Knight	58.5	Jamie Mott (4)	Brendan McCarthy	$31
3rd	1	Doubtful Jack	58.5	Jason Benbow (6)	Peter Moody	$51
4th	2	Rock Classic	58.5	Steve Arnold (2)	Bart Cummings	$51
5th	4	Sound Journey	58.5	Glen Boss (5)	Darren Magro	$101
6th	5	Hollowlea	58.5	Dwayne Dunn (3)	Terry & Karina O'Sullivan	$101

Scratched: Impulsive Dream • Margins: 4¼ lengths, 4½ lengths • Time: 1:09.44 (Last 600m 33.51)

RACE 18

11 February 2012, Caulfield

Sportingbet C.F. Orr Stakes WFA Group 1 $402,000 • 1400 metres • Dead 4

Placing	No.	Horse	Weight (kg)	Jockey	Trainer	Starting price
1st	8	Black Caviar	57	Luke Nolen (5)	Peter Moody	$1.05
2nd	9	Southern Speed	57	Craig Williams (8)	Leon Macdonald & Andrew Gluyas	$16
3rd	2	Playing God	59	Steven Parnham (7)	Neville Parnham	$61
4th	7	Illo	59	Kerrin McEvoy (3)	Bart Cummings	$151
5th	3	Midas Touch	59	Steven King (9)	Robert Hickmott	$101
6th	6	Doubtful Jack	59	Jason Benbow (1)	Peter Moody	$101
7th	5	Danzylum	59	Nicholas Hall (6)	Robbie Griffiths	$101
8th	4	Precedence	59	Steve Arnold (2)	Bart Cummings	$151
9th	1	Efficient	59	Eddie Cassar (4)	Robert Hickmott	$151

All started • Margins: 3¼ lengths, ½ lengths • Time: 1:25.14 (Last 600m 33.39)

RACE 19

18 February 2012, Flemington

Coolmore Lightning Stakes WFA Group 1 $752,500 • 1000 metres • Good 3

Placing	No.	Horse	Weight (kg)	Jockey	Trainer	Starting price
1st	7	Black Caviar	56.5	Luke Nolen (5)	Peter Moody	$1.10
2nd	2	Hay List	58.5	Glyn Schofield (7)	John McNair	$6.50
3rd	3	Buffering	58.5	Michael Rodd (3)	Robert Heathcote	$67
4th	9	Foxwedge	55.5	Nash Rawiller (9)	John O'Shea	$21
5th	8	Lone Rock	56.5	Glen Boss (6)	Robert Smerdon	$21
6th	4	Temple Of Boom	58.5	Danny Nikolic (1)	Tony Gollan	$101
7th	1	Phelan Ready	58.5	Brad Rawiller (2)	Jason McLachlan	$201
8th	6	Metallurgical	58.5	Craig Williams (4)	John P. Thompson	$201
9th	5	Secret Flyer	58.5	Dwayne Dunn (8)	Mark Young	$201

All started • Margins:1¾ lengths, 2 lengths • Time: 0:55.53 (Last 600m 31.82)

RACE 20

28 April 2012, Morphettville

Sportingbet Robert Sangster Stakes Fillies and Mares WFA Group 1 $400,000 • 1200 metres • Dead

Placing	No.	Horse	Weight (kg)	Jockey	Trainer	Starting price
1st	1	Black Caviar	56.5	Luke Nolen (3)	Peter Moody	$1.05
2nd	5	Sistine Angel	56.5	Michelle Payne (1)	Andrew Noblet	$31
3rd	3	Power Princess	56.5	Paul Gatt (6)	Simon A. Miller	$51
4th	2	Lone Rock	56.5	Mark Zahra (5)	Robert Smerdon	$17
5th	7	All Friared Up	56.5	Steve Arnold (8)	Stan Bates	$81
6th	8	Shekinaar	56.5	Justin Potter (2)	David Jolly	$101
7th	4	Just Sybil	56.5	Lauren Stojakovic (9)	Brian Mueller	$101
8th	6	Valentine Miss	56.5	Mark Pegus (7)	Mark Kavanagh	$26
9th	9	Spurcific	56.5	Glen Boss (10)	Robbie Griffiths	$101
10th	10	Tabulated	56.5	Nathan Rose (4)	Jon O'Connor	$501

All started • Margins: 4½ lengths, short ½ head • Time: 1:10.65 (Last 600m 35.37)

RACE 21

12 May 2012, Morphettville

The Distinctive Homes Goodwood 3yo+ Open Group 1 $500,000 • 1200 metres • Good

Placing	No.	Horse	Weight (kg)	Jockey	Trainer	Starting price
1st	1	Black Caviar	57	Luke Nolen (8)	Peter Moody	$1.05
2nd	4	We're Gonna Rock	56	Michael Rodd (6)	Mark Kavanagh	$26
3rd	7	Stirling Grove	54.5	Paul Gatt (4)	Richard Jolly	$31
4th	8	Stanzout	54.5	Dwayne Dunn (5)	Colin Davies	$201
5th	5	Streetcar Magic	56	Justin Potter (9)	David Jolly	$67
6th	3	Outlandish Lad	56	Damien Oliver (7)	Dennis O'Leary	$41
7th	6	Go The Knuckle	55.5	Shayne Cahill (3)	Mark Minervini	$31
8th	9	Weholdtheace	54.5	Joe Bowditch (1)	Craig Stewart	$301
9th	2	Catapulted	56.5	Glen Boss (2)	Mark Kavanagh	$41

All started • Margins: 1¼ lengths, 3 lengths • Time: 1:10.32 (Last 600m 34.06)

RACE 22

23 June 2012, Royal Ascot

Diamond Jubilee Stakes Set Weights Group 1 £500,000 • 1200 metres • Good to Soft

Placing	No.	Horse	Weight (kg)	Jockey	Trainer	Starting price
1st	11	Black Caviar	57.5	Luke Nolen (15)	Peter Moody	$1.16
2nd	12	Moonlight Cloud	57.5	Thierry Jarnet (5)	F Head	$6
3rd	15	Restiadargent	54.5	Maxime Guyon (11)	Ha Pantall	$41
4th	9	Soul	59	Frankie Dettori (8)	Saeed Bin Suroor	$34
5th	8	Society Rock	59	John Murtagh (13)	James Fanshawe	$9
6th	4	Krypton Factor	59	K Fallon (4)	F Nass	$17
7th	7	Sirius Prospect	59	Shane Kelly (1)	D K Ivory	$51
8th	6	Royal Rock	59	T E Durcan (14)	C F Wall	$67
9th	14	Es Que Love	56	Silvestre De Sousa (7)	M Johnston	$51
10th	5	Pastoral Player	59	D Holland (10)	H Morrison	$21
11th	1	Genki	59	George Baker (2)	R Charlton	$51
12th	10	The Cheka	59	T P Queally (6)	Eve Johnson Houghton	$26
13th	3	Jimmy Styles	59	R Hughes (9)	C G Cox	$51
14th	13	Bogart	56	Phillip Makin (12)	K A Ryan	$67

Scratched: Hitchens • Margins: head, neck • Time: 1:14.10 (Last 600m 35.94)

BLACK CAVIAR RACE RECORD

	Group 1	Group 2	Group 3	Listed	Other	Total
2YO				1	1	2
3YO		2		1		3
4YO	6	2				8
5YO	6	3				9
6YO						
Starts/Wins	12	7	–	2	1	22
Win %	100%	100%		100%	100%	100%
% of Races	55%	32%		4%	9%	

Bronwen Healy Photography

The author with Black Caviar.

Notes and Acknowledgments

It was Cox Plate Day 1988 in the Mitty's Store on the first floor of the Moonee Valley grandstand, where the thrill of racing and a passion for words were forever fused. Les Carlyon signed a copy of his compendium *Chasing a Dream* for a thirteen-year-old boy. These years on, that hardback still resonates with me and the carefully protected book is never far from hand. As all who have read him well know, Carlyon had a way of describing a race that made reading the account almost preferable to watching the event. Each year, once the Melbourne Cup was run, I would turn to the next day's front page of *The Age* newspaper that would feature a photograph of the winner above the fold and the words of Les Carlyon below. Only then would I truly know how to feel and what it meant.

Even if the standard is unattainable, it is best to seek inspiration from the great ones. After I had found a career in sports journalism and broadcasting, the lesson of Carlyon for me was to find the words to do justice to the deeds I was privileged to witness and entrusted to capture. If there is an element of his influence in these pages, perhaps Les will recognise another sliver of a grand journalistic legacy.

In my time at the *Herald Sun* and subsequently through ABC online, I have had the joy of writing about such champion racehorses as Might and Power, Makybe Diva and So You Think. It was always in my mind that, when I felt sufficiently moved, that I would attempt to write a book. Black Caviar has proved to be my muse. The idea germinated surprisingly early and I suppose any regular viewer of ABC TV's *Offsiders* would know how quickly and completely she captured my sports-loving heart. I had begun collecting memories, experiences and impressions by the spring of 2010, but with no clear picture of what it might lead to. The direction I would take was decided by the Newmarket Handicap, the afternoon that proved this was a story for the ages.

The practicality of writing this book, at this time, grew from the superb episode of ABC TV's *Australian Story* dedicated to Black Caviar. At the conclusion of months of work by the research team, I was invited to tie together parts of the narrative. Producers Brigid Donovan and Kirstin Murray had done such a sensitive and emotive job with the piece. In a delightful exchange that did not go to air, near the end of a lengthy session with Peter Moody, he quips: 'Remind me never to get into a drinking game with you. There's always just one more.'

Besides Peter Moody, the extensive catalogue of interviewees included Luke Nolen, Rick Jamieson, Meaghan Strickland-Wood, Tony Haydon, Donna Fisher, Pat Bell, Peter Clarke, Pam Hawkes, Jannene Madden, Peter Courtney, Ben Melham, Greg Miles and Alan Thomas.

For much of the racing information I am indebted to my dad for the time we spent together at the races. Those afternoons live on through the collection of race books accumulated from that time and every race day since. My wife has always thought these were useless keepsakes, taking up too much space in the garage.

Finally, I have justification and vindication. I have long recorded races, both feature and random, on the promise they might one day come in handy or simply remind me of great times. Now those videos and DVDs have done both. The specifics have been verified through such racing databases as AAP Racing, Racing and Sports, Racing Victoria, Super Racing (administered by News Limited), and the Fairfax racing sites of *The Age* and *Sydney Morning Herald*. Historical race-day quotes have been sourced from these also.

With all that in mind and the material at hand, the idea was to place Black Caviar in her time. To provide the sense of detail, perspective and texture that was true on each day she went to the races, rather than reflecting in the aftermath of her career and the inevitable blending of events and emotions through memory and hindsight. The collective knowledge here offers a nod to television news reports, radio bulletins, racing programs from TVN and Radio Sport National, and sports programs as varied as ABC Grandstand, radio SEN and *Wide World of Sports*. It is drawn from newspaper articles, blogs, Facebook pages and tweets. It would be impossible to recall and name all the items that contributed to the rich tapestry and thus not all will be named specifically. The beauty of the age is those that are named are likely to be available to view and read online.

The Australian racing media is comprehensively served by talented writers who I read and enjoy every day. Matt Stewart, Andrew Eddy, Adrian Dunn, Pat Bartley, Ray Thomas and Brendan Cormick are among them. The news cycle is thoroughly serviced by the likes of Bruce Clark, Andrew Bensley and Shane Anderson. I am a compulsive listener and viewer.

But what makes the subject of this book exceptional is Black Caviar's crossover appeal – her ability to captivate the sporting landscape and enter the Australian cultural vernacular. For the junkie, there was a Black Caviar fix on every media corner. In my direct experience, I witnessed the Black Caviar effect infiltrate the ABC. Historically, the place of racing within the national broadcaster could be nobbled by a single figure of authority with a personal dislike for it – someone who could see only the gambling and not the sport. Black Caviar transcended such prejudice. She won a regular place for racing not only on ABC Grandstand and *Offsiders*, but the News, *7.30*, *ABC News Breakfast* and ABC News 24. Even with my friend and colleague Jon Faine. She was exalted among the heathen.

Phar Lap was of his time and that makes his legend untouchable. Equally, Black Caviar was of her time, and unlike anything experienced for generations.

CHAPTERS 1 AND 2

On the eve of the 2011 Newmarket Handicap I had the honour of delivering a speech on the career of Peter Moody at the annual Doxa Racing Lunch, a major fundraiser and feature of Melbourne's Festival of Racing. The year prior, the subject had been Gai Waterhouse. She was the topic of, or a key character in, several books documenting the Smith and Waterhouse dynasties. There was a wealth of published material to draw from. By contrast, Moody did not have a reference page on Wikipedia. He remained a relative newcomer on the racing scene whose story was still unfolding.

The principal resources proved to be magazine and newspaper articles documenting Moody's rise to dominance in the Victorian training ranks. There was some lovely material from which to work.

The winter 2008 edition of *The Thoroughbred* magazine carried an extensive Q&A conducted by Ben Collins entitled 'Moody: Rough Diamond'. In September 2008, *R.M. Williams Outback Magazine* provided an insight by Annabelle Brayley into Moody's remote heritage. *Inside Racing* marked Moody's training premiership of 2009/10 with a banner story, 'Shifting the Balance of Power', written by Mark Harding.

Andrew Eddy captured the same sense of history in his 17 July 2010 feature in *The Age*: 'Moody Cruise'. Matt Stewart rounded out the series of stories with an affectionate nod to a popular figure in the *Herald Sun* on 19 February 2011 in 'Early Bird Gets the Worm'. Matt helped me assemble a dossier of newspaper clippings relating to Moody which provided information ranging from instructive to trivial.

My Doxa tribute quoted directly from these sources. Those references have been absorbed into the narrative of the making of Peter Moody. His own words on the day, both privately over lunch and in the formal interview conducted by Bruce Clark, opened the worlds of Wyandra, Charleville and Belgrave South.

Later that year some of those stories were recounted and expanded upon in the ABC News program *One Plus One* in an interview with veteran journalist Joe Pilger.

The Moody family history has been traced through the newspaper archive of the Brisbane *Courier-Mail* from the turn of the twentieth century. And author and friend John Harms was generous in sharing his Queensland local knowledge.

The partnership between Luke Nolen and Peter Moody was perfectly placed in *The Age* by Stephen Howell in his 2005 story 'From Manangatang to the Cup for the Comeback Kid'. It was neatly complemented by Mick Sharkie's feature on Gerald Egan, 'King of the High Country', from the same paper in 2006. On TVN, Bruce Clark's *This Racing Life* episode devoted to Nolen pulled together all the highs and lows.

Two later pieces elicited much enjoyment and inspiration. Ahead of the T.J. Smith Stakes in Sydney, *The Australian Magazine* proclaimed 'The Horse that Stops a Nation', a feature written by Stephen Romei, the paper's Literary Editor. It was said he had been 'following horse racing since his teens and owned a share in a promising three year old filly – but not as promising as Black Caviar'. And I had the privilege of being nominated for a Walkley

Award for Sports Journalism alongside Grantlee Kieza from the *Courier-Mail.* His 'The Horse Whisperer' was the cover story of *QWeekend* on the weekend that Moody took Black Caviar to Queensland.

In my final push to verify and colour in the detail, budding journalist and race caller Edward Sadler assisted with research and interviews. Brett Cavanough and David Power provided the background and texture from Charleville. As did Ian Tyack, the manager of the Cattle Camp Hotel Motel, who plans to erect a Black Caviar tribute in the pub once her career is over, complete with pictures of the horse and Moody. Bill Mitchell spoke of the early years. Lindsay Hatch was an employee at Tulloch Lodge at a similar time to Moody. The reports of Astro Gains' win in the Charleville Cup were captured in the papers of the region. The back page of the *Western Times* carried the action photo of the gelding streaking away with the race. It was also noted Debbie Moody won the $100 prize in the tipping contest while the race was called by Brett Moody.

CHAPTERS 3 AND 4

The story of how five families came to own Black Caviar has been recounted many times with total consistency. As Matt Stewart observed: 'Of all the houseboats, on all the rivers this is the one you should have been on.' Every mainstream media outlet carried the tale at one time or another. But it was also to be found in less obvious places, sometimes with an even finer degree of detail. On a blog called *A White Carousel*, administered by a woman known only as Cate, was a tribute under the moniker: 'Black Caviar + Salmon + Polka dots = the pin-up girl of world racing who puts on breathtaking displays of speed. *She is an iconic Carousel Girl*'. Danny Buttler wrote the story in March 2011 for the *Pakenham-Berwick Gazette* about how some of the local residents found themselves on the 'Ride of Their Lives'.

The Weekly Review, delivered free to inner Melbourne suburbs, published a cover story in October 2011, 'Black Caviar: A Champion's Story'. Peter Wilmoth chronicled the early reticence of Jill Taylor.

Ray Thomas unearthed Neil Werrett's history as an owner dating back to Kotiko for the Sydney *Daily Telegraph*'s 4 November 2011 yarn, 'The Easier it Looks the Tougher it Gets for Black Caviar's Team of Owners'.

A month after *Australian Story* went to air, TVN produced an episode of *This Racing Life* dedicated to Black Caviar that tied together many of the threads. It was the first time I had heard Colin Madden speak of the bonds of his racing partnerships with Werrett forged through grief. And the explanation of the gold coin Madden would hand to Peter Moody just before Black Caviar raced. That program was adjudged by Racing Victoria at its Spring Carnival Media Awards as the best television coverage of the season.

Inglis Bloodstock would forever remain connected to the famous sale it facilitated. At the corresponding event in 2012, the Black Caviar Bar was opened at Oaklands Junction. Pam Hawkes and David Taylor spoke of their good fortune to an audience of prospective owners. Andrew Mayes conducted interviews for ABC Grandstand.

And Troy Corstens never shirked his role in the story and gave his insights here. The man who could have had the champion was never bitter. Corstens did not leave that Melbourne Inglis sale in 2008 empty-handed. Together with associate Brad Spicer, he bought a Choisir colt for $120,000. He raced as Starspangledbanner and, as a three-year-old, won the Caulfield Guineas of 2009 in such commanding fashion that the Irish racing empire Coolmore snared him for $10 million. Transferred from the training of Leon Corstens to Irish master Aidan O'Brien, the smashing chestnut emulated Choisir, winning the Golden Jubilee

Stakes at Royal Ascot. He backed that up with victory in the July Cup at Newmarket.

CHAPTERS 5, 6 AND 7

I had not seen the Cranbourne trial but I was alerted to Black Caviar before her debut run. A well-connected friend in the racing game emailed on Friday urging that I not miss out on a good thing. The commendation was not only that the filly was a certainty on debut, but that this would be the unveiling of a star. It is the only day I ever bet on Black Caviar. *Grandstand AFL* was broadcasting from the Sydney Cricket Ground while it was Doncaster Day at Randwick, just down the road. Our preference most days is to have one television in the box dedicated to the races. I had shared the tip with Drew Morphett and Mark Maclure and during the pre-match program we watched in amazement at the display Black Caviar turned in.

I have found there are two sorts of horses that capture your affection. The first are those that put money in your pocket. You can come to love a middling horse because it always seems to win when you back it. You might never have heard of a sprinter named Holding but I will never forget him. My plasma television is nicknamed HoldingVision. Then there is the horse you adore completely divorced from the punt. I only ever backed So You Think twice. Both were the rare occasions of defeat, in the 2009 Emirates Stakes and the 2010 Melbourne Cup. But for me he exists in the same company as my favourites Better Loosen Up and Northerly. After that first day it was never again practical to back Black Caviar because of her short price. I have never had one moment of regret about this.

The first time I saw her live was in the 2010 Australia Stakes at Moonee Valley. Shameful though it is to admit, I backed Here de Angels to beat her. I've never been happier to lose money in my life.

CHAPTERS 8 AND 9

For years, Drew Morphett has been a constant in the coverage of Australian sport. From Test cricket to AFL to Olympic cycling, more than four decades of prominence in the craft has the effect that everyone knows you. I joined forces with Drew at the ABC in 2004 as he returned and I switched across from commercial television. Together we set about restoring the place of horse racing at the ABC after a grand tradition had lapsed. A Sydney boy who learnt the ropes in Perth before transferring to the hub that is Melbourne, Drew was a late convert to racing but took to it wholeheartedly. His Pakenham South property, Cloverdale Agistment, run with wife Kaz, has been the temporary home for Group 1 winners including Reward For Effort, Typhoon Tracy, Heart of Dreams and, as her first stop, Black Caviar. It has also offered refuge to a few of the slow horses Drew has found himself the owner of. He is the self-proclaimed worst punter in the country.

The combination of profile and involvement put Drew on a first-name basis with nearly everyone in racing. While I learnt to call the races, Drew would provide the bubble of excitement from the mounting yard, able to sidle up to any trainer at the moment of maximum pressure and engage in an on-air chat in the disarming manner that is his gift. We joke that no one can resist a 'wark' with Drew. While the formal pre- and post-race interviews are conducted for television and the big screen on course, Drew had the knack of eliciting wonderful insights in a follow-up interview once the initial glare had passed. These interviews appealed strongly to a sporting audience on ABC Grandstand with no specialist interest in racing. Just as the ABC could tell the story of rowing or gymnastics or wheelchair tennis to an engaged audience, we set out to demystify racing and engage with sports lovers. Anecdotally, it proved popular. Many of the emotion-charged quotes from Black Caviar's owners, trainer and jockey are from those interviews conducted by Drew, beginning with the

Schillaci Stakes of 2010. It was my first time calling Black Caviar live to air and the sense of amazement lives in the tone. I was unprepared for just how startling Black Caviar would be.

Through ABC reporter Guy Hand, we were well schooled on the deeds of Hay List. Guy had struck up an acquaintance with trainer John McNair and produced the story that hinted Hay List might be the best sprinter in the world. I had called Hay List the week before at Flemington and he looked formidable.

Two weeks later, ABC Grandstand preferred domestic cricket to the live call of Black Caviar in the Schweppes Stakes. But as commentators around the country watched her career around Moonee Valley, they instantly switched to talking about the 'Black Flash' rather than the low-tempo cricket in front of them. Once the race replay was aired, a highly tuned audience learnt precisely why.

For the Melbourne Cup Carnival, David Morrow joins our team. He is an institution north of the Murray heading up ABC Grandstand's rugby league coverage and calling track and field at the Olympics. In an earlier time he was a fine Sydney race caller. When I began at the ABC, he passed on his high-powered racing binoculars to me and gently encouraged and supported me while I learnt the craft. Some of the equipment had belonged to his predecessor Geoff Mahoney. He was there at Flemington in 2008 when I called the Melbourne Cup for the first time, becoming the seventh man to fulfil that task for the ABC. I am indebted to David, an elder who has nurtured and guided my career. He was the part owner of Holding. So I owe him more than that still. There is no better week, outside of an Olympic Games, for camaraderie and broadcasting than Cup Week.

The morning after Black Caviar won the Emirates Stakes, I stood in the *Offsiders* office with Barrie Cassidy, John Harms, John Stanley and producer Georgia Stokes to watch the final race of Zenyatta. Like spectators around the world, we were agog and aghast. In hindsight, I read and watched the full story of America's wonder mare from the most prominent of sources. The parallels between her story and Black Caviar's became unmistakable. *Sports Illustrated* carried Tim Layden's piece 'She's the One' on 1 November 2010. The US *60 Minutes* featured 'Is Zenyatta the Best Racehorse Ever?', which can be viewed at cbsnews.com. It concluded: 'Zenyatta is so adored by horse lovers that if she doesn't beat the boys and win one last time, hearts will be broken everywhere. It would be Babe Ruth striking out in his last at-bat.' That very eventuality was magnificently captured by Marcus Armytage on 7 November for the British *Telegraph*: 'Drama Queen Zenyatta Engineered Her Own Downfall'.

CHAPTER 10

A morning at trackwork was beautifully captured in the raw material of *Australian Story*.

I've worked many a Spring Carnival for television, trying to pick horses in the dark to compile a story for the evening news. In the lead-up to the 2003 Cox Plate, I ventured to Flemington on the Tuesday to capture the final piece of work for raging favourite Lonhro. Wayne Hawkes had told me where to be and at what time. Lonhro was a magnificent black stallion. Impossible to mistake. I assured Wayne if I missed him I would give it away. In the half light Lonhro galloped straight past me, recognition dawning too late to salvage the story. I recanted on the pledge.

CHAPTERS 11 AND 12

The build-up to the Newmarket Handicap was of an intensity usually reserved for a Melbourne Cup. As Matt Clinch and I walked into Flemington we had no hesitation pinning the commemorative badge to our suit coats and hanging the 10/10 flag from the broadcast box window.

Greg Carpenter emerged as the central figure in the plot by virtue of holding the title of Victoria's chief handicapper.

Carpenter radically changed the role from that of villain to font of knowledge. His capacity to explain this complex area removed much of the mystery traditionally shrouding methods and giving rise to conspiracy theories. His *Handicapper's Blog* on the RVL website, along with numerous interviews he conducted, were a rich source of information.

Adrian Dunn's report for the *Sunday Herald Sun* on Black Caviar's Lightning demolition appeared under the headline: 'There's Just No Catching Black Caviar after Dominant Lightning Stakes Win'. Matt Stewart's Newmarket Handicap story was entitled: 'Crowd Riding behind Black Caviar in Newmarket Handicap'.

ABC journalist Mary Gearin, regularly honoured for her perceptive sports features by the Australian Sports Commission, was assigned to prepare a story of reflection for the following Monday's *7.30*. She spoke to owners and punters alike, perfectly sampling the joyous mood on track. She followed the link to the sprinter Vain, and interviewed breeding expert Tim Johnson.

Few write about sport with the touch of John Harms. While we had spoken of Black Caviar together on *Offsiders*, he committed his thoughts to print for the first time in the *Courier-Mail* on 30 March 2011 under the headline: 'Spirit of the Bush in Black Caviar'.

Ratings information and supporting opinion was published on the websites of each of the relevant authorities, the International Federation of Horseracing Authorities (horseracingintfed.com) and Timeform Australia (racingandsports.com.au).

The UK *Racing Post* ratings website is racingpost.com. Max Presnell quoted the ratings of Michael McHugh in his column in the *Sydney Morning Herald*.

The sporting calendar demanded I was at the footy rather than the races on William Reid Stakes night. I was calling Geelong, the team closest to my heart, on a pivotal first night under Chris Scott that would lay the groundwork for a premiership, yet I ached to be at Moonee Valley. From that night, Rod Nicholson wrote 'We Love Her, but Black Caviar Bound for a Bigger Stage' for the *Sunday Herald Sun*. Scott Walsh penned 'Black Flash Strikes Again', published in South Australia's *Sunday Mail*. While a personal favourite Anthony Sharwood led his Monday Sports wrap on *The Punch* website with: 'The Fast Black Horse, the Great White Hopes'. Steve Moran's most interesting analysis appeared on his Racing Victoria blog on March 28: 'How Fast Can She Go?'

CHAPTER 13

The sense of fun and adventure surrounding Black Caviar was rich by the time she headed for Sydney. Rank-and-file horse lovers shared their admiration in an uninhibited way. The song, 'The Cav's in Sydney', was uploaded to YouTube by JustHorseRacingAU on 9 April 2011. It was tweeted to me, I suspect, by the author. After a touch too much ridicule, the anonymous creator followed up: 'It's back online! Just to make it clear – it is a joke, not meant in any way as a serious attempt at writing a song or singing!' Ever since Northerly, who I adored, failed to win a race in Sydney, I've always felt apprehension ahead of a Melbourne star's Sydney debut. Makybe Diva made light of the barrier but only after a couple of failed attempts. Her win in the BMW, rounding up Gai Waterhouse's iron horse Grand Armee from a seemingly impossible position, was arguably the win of her career. I watched from the broadcast box at Etihad Stadium and felt the same sharp gasp all at Randwick experienced when Hay List shot away.

Max Presnell pondered Black Caviar's vulnerability on 28 March 2011 in the *Sydney Morning Herald*'s 'A win is a win, but is Black Caviar mortal?' *The Daily Telegraph*'s Tony Thomas published his plea to the racegoers of the Harbour City on 9 April, 'Black Caviar a Rare Star Who We Should All Support'. Sunline's former strapper, Claire Bird, has long been a part of Channel

Nine's racing broadcasts in the spring and autumn. Andrew Eddy wrote 'Now Sydney Gets a Taste of Caviar' for *The Age*. Ken Callander's approval came in a piece for *The Daily Telegraph* entitled 'Savour the Joy of Black Caviar'.

CHAPTER 14

Brisbane was brilliant theatre. It was about this time people started taking videos on their phones of Black Caviar walking by and posting them online. They are utterly unremarkable and yet you will find dozens of them on YouTube. A close encounter with the great mare became something people felt compelled to share. The Brisbane Racing Carnival's advertising campaign, *The Champ Is Here*, lives on at YouTube also.

Among the many pieces carried in the Brisbane press in the lead-up, two stood out as reference points: 'The Greatest Show on Turf' by Phil Lutton in *The Brisbane Times* on 12 May, and 'Black Caviar Rests as Brisbane Buzzes' by Robert Craddock and Bart Sinclair from the *Courier-Mail* on 13 May.

Acclaimed poet Rupert McCall's 'Of Caviar in Black' was originally published in *City North News*, Quest Community Newspapers. The complete poem can be found at http://city-north-news.whereilive.com.au/news/story/legendary-poet-rupert-mccall-pens-poem-horse-black-caviar-exclusively-quest-city-north-news/ and blackcaviar.net.au. A copy of the poem can be requested from rupertmccall.com.au. The final stanza 'Of Caviar in Black' is reproduced by kind permission of Rupert McCall.

In addition to performing it live, in the stirring manner I first experienced with his recollection of Bonecrusher and Our Waverley Star's epic 1986 Cox Plate, McCall subsequently voiced the poem and it can be heard on YouTube.

Craig Young led the coverage of Hay List's near demise in a series of stories for the *Sydney Morning Herald*. By 30 May, things had taken a turn for the better under the headline 'Off the Critical List'.

CHAPTERS 15, 16 AND 17

The interest surrounding Black Caviar's Caulfield Guineas Day appearance was beyond the realms. The association with Phar Lap's best winning sequence was a masterstroke. Anyone with an active involvement with racing felt the increase in demand. ABC News 24 was taking hourly updates from the track. It might be the one time I've said that a horse would win without doubt, fear or equivocation. One producer asked if I thought she would be able to speak with 'Peter Mood'. I suggested that would not be a good opening line.

Moody's sense of exasperation was captured by Dave Lewis on 8 October in *The Australian*: 'Life More than Just Caviar for Restless Moody'. On 6 October Barrie Cassidy, on the ABC website *The Drum,* crafted the notion that having the best horse in the world was a 'dead-set pain in the arse': 'Black Caviar's Down-to-earth Bushie Trainer'. Steve McKee's sense of wonder was quoted by Andrew Eddy on 9 October in *The Age*: 'Priceless Caviar'. Patrick Smith published 'Like Don Bradman, Black Caviar's Remarkable Story is Told in the Seeing' in *The Australian* the day after. Gary Tippett's 'Joy, Relief as the Black Beauty Equals Big Red' appeared on *The Age* website.

The story of Frankel burst to life on the Australian mainstream as the search for a worthy competitor or measuring stick took hold. As in the story of Zenyatta, the similarities were obvious. Will Hayler wrote for guardian.co.uk from Ascot: 'Frankel Triumphs in Queen Elizabeth II Stakes at Ascot's Champions Day' on 15 October. As did Marcus Armytage for *The Telegraph*: 'Frankel Triumphs as World's Best Racehorse on Britain's Richest Ever Race Day at Ascot'.

I was at the Better Loosen Up versus Let's Elope match race, having left school early on a Wednesday afternoon to get to Caulfield in time. I was an admirer of Let's Elope but a dedicated fan of Better Loosen Up, and it was a splendid event for a child's imagination. It resonates far more strongly for me than it does for those journalists who were working at the time.

The English racing commentator Matt Chapman was a feature presence in Cox Plate week. He was interviewed multiple times by Shane Anderson on Radio Sport National and by Mary Gearin on *7.30*.

Growing up, the Raceplay VHS *The King and The Man* was an absolute favourite. That is true not only for an aspiring race caller but also a generation of jockeys. Glen Boss recounted in his autobiography, *The Boss*, how he would picture himself as Gary Willetts when the television echoed '... and here comes Manikato'. Matt Stewart's likening of Black Caviar to the Queen came in the *Herald Sun* on 21 October: 'Cox Plate Meeting Full of Tasty Treats, Not Just Caviar'.

The two very nearly met. Charlie Happell wrote a column for sports website backpagelead.com.au ('Caviar's Curtsey Practice in Vain', 26 October 2011) detailing an attempt by racing officials to get the Queen to view Black Caviar during the Melbourne Cup Carnival. Once it was established that Her Majesty could not attend Flemington, a scheme was considered for Black Caviar to be brought to the Queen: 'There are stables in the grounds of Government House. It was proposed that Black Caviar be brought to the stables with trainer Peter Moody for part of the afternoon.

'The plan was for the Queen, who was attending a reception in her honour hosted by the Victorian Governor Alex Chernov, to take time out from the knees-up to meet the super mare.'

It was not to be. That would have to wait until Ascot.

The four days of the Melbourne Cup carnival is a demanding and thrilling experience. For the past few years Matt Clinch had been my constant companion and support to get through the marathon. It's early to the track and late to leave, talking to as many people as possible, gathering information and texture for the broadcast. Much of that comes through here.

Stephen Howell's carnival retrospective came from industry publication *Inside Racing*. Bruce McAvaney hosts the Channel Seven broadcast of the Carnival and joined the panel of *Correct Weight* on Radio Sport National the Sunday after it wrapped up. I travelled to Qatar with *The Age* football writer Michael Lynch for the Asian Cup in 2011. He has many a great racing story from his English background and brings a lovely sensibility to his turf writing. His piece quoted was 'Daylight Second' on 6 November.

CHAPTER 18

When the world ratings were confirmed, Peter Moody was bombarded by international interview requests. While he professed to treasure peace and quiet, he seemingly obliged them all. *At The Races* was keeping particularly close tabs. 'Mike Cattermole is joined by top Australian trainer, Peter Moody, on the phone to discuss the unbeaten Black Caviar's accolade of being the best female racehorse on the planet.' TVN took to covering Black Caviar's morning jump-outs with the vigour of a race meeting. Bruce Clark's interviews with Moody and Nolen would go on high rotation on the racing channel from lunchtime.

Black Caviar at this point held precedence over all and being released from ABC Grandstand's Australian Open tennis coverage to call the Australia Stakes was an easy assignment. The night was distinguished by a telling sense of camaraderie. Wherever you turned, you walked into a conversation about Black Caviar. Andrew Mayes came to the races for the first time to assist with the coverage and he was given the Cheer Squad beat. Moonee Valley's chief executive, Michael Browell, provided updates to the press and on the TVN coverage as the logistics of the night groaned under the strain. Broadcaster Jason Richardson conducted the official interviews on the course.

Over the weekend, Gerry Collins conducted an expansive interview with Gary Wilkie on ABC Grandstand as the sense of wonder, accomplishment and ambition grew.

CHAPTER 19

Weekend Hussler was the first great horse I called. His three-year-old season was astonishing. I had been sceptical of the spruik on him leading into the Caulfield Guineas but recall saying 'Believe the hype, everything they said was true', as he routed his rivals. He provided some marvellous races, most notably the Oakleigh Plate demolition and Newmarket Handicap triumph. He came to underpin ABC Grandstand's coverage. Like all associated with racing, we knew the bold plan to attack the Caulfield Cup, Cox Plate and Melbourne Cup would fuel the spring narrative. He won the Makybe Diva Stakes at Flemington when the AFL finals action was based in Adelaide. I interviewed Ross McDonald in the aftermath and he laughed that one day they might cast a statue of Weekend Hussler to match the newly unveiled bronze image of the Diva. Brilliant though he was, it was always unlikely, but we never condemned a man shooting for the stars.

Andrew Garvey's excellent analysis of Black Caviar's pedigree came in his *Saturday Age* Breeding column, 'Champion Enters Uncharted Waters', on 11 February.

News of the Dubai option came via *Racing Post* in the early hours of 18 January: 'Black Caviar Given World Cup Night Entries' by Jon Lees.

Former jockey Wayne Harris shared the duties as expert analyst with Simon O'Donnell on Channel Nine's coverage of Orr Stakes Day. Brent Zerafa used the Usain Bolt analogy in *The Daily Telegraph* on 9 February in 'Caviar Will Run Orr Rivals Off Their Legs'.

As the Black Caviar phenomenon reached fever pitch, I received private correspondence from Zeb Armstrong. He was writing his PhD on Bernborough, he said, while awaiting

Hawthorn's next AFL premiership. He made the case through his extensive research that Bernborough, in 1946, was the biggest drawcard racing has ever seen. I bow to his knowledge on the subject: 'The 1946 Caulfield Cup, which Bernborough famously lost carrying 10.10 attracted 108,000 people, over half of which were attending the races for the first time just to see Bernborough. That is 108,000 out of a population of 1.1 million. Therefore just under 10% of Melbourne's population turned up to watch Bernborough. If 10% turned up at Flemington tomorrow to watch Black Caviar the crowd would be over 300,000!

'Similar scenes happened at Doomben on consecutive Saturdays in 1946 where Bernborough won the Doomben 10,000 over 1200 carrying 10.5, then backed up the next Saturday in winning the Doomben Cup over 2200 carrying 10.10.'

Twitter provided an instant and wonderful snapshot of reactions to Black Caviar from all around Australia. Immediately after I had called the Orr victory, those who had listened to the race tweeted me their impressions, from Caulfield, from TABs, from lounge rooms and from cricket matches. On 13 February, Richard Hinds wrote for the Fairfax papers: 'Queen of Turf Unlikely to Be Panacea for Sport of Kings'. Driving to the track that day, I had vowed to colleague Andrew Mayes that we must remember how special the feeling was because soon enough we would be coming and Black Caviar would not be there.

I held back from writing about Black Caviar on all bar one occasion. That night I was moved to post on *The Drum* a piece titled 'A Time to Be Bold': 'Soon enough Black Caviar won't be listed in the form guide. The lawns of Caulfield and Flemington outside the party season will be empty. And the soulless business of punting will again dictate the mood in suburban TABs.

'We will long for these thrilling days and the possibilities contained within them. For these are truly the best of times.'

In the replies to that column came the personal experience of Phillip Tyndall from the aftermath.

CHAPTER 20

In the hours before the Lightning Stakes, I stood in the mounting yard with the VRC's chief executive, Dale Montieth, pondering what lay in store. I asked him about the unthinkable, Black Caviar being beaten. He replied: 'It'd be like Geelong losing a grand final.' With a shared passion for exactly how that felt, we agreed there would be tears and therapy.

Trainer Wayne Hawkes, who I count as a friend, had suggested in the affirmative when I gently inquired whether ABC Grandstand should cover the debut run of All Too Hard to open the program. Host Gerry Collins, a man with a clear affection and knowledge of racing, gave listeners around the country the perfect backdrop before we called the colt to victory.

The quote from Muhammad Ali was chronicled in Alan Goldstein's coffee table photo book, *Muhammad Ali*.

The re-emergence of Hay List was covered in detail by Ray Thomas, culminating in his lovely story 'Hay List Has Overcome a Life Threatening Illness – Now for Black Caviar' from *The Daily Telegraph* on 17 February.

The research of Randwick clocker Craig Thompson, identifying the difficulty of the task coming back in distance from 1400 to 1000 metres inside a week, along with Moody's blunt assessment of how he would be condemned if she got beaten was published by Matt Stewart in the *Herald Sun* on 18 February: 'She Needs to Be Careful'. Adrian Dunn quoted Moody's declaration that Black Caviar was bombproof in the *Herald Sun* on 13 February: 'She Runs Like Lightning There'.

Everybody has their favourite writers and for me there is none better than Greg Baum. When I see him at a sporting event I thrill to the prospect of reading his prose the following day to complete my experience. When I saw him in the Press Room at Flemington before the Lightning, it was with a great sense of delight. He was about to witness what I had come to regard as so precious. His account ran on the front page of *The Sunday Age* entitled 'Black Caviar is All Speed between Smelling the Roses'. He, like her, did not disappoint.

Also on track that day was the French racing television station Equidia filming a documentary on Black Caviar for which I was interviewed. Months later, we saw the trailer for *La perle Australienne*. It's true, even in translation, your words sound better in French.

CHAPTER 21

Moody had become a guest columnist for News Limited and delivered his own verdict on the front and back page of the *Herald Sun* on 22 February: 'Why Peter Moody Won't Race Black Caviar in Melbourne'. John McNair's crotchety turn came through AAP copy carried by ABC News on 28 February, 'Weight Puts Hay List in Doubt for Newmarket', and was reinforced by Chris Roots in the *Sydney Morning Herald* the following morning: 'Melbourne a One-horse Town for Caviar Rival'.

Super Saturday was memorable. Broadcaster Debbie Spillane had developed the same affection for Hay List I felt. We chatted on air about our unabashed hope this would be his day.

The auction of Lot 200 at the Inglis Easter Yearling Sales was televised live on TVN and immediately broke into mainstream news coverage. *Australian Story* had returned to the scene, plotting a follow-up piece on Black Caviar's breeding and creation of a dynasty. They captured the intimate moments with Rick Jamieson. Danny O'Brien conducted interviews for the remainder of the day that were posted as widely as the Bloodstock section of Britain's *Racing Post* website: 'Black Caviar Half-sister Makes A$2.6 Million'.

The Adelaide arm of ABC Grandstand provided a perfectly pitched local coverage of Black Caviar's visit under the direction of

Peter Walsh and Matt Clinch, with producer Andrea Williamson. I had the pleasure of joining them at Morphettville. Through interviews and interaction with their audience came the tone of what this meant. Matt Chapman left Clinch in fits of laughter with his summary of the mare.

One of the great privileges of working for the ABC is the sense of history and the inheritance of responsibility you feel from the generations that preceded you. That work is carried forth. Listening to Alf Guard recount his experiences resonated strongly with the task I was entrusted to perform that day. His recollections of the mechanics of race calling made me smile: 'You've got to know your work. I didn't have a photographic memory. I used to paint the colours on little slips of paper. I'd put them all out on the floor on the night before and I wouldn't go to sleep until I could call the whole lot of them in as many seconds. 120 horses. I'd call them in 120 seconds. I knew my work backwards. I had to. Because I wore spectacles and I couldn't read the race card. You can understand calling a race you're looking through your field glasses, you can't remember a horse, you've got to put your glasses down, put your spectacles on, look at which horse it is, take your spectacles back off, the race is over.' The only thing that's changed is printing the colours from a computer rather than painting them by hand.

The Advertiser warmed to its task with relish from the day of the announcement 'Black Caviar Coming to Adelaide' (12 April) to 'I Love the Spotlight – But Not When it's on My Rear' (27 April).

Bruce McAvaney hosted Channel Seven's coverage of the meeting. He opened with, 'I've been coming here for fifty years and I've never seen it like this.' He rounded up his thoughts in a subsequent interview with ABC Grandstand.

This was the first day of the Black Caviar experience on which I wasn't required to man the broadcast box all day. I took the chance to stand out in the sun and watch. Randomly, people would come over and begin conversations. That was the sort of afternoon it was. I also had the chance to chat with the privileged owners in the surprisingly relaxed environs and flesh out stories of which I knew bits and pieces.

Moody's assessment of the less than glowing reviews was told to Matt Stewart for the *Herald Sun*'s 'Critics of Black Caviar's Performance Baffle Peter Moody' on 2 May.

CHAPTERS 24 AND 25

Royal Ascot was simply unforgettable – a life experience for all of us who were lucky enough to be there. I had a broadcast position in the roof of the grandstand on an outside television gantry, as history unfolded below.

I met so many people that week, from the train to the track and back again. Small details from many of those conversations combine to create the Australian experience, particularly of the Saturday.

One of the great joys of any trip to London is being able to read the full set of British papers of a morning. In *The Daily Telegraph* and *The Guardian*, my guides were J.A. McGrath, Marcus Armytage and Greg Wood. Added to this for the train trip from Waterloo was the specialist paper *Racing Post*, in particular its brilliant Saturday edition dedicated to Black Caviar.

The ABC's London Bureau took me in and facilitated everything, from broadcast equipment to television crosses and the trip to Newmarket for trackwork. Rachael Brown, Emily Smith and Lisa Millar were invaluable.

Every rookie needs a mentor and for me that was Adam Trescowthick.

The full generosity of the owners was on display at Royal Ascot. Their warmth and bigheartedness in sharing their experience and relaying the emotions contributed immeasurably to this story. On behalf of many, I'm sure, I thank Neil Werrett and Lena Attebo, Colin and Jannene Madden, Gary and Kerrin Wilkie, David and Jill Taylor, and Pam and Barry Hawkes.

It was Stephen Silk who came in to manage Black Caviar's burgeoning off-track activities, just as he had done with Makybe Diva. He has been an advocate throughout the writing of the book.

Jeff O'Connor is the racing manager at Moody Racing. He dabbles in a little acting on the side. He shared some of the secrets of Black Caviar with a natural lyrical touch. I am indebted to the trust he showed towards me. No one is more emotional about the mare than Tony Haydon. The intimate moments are owed to him.

Luke Nolen will say he does not have the greatest way with words, but he certainly has a deep understanding of the events he has been a part of. He added the dramatic flourish at Royal Ascot, and as time passes hopefully, he can laugh about it. To relive every detail of an afternoon that did not quite go as planned required a few beers. But Nolen shirks nothing and that is why he is the best in his field.

And to Peter Moody. This story would not have resonated or captivated to the extent that it did without the trainer's commitment to spreading the word and sharing the experience. Many a trainer would have locked Black Caviar away and offered only a reluctant word here or there. Instead, Moody became an evangelist for his sport, and the impact was felt around the world. A couple of weeks after Royal Ascot, he still had the sense that the experience was underwhelming. Hindsight will provide an increasing fondness for one of the great achievements of the Australian turf.

ON A PERSONAL NOTE

Adding a book to a pretty full working calendar required great support at home. I have been in love with my wife Claire since we were teenagers. Of all that she brings to our family, one of her great qualities is that she believes in me. Our lives and projects are shared endeavours. Our girls, Rebecca and Alyssa, have come to love Black Caviar. When she was three, while riding the spring-coiled horse at the local park, Lys shouted: 'Look Daddy, I'm riding Black Caviar, the fastest horse in the world.' Bec has a wonderfully sensitive nature and one day, when the words would not quite flow, she offered: 'Daddy, you're be best journal writer.' She loves the idea that this book will be in the library.

Timing is everything and a partnership with Jason Bakker, director of Signature Sport, has brought order and possibility to my professional life. None of this would have been achieved without him.

Publisher for ABC Books Helen Littleton has been a treasured guide through my first steps into publishing. And the final product owes much to many, including Julia Collingwood, John Mapps, Jo Mackay, Matt Stanton and Graeme Jones.

Thanks to friends Leigh Paatsch, Andrew Holmes and Damian Booth, who all assisted with the manuscript.

At the ABC, Susie Robinson is the rock on whom I rely so much. Craig Norenbergs championed this book. Mark Scott has taken the time to be a source of wise and valuable counsel. Barrie Cassidy is an inspiration and a friend. Rod Law at Fox Footy started as a valuable sceptic of Black Caviar and finished up a believer. But even when he doubted, he always offered his support. Tim Hodges has seen me through the daily grind.

To those who have taken the time to encourage and mould my career, and they will know who they are, thank you.

And to Black Caviar. It has been the honour and privilege of a career.

Index

[Racehorse names are italicised]

A. J. Moir Stakes 210
Abdullah, Prince Khalid 207
Ajax 135, 266
AJC Derby Day 105, 107, 163
AJC Sires Produce Stakes 245, 282
Al Maktoum, Sheikh Hamden bin Rashid 251
Al Maktoum family 249
Albert The Fat 185, 186, 225
Alinghi 135
All Too Hard 268, 269, 282, 283
Allez France 150
Almaraad 251
Alverta 166
Amalfi 28–9
Americain 39, 106, 215
Anacheeva 38, 99
Ancient Song 30
Andy the pony 85
Antidotes 33
Apache Cat 52, 210
Aquinita Racing 46
Arkady 225
Armanasco, Angus 29–30
Ascot Gold Cup Day 315 *see also* Royal Ascot Racecourse
Ashdown, Rod 22
Astro Gains 38–9, 74
At Talaq 251
Australia Stakes 83, 86, 229, 230, 235, 236, 248
Australian Cup 162
Australian Racehorse of the Year award 3, 41, 192, 210
Australian Racing Hall of Fame 245, 297
Australian Story 194, 197
Australian Turf Club 193
Autumn Carnival 86, 100, 163
Avenue 99

Baguette 136
Balavan 212
Barker, Tom 19
Barzalona, Michael 315, 316
Baster, Stephen 140, 141
Baum, Greg 270
BC Thoroughbreds 283
Beaded 140, 141
Beau Babylon 246
Bel Esprit 47, 48, 49–50, 59, 60, 62, 85, 239
  progeny 51, 53, 59, 61, 62, 85, 161
Bel Mer 59–60, 297
Bell, Patrick 120–1, 122, 123, 160, 178, 326, 334, 337-8
Benbow, Jason 30
Bendigo Racecourse 49, 161, 268
Bernborough 135, 140, 198, 253, 295
Berry, Tommy 198, 199–200
Better Loosen Up 207–8, 260, 302
Big Philou 12, 207
Bill Stutt Stakes 40
Billy the goat 85
Bird, Claire 169–70
Biscay 30
Black Caviar
  Australian Racehorse of the Year 192
  career wins 68, 70–1, 72, 74, 78, 81, 98–9, 101, 109, 132, 141, 187, 200, 213, 214, 225, 236, 240–1, 259, 273, 295, 304–5, 332
  compression garment 307–8
  conformation and physiology 5, 7, 50–1, 54, 61–2, 66, 67, 85, 93, 96, 165, 178–80, 237, 245, 290
  foaling of 50

gait analysis 3, 7, 67, 80, 119–20, 121, 122, 169, 171-2, 178–9, 273
handicap 135, 149–50
injury 2, 81, 83, 89–90, 324-5
jockey *see* Nolen, Luke
memorabilia 145, 288
naming of 66
nickname (Nelly) 117
owners 58–63
pedigree 50, 62, 152, 247
Phar Lap compared 137, 194–5, 201, 214, 238, 239, 308
purchase price 62
race colours 66–7
racing performance 78–80, 87, 88–9, 100–1, 110, 132, 133, 139–41, 155–6, 164, 167, 168–9, 186, 199–201, 212–13, 221, 222–3, 225, 239–40, 258, 271, 272–3, 276, 293–6, 304, 329-332
spelling 83–6, 90
temperament 41, 51, 261
trainer *see* Moody, Peter
training regime 6, 67, 84, 86, 88, 96, 118–23, 127
WTR ranking 149–51, 231
Black Caviar Cheer Squad 238–9, 241
Black Piranha 185
Blame 114, 149
Bletchingly 30
Blue Diamond Stakes 33, 48, 67, 72, 95, 139, 208, 246, 268
Blue Sapphire Stakes 65, 73, 74
Bogart 329
Boss, Glen 40, 131, 141, 183–4, 186, 193, 289, 294
Bounding Away 208
Breeders' Cup Classic 113, 114, 148, 149
Breeder's Cup Mile 232
Brereton, Danny 74
Brettell, Jasper 238
Brettell, Paul 238
Brettell, Peter 238
Bridge, Les 101–2
Brief Embrace 49
Brisbane Cup 181
Brisbane Racing Club 177
Brisbane Winter Carnival 175, 178
Browell, Michael 236–7
Browne, Damien 186
Bryant, Bert 207
Bryant, Michael 83, 265, 324, 326, 330, 334, 336
BTC Cup 175, 178, 181, 184–7
Buffering 179, 180, 186, 187, 223, 224, 271–2, 273, 281, 282
Bull, Phil 150
Bullet Train 312
Burns, Des 128, 129
Byrne, Jimmy 25

C. F. Orr Stakes 41, 42, 230, 242, 245, 249, 250–1, 252, 267, 279
C. M. Lloyd Stakes 266
C. S. Hayes Stakes 270
Cadbury Guineas 162
Calaway Gal 49
Callander, Ken 171
Carbine 112, 134, 295
Carbrecel Park 83
Carlton House 314
Carlyon, Les 201–2, 302, 313
Carnegie 27
Carpenter, Greg 135, 136, 148, 149, 150, 231
Carrara 73, 74
Carrick, Peter 61
Casino Prince 161, 162, 268
Cassidy, Jim 108
Cassidy, Larry 187
Catapulted 95
Catip, Terry 19
Caulfield Cup 38, 137, 148, 196, 205, 206, 246, 247, 251, 252, 256, 258, 263, 297, 303
Caulfield Cup Day 28, 253, 255
Caulfield Guineas 33, 49, 73, 77, 99–100, 196, 197, 202–3, 246, 260, 270
Thousand Guineas Day 96, 197, 207–8
Caulfield Guineas Day 96
Caulfield Racecourse 6, 7, 31, 39, 40, 73, 74, 84, 86, 93, 96, 97, 117, 119, 127, 194, 195, 196, 198, 230–1, 260
Caulfield Sprint 205
Cavanough, Brett 17–18, 336
Cavanough, Frank 16, 39
Cecil, Henry 207, 312
Century 136
Challenge Stakes 166
Chapman, Matt 209–10, 213, 290
Charleville Cup 14–15, 16, 39
Chasm 112, 140
Cheltenham Racecourse 285, 287
Chipping Norton Stakes 163, 218
Choisir 131, 321, 328
Christmas Stakes 87
Cinque Cento 38
Clarke, Peter 84–6
Clarke, Michael 208
Cloverdale 65
Colour Vision 315, 316

Combat Kitty 219
Comedy King 134
Comic Court 28, 251
Coming Country 17
Coolmore Classic 40, 166
Coolmore Stud Stakes 41, 106, 107, 140
Corstens, Leon 61, 292
Corstens, Troy 61–2
Cosmic Causeway 292
Courtney, Jim 33
Courtney, Peter 177, 307
Courtza 208
Cox Plate 42, 48, 94, 99, 100, 193, 203, 207, 210, 213, 215, 236, 252, 312
 winners 19, 29, 33, 49, 57, 78, 80, 94, 101, 102, 137, 169, 195, 208, 210, 246, 250–1, 260, 266, 303
Crabbia, Fred 193
Cranbourne trials 67, 70, 96
Crispe, Gary 150
Cromwell Handicap 65, 71
Crystal Lily 139, 140, 141, 154, 155, 156, 168, 192–3
Culminate 40
Cumani, Luca 220, 255
Cummings, Anthony 90, 162
Cummings, Bart 21, 29, 33, 58, 61, 94, 102, 106, 210, 252, 285, 292, 313, 315
Cummings, Jim 251
Currie, Luke 336
Curtana 107, 205

Dalziel, Wally 161
Danehill Stakes 77, 79
Danzylum 42, 256–7
Darley 202, 208, 249
Dato Tan Chin Nam Stakes 58
Davenport family 275, 280
Davenport, Peter 264
Davis, David 57
December Draw 206
Demerit 73
Demetriou, Andrew 302
Desert Sun 46–7, 62, 266
Dettori, Frankie 315–16, 329, 332
Diamond Jubilee Stakes 279, 311, 316, 321, 328-32, 441
Dignity Dancer 21
Dittman, Mick 208
Do Ra Mi 252
Doncaster Handicap 40, 41, 162, 166, 169, 297
Doomben Cup 181
Doomben Racecourse 28, 33, 49, 175, 178, 181, 185
Doubtful 12
Doubtful Jack 212, 213, 239, 240, 257
Dubai Racing Club 248
Dubai World Cup 149, 248
Dulcify 28, 236
Dunaden 220
Dunn, Adrian 133
Dunn, Dwayne 269, 282

Eagle Falls 110, 140, 260
Eagle Farm Racecourse 25, 26, 27, 28, 95, 177, 178, 180, 181
Ebony Way 25–6
Eddy, Andrew 170
Efficient 252
Egan, Gerald 129, 130
El Segundo 33, 80
Elder Stakes 286
Eliza Park Stud 50
Emancipation 225
Emirates Stakes 30, 109, 112, 185, 225
Emjoy Hussey 96
Epsom Derby 149
Eskander, Alan 217–18, 280–1
Estimate 316
European Horse of the Year 232
Exceed and Excel 135
Excelebration 312
Eye Liner 134

Facey, Tony 15–16 *see also* Tony Facey Memorial Plate
Fastnet Rock 219
Ferguson, Stephen 177
Festival Family Day 253
Festival of Racing, 2010 86
Fields of Omagh 78
First Command 97, 98
Fisher, Donna 119–20, 137, 138, 139, 144, 160, 170, 238, 260–1
Fisher Plate 214
Flemington Racecourse 15, 23, 28, 29, 33, 39, 40, 41, 48, 63, 71, 72, 73, 77, 106, 110, 131, 136, 157, 164, 193, 194, 218–19, 220, 221, 222–3, 268, 276
Flight 250
Ford, Peter 46, 47
Foreteller 219
Foxwedge 265, 272, 281
Fraar 251
Frankel 1, 3, 206–7, 209–10, 231, 310, 312–13, 317, 321
Freedman, Lee 30, 33, 97, 111, 118, 248
Fruition 286
Futurity Stakes 41, 230, 249, 279

Galah 219
Gard, Alf 286, 287
Garvey, Andrew 247, 248
Geelong Cup 38
General Nediym 22–3, 26, 78, 102, 135
General Truce 98
Gilgai Farm 46, 50, 143
Gloaming 266
Global Sprint Challenge 131, 134, 193, 264
Go The Knuckle 302
God's Own 202
Godolphin 220, 249, 315, 316
Golden Jubilee Stakes 131
Golden Shaheen 149, 24, 249, 280
Golden Slipper 49, 208, 246, 292
  winners 72, 101, 139, 193, 198, 246
Golden Slipper Day 40
Goldikova 149, 231–2
Goodwood, The 301, 302, 303–5
Grand Duels 140
Grand Flaneur 112, 134
Gunsynd 12, 181
Gurners Lane 15

Habey, Tom 287
Habibti 150
Haley, E. A. 57
Hall, David 285
Hall, Nick 256
Hamilton Racecourse 70
handicapping practice 134, 135–6, 148–51
Hareeba 136
Harms, John 147
Harris, David 247
Harris, Wayne 251–2
Hawkes, D. M. 58
Hawkes, John 108, 161, 162, 268, 285
Hawkes, Michael 161, 268
Hawkes, Pam 58, 63, 65, 66–7, 68–9, 71–2, 73, 80, 89–90, 97, 98, 99, 139, 142, 185, 219–20, 270, 275, 311–12, 333, 335
Hawkes, Wayne 161, 268, 282
Hay List 95–6, 97, 100, 107, 109, 130, 132, 133, 135, 139, 166, 167, 168, 169, 171, 172, 183, 184, 186, 188, 189, 192, 193, 264–5, 271, 272, 273, 274–6, 280, 281, 282
Haydon, Tony 34–5, 67, 117, 121, 122, 123, 124, 142, 159–60, 307, 324, 325, 329, 334, 338, 342
Hayes, Colin 20–1, 33, 251, 285
Hayes, David 33, 87, 209, 251, 259
Hayes, Peter 33
Head, Freddy 330
Headway 38, 41
Heagney, Peter 62
Heart of Dreams 42–3
Heath, Michael 226
Heathcote, Robert 179–80, 272
Helenus 49, 61
Helmet 202, 203, 270, 312
Helsinge 47, 50, 62, 66, 71, 161, 248, 282
Here de Angels 86–7, 211, 212, 213
Heroic 135
Higgins, Roy 33, 151, 161, 181
Highly Recommended 219
Hinchinbrook 140, 154
Hinds, Richard 259
Hong Kong Mile 42
Hong Kong Sprint 149
Hore-Lacy, Rick 268
Hot Danish 100, 101, 189, 192
Howell, Stephen 222
Hurricane Sky 251
Hutchins, John 39, 42
Hyland, Pat 33

Iglesia 142
Illo 252, 256
Ingham, Bob 57
Ingham, Jack 57
Inglis Bloodstock 62
  Australian Broodmare Sale 46
  Australian Easter Yearling Sale 161, 282–3
  Melbourne Premier Sale 51
Instinction 235
International Federation of Horseracing Authorities 148, 231
Iverson, Shane 38

Jamieson, Rick 45–6, 47, 50–1, 54, 66, 71, 143, 152, 161, 162, 163, 282, 283
Janiak, Joe 303
Japan Cup 148, 260
Jarnet, Thierry 329-30, 331
Jeune 251–2
JJ The Jet Plane 149
John's Hope 208
Johnson, Tim 151–2
Johnson, Walter 151
Jordan, Leigh 264
Just Sybil 294

Karuta Queen 198, 199, 200, 212
Kavanagh, Mark 86, 211, 285, 304
Kersley, Fred 136, 137, 145
Kincsem 113–14, 296
King Pulse 140

King's Cup 286
King's Rose 225, 280
King's Stand Stakes 52–3, 131, 210, 328
Kingston Rule 247
Kingston Town 15, 18, 19, 150, 171, 181, 210, 247, 295
Kingston Town Stakes 252
Kiwi 114
Kotiko 60, 291–2
KrisFlyer Sprint 157
Kulgrinda 138, 200, 297
Kwassa Kwassa 72

Lad of the Manor 30
Layt, Neville 198
Lester, Deane 274
Let's Elope 28, 61, 207, 208, 251
Lewis, Dave 196–7
Liberty Rock 269
Lightning Stakes 23, 86, 87, 111, 127, 130–1, 132, 140, 186, 210, 248, 249, 263, 265, 267, 271–3, 281
Linlithgow Stakes 266
Lion Hunter 106
Listed Zeditave Stakes 235
Littorio 246
Lone Rock 271, 293, 294, 295
Lonhro 202, 251
Lost in the Moment 220
Love Song 247–8
Lucas Cranach 220
Lutton, Phil 180
Lynch, Michael 226

McAvaney, Bruce 225–6, 239, 240–1, 267, 287, 296
McCall, Rupert 188
McDonald, Ross 246
McEvoy, Kerrin 32, 203, 270
McEvoy, Tony 34
McEwen Stakes 95
McHugh, Michael 150–1
McKee, Steve 201
McMahon, Bruce 291–2
McNair, John 95, 107, 133, 183, 184, 187, 189, 264–5, 275, 280, 281
McNair, Sue 264
Macdonald, Leon 252
Macedonian 219
Mackinnon Stakes 106
Madden, Colin 58, 59–60, 63, 66, 71, 137, 199, 212, 213, 238, 297, 298, 309, 333, 335
Madden, Jannene 58, 59, 63, 66, 71, 81, 97, 137, 185, 309
Magic Millions Classic 22, 23, 26, 72
Magnus 38, 52–3, 62, 87, 248
Mahogany 128, 136
Makybe Diva 40, 57, 106, 141, 145, 149, 217, 225, 285, 289, 290, 295
Maldivian 246, 250–1
Malua 134
Maluckyday 108
Manawanui 202, 203
Manighar 220, 255–6
Manikato 42, 150, 151, 152, 153, 208, 210, 245, 246, 250
Manikato Stakes 77, 95, 194, 198
Markus Maximus 38
Marshall, Simon 328, 337
Mason, Jim 34
Master Harry 33, 154, 155, 156
Maybe Mahal 136
Mayfield-Smith, Brian 20
media coverage 3, 31, 94, 96, 99–100, 113, 128, 133, 142, 143, 144, 147, 154, 156, 164, 165, 166, 170, 180, 194, 196–7, 201, 206–7, 209, 221–2, 224, 225–6, 227, 232, 239, 247, 252, 259, 267, 288, 290, 291, 310–11
Media Puzzle 106, 141
Melbourne Cup 94, 106, 134, 217, 220
  winners 12, 15, 28, 39, 95, 101, 106, 108, 112, 137, 235, 251, 252, 285
Melbourne Cup Carnival 28–9, 105, 151, 217, 218, 220, 267
  Preview Day 95
Melbourne Racing Club 205, 206, 253
Melbourne Spring Carnival 94, 99, 253
Melham, Ben 109–12
Melito 100, 101, 102
Mercedes Classic 225
Mic Mac 97, 98
Mid Summer Music 205
Midas Touch 257
Might and Power 58, 108, 181
Miles, Greg 79, 152–3, 198, 303
Miller, Trevor 15
Milnes, David 322
Miraculous Miss 78
Miss Andretti 52, 53, 131, 240, 328
Mitchell, Bill 21, 22, 26, 34
Mitchell, Major James 21
Mohammed, Sheikh 316
Mollison 134
Moloney, Jim 33
Monteith, Dale 267–8
Moodie, David 34, 297
Moody, Alf 18
Moody, Breann 26, 142

Moody, Cara 26, 142
Moody, Celine 26, 142
Moody, Charlotte 11
Moody, Garth 12, 13–14
Moody, Jan 12, 14, 27
Moody, John 11
Moody, Peter 25– 7, 29–30, 33, 36, 37, 38–41, 43, 52, 67–8, 74, 77, 80–1, 87–91, 93, 96, 97, 99, 101, 102, 107–8, 113, 115, 117, 128, 133, 135, 136–7, 138, 142, 152, 153, 154, 157, 162, 163, 165–6, 168–9, 170, 175, 177, 178, 179, 180, 182–3, 187, 188, 196, 197, 198, 199, 201, 202, 211, 218–19, 221, 225, 240–1, 242, 245, 248–9, 258–9, 263–4, 267, 269, 270, 274, 280, 283, 286, 289, 290, 292, 293, 297, 303, 321-7, 328, 334, 336, 337-8, 341, 342
  accolades and achievements 30–1, 33–4, 39, 99–100, 111, 144, 145, 192, 231, 317
  appointment as trainer 60–1
  apprenticeship 18–23, 171, 172
  childhood 12–14
  horse selection 52–4, 60–2,
  jockey selection 31–3
  racing industry, introduction to 15–18
  Royal Ascot preparations 237, 249–50, 279–80, 307, 310–11
  running of Diamond Jubilee Stakes 329, 330, 332
  training insights and methods 1-3, 23, 30, 31, 34, 35–8, 39–40, 42, 43, 68–9, 70–1, 77, 79, 83–6, 90, 109, 117–18, 120, 121–5, 132, 138, 155–6, 159, 164–5, 167–8, 189, 192, 194, 213–14, 227, 229–33, 253–6, 265–6, 271, 272, 295, 305
Moody, Sarah (Belcham) 26, 27, 35, 36, 142, 182, 274–5
Moody Racing 20, 26–7, 117, 119, 255
Moonee Valley Cup 215
Moonee Valley Night Racing 235
Moonee Valley Racecourse 28, 40, 58, 72, 77–8, 83, 86, 95, 99, 100, 153–4, 161, 185, 194, 212, 235, 282
Moonee Valley Racing Club 58, 153, 235–6
Moonlight Cloud 330, 331
Moore, George 12–13, 21, 33
Moraitis, Nick 57, 108
Moran, Steve 157
More Diamonds 27
More Joyous 94–5, 99, 102, 157, 193, 198, 205, 304
Morgan Dollar 199
Morphett, Drew 274
Morphett, Kaz 66
Morphettville Racecourse 285, 286, 287, 288–9, 291, 296, 301, 303, 305
Morrow, David 225
Morton, Daniel 210, 211
Moshe 161–2, 268
Mosheen 208, 269
Mummify 251
Myer Classic 41, 194

Newitt, Craig 140, 235
Newmarket Handicap 23, 80, 105, 127, 130, 134, 136, 139–45, 151, 166, 210, 231, 236, 246, 248, 266, 280, 281, 298
Nicconi 87, 88
Nikolic, Danny 140, 269
Nolan, Mick 31
Nolen, Alicia 128, 234
Nolen, Dane 234
Nolen, Kailey 234
Nolen, Luke 7, 31–3, 34, 41, 42, 68, 74, 78, 79, 80–1, 83, 87, 89–91, 97–100, 102, 107–8, 111, 127–30, 132, 133, 138, 140, 141, 142, 145, 153–6, 160, 164, 167–70, 175, 178, 179, 185–8, 195, 197, 199, 200, 201, 212, 218–25, 233–4, 239–41, 255–9, 266, 269, 272–6, 289, 292–6, 298, 304, 305, 317, 322, 323-4, 327, 329-334, 336, 341
Nolen, Shaun 31, 128
Norman Robinson Stakes 28
Northerly 49, 136–7, 145, 164, 302, 303
Noske, Jarrad 71–2, 74
Noske, Jodie 71
Nothin' Leica Dane 28

Oakleigh Plate 87, 140, 246, 280
O'Brien, Aiden 334
O'Brien, Danny 283
O'Brien, Joseph 312, 314, 315
O'Connor, Jeff 7
O'Donnell, Simon 255, 260
Octagonal 57, 128, 225
Oliver, Damien 29, 32, 106, 141, 156
Once Were Wild 108
Only Lord 42
Opinion Poll 315, 316
Ortensia 42

Panipique 138
Paranoia 195–6
Paratroopers 202

Park, Lindsay 20
Parnham, Steve 258
Patinack Farm 161, 282
Patinack Farm Classic 100, 105, 132, 186, 217, 221, 225
Peacock, David 296
Pendant 136
Pepper's Pride 114, 296
Perry, Paul 131
Perth Racing
 Super Saturday 226
Petch, Colleen 224
Petch, Simon 236
Phar Lap 7, 112, 196, 200, 202, 223, 290, 295, 308
 Black Caviar compared 137, 194–5, 201, 214, 238, 239, 308
 career wins 28, 194–5, 214, 217, 286
 public reception of 28, 167, 171, 202, 217, 287, 308
Phelan Ready 72
Pierro 292
Pimlico Racecourse 208
Pinker Pinker 215
Placid Ark 131
Platinum Skye 199
Playing God 252, 258
Point Pain 80
Pompeii Ruler 246
Poseidon 28
Power, David 16, 21, 39
Power Princess 294, 295
Precedence 252
Presnell, Max 164
Price, Mick 59, 235, 271
Price Hike 130
Private Steer 40, 50
Prix l'Arc de Triomphe 148, 149
Prow, Charlie 15
Purse Handicap 17

QTC Cup 248
Queally, Tom 206, 312
Queen Elizabeth II 213, 230, 287, 314, 316–17, 335, 337-8
Queen Elizabeth II Stakes 206, 207
Queen of the South Stakes 293
Queen of the Turf Stakes 41
Queen's Cup 287
Queen's Vase 316
Queensland Oaks 33

racing calls 200, 213, 224, 240, 258, 273, 294, 304, 331-2
racing direction 164
Racing Victoria Limited
 Racing to 2020 207
Rail, Vic 302
Railway Stakes 226
Rain Lover 12, 207
Ramsay, Stuart 30
Ramsay, Trish 30
Rancher 49, 134
Randwick Plate 214
Rawiller, Brad 247
Rawiller, Josh 205–6
Rawiller, Nash 223
Rawson Stakes 266
Razor Sharp 136
Rebel Raider 38
Red Anchor 18–19, 28
Red Anchor Stakes 212
Red Cadeaux 220
Red Ransom 39
Redoute's Choice 53, 202, 268–9, 282
Reset 70
Response 140
Restiadargent 330
Reward for Effort 33, 72, 95
Rewilding 314
Rising Fast 136–7, 246, 251
Riva San 33
River of Life 25
Robert Sangster Stakes 60, 285, 288, 293–5, 297
Robin Hood 314
Roche, Wendy 211
Rock Classic 240
Rocket Man 149, 157, 193
Rodd, Michael 87, 272, 304
Rosehill Racecourse 49, 57, 198, 208, 292
Rous, Admiral 134
Royal Ascot Racecourse 1, 3, 53, 131, 133, 206, 210, 230, 231, 249, 250, 279, 310, 311–12, 317–18, 321
Royal Randwick Racecourse 18, 21, 100, 160, 163, 165, 166, 167, 168, 170, 183, 184, 246, 265
Rubitano 135
Rubiton Stakes 260
Run For Levi 99
Ryan, Gerald 27, 102

S. J. Pullman Stakes 287
Saintly 58, 128, 251
Salinger Stakes 30
Saloon 338
Samantha Miss 54
Sandown Classics 152
Sandown Racecourse 230

Santic, Tony 57
Scandinavia 46, 52, 66, 248
Scenic Blast 131, 210, 211, 213, 224
Schillaci 135, 251
Schillaci Stakes 93, 96, 97–8, 191, 197–202
Schofield 110
Schofield, Glyn 132, 133, 168, 169, 183, 184, 271, 272, 273, 275, 281
Schweppes Stakes 93, 100, 205, 210, 212
Seabiscuit 208
Secret Indulgence 219
Sepoy 198, 205, 208–9, 249, 280
Set For Fame 38, 70–1, 165, 177
Shaftsbury Avenue 131, 136
Shaw, Patrick 157
Sheedy, Kevin 48, 60, 242
Shirreffs, John 113
Shocking 95, 285
Shogun Lodge 170
Shoot Out 102
Shopaholic 269
Shuck, Bill 177, 178, 180–1
Sires Produce Stakes 75
Sister Madly 205–6
Sistine Angel 294, 295
Sky Cuddle 30, 32
Sleep Walker 129
Smart Missile 196
Smerdon, Robert 293
Smith, Ernie 18
Smith, Patrick 201
Smith, T. J. (Tommy) 13, 18–19, 20, 28, 31, 33, 57, 170, 171, 172, 287 *see also* T. J. Smith Stakes
Sniper's Bullet 185
Snitzerland 292
Snowden, Peter 73, 205, 329
So Pristine 293
So You Think 58, 94, 95, 99, 102, 106–7, 149, 196, 210, 313, 314, 315, 316
Song of Norway 248
Soul 329, 330
South Australia Turf Club 285
South Australian Derby 38, 74
South Australian Jockey Club (SAJC) 285, 286, 296
South Australian Oaks 288
Southern Speed 206, 252, 258
Spear Chief 266
Special 276
Spinning Hill 50
Spurcific 294
Stackhouse, Daniel 233
Stanzout 101
Star Kingdom 30
Star Witness 97, 98, 106, 107, 109, 110, 139
Starspangledbanner 87, 202
Steven King 257
Stevenson, Ross 291
Stewart, Matt 142, 210, 266
Stirling Grove 200
Straight Strike 27
Strathalbyn 294
Strickland-Wood, Meaghan 50, 143
Stylish Century 21
Sunline 41, 42, 145, 169–70, 201, 225, 303
Super Impose 302
Super Match Racing 207
Super Saturday 105–6, 127, 280, 282
Surefoot 20
Surround 236, 250
Swettenham Stud 51
Sydney Cup 183, 288
Symons, John 48, 49
Symons, Mick 206

T. J. Smith Stakes 100, 159, 163, 164, 167, 172, 183, 187
T. S. Carlyon Cup 255
TAB Challenge 207–8
Takeover Target 52, 53, 131, 303–4, 328
Talindert Stakes 268
Talty, Martin 248–9
Tan, Dato Chin Nam 58
Taylor, David 63, 73, 160, 225, 267, 275, 298, 305, 336
Taylor, Jill 58, 73, 111, 160, 241, 335-6
Team Corstens Racing 61
Team Hawkes 161, 269
Temple of Boom 272
Testa Rossa 26, 202, 202
Testifiable 38
Thomas, Alan 183, 184, 187
Thomas, Ray 264–5
Thomas, Tony 166
Thompson, Craig 265–6
Tie The Knot 164
Timeform rankings 150
Tinkler, Nathan 161–2, 163, 268
Tobin Bronze 28, 250, 297
Todman 131, 245, 246
Tony Facey Memorial Plate 16
Toorak Handicap 99, 304
Treloar, Wayne 49
Triple Honour 166
Tristarc Stakes 205
True Persuasion 101, 132, 155
Tuesday Joy 162
Tulloch 18, 28, 150, 171, 181, 188, 223, 246, 287, 295, 296

Tulloch Lodge 18
Tully Dreamer 97–8
Turffontein 90
Turnbull Stakes 95, 247
Typhoon Tracy 2–3, 39–43, 117, 120, 144, 165, 192, 250, 324

Umagold 32
Underwood Stakes 246
Ustinov 28–9

Vain 111, 151–2, 245, 246
Valerius 218
Vanity, The 269
Vasil, Tony 73
Victoire Pisa 149
Victoria Derby 19, 28–9, 61, 197, 112, 203
Victoria Park Racecourse 285, 292
Victoria Racing Club (VRC) 193, 209, 267
Viscount 29
Vlahos, Bill 283
Vo Rogue 42, 251, 302
VRC Oaks 54, 269

Waller, Kenny 15
Wanless, Ron 27
Wanted 38, 80, 87, 88
War Admiral 208
Warm Love 132
Warwick Farm Racecourse 52
Waterhouse, Bill 171
Waterhouse, Gai 19, 28, 94–5, 108, 157, 171, 198, 292
Waterhouse, Tom 171–2
We're Gonna Rock 304
Weatherill, Jay 286
Weekend Hustler 52, 135, 202, 246–7
weight-for-age scale 134
Wenona Girl 131
Werrett, Neil 58, 59, 60–1, 62, 63, 66, 98, 153, 161, 162–3, 187, 192, 197, 199, 219, 241, 270, 291, 292, 297–8, 335, 341, 342
Werrett Bloodstock P L Syndicate 58
Whobegotyou 40, 97, 102, 202
Wilander 248
Wilkie, Gary M. 58, 59, 60–1, 63, 66, 67, 69, 88, 90, 144, 162, 170, 241–2, 249–50, 335
Wilkie, Kerrin J. 58, 59, 63, 67, 144
Wilkie, Shannon 66
Wilkinson, Brenton 286, 296
William Crockett Stakes 77, 76
William Reid Stakes 86, 88, 90, 147, 150, 152, 153–6, 236, 282
Williams, Craig 206, 215, 252, 258
Williams, Lloyd 152
Williamstown Racecourse 250
Willow Creek 165
Willowood Equicentre 84–5
Winks, James 110
Winter King 97, 98
Winterbottom Stakes 226
Wonderful World 33
Workforce 149
World Thoroughbred Rankings (WTR) 148, 149, 150–1, 231
  Champion Sprinter of the World 132

Yalumba Stakes 99
Yoshida, Katsumi 283
Young, Marty 226

Zahra, Simon 193
Zarek 29
Zedi Knight 239, 240
Zeditave 30, 49
Zenyatta 113, 114–15, 149, 232, 266, 267, 289, 295
Zipping 95, 102, 152–3
Zipping Classic 153

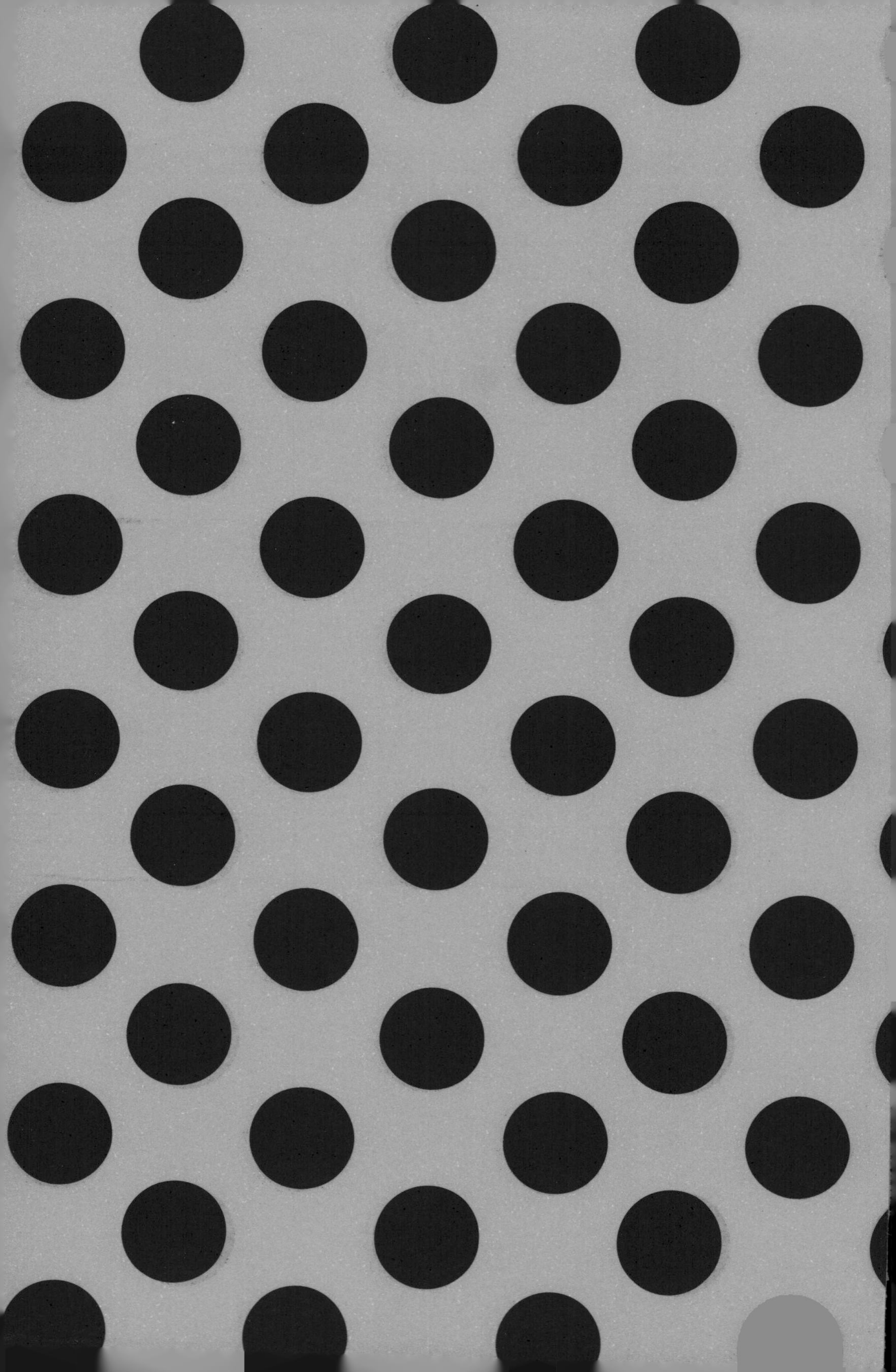

1967

A YEAR TO REMEMBER

1967

A YEAR TO REMEMBER

by
Richard Hease

in association with
British Pathe News
and
Dennis Fairey and Associates

A Year to Remember -1967

First published in book form in Great Britain by Mistral Publishing Ltd. 1991 in association with British Pathe News Ltd.

ISBN - 1 874053 20 0

A CIP catalogue record for this book is available from the British Library.

Printed and bound by Waterside Press, Hatfield, England.

Design and Typesetting by Dennis Fairey & Associates Ltd., Chiltern House, 184 High Street, Berkhamsted, Herts HP4 3AP.

1967

Pathe Review 7

Lifestyle 101

Entertainment 115

War and Politics 123

Births, Deaths and Marriages 133

Disasters 139

Innovation 145

Sport 151

NEWS

Pathe Review

We are all a part of history wherever we are and whatever we are doing. World events shape our memories and for most of the 20th Century those events were filmed and explained by Pathe. Pathe News captured history in motion, creating a living chronicle of a turbulent century.

The following pages contain actual pictures taken from the Pathe newsreels, accompanied by the slightly edited version of the original transcripts which became a very distinctive style through the years.

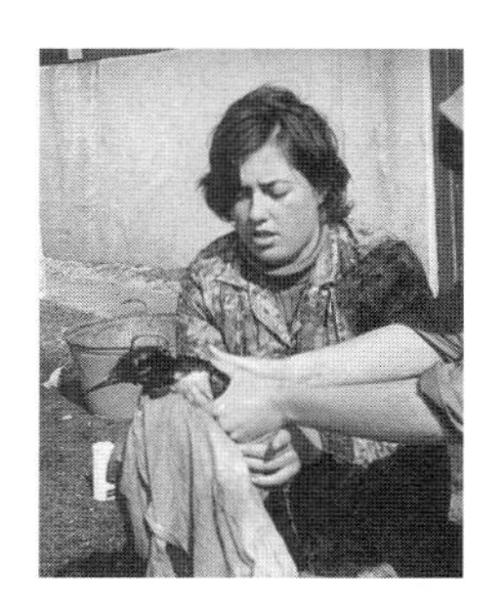

The World in 1967

The Vietnam War dominated world affairs during 1967. The year started with the highest American casualty rate of the war so far: in one week 144 servicemen died in the Vietnamese jungles, 1,044 were wounded and six were listed as missing.

Saturation bombings seemed to be having little effect. The fundamental flaw of American policy, as historians now agree, was that there was little support for the government of South Vietnam among the peasant population. American bombing tactics served to alienate the population further, so giving the Communists greater advantage on the ground.

In the States the war began to cause widespread protest. The young men who were being sent to die at such an alarming rate started to question the reasons for the war. Muhammad Ali, the World Heavyweight Boxing Champion, refused to accept his draft into the army. He argued that no Vietnamese had ever abused him because of the colour of his skin.

Race riots - looting in Newark, New Jersey.

The Civil Rights Movement in the U.S. seemed confused and divided. An increasing number of black activists saw violence as the only means of making significant headway against entrenched racial attitudes. The poverty of many ethnic groups in inner city areas had caused a series of vicious riots in major American cities. In 1967 Detroit erupted into violence.

Vietnam was the first war to be brought on to the nation's TV screens daily and, coupled with the violence on the streets of the country's cities, there was a growing concern about the fate of the nation.

1967 was also the year of the Six Day War in the Middle East. On June 5th General Moshe Dayan launched what was called a "preventative campaign" against Egypt, Jordan and Syria. The cause of the war was Egyptian moves against the U.N. peace-keeping force, which had been established after fighting in Sinai during 1956.

Israel could see that Arab forces were concentrating on her borders and decided to act swiftly to prevent invasion. The Egyptians were also blockading an important sea route to Israel and so Dayan gave the order to attack. On June 5th airfields in Egypt, Syria, Iraq and Jordan were attacked and Arab air power virtually wiped out. In Sinai, Israel moved against Egyptian tanks and by June 7th Israeli forces had reached as far as the Suez Canal. On the same day the whole of the West Bank in Jordan was occupied. Israel had suddenly expanded its territory and now had jurisdiction over another 600,000 Palestinian Arabs. It was a famous victory but one which would leave a legacy of conflict. The Palestinian Liberation Movement could see no other alternative but to fight Israel with ever-increasing levels of violence.

Israel's General Dayan.

FIRE-RAVAGED TASMANIA

February

Food, equipment, clothing and the essentials for living were flowing into the fire-ravaged island. From all over the world, aid in the form of money and goods helped to put stunned Tasmanians back on their feet. Red Cross and other welfare workers continued to restore hope for people who had lost everything in the raging inferno, fanned by high winds which swept across the island.

Scenes such as these were commonplace. Many died. More than 600 homes and farms were destroyed. Desperate efforts to save belongings were futile. Too often all that could be done was to stand and watch as a precious home died in the flames.

When the flames had gone, ships from the mainland took in supplies and the fight for recovery was on, but the Tasmanians can never forget the horror of the enveloping flames that took their homes and loved ones.

Bush fires sweep Tasmania.

Tasmanian family watch helplessly as their home is destroyed by fire.

BOSTON STRANGLER ESCAPES

February

The Boston Strangler's escape from a mental institution sparked a 30-hour wave of terror throughout New England. The escapee, Albert de Salvo, claimed he committed at least 13 murders around Boston.

From the asylum, with de Salvo, went two other inmates. Snow tracks led to their quick recapture but de Salvo avoided the police. The break-out was effected with a duplicate key. Eventually the self-confessed murderer gave himself up. He was transferred to a maximum security prison where he would also receive psychiatric treatment.

Albert de Salvo is re-captured.

LORD SNOWDON IN NEW YORK

March

Pressmen wait for Lord Snowdon to appear, to answer their questions. His private life has been the subject of rumours throughout the U.S. press recently, and, on his arrival from Japan, where he has been on a photographic assignment for his paper, he was beseiged by batteries of probing newsmen. Lord Snowdon displayed admirable self-control as he explained there was no truth in speculations about his personal affairs. He is to join Princess Margaret in the Bahamas for a holiday.

Lord Snowdon beseiged by New York reporters.

RUSSIAN SPACE TRAGEDY

April

Return to earth. The scorching perilous moments faced by spacemen.
Whether Russian or American, the men of space have to meet this final challenge.

For one it meant death. Colonel Vladimir Komarov, the man history books will record as the first cosmonaut killed during a space flight.

As he trained for what Western observers believed was to be a major step towards a moon landing, Colonel Komarov already knew the hazards of space. In 1964 he had piloted a three-man spacecraft.

Vladimir Komarov, like Yuri Gagarin, the first man in space, was a hero. Gagarin had paved the way for all mankind, but his achievement was the start of what is now being quoted as a "senseless space race". All are heroes who leave our planet in the name of progress, but progress has its price. An American Space Program - a Russian Space Program; how much better if mankind pooled its knowledge in the race for the moon instead of nations competing with each other for the same goal.

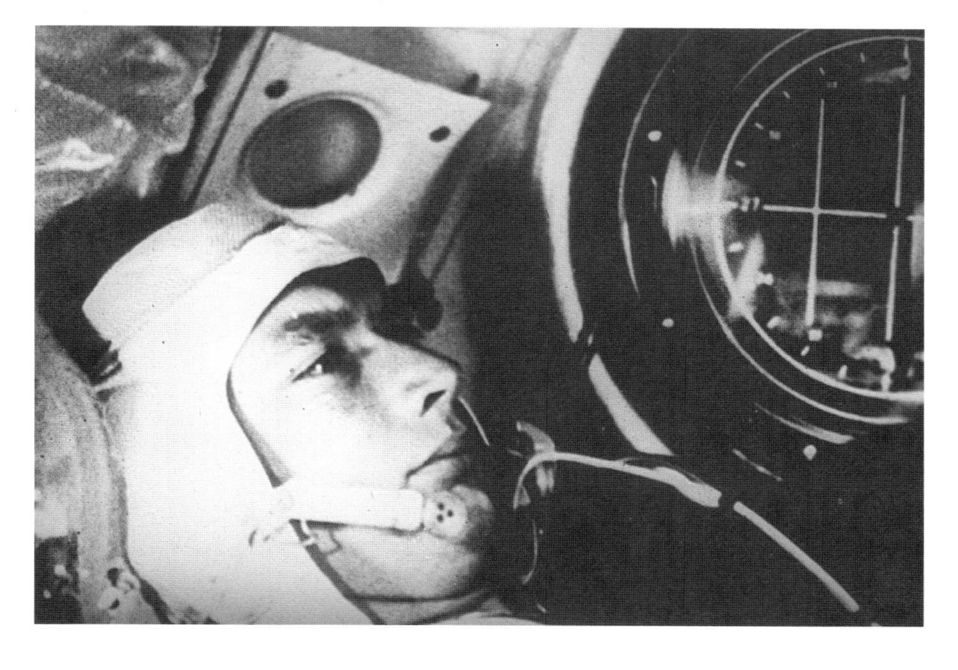

Vladimir Komarov in his Soyuz capsule.

Vladimir Komarov's widow and relatives mourn at his funeral.

Muhammad Ali tells press he refuses to take Army oath.

CASSIUS CLAY REFUSES TO JOIN ARMY

May

Muhammad Ali, previously Cassius Clay, refused to take the U.S. army oath. He maintained that his religion would not allow him to kill people of his own colour in Vietnam.

As his kind of conscientious objection is not recognised in the United States, “Cass the Gas” may have the Law Book thrown at him, with a possible $10,000 fine, or five years in prison.

ISRAEL'S GREAT VICTORY

General Moshe Dayan.

June

Israeli Prime Minister Levi Eshkol must be the proudest man in the world. Especially when he entered into the Jordanian sector of Jerusalem and to stand before the Wailing Wall. To World Jewry, a deeply emotional occasion of great historic importance. Hero of the Jewish Peoples was General Moshe Dayan, Defence Minister and architect of the swiftest, most overwhelming victory of all time.

In the Sinai Desert, in the wake of Egypt's catastrophic retreat, lay Nasser's wrecked tanks - more tanks than were destroyed in the early Alamein campaign. Inspired by General Dayan, four Israeli Commanders achieved the great triumph; Gavish the Commander in Chief, Jaffa, Sharon and Tal. When Sharm al Sheikh, at the mouth of the Gulf of Akaba, fell to the Israeli forces, it shattered Nasser's attempt to blockade the Gulf.

The desert tank graveyard will bear evidence of the sheer futility of Nasser's military aspirations, till the sands of time obliterate the wreckage. The whole world hoped that from great victory and utter defeat wisdom would emerge and bring lasting peace to this part of the world.

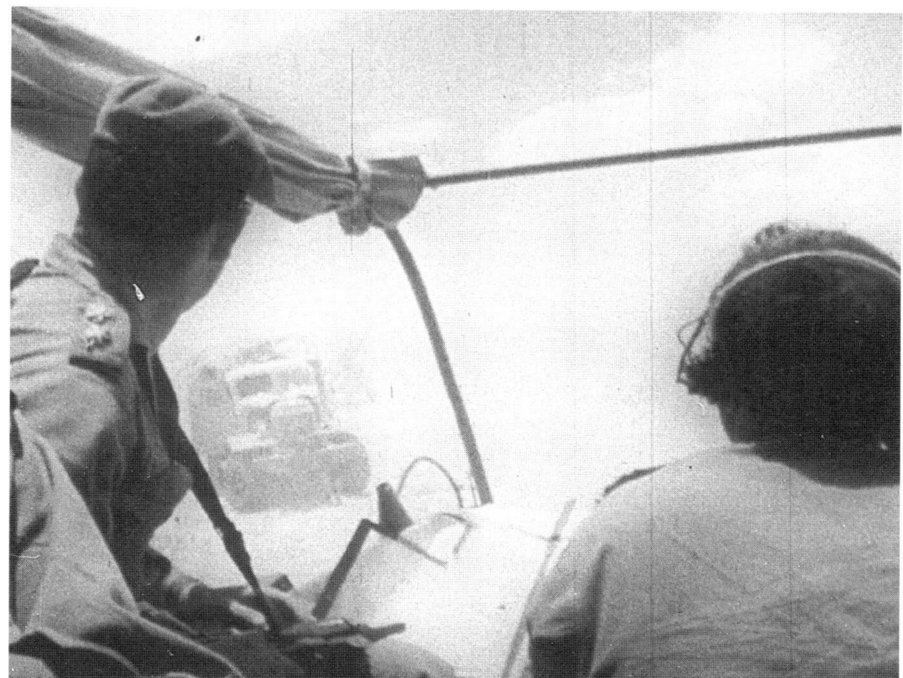

Israeli troops advance past wrecked Egyptian equipment.

SUMMIT CONFERENCE

June

Could it be that a meeting in this homely setting would make the world a safer place for us all? Until recently Glassboro was just a dot on the map. Then, suddenly the world focused on it. Two men, both with enormous power, decided to meet here and talk; exchange views for peace in a troubled world. So with the arrival of President Johnson, history came to the little hamlet, 15 miles from the city of Philadelphia. Far from the White House and much further from the Kremlin, President Johnson and Mr Kosygin had at last met.

Pressmen outside Hollybush.

President Johnson and Mr. Kosygin at summit conference.

Hollybush, a modest Victorian villa, home of the President of Glassboro State College, had suddenly become a summit meeting place. In spite of the mantle of security which immediately settled round the house, the atmosphere of homeliness could not be destroyed. Lunch-time talk included the Middle East crisis, Vietnam, and closer links between the two powerful nations. Away from the corridors of power it seemed that both could talk like friends. Outside, the world waited.

At last they appeared. Two men with the weight of world problems on their shoulders but looking relaxed like men who had enjoyed a good lunch and a useful chat. President Johnson confirmed this. He told the people of Glassboro and the press of the world that the talks had led to progress for better understanding.
Mr Kosygin showed his approval for the way things had gone. This friendly gesture was regarded a welcome sign indeed. It was hoped that Glassboro might earn the name 'The Home of Peace'.

JAYNE MANSFIELD KILLED IN CAR CRASH

July

Jayne Mansfield, one of Hollywood's greatest sex symbols, is dead. At 33, she had been married three times and was the mother of five children. Three of them were with her in the fatal car crash near New Orleans. They escaped, slightly injured, but Jayne, her lawyer friend Sam Brodie and their driver were killed. Throughout her entire career she was rarely out of the headlines. Wherever she went, even at a Royal film performance, she attracted pressmen. No-one can deny she had a flair which gave entertainment to cinema millions.

Jayne Mansfield.

Heavyweight champion Primo Carnera.

July

"Man Mountain", the "Ambling Alp", "Satchel Feet" - whatever the nickname it meant Primo Carnera, the biggest man ever to win the world heavyweight boxing championship.

Now, at 60 he is dead, exactly 34 years to the day after he won the title from Jack Sharkey. When his boxing days were over the huge 18-stone giant returned to wrestling, his first love, but whether it was boxing or wrestling, Carnera was a great entertainer. At last Primo Carnera had lost.

Night-time anarchy grips Detroit.

DETROIT RACE RIOTS

Powerless policeman watches Detroit blaze.

July

It looked like the war-time blitz on London, but this was no war. It was arson, looting; a race-riot blown up into something beyond control. At night time, anarchy took the city in its grip; and with authority powerless, looting by the bands of both races added a new dimension to terror and lawlessness.

Harlem, New York's negro quarter, began to emulate Detroit. Rioting there was nothing new but New York's police feared that this one might dwarf anything known before. All over the country law-abiding people looked to the President for a lead, but Washington was a long way away. For the moment it was a battle; authority against "crime on the rampage".

That the Federal Government was determined to grapple with all this evil had been made crystal clear by President Johnson who said: "We will not tolerate lawlessness. We will not endure violence. It matters not by whom it is done or under what slogan or banner. It will not be tolerated".

Looting and rioting in Harlem, New York.

Queen Mary says goodbye to New York on her final crossing.

QUEEN MARY LEAVES NEW YORK FOR LAST TIME

August

Atlantic travellers said there had never been a ship to equal the Queen Mary. Her sister ship was slightly bigger, the liner United States was faster, but in the affections of millions the Queen Mary has first place. New York gave her the warmest of fond farewells. For the heroine of a thousand Atlantic crossings, Mayor Lindsay had already presented to Captain Trevor Jones a bronze medallion and commemorative plaque. On board was a Pathe camera team to capture the final scenes of a sentimental journey.

Queen Mary arriving in Southampton from New York.

Queen Mary sails from Southampton on her last cruise to Long Beach, California.

The gangplank is removed for the last time at Southampton.

107
QUEEN MARY

GIBRALTAR VOTES BRITISH

September

Two hundred and fifty four years ago the "Rock" became British. A treaty signed then stated that "the Union Jack was to fly over these shores for all time", so naturally the people of Gibraltar had very strong views on Spain's demand that Gib become Spanish territory.

To demonstrate their feelings they smothered their homeland in a mass of red, white and blue; adapted Churchill's bulldog breed slogans and set out en masse for the polling stations to let the world know that they were proud to be British and nothing was going to change that.

So on Sunday, September 10th 1967, Gibraltarians let loose with one of the warmest, most emotional pro-British demonstrations the world had known for many years. The population of this land which has played such a key role in both world wars was making news once more on an international scale by proving its unswerving loyalty to the Crown. It was like a marvellous wildly happy carnival and there was the result, a resounding "yes" to staying with Britain. Of 12,182 votes cast, only 44 were against Britain. Who was it who said, "As solid as the Rock?"

Gibraltar votes to stay British.

Gibraltarians show their loyalty to Britain.

U.S.A. POPULATION EXPLOSION

November

Crowded streets in the city - any city across the breadth and depth of the nation. For the United States is in the midst of the population boom. Every eleven-and-a-half seconds a new citizen received a slap on the back and let the new world know of his arrival to join the ranks of the birth bonanza.

So, at the Washington Census Bureau, President Johnson waited for the population indicator to clock-up the country's biggest all-time score of 200 million people.

Slowly the indicator crept up to the grandest grand total in the history of the United States.

The signs show the dramatic increase of the country's population in less than 200 years. Experts reckon that at the current rate of birth acceleration, a 300 million total is possible by the turn of the century. Each baby could not care less what the figure is or will be - that's for the grown-ups to worry about. His main concern is not millions of mouths to be fed but just one - his.

President Lyndon Johnson watches population reach 200 million.

CURRENT POPULATION
of the UNITED STATES
199 999 998
1967
200 MILLION

First 200,000 Arab refugees cross River Jordan over wrecked Allenby Bridge.

Britain in 1967

In Britain, a sterling crisis in July prompted the Government to seek spending cuts and wage restraint, first voluntarily, then by a compulsory six-month pay freeze. Britain's military commitments East of Suez began to be withdrawn, to save money. Foreign problems and a dock strike at home made economic matters worse.

In November, sterling was devalued for the first time since 1950, from $2.80 to $2.40. In those days of managed exchange rates, the Government was badly harmed by the move. James Callaghan felt it necessary to resign, but Harold Wilson was convinced things would improve in time for the next election. To soften the blow Wilson made his famous statement, that "devaluation would not affect the pound in your pocket". Few believed him and within days General De Gaulle issued another stinging blow, with a "no" to Britain's entry into the EEC.

Jubilant Jeremy Thorpe - new leader of the Liberal Party.

Wilson and Brown meet De Gaulle in an effort to gain entry into the Common Market.

Barbara Castle
visits Tilbury Docks
and talks to dockers.

FATE STEPPED IN

January

It was soon after dawn that 'Bluebird' was prepared for the record attempt.

'Bluebird' rears into the air before somersaulting, killing Donald Campbell.

There was little wind. The water was smooth. The previous evening, Donald Campbell drew the ace and queen of spades, the deadly shadow of remorseless fate. He was a superstitous man, dedicated, his mission in life coming before everything. The Orpheus jet was easily capable of driving 'Bluebird' at 300 miles an hour. British the record had to remain.

He had driven his sports car for the last time, though on that perfect first run there was no hint of tragedy.

They timed him at 297 miles an hour. With luck the new record would be his but luck had run out. Fate was to strike.

Donald Campbell in 'Bluebird'.

LONDON'S CALEDONIAN MARKET

February

The Victorian clock-tower will soon be all that's left of the Caledonian Market. The 32-acre site is being developed. The market was closed in 1939. In its day it was a link with the London of bygone times. Modern ways of marketing made it obsolete.

At one time the Caledonian was a great cattle-market. The stall-holders rushed to get the best pitches like bargain-hunters at sales time. Almost everything was bought and sold. The cattle-market was only part of it.

This was a real bit of old London. Thousands will be sorry when the only reminder of it is the clock-tower.

Stall-holders rush to get the best pitches in the Caledonian market.

The clock-tower in the deserted Caladonian market.

KOSYGIN VISITS BRITAIN

February

Glasgow, the great Scottish city, left it in no doubt that north of the border Mr Kosygin had a host of friends. In St. George's Square it was friendship first, security apparently second. The Soviet Premier seemed to revel in it.

Harold Wilson greets Mr Kosygin at London Airport.

On the programme was a visit to the world's biggest nuclear station, Hunterston, 30 miles from Glasgow on the Ayrshire coast. There, as everywhere during the brief Scottish visit, Alexei Kosygin was almost on back-slapping terms with the crowd, though nobody came forward to hold hands. Even here the visitor was anxious to see as much of the "ordinary people" as time allowed.

When Mr Kosygin went to Kilmarnock football ground to see the home side play Rangers he was taken into every Scotsman's heart - football is football almost all the world over. That Ilyushin airliner at Gatwick meant all too clearly Britain was saying goodbye to Mr Kosygin. In the few days since he arrived at Heathrow, that usually serious face had often broken into smiles.

The two Prime Ministers were on excellent terms. Mr Kosygin had agreed to a hot line between No. 10 and the Kremlin and in every way Britain and the Soviets seemed far more in harmony than before the visit.

Mr Kosygin, for the time being, bade goodbye to Britain. As Scotland might say: "Will you no come back again?"

Mr Kosygin meets the players at Kilmarnock football ground.

Ford

CONCORDE PROTOTYPE

March

London to New York in three hours 17 minutes. That's the promise of Concorde, taking shape at Filton in the Brabazon hangar. The Anglo/French supersonic airliners are pushing ahead towards completion, one in Britain, one in France. They will be the first faster-than-sound airliners in the world -1,450 miles an hour, most of the way at 11 miles high. The present estimate - Concorde will give Britain and France a three-year lead over the U.S.

Also at Filton, a full-scale mock-up of the aircraft. The British prototype will fly in autumn 1968. There was a last chance for prospective buyers to suggest such minor changes as seating in the 186-foot fuselage, accommodating 136 passengers. A new era in airliners.

British prototype takes shape at Filton.

Full-scale mock up of Concorde being shown to press.

TORREY CANYON DISASTER

March

Gone to grief, immovably aground on that graveyard of ships off Lands End, the Torrey Canyon. Spewed out of her, more than 100,000 tons of crude oil, a colossal menace to holiday beaches. Safely ashore at Penzance were taken 32 members of the 61,000-ton tanker's crew. Most of the ship's company were Italians. The captain and three of his men remained aboard. Nobody at this stage could explain how the great vessel came to ground on the rocks, as she was equipped with all modern navigational aids.

Torrey Canyon crew come ashore at Penzance.

First measures taken against the 100 square mile oil slick, initially drifting less than 20 miles off the Cornish coast, were by a small flotilla of vessels spraying detergent. Then the drama took a fatal turn; an engine room explosion blew a hole through the deck. Her flying hatch cover injured the captain of the Dutch salvage crew so severely that he died soon afterwards.

Salvage operations were resumed next day in hope of refloating the ship at high water. Before that it had been suggested that napalm be used to set fire to the oil, both in the tanker and on the sea. In home waters no oil menace on anything like this scale had ever occurred. Britain could pat herself on the back whatever happens for taking such prompt action to protect the beaches.

Torrey Canyon lies with back broken.

Smoke plume after Navy bombs Torrey Canyon.

Cleaning oil from seabirds.

Firemen wash scum from Porthleven harbour at low tide.

Paris fish traders provide free seafood buffet at Les Halles, to prove oil has not affected their produce.

Oil from Torrey Canyon hits Brittany beaches.

FRANCIS CHICHESTER HOME

June

A year to remember, a scene to remember, for Francis Chichester is home. A welcoming armada went out from Portsmouth to greet the hero who had sailed round the world in a small boat, 'Gypsy Moth'. It was one of those truly great events of 1967.

Francis Chichester waves to Plymouth crowds.

Some of the Crown Jewels on display at the Tower.

CROWN JEWELS REHOUSED

July

The Tower of London, a new kind of view. It is not often a place of change and when there is, it makes news. Thousands each year go to see the Crown Jewels. This year the magnificent regalia were in a new setting, an underground stronghold where the precious treasures will be seen to the best advantage. The State Trumpets and Orders of India are set out in the upper chamber, together with maces and the beautiful Sword of State.

It is down two flights of stairs to the heavily-guarded, air-conditioned lower chamber where top-hatted wardens preside over some of the world's most historic and superb treasures. The Coronation regalia, the Ampulla and Spoon, the Queen's orb, symbol of a world dominated by Christianity, and the Sovereign's sceptre, a beautifully jewelled emblem of kingly power, with its 530 carat diamond, the largest of the four Stars of Africa.

The golden spurs made for the Coronation of Charles II together with bracelets and, of course, the magnificent crowns. Queen Mary's Crown, the Crown of India, the small diamond Crown of Queen Victoria and that of the Prince of Wales. St. Edward's Crown, because of its weight worn only briefly during Coronation and exchanged during the ceremony for the Imperial Crown, a crown of gold, diamonds and pearls, and a massive ruby. A crown fit for a Queen.

The world's largest hovercraft makes its public appearance at the Isle of Wight. It weights 165 tons and and can carry 254 passengers and 30 cars at 70 mph.

HOVERCRAFT RALLY

July

Isle of Wight, birthplace of the British hovercraft industry and the perfect place for enthusiasts of the home-built variety, to show just what can be done with enthusiasm - and skill, of course. It was the first national rally for sporting hovercraft ever held on the island; 22 enthusiasts took part in land, speed and obstacle trials.

'Hovernauts', as they like to be called, are in all shapes and sizes, both men and women. There is no such thing as the weaker sex behind the controls of a hovercraft.

Even the do-it-yourself variety of this amazing British invention can take obstacles in its stride. The manoeuvrability is something at which to wonder. Without a doubt there is a very big future for the hovercraft in many fields in transport, even perhaps on the road. Machines like this could be the hot-rods of the future.

'Hovernauts' come in all shapes and sizes.

FRANCIS CHICHESTER KNIGHTED

Gipsy Moth is greeted as she sails up the Thames.

July

Greenwich. There could be no finer setting for the final chapter in the great adventure story of a man and his boat. Thousands had come to see this historic occasion, to greet with a hero's welcome the man who was to be honoured by his Queen and public. With his family, Sir Francis Chichester came ashore from the gallant 53ft ketch, which had bought him alone, but safely, full-circle around the world to home.

Not far from here, 386 years ago, the first Queen Elizabeth knighted Sir Francis Drake. Now it was the turn of Sir Francis Chichester. With Sir Francis Drake's sword, the Queen was to dub the solo voyager Knight Commander of the Order of the British Empire.

The pink riband of the order rested on Sir Francis Chichester's shoulders. How right it was that he should be within sight of his beloved boat; a boat which had brought him 29,000 miles to the greatest honour of all - and there she was, travel-stained but worthy of a Royal visit. Queen Elizabeth II was honouring Gypsy Moth, her proud captain escorting the Queen to inspect her, just as did Sir Francis Drake to the Golden Hind with another Elizabeth.

The Queen knights Sir Francis Chichester at the Royal Naval College.

City of London greets
Sir Francis Chichester.

UFO HOAX

September

It might have been that the Martians had landed - the police were taking no chances. Six unidentified obects were found dotted across the south of England. Fifteen-year-old Neil Batey found this one. It looked like a Flying Saucer and certainly smelt like something out of this world.

A year ago the village of Warminister in Wiltshire hit the headlines. Unusual showers of meteorites rained down, followed by reports of Saucer sitings. Immediately a team from the British Unidentified Flying Objects Association went into action. Loaded with equipment they set up watching-posts and prepared to give a host of, what they hoped would be friendly, little green men, a welcome to earth they would never forget. They waited ... and waited ... and nothing happened. They reckoned that one day something would turn up, or rather come down.

For a time it seemed that predictions were true when the sextet of saucers turned up. They looked genuine at first glance, perhaps a little on the small side, but who could say how big the visitors might be? Then came the moment of truth.

It was a hoax.

UFO watcher at Clevedon, Somerset.

Neil Batey with the UFO he found.

The QE2 under construction, and at its launch.

QE2 LAUNCHED

September

On September 20th at Clydebank, Britain's newest liner was launched. At last the big secret was out; she was to bear the name 'Queen Elizabeth II'. It was a fine tribute to Her Majesty who performed the launching ceremony. The new Queen of the Seas was a proud sight.

PRINCE CHARLES GOES TO CAMBRIDGE

October

Cambridge. Trinity College waited to welcome a new freshman and it's not every newcomer who is greeted by the Master, Lord Butler, but the new boy was the heir to the throne, arriving in a Mini for a major step in his career. The occasion was both informal and formal, with Lord Butler introducing Prince Charles to Mr Denis Marrian, the senior tutor.

It was clear from the start that the college motto, 'Always the same', would not really apply for the next two years while the Prince studied archaeology and anthropology there.

There was even a ceremony of the key; not exactly the Tower of London style but a sign of independence for the Royal teenager. Then with Lord Butler a stroll round Great Court, - a walk which would become familiar to the Prince in the months to come. For more than 400 years countless other students have looked on Trinity as home from home and to help Prince Charles settle in, Robert Woods, a third year student, took him on a short tour.

First the Reading Room and then to the Elizabethan Dining Hall where, with 230 other young men, he would take his meals. The magnificent stained glass window was of special interest to the Prince, for it commemorates his Royal predecessors who studied at Trinity. So a new boy joined the ranks of the freshmen at Cambridge - a student prince.

Prince Charles arriving at Trinity College.

JODRELL BANK LISTENS TO VENUS

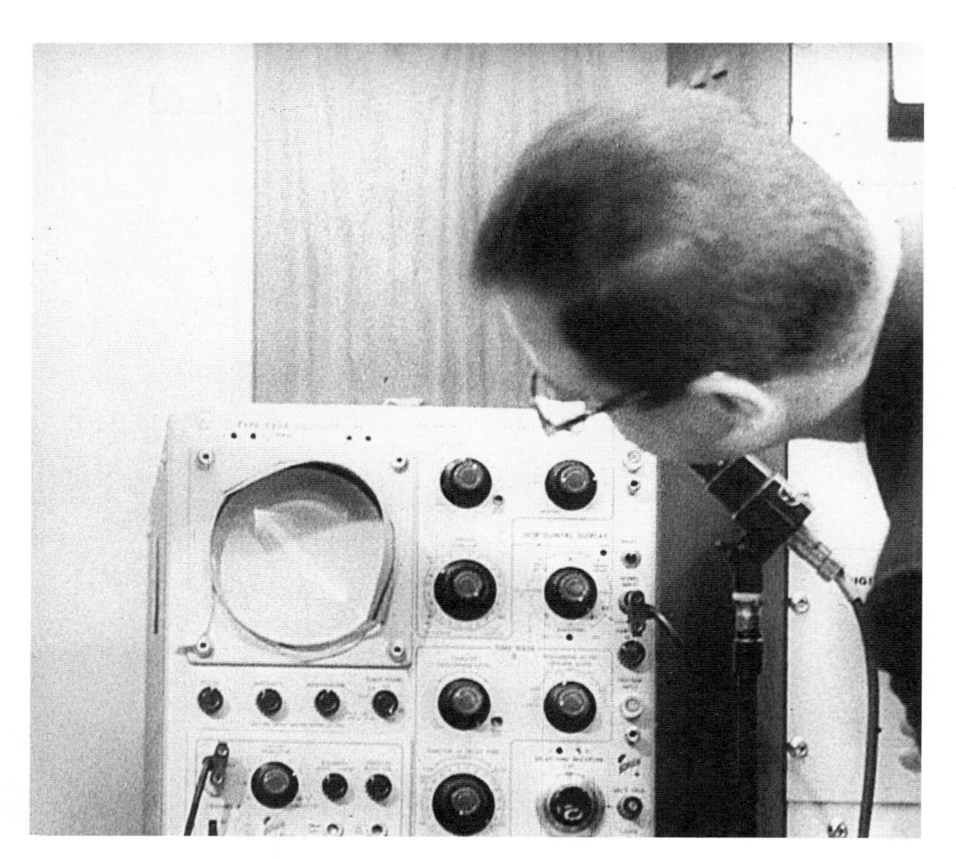

Scientists watch signals from Russian Venus probe.

October

Jodrell Bank. Britain's giant radio telescope listened in across 50 million miles of space to the new voice of the planet Venus. The weird noise was music to the ears of earthbound scientists. It meant that Soviet achievements had taken another step towards the stars.

Flying into Britain, which helped the Soviets achieve that magnificent space spectacular, by lending our ears as it were, came Soviet space hero cosmonaut Valery Bykovsky. The Ilyushin airliner brought the record-breaking marathon space voyager to Britain on a seven-day visit at the invitation of the British Soviet Friendship Association, to celebrate the 50th anniversary of the Russian revolution. Bykovsky made the historic space rendezvous with the first woman cosmonaut four years ago.

The radio telescope at Jodrell Bank.

HITHER GREEN RAIL CRASH

November

Here, in the early light of day, could be seen the full extent of the train crash which claimed 55 lives. The previous night the normal quiet of this London suburb had been shattered. Ambulances, fire appliances and rescue workers had hurried into the narrow streets near Hither Green station. The Hastings to Charing Cross express crash was a bad one.

The death toll mounted. At least 139 were injured - some seriously. The dreaded task of finding victims went on non-stop throughout the night.

Stretcher after stretcher was brought through from the scene of Britain's worst train disaster for 10 years. For some there was nothing that could be done. When the express left the rails, it was travelling at high speed - normal on this stretch of line. Again the unsuspected claimed its victims. They were clamped in the tangled masses of metal.

When day came, the red-rimmed eyes of the rescue workers told as much of the harrowing story as the wreckage itself. In two days 92 people had died. It was a black weekend in Britain.

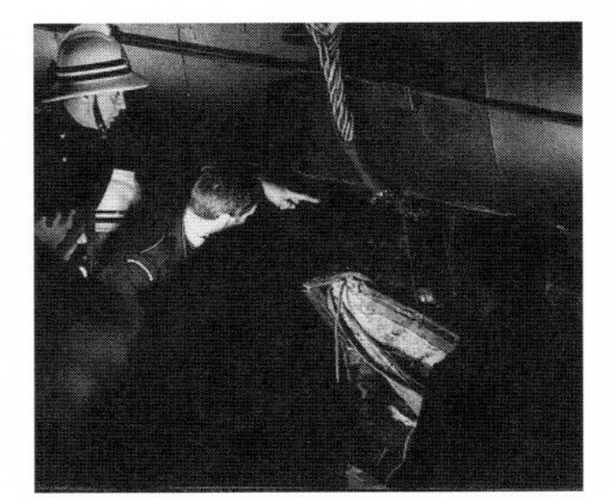

Firemen direct rescue work.

Cranes clear the wreckage of the express train derailed near Hither Green.

Bodies being taken from the wrecked train.

STOCK EXCHANGE CLOSES

November

The newspapers posed questions but facts were facts - the pound had been devalued. On Monday, after the announcement, the Stock Exchange was empty. There was no trading but outside in Throgmorton Street brokers and jobbers crowded together - not to carry on business but to try and sort out what the drop in the pound's value would mean to them when they started work next morning.

There was no point in going to the bank - they were all closed for the day while their staffs made all necessary adjustments. It seemed to be a black, moneyless Monday. We were told devaluation would mean bigger and better export sales, more employment and the chance to get the nation back on its financial feet.

The following day there was plenty of action at the Stock Exchange. The long weekend was over.

Jobbers crowd
Throgmorton Street after
pound is devalued.

EARL ATTLEE'S MEMORIAL SERVICE

November

Westminster Abbey. In the beauty and peace of this holy place, 2,000 people gathered to pay final tribute to Earl Attlee. The ashes of the man who was Prime Minister from 1945-1951 were going to their last resting place.

The procession escorting the casket, carried by the Clerk of Works, solemnly made its way to the shallow grave not far from that of the Unknown Warrior. Earl Attlee's family followed, sadly, but proud in the knowledge that only the truly great rest here; and placing by the grave the Orders and Decorations of the man who became his friend was Charles Griffiths, his former batman.

Earl Attlee's grand-daughter stepped forward to lay a simple wreath by the tomb. The Duke of Westminster, representing the Queen, paid tribute.

Clement Attlee.

RED PANDAS IN LONDON ZOO

December

Two red pandas made their very cute debut before the British public. They were bought recently from a German zoo. Now that routine checks on their health had been carried out they were the first of their breed on view in London for five years. They are called Rama and Suka. Everyone was keen to make a fuss of them. Big cousin Chi-Chi was not used to sharing the limelight but Rama and Suka - male and female respectively - may be able to teach her a few things about marital bliss before she meets An-An again.

Red panda at London Zoo.

CONCORDE DEBUT

Marne Davis' space-helmeted uniform.

December

Toulouse. The giant hangar at Sud-Aviation headquarters was the focal point of the world. Inside was the most exciting new thing in the world of aviation - Concorde number 001. The giant gleaming white dart which points the way to the supersonic future of inter-continental transport was about to make its public debut.

At last the Anglo-French brain-child, born out of the technical and very sensible collaboration of two nations, could be shown to an envious world - at least five years before any rival.

Mr Wedgwood-Benn, Minister of Technology, and Monsieur Jean Chamont, French Minister of Transport, were ready to cut the tapes and launch the greatest airliner ever built. Monsieur Chamont greeted airline representatives, including space-helmeted hostess Marne Davis.
Mr Wedgwood-Benn also had a warm word of welcome for the visitors who came to see this majestic moment as Concorde rolled out into the open.

English and French technicians watched proudly the result of their work being admired - theirs was co-operation on a grand scale. For the two Ministers also, a time of happy unity. Mr Wedgwood-Benn had settled a point of conflict over the 1,500 miles an hour bird - Concorde was to be spelt the French way, with an 'e'.

Concorde was in accord, Britain and France in partnership. Concorde looked good and certainly will be proved good when it flies at the end of February. That job will be up to test pilots André Turcat and Brian Trubshaw. Together Britain and France look set for a supersonic boom time with Concorde.

Visitors inspect prototype Concorde.

Test pilots André Turcat and Brian Trubshaw.

John Lennon at the opening of Apple boutique.

The lighter side of 1967

1967 was the year that "flower-power" came to Britain and the 60s revolution began to change course. Teenagers started to try to put into practice the philosophies emerging from alternative forms of culture. Some made attempts to create new lifestyles. The pop phenomenon of super-groups continued and the U.S. tried to rival The Beatles with its own Fab Four, The Monkees. Pathe News kept cinema audiences up-to-date and ensured that those less interested in the "Swinging 60s" had their fair share of sporting entertainment.

The Monkees arrive at London Airport.

Displaying Mary Quant boot fashionsa.

Patrick McNee
and Twiggy.

AVENGERS, RIGG'S NEW RIG

January

The photocall at Teddington Studios was a gathering of fame and beauty. Patrick McNee posed with Twiggy. The Avengers star did not want to steal the picture - he shared it with the internationally famous model. Similarly, Diana Rigg was photographed with George Mallet. Everybody present had earned distinction. George is an Olympic weightlifter. Lifting Diana was much more pleasant than lifting a barbell. The main object of the call was to display the clothes and fashions the Avengers were wearing in their new series.

Olympic star Linda Ludgrove and champion jockey Josh Gifford were also present.

Diana was in Alan Hughes' designs, for the role of Emma Peel. Pierre Cardin's designs were eminently right for John Steed. The Avengers were already big dollar earners for Britain. Helping to dress the set, Graham Hill, who was photographed as much as the stars. Good luck to all concerned. More dollars wanted urgently.

Patrick McNee (John Steed) and Diana Rigg (Emma Peel).

BRIDE'S NEW LINES

January

Brides-to-be have a good look. Because if you are of a "with it" disposition, this is the kind of outfit you may well want to wear for the great occasion. It's the very latest - a bridal gear gown. Matching outfits, too, featured in a display of new nuptial styles at a London fashion show - bride and bridesmaid, naturally. They call this wedding day special "Soft Shoe Shuffle".

How about this for a Big Day trio? Mod bride, gear groom, and bridesmaid to match. They call this bridesmaid's outfit 'Rave'. Description: frilly pyjama style with ruffs around the sleeves matching those on the pants. Enter the bride, her gown is called 'The Swinger'. It had to come - the time when Carnaby Street-style creations gave a new line to blushing brides.

New bridal fashions.

ELVIS MARRIES PRISCILLA

May

Heart-throb pop singer Elvis Presley is a real-life bridegroom at last. Eight years ago, when he was a soldier in Germany, he met Priscilla Beaulieu, daughter of a U.S. lieutenant-colonel who was also serving there. As she was then only 14 they had to wait for a time. Now, who could say who was the luckier, 'The Pelvis' or pretty Priscilla? The millionaire film star singer, in bride-choosing as in everything else, had terrific success.

JIM CLARK WINS DUTCH GRAND PRIX

June

Jack Brabham was all set in his Repco-Brabham for the Dutch Grand Prix. Driving a Honda, John Surtees. Seventeen cars lined up. Back in the third row, Jim Clark. His first time out in a remarkable new Lotus-Ford. Ninety laps of the circuit, 235 miles in all. Clark biding his time. John Surtees, Denny Hulme, Chris Amon. Graham Hill had to retire with engine trouble. With Graham Hill out of the running, Clark took the lead. At an average of 104.4 mph a great triumph for an untried car. Jim Clark won the Dutch Grand Prix for the fourth time.

Jim Clark acknowledging the cheers of the crowd.

Jim Clark with victory wreath.

HAILWOOD WINS ISLE OF MAN T.T.

June

All set for the battle of the giants. Mike Hailwood's Honda gets a last check-over under the champ's watchful eye. Nearby, ready for action on a MV Agusta, Italian motor-cycle star Giacomo Agostini. The race - the Diamond Jubilee Senior T.T. There was a big line-up of starters but in this event only two men mattered.... Hailwood - number 4 and Agostini - number 9.

It was clear the pace would be hot. Hailwood and Agostini were forcing the field along at a cracking rate. Hailwood was getting every last bit of power out of his big machine and Agostini was closing. The rest of the riders were just making up numbers. Hailwood had rocketed the lap record to 108.77 mph; Agostini was with him but then tragedy for the Italian. On the fifth of the six-lap race the Agusta's chain broke. Agostini was out of the race. There was nothing to stop the great Mike Hailwood. His winning time - a record 105.62 mph.

Mike Hailwood during
Isle of Man T.T.

Sgt PEPPERS
LONELY HEARTS
CLUB BAND

NEW TOY FOR LENNON'S SON

July

Ready to roll to Weybridge, a gipsy-type caravan, a present for a four-year old who probably has everything. The name Julian Lennon, son of John Lennon - who else but the Beatle? It is about £4,000 worth of gaily painted, renovated rolling stock. A big toy for a little boy. It even needed a police escort but it is not every dad who spends that kind of money on his youngster. This might be one occasion when "Money can buy love". So the waggon rolled west - onward towards Weybridge and the Lennon homestead. Sometimes the going got tough.

The pity of it all was that young Julian wasn't there to see his present arrive. He was on holiday with Mum and Dad. If he ever decides to leave home and it seems scarcely likely, he'll be the best-equipped gipsy on the road.

Lennon senior's new toy: £6,000 Rolls Royce Phantom with with £1,000 worth of decoration.

Julian Lennon's gipsy caravan.

MONKEES AT HEATHROW AIRPORT

July

At Heathrow Airport there was no mistaking that Peter, Davy, Mike and Micky were on their way.

What seemed like a highly-trained team of hysterical mini-skirters could scarcely bear the excitement as The Monkees landed. There they were - long hair and "with-it" gear - everything to make the fans go wild. The Monkees certainly could not have been disappointed with the reception. Naturally the press was there - ready for anything to happen. They weren't disappointed. Where there's a will there's always a way through any barrier.

It certainly was "way out" and that's the way one of The Monkees headed. The group knew that their brand of "Monkey Business" means big business and they gave the press the full treatment.

Questions? Well, they were asked a few, but being The Monkees nobody really expected a straight answer. They didn't get one.

Screaming fans greet The Monkees at London Airport.

MONKEES
AT WEMBLEY
Friday June 30
Saturday July 1
Sunday July 2
Peter Tork

Screaming teenagers at one of The Monkees concerts.

ROLLING STONES CLEARED

August

London. It is years since such crowds gathered to await an Appeal verdict but this was the Rolling Stones' case, with the fans out in force.

When Mick Jagger was conditionally discharged and Keith Richard's sentence quashed, the pop idols drove off, the shadow of gaol no longer over them.

Mick held a press conference in Soho soon afterwards. Keith had chicken-pox so could not be there but Marianne Faithfull was present, delighted with the verdict. Mick and Marianne were on top of the world again and so were their millions of fans. For the press their verdict was front page news throughout the Western world.

Marianne Faithfull appears before press with Mick Jagger.

Mick Jagger after his conditional discharge.

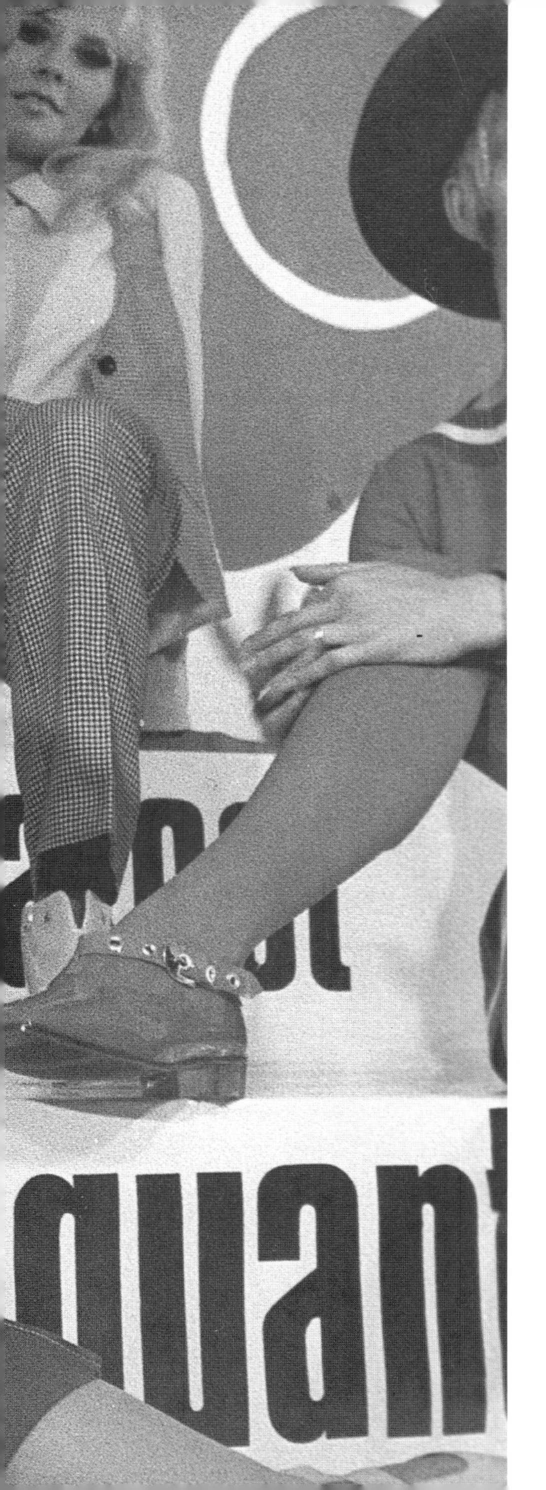

MARY QUANT FASHION BOOTS

August

When Mary Quant invades new realms of fashion, bright young girls are interested and so is the national press. As the outcome of two years' hard work, Mary has perfected the thing for which the new generation has been hoping, boots and shoes that are distinctive, comfortable, washable and almost indestructable. Mary believes that footware should fit like a glove. Wear the latest kind when you're young and in later life you'll never complain that your feet are killing you. That sounds like a wonderful future, viewed from any angle.

Next season's forecast - thigh-length boots, high enough to reach the hem of the skirt. In fashion, new ideas arrive from some of the most unlikely places.

If you think boots must be all in one piece, observe the detachable top which comes off with a zip, either for wearing as shoes or with other tops of different colours. With all the new materials, the saying "There's nothing like leather" is old hat.

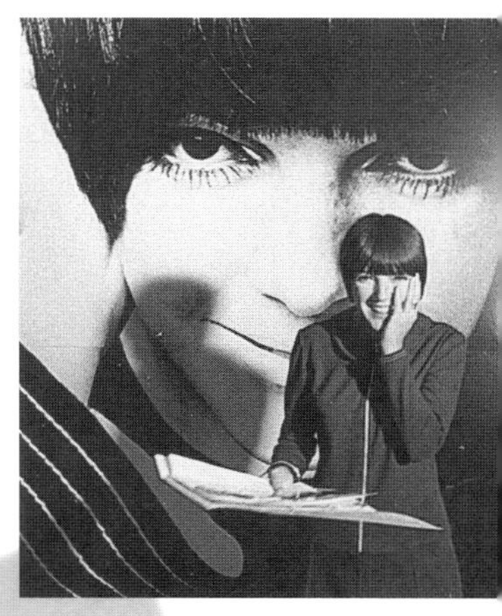

Mary Quant's boot and shoe fashions.

DUNSTABLE FLYING SHOW

August

Revived interest in ballooning was much in evidence at the London Gliding Club's air display. Don Piccard's hot-air variety uses propane burners underneath the bag. It soon becomes lighter than the atmosphere and up it goes. Gas-filled balloons were also there and so were several gliders but undoubtedly what stole the show were the flying machines of World War One vintage, notably the Fokker. A Vickers Gunbus of the same period accepted the German challenge. With crude gun-mountings pilots fought the crucial dog-fights of those days.

Parachutes towed into the air by cars reduce the cost for the learner. He gets the hang of the art without having to hire an aircraft from which to jump in the novice stage. A girl stood up to the 80 mph slipstream on top of the wing, recalling the stunts performed in the1920s. Had she fallen she might have dropped into nearby Woburn Park, seat of the Duke of Bedford, where the flower-power people attended a "love-in" in ducal surroundings.

Standing up to the 80 mph slipstream.

Up, up and away at the Dunstable air rally.

DUKE'S FLOWER POWER

August

Here again, Don Piccard demonstrated the hot air balloon. The idea was first used in France almost 200 years ago. Ascents in hydrogen-filled balloons cost £200 a flight for the gas. Hot air, as every public speaker knows, is very much cheaper.

Teenagers fill the balloon basket with carnations for Piccard to distribute among the flower-people. The flower-people believe that life should be lived in kindness, peace, gentleness and love. For three days at Woburn they paid 30/- each and the weather was wonderful. You really want it fine and sunny for a love-in. Whether the new philosophy will develop into a nation-wide cult or fade away like the flowers remains to be seen.

Flower power at the Duke of Bedford's "Festival of the Flower Children'.

"Be sure to wear some flowers in your hair".

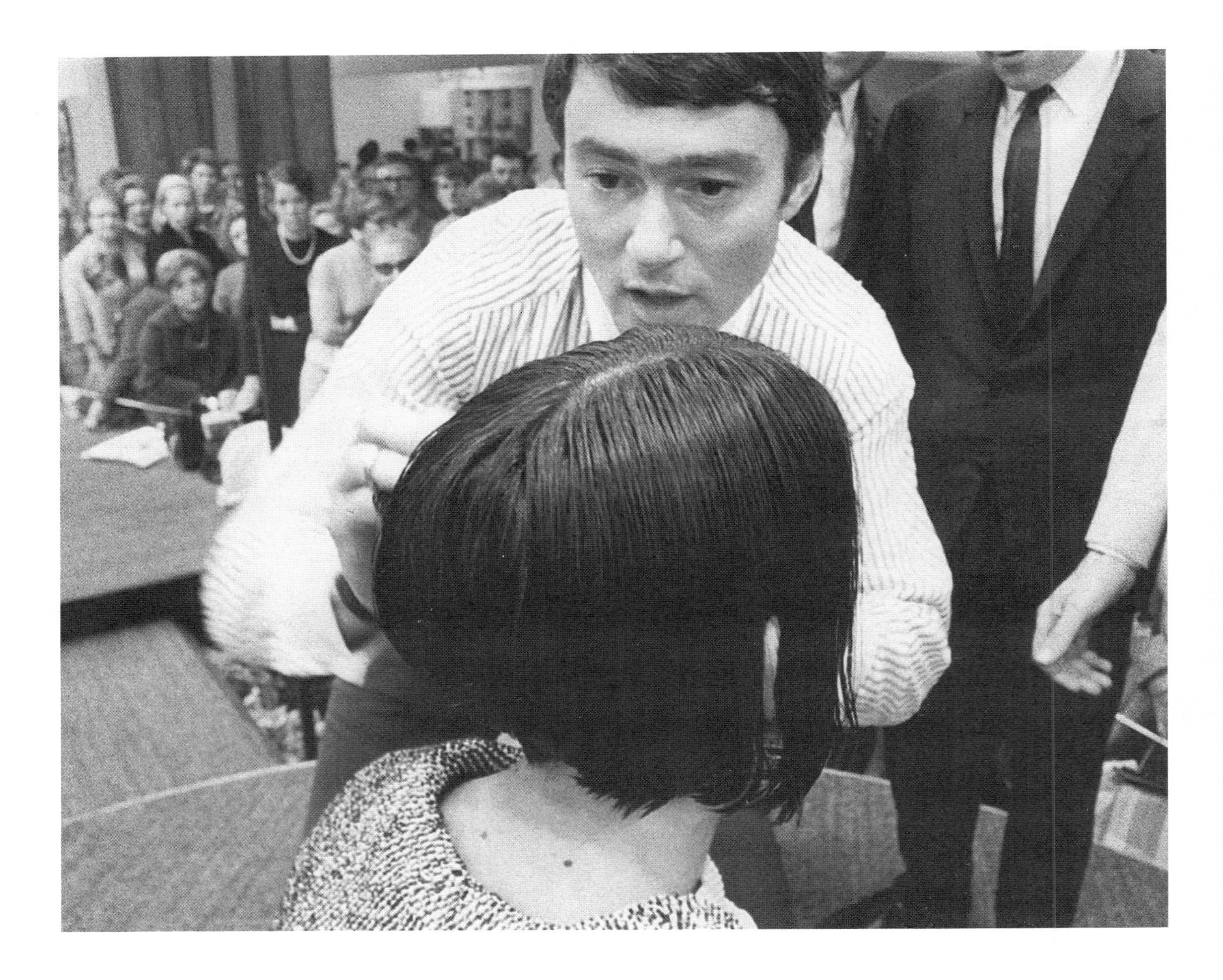

EUROCOIFFURE '67

October

Eurocoiffure '67 they called it and it proved a magnet for some of Britain's and Europe's top mop manipulators. They had gathered at the seaside to make public their crowning glory creations - at a time when female fashions guide the male eye to everywhere but the head. So there was plenty of room at the top to refocus eyes from dresses to tresses.

It is almost pure art the way hairdressers like Vidal Sassoon produce new styles. He, of course, is a world leader in this field but every other exhibitor at the coiffure convention was out to show that they, too, had some heady ideas - both for themselves and their models.

There are some people who are never satisfied. While Samson could really use a little more on top, the Delilah trend these days is ridiculous. A hairpiece for him covers those wide open spaces. For her it is nothing more than an instant hair-do. It is the same old story - the more you have the more you want.

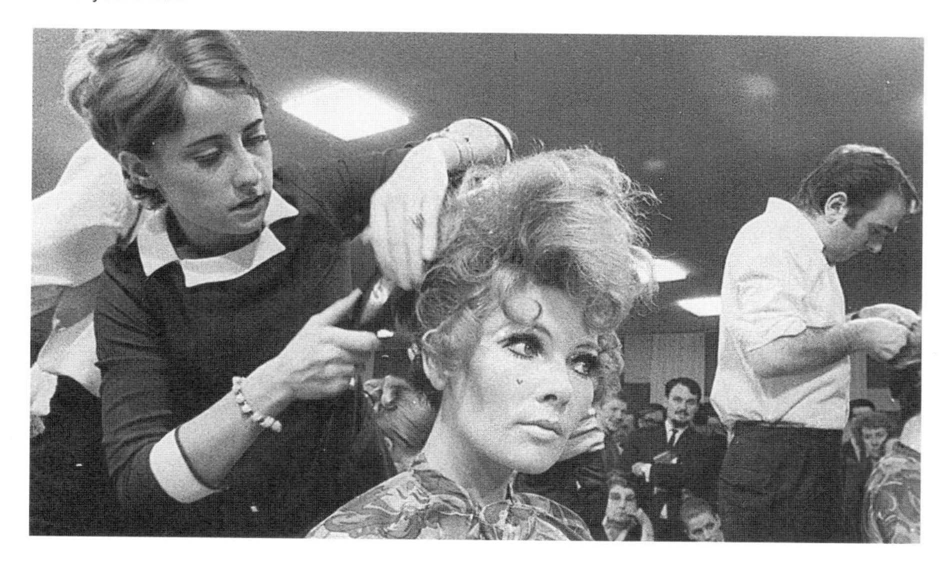

Another competitor uses the 'back-brushing' technique.

Vidal Sassoon at Eurocoiffure '67 in Brighton.

NEW AVENGER'S GIRL

October

London. The unmistakable calling cards of Steed. The immaculate Avenger was introducing his new TV team-mate. She's Linda Thorsen, a 20-years-old goodlooker from Canada, who joins Patrick McNee as his third leading lady in 'The Avengers' series. There is plenty to celebrate for the show is a hit everywhere, especially in the States where it is a big dollar earner for Britain. The press turned out in force to meet Linda, who was chosen from 200 actresses to star as Steed's new playmate Miss Tara King. She follows in the footsteps of Diana Rigg and Honor Blackman but she will not be an Emma Peel or Cathy Gale. Tara will foil the bad men with femininity - she has plenty of that.

New Avengers star Linda Thorsen meets Patrick McNee at the Savoy Hotel.

1967

Lifestyle

The Society of Snuff grinders, blenders and purveyors in session.

Vauxhall Viva Estate - from only £729.

Petrol 'star' grading announced.

'Buy British' girls in Union Jack theme outfits fly to Geneva Motor Show.

Lifestyle

Swinging London continued to promote its youth culture as 1967 became the year of Flower Power, typified by the festival held at Woburn Abbey but the Flower Children had brought their drugs culture from California. The Rolling Stones received prison sentences, later quashed on appeal, for drug offences, and the Beatles were accused of encouraging use of LSD in their songs.

Sex also hit the headlines as the Government legalised adult homosexuality and the Abortion Bill, which permitted medical termination of pregnancy, was passed after months of controversy.

London: Birth control to be supplied on the rates.

More than half a million people sign petition against Abortion Bill.

Experimental open plan office at Beecham House in Brentford.

Plans for the new town of Milton Keynes announced.

Subscriber Trunk Dialling was being introduced, costing 2d per unit.

£1,000 would buy the Comfort Furniture Champagne Suite.

London: Decimal Currency Bill published (finally introduced Feb1971).

After dinner, then what?

ROYAL MINT-CHOCOLATE LIQUEUR
of course!
Unique from France . . . with the luxuriously smooth taste of after-dinner chocolate mints 41/- a bottle : 17/- a flask
From good wine merchants and stores
MAURICE MEYER LTD 1 Crutched Friars London EC3

A three-minute phone call to Paris cost seven shillings.

Most daily newspapers cost 4d; The Times cost 6d.

JWT
DECIMAL CURRENCY
CONVERSION TABLE
OLD NEW PENCE
HEINZ BAKED BEANS
Batchelors BROAD BEANS
Batchelors GARDEN PEAS
HEINZ Curried Beans with sultanas
57 VARIETIES
6 np.
11 np.

Victoria Station, London in the rush hour.

LSD paintwork car.

A letter cost 4d and a postcard 3d.

Disinfected straw on Marlow Bridge to prevent spread of foot and mouth epidemic.

"Colonel Bogey" five trumpet motor horn - only £19 9s 6d.

A television licence cost £5; a radio licence £1 5s.

A three-year driving licence cost 15s.

An annual motor car licence cost £17 10s.

Motique - Barbara Kelly's mobile boutique visits Richmond.

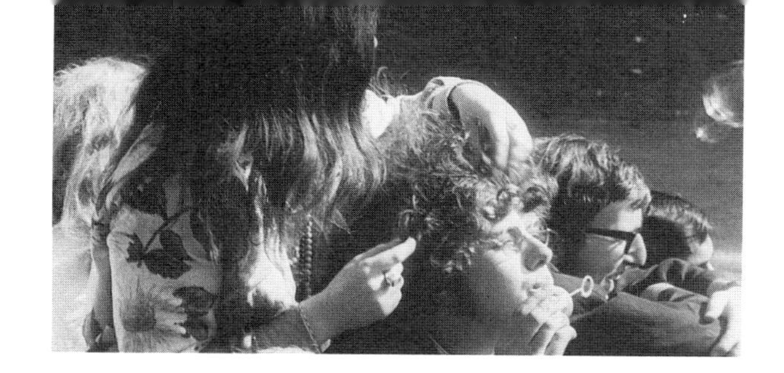

Three hundred flower people at Love-in at Henrietta Park in Bath.

Lunn Poly offered 15 days' holiday in Spain from only 29 guineas.

LSE students staged sit-in protest.

'Legalise Pot' rally in Hyde Park.

Southampton students' rag week stretcher race.

Bruce Forsyth crowns winner of Baby of the Year Competition - Julianne Edith Waterworth.

'Boys' Own Paper' closes down as circulation falls to 24,000.

Bunnies at Playboy Club help Salvation Army raise £3 million for needy children.

Children at Stony Stratford primary school.

Two-month-old pearly 'royal' Kim O'Shea is christened at St.Martin-in-the-Fields.

Society for Protection of Unborn Children formed.

Psychedelic styles for prams and mini skirts.

Fred Titmus, England cricketeer, serving in his sweet shop at Hatfield.

Yves St.Laurent fashion show in Paris.

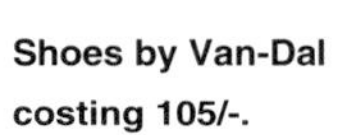

Shoes by Van-Dal costing 105/-.

Ladies broad-fitting high-heel shoes £5.5s.

Shoes by Wildsmith & Co costing £15.15.0.

Carnaby Street mini skirts.

Crowd watching Derby at Epsom.

Way Out Fashions designed by Clive.

1967

Entertainment

Screaming teenagers at pop concert.

TV play 'Cathy Come Home' meets controversy.

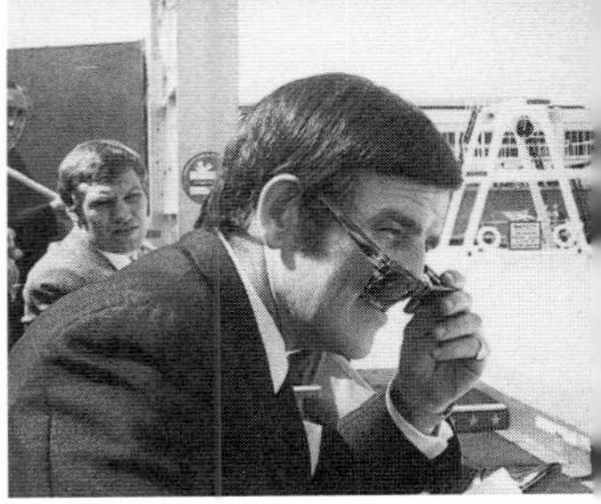

Simon Dee (left) and Alan Freeman (right) Radio 1 DJs

World of Entertainment

Cinema-goers saw Paul Schofield and Robert Shaw play Sir Thomas More and Henry VIII in the award-winning historial drama 'A Man for All Seasons'. Even further back in time was Rachel Welsh in 'One Million Years BC', while David Hemmings and Vanessa Redgrave portrayed the swinging London of the day in 'Blow-up'.

London certainly swung to the beat of The Monkees, the U.S. answer to The Beatles, when they arrived at Heathrow Airport met by their screaming fans. Englebert Humperdinck's, number one hit 'Release Me' stayed in the charts for 56 weeks.

U.K.: BBC1 screens 'The Forsyte Saga' by John Galsworthy.

U.S.: Golden Globe awards go to 'Georgie Girl', 'A Man for All Seasons' and 'Alfie'.

London: Picasso sold for record $532,000.

Michael Caine receives 'Best Film Actor of the Year' award for 'Alfie'.

London: Tom Stoppard's 'Rosencranz and Guildenstern are Dead', opens.

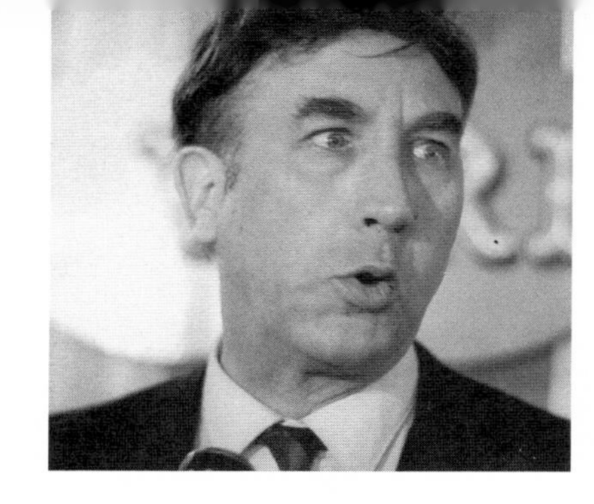

Frankie Howerd - 'Show Business Personality of the Year'.

Academy Awards

Best Picture
'A Man for All Seasons'

Best Director
Fred Zinnemann
'A Man for All Seasons'

Best Actor
Paul Scofield
'A Man for All Seasons'

Best Actress
Elizabeth Taylor
'Who's Afraid of Virginia Woolf?'

Best Supporting Actor
Walter Matthau
'The Fortune Cookie'

Best Supporting Actress
Sandy Dennis
'Who's Afraid of Virginia Woolf'

Richard Burton receiving 'Best British Actor' at the British Film Academy awards.

David Frost attends Show Business Personality awards.

Val Doonican - 'Top BBC TV Personality' - with his wife at Show Business Personality awards.

Elizabeth Taylor receiving 'Best British Actress' at the British Film Academy awards.

The Beatles.

Number 1 singles in 1967

Green Green Grass of Home	Tom Jones	1st December '66	7 wks
I'm a Believer	Monkees	19th January	4 wks
This Is My Song	Petula Clark	16th February	2 wks
Release Me	Englebert Humperdinck	2nd March	6 wks
Something Stupid	Nancy & Frank Sinatra	13th April	2 wk
Puppet On a String	Sandie Shaw	27th April	3 wks
Silence is Golden	Tremeloes	18th May	3 wks
A Whiter Shade of Pale	Procul Harum	8th June	6 wks
All You Need is Love	Beatles	19th July	3 wks
San Francisco (Be Sure to Wear Some Flowers In Your Hair)	Scott McKenzie	9th August	4 wks
The Last Waltz	Englebert Humperdinck	6th September	5 wks
Massachusetts	Bee Gees	11th October	4 wks
Baby Now That I've Found You	Foundations	8th November	2 wks
Let the Heartaches Begin	Long John Baldry	22nd November	2 wks
Hello Goodbye	Beatles	6th December	7 wks

BBC Radios 1, 2, 3 and 4 replace the Light and Third Programmes and the Home Service.

London: 17 DJs from closed pirate radio stations, including Tony Blackburn and John Peel, are to join the BBC.

London: Publishers of 'Last Exit to Brooklyn' sent for trial for obscenity. Found guilty in November.

Grammy awards	
Best record:	'Up, Up and Away' by 5th Dimension
Best album:	'Sgt. Pepper's Lonely Hearts Club Band' by The Beatles

Tickets to Monkees Concert at Empire Pool, Wembley cost 7s. 6d to £1.10s.

U.K.: The Monkees appearance at Heathrow leads to wild scenes.

The Monkees - from left to right Mike Nesmith, Davy Jones, Micky Dolenz and Peter Tork.

The Rolling Stones - from left to right Mick Jagger, Charlie Watts, Brian Jones, Bill Wyman and Keith Richard.

U.K.: Rolling Stones' song 'Let's Spend the Night together' banned from Eamonn Andrews Show.

London: Rolling Stones on drugs charge - they receive prison sentences which are quashed on appeal.

1967

War & Politics

Kinshasa - 10,000 riot and sack Belgian Embassy.

Paris - Wilson and Brown meet De Gaulle in effort to gain entry into Common Market.

War & Politics

Vietnam was the major world battlefield of 1967. The North Vietnamese were not deterred by the escalation of U.S. bombing, while anti-Vietnam protest rallies increased the pressure on the U.S. government.

In June, Israel won a decisive victory in the Six-Day War, following Arab threats of invasion. Army colonels seized power in Greece and King Constantine was forced to flee after his counter-coup failed. Nigeria suffered civil war as its Eastern Region declared its independance as the Republic of Biafra.

In Britain, Prime Minister Harold Wilson's approaches to join the EEC were rebuffed. British troops were withdrawn from Aden as it declared itself the People's Republic of South Yemen but Gibraltar remained British after an overwhelming vote in a referendum.

2nd January
U.S.: Ronald Reagan is appointed Governor of California.

18th January
U.K.: Jeremy Thorpe becomes leader of Liberal Party, after Joe Grimond resigns.

26th February
Vietnam: U.S. launches major attack on Viet Cong HQ.

2nd February
George Brown signs Space Treaty.

Jeremy Thorpe meets press as new leader of the Liberal Party.

Manny Shinwell resigns as Chairman of Parliamentary Labour Party.

1st March
Aden: British troops fire on rioters.

1st April
U.K.: First Ombudsman starts work.

Indira Ghandi wins further term as Prime Minister after close election battle.

15th April
U.S.: 200,000 in protest against Vietnam war.

Bombing of Vietnamese jungle.

2nd May
London: Britain to apply for EEC membership.

18th May
UAR: UN peace-keeping force on Israeli border to be withdrawn.

30th May
Nigeria: Independent Republic of Biafra breaks away from Nigeria.

5th June
Israel: Six-Day War begins.

5th July
Tel Aviv: Moshe Dayan announces that Gaza has been annexed.

7th July
Nigeria: Nigerian troops invade Biafra - Britons and Americans flee.

Hoard of narcotics uncovered by Hong Kong police awaits disposal at city's incinerator.

23rd July
Race riots and
looting in Newark,
New Jersey.

SCHARF'S

London: Biafran demonstration. Biafrans march to Number 10 urging Britain to take neutral line in their dispute with the Nigerian government.

12th August
Washington: North Vietnamese bombing targets announced by President Johnson.

23rd September
Moscow: USSR signs aid pact with North Vietnam.

U.S. ground, air and waterborne forces continue their battle with the Viet Cong.

3rd October
Vietnam: U.S. offer of peace talks is rejected.

21st October
Washington: Violence erupts at Vietnam peace rally.

29th November
London: Jim Callaghan becomes Home Secretary, Roy Jenkins becomes Chancellor.

British pilots released - Captain David Taylor home after being held hostage for 12 weeks in Algeria.

7th December
Aden: Union Jack lowered in Aden as British troops withdraw.

29th October
Israel shells Port Suez oil refinery in retaliation against sinking of Israeli Warship 'Eilat'. £10,000,000 refinery destroyed.

17th December
Australia: Australian Prime Minister Harold Holt drowns while swimming.

Exterior of new building.

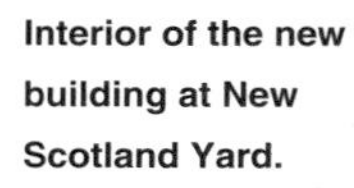

Interior of the new building at New Scotland Yard.

Old New Scotland Yard.

1967

Births, Deaths & Marriages

Tony Hatch marries Jackie Trent

1st January

Michelle Holmes
(British actress
Tina Fowler in
'Coronation Street')

2nd July

Sue Devany
(British
actress/singer)

7th July

Jackie Thorn
(Graphic designer)

Births, Deaths & Marriages

Many famous personalities from all walks of life died in 1967. Some had achieved a full life - others were still climbing upwards in their chosen careers.

Pathe News recorded the funerals of statesmen such as Clement Attlee and provided a tribute to entertainers and sportsmen, including Jayne Mansfield and Primo Carnera.

Pathe cameras were also there at the weddings of the famous, bringing their joy and happiness before the British people.

31st July

Greg Benson
(Australian actor
Matt Wilson in
'Home and Away')

20th October

Susan Tully
(British actress
Michelle in
'East Enders')

21st December

Nicola Cowper
(British actress)

16th November

Lisa Bonet
(U.S. actress)

Actress Susan Tully who plays Michelle Fowler in the BBC soap series 'Eastenders'.

3rd January
Jack Ruby
(U.S. killer)

4th January
Donald Campbell
(British racer)

10th June
Spencer Tracy
(U.S. actor)

8th July
Vivien Leigh
(British actress)

21st July
Basil Rathbone
(British actor)

29th June
Jayne Mansfield
(U.S. actress)

9th August
Joe Orton
(British Playwright)

Joe Orton, watching rehearsals of his first play 'Entertaining Mr. Sloane' in 1964.

27th August
Brian Epstein
(Beatles manager)

8th October
Clement Attlee,
(British statesman)

Adam Faith and Jackie Irving.

1st April

Dennis Fairey

Jo Bradley

14th February

Raquel Welch

Patrick Curtis

1st May

Elvis Presley

Priscilla Beaulieu

24th August

Adam Faith

Jackie Irving

1967

Disasters

Volunteers fight oil pollution from 'Torrey Canyon' on a West Country beach.

U.S.: Three U.S. astronauts killed in spacecraft fire probably caused by faulty wiring.

Disasters

November was a black month for disasters in Britain. A Spanish airliner crashed near London, killing 37 people. The next day an express train left the rails near Hither Green, killing 55 passengers and injuring many more.

Disaster also hit the Space Race; three U.S. astronauts died as a fire swept through their capsule during a rehearsal and a Soviet cosmonaut was killed as his spacecraft crashed during re-entry.

U.K.: 'Torrey Canyon' spills 100,000 tons of oil near Land's End.

New Orleans: 18 die, 40 hurt as jet crashes into motel.

Aden: Nine Arab school children die, 14 hurt when bus runs over landmine.

Street of flames - petrol tanker loaded with eight tons of fuel crashes in Indianapolis street killing four people.

London to Bristol express left the rails at Didcot, causing one death and many injuries.

69 people killed in Stockport as British Midland Argonaut, returning from Majorca, crashed four miles short of its destination at Ringway Airport.

Argonaut airliner being rebuilt six months later in hangar at Farnborough.

Brussels: 322 die in department store fire.

Leaking fuel from fighter on U.S. aircraft carrier 'Forrestal' kills 129 in fires.

U.K.: 134,000 animals slaughtered in foot-and-mouth disease epidemic.

Mediterranean: 66 die as BEA Comet crashes west of Cyprus.

France: 88 die as British DC-4 crashes into the Pyrenees.

Greek ship - 'Emmanuel M' stuck fast on sandbank, mouth of the River Elbe.

London: 53 dead, 90 hurt in train crash at Hither Green, south-east London.

U.K.: 37 die as Iberian Airways Caravelle from Malaga to Heathrow crashes in Fernhurst, Sussex.

1967

Innovation

Dinky Toys produces model of Pathe News camera car.

The Jeltek Flashjac has built-in flashing lights to make road workers more visible.

Innovation

In July, BBC 2 began regular colour television broadcasting with coverage of Wimbledon. BBC Radio launched Radio 1 as the legal alternative to the pirate stations and Radio Leicester introduced local radio.

The first prototype supersonic airliner, Concorde 001, was unveiled.

The first cash dispensers appeared in the high streets, with Barclays leading the way, and breathalysers were brought into use, with new police powers of random testing.

5th May
U.S.: Launch of first all-British satellite Ariel 3.

17th June
China: First Chinese H-Bomb is exploded.

Nobel prizes for 1967:-

Physics	Hans Bethe (U.S.)
Chemistry	Manfred Eigen (West Germany), Ronald Norrish (U.K.) and Sir George Porter (U.K.)
Medicine	Ragnar Granit (Sweden), Haldan Hartline (U.S.) and George Wald (U.S.)
Literature	Miguel Asturias (Guatemala)

Trials to test traffic light time-delays at the Road Research Laboratory, Crowthorne.

Drivotrainer system for learner drivers in Nottingham.

17
18
19

Eleven-year-old Lee Pak Kwan proves abacus can beat new adding machine.

25th September
Paris: European Airbus project agreed by Britain, France and West Germany.

Wallace Manufacturing demonstrates its tricycle, with optional motor.

The Ford Comuta battery-driven runabout is put through its paces.

New European road signs introduced in Britain.

27th June
U.K.: Barclays Bank introduces first cash dispenser.

1st July
U.K.: BBC2 starts broadcasting in colour.

2nd August
London: Dartford tunnel opens.

3rd September
Sweden: Traffic switches to driving on the right.

'Renown', Britain's second nuclear submarine, is launched at Birkenhead.

Scooter Ski - a natty little craft which has a top speed of 25mph and sells for less than £150.

8th November
Leicester: First BBC local radio station opens.

11th December
Toulouse: Concorde 001 prototype unveiled.

Monitoring London's traffic by remote - control TV.

1967

Sport

Epsom: Derby field thunders towards camera.

Mike Keen of QPR receives League Cup after defeating West Bromwich Albion 3-2.

17th August
U.K.: Jimmy Hill quits as Coventry manager for TV career.

Sport

Many new sporting stars emerged, breaking world records galore.

Awards were given to football personalities Alf Ramsey and Bobby Moore in the New Year's Honours List, while Muhammad Ali was stripped of his world heavyweight title after refusing to serve in Vietnam.

Jim Clarke won four Grand Prix motor races - the British, Dutch, Mexican and U.S. - in his Ford-powered Lotus 49, though he failed to gain the world championship that year.

65-year-old Francis Chichester made sailing history as he completed his single-handed round-the-world voyage and was awarded a knighthood by the Queen for his achievement.

Jennings leaps to ball taking Spurs out of danger.

Monaco Grand Prix: Lorenzo Bandini crashes and is critically injured - dies later from injuries.

Tottenham Hotspur win FA Cup Final, beating Chelsea 2-1.

Scotland beat England 3-2 at Wembley.

Two riderless horses cause pile-up in the Grand National.

Scottish left winger David Whyte (above) scores a try which was disallowed.

England (light shirts) beat Scotland 27-14 for the Calcutta Cup at Twickenham.

Jockeys attempt to re-mount at jump 23 following pile-up.

Foinavon, ridden by John Buckingham, jumped clear to win at 100-1.

Karl Mildenberger (right) beats Billy Walker after referee stops fight.

Netherlands: Jim Clark in Lotus-Ford wins Dutch Grand Prix.

Belgium: Eddy Merckx is world cycling champion.

Coniston: Donald Campbell killed in record attempt.

U.S.: Muhammad Ali stripped of heavyweight boxing title.

Wimbledon & U.S. Open	
Mens singles:	John Newcombe
Womens singles:	Billie Jean King
U.S. Open	
Mens doubles:	John Newcombe/Tony Roche
Womens doubles:	Rosemary Casals/Billie Jean King
Wimbledon	
Mens doubles:	Bob Hewitt/Frew McMillan
Womens doubles:	Rosemary Casals/Billie Jean King

Wimbledon: Distinction is abolished between amateur and professional tennis players.

Mary Rand wins 80 metres hurdles in Britain/West Germany match.

Gordon Banks and Bobby Moore skid on snow-covered pitch in 2-2 draw against the Soviet Union at Wembley.

Chris Irwin is pulled from his burning Formula 2 car at Snetterton.

Pathe reports continued into 1968, bringing that year's major world events to its viewers and in its distinctive style also providing a large variety of interesting facts.

In January the U.S. suffered a major set-back in the Vietnam War, as the Viet Cong launched heavy attacks against South Vietnam, even entering the U.S. embassy in Saigon. President Johnson made plans to send in 50,000 more troops, then announced that he would not stand for re-election.

Senator Bobby Kennedy was murdered hours after winning the California Democratic primary election. Richard Nixon was elected President in November, beating Hubert Humphrey. In the last days of his presidency, Johnson ordered a total end to the bombing in Vietnam.

The murder of Dr Martin Luther King, in Memphis, Tennessee, triggered racial riots in many U.S. cities. Britain also experienced racial tension, as Enoch Powell foresaw a river "foaming with much blood", after the Commonwealth Immigrants Bill was passed and the Race Relations Bill was published.

Students across Europe rioted after left-winger Rudi Dutschke was shot and wounded. Paris students tore up cobblestones in a bitter battle with the police and built barricades in the worst street-fighting since 1944. When half the workforce supported the students in a general strike. President de Gaulle was forced to take strong action, regaining full control in a landslide victory in June.

In August Soviet tanks entered Czechoslovakia to suppress Alexander Dubcek's liberal Communist government, finally ending the 'Prague Spring' of 'Socialism with a human face'.

Despite the world tension, Britons continued to be optimistic, starting the "I'm Backing Britain" campaign.

ACKNOWLEDGEMENT

The idea to produce the **Year to Remember** books was born out of the successful **Year to Remember** videos which cover the years 1930-1969.

The British Pathe News library contains some 50 million feet of film dating back to the 1890s. And as such there are probably over 200 million stills of history which could be taken from the film.

Playing stills photographer with movie film is a wonderful task. My thanks go to Ron Saunders of British Pathe News whose knowledge of the library and events is unsurpassable. Special thanks also to the staff of Dennis Fairey and Associates who designed the book. Special mention to Jane Feiven, Jackie Thorn, Sylvia Leigh and Andrew Yeomans for their time, effort and enthusiasm.

Ninety percent of the photographs are taken from the Pathe Film Library and were printed by the Pinewood Stills Department. Inevitably some events which needed to be included were not covered by Pathe - so the following acknowledgements are:

Topham Picture Library
p.121, p.122, p.135, p.137.

Vehicle Art of World War Two

To all the unknown artists.

Vehicle Art of World War Two

John Norris

Pen & Sword
MILITARY

First published in Great Britain in 2016 by
Pen & Sword Military
an imprint of
Pen & Sword Books Ltd
47 Church Street
Barnsley
South Yorkshire
S70 2AS

ISBN 978 1 47383 418 7

A CIP catalogue record for this book is available from the British Library

Typeset in Ehrhardt by
Mac Style Ltd, Bridlington, East Yorkshire
Printed and bound in India by Replika Press Pvt. Ltd.

Pen & Sword Books Ltd incorporates the imprints of Pen & Sword Archaeology, Atlas, Aviation, Battleground, Discovery, Family History, History, Maritime, Military, Naval, Politics, Railways, Select, Transport, True Crime, and Fiction, Frontline Books, Leo Cooper, Praetorian Press, Seaforth Publishing and Wharncliffe.

For a complete list of Pen & Sword titles please contact
PEN & SWORD BOOKS LIMITED
47 Church Street, Barnsley, South Yorkshire, S70 2AS, England
E-mail: enquiries@pen-and-sword.co.uk
Website: www.pen-and-sword.co.uk

Contents

Acknowledgements vi
Introduction 1

Chapter 1 What's in a Name? 7

Chapter 2 The French Army: National Pride and Personal Choice 48

Chapter 3 The British Army: Making a Point 54

Chapter 4 To Name or Not to Name: A National Difference of Opinion 72

Chapter 5 The German Army: A Subtle Approach 78

Chapter 6 Russia: Patriotic Fervour of the Red Army 87

Chapter 7 The US Army: Sometimes Saucy, Often Humorous 90

Appendix 137
Bibliography 178

Acknowledgements

Many people have assisted me in the compilation of this work, especially vehicle owners who have given their time to explain points of detail relating to artwork. I would like to thank Glen Rummery and all vehicle owners from the MVT and IMPS and many others who allowed me to photograph their vehicles. I am also grateful to the owners of kit such as tool boxes, telephones and other equipment, especially Mike Bradley for his jackets, and all the others who provided items for the photographs. I am especially indebted to the many museums including the Tank Museum at Bovington in Dorset, the IWM at Duxford, the Cobbaton Combat Collection in Devon, and History on Wheels near Windsor in Berkshire, where I was able to study artwork on vehicles in close detail. My sincere thanks to Pat Ware of the Warehouse for providing some images, and all the other collectors who also supplied similar images for this work. Without you this would not have been possible.

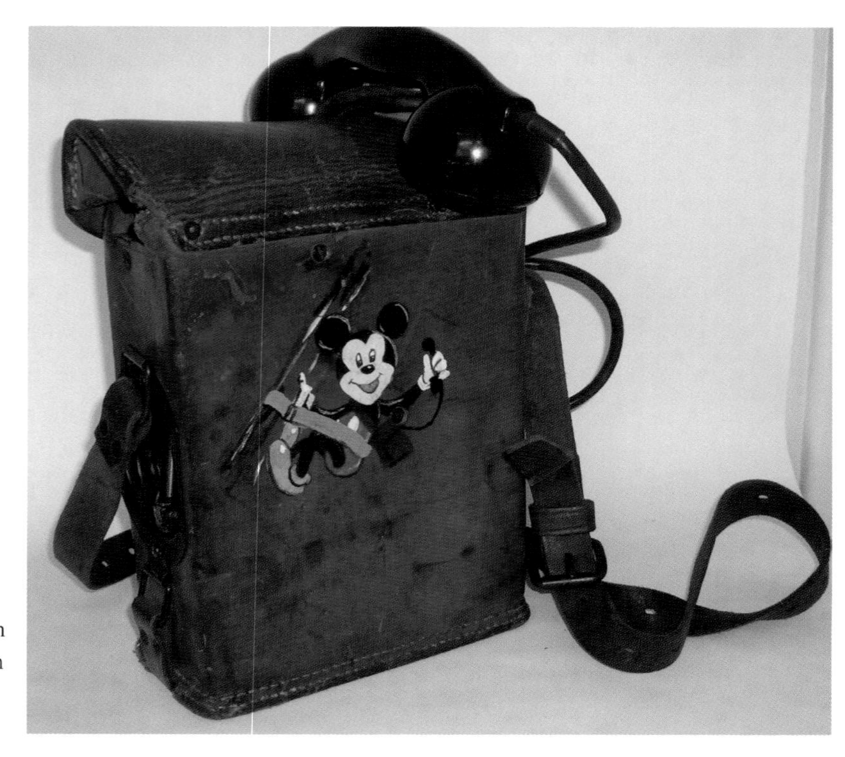

Small items of service equipment, such as this field telephone, were given a personal touch with the application of a familiar motif.

Introduction

Since the beginning of recorded history, men in battle have been known to decorate their armour and, in some instances, even give names to their personal weapons which they carried into war, particularly swords. To reflect the high status of the carrier, such as the king or tribal leader, their weapons were of the finest quality and decorated with embellishments which proclaimed ownership. Named swords appear many times in myth and legend, such as that of King Arthur, whose sword 'Excalibur' was imbued with mystical properties. The Norse god Odin had his sword 'Gram' and similar tales exist in many societies around the world, from a time when warriors believed their weapons had 'special powers' which rendered up great strength in battle.

The sea-faring Viking raiders who sailed to Britain from the Scandinavian countries of Denmark, Sweden and Norway also ventured down to Sicily. They had a tradition of naming their swords, for example 'Hvati' (Keen), 'Langhrass' (Long and Sharp), or the sword of the twelfth century king of Norway, Magnus III, which was called 'Legbit', referred to as 'Legbiter' in some chronicles. Such swords were expensive and had their names etched on the blades. Indeed, such was their value these swords were often buried with their owners, as evidenced during the 1939 excavations at Sutton Hoo in Suffolk. Later, as war became more sophisticated, gigantic stone-throwing machines were developed to lay siege to castles. The men operating these engines of war adopted the practice of naming them. The practice became popular and spread among armies of the Middle Ages. For example, in 1303 when the Bernese army was laying siege to the town of Wimmis, near the canton of Bern in modern-day Switzerland, they deployed two massive trebuchets (catapults) which were called 'La fille de bois' (meaning the girl or daughter of wood) and 'L'ane' (meaning the donkey). The application of names to these machines no doubt also served to inspire the troops who operated them.

The tradition of naming military hardware and decorating equipment with highly elaborate, hand-painted motifs is something which can also be traced back many centuries if not millennia to the very dawn of recorded warfare. During the Classical period of ancient Greece, Rome and Egypt, armies are known to have adorned chariots and shields with religious images, royal emblems and good luck symbols. These armies were among the very first organized military societies and the soldiers stepped onto the battlefield in organized formations wearing helmets, body armour and shields. Helmet styles such as the Greek 'Corinthian-style' enclosed the whole head and covered the

Recreated image showing how Greek hoplites used colours and images to identify individuals on the battlefield.

face, leaving openings only to breathe and for the eyes, meaning that the identity of the wearer was often obscured. As means of identification in battle, commanders would attach brightly-coloured plumes or crests to their helmets. The Greeks carried large, brightly-coloured round shields called 'aspis' to protect their left side leaving their right arm free to wield a sword. In battle formation these shields could be interlocked by the soldiers, overlapping them to form a solid wall behind which the infantry could advance and by using their sheer weight force their way through an enemy's formation. The legionaries of the Roman army employed a more advanced tactic using their shields, called 'scutums', which were painted with symbols of their Legion. This was known as

The Roman Legions also used colours and symbols to identify units on the battlefield, as shown here in this recreated image.

the 'testudo', named after the tortoise whose shell protected it from attack, and allowed them to manoeuvre en masse under cover of the shields.

In such close formation, with heads protected by the all-enclosing helmets, voices would have been muffled and identities lost, making it easy for troops to become disorientated in the melée of battle and lose contact with commanders of units. As means of identifying individuals and leaders on the battlefield the Greeks often decorated their shields with symbols so that men could look to see where their commander was in an instant or who was standing next to them. Some of the designs were heraldic symbols of a particular family and others were a statement of a man's fighting prowess on the battlefield. As such these designs could be in the form of a spider, a scorpion, snakes or the head of a lion, which indicated speed and strength. Some designs were symmetrical patterns and others were mythical creatures such as a griffon or the snake-haired Gorgon 'Medusa', whose look, so legend would have it, could transform men into statues of stone.

While such symbols served to identify the leaders to their own side they also alerted the enemy to the importance of their rank. In such instances he would often be targeted and attacked in force with the intention of either killing him or capturing him so as to render his troops without a leader. In Homer's epic poem *The Iliad*, which tells the story of the Trojan War and the siege of the city of Troy, the mighty Achilles was invulnerable and could not be killed by mortal man unless struck in the one weak spot on his body, his heel. Yet he wore armour, a helmet, and carried a highly decorated shield. Why? The only logical answer is that he wished to be identified to his troops, the Myrmidons. Their allegiance was solely to Achilles and they would have needed to see him on the battlefield in the crush of the fighting. Other legendary figures from the siege of Troy, such as Ajax, Priam, Paris and Hector all wore distinctive armour and carried highly decorated shields for the same purpose; for identification and to announce their status.

Over the centuries men going into war continued to decorate their armour with symbols and sometimes became associated with a particular colour. For example, the exceptional and fearless fourteenth-century military leader, Prince Edward of England, distinguished himself by wearing black armour in battle and carrying a black-faced shield bearing three white feathers with the motto 'Ich Dien' meaning 'I Serve'. Because of this he was certainly conspicuous on the battlefield, but contrary to popular belief the epithet 'Black Prince' does not appear to have been bestowed on him until some 150 years after his death.

One famous example of a named gun comes from the English Civil War. In a unit of artillery in the Parliamentarian Army the crew of a gun named their weapon 'Sweet Lips' after a lady of ill-repute.

By the First World War drivers were naming their vehicles, like this Locomobile named *The Ancre Flyer*.

This British-built Pierce Arrow truck used in the First World War is named *Tigress*.

Heraldic emblems and symbols on shields and helmets with crests continued to be used in armies around the world until the nineteenth century, by which time wars were being fought on an industrial scale with large armies comprising of battalions. There began to emerge the devices which would become regimental cap badges and divisional signs.

Horses have been used in war for thousands of years and the relationships between riders and animals can become close. The names of many military horses are known, one of the earliest being 'Bucephalus' the horse Alexander the Great famously tamed and then rode during his campaigns in the fourth century BC. In the nineteenth century Napoleon Bonaparte rode 'Marengo' on campaign and the Duke of Wellington rode 'Copenhagen'. Horses used in armies around the world are still named, as well as having numbers, because the men can relate more to using a name than a number.

Into the twentieth century, during the great battles which marked both world wars, there, amidst all the bombs exploding and soldiers in their uniforms of drab brown, grey and green, there could be spotted splashes of colour in the form of divisional patches on the vehicles and uniforms. These colours and the patterns they formed were distinctive and allowed soldiers to identify the positions held by their divisions.

For the most part twentieth-century symbols were official, which is to say they were authorized for use by military high commands, and these were accepted as divisional emblems. The design of some of these divisional symbols harked back to earlier days and used lion heads, birds and could incorporate numbers and letters. But there was still room for unofficial symbols and nicknames to be applied to individual pieces of machinery just as individual soldiers were often given nicknames. Aircraft in the First World War were decorated with lucky mascots in bright hues such as playing cards, animals or others items including hats. The practice of naming machines also extended to vehicles, including trucks, which were called after girls, locations – for example *The Ancre Flyer* – or other nicknames, such as *Tigress*.

The images used in this book appear in three categories. Firstly, there are some of the original types, examples of which we have very kindly been allowed to reproduce by the Tank Museum at Bovington in Dorset. Secondly, there are the reproductions of the types of images which were known to be used on vehicles during the war. Lastly, there are the types which are representative of the artwork which featured on vehicles. This book is intended as a reminder of this personal imagery applied to vehicles which was sometimes subtle and always imaginative.

Chapter One

What's in a Name?

The naming of warships is a tradition which can be traced back millennia when the first naval vessels sailed across open water. The ship used by Duke William of Normandy during his conquest of England in 1066 was built at Barfleur in Normandy where it was given the figurehead of a child with a trumpet and named *Mora*, a term which has several meanings and is believed to have Swedish origins. All the warships in William's invasion fleet of 700 vessels were brightly painted, but the *Mora* stood out as the lead vessel. Evidence of this can be seen in the images of the Bayeux Tapestry, and chronicles of the time also record how the ships were painted in bright colours, for the purposes of identifying each ship or to locate them at sea should they become separated in fog during the voyage. William's warships were built in the style of the Viking 'longships' which had also been painted in bright colours and had names, such as *Trana*, built for King Olav Tryggvasson in the tenth century, and who later sailed in the *Ormen Lange* which means long serpent and had a figurehead of a dragon.

Across the centuries the tradition of naming warships continued and even today all ships have a name. Some warships also have a symbolic crest, another tradition which can be traced back many hundreds of years. During both world wars, warships had names which were inspired by mythical creatures, famous battles, or leading military figures, such as the Royal Navy's HMS *Rodney* after Admiral Lord Rodney and HMS *Hood*, named after Admiral Samuel Hood. The German navy, the *Kriegsmarine*, also named some of its capital ships after leaders such as Bismarck, Scharnhorst, Tirpitz and Hipper.

On land, by the twentieth century, armies were increasingly replacing horses on the battlefield with machines, which were to transform warfare out of all recognition to those conflicts which had been fought in the previous centuries. These changes ultimately ended the role of cavalry and the personal association between horse and rider. Artillery and tanks emerged as the dominating forces on the battlefield while the skies were patrolled by aircraft. On the outbreak of the First World War the early designs of aeroplanes were being flown by pilots who saw themselves as an elite group of protagonists, some styling themselves 'Knights of the Air'. Pilots adopted a range of gaudy designs which were painted on the fuselages of their aircraft to mark them out as individuals. In this way they were doing the same as the classical Greeks, but using hats, anchors and dogs to replace scorpions and mythical beasts.

Pilots in the First World War often painted names on their aircraft, like this German aviator who has named his aeroplane *Brunhilde*.

Aircraft at the start of the First World War were usually painted drab brown and green, with national emblems and identifying numbers on the fuselage and wings. The French pilots, who took a more relaxed approach to things, began painting good luck images on their aircraft such as dogs, cats, dice or playing cards. German pilots followed suit and began to paint girls names on their aircraft, and images including flowers such as the Edelweiss, an alpine plant, which appeared on the Fokker Albatros flown by Oberleutnant Paul Bremmer and Leutnant Wilhelm Lehman of Jasta 5. Eventually some pilots painted their entire aircraft in dazzling colours as though to proclaim their presence. This statement was taken to an extreme by Baron Manfred von Richthofen, whose Fokker Dreidecker (triplane) was painted completely red and earned him the nickname 'Red Baron'.

British pilots were no less dashing but they preferred a more subtle approach with emblems such as arrows, tridents or diamonds. American volunteer pilots were already serving with squadrons in Europe before America entered the war, flying with French units such as the Lafayette Escadrille. These volunteers copied their French counterparts and painted lucky emblems on their aircraft. When America entered the war proper in 1917, pilots flew with units such as the 94th Aero Squadron of the American Expeditionary Force, whose aircraft were decorated with symbols such as the 'Hat in the Ring' which showed a top hat with the American stars and stripes inside a red hoop.

Back on the ground, the first tank, developed and built in great secrecy, at the Fosters factory in Lincoln, was given the name *Excalibur*, after King Arthur's legendary sword. The tanks which went onto the battlefield in 1916 were termed His Majesty's Land Ships. The tanks were given designated identification numbers, but it was also decided that their names should be prefixed by the initials HMLS. One of these vehicles was a Mk I 'Male', so-called because it was armed with two 6-pounder guns, which took part in the Battle of the Somme in July 1916. Although it was officially numbered C19, to the crew it was known by the name of 'Clan Leslie'. When deployed on the battlefield the armoured vehicles were identified by official divisional badges painted on them as recognition symbols. The British Army went on to deploy several designs of tank and the naming of individual machines became accepted as part of the army's way of life.

The Germans responded to the problem of the tank threat by resorting to the simple expedient of using British and French tanks, captured intact, which they used against their former owners. Obviously identification markings had to be changed and they were also painted with the national symbol. Regimental badges and divisional numbers meant troops on the ground could quickly recognize friendly vehicles, which also had to carry air identification markings on their upper surfaces to avoid being mistaken for enemy vehicles by pilots.

To the crews of the vehicles, the names they painted on the sides of their tanks and other vehicles were more than good luck symbols. They might be reminders of home with terms such as 'Tea Time'. Female names were popular and names such as 'Hyacinth' or 'Iris' could be seen painted on the sides of British vehicles; they were most likely in reference to a girlfriend or wife of a member of the tank crew. One example was 'Deborah', a tank knocked out in the fighting near Flesquières during the Battle of Cambrai on 20 November 1917. The French followed the British example in naming tanks and trucks and later the Americans copied the practice as thousands more vehicles were used on the battlefield. Canadian troops did the same and some units added good luck charms such as real horseshoes. Painted symbols of horseshoes became popular on French tanks too, also featuring as lucky emblems, in addition to divisional symbols and any other device.

Mostly the tanks were used in France on the Western Front but, as the fighting spread, more vehicles were deployed to other theatres of war such as the Middle East and British East Africa. A special unit known as the Royal Tank Corps was created to operate these machines and battalions were formed and equipped with particular types of tank. In a move which reflected naval heritage, some of these early tanks were given names of the type more usually associated with warships, such as the Mk V tank called *Audacious*. The lighter designs, including the 'Whippet' were also similarly named such as vehicle number A387, used in Africa, was named HMLS *Union* which was painted on its side. In British East Africa the 10th Royal Navy Armoured Motor Battery operated

Tank crews painted the names of their machines on the side, like this Whippet named *HMLS Union*.

Rolls Royce armoured cars, one of which was named *Kifaru* from the native Askari word for rhinoceros. In the Middle East a Mk I 'Female' tank, so-called because it was armed with machine guns, was operated by the Gaza tank detachment of the British Army and called HMLS *Kia Ora*. This was another tribal word, this time from the native Maori language of New Zealand, meaning 'Be Well' or 'Be Healthy'.

It was in France, however, where tanks were used the most. As more appeared the troops saw further examples of names painted on the sides, some of which were more personal in character. For example, a female type Mk II numbered F53, operated by F Battalion of the Royal Tank Corps (RTC), was called *The Flying Scotsman*. Girls' names continued to be universally popular with troops of all armies. This was probably due to the fact that motor vehicles, like ships, are generally recognized as being female and thus referred to as 'She'. That did not stop other terms being used such as the Whippet tank numbered A347, operated by the 6th Battalion RTC, which was named *Firefly*. Another Whippet, also serving with the same battalion, went into action against German positions on 8 August 1918 in support of Australian troops during the Battle of Amiens. The vehicle was named *Musical Box*; it was destroyed in the action. A Mk II 'Male', called *Lusitania*, no doubt in commemoration of the liner of the same name sunk in 1915, was seen in action, while another tank, this time a Mk II 'Female' deployed to the area of Arras in April 1917, was charmingly called *The Perfect Lady*. Some tanks were converted to carry field artillery

'We're All In It' was also designated as an 'HMLS', which became an object of much inspection after it became stuck in the mud in France.

through the mud and the crews also named these; one was called *Merlin*. One tank caught the attention of J.N. MacBean-Ross who was serving as a surgeon on the Somme. He noted in his diary for Tuesday, 23 January 1917 how he and a colleague went out to inspect a tank which was: ' ...stuck in no man's land - HMLS "We're all in it"...' That this was its name, and that it was a female, being armed with machine guns, he concludes that the overall impression was: 'Very interesting indeed'.

The French developed various series of tanks, examples being the light FT17, the much heavier Schneider Char d'Assaut (tank of assault), and the St Chamond. These were built using rivets just like warships and their designs had boat-shaped hulls. An official method of identification symbols based on the suits of playing cards was adopted and painted on the turrets or hulls; some were informally named by their crews.

For their part, the Germans developed two types of tank, the lightest of which was the Leichter Kampfwagen LK II (light battle car) but it never went into series production. The heavier tank was the A7V and around twenty of these were built. As well as the national symbol of the black cross for identification, each one was named, with various titles ranging from girls' names such as 'Gretchen' and 'Lotti' to mythical figures such as 'Wotan' and 'Herkules'; these names were painted on the hulls. Some carried other symbols, for example 'Lotti' was also marked with a grinning skull and cross bones. It looked very piratical and was copied by other tank crews. In fact, the name 'Lotti' or 'Lotte' appears to have been quite popular with German tank crews. It was even

A typical name for a tank in the First World War is recreated here.

applied to at least one captured example of a British 'female' Mk IV tank. While the Germans used the skull, the British tank crews tended to go for symbols less sinister. Often they painted open, staring 'eyes' on either side of the hull. In 1916 the single Cyclops-like 'Ever Open Eye' motif was adopted as the unit badge by the Guards Division and during the Second World War was seen on all the vehicles used by the Guards Armoured Division after the unit was formed in June 1941.

The Guards Division 'Ever Open Eye' was used during both world wars.

Other names used on German tanks included 'Hagen', which was an industrial area where steel was produced, and 'Nixe' which could be a reference to the Greek goddess of the night. These tanks were slow, cumbersome machines and easily destroyed by artillery. Some broke down due to mechanical failure and were captured. At the Battle of Villers-Bretonneux on 24 April 1918 the Germans lost three A7V tanks, one of which was *Elfried* which was later put on display in the Place de la Concorde in Paris. *Nixe* was disabled in battle and later destroyed by the Germans. A third vehicle, *Mephisto*, was later recovered by Australian troops and today is the only surviving example of an original A7V. It can be seen on display at the Queensland Museum in Brisbane, Australia.

Another A7V tank to be left on the battlefield was *Schnuck* which was abandoned by its crew near Bapaume on 31 August 1918. Today there is a realistic replica on display at the Tank Museum at Bovington in Dorset, England, right down to the name *Schnuk* painted on the hull. The name is more or less a slang expression meaning 'So What!'. Some A7V tanks did survive the war, such as 'Lottchen', which was later used to suppress unrest in post-war Germany. Although a girl's name, the meaning has also been interpreted to mean 'Free man'.

Guns of the artillery in all armies have by tradition been named by their crews. During the First World War some of the crews applied affectionate nicknames to the large calibre, long-range guns. For example a crew of the Royal Garrison Artillery operating a 12-inch calibre gun near Louez in France called it 'Bunty' and painted the name on the mounting. Another battery using the same kind of weapon named their gun 'Lucky Jim' which was also painted on the side. Even larger pieces of artillery were the pair of BL 14.5-inch calibre Mk V naval guns converted to railway artillery; they were called *Scene Shifter* and *Boche Buster* in reference to the amount of damage inflicted by their shells, which weighed 1,586 pounds. Two other similar weapons were

Replica of the First World War German A7V tank *Schnuck* seen at the Tank Museum, Bovington, Dorset.

nicknamed 'Gladiator' and 'Piece Maker' (sic). The Germans also gave names to pieces of artillery, such as the M-Gerät 'Dicke Bertha', which translates as Fat Bertha but was more commonly known as 'Big Bertha'. There were two of these huge guns, with calibre of 420mm (16.54 inches); they could fire shells weighing 1,786 pounds out to range of 10,000 yards. They were used to smash the Belgian forts at Liège and Namur. According to some sources the term 'Big Bertha' was in reference to the wife of the industrialist Alfred Krupp whose armament factories built the weapon.

On the battlefield German gun crews followed the example of their British opponents and painted names on the barrels of their weapons, such as 'Irma', which can be seen in some images of the time. Gunners on both sides would sometimes write graffiti messages on shells. They knew full well these messages could not be read because the projectile would explode on the target and all evidence would be destroyed. Nevertheless, the action of writing such messages was good for morale. During the Second World War pilots wrote messages on their bombs and troops scrawled messages on artillery shells, mainly for the benefit of journalists whose photographs appeared in newspapers, to show how upbeat the troops were.

While the giving of names to vehicles and weapons can be seen as being good for morale, the act goes much further. Soldiers of all armies have a unique sense of humour, which can often seem strange, indeed sometimes perverse, to non-military persons. Servicemen the world over enjoy making a 'play on words' which only becomes apparent when said in a particular way. For example, a Firefly aircraft of Naval Air Squadron 1771 flown by Lieutenant Commander W.R. MacWhirter, operating from the aircraft carrier HMS *Implacable*, was painted with the girl's name 'Evelyn Tentions'. A further extension of typical military humour is shown in the way in which the crew of a particular vehicle would paint a slogan on their vehicle and another crew would paint the opposite meaning on theirs. For example 'Miss Behavin' would prompt the reply 'Aint Misbehavin'. Another example might be 'Beatin the Odds' which could be countered with 'Miss Beat' and the image of a girl.

Vehicle designs would often be given a name by either the designers or the military planners and while these were used to identify types, the troops had different opinions and often applied their own nicknames for certain vehicles and weapons. Soldiers the world over can be perfectly blunt and the nicknames they used could range from the affectionate to the downright disparaging. For example, the 56-ton German Tiger I was called 'the furniture van' by their own troops on account of its size. Crews of the PaK43/41 version of 88mm calibre anti-tank gun called the weapon the 'Scheuntor' ('Barn door') because the gun-shield was so large. By contrast, the PaK35/36 with its light 37mm calibre shell was called the 'Door Knocker' by troops because they believed that was all it was useful for 'knocking on vehicles' instead of destroying them. Another German anti-tank weapon was the Panzerschreck (tank fright), a shoulder-

Artillery was also named, like this example named 'Bunty'.

The Germans also named their weapons, such as 'Irma' seen here on the Western Front in France.

'Lucky Jim' was used by the Royal Artillery in France in the First World War.

These Royal Artillery gunners serving in Gallipoli in 1915 have named their gun 'Annie'.

Gunners in all armies of the world wrote messages on shells, in this case using chalk, even though they would never be read.

These graffiti were popular images appearing in newspapers and magazines of the day.

'Miss Behavin' was a saucy phrase with a saucy image.

Other drivers would sometimes reply to a name with an opposite meaning.

Playing cards were considered lucky and often featured in artwork on vehicles.

An example of a play on words with 'Evelyn Tentions'.

'Miss Beat' was another saucy style of image.

fired anti-tank rocket launcher known by the troops as the 'Ofenrohr' or 'Stove pipe', because of its long tubular shape. The British Army called the A11 infantry tank the 'Matilda' after a cartoon duck of the day on account of its apparent waddling motion. The US Army called the M3 light tank 'Honey', because it was sweet to handle. The M10 tank destroyer was nicknamed 'Wolverine' by British troops and the term caught on with US troops; and the 155mm calibre M1 howitzer was nicknamed the 'Long Tom' because of its great length. French troops also used the 'Wolverine' and the crew of one vehicle, serving with the 2nd Regiment of Dragoons, named theirs 'Arc de Triomphe II'. Another unit named one of its Wolverines 'Sirocco' after the prevailing wind which blows up from the Mediterranean Sea. The M4 Sherman tank was called the 'Ronson' by Allied troops, after the brand name of a cigarette lighter, because it caught fire easily when hit by anti-tank guns. The Germans called the same vehicle 'Tommy Cooker' on account of the number of crews killed in them when they caught fire. In typical military humour all crews of tanks called their vehicles 'iron coffins'. One crew of an M4A3 Sherman tank serving with the 5th Battalion of the US Marine Corps on Iwo Jima in 1945 actually painted the name 'Iron Coffin' on their vehicle. Like the French tank crew who named their vehicle 'Friday 13th', Iron Coffin proved unlucky and all the crew were killed when it was destroyed by Japanese anti-tank guns.

Names were not reserved just for vehicles and weapons, sometimes troops would give a nickname to a building being used for special purposes. In Flanders during the First World War, British troops nicknamed a trio of Casualty Clearing Stations, field hospitals, 'Bandagem', 'Dosingem' and 'Mendingem', all examples of play on words using military humour. During the Italian campaign in 1943 a house taken over as offices by the Royal Army Pay Corps was called 'Ye Olde Ackerage'. This was after the slang term 'acker' which the Oxford Dictionary defines to mean money. The word, in use with British troops from the 1930s, is believed to be a corruption or anglicized form of the Arab word *fakka* meaning small change or coins. The British troops would have known this was the office of the pay master who was sometimes referred to as 'The Golden Eagle'.

Some regiments also have nicknames which have been used for centuries and are used as terms of familiarity in armies around the world. In the British Army the Royal Hampshire Regiment was known as 'The Tigers', while the US Army 28th Infantry Division was nicknamed 'The Keystone'. There are many other examples. The padres serving in the Royal Army Chaplains' Department were known to British troops either as 'Sky Pilots' or 'God Botherers'. The chaplains took it in good part and the men knew how brave the padres were on the battlefield. They were often to be seen in the thick of fighting during campaigns such as Normandy, and Operation Market Garden in Arnhem in September 1944.

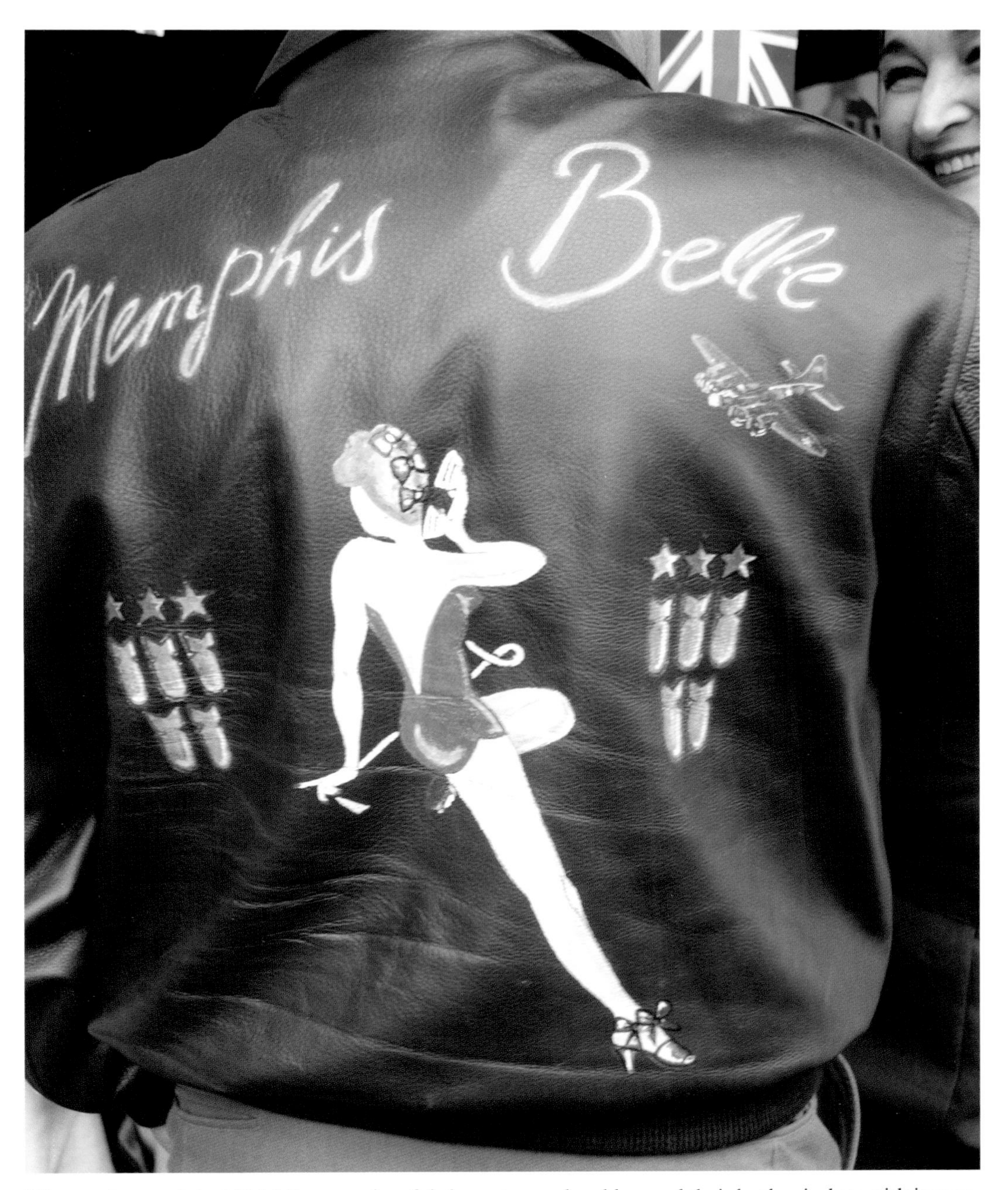

Pilots and crew of the USAAF were colourful characters and emblazoned their leather jackets with images.

Crews of aircraft had their own unique artwork.

Troops also like to personalize items of uniform and even pieces of equipment, if they can get away with it, by adding unofficial images which they could claim was to identify ownership if discovered. In the British Army the practice was not encouraged and the German Army was of the same opinion. American servicemen, in particular the pilots and crew of the United States Army Air Force (USAAF), were more cavalier in their approach. Pilots wore leather jackets called 'A2' and a heavier, fleece-lined type, known as the 'B3'. Both designs were often personalized either by the wearing of individual badges showing unit mascots, such as cartoons, or the whole back of the jacket would be painted with an image or good luck motif. For example, the cartoon character of Daffy Duck was adopted as the mascot for the 600th Bombardment Squadron of the USAAF operating out of bases in England. The image of this rather silly-looking bird was often shown in a vengeful pose swooping down with a bomb held in its webbed feet. Some pilots had the back of their jackets emblazoned with the service emblem or images ranging from saucy female figures to more sedate views. By contrast, the RAF leather flying jacket was not personalized and in the Luftwaffe, only a few pilots bothered to decorate their leather flying jackets.

Other items of issued equipment, such as the leather carrying cases for field telephones, could be decorated with a wide range of images, usually of a humorous nature. Examples of these styles, certainly among the American forces, could be found in all theatres of war from North Africa to the Pacific and certainly all across Europe from 1944. Wooden tool boxes would also be decorated with some kind of image, often as a reminder of home and more peaceful times. Like their air force counterparts, American soldiers were issued with jackets as part of their uniform. The first type was an olive-drab coloured cotton design known as the M-1941 pattern after the year of its first issue. Two years later this was replaced by the M-1943 pattern. The back of the jacket was formed from a single piece of material and some troops could not resist the temptation to decorate these items of uniform with some kind of design. The cotton material was not as ideally suited to such application of artwork as the leather flying jackets, but soldiers being what they are went ahead and produced the best result they could.

The presentation style of artwork ranged from gifted amateurs who had an aptitude for producing simple forms through to truly talented artists who produced some very elaborate designs. Sign writers in units could apply names on vehicles in a range of fonts and styles using freehand technique. For quickness some crews named their vehicles using block capital lettering of the type obtained by the simple use of stencils, mostly in white but sometimes in black lettering and occasionally yellow. Churchill tanks were given various names by their crews, such as 'Penelope', seen in white stencilled lettering, or 'Saturn', in bold letters outlined in white. Churchill tanks were used during the ill-fated raid on Dieppe, Operation Jubilee, on 19 August 1941. The 1st Canadian Tank

Series of replica images as used by USAAF aircrews which were painted on aircraft, vehicles and uniforms.

Cartoon characters from Walt Disney Studios were widely used, such as 'Thumper' from the film *Bambi* which was released in 1942.

Thumper the rabbit from *Bambi*, used on a toolbox in a Jeep.

Other troops tried to copy the USAAF with artwork on uniforms, but painting on cotton jackets did not work very well.

Ink drawings worked much better on cotton jackets, as seen here with 'Grumpy' from the Disney film *Snow White and the Seven Dwarfs* released in 1938.

Brigade lost their Churchill tanks on the beach along with other vehicles. The Germans photographed them for propaganda purposes and one, named 'Backer', is seen being closely inspected by German engineers. Another vehicle lost in the same operation and photographed was a Dingo scout car called 'Hunter'.

With so many vehicles in service and so many troops, names were not the sole property of one particular crew or unit and several examples of the same name or title could be found across various units. Photographic records show this to be true. For instance, a British Churchill Armoured Vehicle Royal Engineers (AVRE) armed with a special 290mm calibre spigot-type weapon which fired a 40lb demolition projectile for destroying concrete emplacements was named 'Liberator', and another AVRE carrying a fascine bundle to span trenches was called 'Mars', after the Roman god of war. These were both commonly-used names. Another spigot-armed AVRE Churchill with 79th Armoured Division, photographed at around the same time, was called 'Fury', and this name also appeared on a Canadian-built M4A5 variant of the Sherman Tank which entered service in late 1943.

In 2014 a war film called *Fury* was released starring Brad Pitt, set against the backdrop of the closing days of the Second World War. The title of the film was in

This Sherman tank was used in the 2014 film *Fury*, seen here during a display at the Tank Museum in Bovington, Dorset.

reference to the name of the vehicle which was central to the storyline. The name of the vehicle is shown roughly painted on the gun barrel and very much looked the part of the role it played. It appears that the film may have been an example of art mimicking life, because apart from the Canadian Sherman and a Churchill AVRE bearing the name, there was an actual Sherman tank named *Fury* serving with Company F of the 66th Armored Regiment with the 2nd Armored Division 'Hell on Wheels'. The 66th Armored Regiment was formed in 1918 and known as the 'Iron Knights' with the motto 'Semper in Hostes' (Always into the Enemy), which suited one of its officers, the future General George S. Patton, right down to the ground. The regiment went on to serve in the campaigns in North Africa and Sicily. On 9 June 1944 it landed on Omaha Beach with the 66th Armored Regiment and other units. It was engaged in heavy fighting and between 25 and 30 July took part in Operation Cobra the action to break out from the Normandy bridgehead. Among the tanks taking part in the action was *Fury*. There are some who believe the real-life tank *Fury* was the inspiration for the film and use the photographic evidence, which has appeared in many publications, to support their claim. Other real-life Sherman tanks which served in combat went into battle with names such as 'Hurricane', which is known to have served with the 746th Tank Battalion, and 'Spiteful'. Each of these vehicles took part in the Normandy landings, and their names could be seen as reflecting the crews' attitude. The name 'Hurricane', like 'Fury', also appeared on other vehicles, such as an experimental anti-aircraft version of the British Mk I Light Tank. The design mounted four Besa 7.92 calibre machine guns in a turret, which could have also been used against ground targets. The weapons proved to be too light in calibre, the design poorly conceived overall, and it was abandoned.

It was not the first time that such a storyline had been developed around a vehicle. The 1943 film *Sahara*, starring Humphrey Bogart as a tank commander in the western desert, is set against the backdrop of the Battle of Gazala, 26 May to 21 June 1942. The tank is an American-built M3 Lee/Grant, nicknamed 'Lulu Belle', a particular design which was used by the British Army during the North African campaign. By naming the tank, the film's producers were showing the audiences that vehicles were named just as they had seen in newspapers.

The 1953 film *Ice Cold in Alex* starred John Mills, Harry Andrews and Anthony Quayle, all of whom had served in the British Army during the war, however the undoubted star of the film was an Austin K2Y ambulance nicknamed 'Katy'. While it was a work of fiction, like *Sahara*, it was set against a backdrop of real events. The K2Y vehicle is referred to as Katy throughout the film but in real life the troops referred to all vehicles of this particular design by that nickname in the same way that the British A12 infantry tank was known as the Matilda Mk II. An example of the latter was photographed showing the name 'Glenor' during the fighting around Tobruk in 1941. Some sources now believe that it may have actually been named 'Glenorchy', and that the last part of the word is obscured by items of kit. It has been identified as serving with either the 7th or 4th Royal Tank Regiment, both of which formed part of the 23rd Armoured Brigade which served at Tobruk. The tanks of the 4th RTR are known to have had their names painted on the hull just below the driver's visor while those of the 7th RTR had their names painted on the upper hull.

When Britain went to war in September 1939 the army had a fleet of some 85,000 un-armoured vehicles, including around 21,000 motorcycles. Between 1939 and 1945 the output of trucks by British motor manufacturers reached almost 920,000 vehicles. The Luton-based company of Bedford built around 66,000 15cwt (.75 ton) MW trucks, and the Ford Motor Company in England built some 60,000 WOT2 vehicles in the 15cwt range. The Commonwealth countries of Canada, New Zealand and Australia also built vehicles, as did India and South Africa. In America the production of trucks, motorcycles and other vehicles by motor companies exceeded 3.2 million between 1939 and 1945. Many of these were sent to Britain and Russia as part of the Lend-Lease Act from 1941. Such numbers meant they were bound to be named by drivers who would have painted the identity on a door, engine bonnet or side panel. The US Government would go on to supply war material and vehicles to forty-four countries under the Lend-Lease programme, the value of which amounted to in excess of $42 billion.

If time permitted and the range of paints was available, then a detailed rendition of an image could be achieved. Alternatively a silhouette or basic image could be produced quickly. Likewise, the result of anything written would depend on time permitting and

British Austin K2Y ambulances were nicknamed Katy by troops during the Second World War. The post-war film *Ice Cold in Alex* starred one of these vehicles.

Austin K2Y ambulances were used in all theatres of the war and drivers had affectionate names for them.

available paint colours. Less time meant a more hurried, usually very simple wording such as a name, no matter how talented the artist. If pastel shades of flesh-coloured pink were available, then female figures showing uncovered arms and legs could be painted, some revealing lingerie, stocking tops and glimpses of garters. These images were never meant to last the rigours of the battlefield and many became faded or scratched. They could be retouched if the crew had a mind to, but largely they became as battered as the troops and vehicles themselves. When vehicles were destroyed in battle the crews were either killed or wounded and the imagery was lost. If another vehicle crew had a mind to it, they might name their vehicle the same in honour as the one destroyed but append the suffix 'II'. This happened with a Cromwell tank serving with 11th Armoured Division during the Normandy campaign, whose crew named their vehicle 'Taureg II'.

Some vehicles, such as the ubiquitous Jeep, had the duty of the operator painted on the front. These small but powerful vehicles, whose speed made them very popular, were used in a range of duties. The chaplains serving with the US Army used Jeeps as transport and sometimes painted their role on the front. Beachmasters (sometimes the title was split up and painted as Beach Masters), who co-ordinated the unloading of vehicles from assault craft during amphibious landings, also had Jeeps and they too often had their role painted in large letters to distinguish them. The Military Police also had their role painted on their vehicles; they assisted the Beach Masters by directing

Example of a Canadian-built Chevrolet C60L truck with the name 'Jane' painted on the bumper (fender).

Close-up of 'Miss Betty' a Canadian-built C15A Chevrolet 4X4 truck seen here in RAF colours.

'Miss Betty', a Chevrolet C15A, dating from 1941.

traffic onto the right roads as the hundreds of tanks and trucks moved inland away from the landing points. Medical units painted large red crosses on white backgrounds on their vehicles which was common to all armies in the European theatre of operations and was internationally recognized. Jeeps were also used by official war correspondents to allow them to travel around. As well as having Press Corps on the vehicle some were named, such as the example known as 'Blue Eyes' which was photographed with its crew. The British recognized journalists' vehicles with the initials 'AFPU', standing for 'Army Film and Photographic Unit', painted on an identification badge.

Many images were copies of popular cartoon characters of the day – for example Donald Duck, Mickey Mouse, Bugs Bunny or Popeye. The studios holding the copyright which regulated the reproduction of these images knew they were being reproduced on vehicles and aircraft without permission being requested. The circumstances were declared to be extenuating and no fees were demanded for such unauthorized reproduction. Indeed, the studios even 'mobilized' these characters and produced morale-boosting cartoon films using them to ridicule the Axis leaders.

The character of Bugs Bunny was created by the studios of Leon Schlesinger Productions, later to become part of Warner Brothers Cartoons, and appeared in the film *A Wild Hare* in 1940. The character, however, had originally appeared in 1938 and went on to be used in a number of productions before America entered the war.

British Army dispatch rider's motorcycle painted in camouflage scheme.

The girl's name 'Lou' is painted discreetly on the fuel tank.

The motorcycle as it looked in the Second World War.

Some drivers used saucy images on vehicles which always raised a smile.

Images of girls painted on vehicles were 'racy' but never rude.

It was the carefree attitude of Bugs Bunny which had been created in his character that appealed to audiences and this popularity led to the studios producing films with a storyline based around him. It was not long before Schlesinger joined the ranks of the Disney Studios and Bugs Bunny was facing up to the Axis forces. A fund-raising production called *Any Bonds Today* was released; Bugs Bunny takes on the Japanese in the 1944 production *Bugs Bunny Nips the Nips;* and in 1945 he ridicules Herman Goering in *Herr Meets Hare*. In some of these films he is joined by other characters such as Elmer Fudd, Porky Pig and Daffy Duck, but it was Bugs Bunny that stood out. So much so, that when he was seen in the uniform of a United States Marine in the 1943 production *Super Rabbit* it resulted in the USMC making Bugs Bunny an honorary Master Sergeant. Many young servicemen would have seen the films before enlisting or being drafted and they took this popularity into the forces with them. The crews serving in the 530 Squadron of the 380th Bombardment Group of the 5th USAAF adopted Bugs Bunny as a mascot, and the Royal Australian Air Force operating B24 Liberators out of bases in Australia's Northern Territories also adopted the character.

The co-characters featuring in films with Bug Bunny were popular with audiences, but of all of them it was only Daffy Duck which really appealed to US servicemen. This

Some vehicles, especially Jeeps, had the operation role painted on them, such as Shore Patrol of the US Navy.

Beach Master was the role of an officer during amphibious landings who directed traffic and troops off the beach. (Inset) Beach Master Jeep in army colours.

Journalists were allocated Jeeps and this one is marked as 'AFPU' – Army Film and Photographic Unit.

Medical units used the Jeep and along with the Red Cross also painted mottos on them.

Chaplains in all armies visited the men in the front line and the Jeep provided mobility. They also painted their role on the vehicle.

cartoon was a natural contender to be adopted by armed forces personnel, probably because of his 'screwball' personality. Daffy Duck first appeared on cinema screens in 1937 and, like Bugs Bunny, his character was mobilized to produce a series of special features which poked fun at the Axis forces. Daffy Duck went to war in such films as *Scrap Happy Daffy* in 1942, about salvaging scrap metal, and *Daffy the Commando* in 1943 when he hits Hitler with a very large mallet. In 1944 he was used to attack the Nazi leaders Herman Goering and Joseph Goebbels in *Plane Daffy* and in 1945 he was used in *Draftee Daffy*. With so much promotion his image, like so many others, was familiar to troops who had seen the films from several years earlier. Some of these men could copy his image on vehicles, aircraft and other flat surfaces.

The Disney Studios mobilized their resources from 1942 and produced a range of films for the US armed forces, including training films and morale-boosting productions. They also used their more familiar characters such as Donald Duck and Mickey Mouse to feature in propaganda films. Disney's involvement lasted for the duration of the war and the characters would become icons to Allied forces as images of the American way of life, just the same as Coca-Cola, chewing gum and candy bars. The characters were used to persuade the American public to accept and understand the need to pay taxes. One of the earliest propaganda films to be produced by the Disney Studios featuring

The Jeep was widely used by all services and drivers would paint images to personalize them using cartoons, such as Mickey Mouse seen here. (Inset) Close-up of Mickey Mouse. The Disney cartoon character also featured in official wartime films.

the irascible Donald Duck appeared in 1943 entitled *Der Fuehrer's Face*, which highlighted the oppression of the Nazi regime. Disney films were widely popular before the war, even Hitler is understood to have enjoyed *Snow White and the Seven Dwarfs*. The images of Donald Duck were painted on vehicles as reminders of normal times, as too was Mickey Mouse, and other characters from films such as *Bambi* appeared on tool boxes for good luck. The characters of all seven dwarfs were painted on the fuselage of a Lancaster bomber with the motto 'Hi Ho' taken from the song which featured in the film.

The irascible Donald Duck was a popular character and the Disney Studios did not charge copyright fees to reproduce such artwork.

Bugs Bunny was another popular cartoon character; his shape changed over time.

Bugs Bunny starred in wartime films and is seen here on a medical Jeep; note his tiny Red Cross armband.

The complete Jeep with Bugs Bunny image.

The Seven Dwarfs from the Disney film appeared on the side of this preserved RAF Lancaster bomber as flown by No 170 Squadron from RAF Hemswell.

The cartoon character Betty Boop was different from other cartoons in that she was based on human rather than animal form. She was created by Max Fleischer and Grim Natwick, first appearing in the 1930 production *Dizzy Dishes*, and was an instant hit with audiences. Over the next nine years she appeared in a series of animated short films produced by Fleischer Studios and released by Paramount. She had a large head with wide eyes framed by curly hair, set on an improbably tiny body supported on spindly legs and featuring the '...most self-confident little bust imaginable'. One of the earliest productions featuring the character of Betty Boop was a cartoon called *Minnie the Moocher* released in 1932. The story has Betty running into a cave where she encounters the vision of a spectral walrus-like creature which appears and sings the eponymous song.

Betty's character, like many cartoon images of the day, became widely known to mass audiences in cinemas and through cartoon strips in newspapers, which made Betty instantly

Betty Boop turned up in all manner of situations in her films, so why not the same on vehicles.

The 'Moocher' character from one of Betty Boop's pre-war films.

Betty Boop was a saucy cartoon character which proved popular with the troops.

Betty Boop lent herself to all sorts of images.

recognizable. Hers was also an easy image to render a reasonable likeness and servicemen who had grown up watching Betty Boop films throughout the 1930s did not forget them and painted her image on Jeeps, trucks and tanks and even aircraft. Despite her being a cartoon her character was spoken about as having 'sex appeal' and was often depicted in a range of poses from demure to provocative, but never crude or vulgar. Unfortunately her popularity was not as strong as believed and Betty Boop was never mobilized by the studios to support the war effort. The last of her short films was released in 1939. One of the reasons cited for Betty Boop falling from popularity is that audiences were developing a preference for animal-based cartoon characters. Despite Betty Boop films not being produced, American troops serving in the war would have remembered her character and she became used as an image on vehicles. Betty did re-appear in post-war years with new films which entertained a whole new generation in the same way as the pre-war generation had grown up with her and gone to war with her.

Another of Max Fleischer's productions to be an instant hit was the character of Popeye the Sailor who was first seen on cinema screens in 1933. Popeye had originally appeared as a cartoon strip in newspapers in 1929 and was best known for gaining instant super-strength powers by eating tinned spinach. Drawn by Elzie Crisler Segar, Fleischer Studios recognized the appeal and began producing short films. These were popular with all demographic ranges, young and old, and servicemen who enjoyed the silly storylines

Popeye was popular with servicemen and easy to recreate.

for the pure entertainment they were. After America went to war, it was not long before Popeye, like other cartoon films, was mobilized by the studios. The first animated wartime short with Popeye appeared in 1942 and was entitled *You're a Sap, Mr Jap*.

In August 1936, Popeye was joined by a curious-looking character which appeared in the comic strip called 'Wha's a Jeep?' The character looked like a cross between a teddy bear and a dog, but with a large bulbous nose. This was the Jeep, and in the story Popeye enquires of a Professor Brainstine, what is a Jeep? It is explained to him that a Jeep is an extraordinary life form from a fourth-dimension world which is now in our third dimensional world. It is highly intelligent, friendly, has the ability to walk up walls and through them and can also disappear. The Jeep does not speak except to sound its own noun, Jeep. It is given the name of Eugene to identify it and appears in a few Popeye films from 1940. It is interesting to note that the term Jeep should be used five years before the vehicle of the same name began rolling off the assembly lines at the production plants of Willys-Overland and Ford. The name for the vehicle was not inspired by the cartoon character but rather from a contraction of the letters 'GP' which is understood to have been to indicate the term 'General Purpose'. The term was popularized by servicemen who did not fail to see that, like Popeye's Jeep, the vehicle could go virtually anywhere. With over 637,000 built during the war and used in all theatres of fighting, the Jeep was an obvious contender for individual vehicles to be named and have some form of imagery painted on them.

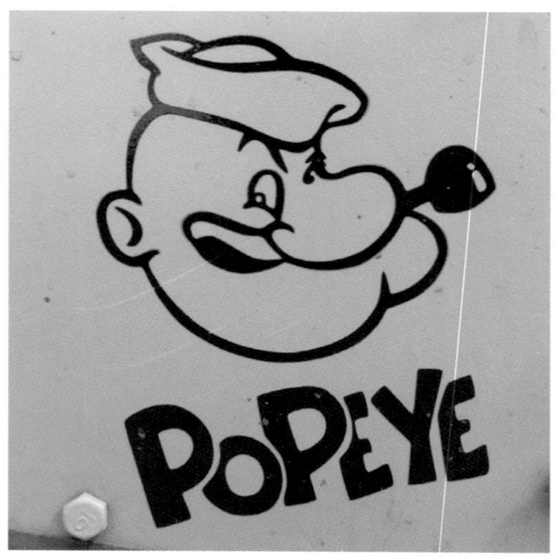

Almost anyone could draw an acceptable image of Popeye.

This recreated image of Popeye was painted on a Dodge WC54 ambulance by Keith Pettit. The vehicle is owned by Glen Rummery and shows how a detailed image could be achieved if the right paint was available.

Showing the position of Popeye on the WC54 ambulance.

The 'Jeep' cartoon character featured in pre-war Popeye films; it was only natural that the image should appear on a Jeep vehicle.

Chapter Two

The French Army: National Pride and Personal Choice

In 1939 the French Army was one of the largest forces in Europe and considered by many to be one of the most powerful in the world. The strength of its armoured units, with some 3,500 tanks of all types, was slightly more than that of Germany, which had 3,379 tanks. Only the Soviet Red Army outnumbered these with an estimated 24,000 tanks, many of which were considered obsolete. Nevertheless it still represented a formidable force. French tanks were formed into divisions, along with a number of smaller units of brigades and battalions. Each of these had its own unit insignia and individual vehicles often had identifying names on the turrets or hulls.

The method of using polygonal geometrical symbols based on playing cards as a means of identification had originated in the First World War. The system had worked well and more than twenty years later the tradition was being continued with the card suits shown in the national colours of France. The colour of the suit indicated the Company, such as blue for 1st Company, white for 2nd Company and red for 3rd Company. Typically the suits represented the section, such as a spade representing 1st Section, a heart being 2nd Section, a diamond being 3rd Section and a club designating 4th Section. In the French territories of Algeria, Tunisia and Morocco, the French Army had deployed armoured units since the 1920s, including vehicles such as the AMD White-Laffly 50AM armoured car which was in service with units of the 7th Regiment des Chasseurs Africaines Levant. Vehicles in this unit carried playing card suits for identification and one was named 'Vendredi 13' (Friday 13), no doubt an attempt at tempting fate because of the implication of bad luck attached to the date. When Italian troops serving in North Africa attacked French units in June 1940 following Italy's declaration of war, one of the earliest recorded casualties in the campaign was Vendredi 13, which was destroyed near to Damascus, thereby proving that Friday 13 was unlucky after all. As well as playing cards, the French sometimes used domino tiles with numbered spots to identify formations. Other symbols included multi-rayed sunbursts in yellow, which was used by the 2nd Cuirassiers. The 18th Dragons of the 1st Division légère mécanique, DLM (light mechanized division), used the emblem of a white 'hippogriffe', a mythical winged creature on a circular blue background. A variation of this badge was a white hippogriffe on a green oval outlined in white.

From the mid-1930s French tanks and other armoured vehicles were being painted in camouflage colour schemes of various hues which were designed to break up the outline of their shape. The patterns were varied, and in some cases quite complex, involving a range of greens, browns and black. In March 1937 one particularly dazzling camouflage scheme was devised which used no fewer than fifteen separate colours in three distinct shades which included blues, browns and darker colours. Colonel (later General) Charles de Gaulle, a leading exponent of armoured warfare in the French Army, recognized the importance of such camouflage patterns which could improve survivability on the battlefield. He also understood that by 'personalizing' vehicles with emblems of the crew's choice it could help morale. Colonel de Gaulle also suggested that as well as vehicles carrying divisional signs and unit emblems, each vehicle should be 'named' after a battle in which French Troops had fought. Presumably these were meant to be those where the French had won a victory, such as Borodino, Austerlitz and Marengo.

One example resulting from this suggestion was the title 'Yorktown', after the siege of the city from 28 September to 19 October 1781, during the American War of Independence, where the Comte de Rochambeau commanded French troops supporting the Continental Army of George Washington against British forces. This particular title of battle is known to have been painted on the turret of a Char D2 tank of the 507th Regiment de Chars de Combat or tank regiment, which in early 1939, before the outbreak of war, was based in the area of Metz. Colonel de Gaulle's suggestion appears to have fitted in well with French national pride and honour. In fact, so popular did it prove that his idea soon caught on with many armoured units. Photographs taken at the time show tanks with a variety of names such as 'Verdun', 'Vauquois' and 'Sedan', painted on their hulls or turrets, after locations where the French Army fought during the First World War. Later on, the names of types of animals were used, along with those of mythical creatures, and historical figures, especially Joan d'Arc.

It was not until after several months of inactivity along the Franco-German border that the German Army launched an attack against France, Belgium and Holland on 10 May 1940. This ended the period known to the British as the 'phoney war', or 'drôle de guerre' to the French. The speed and weight of the attack was unprecedented and the Allies, including the British Expeditionary Force, were forced into a fighting retreat. On 14 May Holland surrendered and on 27 May Belgium surrendered. The French Army continued to fight along with the British Army. Through records it is possible to detail the wartime history and fate of some of these vehicles which took part in the fighting at this time. For example, the tank 'Vauquois' was a Char B1 bis commanded by Lieutenant Pierre Bourgeois of the 41st BCC which was destroyed in fighting in the area of Perthes on 10 June 1940. Many other vehicles were similarly named after regions of France, for example there was a tank named 'Rhône', but its fate is not known.

Before the outbreak of war most French tanks were painted with a 'roundel' or national corcade (cockade) in the tricolour colours of red, white and blue, comprising of an outer circle in red, an inner circle of white and a solid blue centre. These roundels appeared on the sides of the hull and the glacis plates at the front of the vehicles. Turret insignia included a section number, sometimes the rank of the vehicle commander and other designations to identify which company the vehicle served with.

A typical vehicle with these insignia painted on it was a Renault R35 tank, known to have been commanded by Captain Pierre Perat, commanding officer of 21st Battallion de Chars de Combate (Tank Battalion) deployed in the area of Alsace in June 1940. Captain Perat's R35 tank had all the usual regimental symbols, along with a large letter 'P' on the turret, to indicate his name, following the official letter 'V' which indicated the 3rd Company of 21st Battallion de Chars de Combat (BCC). In addition, he also called his tank 'L'Aiglon' (Little Eagle) which was painted on the turret. This was a departure from what Colonel de Gaulle had suggested, but other tank commanders were naming their vehicles in a similar way, such as the FCM36 tank known to have been commanded by Pierre Cassier of the 1st Company of the 7th BCC who named his tank 'Le Téméraire' (The Reckless) while deployed in the region of Sedan in May 1940. One H39 tank serving with a DCR unit during the 1940 campaign was seen in action with the name 'Le Foudroyant' (The Lightning) painted on the side of the hull.

More regimental tank commanders stuck with tradition and named their vehicles after national regions, including 'Champagne', 'Dunkerque', 'Var' or 'Normandie'. Some used the names of French overseas territories such as 'Tunisie', 'Maroc'and 'Algerie'. Other tank commanders were more imaginative in their naming and vehicles were seen called 'Vertus' (Virtue), 'L'Impassible' (The Impassable) and 'Je Grogne' (I Growl). The latter appeared above the head of a wild boar in black painted onto a white shield, which was the unit emblem of the 2/26 Bataillon de chars de combat. It was painted on the sides of tanks serving with the 1 DCR (Division Cuirassée) in May 1940. The names of characters from popular literature also appeared, such as 'D'Artagnan', a central figure in the novel *The Three Musketeers*, by the French author Alexandre Dumas.

When France surrendered on 21 June 1940, the surviving tanks, vehicles and weapons of the army, such as artillery, fell into the hands of the German Army which absorbed into service the most useful types. These vehicles were distributed to units where they were sometimes renamed by their new users who 'christened' them with girls' names, terms of endearment or a simple nickname. Italian troops also took into service a number of captured French tanks, such as Renault R35s, which they deployed elsewhere. Some of these captured tanks were eventually taken to Sicily where around fifty were deployed with the Italian 101 Battaglione Carri which eventually used them to oppose the Allied landings on the island in Operation Husky in July 1943. A number were destroyed and

Images on French army tanks, such as this S35 SOMUA seen on display in the Tank Museum in Bovington, Dorset, were usually regimental symbols.

The French army was later equipped with US-built vehicles such as this M3 Scout Car which is named *Oradour*, after the town in the Haute-Vienne region of France.

others were captured such as the one still known by its French name of 'Le Hérisson' (The Hedgehog) which was painted on its hull.

The surrender of the French army did not mean the end to French resistance, because around 139,000 French troops escaped during the evacuation from Dunkirk and were taken to England. These were formed into the Free French forces commanded by General de Gaulle. They had no vehicles, weapons or replacement uniforms but gradually they were reformed and re-equipped with British equipment. Two brigades of French troops fought in the Western Desert where they admirably proved themselves at engagements such as Bir Hakeim. French forces expanded and in 1943 they began to receive American-produced equipment including uniforms, weapons and vehicles which allowed four divisions to take part in the Italian campaign. The new American-built vehicles, such as M8 armoured cars, replaced the British vehicles and French troops continued the tradition of naming them. More French armoured units took part in the Normandy campaign from June 1944 and in August that year the landings in the south of France, Operation Dragoon, resulted in further French units deployed to Europe. One unit was the 2nd armoured Division of the 1st Free French Army where the crew of a Sherman tank called 'Valmy' was observed taking part in the fighting in the region of Provence. The name was in reference to the 1792 battle where the

The French army also used Jeeps and this example, in the colours of the French Forces of the Interior, is named 'La Guêpe' meaning The Wasp.

French defeated a Prussian army and illustrates a continuation of General de Gaulle's suggestion for vehicle names of French victories. In total some twelve divisions of the First Army commanded by General Jean de Lattre de Tassigny served all the way through to the end of the war.

During the closing months of the war an M7 SPG of the 2ème Batterie de Tir of the 40ème Regiment D'Artillerie Nord Africaine, 2ème Blindée, named 'MdL de Lauzun' was seen serving in the region of Alsace in January 1945. In this region French troops took part in the Battle of the Colmar Pocket which destroyed German forces in the area. The tank 'MdL de Lauzun' had originally been called 'El Moghrabi' but the crew renamed it in honour of their commander Marechal des Logis de Lauzun who had been killed in action in August 1944. The crew of another French M4A2 Sherman tank serving with the 2nd Squadron of the 5th Regiment of Chasseurs called their vehicle 'Vendome' and on 4 April 1945 a Sherman tank of the 2nd Squadron of the 1st Regiment of Cuirassiers was seen entering the German town of Karlsruhe on the side of which was painted the name 'Leopard'. The French may have appeared creative in the naming of their vehicles but when it came to images they preferred to stay with the traditional formula of using recognized names and good luck motifs along with, perhaps, the occasional image of a mythical creature.

Chapter Three

The British Army: Making a Point

Even before the outbreak of war, some units of the British Army were discreetly displaying 'unofficial' artwork on vehicles; but the practice was not widespread and the images or names were not very obvious. Some of the newer, more liberal-minded officers did not mind the practice but those commanding officers of the 'old school' actively discouraged it on the grounds that it was not the 'way of the British Army'. Gradually the regulations were relaxed and personal designs began to appear on vehicles. Dispatch riders on motorcycles had more opportunity to paint titles such as a girl's name on the fuel tank where it was less conspicuous. More obvious were the slogans which appeared chalked on vehicles by troops as they prepared to go 'overseas' to fight in the North African campaign or the Far East. These were temporary and could be washed off to be replaced by other phrases as the mood took the men, but always with an optimistic tone to them such as 'Next Stop the Rhine'.

Typical of the humorous messages chalked on trucks of all armies.

This Austin K3 truck has been named 'Amanda Jane' by the driver.

British Army drivers very discreetly, almost inconspicuously, painted girls names on their vehicles.

Close-up showing the freehand style of painting.

This Austin K3 truck has been named 'Vera Lynn' after the forces' sweetheart who entertained the troops.

Usually when the troops were at the quayside waiting to board their ships newsreel cameramen and photographers from newspapers were present to record the occasion. Much would be made of these scenes and the troops would scrawl sentiments on their vehicles such as 'Khyber Pass to Hellfire Pass' or 'Berlin or Bust', mainly for the benefit of the cameras. Being written in chalk the words were not permanent and if considered too rude for public viewing could be erased. The crew's permanent name for their vehicle would be added but sometimes this would not be chosen until later. Some crews took inspiration from comedians of the day or the work of cartoonists which appeared in newspapers. Cartoonists' work satirized Hitler, Mussolini and Tojo, as well as Goering, Himmler and Goebbels who were all ridiculed with caricatures which over-emphasized certain prominent features. Some of these images were reproduced to prove a point such as Hitler's hair or moustache, the corpulent size of Goering and Mussolini, the skeletal appearance of Himmler and Goebbels and protruding teeth of Tojo. One example of this kind of satirical imagery was photographed on the side of a Jeep probably during the Italian campaign. The Jeep is named 'Shortstop' and driven by a US serviceman. On the side are three discs, each containing an image of Mussolini, Hitler and Tojo. Mussolini has been crossed out and the words 'Benito Finito' written, which would indicate the year 1943 when Italy capitulated and Mussolini was ousted to be replaced

This Jeep was photographed during the Italian Campaign in 1943 and shows the three Axis forces leaders, with Mussolini 'knocked out'.

by Marshal Badoglio. Underneath is the legend 'Uno Abbasso Due Via' which translates to mean 'One down two to go'. This is another reference to Italy's surrender and that only Hitler and Tojo remained.

British humour at the time was usually 'tongue in cheek' and inspired by political situations. Cartoon strips in newspapers were seen as being intended for the younger generation of readers with serials such as 'Pip, Squeak and Wilfred', featuring a trio of animal characters which appeared in 1919 and was published in the *Daily Mirror* newspaper. The strip continued throughout the war, but none of the characters appear to have been used as an inspiration for images drawn on vehicles. The names of the characters were used by the 53rd (City of London) Heavy Anti-Aircraft Regiment of the Royal Artillery when it was deployed to France to provide protection to RAF airfields; the regiment had two gun sites named after each character to give a total of six locations. Other cartoon strips in newspapers included 'Rupert Bear' in the *Daily Express*, and 'Oor Wullie' and 'The Broons' both of which appeared in the Scottish newspaper *The Sunday Post*. The action adventure hero 'Garth' began to appear in the *Daily Mirror* from 1943, but, again none of these had the same wide appeal as the American cartoons such as Daffy Duck and Mickey Mouse.

One cartoon serialization which did have a wide appeal with adult male readers, especially British servicemen, was 'Jane' whose exploits began appearing in the *Daily Mirror* from 1932. Introduced as the 'Misadventures' the wartime storylines in which she became involved featured wartime spies and invariably ended with her losing her clothes except for her underwear, which was always frilly and very scanty. No wonder, then, that such an image should prove popular, but as far as is known the features of Jane never appeared on tanks or vehicles. However, one heavyweight, long-range gun was nicknamed Jane after the character. This had a calibre of fifteen inches and was operated by a coastal battery as part of the 540 Coastal Defence Regiment located at Wanstone in Kent. Along with another gun nicknamed 'Clem', believed to be called after Winston Churchill's wife Clementine, the battery was intended to provide fire support to friendly shipping in the Channel, but with a range of twenty-four miles, the guns could also fire at German installations on the French coast. A similar pair of coastal guns with the slightly smaller calibre of fourteen inches were nicknamed 'Winnie', after Churchill, and 'Pooh', after Winnie the Pooh, the eponymous character of a popular children's book which appeared in the 1920s.

Regular inspections to make sure that all items of equipment and weapons were in good order left little opportunity to decorate tool boxes with any personal embellishments. British Army uniforms being made from wool were not ideal for adding any personal message, unlike leather flying jackets, and had any soldier done so he would have found himself being charged with defacing property. In any case, there was no need for such frippery because divisional badges sewn onto the sleeves were more than sufficient for identification, also they were official. Some of the older officers, those who had served in the First World War, were what the troops called 'Regimental Types' - sticklers for regulation dress code, which also covered equipment.

During the course of the war the British Army increased in size and as it expanded it created a number of new divisions, brigades and smaller units for special operations, all of which had to be identified by their own individual signs and emblems. One of the earliest of these new units was the 6th Armoured Division, created on 12 September 1940, which adopted the emblem of the armoured or mailed right fist as its insignia. The unit was equipped with Matilda and Valentine tanks and was later re-equipped with Crusader and M4 Sherman tanks. The armoured fist was meant to represent the armoured punch to break through enemy defences, which it achieved during the division's service in North Africa, in Italy and later in Europe as part of V Corps. The image of the mailed fist was used by the Germans three years later, when, in October 1943, they created the 17th SS Panzergrenadier Division and named it the 'Götz von Berlichingen'. The name was taken from a sixteenth-century knight who had lost his right hand in battle. The story runs that he employed a blacksmith to make him a replacement hand out of iron. In commemoration of this tough fighter the division adopted the iron fist as its emblem and it earned a fearsome reputation in battle during campaigns such as Normandy.

One of few pre-war units to be raised was the Mobile Division (Egypt) formed in 1938 and commanded by Major-General Sir Percy Hobart, expert in armoured warfare and tank design. In January 1940 the division was given the new title of 7th Armoured Division and it continued its service in North Africa. The unit soon became famous as the 'Desert Rats', a nickname it derived from its new divisional badge which showed the image of an animal called the jerboa in silhouette. The story goes that the wife of the divisional commander had seen this small rodent on a visit to the zoo in Cairo and drew an image of the creature. It went on to appear as the official divisional sign on the vehicles of the unit – a jerboa in red set inside a white circle on a red background. During the war there would be variations on the design as the 7th Armoured Division went on to serve in Italy and North West Europe.

The 43rd (Wessex) Infantry Division which served in the reconnaissance role during the war could trace its origins back to 1915. During the inter-war years it had been reformed but had always retained its divisional emblem of the mythical winged creature known as the 'wyvern', usually in yellow. When the division was deployed to Europe it soon gained a reputation for its tough fighting; the Germans called them the 'Yellow Devils' in reference to the colour of the divisional badge. General Brian Horrocks commanding XXX Corps had a particular fondness for the 43rd Division; as the Allies advanced across Europe he would often exchange cheery greetings with officers of the unit and enquire of them in an informal manner, 'How's the wicked Wyvern today?' Like the vehicles in the 7th Armoured Division, many of these were also named by their crews. In preparation for D-Day it was realized that specialist designs of armoured vehicles would be required to attack the defences along the French coast. The man chosen to create this force was Major-General Sir Percy Hobart, who had commanded the fledgling 7th Armoured Division in 1938 and was General Montgomery's brother-in-law.

Three variants showing the styles of the jereboa of the 7th Armoured Division known as the 'Desert Rats'.

The Wyvern symbol as used by the 43rd Wessex Division seen here on a Daimler 'Dingo' scout car.

The 79th Armoured Division was a specialist armoured unit raised in 1942 and had as its divisional badge a full-faced bull's head in monochrome with red nostrils and horns set on a yellow triangle. It came to prominence during the Normandy campaign in 1944 when its vehicles provided essential support to troops in overcoming obstacles. The emblem appeared on thousands of vehicles from troop carriers to bridge layers, minefield clearance vehicles, demolition tanks, trucks and many other specialist types. As well as having the bull's head divisional badge the crews also gave their individual vehicles a variety of titles which ranged from girls' names to locations, and personality, such as 'Fury'. This title was painted on the front of one of 79th Division's Petard AVREs. It was used to demolish obstacles with a special launcher to fire a powerful explosive projectile. Although not personalized vehicle art in the true sense, the divisional emblem of the 79th was instantly recognizable by troops.

In the Far East a new divisional badge was adopted for a newly-created special unit known as the Chindits. The emblem was a 'Chinthe', a mythical creature in Burmese culture which was half lion and half eagle and appeared on temples across the country. The divisional commander Ord Wingate believed the creature symbolized the co-operation between troops on the ground and the aircraft which would supply them with air drops. Brigadier 'Mad Mike' Calvert stated that 'It was a short step from "Chinthe" to "Chindit". The term caught on and the Chindit force was named. The griffin is a mythical beast being part lion part eagle but the Chinthe, while being similar, is an entirely different shape.

Such divisional symbols while identifying a unit are not markings or a name unique to a particular vehicle. Soldiers would still paint some kind of image on trucks such as ducks, dogs or cats in the age-old traditional style and even a place name which had special meaning to the crew. The Far East campaign was no different and vehicles were named such as an M7 Priest SPG serving with the 18th Field Regiment of the Royal Artillery with the 14th Army in Burma, whose crew called it 'Deepcut', after the depot in Surrey where many units of the British Army had received their basic training.

Naming a vehicle in memory of a member of the crew who had been killed was quite well known among the armies, including the French Army, and also among other branches of the armed forces. The crew of a Lancaster bomber flying with No 467 of the Royal Australian Air Force named their aircraft 'Jock's Revenge' after a flight engineer was killed while flying a mission. It may seem rather a macabre thing to do, but to the survivors it was a tribute to their colleague and a mark of the respect in which they held him.

Sometimes a vehicle could be named for no other reason than the commander liked the title. For example, the Humber Scout Car used by Captain G.E. Gull, the Technical Adjutant of the 1st Battalion Coldstream Guards, serving with the Guards Armoured Division, named his vehicle 'Jack-in-the-Box'. The vehicle had all the other usual unit symbols and numbers, including the Ever Open Eye of the Guards Armoured Division, as well as the name of the vehicle. It was used throughout the European campaign from 1944 until the end of the war. Captain Gull survived and drove back to England in Jack-in-the-Box. The vehicle still survives and today is on display in the Tank Museum at Bovington in Dorset.

To the Canadian troops who served throughout the Italian campaign and across Western Europe it was only natural they too should name their vehicles. For example, the crew of an M7 'Priest' serving with the 55th Field Battery (S) of the 19th Field Regiment (SP) Royal Canadian Artillery of the Canadian 3rd Infantry Division, called their vehicle 'The Wacky Seven'. The M7 was operated by a crew of seven men, hence the number, and the names of each member of the crew was painted on a yellow maple leaf on the side of the vehicle. Other vehicles in the same unit appeared with names such as 'Darling' and 'Doffe' painted on their hulls. During the same campaign the crew of a Sexton SPG serving with the 6th South African Armoured Division named their vehicle 'Hornet II', while the crew of a Sexton serving with the 4th (Queens Own) Hussars with the 9th Armoured Brigade simply called their vehicle 'Ale', no doubt after the crew's thirst for beer, thereby proving that soldiers come up with the strangest of names. Examples of named Sextons can be seen in museums such as 'Alberta' at the Cobbaton Combat Collection at Chittlehampton, near Umberleigh in Devon, and

'Jack-in-the-Box' was used by Captain G.E. Gull of the Coldstream Guards and is on display at the Tank Museum at Bovington in Dorset.

The Humber scout car 'Jack-in-the-Box'.

The Sexton SPG was used by British and Canadian troops; they were named by their crews.

'Beau Brummell' at Fort Nelson, Portsdown Hill Road, Fareham in Hampshire. At the Muckleburgh Collection in Norfolk they have a Sexton SPG on display bearing the name 'Alligator'.

After the invasion of Poland in September 1939 a number of Polish troops fled the country, heading first to France and then to England after Dunkirk. Like a number of other servicemen in exile, including Czechoslovakian, Dutch and Belgian troops, they were all equipped with British uniforms, weapons and vehicles. Many of these expatriates went on to serve in campaigns across Europe. Polish troops fought at Normandy, Arnhem and also during the Italian campaign where they used a range of British equipment including tanks such as the Firefly tank, an M4 Sherman armed with a 17-Pounder gun. Some of these tanks were named by their crews, such as one called 'Zemsta II' which is known to have served with the 1st Krechowiecki Lancers of the II Polish Corps. The name Zemsta means 'Revenge' and presumably when the original Zemsta tank was lost, the crew of the replacement vehicle decided to name it in honour of its predecessor. During the Normandy campaign from June 1944 Polish units used a self-propelled gun known as the Sexton, which comprised a 25-Pounder gun mounted on a Sherman tank chassis. Some of these were named after famous battles, such as

'Raclawice', in honour of the victory over the Russians in 1794, and is known to have served with the Polish 1st Armoured Division. In 1939 the Polish Army had only a few obsolete tanks and armoured vehicles such as 7TP tankettes. They carried identification markings similar in style to those used on tanks of the French army. That is to say a series of coloured triangles or circles to denote platoons and squares to represent the company in which a vehicle was serving. Some vehicles also carried symbols painted on vehicle turrets and were known to include other forms of wild animals such as bison and lynx. In some instances these appeared in red, white or blue and could also be framed by a coloured circle.

Following the success of the Allied landings at Normandy in June 1944 more troops in exile from those countries under German occupation were deployed to serve in Europe. Polish troops had been fighting in North Africa and Italy and French troops had landed on D-Day itself; they were joined by Belgian troops. In August 1944 more French troops landed in the South of France during Operation Dragoon. Other units to deploy included the 1st Independent Belgian Armoured Brigade Group which was equipped mainly with American vehicles and weapons. The Brigade had been formed in 1943, was commanded by Lieutenant-Colonel Jean-Baptiste Piron and during the Normandy campaign it was attached to the British 6th Airborne Division. In August it was transferred to the 49th Infantry Division before going on to serve as part of the British Second Army. Among the armoured vehicles used by the unit were

This Sexton SPG is called 'Alberta' and is on display at the Cobbaton Combat Collection near Umberleigh in Devon.

The Staghound armoured car was used by the British Army and Commonwealth forces. This example is named 'Horsa' and has the badge of the Guards Armoured Division, the Ever Open Eye.

'Staghounds', some of which carried names. One had 'Marlborough' stencilled on the hull. A Staghound named 'Audemer' used by the Brigade is preserved as a tribute to the unit and is on display at the Tank Museum in Kappellen near Brussels in Belgium. The Staghound was an American design known as the T17E1. However, the Americans did not use the vehicle which had been produced for the British Army and was in turn later issued it to other Allied units such as the 1st Belgian Brigade.

The British Army used a range of American-designed vehicles including tanks and the highly versatile Jeep. These had been used in North Africa and Italy, but it was during the European campaign that they really came into their own, and obviously these were named. For example, during the Normandy campaign from June 1944 Lieutenant Michael Trasenster of 'A' Squadron 4/7 Royal Dragoon Guards named his Sherman tank 'Winchester' after his school. The regiment, and A Squadron in particular, went on the serve with great distinction during the campaign and in one action alone on 14 June, just a week after the initial landings in Normandy, A Squadron was heavily engaged by German armour and succeeded in destroying five Panther tanks near the

The Sherman tank was used in all theatres of the war and the crews frequently named the vehicles with a variety of titles such as this 'Lily Marlene', a variation of the spelling of a popular song of that title at the time.

Sometimes a simple title and image summed up everything for a driver.

These symbols could not be more representative of everything that is British. The rider Bellerophon astride Pegasus, the badge of the British Airborne Divisions and the reference to cricket with the British ball knocking down the stumps with the Nazi insignia.

This Daimler Dingo scout car has the badge of the 43rd Wessex Division but is also named 'Benghazi'.

Close-up of the place name where the British Army served in North Africa.

The name Benghazi was popular, especially with the troops who had served there, and was used on a number of vehicles.

village of Lingèvres. The headquarters tank serving with the Sherwood Foresters in the same campaign was named 'Robin Hood' after the outlaw, which legend would have it, lived in Sherwood with his followers. Not perhaps the most original of titles but it was good for morale and the men serving in the unit could identify with it. Unfortunately the tank was destroyed in the fighting around Hill 103 close to the town of Saint Pierre in Normandy. Another named Sherman which stood out during the Normandy landings was 'Beverley' which one of the crew, William Betts, who served with the Essex Yeomanry and landed on D-Day, remembers was painted on the turret.

Some of the tank crews serving in the Normandy campaign had seen service in North Africa and, in a hangover from those days, they named their vehicles after towns in Libya, such as Benghazi. Indeed, the name of this particular town was seen used on many tanks and scout cars.

Armoured engagements became a regular occurrence in Normandy, with some spectacular surprises. At the town of Villers-Bocage, for example, on 13 July a parked column of vehicles from the British 7th Armoured Division was stretched along the road running through the town. Suddenly and completely unexpectedly they were attacked and wiped out almost to the last vehicle. Leading the attack was SS Hauptsturmführer (Captain) Michael Wittmann of the 101 Heavy Panzer Battalion equipped with Tiger tanks. In the space of fifteen minutes the audacious attack destroyed fourteen tanks and fifteen other AFVs. Wittmann was an outstanding tank commander who by the time of his death had claimed 138 tanks destroyed, many on the Eastern Front in Russia. Fate caught up with Wittmann on the 8 August 1944 when he was advancing across open country in the company of two other Tiger tanks near the village of St Aignan de Crasmesnil. From their right flank the three Tigers were engaged by Sherman tanks from A Squadron of the 1st Northamptonshire Yeomanry. At the front was a Firefly version, a Sherman armed with a 17-pounder gun. The gunner Joe Ekins opened fire and destroyed all three Tiger tanks, killing Wittmann. All tanks in A Squadron were named after towns in Russia and Joe's tank, commanded by Sergeant Gordon, was called Velikye Luki.

Joe Ekins, who served with A Squadron, 1st Northamptonshire Yeomanry during the Normandy campaign. He was a gunner in the Firefly version of the Sherman tank named 'Velikye Luki' when he destroyed the Tiger tank commanded by tank ace Hauptsturmführer Michael Wittmann.

Chapter Four

To Name or Not to Name: A National Difference of Opinion

War is a multi-cultural experience which forces together men of all beliefs and political ideologies, either as allies or facing one another as enemies. This was never more apparent than during the Second World War, with France fielding troops from its overseas territories including North Africa, and Britain, with its vast empire stretching around the world, recruiting from South Africa, Canada, New Zealand, India and Australia. There were many other nationalities involved too, including the expatriate troops who had managed to escape across Europe before the Germans invaded and occupied their countries. Each had their own set of ideas about motifs and names which they would apply to vehicles in the hope they would bring good luck. Some of these were superstitious, others used the images as tongue in cheek humour, but it always came back to good luck. Some vehicle crews preferred to keep things simple and use either a place name or a reference to something unique to their country. Canadians, for example, used the maple leaf, which was also a national emblem, along with girls' names and animal names such as bison.

On the other side, Italy was perhaps the most liberal-minded of the three main countries forming the Axis powers. The country was a fascist state under *Il Duce*, Benito Mussolini, who had ordered the invasion of Ethiopia in 1935 and Albania in 1939. As they did not undermine the status quo of European politics, these actions at the time were viewed as nothing more than sideshows and of no real concern to other European states. Many of the slogans appearing on vehicles were declarations of faith in Mussolini and the victory of Italy.

On the other side of the world Japan, which allied itself in an Axis partnership with Germany and Italy, was an ideological state and most slogans appearing on banners of this emergent militaristic state were assertions of victory and power.

Germany was sombre, militaristically ambitious and ideological. Even so, there were some high ranking officers who expressed their unconventional attitudes towards state policy and yet still remained within the boundaries of military convention. For example, the Luftwaffe General Adolf Galland demonstrated his maverick opinions by displaying the image of Mickey Mouse on his aircraft. Hitler was known to enjoy some films released by the Disney studios, but whether or not this extended to Mickey Mouse is not recorded. Hauptmann Hubert Pölz flew some 1,000 missions during the war and

Canadian-built 'Otter' scout car named 'Bison' along with the maple leaf symbol of Canada.

'Sally Ann' is a Canadian-built General Motors C-15TA armoured truck used by the Canadian Army and is shown with the badge of the 79th Armoured Division on the front.

became famous for his Ju 87 'Stuka' dive bomber which was decorated with the image of a snake along its fuselage.

Although America had no overseas territories like France or an Empire like Britain, it was nevertheless a cosmopolitan society with many ethnic groups whose families had immigrated there, mostly from Poland, Germany, Italy, Russia and Ireland, but also from dozens more countries of origin. Some of those serving in the American armed forces in 1942 were second or third generation immigrants from countries against which America was now fighting. Bringing together such a diverse range of cultures was bound to have an effect. There were natural humorists, there were the deeply religious, and there were the superstitious. But interestingly, of all the types of imagery which appeared on vehicles there were no obvious religious references. All of the fighting men had their own ideas about images they would paint on their vehicles and what names to give them. The images could be good luck symbols, from horseshoes to dice; the names were usually those of girlfriends or wives, or perhaps towns where they lived. The crews of some vehicles developed names which were semi-descriptive of their battlefield role, such as 'Fire Buggy', as applied to a flamethrower tank serving in the Pacific. While troops in others armies personalized their vehicles, the masters of the genres were undoubtedly the Americans. It was

Italian M14/41 tank showing the lack of symbols compared to other armies. This example is on display at the Tank Museum at Bovington in Dorset.

Recreated stylized version of Mickey Mouse which appeared on Adolf Galland's Me 109 Bf fighter.

'Macnamara's Band' actually existed. The song about it was performed in the 1940s and the film *Pinocchio* appeared in 1940. The combination of the two themes makes an ideal image for this Jeep.

Saucy and racy, but this typical image is not vulgar.

The skull and crossbones remained popular with some tank crews such as this Russian-built T-26 used during the Russo-Finnish War of 1940-41. This one is on display at the Tank Museum at Bovington in Dorset.

inevitable with so many trucks, tanks and weapons and so many young men that the application of war art should be prolific.

After the Japanese attack at Pearl Harbor the American media increased the jingoism of its propaganda, to stir the nation into action in a way never before imagined. Cartoon strips in the national newspapers, long popular with adults and younger readers alike, showed familiar characters such as Popeye taking on the Axis powers. But it was through the film studios that many of the best results were achieved. Most, if not all of the successful film studios were located in Hollywood, California, including those such as Walt Disney which were producing cartoons with humorous creations Donald Duck and Mickey Mouse. These studios had already produced feature-length cartoon films including *Snow White and the Seven Dwarfs* in 1937, followed by *Pinocchio* and *Fantasia* both in 1940, and *Dumbo* in October 1941, just two months before America became involved in the war. Even after the country went to war Disney studios still continued to produce feature-length cartoon films such as *Bambi* in 1942. The short cartoon films, featuring the Disney favourites of Donald Duck and Mickey Mouse, were still produced and the characters were put to good use in supporting the country's war effort with numerous short films.

Both the Western Allies and the Axis powers had states allied to them either through historic loyalty or for the immediate need of opposing German occupation. From late June 1941 Germany had the support of Finland in its war against Russia. Finland had already fought a costly war against the Red Army between November 1939 and March 1940 and its vehicles had gone into battle bearing the Swastika emblem which had been used by the Finnish Army for many years and was also used by the German Army. Besides carrying this emblem Finnish tanks were also marked with skull and crossbones, sometimes painted in a very haphazard fashion producing a crude finish.

Chapter Five

The German Army: A Subtle Approach

According to many British comedians and cartoonists of the time the Germans were famous for their lack of sense of humour. This opinion may have stemmed partly from the fact that the nineteenth-century Field Marshal Helmuth von Moltke was famously known to have only ever been seen to smile twice in his life. The first time was when he visited some out-dated Swedish defences and the second time when he was told the news of the death of his mother-in-law. Whether or not this story is apocryphal, the long-held opinion of the German lack of humour was certainly exploited on the radio, the stage and in newspapers in an effort to ridicule Germany. However, contrary to what the British public may or may not have believed at the time, the Germans did have a sense of humour, albeit, rather different from that of the British. As mentioned above, there was Adolf Galland who decorated his aircraft with a motif of Mickey Mouse. General Erwin Rommel, who commanded the Afrika Korps in North Africa and the German defences along the 'Atlantic Wall', did have a sense of humour, but drew the line at vulgarity. In this respect he was described by Admiral Friedrich Ruge, the General's naval adviser, as being: '...no prude, but so-called humour of a certain kind was not tolerated in his presence. Once, during a tour, a commander made an attempt in that direction, but stopped cold when he saw the expression on Rommel's face.' Rommel may have smiled inwardly to himself and probably found it secretly amusing to see familiar images and names on vehicles of the units under his command. He may have even accepted some of the more demure imagery, but he would never have tolerated out and out 'toilet wall' humour. The Americans, to a large degree, shared that opinion in accepting 'tongue in cheek' sauciness but never crudities.

Certainly the German Army was very strict and the vehicles it displayed on pre-war parades were all marked in divisional signs and unit identification numbers. Yet, when Poland was attacked on 1 September 1939, some vehicles were seen going into battle on which had been painted various names. One armoured car, for instance, was shown on newsreel film bearing the title 'Saar', no doubt after the coal-rich region of Saarland, which had been re-unified with Germany proper by 1936. This form of naming vehicles after national regions emulated the method used by the French army and would be seen again in later campaigns. The most usual form of application was in the typical German script known as Gothic style. This was elaborate in form, would have taken time to apply and would probably have been applied by the unit sign writer. Less fancy

This SdKfz 138 Hetzer tank destroyer, seen at the Tank Museum at Bovington in Dorset, is named 'Max', a popular name in the German Army.

Gothic lettering denotes the origin of this girl's name.

Recreated SdKfz 223 scout car with Afrika Korps badge on the hull and the girl's name 'Hanne', which would have appealed to Erwin Rommel.

examples were simply painted in ordinary style by a member of the crew, usually in white, but any other colour available would have also been used.

When Germany attacked France, Belgium and Holland in May 1940 the Allied armies confronted German tanks up close for the first time. One of the leading units in the attack was the Panzer Regiment 35 of the 4th Panzer Division, equipped with Panzer III tanks, commanded later in the campaign by Hauptmann Ernst Freiherr von Jungenfeld who had served in German Army in the First World War. Between the wars he travelled extensively across South America, particularly Paraguay, and he wrote a book about his experiences. Because of his travels he was known as 'Unser Pampas' (Our Pampas) by his men. His tank was named 'Pampas' after the pampas grasslands of South America, which were rendered in paint on the turret of his tank. The tank was destroyed near the town of Jandrain on 13 May 1940 when it was engaged by a French Somua S35. As for Jungenfeld, he went on to serve in Russia from 1941 and survived the war.

The speed and ferocity of the Blitzkrieg overwhelmed the French and British armies and they were forced to conduct a fighting withdrawal to the coast where there were plans in place to evacuate them to England. As they retreated the troops abandoned equipment, weapons and thousands of vehicles. Not all of these were destroyed. The German Army repaired some of these vehicles and they were repainted in the colour

This German SdKfz 251 APC is named 'Lo Lo' in the way it would have been during the war.

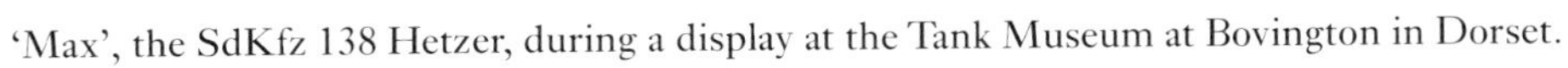

'Max', the SdKfz 138 Hetzer, during a display at the Tank Museum at Bovington in Dorset.

Close-up of the Gothic lettering: 'Max'.

scheme of the German Army. Some drivers applied names to these captured vehicles, usually girls' names.

When the Italian Army in North Africa was routed by the British Army, including tanks of the 7th Armoured Division, in late 1940 they were reinforced by the specially-raised Deutsches Afrika Korps in February 1941. This force was not constrained by convention and was more relaxed in its attitude because of the circumstances and nature of the conditions in which it found itself fighting. A number of the vehicles they deployed were given the names of girls or nicknames and vehicles captured from the British were re-named with German titles. For example, a pair of captured AEC 4X4 armoured command vehicles were named 'Max' and 'Moritz' after two cartoon character boys in popular German literature. They were used as command vehicles by Erwin Rommel throughout the campaign in North Africa and referred to as 'Mammuts' (Mammoths) due to their size; each weighed twelve tons and measured 6.10m in length, 2.36m in width and 2.90 m in height. The British troops had called the design 'Dorchesters' – because they were so well-appointed and comfortable they reminded the troops of the grand hotel of that name in London. The names Max and Moritz were also used on pair of massive railway guns used in Russia. One of these was destroyed but the other was captured at Stalingrad and today is on display at the Kubinka Tank Museum in Moscow. The name Max was also applied to other vehicles used by various units in various theatres of operations and was seen from Russia to France.

A typical example of vehicles being named by the Afrika Korps was that of a Marder III self-propelled gun captured near Fondouk in Tunis in April 1943, towards the end of the campaign in North Africa, which was found painted with the girl's name 'Paula'. Another Marder SPG was discovered the following year in France during the Normandy campaign, when a unit from the US 101st Airborne Division (nicknamed the 'Screaming Eagles') captured a Marder I which had the name 'Lotte' painted on the side.

If the Afrika Korps was relaxed in its attitude towards painting unofficial images and names on vehicles, then the U-Boats flouted it to the hilt. The submarine crews operated in an almost buccaneer manner. At sea the only person to whom the crew were answerable was the captain of the boat (as submarines are known). Flotillas adopted caricature emblems which appeared on the conning towers of the submarines, such as the 3rd Flotilla which had a tortoise, the 29th which had a moose head, and the 29th which had a donkey. Unarguably the most famous emblem of all was that of the 9th Flotilla, with the Laughing Swordfish (*Der Lachende Schwertfisch*) which usually appeared in green but some versions also appeared in red.

Pieces of artillery were given names, especially the large 600mm-calibre heavyweight railway guns. Several long-range weapons known as Karl-Gerät (Karl Device) were built by the armaments company of Rheinmetall between 1937 and 1940 of which six

The 600mm calibre long-range railway gun 'Eva', later renamed 'Wotan', seen here being transported. The graffiti on the canvas covering reads 'Eternal Youth', along with the name of the weapon.

A German Marder III tank destroyer with 'kill rings' on the barrel of its 75mm gun.

The crew of an '88' gun have painted a number of 'kill rings' on the barrel and two ships on the gun shield; an impressive tally by any standards.

were named to distinguish them. They were known as 'Adam' (later renamed Baldur), 'Eva' (later renamed Wotan), 'Thor', 'Odin', 'Loki' and 'Ziu'. The seventh gun was unnamed and never used in combat, being reserved for fi ring for trials. The guns were used variously on the Eastern Front in Russia, being deployed to the Crimea, and later in Poland. Some of the guns were destroyed during the war but Loki and Eva were captured by American forces along with the trials weapon which was taken to the Aberdeen Proving Ground in Maryland before being scrapped. The Russians captured two of the guns, Ziu and Odin, and today one is on display at the Kubinka Tank Museum. The Germans produced two even larger guns, named Dora and Gustav, built by the armaments company of Krupp in 1941. These fired shells of 800mm calibre and represented the zenith of development in heavy-calibre artillery guns.

Smaller calibre weapons were likewise named by their crews. Crews of anti-tank guns or PaK (*Panzerabwherkanone*) were particularly fond of painting names or titles on their weapons. They also painted images of their victims on the protective gun shield or the barrel. Some successful gun crews indicated the number vehicles they had destroyed by painting a 'kill ring' on the barrel of their gun. Leading tank 'aces' such as Hauptsturmführer Michael Wittmann, nicknamed 'The Black Baron' had a total of 138 kills to his credit and Sergeant Kurt Knispel had at least 168, and possibly as many as 195. These tank commanders applied 'kill rings' to the barrels of their tank guns which were photographed for good propaganda and reproduced in publications such as *Der Adler* and *Signal* magazines. The German public also saw these images which gave support for the war effort. It was not uncommon to see 88mm PaKs with many rings on their barrels and some crews painted images of their more unusual targets on the gun shield. For example, guns sited in coastal areas were sometimes presented with a range of targets such as light boats. In such an event, if the gunners were successful in sinking one, this image was also painted on the gun shield.

Chapter Six

Russia: Patriotic Fervour of the Red Army

The Soviet Union, still widely referred to as Russia by most people during the war, had a vast military force known as the Red Army. Apart from an almost inexhaustible supply of troops the country had a massive armoured force of tanks. The Soviet Union had invaded Poland from the east on 17 September 1939 and two months later it attacked Finland. Troops had already gained combat experience in border clashes with Japanese troops in Manchuria and had also sent troops and tanks to support the Republican troops during the Spanish Civil War in 1936–39. Although tanks and other vehicles were used in these engagements none appear to have had slogans or emblems of any particular note except for unit identification symbols.

When Germany attacked on 22 June 1941 the Red Army did stand and fight, but such was the speed and weight of the German assault they were forced to retreat. For six months the Russian troops fell back deeper into the country, all the while losing millions of men and thousands of tanks and other vehicles. Finally, on 6 December the Red Army launched a massive counter-attack which pushed the Germans back for the first time. Among the Russian forces were numbers of a newly-designed tank known as the T-34. It gave the country its first great victory and in doing so restored morale in the Red Army. In Russia, being a Communist Republic, people did as they were directed by the state without question. Army vehicles were usually identified by unit emblems and carried national symbols such as a red star or the crossed hammer and sickle which appeared on the country's flag. Troops were urged on by political leaders, or Commissars, who encouraged troops to shout victory cries as they went into battle, and patriotic slogans were carried on banners. A vast range of patriotic posters were produced for propaganda purposes which carried slogans such as 'For the Motherland, Home and Freedom', 'Let's Crush the Enemy Under an Avalanche of Steel', 'Death to the Fascist Invaders' and 'Glory to the Red Army'. These populist slogans were picked up by some troops and later painted on vehicles in order to serve as inspiration to the army in general.

As the war progressed and the Germans were pushed back the Soviet Red Army began daubing patriotic slogans on the sides of vehicles. These were intended to keep up morale and included phrases such as: 'We will chase the Fascist Beast to its lair' which was seen on the turret of a tank during the Battle of Kursk in 1943.

This example of a Russian KV-1 tank, on display in the Tank Museum at Bovington in Dorset, has a patriotic slogan on the turret from women factory workers.

Some German vehicles had names such as 'Bloodhound' and the very last operational tank in service with the 1st Panzer Division, as it stood within striking distance of Moscow on 4 December 1941, was nicknamed 'Antony the Last' by the troops.

Women working in the factories producing tanks were vehemently patriotic and believed in ultimate victory. Some of them sometimes painted slogans of support on the side of the turret such as 'From the Women of Leningrad to the Front'. An example of this can be seen on a KV-1B tank on display in the Tank Museum at Bovington in Dorset. The KV-1 was named in honour of Marshal Kliment Voroshilov, chief of the Red Army since 1925, and around 1,500 were produced from 1940. Such sentiments served to remind the troops that female factory workers were tirelessly producing tanks to support their fight on the battlefield. They showed how everybody was doing their best for the country's war effort. The Red Army did not expressly paint emblems on its vehicles, beyond unit divisional signs and numbers, because there was no time for such frivolity. In some cases tanks left the production factory without being painted, apart from hastily scrawled good luck wishes or expressions of encouragement, and were sent straight into battle in this same state so that no time would be wasted in getting them into action.

This Russian T-34/85 has a recreated patriotic slogan on the turret which reads 'On to Berlin'.

The style of Russian writing is a form known as Cyrillic which is used in some fifty languages but primarily by Russia. The Red Army expanded to over 34 million men during the war, many of whom came from so-called ethnic areas such as Mongolia. Recruits from these regions were likely to be illiterate and, in the event they could read, they may not necessarily have understood mainstream Russian. Nevertheless they would have been indoctrinated into army methods and followed orders without question. Slogans painted on vehicles, even basic words such as 'to Berlin', could sometimes be spelt incorrectly.

The Red Army was not entirely without a modicum of humour as expressed in its nickname for the 1,386 M3 tanks which America supplied under the terms of the Lend-Lease programme. The Russians called these tanks 'a grave for six men' because they proved inadequate for combat in the extreme conditions in Russia. Britain supplied the Russians with about 1,000 Matilda II tanks which may have been nicknamed the 'Queen of the Desert' from their service in North Africa, but the Russians believed it to be slow and under-armed. Another American-supplied tank was the M4 Sherman. The Russians received around 4,106 of these which they nicknamed 'Emchas' (em chetyrye) in reference to the number four.

Chapter Seven

The US Army: Sometimes Saucy, Often Humorous

On 7 December 1941, America became the last of the main industrialized nations to become involved in the Second World War following the unprovoked attack by Japanese aircraft against the naval base at Pearl Harbor. At the time, America was supplying equipment and vehicles to both Britain and Russia under the Lend-Lease programme, but now it had been drawn into the war directly the armaments companies and vehicle manufacturers were mobilized to produce millions of guns and vehicles. In 1942 American companies produced 20,000 tanks and the following year this increased to over 29,000. By the end of the war America produced around 100,000 tanks and other AFVs of all main types, along with 806,000 trucks of 2.5 tons and more than 2.4 million vehicles of other types, such as Dodge 'Weapons Carriers', of which some 637,000 were vehicles known as Jeeps. A large proportion went to Allied nations as part of the Lend-Lease programme, but the bulk was kept for the American armed forces. Such a range and number of vehicles provided a perfect opportunity for young men to add their personal touch by applying some form of art work. Indeed, one could say the temptation proved too great.

The production of un-armoured vehicles outnumbered armoured vehicles by a ratio of some 10:1 and also in Britain so-called 'soft-skinned' vehicles were produced in greater numbers than tanks. For example, some 100,000 utility or 'Tilly' vehicles were produced. These were more likely to be personalized with names, most often girls' names, which was in keeping with the tradition of referring to a vehicle as 'she'. Jeeps were given all manner of names and titles such as the one photographed at the end of the war as used by the 327th Glider Infantry of the 101st Airborne Division. This is seen marked up with the name 'Doug', presumably the driver's name, along with 'Gilda V II' which presumably meant something to the driver, possibly connected with his girlfriend; this was the second vehicle with that name.

The Americans took the most relaxed, indeed broad-minded, attitude when it came to the individual artwork which was applied to vehicles, aircraft and other military hardware such as tanks and artillery. Some images became legendary and acquired a degree of status when they appeared in periodicals such as *Stars & Stripes*, the official publication of the US Armed Forces, the civilian US *Life* magazine and the British *Picture Post*, which had been founded in 1938 and now sold 1.7 million copies per week. They had a culture of popular cartoon strips, many of which were serialized and syndicated in hundreds of newspapers across the country.

The first American troops arrived in Britain in late 1942, and it did not take long after that for the cartoon caricatures to begin appearing in all sorts of places from walls of barracks to vehicles. One particular image was a curious-looking character depicted with a bald head, bulging eyes and a bulbous nose peering over what looked like a wall, and went on to become one of the most iconic of all images to appear during the war. The image was to be found virtually everywhere and was usually accompanied by the slogan 'Kilroy was here'. Walls, tents, vehicles, aircraft hangars and even some places where access was not immediately obvious could be found daubed with the graffiti. One housewife in Weymouth, Dorset, which was an assembly area for Americans preparing for D-Day, remembered how one day she was returning from shopping when she 'spotted one of those daft little signs that the Yanks chalked up everywhere that year [1944]. You'd find it everywhere on walls, lorries, hoardings, picture houses----everywhere! It was the drawing of a fat-nosed, stupid-looking chap peering over a wall with the words printed below, "KILROY WUZ HERE". I don't know what it was supposed to mean and I have never found out.'

During the Battle of the Bulge in December 1944 in the bomb-blasted town of Bastogne the famous war photographer Robert Capa, who had landed on Omaha Beach on 6 June 1944, wrote how he too saw the image and the phrase in the most improbable of locations: 'On the black, charred walls of an abandoned barn, scrawled in chalk, was the legend of [General] McAuliffe's GIs: KILROY WAS HERE.' Sometimes the middle word was spelled as 'woz' or 'waz', but the sentiment remained the same, which, in military jargon, could be 'Who Cares?'.

Over the years there have been a number of stories concerning the origin of the name of Kilroy and his character ranging from the improbable to the unlikely. Many have put themselves forward to claim the honour of being the originator of the image and slogan. Some claimants were serving in the military, but the strongest case would have to be that of a civilian worker by the name of James J. Kilroy who was employed as a quality control inspector at the Fore River Shipyard at Quincy, Massachusetts. Ships were built using rivet construction to join the huge steel plates together to form the hull. Inspectors had the job of checking that rivets had been inserted properly and that the work was up to standard. Kilroy was an inspector and he would sign his name by the work to signify that he had checked and passed it. Soon his name was appearing on everything. Troops used it as a means of indicating their dissatisfaction and cocking a contemptuous gesture towards the military.

In the early days the Kilroy name did not have an image, but gradually a character did develop and was produced in a simple style which did not require any great artistic skill to draw. It caught on with other armies, even the Soviet Red Army, not generally

A recreated example of the 'Kilroy' slogan, showing the humour of the time.

A recreated example of the British 'Chad' or 'Mr Chad' wartime slogans.

recognized for its levity – Russian troops scrawled 'Vasya was here!' The image of Kilroy is believed to have been copied from the British character known as 'Mr Chad', drawn in a very similar style, and often known simply as 'Chad'. The image is thought to have originated in 1938 and his face peering over a wall was often accompanied by slogans referring to shortages of certain commodities during the war such as 'Wot, no petrol' or 'Wot, no sugar'. Australian troops scrawled 'Foo was here', an expression believed to have originated during the First World War. All of these slogans, and many other forms, appeared on surfaces from buildings to vehicles in all theatres of war. To those who knew the meaning of such graffiti it was humour, but to civilians, especially those countries in theatres of operations, it was baffling.

The saucy pin-up art form is a long-established genre of painting and some artists, such as Alberto Vargas in the 1940s, had the skill and creativeness to produce life-like imagery. The images produced by artists practising this form were titillating and might make the more reserved blush, but they were never vulgar. For the most part they were

This Auster spotter plane, 'Lisa Jane', is typical of the nose art featured on many aircraft. Images of pretty girls and their names were seen on many aircraft.

part of advertizing campaigns, from cigarettes to soap. The style also influenced troops with artistic talent to create similar imagery on vehicles. The USAAF led the way with saucy images on the nose of aircraft from fighters to bombers such as B17s, B24s and B25s. Other aircraft carried slogans such as 'Stinky', 'Ding Dong Daddy', 'Hard t' Get', 'Silver Dollar' and 'Myrtle the Fertile Turtle'. The images accompanying some of these slogans were either good luck charms such as four-leaf clovers or stylized animals such as black cats, birds or dogs.

Another influential artist with the same kind of talent was George Petty, about whose work it was said: 'When you touch the wrist of a Petty Girl, you almost expect to feel a pulse.' Indeed the images were life-like, even if some did have a tendency to being stylized, with certain parts of the female anatomy being exaggerated. In fact, Captain Robert Morgan, who flew the B17 nicknamed 'Memphis Belle', contacted George Petty to officially request the use of an image of a pin-up girl from the men's magazine *Esquire* which would be painted on his aircraft. Petty sent him some artwork and Morgan had an artist on the air base paint the figure on either side of the nose. The effect was an instant hit with the crew and Hollywood film director William Wyler decided to make a morale-boosting film for the American public using the crew of Memphis Belle which was named after Captain Morgan's girlfriend. Morgan later commented on the image

Even fighter aircraft such as this P-38J version of the 'Lightning' could be decorated with some saucy but humorous images.

saying: 'To the German fighter pilots homing in [on] our American bombers, it must have looked sometimes as though they were being attacked by a wave of flying underwear catalogues.' As the war progressed, so the artwork was applied to other types of aircraft, including light 'spotter' planes such as the Auster, long-range reconnaissance types, the PBY 'Catalinas', and fighters including Mustangs and P-38 Lightnings.

There were other artists serving in the armed forces who worked in the same genre including Robert Skemp, Billy De Vorss and Bill Wand. Many of these artists worked for advertizing agencies such as Ruthrauff and Ryan and Benton & Bowles, men's magazines such as *Esquire* and comic book publications which featured scantily clad female forms but were always discreet. To the prudish minds of the day this imagery was decadent but to the young, red-blooded men in the armed forces such images were morale boosters and they were pinned on barrack walls wherever and whenever possible. It was only natural that such images should be replicated on vehicles by talented artists from the ranks. The author Donald L. Miller in his book *Eighth Air Force* states that the 'voluptuous girls' were the favourite subjects of artists painting images on the noses of aircraft. Miller says how these female shapes were: 'Coyly seductive and impossibly beautiful, they were more than idealized versions of girls back home; they were brazen symbols of life on a war front where death was on everyone's mind.' The images were pleasant distractions and the crews loved them. The USAAF did not hold the monopoly on these images and eventually the US Army and US Marine Corps were following their example, painting similar images on their vehicles.

One of the leading exponents of painting what is known as 'Nose Art' on aircraft was Phil Brinkman, who, in 1944, was stationed at the USAAF base Station 174 at Sudbury, Suffolk in England, serving with the 486th Bomb Group. Brinkman was born in St Louis in 1916 and had been working as a commercial artist before the war. He had worked for advertizing agencies in Chicago and St Louis and on being drafted was posted to the Davis-Monthan Army Air Base, Tucson, Arizona. He served there for two years, during which time he was engaged in various duties, but he still managed to keep his hand and eye in use as an artist by painting morale-lifting murals and emblems around the base.

The 486th Bomb Group fl ew B24 'Liberator' bomber aircraft commanded by Winfred 'Jip' Howell and it was he who first recognized the potential of the talents of the young Corporal Brinkman and got him involved with painting many aircraft. This work included a series based on the signs of the zodiac which featured on the twelve aircraft of the 834th Squadron, known as 'The Fighting Zodiac' Squadron. When the Group was posted to Sudbury in England Captain Howell arranged to have Brinkman posted with it in order to further use his talents to maintain morale through his artwork. The Zodiac Squadron went on to fl y forty-nine missions without the loss of a single aircraft. The crews of these aircraft later converted to fly B17 'Flying Fortress' bombers

This example of artwork is on the preserved cockpit of a Lancaster bomber flown by No 405 Squadron of the Royal Canadian air Force.

and they transferred their lucky zodiac symbols with them. The 306th Bomb Group also operated out of Sudbury and the men 'adopted' a 3-year-old girl called Maureen who had been orphaned. They called her 'Sweet Pea' as a term of endearment and for good luck got her to place her paint-daubed hand-print on the nose of a B24 which was named after her.

News of the nose art spread and was much admired by RAF pilots whose own aircraft sometimes sported a name, such as 'Our Beautiful Babe' on an aircraft in No 405 Pathfinder Squadron, or lucky symbols painted on the fuselage by the cockpit, but they were nowhere as elaborate or spicy as the images painted on the USAAF aircraft. High-ranking officers would drop in on an airbase unannounced to conduct an impromptu inspection of a squadron's readiness. Such 'snap' inspections included a check on the aircraft. In such an event the inspecting party would see the artwork. The more liberal or broad-minded might admire such work and be understanding how important such images could be to morale. After all, this was only a continuation of the tradition which had started in the First World War but now, a generation later, was on a much greater scale. Other officers might not be so accepting.

The US military system became more understanding of such art forms and recognized the beneficial value motifs and imagery had on the morale of servicemen. In August 1944, Army Air Force Regulation 35-22, signed by the Secretary of State for War Henry L. Stimpson, authorized the decorating of Army Air Force equipment with individual designs. It actually went one stage further by positively encouraging the use of such artwork because of its morale-boosting effect. This official stance naturally filtered down from aircraft to include vehicles such as Jeeps and armoured vehicles. The USAAF was more liberal-minded than either of its counterparts in the US Navy or US Marine Corps, whose regulations forbade such frippery. Despite all the attempts by the US Navy and USMC to block icons and imagery from appearing on aircraft, artwork was painted on aircraft in an un-official capacity, but it was mostly overlooked and taken in good humour. The US Army followed the example set by the USAAF and overlooked the use of artwork painted on vehicles from motorcycles to tanks. Robert Morgan said of this artwork that: 'It was a way of holding on to our own individuality, or sense of humour, in a war that was overwhelmingly vast, mechanized and brutal.'

The US Marine Corps fought a fierce campaign across the Pacific, battling to retake the islands which had been captured by the Japanese in 1942. Each attack on an island required an amphibious landing in a process known as 'Island Hopping'. Away from all the regulations the US Marines developed a cavalier approach to things and not only named their vehicles, calling them 'Lightning', 'Jungle Jim' and 'Clodhopper', which fought on Kwajalein in 1944, but also applied images of girls like the nose art of the aircraft of the USAAF. Some vehicles were named simply as 'Doris', which was seen in action on Iwo Jima in March 1945, or 'Davy Jones', which was a reference to sinking at sea, something no self-respecting US Marine wanted to do. Some companies of US Marines named their vehicles in alphabetical sequence, with 'A' Company using names beginning with the letter A, 'B' Company having vehicles beginning with B such as 'Betty' or 'Bronco', and so on through the Battalion organization.

Gil Elvgren was another highly talented artist whose technique earned for him the title 'The Norman Rockwell of Cheesecake'. Rockwell was a renowned artist who produced artwork for morale-boosting posters used in the drive to sell War Bonds. Elvgren's more commercial artwork usually showed typical American families enjoying time together, but his imagery, put to good use to support the war effort, was militaristic and inspiring. One of these was his poster of 1942 showing a machine gunner with the rather jingoistic slogan 'Let's give him enough and On Time', in reference to the supply of ammunition. Images of Elvgren's artwork of females appeared on trucks, aircraft and tanks and his style was copied by servicemen who applied their own images, thereby proving the adage that imitation is the sincerest form of flattery. He used live models of pretty young girls to produce the artwork which captured the imagination of so many servicemen all over the world.

Bill Mauldin had been a commercial artist before the war, and after enlistment he went on to serve with the 45th Infantry Division during the Italian theatre of operations in 1943. His work had appeared in many publications before the war, including in advertisements. Mauldin served in Sicily and later in southern France and his artwork

Real life model used as an inspiration for artwork.

How an artist turned the life model into saucy artwork for aircraft and vehicles.

Stylized and over-emphasized female forms were transformed into figures of fantasy using artwork.

was influential. He created the cartoon characters 'Willie and Joe', based on army buddies, which proved highly popular, appearing in cartoon strips in the US Army newspaper *Stars and Stripes*. Among his other work was a cartoon strip called 'Up Front' which appeared in *Yank* magazine and featured soldiers as the characters in various situations. Indeed, there were many young men who had studied art at high school or college and their talents could be applied to painting images on the vehicles in their units. Some vehicle crews in Italy opted for the simple approached and just used a name, such as one unit using M3 half-tracks armed with

75mm guns, serving in the role of self-propelled artillery to provide fire support, which identified individual vehicles by painting the names on the barrels of the guns, such as 'Belching Bella'.

Names and images on the sides of vehicles raised a smile among the troops in the quieter moments, and when they appeared in the heat of battle a named vehicle could raise morale. After being cut off and completely surrounded and attacked for a full week between 20 and 27 December 1944 during the Ardennes offensive, known more familiarly as the Battle of the Bulge, the defenders of Bastogne, who referred to themselves as the 'Battered, bloody bastards', were heartened to see a Sherman of the 37th Tank Battalion of the 4th Armoured Division enter the town. On the side was painted the 'Cobra King'. It provided hope, as well as fire support, to the defenders during the siege. The unit was commanded by Lieutenant Colonel Creighton Abrams whose personal Sherman tank was named 'Thunderbolt'. The unit had a reputation for tough fighting and Colonel Abrams had his admirers, one of whom was General George S. Patton who said of him: 'I am supposed to be the best tank commander in the army, but I have one peer- Abe Abrams.' By the end of the war Colonel Abrams had fifty German tanks destroyed to his credit. Patton was viewed by some as maverick, but he got results and was feared and respected in equal measures by the Germans. He was a man who spoke his mind and led from the front. He wanted to be seen and be where he could see for himself the shape of battle. His personal Jeep, named 'Lucky Forward', was his mobile command post that used to drive him to positions where he could issue orders personally.

Field Marshal Bernard Montgomery used Jeeps also, but he was more often to be seen in Humber 'Super Snipe' cars which he used for liaison duties, such as touring camps to give 'pep' talks. One was called 'Old Faithful', which is on display at the Imperial War Museum at Lambeth in London, and a second vehicle, known as 'Victory Car' is on display at the Coventry Transport Museum in England.

Sometimes a regimental motto such as the US Marine Corps' 'Semper Fidelis' (meaning 'Always Faithful' or 'Always Loyal') was used in a name and shortened to a version 'Semper Fi' for vehicle mottos. Another regimental motto was 'Seek Strike Destroy' which was applied to specialized tank destroyer battalions, especially those equipped with M10 'Wolverine' vehicles. The badge showed a wildcat with a tank crushed in its jaws with the three words arranged around its head. The motto of the 506th Parachute Infantry Regiment of the 101st Airborne Division was 'Currahee' which was taken from the native Cherokee word 'quu-wa-hi' which means stand alone. It was in reference to a peak used in the fitness programme at Camp Toccoa where basic training was undertaken. Some vehicles used by the unit had the name painted on them and would have reminded the troops of what they had been through to become an elite force. The US 17th Airborne Division had a golden eagle's talons as its badge and the

An M-18 'Hellcat' tank destroyer, named 'Bronx Bruiser', with the unit badge and motto 'Seek, Strike, Destroy'.

Detail of tank destroyer unit badge along with the vehicle name applied to the hull.

'Currahee' was a word used exclusively by American airborne troops during training and expressed on vehicles.

Local British dialect 'Ow Bist' from the area known as the Black Country; it means 'How are you?'

Motto of the US Marine Corps 'Semper Fidelis', meaning either 'Always Faithful' or 'Always Loyal', used on a Jeep along with other artwork.

talons were sometimes seen grasping a skull with a Nazi swastika emblem. By contrast some units of the British Army would use forms of local dialect as an emblem such as the term 'Ow Bist' from the Black Country.

The Golden Claws of the badge of the 17th US Airborne Division being used to make a statement.

America entered the war on 7 December 1941 but it was not until November 1942 that a force was assembled to launch an amphibious landing on the North African coast. Operation Torch was the first direct contact US troops had had with enemy forces and one of the units landing was the 34th Division which had the support of self-propelled artillery such as M7 guns. One was named 'The Texas Special' and served during the campaign, ending up in Morocco. During the campaign vehicles had carried the air identification symbol of a white five-pointed star inside a solid blue circle.

While this was taking place more American troops sailed to England to begin the build-up for the invasion of Europe which the Russians had been calling for. These troops brought with them all the things which were familiar to them and in doing so exposed them to the British public and servicemen alike. The vehicles were unlike anything seen before and included new designs such as the Jeep, big, powerful Harley Davison motorcycles, and all manner of other trucks such as the Dodge WC52 'Weapons Carrier', WC54 Ambulances and WC57 Command Cars. Then there were thousands of GMC trucks known to the American troops as either the 'Jimmy', from its initials, or as the 'deuce-and-a-half' from its load rating. These were the wheeled vehicles which the drivers sometimes named and painted images on them.

The British Army developed a series of specialized armoured vehicles which were formed into the 79th Armoured Division and used to support the Allied landings on D-Day. The Americans also developed a series of vehicles for specialized roles one of which was the DUKW called the 'Duck' which served in all theatres of the war and was used extensively by the Allies, including the British Army. The DUKW was

A girl's name was often enough even for the largest trucks.

Slogans could be hopeful, such as 'Agoing Home' on this Sherman.

Jeep drivers would sometimes paint only the name of their girlfriend or wife on the vehicle.

Crews could conjure up all sorts of names for their vehicles and 'Nitro Nick' is a typical example. (Inset) Close-up showing how the name is a reference to the devil or 'Old Nick'.

Troops would have used expressions which were acceptable in the military, such as this which probably summed up the thoughts of many soldiers.

Bugs Bunny with a hand grenade and the words 'Ammo Pulla' which indicate this vehicle supplied ammunition.

Even with a camouflage net covering it the name 'D-Day Doll' can still be made out.

Following the Normandy landings on 6 June 1944 a lot of artwork appeared which referred to the operation.

essentially an amphibious version of the six-wheeled 'Jimmy' CCKW 353 truck, fitted with a boat-like hull to allow it to float, a rudder and a propeller, capable of reaching speeds up to 6mph in water. Several countries developed amphibious vehicles but they never produced them in the same numbers as the American Army which saw the DUKW as having a wide role. The acronym came from the code letters to designate the vehicle with D standing for the year 1942 when the first request for the vehicle was posted, U designated it as amphibious, and K and W denoted all-wheel drive and dual rear axles respectively. By the end of the war over 21,000 had been built and these had carried hundreds of thousands of tons of supplies, troops and other equipment. During Operation Husky, the landings on

Sicily, around 1,000 DUKWs were used. During the Normandy Landings in June 1944 some 2,000 DUKWs carried around forty per cent of all supplies ashore on D-Day itself. There is an example of a DUKW on display in the Tank Museum at Bovington in Dorset which is painted with a duck motif.

The GPA, another amphibious vehicle developed by the American Army, was essentially a floating version of the Jeep. The initials stood for Jeep with the letter 'A' denoting amphibious. The Landing Vehicle Tracked, nicknamed 'Buffalo', was also developed to land troops, stores and vehicles direct to the shore and these were used in the Pacific War and in Europe. All of these types were often named by their crews. In fact, one of the first vehicles to land on Tarawa on 20 December 1943 was an LVT named 'My Delores'. On display at Bovington is an LVT named 'Sevenoaks' which served with 79th Armoured Division.

The Normandy Landings, or D-Day, was launched nineteen months after the Allied landings in North Africa at a time when the fighting was still raging in Italy. At this stage in the war the Allies had more aircraft of all types than the German air force, the Luftwaffe, and exceeded their strength to such a degree that it gave the RAF and USAAF air domination. The fighters flew across the battlefields firing on moving vehicles. To avoid being caught in the open and strafed as the vehicles moved in convoy, they painted warnings on the rear of trucks which read 'Abstand', instructing drivers to keep their distance. As the situation worsened for the Germans so the warning distance

Large amphibious vehicles such as the DUKW carried a simple name.

The DUKW could be named like any ship or boat.

This example of a DUKW is on display at the Tank Museum at Bovington in Dorset and uses a duck motif to reflect the vehicle's title.

The GPA was the amphibious version of the Jeep and, like them, they were also named by their drivers. (Insert) Details of the hand-painted name.

This GPA takes to the water and, like the words to the 1926 song 'Red, Red, Robin', it is bobbing.

Much larger amphibious vehicles, such as this Landing Vehicle Tracked, on display at the Tank Museum at Bovington in Dorset, is named simply 'Sevenoaks'.

The German Army used warning signs to instruct drivers to keep their distance when in convoy to prevent being strafed by Allied aircraft, especially after D-Day.

Instructions on the rear of a German vehicle to remind the following vehicle to keep its distance.

between vehicles was increased. To prevent their own vehicles from being fired on by the USAAF and RAF the Allies painted white stars on their vehicles, and aircraft had black and white stripes painted on the fuselage and wings for quick and easy recognition.

Although the US Marine Corps was well equipped and more than capable as a fighting force, it was not able to repair or build facilities, such as airfields and harbours, which had been destroyed in the fighting. This role required specialist engineers who could restore these installations to allow supplies to be brought in to support the fighting units. It was Rear Admiral Ben Moreell of the US Navy who suggested creating Naval Construction Battalions for these duties. The first training camp to be established for the engineers was Camp Endicott in Davisville, Rhode Island. By the end of the war over 100,000 recruits had passed through the centre. The new force was called the US Naval Construction Battalions, or 'Seabees' for short after the initials 'CB' from Construction Battalions. The unit badge showed a bee holding a machine gun, spanner and hammer in its six legs. It is a caricature of the insect with a determined look and wearing a sailor's cap.

Around 325,000 men served with the Seabees in all theatres, but mainly in the Pacific. Primarily engineers, the men were trained to fight and expected to do so if they were

The Seabees Construction Battalions used their unit badge on their vehicles.

The Seabee badge, showing a bee armed with a machine gun and carrying a hammer and adjustable wrench.

The Seabees had a distinctive badge, as did all units.

The armed Seabee was also used on trucks.

A play on words with Misbeehavin'.

A GMC truck in Seabee markings and colours is also named.

The US Army used Harley Davidson motorcycles, and riders named their machines.

A Harley Davidson with its name 'Wild Breed' on the fuel tank.

The M25 'Dragon Wagon' tank transporter, with M26 tractor unit and M15 trailer, named 'Little Chicken' with M5 Stuart Light Tanks on the trailer.

attacked. This reflected the official motto 'Construimus, Batuimus' (We Build, We Fight), but the unofficial motto 'Can Do!' along with the bee emblem was the more identifiable among the troops. The battalions were equipped with trucks and specialist earth-moving equipment such as Caterpillar bulldozers, Allis-Chalmers HD-15As and International TD-18 'Crawlers'. These were often named and given images, usually of girls, which were painted on the doors and sides just like combat vehicles. Sometimes it could be a play on words with a statement such as 'Misbeehavin'.

As the 'Island Hopping' campaign got underway in the Pacific the US Marine Corps relaxed its once strict code about painting names and images on vehicles and art work proliferated in a way which outdid that in all other theatres of the war. Some of the vehicles carried names which reflected their role, such as the flamethrower versions of the M5 Light Tanks, known as 'Satans'. One unit serving with the 13th Armoured Group fighting in Luzon on the Philippine Islands in January 1945 was seen with appropriate names painted on the side of their Satans' hulls, including 'Flaming Fanny'. Conventional gun tanks, including variants of the M4 Sherman, were used by the 44th Battalion which captured the Philippine capital of Manila in February and vehicles were seen entering the city displaying names such as 'Battle Basic' and 'Ole Miss'. Earlier during the same campaign, in November 1943, M4A2 Sherman tanks of the 1st Corps Medium Tank Battalion included one vehicle named 'Cecilia', which was damaged by gun fire, and 'China Gal' which fired on Japanese positions. The fighting on Okinawa in May 1945 was among the heaviest of the entire Pacific campaign and amidst all of it were to be seen vehicles such as an M7 SPG named 'Waddlin' Willie' which served with the Cannon Company of 383rd Infantry of the 96th Division. As well as having the name painted on the side, an image of a turtle (tortoise) wearing a steel helmet and a gun mounted on the back of its shell also appeared, which no doubt would have raised a few wry smiles among the troops who saw it.

During the earliest of the island landings, such as Taupota on the tip of the east coast of New Guinea in October 1943, there is little in the way of illustrated evidence to show that vehicles and tanks had artwork painted on them. In fact, some of the Sherman tanks seen in some photographs from that operation lack unit markings and appear to be factory fresh. By the following month the 2nd US Marine Division landed on Betio, part of the chain of islands making up the Tarawa atoll, supported by C Company of the 1st Tank Battalion and D Company of the 2nd Light Tank Battalion, equipped with Sherman and Stuart tanks respectively. During the three days of fighting to capture the island, war photographers took pictures of the tanks in action which can clearly be seen with a name painted on them, such as 'Condor' which would indicate 3 Platoon of C Company of the 1st Tank Battalion, along with the image of an elephant painted on the hull. Other tanks from the same unit, also bearing the elephant symbol, were called 'Charlie', 'Colorado', 'Commando', 'Cannonball', 'Cuddles' and 'Cecilia'. This is a typical example of the letter C being used to indicate the third or 'C' Company and platoon of a battalion.

At the time the landings were taking place on Betio, the US Marines were attacking Bougainville in New Guinea where photographers recorded a Sherman tank of the 754th Tank Battalion called 'The Black Orchid'. The name was accompanied by a reclining female figure, and on the turret can be seen the victory tally of the vehicle which shows Japanese flags to indicate it had destroyed five pillboxes and a gun emplacement during the fighting.

War photographers often took great risks and placed themselves in danger in order to take photographs for official use to circulate to newspapers around the world. The photographer would have been too busy trying to avoid being killed and absorbed with taking the images to notice things like the intricacies of the artwork applied to a vehicle. Only now, many years later, can we examine the photographs, study them for details, and analyze why the crews gave the tanks the names they did. For example, 'King Kong', which took part in the fighting on Roi-Namur, part of the Marshall Islands, between January and February 1944 was named after the film of the same name which was released in 1933. Another tank taking part in the same operation was named 'Jungle Jim', a title which proved popular with other tank crews. It is possible

References to native American Indian tribes were common.

Images of native American Indians were also used, such as this badge of the 2nd Infantry Division.

Names of tribes were used, such as 'Cherokee'.

Some tank crews also named the gun, as in this example.

Saucy images were always popular with the troops.

Girls in swimwear were appreciated.

Place names were a comfort to drivers.

This Mack 'NO' gun tractor uses a girl's name and a place name.

to distinguish between the old hands and the 'green' crews, and notice that the newer-looking vehicles, without a name or any artwork, are probably troops without combat experience. Vehicles could also be named in honour of previous vehicles such as 'Another Dinah' or 'Victor III'.

The Japanese had tanks on the islands but they were never in sufficient concentrations to directly threaten American tanks, and the calibre of their armament was outmatched by the guns of the Sherman. Nevertheless, Japanese tanks were a problem to infantry who had to call on the superior firepower of American tanks to neutralize the threats. The main problem facing the US Marines was sustaining manpower levels as casualties mounted due to the tenacity or stubbornness of the Japanese soldiers who fought on with suicidal fanaticism. Each island they attacked proved more difficult to capture from an enemy who would rather die fighting than surrender. The US Marines landed 71,000 troops to capture the Mariana Islands which were defended by 32,000 Japanese and the fighting lasted from 15 June to 9 July 1944. By the time the islands were taken the US Marines had sustained 14,000 killed and wounded while the Japanese lost around 30,000 killed and fewer than 1,000 surrendered. Tanks engaged in the action were seen bearing such names as 'Hothead III', 'Fireball' and 'Apache'. This last name was a reference to American Indians and some vehicles were seen with other similar names such as 'Geronimo' the war chief of the Bedonkohe Apache tribe.

For the most part, names on vehicles were kept simple and often meant something to the crew, even if it was only something for good luck, such as 'Knave', 'Corsair' or 'Blooper'. Some tanks were photographed with unusual names such as 'Inquisitive' or 'Powerhouse Pepper', but for the most part names were easy and humorous. Cartoons still proved popular subjects such as 'Dagwood' which served with the 3rd Tank Battalion, 4th Marine Division on Guam in 1944. Dagwood was another popular comic strip character appearing in American newspapers at the time. References to home remained popular, a tank called 'Monterey', presumably after Monterey in California, was seen serving with the 603rd Independent Tank Company fighting on Biak between May and August 1944. Another was seen called 'Broadway Terror', probably after Broadway in New York. Not all crews chose to name their vehicles, but most did. Indeed, it was considered unlucky not to name one's tank, rather like a ship which has no name is believed to be unlucky.

Crews used names which used the adjective iron to describe their vehicles such as 'Iron Horse', 'Iron Coffin', 'Iron Avenger' or 'Iron Sides'. The adverb 'wild' was also used in naming, such as 'Wild Time', 'Wild Thing' and even 'Wild Gal'. Naming vehicles became standard, but some tank crews applied a separate name to the gun in the turret such as 'Comet' of the 4th Tank Battalion whose main weapon was a flamethrower

Angie is a very lucky emblem with her cards, dice and four-leaf clover.

The talents of amateur artists sometimes produced some very good images of girlfriends or wives.

Sometimes the images 'peeped' out discreetly.

'On the Right Tracks' shown on the side of this International half-track with the unit badge of the 2nd Armoured Division 'Hell on Wheels'.

Some artists were truly gifted, and this motto reflects what the driver must have thought.

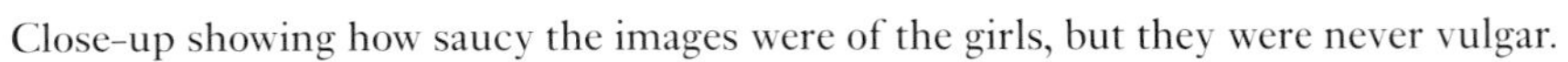
Close-up showing how saucy the images were of the girls, but they were never vulgar.

'Emma' is a cute amateur image and well proportioned.

Images could be based on film stars of the day and this one looks like Marlene Dietrich, who entertained the US troops often very close to the front line.

Girls' names and saucy images remained the most popular form of artwork on vehicles.

Reference to D-Day could not be avoided.

Detail of 'Camilla' showing a racy image designed to raise a smile.

With so many trucks in service drivers often painted images on doors and sides of vehicles.

Images in silhouette and the play on words puts the message across.

The war in the Far East also produced some images inspired by local conditions.

Some slogans said it all, such as 'Meat Hound'.

called 'Widow Maker'. The crew of 'Brassiereless Babe', serving with the 775th Tank Battalion, called the gun of their tank 'Big Mike'.

Crews serving with the 775th Tank Battalion paid particular attention when it came to naming their vehicles and adding the personal touch. Photographs of this unit show that many vehicles had a pair of dice showing various numbers of spots to designate the tank. They also displayed other images of artwork, usually in the form of a reclining female or a girl's head, and the tanks were also named, such as 'Doris', 'Betty' or 'Bronco'. Such a range of artwork on tanks was unusual when the norm was for simplicity. In all theatres of the war girls' names and saucy images of girls remained popular with troops. While saucy, the artist painting them abided by an unwritten self-imposed level of censorship which never went beyond the boundaries of what was acceptable.

In the Philippine Islands tanks displayed good luck charms such as horseshoes, dice, cards and four leaf clovers. One was named 'Battl'n Virgin', and animal names and images were widely adopted, such as 'Lone Wolves' serving with the 44th Tank Battalion in Manila and 'Five Wolves', presumably after the five crewmen in the tank, serving with the 716th Tank Battalion on Mindanao.

The last amphibious landing undertaken in the 'island hopping' campaign of the war took place on 26 March 1945 when US Marines landed on the island of Okinawa. The fighting lasted until 22 June and cost the US Marines 20,000 killed and a further 49,000 wounded; but the Japanese lost 110,000 killed. The Americans had landed 800 tanks on the island, along with other vehicles, against which the Japanese pitted 30 obsolete types. The Marines lost 225 of their tanks while in return they destroyed 743 pieces of artillery and all but three of the Japanese tanks. It had been a hard-fought battle and in view of what they had encountered on the island the US Marines and all the other armed forces were expecting worse when they attacked the islands of homeland Japan. Fate, however, intervened and events overtook any necessity to invade Japan proper. On 6 August 1945 Colonel Paul Tibbets, flying a B29 bomber named 'Enola Gay' after his mother, dropped an atomic bomb, nicknamed 'Little Boy', on the Japanese city of Hiroshima. Three days later on 9 August Major General Charles W. Sweeney, flying a B29 bomber named 'Bocks Car' (sometimes written as Bockscar) dropped a second atomic bomb, nicknamed 'Fat Man', on the Japanese city of Nagasaki. On 14 August, Japan declared its surrender, with the official signing of the end of the war taking place on 2 September 1945. The war was over and the forces in the Pacific theatre were spared another amphibious assault, which undoubtedly would have been costly in lives.

The war was finally over, but that was not the end of images or names being applied to vehicles. During the many post-war conflicts, such as the Korean War and Vietnam, military vehicles continued to be named and personalized with artwork. The act of naming vehicles has become a military tradition in many armies and today examples can

During the Iraq War in 1990–91 vehicles of the Coalition Forces, such as this British Challenger tank, were identified by a large inverted 'V'. This vehicle is also named 'Churchill'.

This Norwegian Army APC serving with the Stabilization Force in Bosnia-Herzegovina is named 'T-Rex' and continues the long tradition of naming vehicles.

The gun of this Swedish Army Stridsforden 90 has been named 'Great Balls of Fire' by the crew.

The crew of this Swedish Army Pansarbandvagn 302 has named it 'Cold As Ice' in the style of typical military humour.

be seen in armies around the world. When British and American forces were engaged in operations in Iraq and Afghanistan some of the vehicles were seen with names and good luck motifs painted on them.

Traditions such as this will never fade and as long as soldiers the world over have their own unique humour we will continue to see vehicles with names painted on their sides or on the guns mounted in the turrets. The soldiers who painted the images on their vehicles during the war remain largely unknown and their work may be considered by some to be ephemeral, but their art was important at the time and some of it is preserved in museums. Their imagery is important to historians and owners of historical vehicles and also serves as a legacy for soldiers of today and in the future.

Appendix

This German Kubelwagen is named '*Kleine Teufel*' – 'Little Devil'.

Detail of the Gothic lettering and the tail forming the letter 'l' at the end.

Although 'Braun' is seen on this PaK47 anti-tank gun it does not mean 'Brown' in this case, but is rather a reference to 'braun ark' the fluid used in the hydraulic systems of guns.

'Hazel' is discretely painted onto the front of this replica SdKfz251/10.

British vehicles seized at Dunkirk were used by the German Army and named, as shown on this representation.

Individuals personalized their kit with images, as seen on this replica kit bag of the USAAF.

The massive German gun called 'Thor' with its 600mm calibre was part of the Karl-Gerät and an example of the type used against Warsaw and Sevastopol.

The wild and wicked nature of Bugs Bunny made him a popular cartoon character with troops.

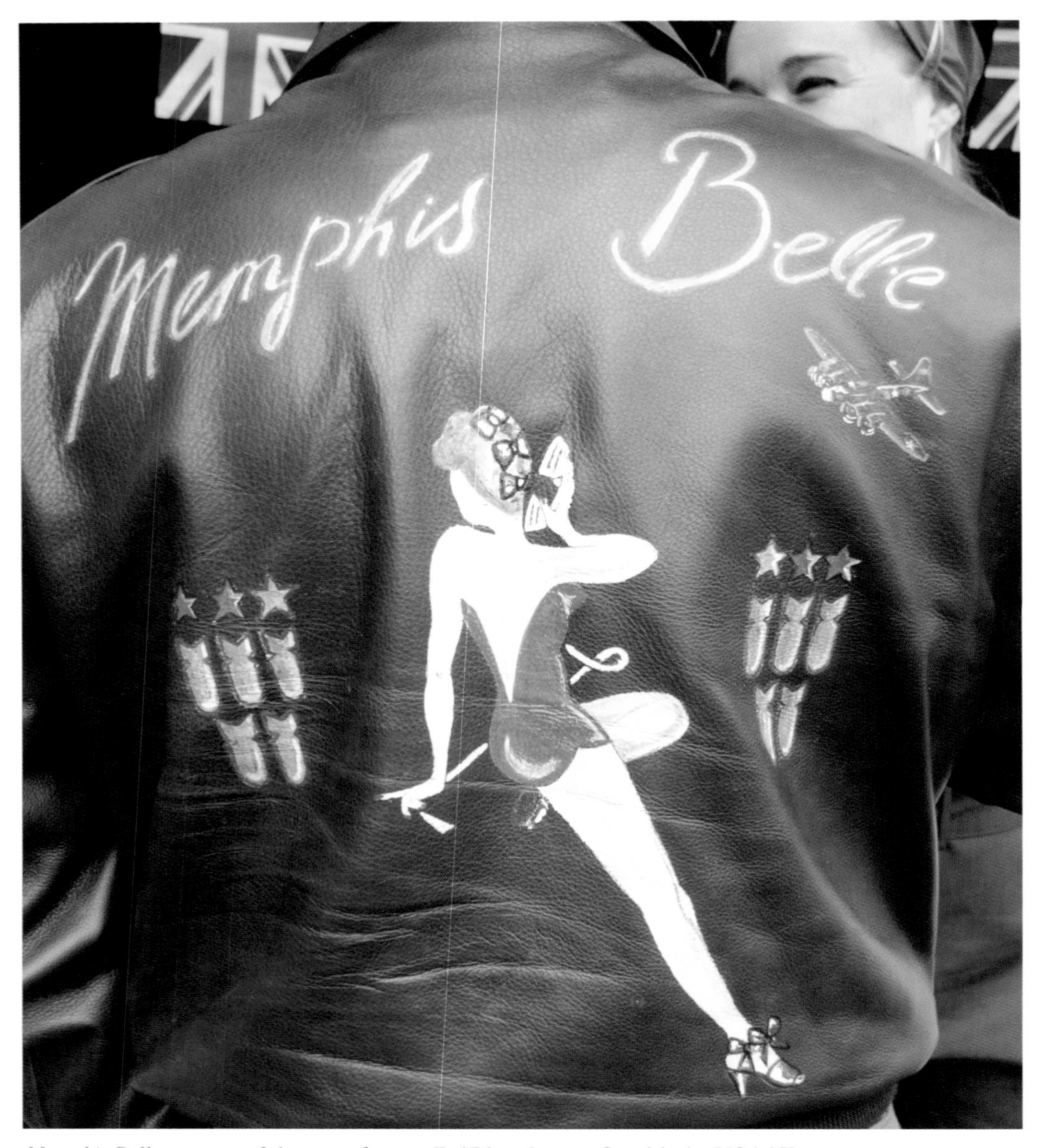

Memphis Belle was one of the most famous B-17 bombers to fly with the USAAF.

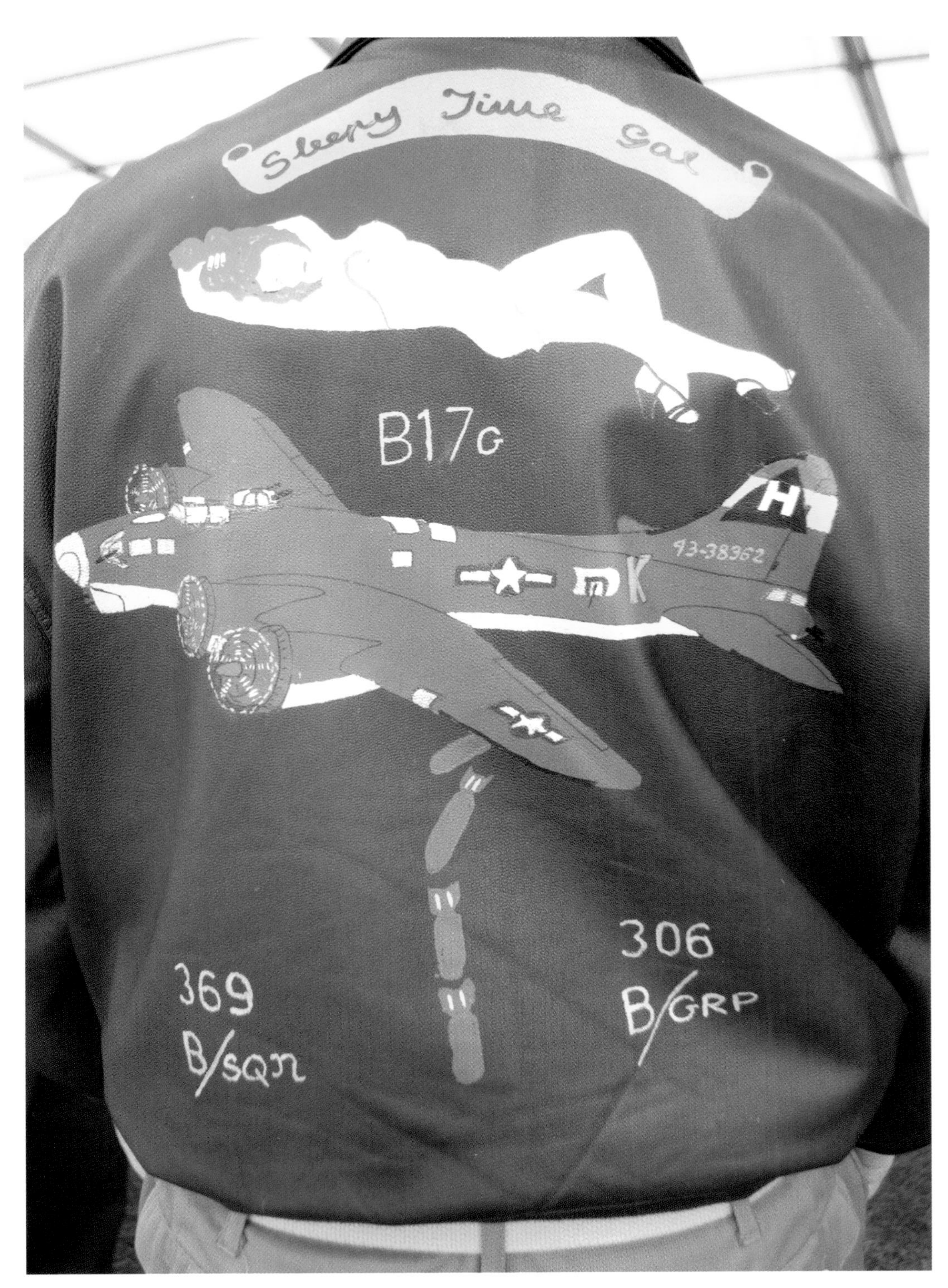

Replica jacket as worn by a crewman of B-17G named 'Sleepy Time Gal' which flew with the 369th Bomb Squadron of the 306th Bomb Group. It was shot down over Stuttgart on 9 September 1944.

Jeep as used by the 4th Fighter Group based in England.

Individual jacket badge as worn by USAAF air crew.

An alternative version of the emblem used by the 4th Fighter Group based in England.

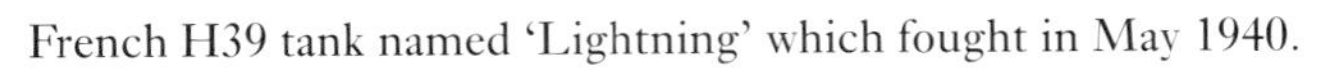

French H39 tank named 'Lightning' which fought in May 1940.

'La Belle' translates to 'The Beauty' from French.

British troops used humour to name vehicles such as 'Puddle Jumper' on the side of this Universal Bren Gun Carrier.

Another example of a variation of the 7th Armoured Division Badge.

This version of the 7th Armoured Division badge on a Daimler Dingo is more traditional.

This Bedford truck of the British Army has the image of a duck which was universally popular.

Close-up of the duck on the Bedford truck.

Simple names like 'Clementine' were used on British tanks, like this American-built M3 Stuart.

Close-up showing how a stencil has been used for the name.

Canadian-built CT-15 truck named 'Miss Betty'.

Style of painting for Miss Betty.

This AEC Matador heavy truck was a venerable vehicle of the British Army as reflected in its name.

This Scammell Pioneer was used to tow artillery and the driver has named it very simply.

Sometimes rhyming words were used to go with a girl's name.

Choosy Suzy seen overall.

The size of the GMC truck made it an obvious choice for images, names and artwork, such as 'My Kerry'.

Detail of 'My Kerry' showing the style of painting.

The canvas covers on vehicles could also be used for artwork like artists' canvases.

M18 tank destroyer 'Nugent' with the unit motto 'Seek, Strike, Destroy'.

Dodge WC54 ambulance with the image of an injured duck, reflecting the humour of the time.

Detail of the artwork on the WC54 ambulance.

Ducks were a lucky emblem, especially Donald Duck, and the cartoon was widely used.

Iconic image of helmet and vehicle artwork.

'On the Right Tracks' is saucy and funny in equal turn.

Command version of the M5 Stuart Light Tank without a turret. This was used in Europe and the Pacific where they were named like other vehicles.

Showing the style of hand-painting.

This half-track has images similar to those seen during the war.

The cartoon character of 'Wile E Coyote' was created by Chuck Jones in 1948, but it is safe to assume that had it appeared earlier it would have been used on vehicles like this.

Some artwork was very elaborate.

Hitler being pursued as the quarry of the hunt.

A very good attempt at amateur art, typical of many such efforts.

Overall view of the M3 Scout Car with 'Ready 'n Able'.

Another very good amateur rendition of artwork.

The cowgirl image reminded American troops of home.

My Kerry, again.

Ready for Duty, again.

'Double Trouble' sums it up for most troops.

Darlin' Doris would have brought a smile to many faces.

D-Day Doll.

Wild Cat.

Very simple and personal wording for the driver.

Lucky Angel, showing style of freehand painting.

This American-built GMC truck is in the colours of the British 2nd Army in Europe. The legend translated from the German reads 'My Lovely Wife'.

Close-up showing style of application.

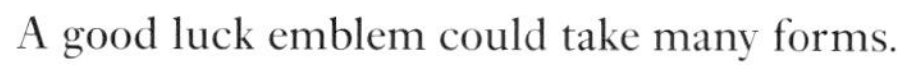
A good luck emblem could take many forms.

Playing cards were popular with all armies.

Images in silhouette had something of mystery about them.

Allentown Annie, again.

Dragon Wagon tank transporter with saucy female figure.

Dragon Wagon transporter with M5 Stuart tanks on trailer. They are named.

Wile E Coyote.

Sherman tanks were usually named, like this example which has the name of the Carthaginian military leader of the third century BC.

The name of the M8 armoured car reflects the crew's opinion of it in 'Mighty Eight'.

Harley Davidson motorcycle named 'Uncle Sam' on the fuel tank.

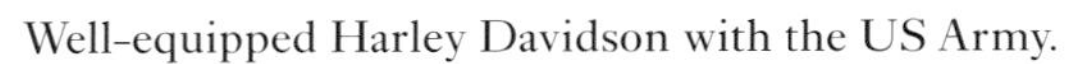
Well-equipped Harley Davidson with the US Army.

Some names were simple terms.

This Jeep called 'Helluva War' has a female figure in silhouette on the front bumper.

Detail of the stencilled sign.

Example of freehand painted sign and artwork.

The British Comet tank was a late-comer to the war and this example, named 'Spud', is seen during a display at the Tank Museum at Bovington in Dorset.

Bibliography

Brighton, Terry, *Master of Battle: Monty, Patton and Rommel at War*, Penguin Viking, London, 2008.
Deighton, Len, *Blitzkrieg*, Jonathan Cape, London, 1979.
Forty, George, *United States Tanks of World War II in Action*, Blandford Press, Poole, Dorset, 1983.
Giuliani, Raymond, *Sherman in the Pacific War 1943-45*, Histoire & Collections, Paris, 2015.
Hart, Dr Stephen (General Editor): *Atlas of Tank Warfare*, Ambers Books, London, 2012.
Miller, Donald L., *Eighth Air Force: The American Bomber Crews in Britain*, Aurum Press Ltd, London, 2008.
Ogorkiewicz, Richard, *Tanks; 100 Years of Evolution*, Osprey Publishing, Oxford, 2015.
Perrett, Bryan, *Tank Warfare*, Arms and Armour Press, London, 1990.
Rolf, David, *The Bloody Road to Tunis*, Greenhill Books, London, 2001.
Smither, J.J., *A New Excalibur*, Grafton Books, London, 1988.
Ware, Pat, *Military Jeep: 1940 Onwards*, Haynes Publishing, Yeovil, Somerset, 2010.
Ware, Pat, *Sherman Tank: 1941 Onwards*, Haynes Publishing, Yeovil, Somerset, 2012.
Winter, Dennis, *Death's Men: Soldiers of the Great War*, Penguin Books, London, 1978.
Zaloga, Steven J., *French Tanks of World War II (1)*, Osprey Publishing, Oxford, 2014.
Zaloga, Steven J., *French Tanks of World War II (2)*, Osprey Publishing, Oxford, 2014.

Index

Page ranges in bold indicate illustrations

A7V tanks, 11, 13
Abrams, Col Creighton, 99
Achilles, 3–4
Alexander the Great, 6
Army Film and Photographic Unit, 34, **38**
Arthur, King, 1
Aspis shield, 2, **2**
Audacious, tank, 9

Bayeux Tapestry, 7
Bern, Switzerland, 1
Betty Boop, 43, **43–4**, 45
Big Bertha artillery, 14–15
Black Prince (Edward), 4
Boche Buster see Scene Shifter
Bourgeois, Lt Pierre, 49
Bremmer, Lt Paul, 8
Brinkman, Paul, 95
Bucephalus, 6
Bugs Bunny, 34, 36, **41–2**
Bunty, artillery, 13, **16**

Capa, Robert, 91
Caricatures, 56, **57**
Chad, 92, **92**
Chindits, 61
Churchill, tank, 25–6, 29
Clan Leslie, tank, 9
Copenhagen, horse, 6

Daffy Duck, 25, 39
Deborah, tank, 9
De Gaulle, Gen Charles, 49–50, 52
Desert Rats (7th Armoured Division), 59, **60**
Disney, Walt (Studios), 27, 39, 77
Donald Duck, 34, 36, 39–40, **40**

Ekins, Joe, 71, **71**
Elvgren, Gil, 97
Evelyn Tentions, 15, **21**
Excalibur sword, 1
Excalibur, tank, 9

Finland, **76**, 77
Foo, 92
Fury film, 29
Fury, tank, 29, **29**, 30, 61

Galland, Gen Adolf, 72, **75**
Götz von Berlichingen Division, 59
Graffiti, 15, **18**, 54, **54**
Gram, sword, 1
Guards Division, 13, **13**, 62
Gull, Capt G.E., 62, **63**, **66**

Hell On Wheels (2nd Armoured Division), 30, **126**
Hippogriffe, 48
Hobart, Maj Gen Sir Percy, 59
Homer, 3
Hoplites, **2**
Horrocks, Gen Brian, 59

Ice Cold in Alex (film), 30
Iliad, The, 3
Irma artillery, 15, **16**
Iron Knights, 30
Italy, 22

Jackets, **23–4**, 25, **28**
Jane, *Daily Mirror*, **58**
Jeep, The, 46, **47**
Jeeps, vehicles, 32, 46

Jungenfeld, Hauptmann Ernst Freiherr von, 80

Karl-Gërat (Karl Device), 83, **84**, 85
Katy (K2Y), 30, **31–2**
Kia Ora, tank, 10
Kill Rings, **84–5**, 85–6
Kilroy, 91, **92**
Kifaru, tank, 10
Knispel, Sgt Kurt, 85–6

Lafayette Escadrille, 8
Legbit or Legbiter, sword, 1
Lehman, Lt Wilhelm, 8
Lucky Jim, artillery, 13, **17**

MacBean-Ross. J.N, 11
MacWhirter, Lt Cmdr W.R., 15
Marengo, horse, 6
Mauldin, Bill, 97–8
Max and Moritz, 79, **81–2**, 83
Mickey Mouse, 34, 39, **40**
Minnie the Moocher, 43, **44**
Memphis Belle, B–17 USAAF, 94
Mephisto A7V, tank, 13
Merlin, tank, 11
Morgan, Capt Robert, 94, 97
Moltke, FM Helmuth von, 78
Mora, warship, 7
Moreell, R Adml Ben, 112
Myrmidons, 4

Napoleon Bonaparte, 6
Native North Americans, **119–20**

Odin, 1

Paint, 31–2, 78, 80
Patton, Gen George S. Jnr, 30, 99
Perat, Capt Pierre, 50
Petty, George, 94
Pölz, Hauptmann Hurbert, 72, 74
Popeye the Sailor, 45–6, **45–6**, 47, 77
Pinocchio, **75**, 77
Press Corps, 34, **38**

Red Cross, 34, **38**
Richthofen, Baron Manfred von (Red Baron), 8
Rommel, Gen (FM) Erwin, 78, 83
Royal Tank Corps, 9–10

Sahara, film, 30
Schnuck A7V, tank, 13, **14**
Scene Shifter, artillery, 13
Scutum, shield, 2, **3**
Seabees, 112, **113–14**, 118
Sign writers, 25
Snow White and the Seven Dwarfs, film, 28, 40, **42**
Stimpson, Henry L. (Secretary of State for War), 96
Sutton Hoo excavations, 1

Testudo, 3, **3**
Title roles, military, 32
Tobruk, 30–1
Trasenster, Lt Michael, 67
Trojan War, 3
Troy, 3

Union HMLS, (tank), 9, **10**
USAAF, 25, 36

Vargas, Alberto, 93
Vikings, 1, 7

Warning signs, 108, **111–12**
Wellington, Duke of, 6
We're All In It, tank, 11, **11**
Wessex Division, 49th Division, 59
William, Duke of Normandy (Conqueror), 7
Wimmis, 1
Wittmann, Hauptsturmführer Michael, 71, 85
Wolverine M10 Tank Destroyer, 22, 99, **100**
Wyvern, 59, **61, 69**